# Tamil Temple Myths

# Tamil Temple Myths

## Sacrifice and Divine Marriage in the South Indian Śaiva Tradition

**David Dean Shulman**

Princeton
University
Press

Published by Princeton University Press, Princeton, New Jersey
In the United Kingdom: Princeton University Press, Guildford, Surrey



Library of Congress Cataloging in Publication Data will be found on the last printed page of this book

Publication of this book has been aided by a grant from the Paul Mellon Fund at Princeton University Press

This book has been composed in VIP Bembo

Clothbound editions of Princeton University Press books are printed on acid-free paper, and binding materials are chosen for strength and durability

Printed in the United States of America by Princeton University Press, Princeton, New Jersey

Designed by Laury A. Egan

FOR

Wendy Doniger O'Flaherty

AND

John Ralston Marr

# CONTENTS

# LIST OF ILLUSTRATIONS


I. Śiva and Pārvatī escape the deluge in a boat. Cīkāḻi. (See II.2 at n. 17.)

II. A cow grieves for its calf, slain by the son of Manunītikaṇṭacoḻan. Tiruvārūr. (See III.2 at nn. 33-34.)

III. The serpent retraces the boundary of Maturai / Ālavāy after the flood. Tañcāvūr, from the *prākāra* wall of the Bṛhadīśvara temple. (See III.3 at nn. 82-91.)

IV. Mahiṣāsuramardinī: Durgā slays the buffalo demon. Tañcāvūr, from the *prākāra* wall of the Bṛhadīśvara temple. (See IV.4 at nn. 1-56.)

V. Ardhanārīśvara: a three-headed androgyne. Tārācuram. (See IV.4-6.)

VI. The Pine Forest: Bhikṣāṭana-Śiva (white with ash) seeks alms together with Viṣṇu as Mohinī. Citamparam, painted ceiling in the Civakāmiyammai shrine. (See IV.9 at nn. 58-95.)


Note: All the illustrations are from the author's private collection.

# ACKNOWLEDGMENTS

THIS STUDY is based on research carried out in England and in India over the years 1972-1976. I am happy to acknowledge the support I received during this period from the British Friends of the Hebrew University of Jerusalem (the Michael and Anna Wix Trust, the Barnett Shine Fellowship, and the John Goodenday Trust). I would like to thank Ms. Charlotte Prince and Dr. Walter Zander from the London office of the Friends of the Hebrew University for their help throughout our stay in England.

A grant from the Central Research Fund of the University of London enabled me to travel to India in search of material unavailable in London.

I wish to record my gratitude to the *devasthānam* authorities in temples all over Tamiḻnāṭu, and to the Tarumapuram Ātīṉam for help in connection with my visits. For much sound advice and kind hospitality, I am grateful to K. Cuppiramaṇiya Aiyar, of the U. Ve. Cāminātaiyar Library in Tiruvāṉmiyūr; V. N. Āṟumukam Mutaliyār; R. Nagaswamy; R. Varadarajan, A. P. Balaiyan, and Pulavarmaṇi Vittuvāṉ Tiru Irattiṉa Tecikar, all of Tiruvārūr; R. Srinivas and Singaram Chettiyar of Kumpakoṇam; Dr. A. Kandiah; and, by no means least, K. V. Rattiṉam Aiyar and family from Nĕppattūr.

Parts of this book have appeared in somewhat altered form in *History of Religions* and the *Journal of Tamil Studies.* For inspiring and illuminating comments on these articles and on an earlier draft of the book, I am grateful to Dr. Tuvia Gelblum, Professors George Hart, Brenda E. F. Beck, and A. M. Piatigorsky, to Dr. Irene Eber, and to Ms. Susie Cohen.

The poem by Dēvara Dāsimayya quoted in Chapter I is reprinted by permission of Penguin Books Ltd. from *Speaking of Śiva*, translated by A. K. Ramanujan (Penguin Classics, 1973), p. 105.

To two people I owe a special debt of gratitude: to Dr. J. R. Marr, who initiated me into the study of Tamil, encouraged me at every step, and shared with me the wealth of his learning, experience, and insights; and to Professor Wendy Doniger O'Flaherty, who not only presented me with copies of the *Mahābhārata* and several Sanskrit purāṇas, but also offered the much greater gift of illuminating these texts with her spirit.

My parents, Herbert and Deana Shulman, first nurtured in me a love of stories; may these pages reflect at least something of the sense of wonder they imparted.

Finally, for a measure of *śāntakalyāṇaguṇa*, for making me say what I mean, and above all for the real gift of her own enthusiasm and love for India, I wish to thank my wife Eileen.

# ABBREVIATIONS

| | |
|---|---|
| *AB* | *Aitareyabrāhmaṇa* |
| *ABORI* | *Annals of the Baroda Oriental Research Institute* |
| *Ait. Ār.* | *Aitareyāraṇyaka* |
| *Akam* | *Akanāṉūṟu* |
| *ALB* | *Adyar Library Bulletin* |
| ASS | Ānandāśrama Sanskrit Series |
| Aṭiyār. | Aṭiyārkkunallār |
| *AV* | *Atharvaveda* |
| *BĀU* | *Bṛhadāraṇyakopaniṣad* |
| *BEFEO* | *Bulletin de l'École française de l'Extrême Orient* |
| Bib. Ind. | Bibliotheca Indica (published by the Asiatic Society of Bengal) |
| *BMGM* | *Bulletin of the Madras Government Museum* |
| *BSOAS* | *Bulletin of the School of Oriental and African Studies* |
| *Cil.* | *Cilappatikāram* |
| *CIS* | *Contributions to Indian Sociology* |
| *CM* | *Cidambaramāhātmya* |
| *CÑP* | *Civañāṉapotam* |
| *CU* | *Chāndogyopaniṣad* |
| *DED* | T. Burrow and M. B. Emeneau, *A Dravidian Etymological Dictionary* |
| *FEQ* | *Far Eastern Quarterly* |
| HOS | Harvard Oriental Series |
| *HR* | *History of Religions* |
| *IA* | *Iṟaiyaṉār akappŏruḷ* (see *Kaḷaviyal*) |
| *IIJ* | *Indo-Iranian Journal* |
| *Ind. An.* | *Indian Antiquary* |
| IO | India Office Library |
| *JA* | *Journal asiatique* |
| *JAOS* | *Journal of the American Oriental Society* |
| *JAS* | *Journal of Asian Studies* |
| *JAU* | *Journal of Annamalai University* |
| *JB* | *Jaiminīyabrāhmaṇa* |
| *JBBRAS* | *Journal of the Bombay Branch of the Royal Asiatic Society* |
| *JIH* | *Journal of Indian History* |
| *JORM* | *Journal of Oriental Research, Madras* |
| *JRAS* | *Journal of the Royal Asiatic Society* |
| *JRASB* | *Journal of the Royal Asiatic Society of Bengal* |

| | |
|---|---|
| *JTS* | *Journal of Tamil Studies* |
| *KB* | *Kauṣītakibrāhmaṇa* |
| *KP* | *Kantapurāṇam* of Kacciyappacivācāriyar |
| *KSS* | *Kathāsaritsāgara* of Somadeva |
| *Kuṟ.* | *Kuṟuntŏkai* |
| *Mai. Saṃ.* | *Maitrāyaṇī saṃhitā* |
| *MBh* | *Mahābhārata* |
| *MBh* (S) | *Mahābhārata*, Southern Recension |
| Nacc. | Nacciṉārkkiṉiyar |
| *Naṟ.* | *Naṟṟiṇai* |
| *Pĕrumpāṇ.* | *Pĕrumpāṇāṟṟuppaṭai* |
| *PICSTS* | *Proceedings of the International Conference Seminar of Tamil Studies* |
| *PP* | *Pĕriyapurāṇam* of Cekkiḻār |
| *Puṟam* | *Puṟanāṉūṟu* |
| *QJMS* | *Quarterly Journal of the Mythic Society* |
| *Rām.* | *Rāmāyaṇa* of Vālmīki |
| *RV* | *Ṛgveda* |
| *ŚB* | *Śatapathabrāhmaṇa* |
| *SII* | *South Indian Inscriptions* |
| SISS | South Indian Śaiva Siddhānta Works Publishing Company |
| Skt. | Sanskrit |
| *ŚRKh* | *Śivarahasyakhaṇḍa* |
| *Tai. Ār.* | *Taittirīyāraṇyaka* |
| Tam. | Tamil |
| *Tāṇḍya* | *Tāṇḍyamahābrāhmaṇa* |
| *TB* | *Taittirīyabrāhmaṇa* |
| *TC* | *Tamil Culture* |
| *Tev.* | *Tevāram* |
| *Tirumuru.* | *Tirumurukāṟṟuppaṭai* |
| *Tiruvāl.* | *Tiruvālavāyuṭaiyār tiruviḷaiyāṭaṟpurāṇam* of Pĕrumpaṟṟappuliyūrnampi |
| *Tiruviḷai.* | *Tiruviḷaiyāṭaṟpurāṇam* of Parañcotimuṉivar |
| *TL* | *Tamil Lexicon* |
| *Tŏl.* | *Tŏlkāppiyam* |
| *TS* | *Taittirīyasaṃhitā* |
| *Vāj. Saṃ.* | *Vājasaneyimādhyandinasaṃhitā* |
| *WZKSO* | *Wiener Zeitschrift zur Kunde des Süd- und Ostasiens* |
| *ZDMG* | *Zeitschrift der Deutschen Morgenländischen Gesellschaft* |

# GLOSSARY

## I. Tamil Terms

*akam*: the inner part; in poetics, the poetry of love
*patikam*: a poem of ten or eleven stanzas, usually in praise of a deity
*pāyiram*: introduction, preface
*puṟam*: the outer part (opposed to *akam*); in poetics, the poetry of heroism and war
*talapurāṇam*: the traditions of a sacred site; *see* sthalapurāṇa
*veḷāḷa*: a non-Brahmin agricultural caste in Tamiḻnāṭu

## II. Sanskrit Terms

*adharma*: disorder; unrighteousness
*amṛta*: the nectar of the gods; the drink of immortality
*apsaras*: a celestial maiden
*ardhanārī*: the androgyne
*āśrama*: a retreat, the dwelling place of a sage in the wilderness; also, one of the four conventional stages in the life of a Brahmin (student, householder, forest-dweller, renouncer)
*asura*: a demon; an enemy of the gods
*aśvamedha*: the horse-sacrifice
*avatāra*: an incarnation (literally "descent") of God on earth
*bhakti*: devotion; love
*bhūta*: a ghost or spirit
*brahmacārin*: a celibate; a student (in the first of the four *āśramas*)
*brahmarākṣasa*: a high class of demons; a Brahmin *rākṣasa*
Brahmin: a priest; a member of the first of the four social classes
*deva*: a god
*dharma*: order (the proper order of the universe); also, the proper conduct demanded of the individual as a member of a social category; righteousness
*dīkṣita*: one who has been consecrated in preparation for ritual performance (e.g., a sacrifice)
*gandharva*: a celestial musician
*gopura*: the gateway into a shrine; often a tall tower set over the entrance
*kāpālika*: Śiva as the bearer of a skull (*kapāla*); a worshiper of Śiva who carries a skull

*karma*: action; by extension, the law by which one's actions determine one's fate

*liṅga*: the phallus; the symbol of Siva

*maṇḍapa*: a porch or pavilion

*mantra*: a sacred utterance

*māyā*: the divine power to create; magic; deception, fraud; illusion, especially the illusory appearance of the phenomenal world

*mūlasthāna*: the original or primary shrine in a temple

*muni*: a sage; an ascetic

*pañcākṣara*: the "five syllables"; the *mantra* sacred to worshipers of Śiva, i.e., *namaḥ śivāya*, "homage to Śiva"

*pāśupata*: a worshiper of Śiva in his form as Paśupati, "lord of beasts"

*prākāra*: the wall surrounding a shrine or temple complex

*pralaya*: the dissolution of the universe; the cosmic flood

*pratiṣṭhā*: stability; the firm basis of creation

*purāṇa*: literally "old, ancient story"; a text in which myths and other traditions are preserved

*purohita*: a domestic priest

*rākṣasa*: an evil demon; a goblin

Śaiva: pertaining to Śiva or the worship of Śiva; a devotee of Śiva

*śakti*: power; the goddess as a source of power

*samādhi*: a state attained through deep meditation

Soma: the elixir of immortality

*śrāddha*: a ceremony in honor of the dead

*svadharma*: conduct prescribed for the individual as a member of society

*svayaṃvara*: a bridegroom test; a ceremony at which a young woman chooses her husband

*sthalapurāṇa*: the traditions of a sacred site; the *purāṇa* of a shrine

*tapas*: literally "heat"; austerities; penance

*tīrtha*: a sacred site or shrine; originally, a ford or bathing place

*tulasī*: holy basil, sacred to Viṣṇu

*vāhana*: a divine vehicle

Vaiṣṇava: pertaining to Viṣṇu or to the worship of Viṣṇu; a devotee of Viṣṇu

*vimāna*: an aerial chariot; a temple structure

*yakṣa* (fem. *yakṣī, yakṣiṇī*): a class of semidivine beings; a nature spirit

*yogī* (fem. *yoginī*): a practitioner of yoga

*yoni*: the vulva or the womb

# Tamil Temple Myths

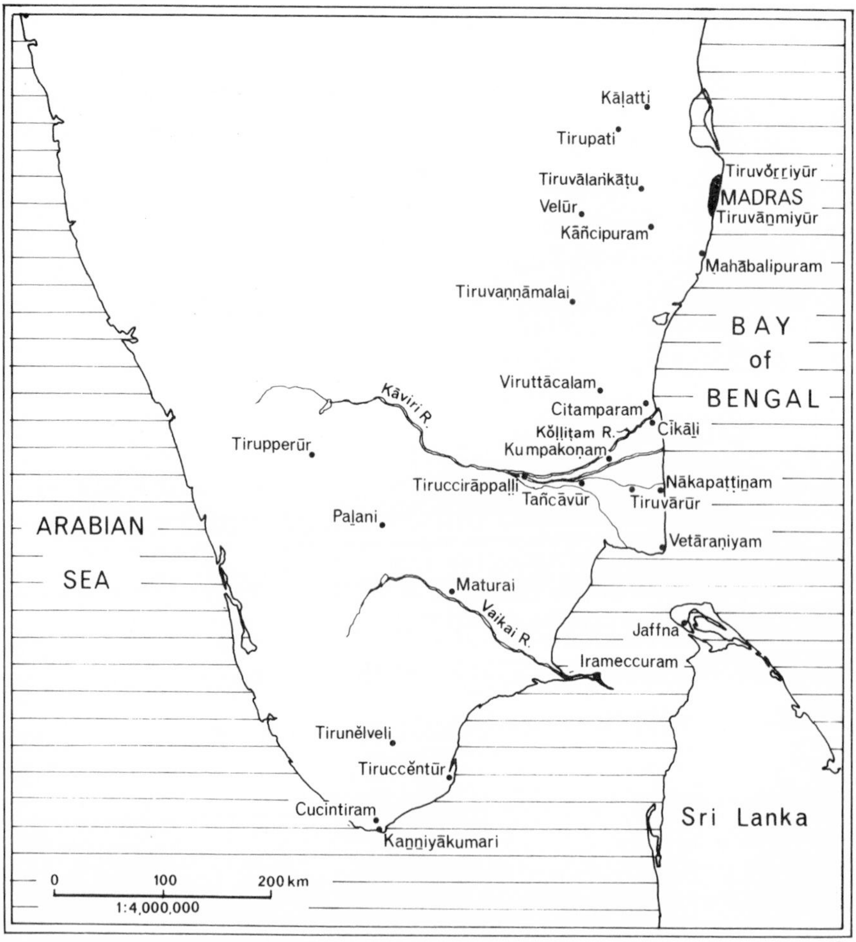


Tamiḻnāṭu, Major Shrines

CHAPTER I

# Introduction

On this earth circled by the sea,
is there another land ruled by
the three great gods?
The heaven of the gods is here.[1]

## 1. Tamil Mythology and the Indian Tradition

From earliest times, India has given form to many of its most vital ideas through the medium of myth. The labyrinthine world of Hindu mythology has always been known to us principally from classical texts in Sanskrit—the Vedas, the Brāhmaṇas, the two epics, and the major purāṇas. It is in the works of this last category, the purāṇas (the name means "old," "ancient story"), that Hindu myths have crystallized in their classical forms. Yet within this vast world there exist, and no doubt have for long existed, individual traditions of mythology proper to the various historic centers of Indian civilization. One of the most extensive of such traditions is that of the Tamil region (Tamiḻnāṭu) in southern India. This area is the home of an ancient culture revealed to us by a large corpus of Tamil literary texts dating back to the first centuries of this era; these poetic texts—known as "Caṅkam" literature, since they are said by legend to have been submitted to an "academy," Caṅkam, of poets in the city of Maturai—were clearly produced by a flourishing south Indian civilization with its own distinctive character and world view.[2] Tamiḻnāṭu is also the birthplace of two powerful devotional movements, connected with the worship of the gods Śiva and Viṣṇu, which, from approximately the seventh century onwards, left an enduring imprint on Hindu culture generally. The Tamils have thus made a major contribution to Indian civilization; yet many aspects of this contribution are still largely unknown. This study is intended to fill an important gap in our knowledge of south India—for Tamiḻnāṭu has recorded a local tradition of mythology extraordinary in its variety and imaginative range, and differing in many respects from the classical northern tradition. These Tamil myths provide us with a regional variant of Hindu mythology of peculiar interest and importance, not least because of the long tradition of continuous cultural activity in this region. Despite the enormous extent and the intrinsic importance of this Tamil literature of myth, it has so far been virtually ignored by Western scholars.

The following pages are an attempt to explore some major themes of this literature. One outstanding feature must be mentioned at once: the Tamil myths were written down in texts attached to individual shrines in the Tamil land. Tamiḻnāṭu is graced by hundreds of such shrines, some of them very old, most of them popular sites of pilgrimage. Nearly all such shrines have produced one or more works in which their traditions have been given poetic form. These works are known in Sanskrit as *māhātmyas* ("majesty," "greatness") or *sthalapurāṇas* ("ancient stories of a sacred site"); in Tamil they are generally referred to as *talapurāṇam*.[3] Every work of this class records the traditions that have grown up around a shrine and its locale, and that are used to explain and to sustain the shrine's claim to sanctity. Taken together, these texts, whether composed in Sanskrit, Tamil, or in rare cases Telugu, embody a rich tradition of mythology unique to the Tamil area.

The Tamil myths are, nevertheless, a part of the wider world of Hindu mythology; however different their orientation, however local their concerns, they are by no means independent of the classical Sanskritic tradition. On the contrary, they have taken many of the most famous northern myths (and at least as many of the lesser-known stories as well) and adapted them to their own purposes, often transforming them considerably in the process. The Tamil myths share a common pantheon with the classical Sanskrit purāṇas and with other regional literatures—although purely local, Tamil figures, such as Vaḷḷi, the beloved second wife of Murukaṉ, do exist. Clearly, the Tamil tradition is complex and multilayered. Northern and indigenous elements have merged in the tradition of every major Tamil shrine. The deity of each shrine will have both a local name and mythological history, and an entire complex of names, attributes, and myths derived from the northern, classical deity with whom he is identified. For example, Śiva at Maturai is known as Sundareśvara, "the beautiful lord" (Tamil Cŏkkaliṅkam or Cŏkkecar); his bride there is Mīnākṣī, "the fish-eyed" (Tamil Mīṉāṭciyammaṉ). The myths told about Sundareśvara and Mīnākṣī are replete with local elements, some of which no doubt have prehistoric roots; the stories all take place in Maturai and the surrounding region. Yet Sundareśvara is clearly identified with Śiva, and Mīnākṣī with Pārvatī, Śiva's consort in the classical purāṇas; both deities are often described in terms directly borrowed from the northern tradition. This situation is typical of the shrines we will study; the tradition of each sacred spot has developed through the fusion of local and imported elements. This is, in fact, an ancient process in this area. Already in the "Caṅkam" anthologies of bardic poetry, *Ĕṭṭuttŏkai* and *Pattuppāṭṭu*, the assimilation of northern, Sanskritic elements by the Tamil tradition is readily apparent; it is yet more pronounced in the early Tamil epic, the *Cilappatikāram* (fifth-sixth centuries A.D.?), and by the time of the devotional movements, it has come to provide the very structure within which the mainstream of local myth and legend is subsumed. The Tamil local purāṇas are thus a subcategory of the purāṇic literature generally, as incorporated in the Sanskrit "great" purāṇas (the so-called *mahāpurāṇas*),[4] and a seemingly endless series of related works; our task is to delineate the characteristic features of this distinct, fairly homogeneous south Indian variant of Hindu myth.

The boundaries of the regional tradition with which we are concerned may be defined as the area of Tamil speech. Tamiḻnāṭu is the home of the oldest articulate culture in south India, and the degree of cultural continuity in this region is one of south India's most outstanding features. No other Dravidian language can claim so long and uninterrupted a tradition. Nevertheless, medieval Tamil culture shares much with neighboring cultures expressed in other Dravidian languages. We must, therefore, distinguish between the specifically Tamil and the generally south Indian. For example, the goddess Mīnākṣī is firmly rooted in the Tamil tradition of Maturai, while the Vaiṣṇava saint Āṇṭāḷ (Godā) is common to both Tamil and Telugu sources.[5] Often a pattern will be general throughout south India, while its individual expressions will be specifically located: thus the idea that a deity must have a second, local bride is very widespread in the south; but the Tamil myths of Vaḷḷi, the second wife of Murukaṉ mentioned above, are fully intelligible only against the background of early Tamil literary conventions. On the level of village religion, there is an impressive similarity of practice and concepts over a wide area of south India;[6] as we shall see, village cults often seem to preserve features known from the oldest layer of Tamil civilization.

The basic texts for this study have thus been recorded within the present boundaries of Tamil speech, although other south Indian myths have sometimes been cited in support of an argument or for purposes of comparison, and classical northern mythology is always present as a factor in our discussion. The Tamil myths themselves often emphasize the importance of the Tamil language, and in this connection they mention the Vedic sage Agastya, who is believed to have come from the north to reside on the Pŏtiyil Mountain near the southern tip of the subcontinent.[7] The Agastya legend is in essence an origin myth explaining the beginnings of Tamil culture: according to a widespread tradition first found in the commentary ascribed to Nakkīrar on an early work of rhetoric, the *Iṟaiyaṉār akappŏruḷ*, Agastya was the author of the first Tamil grammar.[8] This assertion is made in the context of the Caṅkam legend mentioned earlier, which describes the composition of the earliest Tamil poetry; this legend is firmly attached to Maturai, one of the historic centers of Tamil culture, and has a prominent place in the Maturai purāṇas. We will return to the Caṅkam story in connection with the Tamil flood myths, for the "academy" of poets situated in ancient times in present-day Maturai is said to have been the last of a series of three; the first two "academies" were located in cities swallowed up by the sea. Agastya is connected by the legend with the first two Caṅkam. The gods Śiva, Murukaṉ, and Kubera are said to have been members of the first Caṅkam, and Śiva and Murukaṉ appear again in popular myths about the third Caṅkam, in Maturai.[9] The entire cycle, with its depiction of the gods as Tamil poets, may be seen as an expression of love for Tamil and belief in its divine nature.[10] But it is difficult to estimate the age of the legend, or even of that part of it connected with Agastya's southward migration; the Sanskrit epics are already familiar with the sage's journey to the south, including his exploits of stunting the growth of the Vindhya Mountains and destroying the demon Vātāpi (eponymous with the town of Vātāpi/Bādāmi in the western Deccan).[11] For our purposes, it is essential to realize that in its myth of cultural origins the Tamil tradition has fastened on a Vedic seer explicitly said to have come from the north. In other words, the tradition clearly sees itself as derived in the first instance from a northern source. This orientation toward the north as a source of inspiration and prestige is quite characteristic of Tamil culture in its development after the "Caṅkam" period, that is, after the process of fusing local and imported elements had reached an advanced stage and a rich, composite tradition had emerged. The myths of Agastya offer us a vantage point from which to consider this process; they also demonstrate the understanding the Tamils had of their own cultural history. Let us look, for example, at one later

Tamil myth that explores Agastya's association with both Tamil and Sanskrit:

> Nārada asked the sages who were gathered to the southwest of Śivagiri: "Who among you is best? Who has performed austerities in the Vedic Śaiva path? Who has attained the truth and gained the grace of Śiva? Such a one is equal to the godhead (*civam*), and him I praise. Now let me have freedom from rebirth." So saying, he disappeared and reached heaven. The sages agreed that Agastya fitted the description and merited the blessing of Nārada, but at this Vyāsa became angry: "What have you said? You must be speaking only out of politeness (*mukamaṉ urai*). Your praises should go to Sarasvatī (*kalaivāṇiyaṉṉai*); she will grant release (*vīṭu*)." Said Agastya: "Did not Śiva (and not Sarasvatī) collect the Vedas and other arts (*kalai*)?" Vyāsa retorted, "You too once acquired a good knowledge of those Sanskrit works (*vaṭa nūl*) sung by me. Is there anything else (of which you can be proud)?" At this Agastya fell silent and left the sages, who were now greatly perplexed as to which of the two was greater—Agastya, who was a form of Śiva, or Vyāsa, a form of Viṣṇu.
>
> Agastya worshiped Śiva until the god appeared and taught him a sacred *mantra*, saying, "This is sweet Tamil. Murukaṉ will teach it all to you without leaving anything out. First worship for one year in the *āśramas* of Ādikeśava and Parāśara, and then return to Śivagiri." Agastya followed this command; Murukaṉ instructed him in the Tamil syllabary and the other parts of grammar, then disappeared into his shrine.
>
> When Agastya returned to the sages, he was welcomed by Vyāsa and the rest: "You have brought mountains here so that the south will flourish,[12] and you have enabled all to taste the divine drink of Tamil." Agastya put Tamil grammar in the form of aphorisms for the benefit of the land between Vaṭaveṅkaṭam and Tĕṉkumari, and he expounded his book to his twelve disciples.[13]

The boundaries mentioned are the traditional northern and southern borders of the Tamil land: Vaṭaveṅkaṭam is Tirupati, the site of a major shrine to Viṣṇu-Veṅkaṭeśvara, whose myths are studied below; Tĕṉkumari is invariably glossed by the commentators as referring to a river, apparently far to the south of the present Kaṉṉiyākumari (Cape Comorin) at the limit of a territory that was later swallowed up by the sea.[14] Agastya, the champion of Tamil, is honored by the sages, and even his rival, Vyāsa, acknowledges his superiority in the end; but it should be noted that the sage learns Tamil only after being sent to the *āśrama* of Parāśara, Vyāsa's father. Vyāsa, the master of Sanskrit learning, insists on the preeminence of the goddess of learning, Sarasvatī; but Vyāsa is himself seen as an incarnation of Viṣṇu,[15] and the Śaiva author of our text must therefore see him defeated by Agastya, here regarded as a form of Śiva. Other Tamil myths also make Agastya a hero of militant Śaivism as well as the author of Tamil grammar.[16] Yet the image of Agastya in the above myth is a complex one. Agastya's greatness appears to lie in his command of *both* traditions: he is well trained in the Sanskrit works of Vyāsa, and he learns the science of Tamil from the god who is master and examiner of Tamil, Murukaṉ.[17] Agastya is thus a symbol of Tamil learning, not as independent from or opposed to Sanskrit, but rather in harmony and conjunction with it. This cultural merger represented by the Vedic sage who teaches Tamil is perfectly apparent in the Tamil purāṇic literature, in which Sanskrit myths, motifs, and deities are the carriers of a *local*, south Indian tradition with its own characteristic ideas and concerns.

How was a unified tradition created out of these different elements? The process was undoubtedly lengthy and complex. On the one hand, the classical culture of the "Caṅkam" period certainly did not disappear without trace; many ancient cultural traits have survived, notably in village rituals, folk poetry, popular tales, and so on. I will return to this point below. On the other hand, a major contribution to the formation of Tamil culture was undoubtedly made by the Brahmins, who became the custodians, and in some cases the creators, of the traditions of Tamil shrines. Many Tamil purāṇas describe the migration of a group of Brahmin priests from some site in the north to the Tamil shrine, and it is certain that such migrations were an important historical force extending over many centuries. Brahmins were often settled on lands by royal grants, for the king could gain a much-needed form of legitimization by such a gift to the Brahmins.[18] Those Brahmins who became attached to local holy places brought with them their own traditions, which were part of the wider Brahminical culture; but they were also influenced by local factors, the most powerful of which could become central to the cult in its final, Brahminized form. In those literary sources that were either written by Brahmins or composed under significant Brahmin influence—and all Tamil *sthalapurāṇas* fall into this category—a standard, all-Indian framework could be made to absorb local themes. Here, as in other areas, we glimpse the unifying, synthesizing, fertilizing force that Brahminism has represented in the history of Tamil̲nāṭu. It is largely this force that allows us to speak of a single, distinctive system of Tamil mythology incorporated in literary texts composed over a period of some one thousand years.[19]

Let us take a closer look at this phenomenon. It is by no means enough to divide the composite tradition with which we are dealing into northern and southern branches that have merged in the course of the crystallization of the cult. We must also notice the existence of internal processes of change accompanying the process of assimilation. Change has occurred both within individual elements of the tradition and within the mature tradition as a whole. One of the major themes of this study illustrates the complexity of the problems that confront us in this area: it appears that an early ideology of sacrifice, which strongly recalls and was perhaps assimilated to the Vedic sacrificial cult, lies at the basis of the tradition of many shrines. In Chapter III we will explore the symbols that convey this idea, especially in relation to the main god, whose blood first reveals the shrine. Perhaps from very ancient times the idea of sacrifice was associated with the worship of the goddess, who is closely identified with the sacrifice as the source both of death and of new life, and who embodies basic south Indian concepts of woman and sacred power. The marriage myths we find in nearly every shrine clearly demonstrate this connection between sacrifice and love; they are discussed at length in Chapter IV. But the marriage myths also show us a second stage in the elaboration of the cult, a stage in which the myth of sacrifice has been radically reworked so as to exclude the participation of the main god, the consort of the goddess. In the concluding chapter we will study the implications of this development for the orientation of Tamil Śaivism in its most recent form. The evolution I will seek to establish is in the direction of a deity ever more removed from the realm of death and rebirth, specifically from the violent death and restoration of the sacrifice: the god becomes *nirmala*, without taint. In order to do so, however, he must first transcend his own mythology; for, as we shall see, the symbols that recur in the myths leave little doubt that the god himself enacts the sacrifice.

We will be concerned in the following chapters with the mechanics and the meaning of this evolution. For the moment let us note two relevant explanations of the trend away from violence. The process of Brahmin accommodation to ancient Tamil religion has been described by George Hart in the following terms:

> "It must be remembered that, to the ancient Tamils, sacred forces were dangerous accretions of power that could be controlled only by those of low status. When the Brahmins arrived in Tamilnad, it was natural for them to dissociate themselves from these indigenous forces and to characterize themselves as 'pure,' that is, isolated to the greatest possible extent from polluting sacred forces; indeed, if they were to gain the people's respect, they had very little choice. It was also natural for the Brahmins to characterize the gods they introduced as pure and unsullied by pollution. . . . It follows that the Brahmins had to adopt from the high-caste non-Brahmins many of the customs whose purpose was to isolate a person from dangerous sacred power."[20]

The idea that the sacred is dangerous and potentially polluting is undoubtedly ancient in the Tamil area, and there is every reason to believe that the Brahmins who settled there came to terms with this idea in a manner that guaranteed their own claim to purity. But it is noteworthy that within the Vedic sacrificial cult itself we find an evolution away from contact with the dangerous forces of violence and death that are at work in the sacrifice. This development has been described by Heesterman[21] in terms of the emergence of the *prāṇāgnihotra*, the "sacrifice of the breaths," as a substitute for the original blood-sacrifice: by a studied system of symbolic equivalences, the arena of the sacrifice is transferred from the sacrificial pit to the mind of the Brahmin "who knows thus," and who offers up his own breaths (*prāṇa*) in place of the original victim. The entire ritual is internalized, with the result that the actual slaughter of a victim is eliminated. Death and destruction are relegated to the chaotic world outside the individual performer of the ritual (just as they are made to rest beyond the confines of the sacred shrine in the Tamil myths). In other words, within the Brahmin tradition itself there was a powerful impetus toward freedom from the burden of death, which was an unavoidable part of the sacrificial ritual in its early form. It is this transformed tradition that was imported into south India, and that both crystallized and ultimately reinterpreted a local myth of violent sacrifice. Yet we shall see in the following pages how vital and enduring the underlying myth has always been, and how quickly the religious ideology superimposed upon it crumbles before the inherent force of the ancient symbols.

## *Note on Method*

In view of the complex nature of the tradition being studied, I have adopted a somewhat complex approach to my sources. I have, to begin with, attempted to understand the myths as they are today, or as they might be understood by the millions who regard them as living truths about their god. This is, in itself, a difficult task. But a comparison of the myths of many shrines revealed a number of recurrent patterns and symbols, which seemed to express ideas at variance with the declared themes of the authors. I have brought these patterns together and interpreted them with the help of all the sources available to me. Myth is by nature a conservative medium; symbolic images survive in late versions, where they may be given a completely new role or left incongruously opposed to the new context.[22] How, then, is one to know which elements are more archaic than others? In our case there is, first of all, the aid offered by classical sources in Tamil (such as the bardic anthologies and the two epics, the *Cilappatikāram* and *Maṇimekalai*), which tell us a good deal about the ancient religion of the Tamils. As I have stated, some features of the classical culture seem to have survived in village cults in the Tamil area; the villages often seem to have preserved a direct link to the ancient past, and village myths often shed light on the underlying themes of Tamil purāṇic myths. We will see a number of examples of this phenomenon. To name but a few in advance of their discussion: there is the village cult of blood-sacrifice, which explains many persistent features of the purāṇic myths of Mahiṣāsura (the idea of the transfer of power, the role of the buffalo, and so on); the transvestite worship of the goddess, which helps us to understand the purāṇic myths of sex reversal; the village cults of demon-worship, which are akin in some ways to the purāṇic myths of the demon-devotee; the identification in folk myths of Mīnākṣī, the goddess of Maturai, with Kaṇṇaki, the heroine of the *Cilappatikāram*, and of the god of Maturai with the serpent. These and other examples of the link between folk tradition and Brahminized myths will be studied at length below. There exist a number of useful descriptions of south Indian village religion;[23] in addition, much of the folk mythology of the Tamil region was written down in the form of folk epics or ballads during the eighteenth and nineteenth centuries. Almost all of these compositions are clearly oral in origin, like the oral epic recorded by Brenda Beck in the Coimbatore region;[24] other such oral narratives are still in circulation. The rich mythology of the Tamil folk epic deserves a separate study; I have cited the sources that exist today in print when they are relevant to our discussion. I have also included a number of oral myths collected during a period of research in Tamilnāṭu; like the folk epics, these oral traditions often appear to have preserved archaic features with more fidelity than the Brahminized literary texts.

In order to avoid the dangers of tautology and circular reasoning, the village myths must, of course, be used with some care. Not all elements of the folk tradition are necessarily "archaic." Although the oral transmission of south Indian mythology was basically a conservative process, the folk tradition was by no means independent of purāṇic sources or of the processes of change within the Tamil Śaiva tradition generally. One prominent example of purāṇic influence on folk mythology—in the Maturai myths of Mīnākṣī and the Pāṇṭiya king—is discussed below. Clearly, the village traditions are most helpful when they support a conclusion already postulated on the basis of the internal evidence of the purāṇas—in other words, when an underlying theme related to a folk theme emerges from the literary texts *despite* obvious attempts to obscure it. The folk sources cited in the following pages do, in fact, support the existence of an underlying layer of Tamil myth that has been hidden under later attempts to isolate the deity from impurity.

We may also seek help from literary sources produced after the "Caṅkam" period—both the medieval "epi-purāṇic" literature of poems sung in praise of local deities and their shrines, a literature more or less contemporaneous with the Tamil purāṇas themselves;[25] and, more important, the earlier classics of the Śaiva tradition, especially the *Tevāram* hymns. The *Tevāram* constitutes the first seven books of the Tamil Śaiva canon; it consists of poems sung, according to the tradition, by the three early saints of Śiva, Tiruñāṉacampantar, Appar (both probably of the seventh century), and Cuntaramūrtti (ninth century?). Like the Tamil myths, the *Tevāram* poems are associated with individual shrines.[26] As the Śaiva tradition itself recognized,[27] the textual tradition of the hymns is not always reliable; nevertheless, the *Tevāram* poems of any given shrine usually reveal the local cult in a mature form, with the names and in many cases the major myths of the local deities already established. The poets often allude to prominent features of the local cult, and in this way they sometimes offer clues to the original basis of the local myths.

Many elements of Tamil mythology have close analogues in the Tamil hagiographic tradition. The lives of the sixty-three Śaiva saints (*nāyaṉmār*) were codified in the twelfth century by Cekkiḻār in the *Tiruttŏṇṭarpurāṇam*, usually known as the *Pĕriyapurāṇam* (the twelfth book of the Śaiva canon). At many points these hagiographies are important aids to our understanding of Tamil myths: an outstanding example is the story of Kāraikkālammaiyār, which is in effect a hagiographic variant of the myth of Nīli, the ancient goddess of Tiruvālaṅkāṭu.[28]

I must also mention here one of the best-loved of all Tamil literary works, Kampaṉ's Tamil adaptation of the *Rāmāyaṇa*, the *Irāmāvatāram*.[29] The Tamil cultural achievement, and the decisive themes and problems of Tamil devotional religion, receive perhaps their finest expression in Kampaṉ's verses. I have referred often to Kampaṉ in the course of this study, and in Chapter V an attempt is made to interpret in some detail Kampaṉ's version of an important myth of a demon-devotee.

In the end, however, all the above are no more than auxiliary sources, and one must rely above all upon the internal evidence of the purāṇic texts. The principles that have guided my analysis may be simply stated. When the evident force of a symbol appears to conflict with the interpretation offered by our source, we may suspect that a historical change has taken place. For example, the constantly recurring theme of the wounding of the deity[30] is never, to my knowledge, explicitly related by the Tamil purāṇas to the god's death in sacrifice; it is, in fact, never really explained at all, except as a common sign of the divine presence in a site. Nevertheless, when seen together with its related motifs, this theme can hardly be separated from the ancient concept of sacrifice. The myth most closely linked with the theme of wounding the deity is that of Śiva's marriage to the local goddess; as I will attempt to demonstrate, this union is characterized by the god's violent death and rebirth. Yet such is not the standard understanding of the divine marriage in the purāṇic texts, which usually describe Śiva's marriage in very different terms, as a harmonious union with a meek, submissive bride. The violent aspects of the marriage have been projected on to the battle between the goddess and her demon enemies. This conclusion is not simply a case of imaginative interpretation: it must be stressed that the *texts themselves* preserve traces of the identification of Śiva with the demon-victim. I have operated on the working assumption that even late texts retain evidence of earlier stages in the development of the tradition, and that such earlier stages, even when obscured by a later ideology, proclaim their existence through apparent anomalies in the narration. It is, on the whole, better to assume that all elements in the myths are meaningful and can sustain interpretation than to believe that chance alone has produced such anomalies—let us at least assume that our texts have meaning! In studying these myths, I have thus tried to isolate those symbols that stubbornly persist despite their apparent incongruity or inconsistency with the general tenor of the myths; I have then attempted to discover whether these symbols are related to one another in a coherent manner, and whether they point to the existence of an earlier level of meaning than that suggested by the explicit statements of the texts. As will become clear, the Tamil authors are, in fact, particularly fond of rationalizing older, inherited patterns whose original force is still quite evident from the mythic images used by the narrative.

Another element in the analysis is important here. I have already noted that many Tamil myths are reworkings of classical Sanskrit myths. For example, the marriage myths that are so prominent in the Tamil tradition are directly related, in their present format, to the Sanskrit myths of Śiva's marriages (to Pārvatī and Satī / Umā). But the import of the Tamil myths is, in general, very different from that of the Sanskrit models. Here local south Indian ideas have been absorbed within the framework of Sanskritic myths of the divine marriage. Clearly, it is necessary to define the changes made by the Tamil versions in their inheritance, especially since such changes often coincide with the anomalies and inconsistencies mentioned above. Thus when the Tamil myths declare Mahiṣāsura to be a devotee of Śiva who offers a *liṅga* to the goddess,[31] we must note (a) the discrepancy between this description and the standard Sanskrit accounts of Mahiṣāsura, and (b) the unusual relationship—a symbolic marriage—between the demon and the goddess, who subsequently marries Śiva at a local shrine. Both of these elements are part of a basic, hidden pattern of myth.

Such a pattern becomes readily apparent from a comparison of the myths of many shrines. No single shrine offers a complete picture of the major elements and concerns of Tamil mythology; it is only by comparing the many variants of a myth that we can arrive at an understanding of the true importance of the motifs and the underlying conceptions that they convey. When we find the same elements recurring consistently, albeit in varying forms, in the traditions of many shrines, we approach a definition of the basic components of Tamil mythology. I have therefore surveyed a fairly wide sample of the literature and have avoided concentrating too heavily on the traditions of any one spot.

Although I have always tried to find a "primary" literary source for each myth—that is, a narration of the myth in verse, in either Sanskrit or Tamil—I have not hesitated to rely on other sources as well, such as prose retellings, commentaries, popular devotional hymns, and folk sources. In fact, the distinction between "primary" and "secondary" is in this case largely irrelevant, since even the verse originals of the Tamil purāṇas are nearly always derivative: the myths antedate the written versions, often by many centuries. As I have already hinted, the literary sources of Tamil mythology have always existed alongside, and indeed been nourished by, an unbroken oral tradition. Local traditions handed down by word of mouth have been recorded in different periods in various forms. Today, for example, the poetic texts of the purāṇas are no longer available in most shrines; their place has been taken by a popular literature (in prose) of pilgrims' handbooks, in which the main myths and rituals attached to the shrine are summarized. These works, which are usually produced by the temple authorities (the *devasthānam*) in limited editions run off local printing presses, embody an essentially oral tradition, although in some cases they have merely summarized or abridged the *sthalapurāṇa*. I have used these pamphlets to supplement the information of the purāṇas; in a few cases, when I was unable to obtain a copy of the original purāṇa, I have cited these prose versions instead. I have also recorded a number of oral myths from Tamil shrines. The fact that many of the myths cited below were written down only in the fairly recent past says little about the date of their origins. Moreover, many would argue today that any version of a myth, however late, deserves consideration as evidence of the living power of the myth and its meaning for the narrator.

In the interests of economy, I have for the most part summarized myths instead of translating them. Extensive translations would have meant a work several times the length of the present study.[32]

For the same reason, versions extracted from modern, secondary sources have been summarized, and have been printed as extracts. Direct quotations from secondary sources will be in quotation marks. In reducing the prolix narratives of the purāṇas to more manageable size, I have at times had to omit whole episodes as well as material extraneous to the plot (such as hymns of praise, allegorical interpretations, lists of ritual rewards to be gained from worship at a shrine, and so on); but I have always striven to record the essential elements of each myth as accurately as possible. I have, however, introduced one major change for the benefit of the non-Tamilist: I have replaced the Tamil names for the gods with their standardized Sanskrit equivalents (for example, Śiva for Civaṉ, Viṣṇu for Tirumāl, and so on) in the case of figures drawn from the common stock of Hindu myth. Names that are unique to Tamil mythology, and place names generally, have been retained in their Tamil form.[33]

In referring to the Sanskrit epics and the *mahāpurāṇas*, I have used the recent "critical" editions, relying not only on the text in its "reconstituted" form, but on the possibilities made available by the apparatus. Thus in citing these texts, I often refer to lines or verses deleted by the editors. For the *Mahābhārata*, however, I have usually studied the text of the Southern Recension before referring to the Poona edition, and in some cases Southern Recension is cited in addition to the Poona text. The major exception to the practice outlined above is my use of a more traditional text of the *Harivaṃśa*; here, one feels, the "critical" edition has gone too far in excising essential material from the text. No truly critical editions exist of any of the Tamil purāṇas or of the related folk sources mentioned earlier.[34]

Throughout this study I have concentrated on explaining the myths in their Indian context. Many parallels to these myths exist in the mythologies of other peoples, but I have felt that it is important first to understand the tradition within its own terms. Those who might wish to explore structural or thematic comparisons with the myths of other cultures, or who bring to the study of myth the particular biases of their own disciplines, will, it is hoped, be able to make use of the summaries of the Tamil sources. But I must confess to having followed my own interests and instincts in exploring the uncharted world of the Tamil purāṇas. I have not hesitated to pursue those themes that appeared to me to be of crucial importance for understanding Tamil culture. For the following chapters are an attempt not only to describe but also to interpret the Tamil myths in the light of what appears to be their major concerns; and no doubt in the study of myth, as in the writing of history, the very act of selection implies the existence of a personal interpretation.

## 2. The Ritual of Pilgrimage

Since the major sources of Tamil mythology are so closely tied to local shrines, the Tamil myths are naturally associated with temple worship and, in particular, with the ritual of pilgrimage (*tīrthayātrā*). It may, therefore, be helpful to take a preliminary look at this phenomenon in its classic south Indian form before turning to the myths themselves. The Tamil land is crowded with sacred sites, which are regularly visited by thousands of devotees; each Tamil *talapurāṇam* seeks to justify pilgrimage to the particular shrine to which it is attached. This is a pilgrim's literature, produced for the benefit of worshipers in living centers of pilgrimage, often by pilgrim-poets.[1] The first extensive examples of this kind of literature are found in the *tīrthayātrāparvan* of the *Mahābhārata*, where localized myths are cited to glorify individual shrines.[2] By the time of the Tamil *talapurāṇam*, we find a standard literary form in which the pilgrim is offered essential information about the shrine to which he has come.

What does the pilgrim need to know? Above all, he is concerned with the specific powers and individual features that have given the site its sacred character. The purāṇa composed at this spot will therefore provide him with the traditional history of the shrine, including its (usually miraculous) discovery and the adventures of those important exemplars (such as gods, demons, serpents, and men) who were freed from sorrow of one kind or another by worshiping there. Basic elements of the sacred topography will be identified, and subsidiary shrines may be brought into relation with the main deity of the site. Any local idiosyncrasies in ritual or in the structure of the cult (for example, the Monday fast at Maturai, the forty-day women's vow at Cucīntiram, the exact plan of festivals in many shrines) will be explained by a myth. The purāṇa will also offer lists of the ritual benefits to be gained from worship at the shrine. In most cases these are fairly standard: the site frees one from evil of various sorts, from ignorance, disease, the consequences of one's misdeeds, and so on. Occasionally a shrine will establish a reputation as "specializing" in the treatment of a particular sort of evil: thus Vaittīcuvaraṉkoyil, for example, is renowned as the site where Vaidyanātha-Śiva, "the lord who is a physician," cures his devotees of all diseases.

Nearly always the "home" shrine, the subject of the purāṇa, is glorified at the expense of all others; each shrine claims to be the site of creation, the center of the universe, and the one spot where salvation is most readily obtainable. Many stories illustrate these claims of superiority: for example, we are often told that the Ganges itself is forced to worship in a south Indian shrine in order to become free of the sins deposited by evildoers who bathe in the river at Kāśī (Benares).[3] A man who was bringing the bones of his father to Benares for cremation stopped at Tiruvaiyāṟu for the night; in the morning he discovered that the bones had grown together into the shape of a *liṅga*. When he set off again for Benares, they were separated again—and thus he realized the greater sanctity of Tiruvaiyāṟu.[4] The shrines of the Tamil land define themselves in contrast to (or in imitation of) famous shrines of the north: thus we have a Tĕṉkāci, a Dakṣiṇaprayāga (Tirukkūṭalaiyāṟṟūr), a Dakṣiṇadvārakā (Maṉṉarkuṭi), a Dakṣiṇamānasā (at Vetāraṇiyam), several Dakṣiṇakailāsas, etc. These claims are typical of a pilgrim's literature.[5] They might also be seen as the pilgrim's equivalent of what has been termed "henotheism," that is, the worship, in the context of a plurality of acknowledged gods, of each god *in turn* as supreme.[6] The denigration of other gods/shrines is the simple corollary of praising the momentary favorite; the same principle operates in relation to the praise (*praśasti*) offered to kings, patrons, and gurus.

What is the pilgrim's experience in this land of temples? There is often, to begin with, the long, uncomfortable journey to the shrine, which may be defined as a form of asceticism, *tapas*.[7] The journey is, however, only the prelude to a deeper sense of self-sacrifice. Once the pilgrim arrives at the shrine, he sees before him the towering *gopuras* or gates set in the walls that enclose the sacred area. He leaves his shoes outside the gate; he will also usually undergo an initial purification by bathing, which prepares him for contact with the powerful forces inside.[8] Once the pilgrim is through the *gopura*, the real journey begins. This is a journey into the self, and backwards in time. The tall *gopuras* of the south Indian temple create a sense of dynamism, of movement away from the gate and toward the center, which is locked inside the stone heart of the main shrine. There lies the sacred force contained within the walls, rendered accessible only through the strong ties that bound it, and through the ritual ordering of the universe within. The worshiper first circles around the temple compound, offering obeisance at minor shrines, always keeping the main sanctuary on his right; he circumscribes the center in an individual act of demarcation, just as the stone walls forever mark its limits. At length he will penetrate into the recesses of the main shrine and come to rest before the *garbhagṛha*, where the image of the deity is located. Here he has arrived at the farthest reach of his wandering; hidden away in stone and darkness, as in a cave in the bowels of the earth, lies the symbol of the god, which is imbued with the divine power whose deeds are narrated in our myths. Knowledge, or truth, is, in the eyes of the Hindus, by nature esoteric; it is buried, lost, to be recovered from the depths of the sea or from the darkness of the earth.[9] The temple expresses in its very structure this search for hidden wisdom: the *gopuras* point us inward, to the cave. But the *garbhagṛha* is, literally, a "house of the womb"; at this spot the pilgrim is conceived afresh, to be reborn without taint, with all the powers latent in the newborn child.[10] He is not, indeed, alone in this experience; as we shall see, the very deity whom he worships also suffers in this site a new birth preceded by violent conception. Life enters the womb in darkness, out of the disintegration into chaos and death of an earlier existence.

This interpretation is applicable to the structure of the south Indian temple in its most mature form, which it attained only in the late stages of Coḻa temple architecture. Earlier, the *gopuras* are not as high as the central *vimāna*, which houses the inner sanctum; in the Bṛhadīśvara temple at Tañcāvūr, for example, the central *vimāna* rises to a height of over two hundred feet—several times the height of the gates. In cases such as this, the pilgrim's passage through the *gopuras* toward the central shrine is a form of ascent—as, of course, it is in the many shrines built upon hills or mountains. Yet even here the *garbhagṛha* remains remote, in the chamber of stone, and the worshiper seems to enter and reemerge from a womb.

What are the pilgrim's goals? Usually there is a practical aim to be furthered by the pilgrimage; the worshiper comes in contact with a power that aids him in his mundane existence. How is this accomplished? On one level, we seem to find an archaic concept of exchange: the pilgrim gives something of himself to the god or goddess, and the deity returns this offering in a renewed form. We will explore this concept further in the context of the myths of marriage. More generally, the pilgrim seeks the help of the god in response to his devotion, *bhakti*. The act of pilgrimage is itself an expression of *bhakti* for the god in his specific, located home. If I have stressed the pragmatic orientation of the worshiper, it is, of course, through no wish to doubt the intensity of his encounter with his lord; rather, my intention is to clarify an important issue. Again and again we are told that a shrine provides the devotee with both material reward (*bhukti*) and release (*mukti*). The former is a clear enough goal, while the latter would, on the surface, appear to coincide with the ideal of renunciation as proclaimed in the Upaniṣads and later texts. This is not, however, the case; it is important to realize that no one in Tamiḻnāṭu goes on pilgrimage to attain release. What has happened in the Tamil tradition is that the world-renouncing goal of the ascetic has been redefined as equivalent to *bhakti*. Pilgrimage comes to substitute for *sannyāsa*.[11] To illustrate this development, we may turn to a Tamil variant of a well-known theme—the problem of overcrowding in the *muktipada*, the zone of release:

> The gods complained to Śiva that evil people without merit were going to Viruttācalam and reaching Śiva's feet. "What is the use of the preeminence you have given us?" they asked. "No one worships us, we receive no sacrificial portions, no one offers anything to the sun or to Yama, hell is deserted and the positions reached by *tapas* are ruined. Help us!" Śiva answered: "You yourselves reached your present status by performing *tapas* at Mutukuṉṟam. Would it be right (*nīti*) to stop others from worshiping there? You too should worship at Mutukuṉṟam and reach the *muktipada*." The gods went to the shrine, bathed in the Maṇimuttā River, which is the river of the liberated (*muttanati*), and meditated on Śiva, who granted them a vision of his dance of knowledge.[12]

Śiva shows himself to be quite indifferent to the gods' distress. In fact, his suggestion to them implies that everyone should attain *mukti*—a direct reversal of the basic assumption of the Sanskrit myths about the *muktipada*.[13] This reversal causes a theoretical problem: if everyone goes to the zone of release, a dangerous imbalance results, with heaven overflowing and hell empty.[14] Yet these considerations, so basic to Sanskrit myths, are largely disregarded by the Tamil text: the power of the shrine has become an absolute. The shrine must offer salvation to all, whatever the consequences. But let us take a closer look at the meaning of this story. The gods descend from heaven to earth, to the shrine, where they are granted a vision of Śiva's dance of knowledge. It is this vision that, by implication, is equated with salvation; and there is no reason why all cannot possess it, without threatening the gods in their celestial bastions. In other words, the myth directs us not to heaven but to earth, which has become the locus of *mukti*: even before witnessing the dance, the gods bathe in the River of the Liberated, which flows through the sacred site. *Mukti* is present for the devotee within the conditions of his life on earth. This is a development of particular importance. Tamil devotional religion can dispense with heaven altogether, for the shrine is superior to any world of the gods. When King Varakuṇapāṇṭiyaṉ asks to see the world of Śiva, the god brings *his* world to earth (*avv ulakai ivv ulak' iṭai varuvittu*);[15] afterwards the king is said to have ruled the city of Maturai, which was wealthier than Pŏṉṉakar, the golden city of the gods, and which was famed as "the world of Śiva on earth" (*pūvulakiṟ civalokam ĕṉṉav icaippaṭa*).[16] The same title (*pūloka-civalokam*) is attributed to Tiruvŏṟṟiyūr, Tiruviṭaimarutūr, and other shrines.[17]

One might go still further and maintain that *bhakti* movements in general, and certainly the mainstream devotional movements of southern India, are oriented toward life in this world, with its conventional social categories; far from being revolutionary in a social sense, *bhakti* religion—except in its most extreme manifestations—tends toward the preservation of the social order through the sanctification of the present.[18] Having inherited the goal of world-renunciation from an earlier stage of Indian religion, *bhakti* stands it on its head and directs man back to life on earth. The *bhakta* is commanded to live not in some future heaven but *here*, in the present moment, through a recognition of the divine within him and within the world in which he lives. Already in the *Bhagavadgītā*, *bhakti* provides in effect a practical answer to the fascination of renunciation; Kṛṣṇa reveals himself to Arjuna, and thus convinces him to return to the battle, to his socially prescribed role. In Tamil mythology, the world—and in particular the Tamil land—is clearly consecrated as the realm of the divine. The myths never tire of describing the god's participation in our lives; Śiva's "amusements" (*tiruviḷaiyāṭal*) at Maturai often take the form of a sudden revelation, in which men are made to confront the divine presence that pervades their universe. The *bhakta* poets cannot help celebrating the world. See, for example, how Kampaṉ describes a sunrise:

> The sun whose death the day before
> recalled the death of all who suffer endless rebirths,
> that sun which is without birth
> was born again
> and thus made one forget heaven and all other pure worlds.[19]

Why did the sunrise make those who beheld it forget heaven? According to the commentators on this verse, the point is that the sun, which is not born and never dies, provides a contrast to the lives of creatures who suffer endless rebirths and recurring death; the use of the verbs *iṟa*, "to die," and *piṟa*, "to be born," to describe the previous day's sunset and the present sunrise, respectively, is therefore pointed and ironic, intended to drive home the contrast. The clue to this notion lies in the epithet *piṟavā*, "the unborn," to describe the sun; the sun thus makes us think of *mokṣa*, of a state beyond birth and death, and forget heaven and other worlds which, however superior to life on earth, would still implicate us in the process of creation. "Everyone must seek *mukti*, in which there is no birth."[20] But is this really the point? The verse is a celebration of sunrise as seen on earth; and this spectacle that the poet praises involves, in his words, a kind of birth for the sun. We forget heaven not because we are reminded of the transience of pleasures and wish to renounce them, but because life on earth is beautiful. And the essence of this joy in mundane existence is explained by the following verse, in which Rāma—the god Viṣṇu incarnate, to whom the poet turns in worship—is (as often in Kampaṉ) compared to the sun (he is the black sun brighter than the sun itself). The presence of Rāma in the world makes life in this world full of wonder and happiness.

At this point a problem arises. If the god is present everywhere, within the recognized conditions of our life, what purpose is served by the shrine? Why need the devotee take the trouble to go on pilgrimage? The boundaries between the shrine and its surroundings disappear in the light of the consciousness of god. Iconoclastic poets stress this point:

> To the utterly at-one with Śiva
>
> there's no dawn,
> no new moon,
> no noonday,
> nor equinoxes,
> nor sunsets,
> nor full moons;
>
> his front yard
> is the true Benares,
> O Rāmanātha.[21]

Nevertheless, the Tamil purāṇic myths insist that there *is* a difference between the shrine and the outside world. The shrine is consistently idealized as a place outside of and opposed to the sway of time and the corruption that time brings about. Yama, the god of death, has no power over men who reside in the sacred area.[22] Nor does the Kali Age, the degenerate period of time in which we live:

> The sage Sarva was worshiping Śiva on the bank of the Sarasvatī River when the Kali Age began. "*Adharma* now appears to me as *dharma*," he said; "where can I escape the power of Kali?" A voice from heaven directed him to Tiruvāñciyam. Kali, seeing him heading in that direction, pursued him, calling, "Stop! You are in my power!" The sage began to run, and Śiva sent the Kṣetrapāla (the guardian of the sacred site of Tiruvāñciyam) to arrest Kali. Kali begged to be allowed to dwell near the shrine and to come one night a year to expiate his faults. He dwells there still, and the Kṣetrapāla is now known as Kalinigraha ("he who restrains Kali").[23]

The shrine is beyond the power of Kali, the personification of the age with all its faults. Kali's task, his *svadharma*, involves him in evil, and the shrine, which is opposed to his nature, offers him a means of absolution. Note that Kali remains on the edges of the shrine near the Kṣetrapāla, and thus becomes, together with the latter, a kind of guardian figure on the border of the sacred zone. Kali at Tiruvāñciyam is thus one of a remarkable series of gatekeepers, whose presence at the border of the shrine seems to serve several purposes: the gatekeeper marks the transition from this world, a realm of sorrow, to the other-worldly shrine. Sometimes his presence is said to be intended to deter undesired visitors from entering: thus Yama is stationed by Śiva at the entrance to this same shrine, Tiruvāñciyam, to keep evil men away.[24] Sinners who die at the shrine attain an undeserved salvation; hence Yama is made to punish them not with death—as he usually does—but with life, outside the shrine. Still, the implication of this myth is that if a man, be he righteous or evil, can succeed in getting past the gatekeeper, he is assured of salvation. The gatekeeper thus comes to represent a trial of inner strength; the devotee must overcome his fears, his doubts, his human weakness, in order to accomplish his pilgrimage. The following myth from Tiruvārūr makes this idea clear:

> Indra saw that all evil men were going to heaven and reaching *mokṣa* by worshiping at Acaleśvara (at Tiruvārūr). He therefore called Anger, Lust, Covetousness, Hatred, Fear, Sexual Pleasure, Delusion, Addiction, Jealousy, and Desire and said: "You must prevent any man or woman who is going to the shrine from reaching it." They went and destroyed its reputation on earth.[25]

The vices employed by Indra are exactly analogous to the gatekeepers ordered to keep men away from a shrine. The gods have a clear enough interest in such a goal; as we have seen, the shrine supersedes the rituals upon which the gods depend, and offers a short cut to heaven. Although Indra's initial concern is with the dangerous and unjustified salvation of the wicked, he acts against man in general: no man or woman must be allowed to reach the shrine. The security of the gods depends upon the corruption of men.[26] Nevertheless, we must not forget that this is a myth that extolls the power of a shrine; the lesson that the readers or listeners were no doubt intended to draw was that if they could only master the vices sent by Indra, and concentrate on the importance and power of the shrine, they could achieve final happiness by going there. The myth thus offers both an explanation of the fact that people are no longer flocking to Acaleśvara—because they have been corrupted by Indra's messengers—and an implicit recommendation to the listener not to succumb to evil, or at any rate not to the evils commissioned by Indra to keep men away from the shrine.

In some cases the test represented by the gatekeeper has a violent conclusion: the devotee slays the guardian in order to unite with the god. Thus Śiva as Bhairava impales Viṣvaksena, the gatekeeper of Viṣṇu, on his trident.[27] Or, the terrifying guardian may be appeased by the prior worship of the devotee: Śani, malevolent planet of suicides, is worshiped in a shrine at Tirunaḷḷāṟu before one enters the inner sanctum of Śiva;[28] and the fierce image of Brahminicide that stands on the east *gopura* at Tiruviṭaimarutūr receives offerings of salt and spices.[29] Let us look for a moment at the myth told in connection with the latter figure, for it serves to illustrate the idealized nature of the universe within the gates:

> Varakuṇapāṇṭiyaṉ was returning from the hunt when his horse inadvertently stepped on and killed a sleeping Brahmin. The king was afflicted by Brahminicide, and nothing he did by way of expiation was effective. Śiva answered his prayers with a voice from heaven: "King, do not fear. The Coḻa king is planning to go to war against you. You will defeat him and pursue him, and in this way you will reach the shrine of Tiruviṭaimarutūr, where your sin will be healed." It came to pass as Śiva had said. When the king reached Tiruviṭaimarutūr, he entered the temple through the eastern gate, and his sin stayed outside. Śiva said to him, "That shade (*piramacāyai*) is still outside the eastern gate; return to Maturai through the western gate." The king came out through the western *gopura*, which he called by his name.[30]

The king's *brahmahatyā* still stands, waiting for him, at the eastern gate. Evil cannot penetrate the sanctuary, which represents, through opposition to the evil and suffering lurking outside, a zone of safety and freedom. Many myths describe the shedding of evil beyond the limits of a shrine; to cite only one more example: Rāma is freed of the ghost of Kumbhakarṇa when he approaches Tiruvāṉaikkā; from the sages there Rāma learns that no demon, Brahmarākṣasa, or disease can enter the sacred bounds; but in order to be rid of the shadow upon leaving the shrine, Rāma must atone for his acts of slaughter by setting up a *liṅga* there.[31] The devotional rite cuts the bonds between Rāma and the ghost forever, but we are never told that the ghost ceases to exist. Indeed, in the closed Hindu cosmos evil cannot cease to exist; it can only be distributed among other vehicles (as Indra distributes *his* crime of Brahminicide[32]) or transmuted into something else.[33] The shrine exists as an island surrounded by the chaos of the unredeemed; outside it, evil, death, and the Kali Age persist unchanged. The cost of maintaining a refuge from the world is isolation.

How does the pilgrim bridge this gap? What does he derive from his brief sojourn in the shrine? And how, indeed, are we to understand the shrine's peculiar freedom from taint? Let us recall the ritual nature of pilgrimage; like ritual generally, the shrine possesses a conventional, formal structure. It is, above all, ordered. Fences have been erected around the sacred, which in this way becomes manageable and accessible. The ritual ordering of the universe within the confines of the shrine creates an ideal opposed to the disorderly world of nature. At the heart of the shrine lies a concentration of sacred power; but this power is restricted, channeled, forced into an inherited pattern of symbolic relations. Chaos is represented through symbols that reflect its subjugation: the primeval water of the flood, the water that threatens to destroy the created universe and out of which the universe has emerged, exists within the shrine or in its vicinity in the form of a temple tank, a river, or the sea; similarly, the ancient forest, the dwelling of chaos that opposes the ordered life of society, is represented in the shrine by the sacred tree.[34] The shrine is a microcosm of the whole of creation, but it differs from the surrounding world by the strict ordering of its component elements. The pilgrim who enters this world is transformed in the direction of harmony. For a moment, he has left his world and entered an idealized cosmos, in which violent forces act within the limits imposed upon them; he touches these forces and is strengthened by them and is then redirected to the chaotic world outside. Through his contact with the bounded power of the shrine, the pilgrim brings to the sphere of his usual activity a new sense of borders and control. From the substratum of violent energy that gives life to the universe and that inheres in limited form in the shrine, the worshiper derives a new vitality—and with it an ideal of order that he retains in the disorderly but still divinely appointed realm beyond the temple bounds.

Order and limitation are not, however, the only clues to the role of the shrine. Another principle, no less important than the idea of limitation, is at work here, in a way that brings the Tamil purāṇic myths into the mainstream of Hindu tradition. This is the principle of separation, the logical consequence of the concern with the contamination of power, and especially the power tied up with the sacrifice. Separation may be regarded as the Brahminical ideal *par ex-*

*cellence*, the very basis of the Brahmin preeminence: the Brahmin who performs the *prāṇāgnihotra*, the "sacrifice of the breaths," detaches himself from his surroundings (and, of course, from the burden of evil produced by the performance of actual blood sacrifices) and becomes an independent island of purity in the midst of a world corrupted by the exercise of power and the dependence upon power. From this point, the road to world renunciation is not far, and the religious ideal becomes one of absolute transcendence and purity, or of *mokṣa*—release from life in this world with its inherent evils, its unending cycles of death and rebirth, its inevitable pollution through contact with the violent forces that motivate these cycles.[35] I shall refer to this ideal of freedom as "Upaniṣadic," since it reaches its first mature expression in the Upaniṣads. Hart has described a parallel process in the south Indian tradition, with the same goal of separation from the inherently dangerous and polluting centers of sacred power.[36] This quest for purity finds an expression in the idealization of the shrine. Of course, the pure principle of the Upaniṣads—the *brahman* that is the hidden essence of all things—differs from the ideal of the shrine in refusing limitation of any sort; its universality would seem to contrast with the limited manifestation of the shrine. Nevertheless, as we shall see, the Tamil purāṇic myths do proclaim a universal ideal of absolute purity, and the Tamil shrines often appear as individual foci of this freedom—as tangible symbols of an other-worldly goal of total independence. This is very different from the notion of control and ordered power; the idealization of the shrine, when taken to its farthest reaches, severs the link between power and pollution, thus removing the shrine totally from the unclean world of death and rebirth, of evil, of dynamic change. The shrine comes to symbolize an unlimited, unchanging absolute. This ideal need not be described in this case as a final negation or transcendence of power, for a sense of the power that inheres in the sacred spot is never really lost, not even in the context of the search for utter purity; nevertheless, this power, if completely isolated, could in theory become independent of the general processes of creation out of violence and destruction. The shrine is depicted to the pilgrim as a self-contained entity unaffected by the violent forces of chaos at work outside its borders. Separation is the key to this ideal state, as it is in the case of Upaniṣadic idealism; the shrine shares with the Brahminical tradition the desire for purity based on the exclusion of evil and on complete independence of the contamination of power.

A basic ambivalence thus seems to be attached to the Tamil shrine, which is both a locus of power—albeit power controlled and contained—and a symbol of freedom and other-worldly detachment. The ambivalence is all the more striking in view of the "this-worldly" orientation of Tamil devotional religion and the rejection of *mokṣa* as a primary goal.[37] Despite this turning away from the Upaniṣadic ideal, the latter has left its mark on the Tamil purāṇic tradition, both in the concept of the deity and in the depiction of the shrine where he is worshiped. We will return to this problem at a later stage, but it should already be apparent that Tamil *bhakti* religion does not lack the tension between the goals of power and purity—we might even say between the real and the ideal—that seems to be characteristic of Hinduism generally.[38] In the classical Hindu tradition, there is little doubt of the theoretical superiority of the ideal of purity, which, as has been noted, underlies the Brahmin claim to prestige. The Tamil purāṇic texts often appear to follow this pattern as well; we shall see how consistently they strive to purify the image of the deity by detaching him from the symbolism of power (death and rebirth). Yet if one looks at the Tamil tradition as a whole, one cannot but notice how the ideal of purity is constantly compromised by the demand for power. The world always encroaches on the islands of independence. The Tamil tradition is, in fact, cognizant of this fact: we shall see that one of the most important motifs in the goddess myths is that of the intrusion into the sealed shrine, in which the powerful virgin has been isolated and contained; in the myths of most Tamil shrines, the separation of the goddess is fatally damaged and a divine power unleashed upon the intruder (usually her bridegroom Śiva). Moreover, this intrusion is, ultimately, necessary. Despite the persistent search for order and limitation, the myths suggest that it is in *disorder* and chaos that one meets the divine. God is reached precisely at the point where his isolation is breached and the ideal brought back to earth, or where the creative forces of chaos break through their bounds.[39] This immediate, perhaps explosive encounter takes place at the shrine, the dwelling place of a sacred power. This power can never be finally contained or transcended so long as one accepts life and yearns for the god who gives life. Vitality is tied up with death, with the chaos of the nether world (just as *ṛtá*, the cosmic order, is said in the Vedas to be hidden in the nether world[40]); this connection raises a problem that is never fully resolved, as the tradition struggles to free itself, and its god, from death and from evil; but in a religion that ultimately asserts the divine nature of terrestrial existence, power—however dark or mysterious its workings, however terrible its effects—never loses its sacred character.

## 3. The Tamil Purāṇas: Types and Prototypes

If we are to believe the Tamil literary tradition, the composition of purāṇas in Tamil goes back to the very earliest period of literary activity: the commentary ascribed to Nakkīrar on *Iṟaiyaṉār akappŏruḷ*—where we find the first complete account of the Caṅkam myth of cultural origins—mentions a *Māpurāṇam* and a *Pūtapurāṇam*, both allegedly composed during the period of the "middle Caṅkam."[1] Both works are lost except for stray verses quoted in medieval commentaries.[2] Although nothing more is known of these books, it is not improbable that purāṇas were composed in Tamil at an early period. Several of the *mahāpurāṇas* in Sanskrit were probably extant by the end of the fifth century A.D. (the *Brahmāṇḍa*, *Mārkaṇḍeya*, *Vāyu*, and *Viṣṇu* purāṇas).[3] Tamil adaptations of a number of these works were made in the late medieval period, but it is likely that the *idea* of composing a purāṇa, perhaps on the basis of earlier Sanskrit models, would have been carried to the Tamil area at the same time other literary forms (such as the *kāvya*) were borrowed. Here, as in other areas of Tamil literature, the Jains may have made an early contribution, for we hear of a *Cāntipurāṇam* and a *Purāṇacākaram*, both Jain works no longer extant, apparently belonging to the tenth century.[4] Other early Tamil purāṇas that have been lost include a *Kaṉṉivaṉapurāṇam* and *Aṣṭātacapurāṇam*, twelfth-century works known from inscriptions.[5] The first would appear to have been a *talapurāṇam*.

The purāṇic literature in Tamil is usually divided into three categories: 1) adaptations of the Sanskrit *mahāpurāṇas*; 2) hagiographic purāṇas; and 3) *talapurāṇam*.[6] The first extant Tamil purāṇa would then be the *Pĕriya purāṇam* of Cekkiḻār.[7] This division is, in fact, rather unsatisfactory. The *Pĕriya purāṇam* and similar works, such as Kaṭavuṇmāmuṉivar's *Tiruvātavūraṭikaḷpurāṇam* on the life of Māṇikkavācakar, share very little with the classical purāṇic literature; they are put in this class only by virtue of their name, which in this case is a misnomer. Hagiographic material is common enough in both the Sanskrit *mahāpurāṇas* and the *māhātmya-sthalapurāṇa* literature; the *Tiruviḷaiyāṭaṟpurāṇam* from Maturai, for example, includes many stories of the lives of the devotees of Śiva, but these stories appear in a work essentially devoted to myths of the god and his consort. The *Pĕriya purāṇam*, on the other hand, is almost solely taken up with "biographies." Adaptations of the *mahāpurāṇas* include such works as Cĕvvaiccūṭuvār's much-loved *Pākavatam* (a work of the late fifteenth or early sixteenth century),[8] the Tamil *Kācikāṇṭam*, *Kūrmapurāṇam*, and *Iliṅkapurāṇam* of Ativīrarāmapāṇṭiyaṉ (sixteenth century),[9] his cousin Varatuṅkarāmaṉ's *Piramottarakkāṇṭam*, and the *Maccapurāṇam* of Iracai Vaṭamalaiyappapiḷḷaiyaṉ (1706-1707).[10] Although these works are based directly on Sanskrit prototypes, they differ greatly from the Sanskrit originals both in style and in their perspective on the mythological materials; unlike the Sanskrit purāṇas, the Tamil adaptations are polished and compressed, and thus belong, in effect, to the *kāvya* genre.[11] I have not included them in this study, as they are almost entirely lacking in material which is peculiarly southern (or have merely taken over such material from their source, as may be the case with the *Pākavatam*—since the *Bhāgavatapurāṇa* is often thought to have been composed in the south). In two cases, however, I have used texts conventionally assigned to this category. Kacciyappamuṉivar's Tamil version of the *Vināyakapurāṇam* was clearly based on a northern Sanskrit original,[12] but has assimilated local material. And the *Kantapurāṇam* of Kacciyappacivācāriyar is one of the basic texts of this study.

The *Kantapurāṇam* is, in fact, wrongly assigned to the category of adaptations of the *mahāpurāṇas*. It bears no relation to the *Skandapurāṇa* in its printed form, while its affinities are clearly with the class of *talapurāṇam*: it celebrates Kāñcipuram, and in particular the god of the Kumārakoṭṭam shrine there (where Kacciyappacivācāriyar is said to have composed the work), and it gives us in effect the myths of Murukaṉ in the form current in the Tŏṇṭai region.[13] The complete localization of the mythic action in the major shrines of the Murukaṉ cult in Tamiḻnāṭu is apparent throughout the work. The *Kantapurāṇam* claims, however, to belong to the *Skandapurāṇa*.[14] The Sanskrit text on which it was based is known from manuscripts and one recent printed edition; it too appears to have been composed in Kāñcipuram.[15] This text has never been studied critically, and the possibility that the Tamil *Kantapurāṇam* was earlier has been raised.[16] Nevertheless, the evidence of the two texts indicates that the Sanskrit *ŚRKh* was indeed the prototype for Kacciyappar's composition; the latter bears all the signs of a unitary work written by a single author, while the *ŚRKh* seems to be a composite text.[17] Kacciyappar has clearly taken liberties with his model: for example, the myth of Murukaṉ's second marriage (to Vaḷḷi, Sanskrit Lavalī, his local south Indian bride) has been removed from its natural context in the fifth *kāṇḍa* of the *ŚRKh* and used to provide a powerful, climactic ending to the *Kantapurāṇam* as a whole.[18] This is but one example of a skilled artist's sense of fitness and order; in many ways Kacciyappar's work is much richer and more interesting than the Sanskrit original. The Tamil text gives us a far more complete account of the Murukaṉ myths of the south, and is particularly faithful to the ancient sources of the tradition.[19] The Murukaṉ myths themselves are, of course, older than either of these texts. The *ŚRKh* offers a standard medieval version of the myths, but it was probably the great popularity of the Tamil *Kantapurāṇam* which was responsible for the extreme regularity and lack of variation in the Murukaṉ myths recorded in the Tamil *talapurāṇam* literature as a whole. This standardization distinguishes the Murukaṉ corpus from all other areas of Tamil mythology.

The date of Kacciyappar has been the subject of much discussion, with estimates ranging from the eighth to the eighteenth centuries. Mu. Aruṇācalam has ably presented the evidence.[20] He concludes that Kacciyappar belongs to the end of the fourteenth century. Zvelebil[21] follows his argument, but then admits that it is weak and that 1625, the date put forward by Nilakanta Sastri, is "almost equally acceptable."[22] As with so many cases in Tamil literature, the dating of Kacciyappar depends upon imprecise allusions and circumstantial evidence. Two things are clear to any student of the purāṇa: Kacciyappar took Kampaṉ's *Irāmāvatāram* as his model,[23] and he was familiar with the terminology and concepts of Śaiva Siddhānta. It would appear likely that he lived after the great scholar Umāpaticivācāriyar (first half of the fourteenth century), whose works helped crystallize the language of the Siddhāntin theologians.

Any attempt to narrow down the date of Kacciyappar may hinge on the dating of his pupil Ñāṉavarotayar, who praises Kacciyappar in the thirteenth invocatory stanza of the *Upatecakāṇṭam* (the sequel to the *Kantapurāṇam*). To some, this reference (*kāñci vaḷar kacciyappa kkaṟpaka ttāru*) suggests that Kacciyappar was still alive at the time of writing.[24] The phrase should not, however, be forced to bear the full weight of such an argument. Still, there is a strong tradition that Ñāṉavarotayar was a direct pupil of Kacciyappar. Ñāṉavarotayar has been dated in the first quarter of the fifteenth century on the basis of rather slender evidence.[25] Another pupil of Kacciyappar, according to the tradition, was Koṉeriyappar, who wrote another Tamil version of the *Upatecakāṇṭam*. Unfortunately, we have no means of determining his date.[26] It does appear likely, however, as later sources suggest,[27] that Koṉeriyappar's version of the *Upatecakāṇṭam* is later than that of Ñāṉavarotayar. Certainly Ñāṉavarotayar adheres much more closely to the Sanskrit original, including the *adhyāya* divisions.

Kacciyappar is mentioned in the works of three poets of the seventeenth century.[28] We therefore have a safe *terminus ad quem*. If the later literary tradition is correct, we would be able to push his date back approximately two centuries from this limit. In the present state of our knowledge, further precision is impossible.

The golden age of purāṇic composition in Tamil begins in the sixteenth century. There are earlier purāṇas extant, such as the *Koyiṟpurāṇam* of Umāpaticivācāriyar (early fourteenth century), a close adaptation of the *Cidambaramāhātmya*, and the "old" *Tiruviḷaiyāṭaṟpurāṇam* (on the Maturai shrine) by Pĕṟumpaṟṟappuliyūrnampi.[29] Other early purāṇas have been lost, as we have seen. But it was only in the sixteenth century that purāṇas began to be composed on a wide scale—a process that has continued right up to the present day.[30] Our main sources for the study of Tamil mythology are thus very late, although much of the related *māhātmya* literature in Sanskrit is somewhat older;[31] and in any case the myths themselves, as distinct from the form in which they were finally recorded, are often very ancient, as I hope to show. The sixteenth century also witnessed the establishment of two of the most prominent surviving Śaiva mutts (Tamil *maṭam*, Sanskrit *maṭha*) in Tamiḻnāṭu, at Tarumapuram and Tiruvāvaṭutuṟai; this fact is closely related to the vogue in purāṇas noticeable from this period, for a majority of these works were composed by scholars associated with these institutions of religious learning.[32]

The character of the versions of the Tamil myths now available to us is scholastic, erudite, saturated with allegory, and ornate in language and style. The format of the works is conventionalized: beginning with invocations to the deities of the shrine, the author proceeds to pay obeisance to Naṭarāja-Śiva, the sixty-three Śaiva saints (*nāyaṉmār*) as a group (perhaps with a special verse on one of them connected with the shrine, such as Kāraikkālammaiyār at Tiruvālaṅkāṭu), and the servants of Śiva generally; Caṇṭecuranāyaṉār, who cut off the legs of his own father when the latter committed an offense against Śiva, is often singled out for special praise.[33] In the *avaiyaṭakkam*, a brief resumé of the contents of the purāṇa, the number of cantos, and so on, is presented. The author apologizes for his presumption in composing the work, usually refers in a general way to his source (more often than not, the *Skandapurāṇa*),[34] and may name a patron who commissioned or supported the work. Devout authors from the mutts will also praise their *guru* and the founder of the line of teachers (*guruparamparā*). Inevitably, there will then be one or more cantos singing highly conventionalized descriptions of the beauties of the town or village in which the shrine is located (*tirunakaraccarukkam*), the river that flows through it or the sacred tank within the walls of the shrine (*tīrttaviceṭam*), the region as a whole (*tirunāṭṭuccarukkam*), and perhaps a central image worshiped in the temple (*mūrttiviceṭam*).[35] The actual myths are often introduced by the story of the creation of the Naimiṣāraṇya, where the sages are performing *tapas*,[36] or simply by an account of the arrival there of the narrator, Sūta, and the request made of him by the sages to hear the stories of a holy place (usually the most sacred place in the universe). The Sūta then proceeds to narrate the purāṇa. Sometimes another narrator is interposed: in the *Tiruviḷai.*, for example, the Sūta recites the purāṇa as narrated by the sage Agastya, who learned it from Murukaṉ.[37]

Although the Tamil purāṇas are repetitive in structure and learned in style, they are not necessarily dry or devoid of poetry. One often feels that the authors were deeply moved by the myths, and this sense of the underlying poetic power of the stories does break through the long, sometimes monotonous chain of *viruttam* verses. Such is the case, for example, in Kacciyappar's account of the myth of Vaḷḷi and Murukaṉ;[38] and Parañcoti's *Tiruviḷai* is justly cherished for its lyrical, captivating language as well as for the stories it relates. The fact that leading scholars and theologians were responsible for the production of many of the Tamil purāṇas is an indication of the seriousness with which the endeavor was regarded.[39] The stories were no doubt always beloved in their own right, as they are today, for their wealth of imagination and invention, for their humor, and for the expression they gave to the love of a people for its land; but they were also regarded as carrying a message of the highest importance. In its mythology, Tamil civilization has given us a powerful expression of some of its most basic and enduring ideas.

Many of the Tamil purāṇas, like the Sanskrit *māhātmyas*, are of unknown authorship; many have never been printed. Indeed, the full extent of this literature is not yet known. Kiruṣṇacāmi, who has prepared much the best bibliography of these works available, lists 581 items;[40] but his list is far from complete. Zvelebil has estimated that there may be nearly 2,000 Tamil purāṇas.[41] Only a few have achieved popularity outside the shrines they celebrate. A list of the better-known authors and their dates is given in Appendix I. I have not, however, limited my study to these titles, but have tried rather to sample as many Tamil purāṇas as possible. Some of the most fascinating myths are, in fact, buried in obscure, anonymous works from small, out-of-the-way shrines.

In order to convey something of the atmosphere surrounding the composition of a Tamil purāṇa, I wish to cite two examples, one a fairly typical literary "hagiography" of the premodern period, and the second a documented historical instance. We begin with the story of the *Tiruccĕntūrttalapurāṇam* as preserved in the local tradition of this shrine. The Tamil purāṇa dealing with Tiruccĕntūr, an elegant composition of 899 verses, is ascribed to Vĕṉṟimālaikkavirāyar, who lived in the seventeenth century. When the Tiruccĕntūr temple authorities published an edition of the Tamil purāṇa in 1963, they included a brief history of the author in prose, based on the inherited traditions about him (*vĕṉṟimālaikkavirāyar varalāṟu*, pp. 9-15). Here is a resumé of this "biography":

> One of the two thousand Brahmins of Tiruccĕntūr, who are known as the Tiricutantirar,[42] was blessed with a son. When the child was five years old, his parents tried to have him educated, but the boy was unable to master anything except the ways of worshiping Lord Murukaṉ: he learned to circumambulate the shrine, to fix the image of the lord in his heart, to say "Murukaṉ is my helper," to prostrate himself before the god. He retained nothing else of his instruction, and, as he grew older, he was found fit only to serve in the temple kitchen, where the offerings of food to the god were prepared. As he worked in the kitchen, he used to lose himself in meditation on the lord.
>
> One day while he was thus sunk in worship, he forgot that the moment of offering was near. The image of the god had already been adorned, and the Brahmin priests were angry: "Where is the offering? The auspicious moment must not be

missed!" They dragged the cook from the kitchen, beat him severely and dismissed him from his post.

The unhappy devotee, unable to bear the distress caused by faltering in his duty to the lord, resolved to kill himself. At night he approached the sea and called out to Murukaṉ: "Lord, I have failed in your service. This body, the site of my failure, must be destroyed." As he was about to throw himself into the sea, a voice called out, "Stop! Stop! (*nil nil*)." He did not look back to see who was trying to save him, for he truly wished to die. He entered the water, and the waves covered his body.

But a great wave threw him back on to the shore. With an effort he stood up. His body shivering, he wept as he called out, "O bridegroom of Vaḷḷi![43] I have failed you; have I not even the freedom to die [*iṟakka kkūṭavā cutantiram illai*, a pun on the name of the Brahmins of Tiruccĕntūr, the Tiricutantirar]?" A voice replied, "Those who love the lord must live until their appointed time, to aid all who live in this world. Sing the purāṇa of Tiruccĕntūr in Tamil. Go and see Kiruṣṇa Cāstiri of Cevalūr."

He looked about him—and there stood Murukaṉ, with his six faces and twelve arms. "My lord," cried the man, "I am without learning. How can you command me to compose this work?" At this, the image of the lord disappeared.

At dawn, the devotee bathed and went to Cevalūr. There he found Kiruṣṇa Cāstiri. "Swāmi," he said, "do you know the *māhātmya* of Tiruccĕntūr?" "Oh, so you are the one," replied the learned Brahmin in joy; "in a dream I was ordered to translate the Sanskrit purāṇa[44] for a devotee who would come at dawn. Now you have arrived, and I have found a reason to live." He seated the man before him and, taking a copy of the *māhātmya*, explained its meaning to him. The devotee was overcome by a flood of poetry, as if a sluice gate had burst open; thus each Sanskrit verse took shape in Tamil poetry, until some nine hundred verses had appeared. Amazed, the learned Brahmin gave him the name Vĕṉṟimālaikkavirāyar ("king of poets having a garland of victory").

The poet took leave of Kiruṣṇa Cāstiri and returned to Tiruccĕntūr, where he wished to recite the purāṇa (*araṅkeṟa*) in the presence of the lord. He went to the authorities of the temple, and they laughed at him: "This man, who was not fit even to be a cook, now says he has composed a purāṇa!" They did

> not bother to look at his work. The poet took the manuscript to the sea-shore and cast the palm leaves into the sea. Then he went away and lost himself in meditation. A voice called to him: "Your service has been accomplished. Come!" The soul of the poet merged in the shadow of the grace of God.
>
> Like the leaves of the poem that Tiruñāṉacampantar cast into the Vaikai River,[45] the palm leaves floated on the waves until they reached a place on the coast of Ceylon; that place is still known as Paṉaimuṟi ("point of the palm [leaves]"). There a devotee of Lord Murukaṉ found them and read them with joy; he took them home and recited them daily. One day a hurricane devastated that town—except for the street where the manuscript was kept. Learning of this in a dream, men rushed to the site and discovered the purāṇa. They made many copies of it and recited it there, and the hurricane departed. The Tiruccĕntūrppurāṇam melted the hearts of the Otuvār (the professional reciters of the Śaiva *Tevāram*-hymns), and thus its fame spread to all the (Tamil) country.

This legend has absorbed a number of well-known motifs, including that of the simpleton who composes a learned work (the purāṇa itself, it should be remarked, is replete with the usual ornate rhetorical devices of medieval Tamil literature). The ignorant, the childlike, the simple-minded become great: this motif appears in slightly different form in the story of the great poet Kumarakuruparar, who is said to have been born a mute and to have received the gift of inspired speech when, at the age of five, he was brought before Murukaṉ at this same shrine, Tiruccĕntūr.[46] The story of Vĕṉṟimālaikkavirāyar gives us a conventional demonstration of the superiority of *bhakti* over ritual conventions: the cook's "fault" in missing the proper time for the offering is clearly not serious in the eyes of the god, who grants him grace after saving his life. The Brahmins of Tiruccĕntūr are portrayed as lacking in true understanding and compassion, just as the Brahmin priest at Kāḷatti has to be taught the greatness of the crude but devoted worship of Kaṇṇappar.[47] Note again the "this-worldly" orientation of *bhakti* as revealed by the legend's explicit rejection of suicide. This episode may, in fact, be derived from the popular story of the poet Aruṇakirinātar, who became disgusted with his dissolute life and tried to commit suicide by leaping from the tall *gopura* of the temple at Tiruvaṇṇāmalai; Murukaṉ caught him in his arms and, as in the

Tiruccĕntūr story, commanded him to sing his praises.[48] The palm leaves carried by the waves, which the story associates with the incident of Tiruñāṉacampantar's contest with the Jains at Maturai, recalls the very widespread theme of hidden knowledge recovered from the depths.[49] The greatness of Tiruccĕntūr, and the true stature of the despised cook who becomes the vessel for divine inspiration, are revealed by the text that is carried miraculously across the sea to the devotee who is capable of responding with joy. Yet even at this stage the sacred text remains hidden from sight, locked in the house of the single devotee, until a further miracle leads to a more general revelation.

Such is the picture that, in the absence of reliable historical sources, a shrine retains of the composition of its purāṇa. Somewhat more prosaic is the story of a nineteenth-century author's actual activity. We are fortunate in having a fine biography—indeed, the first true representative of this genre in Tamil—of the great poet-scholar Tiricirapuram Mīṉāṭcicuntaram Piḷḷai. This biography was composed by Mīṉāṭcicuntaram Piḷḷai's outstanding pupil, U. Ve. Cāminātaiyar, who was himself one of the great figures of modern Tamil scholarship. Cāminātaiyar's rather dry style hardly disguises the intense devotion he brought to this memorial to his teacher at the Tiruvāvaṭuturai mutt. In the fascinating pages of this work we have many precious details about the veritable "purāṇa industry" that Mīṉāṭcicuntaram Piḷḷai ran—for throughout his life this gifted scholar was engaged in producing to order Tamil purāṇas and similar works in praise of the gods of various shrines. We learn of the way a Tamil purāṇa would be commissioned by a wealthy patron; the subsequent search for manuscripts containing Sanskrit versions of the myths of the selected shrine; the preparation of Tamil prose renderings of the myths; the author's visits to the shrine in order to see the site with his own eyes and gather the traditions of the older residents there; the actual composition of the verses and the first formal recitation of the work (*araṅkeṟṟam*). Mīṉāṭcicuntaram Piḷḷai composed no fewer than twenty-two purāṇas in this way.[50] As an example of the process of composition, we may look at the history of the *Tirukkuṭantaippurāṇam* on Kumpakoṇam as described by Cāminātaiyar:

> "At that time Civakurunātapiḷḷai, who was the *taḥṣīldār* in Kumpakoṇam, and other Śaiva dignitaries thought, 'Let us ask this master poet to compose the purāṇa of Kumpakoṇam in

Tamil verse.' At their request he [Tiricirapuram Mīṉāṭcicuntaram Piḷḷai] came to Kumpakoṇam from Tiruvāvaṭuturai in 1865 and took up residence with his retinue in the building of the Tiruvāvaṭuturai mutt in Peṭṭai Street. He first had the Kumpakoṇam purāṇa translated from Sanskrit into Tamil prose; in this he was aided by Maṇṭapam Nārāyaṇa Cāstirikaḷ Mutaliyār, a scholar of the Caṅkarācāriyar Mutt. Afterwards he began to compose the purāṇa in verse form. He would compose the verses orally, and from time to time one of his pupils, Tirumaṅkalakkuṭi Ceṣaiyaṅkār, would write them down. Short parts of the purāṇa used to be prepared each day in the morning and given their first formal recitation in the afternoon in the *maṇḍapa* in front of the shrine of Ādikumbheśvara (Śiva at Kumpakoṇam). Many came to take pleasure in the recitation. . . .[51] One day the verses were not composed, because some of his friends came in the morning and spent a long time in conversation with him. Then, because he was very tired after the midday meal, he went to sleep. His students and others were afraid: 'The verses for this evening's recitation are not ready; when he wakes, he will be angry at Ceṣaiyaṅkār for not having reminded him.' When he awoke, he refreshed himself and spoke unconcernedly with several people who had come there. Ceṣaiyaṅkār came and stood there. 'What is the matter?' he asked. 'The verses for this evening's recitation have not been composed; it was impossible to remind you earlier; there was no opportunity to remind you this morning,' he said with some anxiety. 'Bring the palm leaf,' he [Mīṉāṭcicuntaram Piḷḷai] said without worry. Ceṣaiyaṅkār brought the manuscript of the purāṇa; he had him read out the last verses composed, picked up the thread of the story, thought a while, and then recited fifty verses so quickly that his (Ceṣaiyaṅkār's) hand had no time to rest from writing. People used to speak of this amazing feat in that city and the surrounding villages.

When the *araṅkeṟṟam* of the Kumpakoṇam purāṇa was completed, the dignitaries of that city gave him a shawl, a silk upper garment, [other] garments and gifts, and two thousand rupees collected from the public. They had the manuscript of the purāṇa mounted upon an elephant and taken around the town in state. Then several of the dignitaries purchased and donated a covered palanquin, made Piḷḷai sit in it, and carried it

> themselves for some distance. Thus they demonstrated the love they felt for the Tamil language and the custom of olden times."[52]

Clearly, not all authors of purāṇas had to suffer in the manner of Vĕṉṟimālaikkavirāyar of Tiruccĕntūr. In the late nineteenth century, the composition of a purāṇa was still a rewarding occupation, and not only in spiritual terms. Mīṉāṭcicuntaram Piḷḷai was very much the traditional Tamil scholar, a man of immense learning to whom verse composition was a natural and easy activity. As one can see from this passage, in Tamiḻnāṭu, as in many other traditional cultures, skill in rapid extempore composition was highly regarded. Kampaṉ, according to one tradition, composed the whole of his *Irāmāvatāram*, a work of some ten thousand verses, in two weeks. We may be sure the latter story is untrue; but by the time of Mīṉāṭcicuntaram Piḷḷai, the creation of a long narrative poem such as a purāṇa was clearly a highly conventionalized endeavor, and originality in expression was hardly valued *per se* so much as the mastery of versification and a normative use of the conventions.[53] The response of the poet's audience reveals the reverence felt by the people for the myths told about their local shrine, and for the work of the poet who retold them in their language; this basic, enduring attitude was undoubtedly a decisive factor in the creation of the vast purāṇic literature in Tamil during the last five centuries.

CHAPTER II

# The Phenomenon of Localization

> Every inch of ground on earth . . . has a divine association. Mother Earth has been there since the beginning of creation, being one of the five primeval elements. She has seen countless pairs of feet running about on thousands of aims and pursuits, both evil and good, and will continue until Time ("Kala") swallows and digests everything. Even after the participants have vanished, every inch of earth still retains the impress of all that has gone before. We attain a full understanding only when we are aware of the divine and other associations of every piece of ground we tread on. Otherwise it would be like the passage of a blind man through illuminated halls and gardens.[1]

## 1. The Shrine as Center

The feature that most conspicuously distinguishes the Tamil myths from the classical corpus of Sanskrit myths is the persistent localization of the mythic action. *Sthalapurāṇas*, as collections of stories that have clustered around individual shrines and their environs, are by definition repositories of localized myths and legends; yet this definition by itself tells us nothing of the religious conceptions that underlie the phenomenon of localization. This chapter attempts to analyze these conceptions as they appear in a set of recurring symbols and in a number of stories, in which the tension between the limitation implicit in the localization of the deity and the universalism proclaimed by the god's devotees is made clear. We begin with a survey of cosmological motifs attached to the Tamil shrines.

These motifs are not, in fact, unique to Tamil Hinduism. On the contrary, they are for the most part simply the south Indian variants of very widespread types. Most basic of them all is the identification of the sacred site with the center or navel of the universe, the spot through which passes the *axis mundi* connecting heaven and earth and the subterranean world of Pātāla. Let us look, for example, at Śiva's description of Citamparam to his disciple, the cosmic serpent Ādiśeṣa:

> That day I danced in the forest while Viṣṇu looked on,[2] I saw that the spot could not support me.[3] . . . But there is a site (*maṉṟu*) which can sustain the dance. . . . The world is analogous to the body (*alaint'iṭum piṇṭam aṇṭam camam*). The left channel (of the "subtle" body—*iṭai nāṭi*) goes straight to Laṅkā, and the right channel (*piṅkalai nāṭi*) pierces the Himālaya. The central channel (*naṭuviṉ'āṭi*) goes directly through great Tillai . . . the site of the original *liṅga* (*mūlakkuṟi*).[4]

Tillai is the ancient Tamil name for Citamparam, the site of Śiva's dance of joy (*ānandatāṇḍava*); so powerful is this dance, which represents the entire cosmic process of creation and dissolution, that it can be performed only at the very center of the cosmos. The imagery used by the text is shared with the physiology of Haṭhayoga, which defines the *suṣumṇā* (*cuḻumuṉai, natuviṉ'āṭi*) as the central "conduit" of the "subtle" (*sūkṣma*) body—the invisible body that is hidden within our gross (*sthūla*) material body.[5] This axis pierces the center of the universe, which, if the body symbolism is retained, may be described as the *mūlādhāra* ("root," base of the spine)[6] or as the *hṛdayakamala* ("heart-lotus")[7] of the cosmic man, and which is equated with the shrine. The image of the human body thus provides a microcosmic model of the universe; and just as in the Upaniṣadic speculative tradition the heart of man is the site of the unfathomable space (*ākāśa*) mystically identified as the dwelling-place of *brahman*,[8] so Citamparam, which sees itself as the heart of the universe, locates an invisible Ākāśaliṅga in its innermost sanctum, the Citsabhā ("room of consciousness").[9] The shrine thus proclaims its identity as the center which, like the hidden source of life within man, is directly linked to the infinite.

The situation of the center on the *axis mundi* is frequently expressed by dynamic images of the link between the shrine and the worlds above and below: thus the *sūkṣmaliṅga* at Tañcāvūr went on growing in the palm of the founding king;[10] similarly, the stone image of the bull Nandin at this shrine continued to grow until a nail was driven into its back.[11] The image that grows forever, or until some way can be found to stunt its growth, is a common motif: Nĕllaiṉātar (Śiva at Tirunĕlveli) in the form of a *liṅga* outgrew twenty-one pedestals (*pīṭha*) until a king, fearing that worship would soon become impossible, threatened suicide unless the god stopped.[12] The goddess Kālī at the edge of the temple compound in

Tiruvŏṟṟiyūr is covered with earth up to her breasts, but she is believed to be slowly emerging from the ground and growing from year to year; the Ākāśaliṅga at the same site is thought to be growing still, despite a nail that was driven into it to stop it. The nail is still pointed out.[13] The Ākāśaliṅga here recalls the invisible *liṅga* in the Citsabhā at Citamparam; at Tiruvŏṟṟiyūr, however, the *liṅga* is visible and immediately adjoins the shrine of Aṇṇāmalaiyār, the god as a pillar of fire. This, too, is a famous instance of the localization of the *axis mundi*:

> Brahmā and Viṣṇu quarreled over who was superior. Śiva appeared to them in a *liṅga* of fire. Viṣṇu tried to find its base by digging in the form of a boar, while Brahmā became a goose and flew toward the top. Neither could find any limit to the *liṅga*. They recognized it as a form of Śiva, who made the fiery *liṅga* into the mountain Tiruvaṇṇāmalai.[14]

The *liṅga* of fire is petrified in the form of the cosmic mountain reaching from the shrine to heaven. This mountain may be present under different names: the mountains at Tiruccĕṅkoṭu and Tirukkoṇamalai are identified with Mount Meru (or fragments of Meru);[15] at Tiruviṭaimarutūr, Śiva's mountain Kailāsa became the *marutam* tree, a representative of the cosmic tree joining heaven to earth and the nether world;[16] both Meru and Kailāsa follow Devī when she leaves with her two sons and other gods to join Śiva at Kāḷatti.[17] Agastya, making his way southward, saw a mountain and a tree melting from the beauty of the hymns sung to the lord of Citamparam by Nārada and other heavenly musicians; he took a piece (*paṭika ttuṇṭam*) of the mountain and set it up as the pedestal (*pīṭha*) in the shrine of Comacuntarar in Maturai.[18] Crystal (*sphaṭika*) *liṅgas* elsewhere (Tiruvaṇṇāmalai, Caṅkaranārāyaṇacāmikoyil)[19] may be associated with the world axis through the thunderbolt (*vajra*).[20] The *liṅga* at Tiruppuṉavāyil touches heaven.[21]

The connection of the shrine with the nether world is no less important than its link to heaven. Pātāla, the dark region under the earth, is a zone of terror and death, the abode of the serpent, a realm of chaos. Yet in Hindu thought creation is possible only against the background of chaos and death; life is born out of darkness; Death himself is the creator.[22] The universe is created, or created anew, out of the waters of the *pralaya*, the cosmic flood into which all earlier worlds have dissolved. Chaos gives way to order, and to a new birth; but this new life needs still to be nourished by the violent forces from which it was born. Hence Pātāla, no less than the celestial worlds of the gods, comes to be regarded as a transcendent source of vitality; and most shrines see themselves as the *biladvāra*, the door to the nether world. The water of the sacred tank or river is commonly thought to well up from this region; the Pātālagaṅgā, the Ganges of Pātāla, flows at Śrīśaila,[23] at Tiruvārūr,[24] at Tiruvālaṅkāṭu,[25] and many other shrines.[26] Tiruveṇkāṭu, which is situated in a plain (the flat landscape common throughout the Kāviri delta), claims to lie astride a subterranean mountain—the Pātālakailāsa;[27] and Ādiśeṣa/Patañjali, Śiva's serpent-devotee, can reach Citamparam only by way of the nether world (Nāgaloka), at the center of which he discovers a mountain limitless in either direction.[28] Again, this is the *axis mundi*, which the myth firmly locates in Pātāla under the shrine; another myth, from Tiruvārūr, stresses the passage along this axis from the nether world to the world of the gods:

> Many people worshiped Śiva at the entrance to the nether world (the Nāgabila) and in this way reached heaven. Alarmed at the imbalance produced by this influx of men into heaven, Indra stopped up the entrance with a mountain. The demon Tāraka conquered Indra, destroyed his city and plundered its wealth; he drove him and the other gods away and, taking possession of their world, ruled from Mount Krauñca. The gods sought the help of Śiva, who dispatched his son Murukaṉ to fight the demon. Murukaṉ threw his spear (*vel*) at the mountain home of the demon and reduced it to dust, killing Tāraka; but from the noise that was produced all the mountains of the earth began to sway and tremble, including the one over the Nāgabila. The sages there pleaded with Murukaṉ for protection, so he placed his spear and four *śaktis* on top of the mountain to steady it and to guard the town.[29]

The devotees at first proceed directly from Pātāla, or the entrance to Pātāla, to heaven; their route is symbolized by the mountain that Indra uses to cover the entrance. Indra's concern in this myth stems from the conventional fear on the part of the gods of overcrowding in heaven—a theme which we noted earlier with reference to the shrine of Viruttācalam.[30] The gods seek to destroy overly powerful shrines, just as they corrupt men who threaten them by an excess of virtue, asceticism, or piety;[31] the myths are ostensibly concerned with the question of balance in the universe, for the shrine, like the anomalous ascetic who becomes more powerful than the gods, upsets the established hierarchy of forces and allows a dangerous imbalance to be created. Yet here, as in other myths about overcrowding in heaven, the attempt to hide the shrine is ultimately futile, for the mountain that rests upon the Nāgabila becomes in itself a sacred site. This development is associated with two important themes—the attack upon the mountain, and the idea of holding down the shrine. Murukaṉ's war against the mountain belongs to an entire series of myths, in which a symbol of the *axis mundi*—a mountain or tree—is destroyed by a god; a major example is the ancient Tamil myth of Murukaṉ's attack upon the mango-demon Cūr.[32] In these myths the mountain or tree becomes a menacing force filling and blocking the space necessary for creation, and the god acts to restore the universal order; the destruction of the demon who inhabits the tree or mountain may thus take on the aspect of a sacrifice needed in order that creation can take place. These ideas appear already in the Vedic myth of Vṛtra, the serpent coiled around the mountain who is slain by Indra.[33] Indra is also associated with another act of violence against the mountains: by cutting off the mountains' wings, he made them stick fast to the earth.[34] In the latter instance we see the second theme found in the myth from Tiruvārūr—the idea of holding the mountain in place. Murukaṉ places four *śaktis* on top of the mountain to keep it from trembling; they cover the four cardinal points while Murukaṉ's spear steadies the center. The four *śaktis* were certainly worshiped as goddesses by the time our myth was recorded; the *Skandapurāṇa*, in a variant of this myth, gives their names as Āmbavṛddhā, Āmrā, Mahitthā, and Camatkarī.[35] But the *śaktis* may originally have been spears (another meaning of the word *śakti*);[36] a stake or spear is in any case a common symbol of the village deity (*grāmadevatā*).[37] The god, in effect, thus nails the mountain in place; this image is derived from the archaic motif of holding the earth down after creation.[38]

The importance of the shrine's connection to the nether world should now be clear. Pātāla and heaven are two ends of a single spectrum, in the center of which sits the shrine. It is in the subterranean zone of death—and of the fertility derived from death—that the tree (*sthalavṛkṣa*) present in each shrine has its roots. The tree, of course, also represents the *axis mundi*. Around its base are scattered the *nākakkal*, the serpent-stones depicting the Nāga deities who inhabit the nether world; pilgrims pray for fertility before these images of the serpent, in the shade of the tree that is itself a symbol of the fertility they seek. The temple tree thus serves as a focus for several related ideas: as in the myths of the ever-growing *liṅga*, the tree is a dynamic symbol of the connection between heaven and the worlds below; the tree reaches down to the realm of primordial chaos and also, as we have seen,[39] recalls the chaos of the wilderness in its opposition to order and culture; and, most significantly, the tree epitomizes the process of growth from a seed embedded in the substratum of darkness and death. This final element links the tree to classical images of the birth of the divine seed, as the following myth from Tiruvāṉaikkā (Jāmbukeśvaram) makes clear:

> In a grove of wood-apple (*nāval*) trees near Tiruvāṉaikkā, an ascetic was performing *tapas* in order to obtain release. One day a fruit fell in front of him. Thinking himself unfit to eat so beautiful a fruit, he took it to Mount Kailāsa and offered it to Śiva. The god ate the fruit and spit out the seed. The ascetic quickly swallowed the seed which, watered by the saliva of Śiva, immediately grew into a tree which split open his head, giving shade to the entire world of the gods. The ascetic begged Śiva to stay forever in the shade of the tree; the god agreed but ordered him to return to the spot where the fruit had fallen. As he walked there, stopping to worship at holy sites along the way, people could not believe their eyes. "Look, a walking tree!" they cried. "Is this some amusement of Śiva?"
>
> At last he arrived back at Tiruvāṉaikkā, where he resumed his *tapas*, living on roots, dried leaves, and the wind. When the goddess created the *liṅga* of water at that spot, she positioned the sage of the *nāval* tree nearby to give it shade.[40]

Śiva keeps his promise to the sage: the goddess fashions his symbol from the water of the shrine, at the center of the universe, the spot where the Tree of Life must be forever located. This myth recalls in several ways the story of the infant Skanda's birth from the seed of Śiva: in the post-epic versions of that myth, Śiva delivers his seed to the fire-god Agni; because Agni is the mouth of the gods (the fire that brings them the sacrificial offerings), they are impregnated by the seed; but the seed is itself fiery and uncontrolled, and the gods cannot bear it—it splits open their stomachs and pours out to form a lake.[41] In other versions the same motif applies to the Kṛttikās, the six wives of the sages who become the foster-mothers of

Skanda: the seed enters them through their buttocks and is torn from their stomachs.[42] Skanda is sometimes said to have burst from Pārvatī's womb after she drank the golden water of the lake formed from Śiva's seed.[43] Śiva himself swallows and then emits as seed from his penis the *guru* of the demons, Kāvya Uśanas, who is called for this reason Śukra ("seed"); Śukra causes the god pain by performing *tapas* in his (Śiva's) stomach, just as Śiva's seed burns the stomachs of the gods, and because Śukra emerges from Śiva's body, he too is made a son of the god through the intercession of Pārvatī.[44] As in these myths of Skanda and Śukra, the goddess at Tiruvāṉaikkā does not give birth to the divine child, the sacred tree that replaces Skanda in this myth; rather, she adopts the tree and connects it with the *liṅga* of water which she has created. The divine seed bursts not from the stomach of the sage but from his head. Note the suggestion of self-sacrifice implicit in this tale: the sage appears to lose his human identity and form when the seed rips through his head and flowers into a tree. It is as a walking tree that he returns to the shrine, and it is as the *sthalavṛkṣa* that he resides at Tiruvāṉaikkā today. The idea of self-sacrifice is connected here with a reversal of the usual norms of purity and pollution; nothing in India is more impure than food that has been touched by another person's saliva, but here the sage swallows without hesitation the seed spit out by the god. The context of worship requires this reversal. The same notion is found in the practice of giving *prasāda*—the gift to the devotee of the god's leavings, the food or other items left over from the offerings and regarded as a sign of the god's grace to his worshipers. In our myth, the left-over seed transforms the devotee into a tree that shelters the entire world of the gods, just as Skanda, the child-turned-warrior, protects the gods with his military might. The substitution of a tree for the infant Skanda is not unique to this myth: Pārvatī nourishes the sprout of an *aśoka* tree as a substitute for a child, and when she is questioned about this she says, "A tree is equivalent to ten sons."[45] Skanda / Murukaṉ becomes a tree in the myth of the wooing of Vaḷḷi,[46] and Śiva is also at times described as a tree.[47] All of these stories owe much to the Vedic image of the golden seed of creation (or the golden embryo, Hiraṇyagarbha).[48] We will return to this image and to the myths of the seed born in violence. The confusion of seed and fruit is common: the wind brought the Lady Añjanā a fruit each day; one day he infused the fruit with his seed, and she ate it and gave birth to a child (Hanūmat) who mistook the rising sun for a red fruit and tried to catch it.[49] A barren woman was given a mango by Śiva; she swallowed the pit and gave birth to a son.[50] The Tiruvāṉaikkā myth may also have borrowed from the folk theme of the yogi who grows a tree from a seed within seconds, a theme that may go back to the story in the *MBh* of the sage Kāśyapa's sudden revival of a banyan tree burned by the bite of the serpent Takṣaka.[51]

Thus the tree, like the stone image of the deity, or its analogue, the mountain found in some shrines, represents the vital link between the shrine and the transcendent worlds above and below; but the symbolism of the tree is more complex because of the tree's implicit association with primeval chaos and the notion of a violent birth and growth. In this association there is a close tie between the tree and the sacred waters, which reach the shrine from the dark world of Pātāla and which, like the tree, are confined and thus controlled by the ordered universe of the shrine. Together, all these elements constitute a regulated microcosm, or an "ideal landscape" of water, rock, and tree.[52] What has to be stressed in this arrangement is the absolute localization of all the symbols. The importance of this phenomenon may be seen by the striking contrast it provides with an earlier phase of Indian religion, that is, the sacrificial cult of the Vedic age. In Vedic religion the site of the sacrifice marked the center of the universe, through which passes the *axis mundi* (symbolized by the *yūpa*, the sacrificial stake); but, in contrast to the Tamil myths, the Vedic sacrificial system was not tied to specific localities. The mobility of the sacrifice has been noted by Renou:

> "It must be remembered that there were no temples at the Vedic period: 'the sacrifice takes place within the officiants themselves,' says one of the *Brāhmaṇas*. The term *āyatana*, which later came to mean 'sanctuary,' merely designates the ordinary domestic hearth in Vedic times. The temple cult of the classical period must have grown out of the domestic cult. Sacrifices took place on a specially prepared piece of ground, but the same spot was not necessarily used again for subsequent ceremonies. There was no building other than temporary huts."[53]

There seems little reason to assume that the localized worship of Tamil devotional religion was an outgrowth of the "domestic cult"; already in the Tamil epics we have clear instances of localized cults,[54] and the notion of a divinity inhering in a particular place or object seems to belong to the very oldest stratum of Tamil civilization.[55] In any case, there is a decisive distinction between the Vedic concept of a movable ritual applying a set of standard symbols to any newly chosen site, and the Tamil belief in a rooted, totally localized godhead.

This belief attains a particularly graphic expression in a series of Tamil myths, which describe attempts to remove the deity from its proper spot. The god is essentially immovable—even when he has been "imported" into the shrine from somewhere else (often the prestigious north). A common ritual of consecration causes the divine presence to reside in an image or a shrine;[56] in the myths, however, this action merely reflects a preexistent relationship between the god and the site. A divine power is felt to be present naturally on the spot. The texts are therefore concerned with the manner in which this presence is revealed and with the definition of its specific attributes. Often the divinity is revealed by a self-manifest image, usually a *svayambhūliṅga*;[57] when this is not the case, the sacred force that seems to radiate from the very soil may make itself felt by attracting and holding on to a predestined, proper form. A myth from Paḻani associates this idea with the origin of the shoulder-pole (*kāvaṭi*) that devotees of Murukaṉ carry up the mountain there:

> Agastya was given two hills, Śivagiri and Śaktigiri, as sites of worship, with permission to take them south. One day he met the demon Iṭumpaṉ, who had survived the slaughter by Murukaṉ of the hosts of Cūr. Since all the other demons had reached heaven by virtue of having been killed by Murukaṉ, Iṭumpaṉ spent his time performing their *śrāddha* rites. Seeing he was of good nature, Agastya sent him to bring the hills.
>
> When Iṭumpaṉ arrived at the hills, a *kāvaṭi* appeared, and the eight serpents which support the world took the form of ropes so he could tie the hills to the support. In this way he lifted the mountains and carried them southwards until he reached Āviṉaṉkuṭi (Paḻani). Suddenly he felt faint; he put the hills down and rested, but when he tried to lift them again he could not move them.
>
> Puzzled and sorrowful, he climbed one of the hills, and there he noticed a child under a *kurā* tree. "Go away," he said to the child, and added that he was a murderous demon. "This is my home," said the child; "pick it up, if you can!" "You may be

> small in size, but you tell big lies," cried Iṭumpaṉ as he leaped at the boy. But the child was Murukaṉ, playing his games; he killed Iṭumpaṉ at a stroke. When Iṭumpaṉ's wife Iṭumpi heard of her husband's death, she prayed to Murukaṉ, who revived him. Agastya came to worship Murukaṉ at that spot, and he ordered the demon to serve Murukaṉ there for his salvation.[58]

The child-god under the tree recalls a well-known myth about the sage Mārkaṇḍeya: Viṣṇu, who holds the entire universe within him, let Mārkaṇḍeya slip out of his mouth into the waters of the cosmic flood; later Viṣṇu revealed himself to the sage in the form of a child asleep under an *aśvattha* tree on an island in the midst of the ocean.[59] In this way Mārkaṇḍeya learns that the perceived world is in fact illusory, completely contained within the god; but in the myth from Paḻani, Murukaṉ demonstrates rather the uncompromising reality of his dwelling at a specific site, the shrine to which the two hills belong and from which they cannot be uprooted. Similarly, the white image of Gaṇeśa (Śvetavināyaka) that Indra brings with him on his pilgrimage to atone for his adultery with Ahalyā refuses to budge when Indra wishes to return from Tiruvalañcuḻi to heaven.[60] The motif recurs in the origin myth of Śrīraṅkam:

> The shrine of Viṣṇu-Raṅganātha (the Śrīraṅgavimāna) emerged from the ocean of milk and was kept by Brahmā. Ikṣvāku performed *tapas* to bring it down to earth, and Viṣṇu ordered Brahmā to part with it, much against his will. Ikṣvāku brought it to Ayodhyā, where it remained until the time of Rāma Dāśarathin. Rāma entrusted it to Rāvaṇa's pious brother Vibhīṣaṇa, who wished to take it to Laṅkā. On his way he set it down at the Candrapuṣkariṇī *tīrtha* on the Kāverī River and celebrated a festival together with the Coḷa king. When he tried to pick it up, he could not move it. Raṅganātha appeared and informed him that the Kāverī River had performed *tapas* to keep the shrine in her bounds, and that he intended to stay there for the good of men, not of Rākṣasas![61]

This story gives us the important theme of the demon who wins but then loses a shrine: at Śrīraṅkam this is Vibhīṣaṇa, the virtuous Rākṣasa-king of Laṅkā, but the motif is often associated with Vibhīṣaṇa's brother Rāvaṇa, who must be tricked into setting down the *ātmaliṅga* given him by Śiva.[62] The *liṅga* is locked in place, and the demon king goes off empty handed. The demons, however pious, cannot be allowed to retain possession of an important shrine; the myth from Śrīraṅkam states explicitly the god's preference for men over demons, just as in other myths men take precedence over the gods, and the shrine on earth supersedes the heavenly worlds of the gods in power and magnificence.[63]

The deity is located, rooted to the spot. One shrine at Tiruvārūr is named Acaleśvara, "the immovable lord," because Śiva promised never to abandon it:

> King Camatkāra performed *tapas* and, when Śiva appeared to him, begged him to be present forever in the holy site. The god said he would remain, immovable, in that place (*acalo 'haṃ bhaviṣyāmi sthāne 'tra*). The king set up a *liṅga*, and a voice from heaven announced: "I will dwell eternally in this *liṅga*; even its shadow will never move." So it happened: the shadow of the Acaleśvara-*liṅga* is ever stationary. Only he who is to die within six months is unable to perceive this marvel.[64]

Even the shadow of the god is frozen in place, while the miracle is made secure by terror—he who doubts it will die! The futility of attempting to move the deity or his image is illustrated by several explicit examples:

> Rāma was advised by sages to set up a *liṅga* in an auspicious moment in order to rid himself of the sin of killing Rāvaṇa and other demons. He sent Hanūmat to Mount Kailāsa to bring a *liṅga* from there. Hanūmat went there but could not see Śiva in the form of a *liṅga*, so he performed *tapas* to win the god's grace. When the monkey failed to return, the sages, afraid that the auspicious moment would pass, advised Rāma to install a *liṅga* of sand made by his wife Sītā. Rāma accepted this suggestion. But no sooner had this *liṅga* been consecrated than Hanūmat arrived with a *liṅga* given him by Śiva. Seeing Rāma worshiping the *liṅga* of sand, he became dejected: his effort had been in vain. He threatened to kill himself because of the dishonor shown him by Rāma. Rāma instructed him in the virtue of detachment; then he told the monkey that he could remove the *liṅga* fashioned by Sītā and install in its place the one he had brought.
>
> Hanūmat took hold of the sand-*liṅga* with his hands and tried to move it; it would not budge. Then he wrapped his tail

around it, touched the earth with his hands and jumped high into the heavens. The earth with its mountains and islands shook, and the monkey fell senseless near the *liṅga*, his mouth, eyes, nostrils, ears, and anus streaming blood. Sītā wept over the fallen monkey; Rāma picked up his body and stroked it as he wept, covering Hanūmat with his tears. Hanūmat awoke from his faint and, seeing Rāma in this state, sang his praises and those of Sītā. Rāma said: "This act of violence was committed by you in ignorance. None of the gods could move this *liṅga*; you fell because you offended against Śiva. This place where you fell will be known by your name; the Gaṅgā, Yamunā, and Sarasvatī will unite there, and whoever bathes there will be free of evil."

At Rāma's command Hanūmat set up the *liṅga* he had brought. The other *liṅga* still bears the marks of the monkey's tail.[65]

The scars on the *liṅga* bear witness to the doomed attempt to move the image; the *liṅga* of sand cannot be shaken. It is important to note that the sand-*liṅga* is fashioned by a woman, Sītā (who is the goddess Śrī incarnate). We have here a decisive link with the *liṅga* of sand (or earth)[66] created by the goddess Kāmākṣī at Kāñcipuram.[67] There Kāmākṣī protects the *liṅga* from the waters of the flood that could sweep it away. In both cases a goddess creates the image of the god out of the earth, and this image is rooted to the spot from which it is made. We may regard both stories as instances of the important theme of the chthonic goddess who attracts the god to the shrine and locates him there forever.[68] This observation allows us to bring our initial perspective into sharper focus: it is the goddess, who is identified with the earth and with all that is indigenous and unique in the site of the shrine, who is responsible for effecting the link between the deity and his local home. In this sense the goddess is associated with the ancient concept of *pratiṣṭhā*, the firm ground of stability that makes life possible in the midst of chaos;[69] the goddess provides the god with *pratiṣṭhā* in the one spot that is not subject to change or destruction, the center of the universe, the shrine. We will return to this theme in discussing the myths of marriage. Another part of the sand-*liṅga* myth from Irāmeccuram quoted above is mirrored in the traditions of Kāñcipuram: the monkey Vālin tried to uproot the Vāyuliṅga there by wrapping his tail around it and pulling with all his strength; the *liṅga* could not be moved, and the monkey's tail broke in two.[70]

The goddess is assigned a major part in another myth belonging to this series:

> The demons came to make war on Indra in the world of the gods. Afraid, Indra fled without their knowledge to Vĕṇkāṭu (on earth); after worshiping the god there, he bathed in the spot where the Kāviri joins the sea at Pūmpukār. "This place is more glorious than heaven," he thought, and he commanded Maya to build a shrine for the worship of the *ātmaliṅga* to the west of Pallavanīccuram.
>
> While Indra was worshiping there, the demons were searching for him everywhere. Nārada informed them of his hiding place; the demons hastened to earth to fight, but were vanquished and slaughtered by Indra through the grace of Śiva.
>
> Indra then wished to return to his kingdom, but when he tried to pick up the *liṅga* to take it back with him, he was unable to move it. He harnessed his horses to the shrine; they pulled, but it would not budge. When his elephant Airāvata tried to dislodge it, the goddess, afraid, cried out (*kūviṉāḷ*). Śiva heard the sound *kū* and said, "Do not fear." With his toe he pressed down on the earth so that the golden shrine would not move. The elephant then tried to dig up the shrine with his tusks, which scraped the nether world, and the reflection (*cāyai*) of the jewels in the hoods of the serpent Ādiśeṣa (who holds the earth on his heads) fell on to the earth by way of that hole. Seeing this, the gods named that spot Cāyāvaṉam. Finally, Airāvata wrapped his trunk around the shrine and pulled with all his might; still there was no movement, and the elephant grew tired. Indra realized that this was an act of Śiva. He bowed to the god and complained, "Is this right?" Śiva appeared, and Indra begged to be allowed to take the *liṅga* to heaven. Said Śiva: "This site is eight times greater than the world of Śiva. We wished to reside in this *liṅga* to give knowledge and liberation to our devotees. Hence we refused to allow it to be shaken." At the command of the god, Indra celebrated a festival at that site.[71]

Śiva holds the shrine in place with his toe, just as he presses down with his toe on Mount Kailāsa when the demon Rāvaṇa—who is also connected with an *ātmaliṅga*—tries to uproot the mountain.[72] In the end the shrine remains on earth, and Indra returns empty handed to his world after celebrating his festival.[73] The image of

Indra's horses straining to move the shrine has an important iconic parallel in the carvings of horses pulling wheeled stone chariots (*rathas*) in several shrines.[74] There, however, the intention may be opposite to that of the above myth; it is difficult to avoid the feeling that the *rathas* are an attempt to free the god from his frozen position and endow him with the faculty of movement. Several folk myths deal with the related theme of moving the processional chariot of the god: when the chariot was arrested at Kāñci in the course of a procession, the sacrifice of a woman pregnant with her first child induced the goddess Kāmākṣī to make the chariot move again.[75] In the shrine of Tillaikkāḷi at Citamparam, one finds the images of Vīrappĕrumāḷ and seven of his followers, all holding swords; when a *ratha* became stuck during a procession, Vīrappĕrumāḷ was on the point of cutting off his own head, but Mahākālī intervened and stopped the sacrifice.[76] In these stories sacrifice or the threat of suicide is necessary to move the god (with the help of the goddess!), just as in other cases a sacrifice stabilizes the shrine in one spot.[77] The ponderous wooden *rathas* used in many places to take the god in procession around the shrine are, of course, apt to become stuck in the course of the procession.[78] Note that the *ratha* allows the deity to circumnavigate his shrine: this, it may be suggested, is the extent of the god's freedom. The local lord is allowed to complete an orbit around the center to which he is still felt to be irrevocably tied.

In the myth from Cāyāvaṉam (Tiruccāykkāṭu), the goddess cries out when Airāvata attempts to move the shrine—hence her name at this site, Kūv ĕṉṟa kotaiyār, "the Lady who said *kū*." It is not clear why she cries: is it simply from fear of the elephant, as in the myth of Śiva's slaying of the elephant demon, when the god dresses himself in the flayed skin of the elephant in order to give Devī a fright?[79] Or is it because Devī fears that the shrine will be uprooted and wishes to prevent this result, just as Kāmākṣī embraces the *liṅga* to keep it from being swept away in the flood? Airāvata wraps his trunk around the shrine, just as Hanūmat winds his tail around the sand-*liṅga* at Irāmeccuram. The elephant's failure to move the image reverses the pattern of another myth, in which the sages of the Pine Forest, unable to move the dangerous fallen *liṅga* of Śiva, call upon Śiva to help, and the god takes the form of an elephant and transfers the *liṅga* to a shrine.[80] In the myth from Cāyāvaṉam, Indra flees to the world of men out of cowardice; but why does he choose the area of Tiruvĕṇkāṭu in the first place? An oral variant of the myth offers a different explanation of Indra's exile from heaven:

> The inhabitants of the world of Indra had no way of reaching *mokṣa* there. Indra's mother used to worship the *Ratnachāyāvaneśvaraliṅga* (at Tiruccāykkāṭu) each day, because only it could grant *mokṣa*. Indra was in the habit of circumambulating his mother and prostrating before her each morning. One day she was late because of her worship on earth. Indra found out why, and decided to bring the *liṅga* she worshiped to his world (Indraloka) to save all the trouble of going and coming.
>
> When Indra tried to pick up the *liṅga* to put it in his chariot, the entire universe rocked, and the jewels in the head of Ādiśeṣa were scattered. Devī called out "Kuhu!"—hence she is named Koṣāmpāḷ (from Sanskrit *ghoṣa*, "noise," "cry") or Kuyiliṉ iṉmoḻiyammai ("the lady whose speech is sweeter than that of the hawk-cuckoo"). At her call, the god righted the universe. A voice from heaven said: "Indra, worship the god within yourself (*ātmastha*). We shall stay here on earth for the sake of others (*parārtha*)."[81]

As in the myths of the *muktipada* cited earlier,[82] men are more fortunate than the gods, for *mukti*—in the sense of the salvation attained by, or indeed equivalent to, the worship of Śiva—is readily within the grasp of the inhabitants of the earth. The shrine offers immediate redemption. Note again the essential role of the woman: the call of the goddess brings about the intervention of Śiva, while another woman, the mother of Indra, inadvertently brings Indra to the shrine and prompts his attempt to uproot it. In the related myths of Rāvaṇa and the *ātmaliṅga*, it is sometimes the pious mother of the demon who forces Rāvaṇa to bring the *liṅga* from Kailāsa to earth.[83] At Tiruccāykkāṭu the *ātmaliṅga* mentioned in the written version of the myth is replaced in the oral variant by the god within oneself (*ātmastha*) as the final object of Indra's devotion. Indra is left with the hidden god who must be sought by knowledge of the Self; men have an easier path to release in the worship of the god manifest in his shrine. The attempt to remove this shrine shakes the earth to its foundation; Śiva restores balance and chooses to remain in the sacred site in the interests of others—specifically of men rather than of gods, just as Viṣṇu stays at Śrīraṅkam to benefit men rather than Rākṣasas. Śiva's concern for others, as illustrated by his readiness to dwell forever in the shrine, is no doubt meant to contrast with Indra's more selfish goal of an individual salvation. Indra's search for the lord of the Self may even reflect the old goal of *mokṣa*, in the classic sense of liberating the *ātman* from its state of bondage on earth and identifying it with *brahman*; in this case the myth would be stating the characteristic attitude of Tamil devotional religion, which, as we have seen, regards this notion of liberation as definitely inferior to the worship of God in this life.

Finally, we may note one more iconographic parallel. According to a well-known story, the *liṅga* at Tiruppaṉantāḷ was leaning to one side; a Coḻa king wished to straighten it, so he tied men, horses, and elephants with ropes to the *liṅga* and ordered them to pull. They were unable to straighten it. Kuṅkuliyakkalayanāyaṉār tied his neck to the *liṅga* and made it stand properly with only a slight tug.[84] Depictions of this scene show a figure pulling the *liṅga*, as in the myths quoted above—but here the devotee is fixing the image in place by the power of his devotion.[85]

All the above myths illustrate the prime importance of *place*. Each shrine sees itself as the only center of the universe, the one spot that is directly linked to heaven and the nether world; the deity of the shrine can hardly be moved from a spot endowed with this characteristic. Moreover, just as the shrine can never be detached from its place, so it can never be destroyed. As we have seen, the gods have good reason to wish to destroy a powerful shrine: all who worship at the shrine go directly to heaven, and the gods are crowded out of their own homes.[86] Hence the common motif of the gods' war against a shrine. Yet the gods' attempts to hide or destroy a shrine usually fail: at Puṣpagiri ("Flower-Hill") a drop of *amṛta* fell from Garuḍa's pot into the temple tank, whose waters then granted everyone immortality. Brahmā was alarmed, and Nārada told Hanūmat to drop a hill on the tank, but the hill simply floated on the water like a flower (hence the name of the shrine).[87] The shrine survives not only individual attempts to destroy it, but even the universal destruction of the cosmic flood, the *pralaya*. Indeed, the Tamil myths of the flood are the most important examples of the theme of the shrine's indestructibility. These myths also clarify another major element in the symbolism of the center—the link between the center and the creation of the world. We must now turn to these myths of the flood and of creation from the primeval waters.

## 2. Surviving the Flood

Tamil tradition has long been famous for an origin myth based on the idea of a destructive flood. The story first appears in the commentary attributed to Nakkīrar on the *Iṟaiyaṉār akappŏruḷ*.[1] There we learn that the ancient Pāṇṭiya kings established three kinds (*mūvakaippaṭṭa-*) of Caṅkam or literary "academies" to judge the compositions of the early Tamil poets. The first Caṅkam, in which the gods Śiva and Murukaṉ were included, sat for 4,440 years in "the Maturai which was flooded by the sea" (*kaṭal kŏḷḷa ppaṭṭa maturai*). The second (*iṭaiccaṅkam*) sat for 3,700 years in Kapāṭapuram, and "it seems that at that time the sea flooded the Pāṇṭiya land" (*akkālattu ppolum pāṇṭiyanāṭṭai kkaṭal kŏṇṭatu*). The third Caṅkam studied Tamil for 1,850 years in Upper Maturai (*uttara maturai*). This tradition is repeated with some elaboration in the commentary by Aṭiyārkkunallār on *Cil*. 8.1-2. Aṭiyārkkunallār informs us that the sea swallowed up forty-nine provinces (*nāṭu*) of the old Pāṇṭiya land from the Pahṟuḷi River to the north bank of the Kumari River. In other words, the medieval tradition of the commentators regards the ancient, antediluvian Tamil land as stretching far to the south of the present southern border at Cape Comorin.[2] The story of the three Caṅkam as it appears in our sources is suspect on many counts,[3] and there is no geological evidence of any deluge affecting the area in historical times.[4] Nevertheless, the Caṅkam legend is by no means the only instance of the flood motif in Tamil literature: the epic *Maṇimekalai* describes the destruction of the ancient Coḻa port city Pukār (Kāvirippūmpaṭṭiṉam) by a flood[5]—although Pukār exists today as a village by the seashore, near the spot where the Kāviri pours into the Bay of Bengal. And, as we shall see, nearly every Tamil shrine claims to have survived the *pralaya*, the cosmic flood that puts an end to the created universe.

All of these flood myths may well go back to a single archetype. Already in the story of the three Caṅkam we may detect the conflation of two basic elements—the idea of a complete destruction (of the ancient cities of Maturai and Kapāṭapuram), out of which a new creation emerges; and the belief that something (here the Caṅkam, the institution that symbolizes the beginning of Tamil culture) survives the deluge. These ideas are, of course, somewhat similar, for even the notion of rebirth out of a total destruction implies a degree of continuity. I will argue below that it is this concept—the renewed creation that follows upon the deluge—that underlies both the Caṅkam legend and the corpus of flood myths attached to the shrines. Tamil mythology depicts the creation of the world as a recurrent moment in the cosmic cycle, a moment that arrives after the universal deluge, and is always linked to the shrine as the center of the cosmos, hence the proper site from which to create; the connection between this conception and the Caṅkam story emerges in the local tradition of Maturai, the probable source of the Caṅkam legend, and the home of the third, possibly historical Caṅkam.[6]

Before we turn to the Maturai flood myths, let us survey the two broad categories of Tamil flood myths, which correspond to the two basic ideas isolated above—myths of creation and myths of survival. We begin with the latter category, which seems at first glance to be more prevalent in Tamil. Most Tamil purāṇas contain a myth describing the shrine's survival of the cosmic flood. The idea of surviving the deluge may go back to the earliest flood myth in India, in which Manu, the progenitor of the human race, is saved from the flood by a fish:

> A fish warned Manu of an impending flood. Manu built a ship and, when the waters began to rise, tied it with a rope to the horn of the fish. The fish carried him over the northern mountain and instructed him to bind the ship to a tree. The waters gradually abated. Manu offered ghee, sour milk, whey, and curds into the water, and, in a year, a woman was born. She came to Manu and told him to use her in a sacrifice, and by her he had offspring.[7]

This myth has been much discussed, often in the light of the well-known Middle Eastern parallels; the possibility of borrowing cannot be ruled out.[8] Eventually this myth becomes the background to Viṣṇu's fish-avatar.[9] It is interesting to note that two purāṇas place the beginning of the story in south India: the *Matsyapurāṇa* begins with Manu practicing *tàpas* on Mount Malaya,[10] and the *Bhāgavata* gives the role of Manu to Satyavrata, lord of Draviḍa.[11] Perhaps these identifications reflect an awareness of the hypertrophy of the motif in south Indian mythology; or they may indicate no more than the provenance of these particular versions. In the version quoted above, as well as in later purāṇic texts, Manu's survival is a key element, for the flood is the reason for a *repetition* of the creation story, a second creation similar to the first (note the appearance here of the incest theme), and also to some extent dependent upon it. The same pattern appears in many tribal flood myths in India: no sooner is creation accomplished than it is threatened with disaster.[12] Note the idea of sacrifice in the text quoted above: the postdiluvian creation is connected with a sacrificial rite; the horn of the fish that saves Manu may be a multiform of the *yūpa*, the sacrificial post.[13] A deep level of meaning may be hinted at here: the universe is created anew out of the havoc of the deluge, just as new life is attained through the violent act of sacrifice.[14]

Other Sanskrit accounts of the flood include among the survivors the Seven Sages with the seeds of creatures,[15] Brahmā, the sage Mārkaṇḍeya, the Narmadā River, Bhava (Rudra), the fish-Viṣṇu, and the Vedas, purāṇas, and sciences.[16] The *Matsyapurāṇa* mentions a "boat of the Vedas" in which the survivors escape; this motif is developed in an important Tamil flood myth, in which the survival of Manu and the others is replaced by two related elements—the escape of Śiva and Umā in a boat fashioned from the *praṇava* (the syllable *Om*), and the continued existence of the shrine:

> All creatures except Śiva, who is the First Principle, perished in the deluge that covered the universe. In order to create the worlds anew by the power of his grace (*aruḷ valiyāṉ*), Śiva, clothed only in the sixty-four arts, without his serpent ornaments, his crescent moon, his garland (of *kŏṉṟai* flowers), or his tiger skin, made the *praṇava* which is the sound of the Vedas into a boat (*toṇi*). With the name Pĕriyanāyakaṉ ("the great lord"), together with Umā he entered the boat and sailed through the waters. They found a shrine standing firm as *dharma*, undestroyed by the flood. "This shrine is the 'root' of the universe (*mūlātārakettiram* = Skt. *mūlādhārakṣetra*)," cried Śiva in joy, and he remained there in the boat. The guardians of the quarters found him there and said, "He has dried up the waters with his third eye!" Varuṇa, the lord of the sea, came there and worshiped the god who saves those without egoism from the sea (of rebirth).[17]

This story provides the explanation for one of the names of Cīkāḻi—"Toṇipuram," city of the boat. The shrine is not destroyed by the flood because it is the center of the world, the "root" or base of the spine of the cosmic man whose body symbolizes the created universe.[18] Śiva arrives at this spot with his bride, without his usual attributes, in a boat made from the sound of the Vedas; the indestructible shrine becomes the god's refuge from the flood, and the spot from which he can begin the work of creation once more. The sound of the Vedas will guide the god in this work, for sound (*śabda*) is traditionally an important instrument of creation.[19] The first step in this process is taken when Śiva burns up the waters with the fire of his third eye. Water must give way to land, so that

I. Śiva and Pārvatī escape the deluge in a boat.

creation can take place; elsewhere, however, Śiva's third eye creates not land but the flood—in the form of ten rivers—from the sweat of Pārvatī's hands when the goddess covers his eyes.[20]

The myth from Cīkāḻi clearly reveals the link between the shrine's survival and its role as the site of the new creation. The progression is not, however, always so clear; many texts content themselves with the first notion, and say nothing of the cosmogony. The shrine is eternal and has never been destroyed (hence the use of such common epithets as *maṉṉum ūr*,[21] *mūtūr*,[22] *paḻaiyapati*,[23] *nirantarapuri*,[24] and so on, all indicative of the shrine's antiquity and indestructibility). All the holy places near Maturai disappeared during the deluge except that worshiped by Kubera at Uttaravālavāy.[25] Gaṇeśa at Tiruppuṟampayam is known as Piraḷayam kātta vināyakar because he saved the world from the flood.[26] A folk etymology explains the name of a shrine mentioned in the *Tevāram*, Paravaiyuṇmaṇṭaḷi, as the temple (*maṇṭaḷi*) that swallowed (*uṇ*) the sea (*paravai*) sent by Varuṇa.[27] The Nāgagiri at Tiruccĕṅkoṭu is never destroyed during the deluge,[28] and the inhabitants of Tiruvāñciyam need not fear the end of the world—for all the worlds come to Tiruvāñciyam and enter into the goddess there.[29] Similarly, the Vedas and other holy scriptures enter into the *liṅga* at Vetāraṇiyam at the time of the universal destruction, for that *liṅga* is never destroyed.[30] Śiva surrounded Tiruttеṅkūr with a great rampart so that the waters of the flood could not overwhelm it.[31] The motif is known in other literatures, as well: Palestine is higher than other lands and was therefore not submerged by the flood.[32]

An unusual development of the motif of surviving the flood is found in the story of the sand-*liṅga* at Kāñcipuram, which is one of the most popular of all Tamil myths:

> The goddess Umā came to earth to expiate the sin of hiding the eyes of her husband Śiva. She worshiped the god of Kāñci in the form of a *liṅga*, and he, in order to test her, gathered all the waters of the world into the river Kampai, which flooded the town of Kāñci. Umā embraced the *liṅga* to save it from the flood, and the *liṅga* grew soft in her embrace. Śiva arrested the flood, and ever since the *liṅga* at Kāñci bears the marks of Umā's breasts and the bracelets she wore on her arms.[33]

Here the flood motif is put to the service of the myth of Śiva's marriage to the goddess at Kāñcipuram. Other versions state that the *liṅga* was fashioned by Pārvatī from sand on the bank of the river,[34] and this idea brings us even closer to one of the possible sources of the myth, the mention in the *Cilappatikāram* of a woman who embraced a sand image of her husband on the bank of the Kāviri to protect it from the flood.[35] V. R. Ramachandra Dikshitar notes in this connection that "even today it is a custom among some classes for the chaste wife to go to the river bank, make an image of her husband in sand and after making offerings to it, to cast off the clothes she was wearing and to put on new ones."[36] The *Pĕriya purāṇam* expressly states that the image embraced by the goddess became the wedding form of the god (*maṇavāḷa naṟ kolam*), although Pārvatī leaves the imprint of her breasts and bracelets not upon sand but upon stone, which is melted by her love.[37]

In one variant of this myth, Devī at Kāñcipuram is aided by Durgā, who wins the name Pralayabandhinī, "she who holds back the *pralaya*," by forcing the flooding river into a skull (*kapāla*).[38] The goddess is associated with the flood in other sites as well:

> The gods praised the goddess Kanyākumārī after her defeat of Bāṇāsura; they asked her to remain forever at the site of the battle, on the shore of the sea. They wanted fresh water, not salt water, to pour over her image, so the goddess split the

> earth with her spear, and a great flood welled up from the seven Pātālas and covered the earth. Alarmed, the gods prayed for help, and the goddess made the water remain in the cleft of the earth: that is the Mūlagaṅgā at the shrine of Kanyākumārī.[39]

Devī first creates and then controls the flood. Note that the Mūlagaṅgā at this shrine emerges from the nether world, the zone of chaos. The raging river is then contained within the borders of the shrine by the goddess, just as Durgā swallows up the flood at Kāñci. The goddess creates order from the materials of chaos, through the imposition of limits; at Kāñci she herself braves the flood in order to save the image of the god. In these myths we see again the importance of Devī as a source of *pratiṣṭhā*, the firm ground in which the deity and the shrine built around him are anchored.

The idea that the shrine must survive the flood found its way into the post-epic versions of the story of Dvārakā, the city carved out of the sea by Kṛṣṇa. According to the *Harivaṃśa*, Kṛṣṇa—who is known in another context as an enemy of the sea[40]—requested the sea to recede in order to make room for the building of Dvārakā ("the Gate"—to the nether world?).[41] After the Bhārata war and the deaths of Balarāma and Kṛṣṇa, Dvārakā was submerged by the sea.[42] But the *Viṣṇupurāṇa* explicitly excepts the shrine (*gṛha*) of Kṛṣṇa from the destruction: "On the day Hari (Kṛṣṇa) left the earth, strong black-bodied Kali came down (*avatīrṇo 'yaṃ kālakāyo balī kaliḥ*). The ocean covered the whole of Dvārakā except for the temple of Vāsudeva. The sea has not been able to violate (*atikrāntum*) it; Keśava (Viṣṇu) dwells there always."[43] The *Bhāgavata* repeats this statement: "The sea submerged in a moment Dvārakā, which was abandoned by Hari, except for the temple (*ālayam*) of the lord; Madhusūdana (Viṣṇu) is always present there."[44] Kṛṣṇa's death is thus the prelude to the destruction of his city and to the beginning of the Kali Age, the corrupt, unhappy period that is our present moment in time; but the god remains even now in his shrine, which no doubt offers its pilgrims an immediate salvation. Dvārakā, of course, is said to exist still today in Gujarat.[45]

There seems little reason to believe that the idea of the shrine's survival belongs to the earliest layer of the Dvārakā story; more probably, it was simply introduced by the purāṇas into the older legend. In the *MBh*, the destruction of Dvārakā is complete; indeed, this episode in the epic seems to revolve around the idea of a total devastation—it follows immediately the story of the Yādavas' fratricidal massacre—and raises the question of the god's responsibility for the existence of death.[46] This version of the story has a parallel in Tamil tradition in the myth of the flooding of Pukār:

> King Nĕṭumuṭikkiḷḷi fell in love with a girl he saw one day in a garden. She lived with him for a month and then disappeared. The king learned from a messenger that the girl was Pīlivaḷai, daughter of the Nāga king Vaḷaivāṇaṉ, and that she was to bear a son to a king of the solar dynasty. When Pīlivaḷai had given birth, she sent her son to his father on a merchant's ship, but the ship foundered and the baby was lost. In his grief the king forgot to celebrate the festival of Indra, and as a result the goddess Maṇimekalai destroyed the city by a flood.[47]

As in the *MBh* version of the Dvārakā story, the destruction of the city is complete, although Pukār, like Dvārakā, is still pointed out today. In this myth the flood is attached to the important theme of the king's marriage to a Nāga princess; ultimately it is the king's love for the Nāginī that brings ruin to the city. Union with the Nāga serpent deities, who represent the indigenous possessors of the earth, may legitimize a dynasty, but it is very often a source of danger as well: a Kashmiri legend tells of a king who burns a Nāginī in an oven in order to free himself from her magic control.[48] The basic pattern of the Pukār myth survives in a number of popular variants from northern Tamiḻnāṭu, especially the Tŏṇṭai region: for example, the purāṇic tradition of Mahābalipuram near Madras describes the destruction of the site through a flood sent by Indra, who becomes jealous of the splendor of this city of men.[49] In the Mahābalipuram tradition, the role of the serpent temptress is given to a celestial *apsaras*—the usual accomplice of the gods in their attempts to corrupt powerful mortals.[50] Another variant from this region retains the Nāginī and reverses the whole force of the myth: the Tŏṇṭai ruler Tiraiyaṉ is said to have been born from the union of a Coḻa king with a serpent maiden, who tied a *tŏṇṭai* creeper to her son as a sign of his lineage and sent him on the waves (*tirai*) to receive his kingdom.[51] This attempt to explain the name Iḷantiraiyaṉ retains the Coḻa hero of the Pukār myth, and thus hints at the provenance of the story; but here the infant prince is carried safely by the water, and there is no violent deluge. Other variants support the positive role of the water, which now brings a ruler instead of destruction.[52] The king rises from the ocean like the goddess Śrī from the ocean of milk,[53] and like the daughter of Manu after the flood recedes; the appearance of the dynasty may replace the motif of the *city* won from the sea. Order, in the person of the king, replaces the inchoate powers of the ocean, and the flood provides the background to the dynastic foundation—or, in other words, to a renewed creation. Again we are led back to the theme of creation from the water. We must now examine in more detail the Tamil cosmogonic myths, which begin at the moment of the universal deluge.

### *The Creative Flood: The Kāviri and the Lord of the Pot*

For a typical example of a shrine's picture of creation, we may turn to the tradition of Tiruvŏṟṟiyūr:

> Brahmā was born on a lotus growing from the navel of Viṣṇu during the universal flood. The lotus swayed under his weight, and he fell into the water. He prayed to Śiva and Devī, and the goddess interceded on his behalf with Śiva. The lord agreed to his request not to be reborn, and then disappeared with the goddess.
>
> Left alone, full of sadness, Brahmā performed yoga to burn his body with his inner fire (*mūlattiṉ kaṉal*). This fire burnt the world and dried up the flood, and by the grace of Śiva the waters gathered in a heap. To grant Brahmā release, Śiva appeared as a square painted plank (*caturacciṟpam ākiya palakam*) in the midst of the fire, and he dwells in that form to this day at that spot, which is known as Ātipuri, since the lord came there at the beginning (*ātiyil*). The waters of the deluge became a deep lake to the northeast of the *liṅga*.[54]

The beginning (*ādi*, Tam. *āti*) celebrated in this myth is the start of creation, the reemergence of the world after the flood is burned away. This is a process that must involve the shrine: Brahmā dries up the waters with his internal fire, thus causing the shrine, the site of creation, to be revealed through the appearance of the *liṅga*/plank. Ironically, Brahmā, who traditionally performs the actual work of creation, here initiates the creative process while seeking release from existence and from the sorrows of having a body! Brahmā is, in fact, said to have gained his wish: Śiva appears to grant him release. In this case, however, release seems to be identified with the divine epiphany itself; once again, it is not the old goal of *mukti* that is praised, but the "release" that comes from worshiping the god in his local home, in this very real world. Brahmā thus attains his desire without ceasing to exist, in his present incarnation; the salvation he achieves in the shrine on earth presumably obviates any future births, so that Śiva can promise that he will not be reborn. The same immediate salvation is, of course, offered to all who come to worship at Tiruvŏṟṟiyūr. In the eyes of the Tamil author, creation is thus a positive, beneficent process leading to the possibility of happiness in the circumstances of our life on earth.[55] The waters of the flood out of which the world is created persist in a controlled, circumscribed form near the central image of the shrine—an eternal reminder of the creative act that has taken place at this spot.

Somewhat more complex is the cosmogonic myth at Kumpakoṇam, where Śiva is Ādikumbheśvara, "lord of the pot":

> When the time of the universal deluge drew near, Brahmā came to Śiva and said, "Once the world has been destroyed, how will I be able to create it anew?" Śiva instructed him to mix earth with *amṛta*, fashion a golden pot (*kumpam*, Skt. *kumbha*), and put the Vedas and other scriptures into the pot along with the Seed of Creation (*ciruṣṭipījam*). Brahmā made the pot and decorated it with leaves, and, when the flood began to rise, he put the pot in a net bag (*uṟi*) and sent it off on the waters. Pushed by the wind and the waves, the pot floated southwards; the leaves fell off and became holy shrines, and the pot came to rest at a spot proclaimed sacred by a heavenly voice. Lord Aiyaṉār tried to break the pot with an arrow, but his arrow missed. Śiva took the form of a hunter and shot an arrow, which hit the pot and let loose a flood of *amṛta*. When the waters of the deluge receded, Brahmā fashioned a *liṅga* from earth mixed with *amṛta*, and Śiva merged into the *liṅga* in the presence of the gods.[56]

Once again Śiva's appearance at a shrine after the cosmic flood marks the start of a renewed creation. The god frees the seed from its container and thus allows the world to be formed afresh. Note that Śiva's action is a violent one: the hunter god shatters Brahmā's pot with his arrow. The basic images of this myth—in particular, that of the creative seed carried in a pot—are drawn from well-known Sanskrit myths. In one version of Prajāpati's creation, Dawn appears before the gods in the form of an *apsaras*; they shed their seed at the sight of her, and Prajāpati fashions a sacrificial vessel out of gold in which he places the seed, from which Rudra is born.[57] In one of the classic myths of the creative sacrifice, Prajāpati, who is identified with the sacrificial victim, lusts for his daughter; to punish him, the gods create Rudra from their most fearful forms, and Rudra pierces Prajāpati with an arrow. The seed of Prajāpati pours out and becomes a lake.[58] In later versions Brahmā spills his seed "like water from a broken pot."[59] Rudra, the archer and sacrificial butcher, has become the hunter Śiva at Kumpakoṇam; the pot that holds the seed is, in the Tamil myth as well as in the Sanskrit sources, a symbol of the womb.[60] This conjunction of seed and the pot/womb is implicit in the *kumbhābhiṣeka* ritual of consecration, in which a shrine is bathed in water from a pot. Kumpakoṇam, of course, derives its name from the pot (*kumbha*). Siva is also known as Kumbheśvara in Nepal, where he is said to have been established by Agastya, the sage whom we have seen to be prominent in traditions about the origin of Tamil culture;[61] Agastya is himself called Kumbhayoni, "born from a pot," because of the following myth: Mitra and Varuṇa saw Urvaśī at a sacrificial session; they spilled their seed, and it fell into a jar containing water that stood overnight. Agastya was born from the seed in the jar.[62] As we shall see in a moment, Tamil tradition connects Agastya with another pot, and one Tamil myth explains his title Kumbhayoni not by the above story but by the "survival" motif: Agastya was given this epithet because he escaped from a pot during the universal flood.[63]

In the myth from Kumpakoṇam, the seed that Brahmā places in the pot may be understood in two ways—either as the actual seed of the creator (and thus a multiform of the *amṛta* that is used in fashioning the pot), or as the creative sound (the "seed-*mantra*") that helps give form to the universe, like the *praṇava* in the myth from Cīkāḻi cited above. The sound of the Vedas becomes the boat that carries Śiva and Umā to Cīkāḻi; in the myth from Kumpakoṇam, the Vedas and other scriptures are carried with the seed in the pot. When the pot is broken, a stream of *amṛta* pours forth, so that we have in effect a second, creative flood that contrasts with the destructive *pralaya* covering the earth. This motif is developed further in a popular myth about the origin of the Kāviri River:

When Śiva sent Agastya to the south, he gave him at his request the river Pŏṉṉi so that he could have water for his ablutions. The river protested that it was not right for her, a woman, to follow a man, but Śiva assured her that the sage was in complete control of his senses. Agastya put the river in his water pot (*kuṇṭikai*) and headed south.

Indra, who was hiding from the demon Śūrapadma and his brothers, had taken the form of a bamboo in a pleasure-garden he had created for the worship of Śiva at Cīkāḻi. Śūrapadma's spies were unable to find him, so the demon king sent a drought to devastate the world. The garden at Cīkāḻi shrivelled up in the blazing heat of the sun. Indra, distressed at the loss of flowers for worship, was advised by Nārada to worship Vināyaka, who would bring the waters of the Pŏṉṉi to Cīkāḻi.

Indra worshiped the elephant-headed god, and Vināyaka took the form of a crow and perched on Agastya's water pot. The sage raised his arm to drive the bird away, and the crow upset the pot. The Pŏṉṉi poured on to the earth with tremendous force, shaking the worlds.

Vināyaka took the form of a Brahmin lad and fled from the enraged sage, but at length he revealed to him his true form. The sage asked forgiveness, but complained that he was now without water for his worship. The god took some water in his trunk and poured it into the pot, which immediately overflowed again. Agastya thanked Vināyaka and proceeded southwards, and the Pŏṉṉi flowed toward Cīkāḻi, where it revived Indra's garden.[64]

This story bears a superficial resemblance to that of the descent of the Ganges from heaven to earth; Indra's worship of Vināyaka-Gaṇeśa ultimately brings the river to earth to revive his garden, as Bhagīratha's worship of Brahmā and Śiva brings the Ganges to cover the ashes of the sons of Sagara and gain them entrance to heaven.[65] A further connection is the episode of the sage Jahnu who, seeing the Ganges sweep over his sacrificial site, drank up the water of the river, just as Agastya, the central figure of the Tamil myth, is said to have drunk the waters of the ocean.[66] There is, however, an important difference between the stories of the two rivers: Bhagīratha must persuade Śiva to sustain the Ganges in its descent, since the earth could not bear its violent force; but although the Kāviri descends violently, shaking the worlds, the sacred ground of the Tamil land can bear it. The text makes this point by recalling the flood at Kāñcipuram, which we discussed above: "The Pŏṉṉi fell to earth in a flood like the Kampai, which our lord called to Kāñci to demonstrate the love of the Lady who gave birth to the world";[67] by implication, the earth can survive, as did Kāñcipuram.

The Kāviri myth has, however, borrowed more significantly from other sources. Its basic image is once again that of the creative seed / flood carried in a pot. Agastya's appearance in the myth is natural for at least two reasons: first, Agastya is himself born from a pot (Kumbhayoni); and second, this sage is the major figure in the Tamil myth of cultural origins, and thus belongs by right in other myths of creation—especially creation from a flood. Both the Caṅkam and Kāviri myths seem to belong to this category, as we shall see. Agastya figures already in a much older version of the Kāviri myth: at the request of Kāntamaṉ the Cōḻaṉ, Agastya tipped over his pot (*karakam*), and Lady Kāviri flowed eastwards to the sea; she joined the sea at the spot where the ancient goddess Campāpati was performing *tapas*, and the goddess declared that the city would be known thereafter by the name of the river (Kāvirippūmpaṭṭiṉam).[68] Here the Śaiva veneer of the *Kantapurāṇam* is lacking, and Indra's catalytic role is fulfilled by the Cōḻa king; yet both Agastya and the origin of the river in the water pot are mentioned. They might be said to be the primary constituents of the story, and to suggest in themselves the identification of the river with the divine seed. This identification is strengthened in the *Kantapurāṇam* by the addition of several elements drawn from the myth of Skanda's birth. There, too, the seed (of Śiva or Agni) is often put into a pot (or pit);[69] or it is placed in the Ganges,[70] or in a golden lake,[71] or in a clump of reeds.[72] In the Tamil myth the clump of reeds appears as the bamboo in which Indra hides[73] until Cīkāḻi is flooded by the river. The bamboo and other trees of Indra's garden are burned—not by the fiery seed of Śiva, which burns any vehicle or receptacle in which it is placed, but by the sun, which consumes them "as the Triple City was once burned by Śiva."[74] Indra instigates the descent of the river, just as he interferes with Śiva's *tapas* to seek the birth of Śiva's child. The very name of the river that appears most often in this account—Pŏṉṉi, the Golden, "the Kauvery river, as having golden sands"[75]—recalls the constant recurrence of gold in the Skanda birth myth: the seed itself is golden[76] (an inheritance from the Vedic Hiraṇyagarbha), as are the pot,[77] the mountain on which it is placed,[78] the reed forest or lake (with trees or lotuses),[79] the twins born by Agni's wife Svāhā,[80] the cup with which Pārvatī nurses the infant Skanda,[81] and all that the brilliant seed illuminates (grass, creepers, shrubs, mountains, and forests).[82] Moreover, the Pŏṉṉi is compared to "*amṛta* drunk by starving men";[83] *amṛta* or Soma is a common equivalent for seed in Śaiva symbolism,[84] and let us recall that the Seed of Creation flows from the broken pot at Kumpakoṇam as a river of *amṛta*.

Gaṇeśa's appearance in the myth, first as a crow and then as a Brahmin boy, also has important precedents. The first image goes back to the ancient concept of the fire-bird carrying ambrosia;[85] the conjunction of birds and seed is common in Hindu mythology.[86] Birds are usually present in the Skanda myth: Agni takes the form of a parrot,[87] turtle-dove (*pārāvata*),[88] or goose[89] to interrupt Śiva and Pārvatī in their love making; Kāma comes in the form of a *cakravāka* to wound Śiva;[90] and Svāhā as a Garuḍī bird carries the fiery seed to the mountain peak.[91] In the Kāviri myth, the crow-Gaṇeśa liberates the seed/river from the pot. Gaṇeśa then takes the form of a young Brahmin and flees from Agastya; this element in the myth may be related to the following, somewhat unusual account of Gaṇeśa's birth:

> Viṣṇu in the form of a Brahmin ascetic, tortured by thirst, interrupted Śiva and Pārvatī when they were making love. Śiva spilled his seed on the bed. Śiva and Pārvatī offered the Brahmin food and drink, but he took the form of a child and went to the bed, where he became mingled with Śiva's seed. Seeing a baby lying on the bed and looking up at the roof, Pārvatī nursed him as her son (and he was named Gaṇeśa).[92]

The interruption of Śiva and Pārvatī's love making, which is basic to the Skanda birth myth, here produces their other child, Gaṇeśa. Gaṇeśa, instead of taking the form of a young Brahmin, is here born *from* the Brahmin, whose thirst is quenched not by water but by Śiva's seed, just as the river/seed restores the parched plants of Indra's garden in the Tamil myth.

The creative force of the Kāviri flood becomes clear at the conclusion of the myth: Cīkāḻi, which has been desiccated by the drought sent by Indra's demon adversaries, is revived by the river. We have here, in effect, a reversal of the other flood myth from Cīkāḻi, in which Śiva, who has escaped to this shrine in a boat, begins creating the world at this spot by first drying up the waters of the flood. Both myths, however, contain the same basic idea of a new creation proceeding from a flood. In the Kāviri myth, the flood is itself an equivalent of the divine seed carried in a pot; in the more conventional cosmogonies, such as the myth from Tiruvŏṟṟiyūr, the creation follows the great flood and opposes it as land is opposed to water, order to chaos. Nevertheless, the destruction of the deluge is the necessary prelude to the rebirth of the world; the violent flood holds within it the seed of a new creation. This idea is clearly conveyed by the Kumpakoṇam story, in which the creative seed is carried over the waters in a pot, just as the sound of the Vedas, Śiva's guide to creation, brings the creator god to Cīkāḻi. It now remains for us to study the relevance of these symbols for an understanding of the myths of Maturai and the Tamil Caṅkam.

## *The Maturai Flood Myths and the Caṅkam Story*

Of all Tamil shrines, Maturai can claim the greatest number of flood myths. There are two major myths of a flood in the Maturai purāṇas;[93] in addition, we have a story about the rediscovery of the boundaries of the city after the *pralaya*;[94] a related story in which the Vedas, newly emerged from the *praṇava* after a universal destruction, are expounded to the sages of the Naimiṣa Forest in Maturai;[95] the arrival of the seven seas in Maturai for Kañcanai's ablutions;[96] the myth of the Kubera-*liṅga*, which never perishes in the flood;[97] the flooding of the Vaikai River;[98] and three examples of the closely related theme of surviving not a flood but its opposite, a drought.[99] The flood myths relating to the first two Caṅkam also belong here, as we shall see. Let us begin with the first of the flood myths in Pĕrumpaṟṟappuliyūrnampi's *Tiruvālavāyuṭaiyār tiruviḷaiyāṭaṟpurāṇam*:

> Varuṇa, the lord of the sea, wished to test the greatness of Śiva, so he ordered the ocean to flood the world. The gods, men, Nāgas, and others took refuge with the lord of Ālavāy (Maturai), to whom the panic-stricken Indra called for help. Śiva sent the doomsday clouds (Puṣkalāvarta and three others) to drink up the waters of the ocean. Varuṇa was incensed at this action, so he sent his own clouds to destroy the city with their rain. Śiva made the doomsday clouds into buildings and sent them to protect Maturai from the rain. They towered

> over the city until Varuṇa's clouds dried up, and they then remained in Maturai as four buildings (*māṭam*). Hence Maturai is known as Nāṉmāṭakkūṭal ("the junction of four buildings").[100]

This story is in explanation of one of the old names of the city, Nāṉmāṭakkūṭal, which probably derives from four ancient temples (to Kaṉṉi, Kariyamāl, Kāḷi, and Ālavāy) in the town. The name appears in the classical sources,[101] and the identifications of the four temples given by Nacciṉārkkiṉiyar (on *Kalittŏkai* 92.65) survive in the names of the protecting divinities cited in the introduction to Pĕrumpaṟṟappuliyūrnampi's text.[102] This, then, is an origin myth: the four great temples of Maturai were the doomsday clouds sent by Śiva to defend the city from the flood. The doomsday clouds, which are said to have been born from the seed shed by Brahmā at the wedding of Śiva and Satī,[103] connect this story with that of the Pāṇṭiyaṉ, who imprisoned the four doomsday clouds in response to a drought caused by Indra.[104] In our myth, the flood is checked by the doomsday clouds, which then protect the city from the flood of rain sent by the angry Varuṇa; here the clouds are analogous to the mountain (Govardhana) that Kṛṣṇa holds up to protect Gokula from the torrential rains of Indra.[105] In the slightly expanded version of the flood myth in the *Tiruviḷai.* of Parañcoti, Indra is also the instigator of the flood at Maturai:

> Once when Indra came to worship in the temple at Maturai, he found Apiṭekapāṇṭiyaṉ engaged in worship there. Indra had to wait to offer his devotion. When he returned to heaven, Varuṇa came to visit and found him feeling sad because his prayers had been delayed. When Varuṇa saw how devoted Indra was to Cŏkkaliṅkam (Śiva at Maturai), he asked if the god of Maturai could cure the pain in his stomach. "Try him and see for yourself," said Indra, so Varuṇa sent the sea to destroy Maturai. The Pāṇṭiyaṉ sought the help of Śiva, and Śiva sent four clouds from his matted locks to dry up the sea. Furious at this check and unable to understand the amusement of the lord of Maturai, Varuṇa sent seven clouds to destroy the city with rain. Rain fell in streams like crystal pillars, and the inhabitants of Maturai thought the end of the world had come. To remove their distress Śiva commanded the four clouds to cover the four corners of the ancient city in the form of four buildings. The clouds of Varuṇa exhausted their rain on these buildings,

> and Varuṇa became ashamed. He worshiped the lord of Maturai, and the pain in his stomach disappeared.[106]

Here it is specifically Maturai rather than the world as a whole (*ñālam*) that the sea attacks. Note that the stock idea of the rivalry between Indra and a virtuous mortal (king or sage) is transferred to a competition in devotion to Śiva: Indra must wait until the king finishes his prayer. Moreover, as in the earlier version, the idea of testing the devotee is reversed, and Varuṇa tests the god. Indra's inspiration of the test might be seen as an interesting extension of his role in opposing Śiva in other myths, for example by sending Kāma to disturb the god's meditation—an action that, like Varuṇa's trial by water, is ultimately benevolent in intent. There is also an echo of the myth of churning the ocean, which in any case shares several motifs with the cosmogonic flood (such as the emergence of *amṛta*, a multiform of the divine seed, from the waters): there Śiva neutralizes the poison that rises from the depths of the sea, as at Maturai he heals the pain in the sea-god's stomach.[107] The idea that *bhakti* can cure stomach pains is a common motif in Śaiva hagiographies.[108]

The second flood story is a multiform of the first:

> Once the sea rose against the ancient city of Maturai. The gods were alarmed and, seeing this, Śiva appeared to Ukkirapāṇṭiyaṉ in a dream and told him to throw the lance which he (as his father, Cuntarapāṇṭiyaṉ) had given him against the fearsome sea (*nām aḷitta velaiy aṟa nām aḷitta velaiy ĕṟi*). The Pāṇṭiyaṉ awoke and, after being urged again by the god, threw his spear at the sea, which became calm and lapped at his feet. Tamiḻccŏkkaṉ (Śiva) appeared, erected a *maṇḍapa*, and said, "This will be the site of the first and second Caṅkam; the third will be on the bank of the Ganges."[109]

Aravamuthan has shown that the notion of the sea lapping the feet of the king became a cliché of the commentators.[110] The bank of the Ganges is taken to be a reference to the Pŏṟṟāmarai Tank at Maturai.[111] The *Tiruviḷai.* adds a pretext for the flood: Indra became jealous of the Pāṇṭiyaṉ, who was ruling virtuously and had performed ninety-six horse sacrifices, so he told the lord of the sea to flood Maturai as if it were the time of the universal deluge.[112] Instead of the god's building a *maṇḍapa* for the Caṅkam, the *Tiruviḷai.* has the king consecrate to Śiva all the area of fields and villages between the walled ancient city of Maturai and the retreating sea (verse 20).

It is this last element, the consecration of the land relinquished by the sea, which, one might suggest, is the focal point of the myth. Not only does the city *survive* the flood; it is in part (fields and villages or, in *Tiruvāl.*, the site of the Caṅkam) created from the flood by the casting of the spear. The same motif occurs in a number of other myths. Aravamuthan has suggested that the idea of throwing a spear at the sea goes back to Agastya's drinking the ocean[113] or, more convincingly, to Kārtavīrya's showering arrows at the ocean[114] and Skanda's hurling his lance at Mount Krauñca.[115] There is also the story of Bhīṣma, who dries up the Ganges by shooting arrows at it.[116] But the idea of a creative attack upon the ocean is perhaps most clear in another well-known origin myth in south India: Paraśurāma created the land from Gokarṇam to Kanyākumārī by throwing his axe at the ocean.[117] The prototype of this tradition appears in the *MBh*:

> Paraśurāma cleared the earth of Kṣatriyas and gave it to Kaśyapa as a sacrificial fee. Kaśyapa said to him, "Go to the shore of the southern ocean; you must not dwell in my territory." The sea measured out for Paraśurāma a country called Śūrpāraka. Kaśyapa made the earth an abode of Brahmins and entered the forest.[118]

The Kōṅku and Tuḷuva regions have a similar myth of origins.[119] We may recall here Kṛṣṇa's war against the ocean and his building of Dvārakā on land relinquished by the sea.[120]

Another variation on this theme is the myth of the bridge at Irāmeccuram: Rāma asked the sea to help him cross to Laṅkā; when the ocean did not appear in answer to his appeal and three days had passed, Rāma began to shoot arrows at the sea. The sea came up from Pātāla and sought refuge with Rāma, begged not to be forced to transgress the laws of creation by drying up its waters, and suggested that instead the monkey Nala build a causeway.[121] Like Paraśurāma, Rāmacandra attacks the sea; and, although the sea does not recede, it provides the means of crossing over it by land.

Perhaps the most important parallel is found in the Tamil myths of Murukaṉ. Ukkirapāṇṭiyaṉ, who casts his spear against the sea in the Maturai flood myth, is himself an incarnation of Skanda / Murukaṉ, for he is the son of Śiva / Cuntarapāṇṭiyaṉ and Pārvatī /

Mīnākṣī.[122] In Tamil mythology, Murukaṉ casts his spear twice—once against Mount Krauñca, as in the Sanskrit sources, and once more against the demon Cūr (Śūrapadma), who has taken the form of a huge mango tree in the midst of the sea. It is this latter episode that is particularly celebrated in Tamil literature: "We praise the wielder of the spear that killed the mango (demon) in the ocean."[123] Moreover, Murukaṉ's war against Cūr may be part of an ancient myth of creation: the spear dries up the waters of the ocean as it flies toward the mango, and the destruction of the mango creates space for the world and liberates the sun from the darkness of chaos.[124] In casting his spear in the ocean, the god thus overcomes the forces of disorder and uncontrolled violence, just as the king of Maturai subdues the threatening sea with his spear.

There is another set of references in ancient Tamil literature to throwing back the sea. The hero of the fifth decade of *Patiṟṟuppattu* is Cĕṅkuṭṭuvaṉ "who drove back the sea" (*kaṭal piṟakk' oṭṭiya cĕṅkuṭṭuvaṉ*). He too is said to have lifted his spear (*vel*) against the sea,[125] but the old commentary takes this to mean he fought against people whose stronghold was the sea (*taṉṉuḷ vāḻvārkku araṇ ākiya kaṭal*). Probably the verses refer to pirates, although this is not stated explicitly.[126] There remains a strong possibility that the epithet *kaṭal piṟakk' oṭṭiya-* contributed to the later flood myths from Maturai.

Let us return to the Maturai myths. We have seen that both *Tiruviḷai.* end the second flood myth with an act of creation after the deluge, and *Tiruvāl.* (the earlier of the two) connects this with the story of the Caṅkam. Aravamuthan has argued that the last verse of *Tiruvāl.* 21, which tells us that the site established by the god served as the home of the first two Caṅkam, is spurious.[127] Certainly the verse presents difficulties if one is to attempt to put together a chronology based on the *Tiruvāl.*; this, in effect, is what Parañcoti (or rather his probable source, the Sanskrit *Hālāsyamāhātmya*) has done,[128] and it is perhaps significant that he speaks throughout of only one Caṅkam. However, the *Hālāsyamāhātmya* follows the earlier tradition in this case, and mentions three "academies," the first two in the city saved from the flood, and the third on the bank of the Ganges.[129] Evidently Parañcoti has replaced this tradition with a more consistent scheme, based on the existence of a single Caṅkam. Perhaps he was closer to the original Caṅkam legend than he knew.

The first complete account of the three Caṅkam and the two destructive floods appears, as we saw earlier, in the commentary ascribed to Nakkīrar on *Iṟaiyaṉār akappŏruḷ*. But there are still older allusions to an ancient flood in the Pāṇṭiya land. *Kalittŏkai* 104 tells us that when the sea rose and took his land, the Pāṇṭiya king (*tĕṉṉavaṉ*) carved new lands for himself from the territories of his enemies, removing the (Coḻa) tiger and the (Cera) bow, and substituting the (Pāṇṭiya) emblem of the fish.[130] Does this not confront us again with the familiar motif of land created in opposition to water? Perhaps not. The *Cilappatikāram*, which also knows the flood legend in relation to the Pāṇṭiyas, reverses the usual order: "May the *tĕṉṉavaṉ* prosper who ruled the South and took the Ganges and the Himālaya of the North when once the sea, refusing to bear the prowess he demonstrated to other kings by throwing against it his sharp spear, swallowed the Kumarikkoṭu together with the Pahṟuḷi River and several nearby mountains."[131] According to the old, anonymous commentary (Arumpatavurai), Kumarikkoṭu refers to the bank of the Kumari River, while Aṭiyārkkunallār takes it to mean a mountain peak. This text is unique in explaining the flood as revenge for the casting of the spear rather than its occasion, although it also implies that the Pāṇṭiyaṉ conquered new lands because of the flood. Aṭiyārkkunallār supports this: the *tĕṉṉavaṉ* ruled Muttūrkkūṟṟam in the Coḻanāṭu and Kuṇṭūrkkūṟṟam in the Ceramānāṭu in exchange for the lands he had lost in the flood.[132]

What, then, is one to conclude about the legend of the three Caṅkam and the lost lands of the Pāṇṭiyas? We have seen that the *Tiruvāl.* connects the origin of the Caṅkam with the flood, while the references in *Cilappatikāram* and *Kalittŏkai* suggest that the flood is used, as in much later purāṇic myths, to explain the origin of the present boundaries of the Pāṇṭiya land. The commentators' information on the lands that were allegedly lost in the deluge hardly inspires confidence, and early references in the literature[133] know only one Caṅkam, that which is said to have been situated in present-day Maturai. Given the prevalence of the flood motif in south Indian mythology, its particular prominence in Maturai, its association with the idea of creation, and the absence of any geological evidence of a real flood, it would seem that the story of the *first two* Caṅkam is an expansion of an early origin myth centered in Maturai.[134] Like other Tamil shrines, Maturai sees itself as the indestructible center of the universe, the site of creation, the survivor of the *pralaya*; to these notions Maturai has added its claim to be the ancient home of Tamil poetry and the site of the "academy" linked by a persistent tradition to the first flowering of Tamil culture. Literary origins have been described in terms borrowed from the cosmogonic myth; the flood that precedes the creation of the world has been used as the background to the establishment of the Caṅkam, as well. But creation in India is not a unique event at the beginning of time, but an ever-recurring moment, a repetition of something already known; and thus the academy of poets in historical Maturai is not, in the view of the tradition, the first of its kind, but rather a rebirth of an earlier model after a cataclysmic flood.

To summarize: the Tamil flood myths are essentially myths of creation. At the end of each cycle of time, a flood destroys the world—except for the shrine situated at the world's center and linked directly to the transcendent worlds above and below. At this spot God creates the universe once more by throwing back the waters of the flood, or by substituting for them a creative flood of seed or *amṛta*. The cosmogony implies the institution of order in the face of primeval chaos; hence the close connection between the Tamil flood myths and the legend of the birth of Tamil poetry and culture. Civilization and order oppose the forces of chaos out of which they emerge. Yet these forces are never wholly conquered; the violent flood will one day return to destroy the world, and it may survive inside the shrine in a limited, bounded form as part of the idealized, ordered microcosm at the center of the universe.

## *The Walls of the Shrine*

The idea of imposing limits on a violent power is often attached to the common motif of erecting ramparts or embankments. Every important shrine is surrounded by a wall, which defines the boundary of the sacred zone; the wall serves to isolate the shrine from the surrounding realm of chaos and evil, and also to restrict the operation of the powerful forces situated within. The idealized universe of the shrine can exist only through a rigid ordering and limitation, and by the exclusion of external disorder. Hence the importance of the divider: the wall safeguards the shrine; the waters of the flood are often said to lap against the wall, which prevents them from overpowering the sacred site.[135] Historically, it is the Kāviri River that has attracted the largest number of stories about the building of embankments; many of these stories involve the Coḻa king Karikālaṉ.[136] But it is frequently the god himself who helps build a wall to protect his shrine:

> Koccĕṅkaṇār and other kings came to build the walls of the temple at Tiruvāṉaikkā. A voice from heaven said, "Make everything ready but do not build the walls." Śiva took the form of an ascetic and put carpenters and other craftsmen to work on the wall. He paid them in ashes that turned to gold. They worked diligently, but whenever the wall began to grow high, the ascetic put his foot on it and pressed it into the ground. After doing this (several times), he raised the wall to heaven as a great rampart for the benefit of his devotees.[137]

Śiva, the deity worshiped at Tiruvāṉaikkā, first emulates and then reverses the act of his disciple Agastya, who presses the Vindhya mountains into the earth.[138] This myth belongs to a wider category of depictions of the god as a laborer;[139] as in many of these myths, the god who comes to earth to perform manual labor is also a prankster who refuses to work in a normal fashion, and yet accomplishes more than all his fellows. The god's apparent opposition to our notions of propriety and order is illustrated by the wages of ash paid to his workmen; yet Śiva's ashes turn to gold. Another myth from Maturai connects this pattern with the flood, which comes this time not from the ocean or the ocean's lord, but from the Vaikai River:

> Because of the sufferings inflicted on his devotee Vātavūrar, Śiva caused the Vaikai to flood. The king ordered the inhabitants of Maturai to build dykes to hold back the raging river. An old woman named Vanti sought a workman to do her portion of the work for her; in her weakness and distress, she cried to Śiva. A worker appeared, carrying a basket on his head and a spade on his shoulder, and agreed to work for her in exchange for the rice cakes (*piṭṭu*) she sold for a living. He ate all her cakes and went off to work, but he labored at the dyke in a most erratic manner: he would fill his basket with earth and put it on his head, then he would cry, "It is too heavy!" and pour it out again; he would dance, sing, laugh, kick up a shower of sand as he ran about; then he would sigh as if he had been laboring long and go back to Vanti with a demand: "I am hungry. Make some more cakes quickly!" He would stuff himself in a second and return to the dyke with new energy, but soon he would be tripping the other workers, or jumping into the river for a swim, or lying down for a nap. The overseers noticed that the work was progressing in all parts except

> that assigned to Vanti, and they reported this to the king. He flew into a rage and struck the mad laborer—and the entire universe reeled from the blow. When the workmen raised their eyes, they saw that Vanti's laborer had disappeared and the dyke had risen up to heaven.[140]

Here Śiva himself sends the flood as a pretext for another of his amusements which, as throughout the Vātavūrar cycle, contrasts the duties of life in the world with the overriding imperative of love for the god. The myth ends with the dyke complete, the flood contained, the city saved; as in other Tamil myths, the city-shrine survives the deluge. The dyke that touches heaven completes the isolation of the holy site, situated on the *axis mundi* and opposed to the surrounding realm of disorder. Such isolation is not, however, achieved without cost. We must now investigate the religious implications of a concept of the deity as localized, endowed with specific, limited forms and attributes, and in some sense opposed to the world outside his shrine.

## 3. The Specialization of the Divine: Divodāsa and the Dance of Śiva

The localization of the divine presence is not a simple matter. Even if each shrine sees itself as the center of the world and the natural site of creation, the tenacity with which it claims a specific, unchanging form of the deity raises difficult questions for the authors of our myths. Why must the god be so closely bound to the shrine? Is he limited by its limitations? How does he transcend his individual incarnations? These problems come to light in the myth of Divodāsa, the king who competes with Śiva for possession of Kāśī (Benares). Divodāsa appears in the *RV* in association with Indra's destruction of a hundred cities of stone.[1] In the epic he is said to have fortified the city of Vārāṇasī (Benares),[2] and to have taken away the sacrificial fires of his enemies.[3] In the Sanskrit purāṇas, Divodāsa's attachment to Kāśī brings him into conflict with Śiva, who is himself fond of the city and wishes to dwell there with his wife:

> After his marriage to Pārvatī, Śiva lived with his bride in the home of his in-laws. His mother-in-law, Menā, expressed distaste for the habits of Śiva and his fearsome attendants, so Pārvatī asked that he find them another home. Śiva looked

> through the world and decided upon Kāśī, but the city was inhabited by Divodāsa. Śiva sent Nikumbha (Gaṇeśa) to evict Divodāsa by subtle means. Nikumbha appeared in a dream to a Brahmin in the city and instructed him to erect a shrine containing his image. When the shrine was established, many people worshiped Gaṇeśa and received sons and gold and other boons. Suyaśā, the wife of the king, asked the god for a son; when, after a long time, she still had not had her wish fulfilled, Divodāsa destroyed the shrine in anger. For this Gaṇeśa cursed him, and the city became empty. Śiva came there with Devī and declared that he would never again depart from Kāśī.[4]

Clearly, there is no room for both god and man in Kāśī; the king must be driven out along with the other inhabitants before Śiva can take up residence there. Our texts add that Śiva dwells in Kāśī in the first three *yugas*, and in the fourth (the Kali Age) *that* city goes into hiding while the city (of men) exists again.[5] Here the motif of hiding the shrine explains the existence of the historical Kāśī, the city of men, which—in contrast with the usual pattern of the south Indian myths—is considered problematic. The Kāśī inhabited by men can exist only if Śiva's Kāśī is hidden. This idea is closely linked to the motif of destroying (rather than hiding) a shrine—the act that is used here as the pretext for Divodāsa's removal from Kāśī. Gaṇeśa, who is worshiped in order to avoid obstacles, here *creates* an obstacle to Divodāsa's rule; the king falls victim to Gaṇeśa's plot, and Śiva is thus given a chance to take the city for himself.

The dilemma posed by the incompatibility of a divine and a human presence in Kāśī is intensified in other versions of the myth, which stress the righteous nature of the king:

> For six years the world suffered a terrible drought. Brahmā asked the ascetic prince Ripuñjaya, who was performing *tapas* in Kāśī, to become king in order to bring relief to the world. Ripuñjaya agreed, on condition that the gods depart from earth, leaving him the sole provider of happiness for men. Brahmā persuaded Śiva to leave his beloved Kāśī, and Ripuñjaya took the name of Divodāsa and ruled as a righteous (*dharmiṣṭha*) king in Kāśī.
>
> After eight thousand years the gods complained to Bṛhaspati: "Divodāsa is ruling his kingdom flawlessly. We gods will suffer if he alone reaps the fruit of his righteous ways." Meanwhile, Śiva was homesick for Kāśī and complained about his

absence from the city to Pārvatī. He sent seductive *yoginīs* to make the king fall from his *svadharma*, but they were happy in Kāśī, and refused to return to heaven. Sūrya then took many forms and preached heresy to the citizens of Kāśī, but he failed to find a chink (*chidra*) in the city's righteousness. Brahmā, too, was sent and failed. Gaṇeśa took the form of an astrologer and deluded people in their sleep; but when Divodāsa called him to the palace, he merely praised the king's righteousness and promised him that in eighteen days an old Brahmin would come to tell him what to do.

Viṣṇu took the form of a teacher named Vinayakīrti, while Lakṣmī became the *bhikṣuṇī* Vijñānakaumudī. They corrupted the inhabitants of Kāśī with Buddhist ideas. Divodāsa sent for the teacher and said, "I am weary of ruling and wish to withdraw from the world. What shall I do? My only offense has been to regard the gods as mere blades of grass, and even that was for the good of my subjects, never for my own benefit. I have ruled righteously, and my subjects are devoted to *dharma* and truth, but I know many (of the righteous) have been destroyed through the enmity of the gods. The heroes of the Triple City were supreme in their devotion to Śiva, yet Śiva reduced them to ashes as an amusement (*līlayā*). Bali, most excellent of sacrificers, was deceived and sent to Pātāla by Viṣṇu; Dadhīci was slain by the gods in order to make a weapon from his bones; Hari cut off the thousand arms of the virtuous Bāṇa—through what fault of Bāṇa's? I do not wish to struggle against the gods, but I am not afraid of them; they reached their position through sacrifices, but I am superior to them in sacrificing, charity, and *tapas*." Viṣṇu said, "The gods are pleased with your virtue. Your one flaw (*doṣa*) appears to be in your heart: you have kept the lord of Kāśī far away. You can redeem yourself by setting up a *liṅga*." Divodāsa installed his son as his successor, built a Śiva temple and worshiped the *liṅga*. After acquiring the appearance of Śiva himself, he was taken up to heaven in a divine chariot.[6]

The rivalry between the king and the god is more complex in this version; in addition to the competition between Śiva and Divodāsa for control of Kāśī, we have the gods' fear of overly righteous mortals, a fear that belies their ostensible support for righteousness on earth. Divodāsa is able to realize his somewhat arrogant wish to be the sole source of happiness for men; thus the gods, and the worship of the gods, are rendered redundant, and Śiva is kept in exile from his city. Hence the need to corrupt the human exemplar of virtue. The attempts to corrupt Divodāsa belong to two main types: Śiva's *yoginīs* replace the usual troops of divine temptresses sent by Indra; and preachers of heresy are dispatched to destroy the right beliefs of the city's populace. Divodāsa himself is incorruptible, but he appears to be weakened by a moral sensitivity; he knows that devotion to *dharma* is no guarantee of safety, and he even cites as proof the destruction by Śiva of the pious *tripura* demons along with other examples of unmerited punishment by the gods. In the end he is reluctantly rewarded by being promoted to heaven at the cost of surrendering his claim to Kāśī, and his defeat is rationalized by reference to his lack of devotion to Śiva—a charge meant to obscure the root cause of the problem, Śiva's uncompromising desire for Kāśī.

The devotional aspect of the myth is further developed in Kacciyappar's *Vināyakapurāṇam*, which has a version of the Divodāsa myth largely dependent on that of the *Skandapurāṇa*. There is no significant divergence until after the failure of the *yoginīs* to corrupt the king, when Śiva sends Gaṇeśa to Kāśī:

> Vināyaka took the form of an astrologer with a book under his arm. He gave the town's citizens bad dreams, and then appeared and interpreted the dreams and the position of the stars as auguring the impending ruin of the city. The people fled, forgetting to perform their rites. The king learned of the astrologer's activities from his wives; he invited him to the palace and told him he was tired of ruling. The astrologer told him that a Brahmin would come to tell him what to do.
>
> Viṣṇu and Lakṣmī came and corrupted the people with Buddhist ideas. The king summoned the Brahmin teacher of heresy and said, "I know you are really Viṣṇu, and I know you have corrupted my people. This is a plot of the gods against me. I also know it was Vināyaka who came earlier to dispel my ignorance (*aññāṉam*). Forgive me for driving away the gods."
>
> Viṣṇu took his old form, since he saw that Divodāsa deserved to hear the truth. He told him to restore Kāśī to Śiva. Divodāsa turned the city over to his son, built a temple to Śiva, and worshiped the *liṅga*, and Śiva caused him to merge into the *liṅga*.[7]

This version adds to the righteousness of Divodāsa the attribute of superhuman wisdom: he sees through the disguises of Gaṇeśa and Viṣṇu. Divodāsa boldly proclaims the rivalry between himself and the gods and even speaks of a plot (*cūḻcci*) against him. Yet this element is largely subordinated to a moralizing note that suggests the late character of this version: Divodāsa recognizes in the plot of the gods a purpose that transcends questions of rank and competition. Vināyaka has come down to Kāśī to enlighten the king rather than simply to corrupt him, and Viṣṇu puts off his disguise when he sees the king's sincerity—for Divodāsa seeks forgiveness instead of continued confrontation. In the end, instead of being translated to heaven with the aspect of Śiva, Divodāsa merges with the *liṅga* in Śiva's temple; and it is in this form as the *liṅga*, in the shrine built for him by his mortal rival, that the god succeeds in coming home to his city on earth.

Let us return for a moment to the version of the Divodāsa myth in the *Skandapurāṇa*, where an important problem is formulated. Śiva has been lamenting his forced exile from Kāśī, and Pārvatī demands an explanation of his homesickness: "You who are all-pervading (*sarvaga*), everything is in your hand. How can you be affected by junction or separation (*yoga-viyoga eva kas te*)? Your power creates, destroys, and sustains creatures; if you look away for but an instant, the worlds are annihilated. . . ."[8] To this Śiva answers cryptically: "The eight-fold form (of god: *aṣṭamūrti*) is called Kāśī; the world arose in an eight-fold form."[9] Is the sacred city thus equated with the created universe? If so, why is the god said to suffer exile from this one specific spot? Although Śiva appears to evade the issue, his reply is interesting in the light of the Tamil tradition of eight major shrines (the *aṭṭavīraṭṭāṉam*) sacred to Śiva. The *aṣṭamūrti* is a well-known symbolic set that appears already in the *Brāhmaṇas*, and that expresses the god's presence in (and perhaps identity with) the world.[10] As such, it frequently appears in the Tamil hymns of the *Tevāram*. But the *Tevāram* poets were also familiar with at least some of the identifications that make up the derivative set of the *vīraṭṭāṉam*, a popular classification of eight major events in the mythology of Śiva in terms of their localization in the Tamil land. An anonymous verse lists the identifications as follows: 1) the decapitation of Brahmā (took place at) Kaṇṭiyūr; 2) the impaling of Andhaka—at Kovalūr; 3) the burning of the Triple City—at Atikai; 4) Dakṣa's sacrifice—at Paṟiyalūr; 5) the war with Jalandhara—at Viṟkuṭi; 6) the skinning of the elephant—at Vaḻuvūr; 7) the burning of Kāma—at Kuṟukkai; and

8) the killing of Yama—at Kaṭavūr.[11] The Tamil purāṇas provide the mythology to support these identifications, some of which apparently go back at least to the seventh century A.D.; all in all, they represent an unusual popular reinterpretation of classical cosmological notions. Similarly, the five constituent elements—earth, air (or wind), fire, water, and "ether" (*ākāśa*)—have been distributed over a set of five shrines, each of them distinguished by a *liṅga* associated with one of the elements (Kāñci, Kāḷatti, Tiruvaṇṇāmalai, Tiruvāṉaikkā, and Citamparam, respectively).[12] The very elements of the universe are thus, like the deity, localized in individual shrines in the Tamil land.

Still, we are without a satisfying answer to Pārvatī's question: how can the god, who is affirmed to be omnipresent, suffer exile? Even if Kāśī is considered to be somehow equivalent to the *aṣṭamūrti*, and hence to the world, Śiva still cannot go there without removing Divodāsa. All of Śiva's actions after he convinces Pārvatī of Kāśī's unique greatness indicate that for the purposes of the myth, the idea of divine omnipresence is completely subordinated to the idea of the god's special yearning for a particular place.

The same wavering between notions of universality and a specific presence is evident in the tradition that Śaṅkara, the *advaitin* philosopher, sought forgiveness on his deathbed for having spent much of his life in pilgrimages to shrines, since worshiping at holy places might imply that god is not everywhere.[13] This story reflects the tension between *advaita-vedānta* and *bhakti* religion, which claims Śaṅkara as the author of many popular texts,[14] and as a prominent figure in the history of several shrines.[15] But the question can be put in more general terms: what does it mean to say that the god has a particular form, name, mythological history, and mode of worship in any given place? Hart has outlined an historical aspect of the problem: the basic orientation of Tamil religion since earliest times has been toward deities that inhere in a place, or that are, in Hart's terms, "immanent" rather than "transcendent"; the Upaniṣadic Absolute (or the *brahman* of the *advaitins*) is, on the other hand, an unlimited, underlying reality existing equally everywhere.[16] What must be stressed here is that the god of the Tamil purāṇas stands at the end of a long period of development, in the course of which the contrasting ideals of earlier stages of Indian religion have merged. The god has thus absorbed the nature of the Upaniṣadic Absolute as well as of the fearsome ancient Tamil deities; he also focuses in his person the symbolism of the Brahminical sacrificial cult.[17] The Tamil Śiva is a complex, composite figure, and there is no reason to believe that the currents that mingle in his worship have resolved their contradictions. On the contrary, their incompatibility is evident in the synthetic image of the god that emerges from their union. As the inheritor of Upaniṣadic idealism, Śiva becomes a symbol of *mokṣa*, and thus embodies the universality, the freedom, the purity of release—and this despite the fact that *mokṣa* as a practical goal is virtually eliminated, or rather redefined to coincide with devotion to the god. Renunciation is rejected, while life on earth and within society is sanctified through *bhakti*, as we have seen. One wonders if this development was facilitated by the idealization of the shrine, the site of the divine revelation; it is almost as if the tension between the absolute freedom and purity sought by the renouncer and the reality of the world of relations that he rejects persists in Tamil devotional religion in the isolation of the other-worldly, idealized shrine from the surrounding realm of conflict and evil. In other words, the sanctification of man's life on earth takes place through the preservation on earth of an other-worldly refuge characterized by harmony and freedom from evil.

Such a view would help explain the constant preference of the myths for the particular rather than the universal aspect of the deity: it is precisely in his specific, located form inside the shrine that the god is most isolated and hence most pure. The particular is the only sure path to a universal ideal of freedom. But this is only part of the picture. It is important to remember that the god in his shrine is still a source of power—indeed, of dangerous, violent power—and, as we shall see, an exemplar of the sacrifice. This is the other side of the Tamil Śiva—a god of chaos and caprice, of darkness and of violent birth, both victim and master of the sacrifice. As such he is totally located, possessed of distinct and seemingly independent incarnations in each sacred spot. The shrines in which he is revealed thus become the scenes of a more intense reality, or of a more extreme expression of chaos, than the surrounding, everyday world; only in the shrines the revelation of power is controlled by the ritual order, and made accessible through the boundaries imposed upon it. The shrine thus becomes preeminent both as a transformation of the ideal of isolation and purity and as an epitome of terrestrial existence and power.[18]

It now becomes clear why the Tamil myths, even when they wish to avoid compromising the universality of the god, invariably proclaim the decisive importance of his local incarnations. One text puts it in terms of a familiar image: "Even if a cow's entire body were filled with milk, it could secrete it only through the teat; in the same way the Supreme Lord (*paramaṉ*), who pervades the universe, manifested himself in the Picture-*liṅga* for the salvation of those who dwell in the world."[19] The comparison of a shrine with milk is not fortuitous, as we shall see; milk is a multiform of the divine seed of creation. Elsewhere, entire myths deal with the problem of the particular revelation and its relation to a universal presence. Observe, for example, how the Tamils transform the well-known story of Skanda's competition with his brother, Gaṇeśa:

> When Gaṇeśa and Kārttikeya reached manhood, their parents decided to find them brides. The brothers quarreled over this, so Śiva and Pārvatī devised a test: whoever went around the world first would be married. The valiant Kārttikeya immediately started off, but the clever, obese Gaṇeśa thought to himself: "I will never succeed in circling the earth; I doubt if I can go farther than a single *krośa*!" He asked his parents to sit down and walked around them seven times; then he asked them to find him a bride. "First try to go around the world," they said. "Look, Skanda has already left." Gaṇeśa replied, "By going around you I have gone around the world. Parents are the world of a devoted son." Śiva and Pārvatī were impressed with their son's wisdom, and they married him to Siddhi and Buddhi, the daughters of Prajāpati.
>
> When Kārttikeya returned he found his brother already married. He left in anger for Mount Krauñca, where he has dwelled as a bachelor ever since.[20]

This myth has an older form based on the importance of the sacrifice: Indra and Ruśamā had a contest to see who could first go round the world; Indra ran round the earth, Ruśamā ran round Kurukṣetra (the archetypal site of the sacrifice). Both claimed to have won, but the gods said: Kurukṣetra is as great as the altar of Prajāpati. So neither of them won.[21] The purāṇic myth plays on the image of the ponderous, obese Gaṇeśa who must live by his wits, especially in his confrontations with his more vigorous brother and threatening father. Parents constitute the world of their child; other versions state the lesson slightly differently: since Śiva with his Śakti constitutes the world, to circumambulate the god is to go round the world.[22] But the Tamil version qualifies this conclusion:

Nārada won a pomegranate (*mātuḷam*) from Brahmā by playing music. He gave it to Śiva, who promised it to whichever of his sons could go round the world in a moment. Murukaṉ left Kailāsa on his peacock for the world of men, but Vināyaka went around the mother of all life and the lord who pervades the universe, and Śiva gave him the fruit.

When Murukaṉ returned, he saw the fruit in the hand of his brother and, understanding what had happened, left for the south. He chose to dwell as the great lord (*makecaṉ*) who is formless and yet with form[23] at Tiruvāviṉaṉkuṭi. Soon Śiva became lonesome for his son, so he went there with Umā. She said to Murukaṉ, "Come back to us, dear son, and drink the milk from my breasts," and Śiva said, "You who are eternally a child and yet a man, is a pomegranate a fruit? *You* are the fruit (*paḻa'nī*)!" Murukaṉ bowed to his father, and Śiva agreed to his wish that they dwell together at that place, which has ever since been known as Paḻani.[24]

Although the premise of the first myth is nowhere denied, it is overshadowed by an obvious preference for the local incarnation. The very prize of the contest—the pomegranate here replacing the bride of the Sanskrit version—is superseded by the identification of Murukaṉ in his shrine at Paḻani as the ultimate reward: the god is the fruit (of his servants' devotion). In view of this conclusion, the contest for a mere pomegranate pales in significance. Although the text states that Śiva pervades the universe, this statement remains on a rather theoretical, formal plane; in emotional terms—and Tamil Śaiva myths are, above all, characterized by their emotional nature and concerns[25]—even Śiva is dependent on the shrine. The Sanskrit version, too, has a sequel in which Pārvatī longs for her son and takes Śiva to meet him at Mount Krauñca, but there is no reconciliation—the still indignant Kārttikeya moves away.[26]

Another attempt to confront the problem of universality as opposed to the local, limited form of the deity focuses on the most famous of Śiva's dances—the *ānandatāṇḍava*, the dance of bliss, which tradition places in Citamparam.[27] As in the Citamparam stories, this dance is here associated with two important devotees, the tiger-footed Vyāghrapāda and the sage Patañjali, who is an incarnation of the cosmic serpent Ādiśeṣa:

After his wedding with Pārvatī, Śiva took his bride to Vedagiri. Patañjali and Vyāghrapāda came to pay their respects to

> the bride and groom, but they soon excused themselves in order to return to Citamparam, for already they longed for the sight of the lord's dance. Śiva laughed at them and said, "You are speaking like fools lacking discrimination. Do you not know that Śiva is all-powerful, ever-present, the eternal spirit? I will show you the dance right here."
>
> Patañjali apologized for his ignorance and went back to his *āśrama*, but Vyāghrapāda insisted on leaving at once for Citamparam, since he had taken a vow always to behold the dance there. Śiva gave him leave to go, and then instructed Varuṇa to prepare a storm to block his way. Vyāghrapāda was trapped by the storm not far from Tirukkaḻukkuṉṟam. Soon he was hungry, thirsty, and above all full of longing for the dance of the lord. Śiva appeared to him in the form he takes in the Ciṟṟampalam (at Citamparam), and performed the dance of bliss. In memory of this event, Vyāghrapāda asked that that spot be known as Vyāghrapādapura; until this day Śiva dances there in his form in the Ciṟṟampalam.[28]

The myth poses the question in all its severity: why does the devotee need to go to Citamparam to see his god? Is Śiva not present everywhere? How can one part from him in one place in order to seek him in another? Once again, however, the resolution is incomplete. Śiva affirms his omnipresence, but instead of accepting this at face value the myth proceeds to set up a new shrine, endowed with specific local characteristics, devoted to a god who is given a particular name and a single form and, of course, a mythological history in this spot. Vyāghrapādapura (also known as Pulipparkoyil, five miles west of Tirukkaḻukkuṉṟam) is not the place where the god demonstrated that he is (or can be) everywhere; it is the place where he proved that he could assume a particular form, namely the one for which he is famous at Citamparam, at any other specific, located spot. Instead of transcending the limitation inherent in the shrine (and admitted by Śiva's initial statement), the myth engenders a *second* shrine no less circumscribed and individual than the first. Of course, in a sense we are looking at the problem backwards: it is the shrine that has engendered the myth, and not vice versa. Worship at Vyāghrapādapura was influenced by, perhaps even initiated because of, the diffusion of the Naṭarāja cult of Citamparam—perhaps during the period of the Coḻas, whose family deity (*kuladeva*) was Naṭarāja;[29] the myth strives to explain this connection with Citamparam. Nevertheless, we have regarded the problem from the point of view of the myth itself. The question it raises is a serious one, and the answer suggested by the myth testifies to the power of an enduring and widely shared conception. It may be noted that the *ānandatāṇḍava* is not the only dance of Śiva's to be grounded in a single shrine; there is a series of six important dances, each of them tied to a specific locality, indeed to a particular hall (*sabhā*) in their respective shrines.[30] Like the five elements and the eight forms (*aṣṭamūrti*) of the god, the dances of Śiva have thus been separated and distributed among prominent shrines in the Tamil land.

Yet while the shrine seems always to triumph in these myths, one could take the notion of localization too far, as an anecdote from the time of the great commentator and author of the *Kāñcippurāṇam*, Civañāṉayoki, reveals:

> At the first recitation (*araṅkeṟṟam*) of the *Kāñcippurāṇam*, those who were jealous of Civañāṉayoki tried to embarrass him. Acting under their instructions, an *otuvār* (one trained in reciting the Tamil hymns of the *Tevāram*) raised an objection to the third invocatory verse, which was addressed to Naṭarāja. "A purāṇa about Kāñcipuram should begin with an invocation to Ekāmparanātar (Śiva at Kāñcipuram), not the god of Citamparam," he said with scorn. Kacciyappar, a pupil of Civañāṉayoki, asked the *otuvār* to recite the *Tevāram* hymns proper to Kāñcipuram. The *otuvār* readily agreed. Solemnly he began to recite; but no sooner had he intoned the customary opening formula, "*tirucciṟṟampalam*,"[31] than Kacciyappar stopped him. "Should you not say '*pirutiviyampalam*'[32] if you are reciting the *Tevāram* of Kāñci?" he asked. "It is the custom to say '*tirucciṟṟampalam*' before the hymns of all sacred shrines," said the *otuvār*. "Yes," replied Kacciyappar, "and it is likewise the custom to invoke Naṭaraja at the beginning of all Śaiva compositions, as you would have known had you read any!"[33]

Here the border between convention and the concern of the myths is clearly drawn. For the authors of our texts, any attempt to restrict too drastically the revelation of a particular form of the deity would have been unacceptable; Naṭarāja and Ekāmparanātar are, after all, forms of the same god, even if each of them has his own, separate shrine. One must remember that the assertions of the myths need not always have coincided with the beliefs of the authors of the Tamil purāṇas, who were for the most part not the originators of these myths, but poet-scholars who gave them a literary form, usually on the basis of much older materials. Civañāṉayoki and his pupil Kacciyappar were both Śaiva Siddhāntin scholars, and the Śiva of the Siddhāntins is a limitless, universal god whose myths the theologians often interpret allegorically.[34] Yet the myths' obsession with the local history and attributes of the deity usually shines through the works even of those who believed that "God does not occupy space and is in no way limited by it."[35]

A corollary to the belief in the localization of the divine presence is a fear of the god's *absence* from a shrine: Ceramāṉ Pĕrumāḷ used to hear the jingling of the lord's anklet each day at the conclusion of his daily worship; one day he nearly cut off his head when the sound was delayed—because the lord was listening to Cuntarar's songs at Citamparam.[36] When the Pāṇṭiyaṉ slighted the poet Iṭaikkāṭaṉ, Śiva and Umā left Maturai for another shrine to the north, thus depriving the city of all its glory.[37] When a king ordered Tirumaḻicaiyāḻvār to leave his city, the saint asked the god (Viṣṇu) reclining in his shrine to roll up his mat and come with him; the god followed his devotee out of the town.[38] The idea that a deity may abandon his dwelling place is found already in ancient Tamil poetry;[39] the belief that a sacred power inheres in, and may depart from, a specific object or place thus goes back to the earliest period of Tamil civilization. In Brahminical temples today, it is feared that any ritual mistake or polluting influence may cause the immediate departure of the god.[40]

To summarize: the myths of the Tamil purāṇas are imbued with the belief that a sacred presence is revealed in individual, localized manifestations. The history and nature of these manifestations form the subject matter of the Tamil myths. While conscious of the theological issues implicit in this belief, the myths insist upon the overriding importance of the shrine. Gods and men alike need and long for the holy site, the sanctity of which both anticipates and results from their love. This concept is ancient and pervasive. The power residing in the shrine is isolated and thereby controlled; this isolation ultimately links the shrine to the Brahminical ideals of independence and freedom from evil, but the idealized shrine nevertheless serves the devotee in his everyday, mundane existence. Although the deity has absorbed the universalism implicit in the Upaniṣadic goal of *brahman*, the myths are concerned with the specific rather than the universal, with the present rather than the apocalypse (the *pralaya*, which has no power over the shrine), and with life on earth as opposed to release or to life in heaven.

CHAPTER III

# The Creative Sacrifice

## 1. Introduction

The cosmological motifs studied in the previous chapter derive their particular character in Tamil mythology from their association with a fundamental conception, which appears in the tradition of most Tamil shrines. We may call this conception the "creative sacrifice." As we have seen in the myths of the cosmic flood, the world is born, or reborn, out of the violent destruction of a former creation; the deluge holds within it the vital seed of new life. The flood myths reveal on the level of cosmic processes the basic Indian notion of sacrifice: life is born out of death, out of chaos and darkness. This notion is found both in the classical Brahminical system of sacrifices and in the village cults of southern India; we will be concerned in this chapter with its meaning and history in the tradition of the Tamil purāṇas.

Let us begin by summarizing the Brahminical concept of sacrifice as it appears from classical Sanskrit texts. Man and other creatures live by devouring other forms of life; the dead make the earth fertile and, by dying, create space for the living. In the *BĀU* it is Death himself who creates, and who consumes his creation in order to produce more life.[1] The sacrifice is, in essence, an attempt to force the process of creation: one kills, and in killing creates a vacuum that must attract more life. That this act of violence may have serious consequences for all the participants is a given; yet the ritual proceeds logically from the assumption that life is won from death. The Hindu universe is a closed circuit: nothing new can be produced except by destroying or transforming something else. To attain more life—such as a son, or the "rebirth" of the sacrificial patron himself—the life of the victim must be extinguished. Life and death are two facets of a single, never-ending cycle: thus a son may be born to a childless king on condition that this same son will in turn be sacrificed.[2]

The symbol of the new life produced from the sacrifice is the fiery seed, which is equated to the remainder (*vāstu*), that part of the sacrifice which is left after all the oblations have been made.[3] The remainder contains the germ of a new birth. Like leavings generally in Hinduism, the remnant of the sacrifice is impure and polluting;

at the same time, it is a fertilizing, life-giving substance. Hence the remnant is praised in *AV* 11.7 as the foundation of the universe; later this idea is attached to the cosmic serpent (Ādi-)Śeṣa, the Remnant (*śeṣa*) upon which the universe rests.[4] The remainder of the sacrifice belongs by right to Rudra, the sacrificial butcher; the *vāstu* is thus symbolically identified with the *prāśitra* portion, the impure first cut offered to Rudra.[5] The god who performs the violent act of sacrifice wins the *vāstu*, the residue as seed, and the titles Vāstavya and Vāstoṣpati; ultimately, however, Rudra-Vāstoṣpati becomes the Vāstupuruṣa, the sacrificial victim whose figure is traced on the site of each new shrine. The temple is erected upon the foundation of this symbolic sacrifice; just as Ādiśeṣa supports the universe, the Vāstupuruṣa sustains the shrine. Here the *vāstu* epitomizes the entire process of sacrifice: the slain victim is the remainder/seed from which the sacred edifice is produced.[6] Today, of course, no sacrifice is actually performed in the course of building a temple; instead, the form of the Vāstupuruṣa is simply mapped out over the consecrated area. In the Vedic sacrificial cult, however, real sacrifices were needed to build the altar,[7] and the Tamil folk tradition offers numerous examples of the theme of the blood-sacrifice needed in order to build a shrine or accomplish some other difficult task.[8]

The Tamil purāṇic tradition has, in fact, combined the inheritance of Brahminical sacrificial concepts with ancient Tamil notions. The Tamils of the Caṅkam period regarded blood as the source of life. Life (*uyir*) resides in the blood, and escapes with the blood poured out from a wound.[9] As Hart has shown, the Caṅkam poems frequently compare the shedding of blood in war to the harvest of grain, that is, to the production of food from the soil;[10] the war sacrifice thus comes to epitomize the process of creation from the chaos of death and destruction.[11] Sacrifice offers a ritual expression of the identification of life and blood. In ancient times blood sacrifices were offered to Murukaṉ, to the king's drum, and (together with toddy and paddy) to the memorial stone (*naṭukal*) erected in honor of a dead hero.[12] Blood sacrifices are still common in village rituals in south India; here the blood of the victim is often drunk by one or more of the participants, or poured into the mouth of the image of the goddess.[13] In this way the power and life-force of the victim are transferred to the goddess or to the participants in the ritual. We will return to the goddess's part in this scheme in Chapter IV. For the moment, it is important to note that the blood sacrifice in the villages includes an implicit notion of the exchange or transfer of power.

This notion of exchange survives in various forms in the Tamil purāṇic myths, as well. In essence, the myths suggest that the devotee brings to the arena of sacrifice an offering that is returned to him, in a new form, through the ritual. As we shall see, the donor is ultimately identified with his gift; in other words, the devotee sacrifices himself or a part of himself in order to win the reward of the sacrifice—more life, renewed strength, rebirth. The deity receives the offering and then restores it to the donor. But the role of the god is not limited to this side of the cycle. In the myths the god serves as a model for the pilgrim's part in the ritual: the deity offers up his own life in order to be reborn from the sacrifice. The devotee sees before him a divine exemplar. This is the underlying theme that we will trace in the Tamil myths.

This theme is not, however, explicitly stated in our texts. On the contrary, it has been submerged by a later ideology, which wishes to exonerate the deity from the burden of death. I have mentioned that the sacrificial act is considered to have serious consequences; those who bear responsibility for the slaughter are loaded down with evil, however beneficial or necessary the sacrifice may appear in the long run. Killing implicates the killer in evil; blood, like other excretions of the body, is impure and defiling.[14] In the Brahminical sacrificial cult, the Brahmins come to represent the force that sustains the burden of slaughter; they alone are regarded as innately prepared to accept this charge, and thus they alone permit the sacrifice to go on. The Brahmins of the Vedic cult thus share, by their collective association with violence and death, something of the collective burden borne by the outcastes—the low groups such as the Paṟaiyaṉs who already in ancient times seem to have performed duties connected with death or related manifestations of contaminating power.[15] In the myths, this aspect of the sacrifice appears in relation to the theme of expiation; as we shall see, each act of killing requires a ritual expiation, usually by worshiping in a shrine. But there is a further development to be observed in this context: just as within the Brahminic tradition itself one finds an attempt to break out of the cycle of violence rooted in the sacrifice, in order to arrive at a state of purity and freedom independent of the processes of death and rebirth,[16] so the Tamil purāṇic tradition seeks to purify the deity by denying his participation in the sacrifice. The god is isolated and without evil, never slain or reborn, neither victim nor butcher at the gruesome rites of his devotees. An attempt is made at detaching the deity from the polluting locus of power. Yet the sacrifice itself persists as long as life—or the will to live—survives: for in a culture in which the source of vitality is so closely bound up with chaos and death, the god who gives life to his servants can never completely sever his tie to the sacrifice.

## 2. Milk, Blood, and Seed

It is with these ideas in mind that we turn now to the origin myths of the shrines. Here we find a striking, recurrent combination: the Tamil myths insist on the presence of both blood and milk at the moment when the sacred site is discovered. Let us take a representative example, in this case a folk tradition about the temple at Cucīntiram (Śucīndram):

> A shepherdess used to cross the Jñānāraṇya ("the forest of knowledge") each day to sell milk and curds. Each time she passed a clump of bamboo, her feet would become entangled, and she would spill the milk and curds. After this had gone on for some time, she told her husband, and he rushed to the spot with his friends and cut down the bamboos. To their amazement, blood flowed from the cut bamboos. Impressed with the sanctity of the spot, they erected a shrine, which became the nucleus of the Cucīntiram temple.[1]

The spilling of milk first marks the sacred site, but the actual revelation depends on the flow of blood. Why does this conjunction occur? On the simplest, most immediate level, the myth asserts the tangible reality of the god, whose blood reveals the site of a living incarnation. But there is much more to the imagery than this. Blood and milk are frequently associated in south Indian symbolic schemes. One dramatic example appears in a Lingāyat folk version of the *Cilappatikāram* story. Here the heroine (the Kaṇṇaki of Iḷaṅko, known in this version as Chandra) first learns of her husband's death when milk turns to blood:

> "Early the very morning this happened, the old milk-seller (at whose house, which was a little out of the town, Chandra had been sleeping), took her guest a bowl full of milk to drink; but no sooner had Chandra tasted it than she began to cry, saying,

'Good mother, what have you done? My mouth is full of blood!' 'No, no, my daughter,' answered the old woman; 'You must have been dreaming some bad dream. See, this is pure, fresh, warm, milk I have brought you; drink again.' But when Chandra tasted it for the second time, she answered, 'Oh no! Oh no! it is not milk that I taste, but blood. All last night I had a dreadful dream, and this morning when I woke I found that my marriage necklace had snapped in two; and now this milk tastes to me as blood. Let me go! let me go! for I know my husband is dead.' "[2]

A few more examples of this association may be cited: a Kond tribal myth states that in former times the hills and mountains lived on a diet of blood and milk in the Upper World; they came down to earth when Mahāprabhu promised them blood, but the British stopped the practice of giving them blood (sacrifices), so now the hills are angry and give men fever.[3] In non-Brahmin wedding rites in Mysore, a twig of the *nerale* tree, which yields a red sap when cut, is "married" to a twig of the *kaḷḷi*, the "milk-post," which exudes a milk-like substance.[4] In a myth from Kerala, a woman gave birth to a boy, and her attendant asked a neighbor for milk for him; she was refused, and the neighbor's cow then gave forth water, milk, charcoal, and blood.[5] These examples, drawn from all over south India, could easily be multiplied.

The alternation of blood and milk is not entirely unknown to Sanskrit mythology: in his journey through a symbolic landscape, Bhṛgu comes to a river of blood guarded by a naked man with a club, and flowing beside a river of ghee, from which golden men draw up all desires with golden cups.[6] One may also recall the combination of white Soma with red *surā* (liquor) in the Sautrāmaṇī ritual; it has been suggested that they are assimilated there to the Soma mingled with the blood of the demon Namuci.[7] Nevertheless, this combination is rare in the northern Sanskritic tradition. Red and white often appear together in Tamil rituals, as Brenda Beck has noted;[8] in general, the "cool" white is needed to surround and contain the "hot" red. This idea recurs in Tamil medicine—"cool" foods, such as milk, must be taken along with "hot" medicines, such as Western drugs[9]—and many other instances of the red/white, hot/cold pattern exist. Even if we restrict ourselves to the field of temple ritual, we have the red and white stripes that almost inevitably cover the walls of shrines; and the white ash (*vibhūti*) given as *prasāda*, "grace," by the god to the pilgrim, alongside the red *kuṅkuma* powder more often given by the goddess.

In this context, milk may be seen as the cooling antidote to blood, which is considered extremely hot. The myths offer many examples of the cooling effect of milk, as in the following Badaga story:

> A man found on the river bank a stone shaped like an ox. He took it home as a present for his children, but forgot to give it to them; when he next went to the river for worship, he found it in his pocket and put it on the ground. When he returned, the stone was gone. The next morning he discovered that it had turned into a live ox that attacked another ox in a nearby village and was killed by its owner—but this man was suddenly paralyzed upside down.
>
> When the man who had first found the stone returned home, there was the stone ox again, with one horn broken and a spear wound on its left side. The villagers offered the stone ox milk each day. One day they forgot, and the ox became alive and attacked them, refusing to allow them to come into its shed. They made a hole in the roof and poured milk on it from above, and it turned back to stone.[10]

The ox, which becomes a deity worshiped by the Badaga, is known as Basavanna (from Sanskrit *vṛṣabha*). His transition from stone to flesh and back again recalls the common motif of Śiva's emergence from and absorption into the stone *liṅga*; indeed, as we shall see, the wounded ox whose power is somehow contained within stone is an exact analogue of the wounded deity residing in the *liṅga*. The major element in keeping the god's power contained is clearly the libation of milk poured over the stone; it is this offering that keeps the dangerous animal—which, when alive, attacks and suffers wounds, and stands its slayer on his head—pacified and paralyzed. Milk holds the violence in check. The pacifying influence of milk is a prominent theme in the mythology of the goddess, whose bloodthirsty nature can be transformed by the presence of her child: thus Śiva becomes an infant and delivers her from anger by sucking the milk from her breast.[11] The oral tradition of Śrīvaiṣṇavīkoyil (near Tirumullaivāyil) states that an image of Gaṇeśa was stationed within sight of the goddess there, to keep the feeling of maternal love (symbolized by the flow of milk from her breasts) ever dominant in her; otherwise, evil people of strong concentration could use the goddess to gain power (*śakti*) for their own violent ends.[12]

This background of color symbolism with its related ideas of heat and power does not, however, suffice to explain the prominence of the milk-blood motif in the origin myths of the shrines. The appearance of milk and blood in the myths provides another instance of the conjunctions we are exploring, but they alone fail to define the basic meaning of the motif. Even if we assume that the shrine constitutes a concentration of potentially violent power that must be held in check by the cooling libation of milk, just as it must be circumscribed by high walls and ritually ordered, still we are left with unanswered questions. If the milk is essentially a cooling antidote, why does it usually appear *before* the revelation of blood? If this is an attempt to prepare the ground, as it were, for the violent manifestation of the deity, or to create a safe "boundary" of whiteness and coolness—as one finds in the structure of Tamil life-cycle rituals, or indeed in the ideal pattern of any auspicious event[13]—why do the purāṇic texts never relate to it in these terms? Why, in particular, must the god himself be wounded, so that it is his blood that soaks the shrine? A deeper level of symbolism is suggested in the myths. Moreover, one must note the persistent link between the wounding of the god and the *source* from which issues the milk offered to him. In this connection there appears one of the stock figures of the origin myths—the Kāmadhenu, the wishing-cow of the gods and sages:

> The sage Vasiṣṭha wished to worship Viśvanātha-Śiva at Kāśī. In order to obtain milk for bathing the *liṅga*, he asked Indra for the Kāmadhenu. One day while he was worshiping at Kāśī, the cow wandered outside the city and reached the slopes of Kailāsa, where she stayed for the night. This meant that the sage was without milk for worship for one day, so when the cow returned the next day, he cursed her to become wild.
>
> The cow wandered from place to place until she reached Tiruvāṉmiyūr. As soon as she entered the bounds of that site, her former (peaceful) nature returned. Feeling that there was something special about the place, the cow searched among the bushes and discovered a *liṅga*. From that day she bathed the *liṅga* with her milk, and the *liṅga* became white.
>
> A king came to hunt animals that were destroying his

people's crops. During the hunt, a lion was frightened off and fled to the thicket where the Kāmadhenu was lying. The cow jumped on it and tore it to pieces with her horns. When the king heard of this, he wished to catch the cow. He sent soldiers to cut down the thicket; the cow sprang at them, and in so doing her hoof struck the *liṅga* and left a deep scar. After slaying the soldiers, the cow returned to find the *liṅga* marked with gaping wounds. "Alas, what evil have I done!" she cried. But the voice of Śiva spoke to her, saying, "Beloved! Be not sorrowful. You need not fear anything. We disregard evil committed in ignorance by our devotees. To us your hoof has become like the golden foot of our Skanda. From the milk you poured over us, we have become the color of milk (*pālvaṇṇar*)—and this *liṅga* will be called by this name. Your curse is now over; return to heaven."

The king heard all this, abandoned his kingdom to his son, and worshiped the god of this shrine.[14]

Although the *liṅga* itself is not said to have bled, the god must still be wounded—this time by the cow, which has first killed a lion and subsequently slays the king's men. The wounding of the god is, in fact, the redemptive act: entry into the sacred bounds of the shrine is said to cause the wild cow to become tame again, but the cow remains fierce enough to kill lions and men; her curse ends only when Śiva comforts her for her grief at striking the *liṅga*. Vasiṣṭha's curse takes a different form in another myth: when he missed the Kamadhenu at a sacrifice, he cursed her to become a goat; by worshiping at the shrine, she regained her old form; but Vasiṣṭha was also required to worship there in order to expiate his fault in depriving the gods of their sustenance (the milk of the Kāmadhenu).[15] That the Kāmadhenu is capable of shedding blood is clear from the tale of Viśvāmitra's attempt to seize by force Vasiṣṭha's wishing-cow Nandinī (or Śabalā): the cow created from its body armies of barbarians who drove off Viśvāmitra's soldiers.[16] The myth from Tiruvāṉmiyūr goes further by making the cow itself a killer. This is instructive: the myth combines rather than opposes the two fluids, blood and milk, in the figure of the wild cow. The combination recalls an ancient image of great importance in the Tamil tradition—the breast that is both life-giving and lethal.[17] Kaṇṇaki casts off her breast in order to burn the city of Maturai.[18] I shall have more to say of this story.

The myth from Tiruvāṉmiyūr is instructive in yet another way; it hints of the unspoken equivalent of blood and milk, the seed of Śiva that produces Skanda. The cow that both waters and wounds the *liṅga* is equated by the god with his golden-footed child.

There are many permutations of this story; in view of the importance of the Kāmadhenu for an understanding of Tamil symbolism, we may briefly review several of the more important Tamil variants. The combination of milk and blood in the wishing-cow is even more striking at Cikkal, where the Kāmadhenu herself becomes a tiger.[19] Usually, however, the cow opposes a tiger, as in a myth from Tiruvārūr that eliminates the blood altogether in favor of a lesson in nonviolence (*ahiṃsā*):

> King Kulicaṉ (Skt. Kalaśa, "pot")[20] mixed meat with food he gave to Durvāsas, and the sage therefore cursed him to become a tiger. He roamed the forest devouring creatures until he came to Tiruvārūr, where Nandinī the Kāmadhenu was worshiping a *liṅga* with her milk. The tiger was about to pounce on the cow, but she pleaded with him to let her first feed her calf and worship the god. "What, you wish me to let you go while I stand waiting to see if you return?" asked the tiger incredulously. "Even those who seek release (*vīṭu*) tremble when the hour of death approaches—will a cow give up its life for a tiger?" The cow swore she would return, and at length the tiger let her go. She fed and comforted her calf and worshiped the *liṅga*; then she returned to the tiger. Seeing her, the tiger's ignorance was suddenly dispelled. "I have shed the blood of many animals, evil creature that I am, but you have brought me enlightenment," he said. The cow showed him the *liṅga*, and he regained his proper form.[21]

Violence is averted by the cow's readiness to sacrifice herself.[22] A similar story is told at another shrine: the Kāmadhenu, caught by a tiger, asks to be excused to feed her calf. When the cow returns, the tiger falls upon her but suddenly faints; when it awakes after five hours, it understands the truth (of nonviolence).[23] Both stories show a progression from the pattern of violent confrontation—the murderous tiger opposing the milk-giving cow—to a nonviolent resolution based on the principle of *self*-sacrifice (the Kāmadhenu prepares to give up her life). As we shall see, this progression has a more general scope in the history of the Tamil purāṇic tradition, which seeks ultimately to substitute for the original violence of the blood sacrifice an internal act of self-sacrifice on the part of the devotee.

The *Padmapurāṇa* has a version of the above myth in which the king is turned into a tiger for a different reason: he shoots a doe nursing her fawn, and the dying doe curses him to become a tiger.[24] This episode also turns up in the myths of Tiruvārūr, but there it has been elaborated into a separate story:

> King Camatkāra came upon a deer nursing her child in the forest. He shot an arrow that pierced her in a vital spot. She saw the king and said, "What you have done is not right (*ayuktam*). I do not grieve at my death, but I feel sorry for this poor fawn hungry for milk. Because you have committed this cruel deed, you will become a leper (*kuṣṭhavyādhisamāyukta*) from today."
>
> The king said, "The destruction of animals is the *svadharma* of kings. You should not curse me, for I was only performing my *svadharma*." Replied the deer: "True—animals were created by Svayambhū in order to be killed by warriors. But evil attaches to a man who kills an animal that is sleeping, uniting with its mate, nursing, or drinking. Therefore I have cursed you." Then she died, and the king became a leper. He called his advisers and said, "I will perform *tapas* and worship Śiva to rid myself of the disease. Men may gain anything they desire through *tapas*." He wandered over the earth on pilgrimage to sacred sites until he reached the Śaṅkhatīrtha ("tank of the conch") at Hāṭakeśvara (= Tiruvārūr). After bathing there, he was at once freed of his disease.[25]

The transformation of the hunter-king into a bloodthirsty tiger—an example of a curse that heightens or perpetuates the effect of its cause—is replaced in this myth by the curse of leprosy, the white of the disease corresponding to the white milk of the slain doe.[26] The use of color is consistent to the end: the king loses his diseased white skin by bathing in a tank named after the white conch. Three white substances are thus juxtaposed with the red blood of the deer. The victim is again stoic in the face of death: the deer admits that a king's duty is to kill, but insists that this duty is limited by specific conditions.[27] Thus the king is forced to expiate his transgression; note that here, as in other myths we have seen, pilgrimage is defined as *tapas*, but in effect takes the place of more traditional austerities. The child hungry for the milk of his mother is a focal concern of both versions of the myth: the king as hunter deprives the child of the mother's breast, while as tiger he merely allows the cow to feed its calf a final time before returning to face death. In the latter episode, however, the sacrifice is averted; the tiger learns a higher ethic, and the myth achieves a happier resolution. Similarly, in a myth from Maturai a hunter kills a doe that has come to drink at a tank; Śiva, who is mother of all, makes a tiger give milk to the motherless fawn.[28] The pacified, milk-giving tiger is the reversal of the murderous Kāmadhenu of Cikkal and Tiruvāṉmiyūr (and many other sites): in both images we see the combination of violence and sustenance, or of blood and milk.

There is another way of averting the loss of the mother: by sacrificing the tiger instead. This is the solution of a Bengali variant of this myth:

> Brahmā shed his seed at the sight of the little finger of Caṇḍī. The seed entered her body, but she cast the embryo out into the river. The cow Kapilā drank from the river and gave birth to a calf. One day while on her way to feed the calf she was stopped by two tigers, who were persuaded to let her go until she had nursed her child. When the calf heard of its mother's promise to return, it became furious and defeated the tigers.[29]

The battle with the tigers is set against the image of the calf sucking the milk of its mother, but here the violent calf replaces the murderous cow of other myths. Similarly, in a myth from Tirupperūr it is the calf of the Kāmadhenu rather than the wishing-cow herself who wounds the *liṅga* and causes the flow of blood.[30] Nevertheless, the image of the violent mother—the wild cow of Tiruvāṉmiyūr and Cikkal—survives in the Bengali variant in the "original" bearer of the seed, the fierce goddess Caṇḍī. A tribal myth reverses the outcome of the Bengali version: incited by Śiva, Nanga Baiga killed a tiger created by Pārvatī; as Nanga Baiga was burying the tiger under a tree, he cut a root, and the tiger drank milk from the root and was revived.[31] As in the south Indian rituals connected with a "milk-post,"[32] a latexiferous plant here provides milk, whiteness, and, in this case, new life.

Tiruvārūr is again the site of another, better known myth based on the same elements as the above examples. Here the king is again a source of violence, as in the case of the hunter turned tiger; but here, too, the sacrifice is ultimately superseded:

> The son of King Manunītikaṇṭacoḻaṉ inadvertently ran over a calf with his chariot. The calf was killed, and its grief-stricken mother rang the bell of justice by the palace of the king. To give justice, the king ordered that his son be run over by the same chariot. When his minister committed suicide so as not to have to carry out the order, the king himself drove his chariot over his son. Vītiviṭaṅkappĕrumāṉ (Śiva at Tiruvārūr),[33] unable to endure this sight, appeared and restored the calf, the king's son, and the minister to life.[34]

Unlike the myths cited earlier, this myth makes the calf (child) the direct rather than the indirect victim. The king's son is slain in expiation of the death of the calf.[35] In the corresponding story from the Sanskrit dynastic lists, Pṛṣadhra, the son of Manu, kills a cow by mistake and is cursed to become a Śūdra.[36] The Tamil king-lists have the more dramatic Tiruvārūr myth in this slot of the genealogy.[37] A closely related story is that of Dilīpa, who offers his life to the lion Kumbhodara in exchange for that of Nandinī, the daughter of the wishing-cow Surabhi.[38] In the Tiruvārūr myth, the intervention of Śiva after justice has been satisfied nullifies the effects of violence; the sacrifice is performed and then reversed. The god becomes manifest in response to the acts of slaughter, which in this case he cannot allow to go unanswered; the role of the righteous man here requires an initial sacrifice, or self-sacrifice (the father offering up his own son), but leads to a subsequent restoration and victory over death.[39]

In all these stories, the image of the milk-giving mother combines and contrasts with elements of blood and violence, threatened or real. The Kāmadhenu may be taken as a form of the goddess, who, as we shall see, is a source both of death and of rebirth for her devotees—and for her husband Śiva as well. The cow's association with blood reflects the lethal side of her nature; her milk symbolizes her power to give and sustain life. But this is not all. Both blood and milk have further associations that help explain their constant union in the Tamil origin myths. In Hindu mythology generally, both blood and milk are creative media linked with a number of other substances. Milk appears in a series of positive transformations: the gods and demons churned the ocean of milk to produce *amṛta*, the drink of immortality; at the same time they brought forth poison (the opposite of *amṛta*), the sun, the moon (the re-

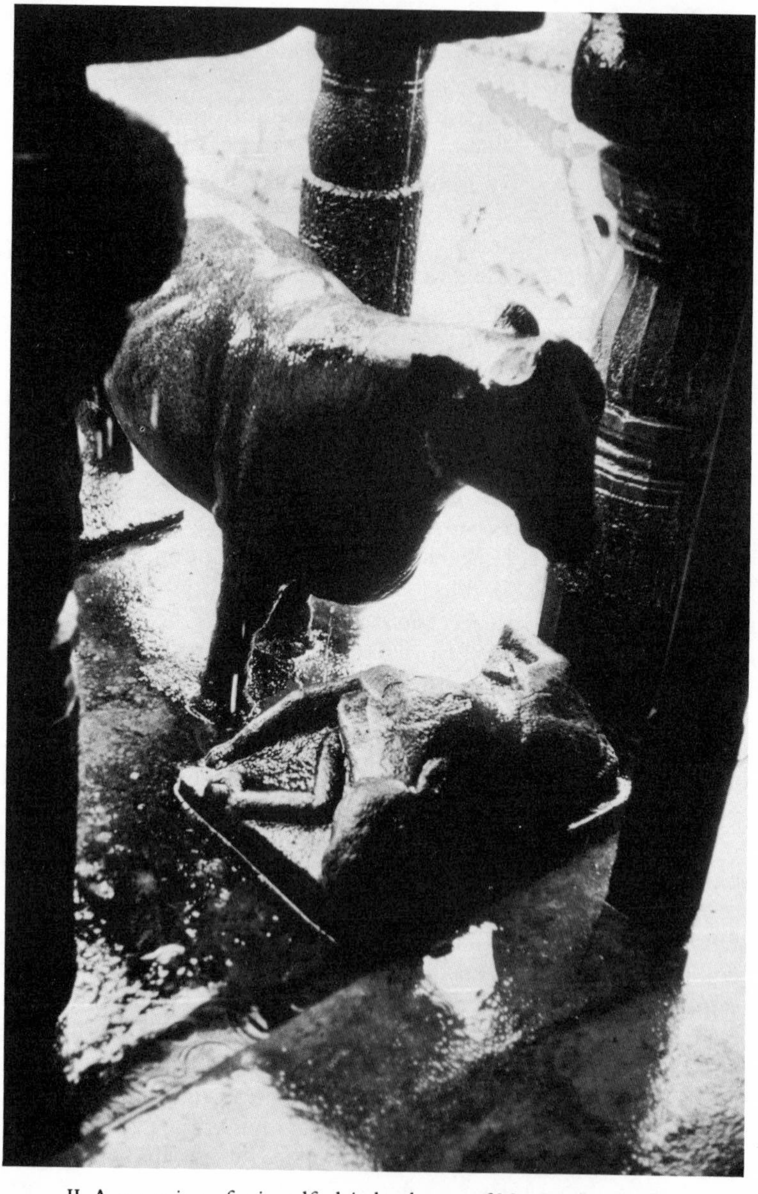

11. A cow grieves for its calf, slain by the son of Manunītikaṇṭacoḻaṉ.

pository of Soma), the goddess Śrī, liquor (*surā*), the horse Uccaiḥśravas, the physician Dhanvantari, and the Kaustubha jewel. Pṛthu milked the earth and thereby revived the plants that support life.[40] Milk is equated to *amṛta*:

> Dakṣa created the divine cow Surabhi from *amṛta*, and Surabhi gave birth to cows whose udders poured forth milk. Some froth (*phena*) fell from the mouths of the suckling calves onto the head of Śiva, who burned them with his third eye. Dakṣa pacified him with the argument that what partook of the nature of *amṛta* could not become impure. Śiva made the cows the support of all life.[41]

Milk is also seed: "Father of calves, lord of the inviolable (kine), also father of great gulfs; calf, afterbirth, fresh milk, beestings, curd, ghee—that (is) his seed."[42] Manu offered ghee, sour milk, whey, and curds into the water, and in a year a woman was produced.[43] Brahmā offered his seed into the fire as if it were consecrated butter (*ājya*).[44] Milk is Soma,[45] and the light of the moon, the storehouse of Soma.[46] Milk is knowledge, that is, immortality: Tiruñāṉacampantar drank the milk of divine wisdom (or the mantic wisdom of the poet[47]) from the breasts of the goddess Pārvatī.[48] Gaṇeśa and Skanda remain young (*kumārau*) because they drink the milk of Pārvatī's breasts, and have never known women.[49] Of all these correspondences (milk, butter, seed, mead, Soma, *amṛta*), it is perhaps seed that is most closely associated with images of milk in south Indian shrines: at Cikkal the *liṅga* itself was formed from the cream floating on the *tīrtha*, which was the milk of the Kāmadhenu.[50] Hence the god is known as Navanīteśvara, "lord of fresh butter." At Tiruvāṉmiyūr, too, the *liṅga* is white as milk, and the god is therefore Pālvaṇṇanātar, "lord with the color of milk."[51] At Tirukkūvam the *liṅga* becomes white when there is an abundance of rain, red when war breaks out; the red obviously indicates blood, while the rain will be another form of seed.[52]

Blood, too, is seed: from each drop of the blood of Raktabīja, whose name means "seed of blood" or "having blood as seed," demons were born.[53] The same motif recurs in the stories of Andhaka[54] and Dāruka.[55] A warrior is created from the blood of Viṣṇu's left arm, which pours into the skull in Śiva's hand.[56] Elsewhere Śiva creates the world from a drop of blood.[57] The creative drop of blood from the finger of God is referred to as *amṛta* (an allotrope of Soma and seed) in one folk source.[58] The creative potential of blood is highly developed in tribal myths: a girl (or goddess) is born when the shadow of a hawk falls on the menstrual blood of sixty-four *yoginīs*,[59] and trees grow from the blood that drips from the heads of ascetics hanging upside down.[60] In south Indian village myths, creation from blood is an alternative to sexual procreation.[61]

It should be noted that both breast milk and blood are, like other bodily excretions, polluting. In ancient Tamil poetry, the hero is sometimes said to avoid contact with his wife's breasts during the period when she is nursing;[62] he fears contamination from her milk.[63] More generally, however, milk is associated with whiteness and purity, even if it is capable of being transmuted into its opposite—poison.[64] Blood, according to both Sanskrit and Tamil sources, is dangerous and polluting: in the Brahminical sacrificial ritual, the victim was slain by strangulation so as to avoid pollution by blood.[65] Many myths illustrate this view: Brahminicide pursues Indra in the form of an old outcaste woman with garments covered with blood.[66] Viśvāmitra curses the Sarasvatī River to be mixed with blood because it has carried his rival Vasiṣṭha beyond his grasp.[67] At this point, however, an important difference must be noticed—for while milk has a basically positive value in both the classical Sanskritic and Tamil traditions, the Tamil attitude toward blood is more complex than that found in northern sources. In the latter, blood is clearly an inferior substance. Forty drops of blood are said to be needed to form one drop of semen.[68] A folk tradition holds that from the wounds of a *brahmacārin* flows semen rather than blood;[69] the blood of the Jain Tīrthaṅkara is white as milk.[70] Blood is transformed within the body into more powerful substances—in the man it becomes seed, in the woman it turns to milk (and, according to some, to the red "seed" of the woman that is mingled with the male semen to create a child).[71] This preference for other fluids is perhaps most clearly expressed in the myth of Maṅkaṇaka:

> The sage Maṅkaṇaka cut his finger on a blade of grass, and vegetable sap (*śākarasa*) flowed from the cut. Full of pride at this event, he began to dance, and his dance shook the universe. Śiva came and asked him why he was dancing, but when Maṅkaṇaka explained, he merely said, "That does not surprise me at all;" he pressed his thumb with the tip of his

finger, and ashes white as snow (*himasannibha*) flowed from the wound. The sage begged forgiveness for his pride.[72]

A modern commentator on this myth identifies the sap with Soma and the ashes with Agni.[73] The ash could also be regarded as Śiva's seed (which is fire in the myths of the birth of Śiva's child Skanda); ashes are the substratum of death from which new life arises; Śiva covers his body with the ashes of Kāma, which acquire an erotic force in the context of Śiva's marriage.[74] The ash (*vibhūti*) given as *prasāda* by the god in his temples may thus represent his seed; it is also assimilated to Soma / *amṛta*, and eaten by the recipient. For our purposes, the point is that none of these substances is blood, which obviously belongs to a lower, nonmiraculous order. Plant sap or Soma is clearly superior to blood, and ashes better still! It is as if blood existed only to be transmuted into something more desirable—the sap of plants,[75] ashes, milk, Soma, *amṛta*, or seed.

The Tamil myths appear to have reversed this tendency. Blood remains dangerous and polluting, but it is also a sacred fluid. Blood is the source of life, a substance inbued with power, a dynamic, creative medium; hence, like other dynamic elements linked with chaos and death, it is potentially dangerous and must be controlled.[76] But, like the tree rooted in Pātāla or the *tīrtha* welling up from the nether world, it is also a locus of sacred forces. Moreover, as we have seen, blood is the very instrument of revelation in the origin myths of the shrines. The contrast with the Sanskritic tradition becomes especially clear in two myths from Tiruppātirippuliyūr, the first of which is a Tamil version of the Maṅkaṇaka story:

The devoted sage Maṅkaṇār (= Maṅkaṇa, Maṅkaṇaka) went to pick flowers for worship, and in the process received scratches on his hands and legs. To his surprise no blood flowed, only green fragrant sap of plants. "Who is my equal?" he thought with pride, and started to dance. He danced for a month; then he jumped high over the forest, and his foot hit the head of Tūmappar, who was performing *tapas* there. Tūmappar cursed him to become a hare, and directed him to Tiruppātirippuliyūr, where after one hundred years he was granted *mukti* by Śiva.[77]

Although there are several minor alterations in the story—here the protagonist *begins* as a devotee of Śiva, while in the Sanskrit versions he *becomes* a devotee because of the events of the story—the basic attitude toward blood is unchanged from the Sanskrit prototype, at least as far as Maṅkaṇaka is concerned. The flow of vegetable sap instead of blood intoxicates the sage, and sparks off his ecstatic dance. The second transformation—of blood to ashes in the veins of Śiva—is, however, missing, and the sage is enlightened only after suffering the effects of a curse. His transformation into a hare is duplicated in the second myth, which is an obvious multiform of the first:

> Vyāghrapāda's son Upamanyu was worshiping Ambikā when by chance he struck her (or, according to the commentator, the pedestal of her image) with his foot. She cursed him to become a hare to expiate this offense, but promised him that he would regain his true form at the touch of a branch of the Pātiri tree. One day Ādirājendra was hunting in the forest; he wounded the hare with an arrow. The hare, bleeding from his wound, touched the Pātiri tree, and at that instant he regained his old form and won release (*vīṭu*).[78]

Devī (Ambikā) replaces the sage Tūmappar of the former myth as the author of the curse; she also takes the blow usually reserved for the *liṅga*. We thus have a reversal of the pattern discussed earlier, in which Devī as the Kāmadhenu is the *cause* of the god's wound. The wounded Upamanyu takes the role of Maṅkaṇaka in the Tamil version of his story, but here real blood, not the sap of plants, pours from his body. The cult site is covered with blood (that of the transformed devotee),[79] as in earlier examples; in this case the devotee is wounded instead of the god. That there is a trace of the original combination of milk and blood is less obvious but nonetheless certain, for Upamanyu is famous precisely for his connection with milk: he was brought up on the milk of the Kāmadhenu at the *āśrama* of Arundhatī; when he returned to his parents, he refused to touch the food prepared for him, and Śiva brought him the ocean of milk (*pāl alaiyuṅ kaṭal*).[80]

The tradition of Tiruppātirippuliyūr has probably borrowed Upamanyu and his father Vyāghrapāda from Citamparam, where they appear in connection with the discovery of the *mūlasthāna*, the earliest shrine to Śiva at that site;[81] the "tiger-footed" Vyāghrapāda and his son nourished by the ocean of milk may provide the necessary conjunction of blood and milk in the Citamparam myths. At Tiruppātirippuliyūr, this conjunction is found within the single figure of Upamanyu, whose blood soaks the base of the Pātiri tree. In both cases the Tamil myths assert the necessary and sanctifying role of blood, in marked contrast with the Sanskrit myths of Maṅkaṇaka.

Blood, then, comes to be a conventional symbol of sanctity in the Tamil origin myths. It appears because of an act of violence, usually an attack upon the deity himself. The god is in some way wounded, and this fact acquires a decisive significance in defining his local character and the manner of his revelation. To cite another few examples simply to drive home this point: the main god of the Vaiṣṇava shrine of Tiruvallikkeṇi (Madras) is Pārthasārathi, Kṛṣṇa as the charioteer of Arjuna; while serving in this capacity, Kṛṣṇa is said to have been badly wounded in the face by arrows shot (at Arjuna) by Bhīṣma. Kṛṣṇa's face was covered with blood; the scars are still visible on the image in the shrine.[82] As has been noted by U. Ve. Cāminātaiyar, the neighboring shrine of Tiruveṭṭīcuvaraṉ has a Śaiva parallel to this theme: when Arjuna was performing *tapas* to gain possession of the great Pāśupata weapon, Śiva appeared to him in the form of a hunter; they fought, and Śiva was struck by Arjuna. The entire universe reeled from this blow.[83] The *liṅga* at Tiruveṭṭīcuvaraṉ bears the mark of the wound to the head of the god.[84] Both these myths make the god suffer on account of Arjuna; both explain the presence of a blood-stained image as the central object of worship in the shrine. The sanctifying character of blood is nowhere more clear than in these two sites;[85] the self-sacrificing role of the deity recurs in many other myths. In the origin myth of Tirupati, a shepherd tries to prevent a cow from pouring her milk on an anthill in which the god is hiding; the cow is struck, the god takes the blow and bleeds, and the shepherd dies.[86] Here the deity serves as a surrogate for the cow, whose milk he drinks in his anthill home; the blood of the deity mingles with milk from the cow. The god is revealed to his worshipers through violence: at Tirumullaivāyil, King Tŏṇṭaimāṉ cut at a *mullai* creeper in which his elephant's foot was caught; the sword struck a hidden *liṅga*, which poured forth blood.[87] The *mullai* plants[88] covering the *liṅga* are jasmine, with its white flowers; thus we have the conventional red/white combination at this site, too, the white of the jasmine substituting for the white milk of the wishing-cow.[89]

We may now attempt to make the meaning of this combination explicit. We have uncovered several layers of symbolism that may be linked by an underlying ideology of sacrifice. The god is pierced by an arrow, cut by a sword, or scarred by the hoof of the Kāmadhenu; his blood gushes out to mix with the milk / seed which bathes the site. Blood is itself a form of seed; life is born out of the disintegration of an earlier existence. The blood sacrifice produces the creative seed. In many myths this entire process depends on the Kāmadhenu: the cow/goddess initiates the sacrifice by a violent attack on the god or his symbol, but the cow is also the source of the life (white milk, the divine seed) poured out at the site of the sacrifice. Note that in the Tamil origin myths both blood and milk serve as allotropes of the seed won from death; this convergence of symbols takes place against the background of violent action, and relates directly to the Tamil view of blood as powerful and sacred. The deity of the Tamil shrine is nearly always revealed—we might say born[90]—in violence. The persistent theme of aggression against the deity as it appears in the Tamil origin myths becomes immediately intelligible in the light of sacrificial concepts. At times the wounding of the god is juxtaposed with symbols of seed familiar from classical Brahminical sources; let us look at one more, rather dramatic example:

> King Āryarāja ruled righteously over the Ārya land (*āriyanāṭu*). One day his crown of jewels was found to be missing. The king retired to his room and said to Śiva: "Is this fair? I have served you righteously, yet my priceless crown has disappeared. If it is not returned to me, I will abandon the kingdom." When he opened the door, Śiva in the form of a Brahmin was there. The Brahmin told the king he had seen the crown at Tiruvāṭpokki. The king went there and heard the local purāṇa recited; thus he learned that the mountain was the body of the god. A voice from heaven directed the king to climb the mountain, despite his reluctance to tread on the deity.
>
> He went up and entered the shrine there, and Śiva took the form of a Brahmin, and appeared from behind the *liṅga*. "Oh king," he said, "the god told me in a dream to give you the crown kept in his treasure room if you can fill this golden vessel (*kŏpparai*) with water from the Kāviri." The king took a pot (*kuṭam*) and carried water from the river up the mountain many times, but the golden vessel was never full—it seemed that the water kept flowing out of it. "How can you ask me to fill a vessel with a hole in it?" asked the king. "Try once

more," said the Brahmin. The king took the heavy pot and filled it with water, carried it up the mountain and poured it into the vessel, but still it was not full. "I am sorry," said the Brahmin, "I cannot give you the crown." At this the king became very angry and, taking his sword, lunged at the Brahmin, who hid in the *liṅga*. A spurt of blood came forth from the *liṅga*'s crest. The king cried out, embraced the *liṅga*, wiped the blood with his garment—but the flow did not stop. He ran over the mountain gathering fresh leaves, then squeezed their sap out over the *liṅga*, but still the blood gushed higher and higher. In despair he determined to kill himself: "I cannot bear to behold the apple of my eye (*kaṇmaṇi*) bleeding," he cried as he dashed his head against a rock. Śiva came out of the *liṅga* and restrained him with his hands.

The god granted the requests of the king—that the *liṅga* be worshiped with Kāviri water, that those who offered golden pots to the god be rewarded, that the mountain be named Maṇivarai, that the *liṅga* be called Tirumuṭittaḻumpaṉ ("having a scar on its crest"), and that the king receive *mukti* after a period of rule. The god then took his crown off his head and put it on the head of the king.[91]

The central image of the king's test, as of later worship at this shrine, is the seed carried in the (golden) pot. As in the myth of the Kāviri's descent,[92] the sacred water of the river is symbolically equated with seed. But seed alone is not enough: the king's perseverance is unrewarded, and another sign of the divine presence is needed; Śiva seems deliberately to goad the king into striking out with his sword, so that a river of blood can join the golden river of seed. The wounding of the god drives the king to suicide and precipitates the revelation. Note that blood is again more powerful than vegetable sap: once again, a Tamil myth reverses the import of the Maṅkaṇaka story. Only the threat of another sacrifice can check the flow of blood. As in the story of Kaṇṇappar, who tears out his eye to stanch the bleeding from the eyes on a *liṅga*,[93] the wounded *liṅga* at Tiruvāṭpokki is associated with the eye, and this identification gives the mountain its name. The king who at first blackmails the god with the threat of renunciation—he will abandon his kingdom if his crown is not restored!—in the end goes back to his duties with the god's crown and the promise of ultimate release, the rewards of devotion after his inadvertent attack upon Śiva. Pilgrims to this shrine still offer golden pots filled with Kāviri water, which is poured out over the *liṅga* with its eternal scar: the symbolism of the sacrifice is reenacted in local ritual.

### 3. Serpents and Anthills

Having isolated within the Tamil origin myths a set of symbols suggestive of a latent concept of sacrifice, we may now turn to a myth that deals explicitly with a sacrifice. This is the myth of the *mūlasthāna* at the famous shrine of Tiruvārūr, where Śiva is Valmīkanātha, "lord of the anthill":

> Once the gods, Viṣṇu, Indra, and the rest, performed a sacrifice at Kurukṣetra, having determined that he who would complete the sacrifice without hindrance would be foremost among them. After a thousand years, the gods grew weak. Then Viṣṇu completed the sacrifice and became proud (*akantaiy uṟa*). By the command of Śiva, the sacrificial fire spurted up toward heaven, and a bow appeared in it; Viṣṇu proclaimed himself first among the gods and, taking the bow in hand, showered the gods with arrows. The gods fled to Śaktipura, as once before they had fled from the poison produced from the churning of the ocean. Viṣṇu followed them there, but on entering that site he lost all his strength and fell asleep, resting his neck on the end of the bow.
>
> The son of Bṛhaspati said to the gods, "It is improper for anyone to come here full of conceit; therefore Viṣṇu fell asleep through the power of Parāśakti. Hāṭakaliṅgamūrti (= Śiva) dwells beneath this spot, sacred to the goddess; this bow is the bow of Śiva (*ñāṉavīcaṉ ṟūyavar cilai*) and has the form of sun, moon, and fire, and it will cut off the head of him who made an obstacle to your sacrifice and who was disrespectful to this place. Dig an anthill (*puṟṟu*), take the form of white ants (*cĕllu*), and gnaw through the bowstring."
>
> The gods did as he suggested, and when the bowstring snapped, the bow cut off the head of Viṣṇu; by the command of Śiva, the head fell into the vicinity of the sacrificial pit at Kurukṣetra. Portents of the end of the world appeared, and Mount Meru itself was shaken. Suddenly a great light arose in the form of a *liṅga* from out of the anthill. The portents ceased, and the gods worshiped the *liṅga*. Śiva appeared with Umā in

that *liṅga* and said to the gods, "Because Viṣṇu had no respect for this site of our Parāśakti, he has lost his head. If his head is placed on the body again, he will come to life (*ĕḻuvaṉ*)." Śiva gave the bow to Indra, and if Indra places it near a cloud, rain comes. The gods returned to Kurukṣetra and completed the sacrifice. By the command of Śiva, the body of Viṣṇu appeared there, and the Aśvins (*maruttuvar*) replaced the head on the body. Viṣṇu came back to life. He returned to Śaktipura to worship there.[1]

As the myth suggests, the *liṅga* in the *mūlasthāna* at Tiruvārūr rises up from an anthill.[2] The source of this myth is a series of ancient myths that describe the removal and subsequent restoration of the "head of the sacrifice."[3] The *Śatapathabrāhmaṇa* tells the story as follows:

The gods, Agni, Indra, Soma, Makha, Viṣṇu, the Viśvedevas, and others except for the Aśvins, were present at a sacrifice at Kurukṣetra. (They thought:) "Let us attain excellence (*śrī*), glory (*yaśas*), and food." They said, "Whoever comes first to the end of the sacrifice (*yajñasyodṛc*) by effort, *tapas*, faith, sacrifice, and oblations, shall be the most excellent among us." Viṣṇu attained the end first and became the most excellent of the gods. (Viṣṇu is the sacrifice; the sacrifice is the sun). Taking his bow, he rested his head on the end of it. The gods, unable to overcome him, sat down around him. The ants (*vamryaḥ*), being promised food and the ability to find water even in the desert, gnawed the bowstring, and the ends of the bow sprang apart and cut off Viṣṇu's head. The head fell and became the sun. Indra reached him first as the gods rushed toward him; Indra embraced him and became glory (*yaśas*); therefore Indra became Makhavat, but they call him Maghavat, for the gods love secrets.[4]

Other versions replace Viṣṇu with Makha[5] (Makha Vaiṣṇava)[6] or Rudra.[7] The identification is less crucial than the fact that the myth connects the most excellent (*śreṣṭha*) of the gods with the end of the sacrifice, and then with the sacrifice itself.

At first glance the myth from Tiruvārūr follows the earlier myths quite closely. The sacrifice takes place at Kurukṣetra (the archetypal sacrificial site); Viṣṇu completes the sacrifice first, grows proud, and is beheaded. The ants are the gods themselves, but this idea, too, goes back to the older myths, where Indra in the form of an ant cuts the bowstring of Rudra.[8] The restoration of the head by the Aśvins is carried out in exchange for a part of the oblations[9]—indeed, a major part, for the texts addressed to the Aśvins then become of primary importance in the *pravargya* ritual associated with this myth. The presence of the Aśvins who restore the head of the sacrifice is also clearly linked with the myth of Dadhyañc, the immediate sequel to the sacrificial myth in the *Śatapathabrāhmaṇa*: Dadhyañc knew the secret of the sacrifice, the *madhu*, the completion of the sacrifice by restoring the head. Indra threatened to cut off his head if he taught the secret to anyone else. The Aśvins became his pupils; they cut off his head and replaced it with a horse's head with which he taught them the secret; Indra cut off the horse's head, and the Aśvins then restored his own head.[10] The horse's head remains in Lake Śaryaṇāvat, at Kurukṣetra, the site of the gods' sacrifice.[11] As we shall see in a moment, Dadhyañc is also present at Tiruvārūr. Note that the horse-headed Dadhyañc is analogous to Viṣṇu's horse-headed form (Hayagrīva), and one relatively late text actually combines our myth with the Hayagrīva story:

> After fighting demons for ten thousand years, Viṣṇu grew tired; he seated himself in the lotus position, leaned his head on his strung bow, and fell asleep. The gods were unhappy, for they wished to perform a sacrifice. Brahmā created an ant to eat the end of the bow; it agreed to do this on condition that the part of the oblation which fell outside the sacrificial pit would belong to the ant. The string gave way and the bow snapped, decapitating Viṣṇu. Now the gods were even more distressed. They worshiped Devī, and she explained that this had happened because of a curse uttered in jealousy by Lakṣmī when Viṣṇu once laughed in her presence. She also explained that a demon named Hayagrīva had won a boon to the effect that he could be killed only by someone with a horse's head. Viśvakarman cut off the head of a horse and fixed it on Viṣṇu's head, and Viṣṇu as Hayagrīva killed the demon.[12]

Here the horse-headed god[13] confronts a horse-headed demon; the *Bhāgavatapurāṇa* knows Hayagrīva as a demon who stole the Vedas from Brahmā and hid them in the sea, whence they were recovered by Viṣṇu in his fish avatar.[14] The episode of the ant leads again to the decapitation of Viṣṇu, but here this result appears to be an accident—until Devī reveals its higher purpose.

The role of the goddess is also central to the Tiruvārūr myth. The decapitation of Viṣṇu is explained in terms of his disrespect for the goddess, who deprives him of strength the moment he enters her sacred site. The city itself is called Śaktipura—city of *śakti*, the "power" usually identified with the goddess—in the first and subsequent references in the text. Yet the goddess here *drains* Viṣṇu of power! In this idea, and in other ways, the anthill myth is closely linked to the well-known myth of Dakṣa, Śiva's antagonistic father-in-law who excludes Śiva from his sacrifice:

> Śiva married Umā (Satī), the daughter of the Prajāpati Dakṣa; but Dakṣa did not like his son-in-law, and refused to honor him. Dakṣa performed a great sacrifice, but he did not invite Śiva or reserve a portion for him. The sage Dadhīca tried in vain to convince Dakṣa to invite Śiva. Umā, hearing of the sacrifice, begged to be allowed to go there, and Śiva gave her permission. She upbraided her father for not inviting her husband; then, in great anger, she entered the fire and died. Śiva came as Vīrabhadra (in some versions, together with Bhadrakālī) to destroy the sacrifice; he uprooted the sacrificial stakes, plucked out the eyes of Bhaga, knocked out the teeth of Pūṣan, and cut off Dakṣa's head with the sacrificial knife. When the wrath of Vīrabhadra was appeased, and Dakṣa had acknowledged the greatness of Śiva, Śiva restored the sacrifice and put a ram's head on Dakṣa.[15] Then Śiva took up the corpse of Satī and danced with it over the face of the earth. Viṣṇu, fearing that the wild dance would destroy the world, cut Satī's body into pieces. Wherever a part of the corpse fell, a shrine was consecrated.[16]

This complex myth is largely derived from one of the classic myths of sacrifice—the piercing of Prajāpati by the sacrificial butcher Rudra. There, Rudra wins his unique portion—the remainder (*vāstu*), that part of the sacrifice left after all the oblations have been made—in return for punishing the incestuous lust of the creator for his daughter.[17] The original sexual sin survives in the Dakṣa myth in the form of Dakṣa's jealous desire for his daughter Satī; and the rivalry between Śiva and Dakṣa for the favors of this goddess comes to a head at the moment of sacrifice.[18] Note that Śiva is deprived of his *śakti*—the "power" residing in his wife—when Satī leaves to attend Dakṣa's sacrifice, where she burns herself to death. In one Tamil version of the myth, Devī actually stalks out of the androgyne in a fury, leaving Śiva with half his body aching.[19] Let us recall, too, that Satī is the prototype of the pious Hindu widow who burns herself with the body of her husband, even though she dies before her husband, according to the myth.

There are other connections between the anthill sacrifice and the Dakṣa myth. Dakṣa's head is first cut off, then replaced by another, like Viṣṇu's in the sacrifice. Dadhyañc confirms this connection, for he appears (under the name of Dadhīca or Dadhīci) at the start of Dakṣa's sacrifice to warn him of his impending doom. The presence of Dadhīca, a sacrificial figure *par excellence*, adumbrates the fate in store for Dakṣa; and we have just seen the close tie between Dadhyañc and the anthill sacrifice. Dadhyañc turns up in Tiruvārūr in the sequel to the anthill myth in which Vṛtra is slain by Indra with a weapon made from the backbone of the sage Dadhīci.[20] This, too, is an ancient element drawn from the Ṛg Veda.[21] The bow that appears from out of the sacrificial fire in the Tiruvārūr myth—clearly identified with the rainbow popularly believed to originate in the anthill—is prominent in some versions of the Dakṣa myth: here too Viṣṇu, exhausted, rests his head on the bow and is decapitated.[22] One Epic version of the Dakṣa myth makes the sacrifice the prelude to the destruction of the *tripura*, the Triple City of the demons; Śiva's first act following the dispersal of the sacrifice is to make the divine bow and arrows with which he shoots and destroys the *tripura*.[23] Even more striking in the context of the parallel we are pursuing is a version of the Dakṣa myth from the Sauptikaparvan of the *MBh*:

> The gods made a sacrifice but gave no portion to Sthāṇu (= Śiva); he therefore made a bow composed of forms of the sacrifice and, angry and with his bow drawn, approached the sacrificial site of the gods; he pierced their sacrifice, which fled as a deer into the sky, pursued by Rudra. With the end of the bow, Tryambaka then blinded Bhaga, cut off the arms of Savitṛ, and broke the teeth of Pūṣan; then the dark-throated god (*śitikaṇṭha*) rested on the end of the bow (*avaṣṭabhya dhanuṣkoṭim*). A cry uttered by the gods (*vāg amarair uktā*) cut through the bowstring, and the bow sprang apart. The gods took refuge with the most excellent of the gods (*devaśreṣṭha*), now without his bow, and he cast his anger into the water, where it burns and dessicates all. He restored the missing limbs of the gods, and they offered him all the oblations.[24]

This version has clearly borrowed from the anthill sacrifice, even to the extent of echoing entire phrases from the texts of that myth.[25]

Only the culmination of the myth in the decapitation of the "most excellent of the gods" (Śiva here replacing Viṣṇu, Makha, Rudra) seems to be missing. Still, the god leaning on the bow is Śitikaṇṭha, "the dark-throated"; this epithet is explained by another myth, but, as I will attempt to show later, the use of the name in this context is no accident. Śitikaṇṭha belongs in the series of sacrificial victims whose heads are removed and subsequently restored. Sāyaṇa, commenting on the version in which Rudra is beheaded by Indra as an ant, has Rudra rest the end of the bow on his neck (*rudrasya galam avaṣṭabhya*).[26] The bow is snapped when the word of the gods cuts the string: here we may recall that Dadhyañc is identified with Vāc[27] (the word that reveals the secret of the sacrifice, how the head is restored, and so on), while in place of the horse head under the waters of Śaryaṇāvat (which may be assimilated to the fire-breathing submarine mare)[28] we now have the anger of the god-victim. This substitution survives in later texts, where the submarine fire comes from the eye of Śiva-Kāmāntaka, the destroyer of Kāma;[29] the fire is also the symbolic coordinate of the divine seed that engenders Skanda, carried by the Ganges. Here we may have reached the heart of the sacrificial myth, the element that binds together apparently disparate and conflated accounts. The sacrifice is itself, or produces by its performance, the fiery, dangerous, creative seed. It is the brilliant seed, or its analogue, the portion given to Rudra, which blinds Bhaga, knocks out the teeth of Pūṣan, and so on, in early versions—precisely the actions attributed to Śiva in the Epic and subsequent versions; their parallel in the anthill myth is the showering of the gods with arrows from the divine bow by Viṣṇu. Sometimes the seed is specifically stated to have produced Rudra, just as later it produces Skanda.[30] Rudra's portion is equivalent to the seed and to the remnant, the *vāstu*, the end of the sacrifice (in the anthill myth: *udṛc*).[31] It is this concept of the primary importance of the remainder that underlies the statement in the Epic myth that the gods gave to Śiva "all the oblations" as his portion.[32] What is important for our purposes is that this point can only be reached after the sacrifice is in some sense performed. Although the text fails to state this clearly, we must assume that the god resting on the end of the bow is, like his counterpart in the anthill myth, identified with the sacrifice.

The rivalry between Śiva and Dakṣa thus takes on a new dimension: they vie not only for the goddess but also for the position of sacrificial victim! Dakṣa is not mentioned in the myth in *MBh* 10.18; the sacrifice flees as a deer after being pierced by the destroyer, just as Prajāpati takes the form of a stag to pursue his daughter (fleeing as a deer).[33] But the destroyer is himself sacrificed, if our analysis is correct. The myth has hidden this element. In the chapter that directly precedes this myth, however, Dakṣa and Śiva confront each other as Prajāpati and Sthāṇu; seeing Dakṣa's creation, Sthāṇu castrates himself.[34] The two myths are surely part of a single sequence.

Why does the myth suppress the sacrifice of Śiva? This is only one example of a very widespread tendency, which I have already hinted at more than once. The myth strives to break out of the cycles of death and rebirth implicit in the sacrificial scheme. Specifically, it wishes to spare the divine victim the need to die. The creator does not suffer death and need not be reborn—indeed, he *must* not die. His role as victim must be obliterated. Hence he destroys the sacrifice which is his death, just as Śiva-Kālāntaka may be said to evade his own destruction by killing Yama, the lord of death.[35] The victim has good reason to want to disperse the sacrifice; this is precisely the reasoning of the serpents who, faced with the prospect of being slaughtered *en masse* at Janamejaya's sacrifice, discuss ways to prevent its taking place: they could bite and kill the officiating priests, extinguish the sacrificial fires by becoming clouds and raining on the site, steal the offering ladles, bite all the people attending the rite, befoul the prepared food with excrement—or become priests themselves and stop the sacrifice by demanding their fees![36]

There are other elements in Śiva's attempt to subvert the sacrificial ritual; we will return to this theme. But we are concerned here with the underlying, older level of the myth, and it is my contention that this level is preserved, albeit in a new form, in the myth from Tiruvārūr. There Viṣṇu is the sacrificial victim, and Śiva is the destroyer—through the agency of the gods and on behalf of Devī. In other words, Śiva sacrifices Viṣṇu to the goddess. But we may go further than this. Śiva rises from the anthill in Tiruvārūr. Why is the anthill the dwelling of the god? No doubt there is an important element here of chthonic claims on the deity. The anthill is closely connected with ideas of the earth and fertility; the god is localized in his uniquely local, earth-bound home.[37] Yet it is the subterranean associations of the anthill that seem most profound: the anthill is the entrance to the nether world, the abode of snakes and demons,[38] the realm of the dead.[39] This is the world with which Śiva is linked by the anthill. But the anthill is also the depository of remnants of the sacrifice;[40] the anthill is associated with Prajāpati or the ear of Prajāpati (the earth);[41] an anthill with seven holes replaces the head of the human victim.[42] The anthill is clearly the locus of the *vāstu*, the end of the sacrifice, the divine seed.[43]

It is beginning to look as if Viṣṇu is not, after all, the only, or even the most important, victim of the sacrifice at Tiruvārūr. It is Śiva who is identified with the anthill and thus, by implication, with the whole set of sacrificial concepts—and particularly with his peculiar portion, the *vāstu*. One wonders if Viṣṇu has entered the Tiruvārūr myth as a scapegoat, just as in other myths he takes upon himself the unwanted burden of corrupting the *tripura* demons, thus allowing Śiva to escape blame in killing them.[44] Viṣṇu's role in the anthill myth can, of course, draw on impeccable sources, but we have already seen the concern of other myths to remove the status of sacrificial victim from Śiva. The same process may have operated here. (Note, too, that the Tiruvārūr myth, by identifying the gods as the ants, is closest to the earlier myths that refer the story to Rudra rather than Viṣṇu.)

Further support for this view can be drawn from another set of images. The *liṅga* implanted in the anthill may represent the *liṅga* in the womb. In the old Tamil love-poems, the plundering of an anthill by a bear suggests the rape of the virgin.[45] We have seen that the castration of Sthāṇu / Śiva directly precedes the complex Dakṣa myth in *MBh* 10.18. It is therefore of interest that the castration theme appears in an apparently earlier origin myth for the Tiruvārūr shrine:

> Śiva, grieving at his separation from Satī, wandered naked and with a skull in his hands into the *āśrama* of the sages (of the Pine Forest). Having never seen such a sight, the wives of the sages fell in love with him. He begged for alms as he went down the street, and the women followed, gaping at the beggar. The sages, their husbands, saw this and cursed him for desecrating the *āśrama*; at their curse, his *liṅga* fell and, cleaving the earth, entered Pātāla. Ashamed, Śiva entered a deep cave (*gartā*) and fell asleep.
>
> But the worlds were troubled and the seas burst their bounds, and the gods, fearing the end of the world had come, sought the aid of Brahmā. He thought hard and realized what had happened: "This is because the *liṅga* of Śiva has been made to fall; we must get him to take it back." The gods went to the

> cave and found Śiva asleep; they begged him to take back his *liṅga*. "The real reason it fell," said Śiva, "is the absence of Satī; the sages' curse was only a pretext. What would I do with a *liṅga* now?" They said, "Satī has entered the womb of Menakā. Soon you will have a wife once more; take back your *liṅga* and give us security." Śiva agreed on condition the *liṅga* be worshiped. The gods hastened to Pātāla and worshiped it there; they asked for another *liṅga* for their devotion, and the god showed them the shrine (of Hāṭakeśvara = Tiruvārūr); Brahmā installed there a golden *liṅga*.[46]

The myth of the anthill sacrifice with which we began refers to the Hāṭakeśvara shrine as older than the anthill;[47] today Hāṭakeśvara is a subsidiary shrine inside the Tiruvārūr temple complex, but the local priests still refer to it as the *biladvāra*, the door to the nether world. The Hāṭakeśvara *liṅga* remains in Pātāla underneath this shrine; the cleft it opens in the earth in descending to the nether world allows the Ganges to emerge on to the surface of the earth from Pātāla,[48] but the original passage, the Nāgabila, is hidden by Indra—until, after a long time, an anthill appears, and the serpents can come forth on to the earth.[49] Hāṭakeśvara is thus linked by an anthill to the realm of chaos and vitality under the earth; since Hāṭakeśvara may well be the older site, one wonders if its myths were at some point transferred to the present *mūlasthāna* of Valmīkanātha, the lord of the anthill. The castration of Śiva takes the place of the sacrifice in this text. Śiva echoes the words of Sthāṇu in the Epic Dakṣa myth: Satī is absent, so he does not need his *liṅga*. (In the Epic: *prajāḥ sṛṣṭāḥ pareṇ'emāḥ kiṃ kariṣyāmy anena vai*).[50] But the castration is ultimately creative: Śiva takes back his *liṅga* in order to marry Pārvatī (and beget the divine child Skanda), and the shrine, in which Śiva will be worshiped in the form of a *liṅga*, has been created and provided with the sacred, life-giving waters because of the castration. The basic pattern of the sacrifice is present here: Śiva is castrated in order to be fertile, just as the sacrificial victim dies in order to be reborn.

Our results so far coincide remarkably with an extensive series of myths in which an anthill, the site of the divinity, is pierced or stepped upon, and the god or goddess dwelling in it wounded. Thus the goddess Mātaṅgī is said to have been discovered when a king pierced her anthill home with his lance; Mātaṅgī rose from the anthill bleeding, with the heavens in her left hand and the cosmic serpent Adisesa in her right.[51] The shrine at Ceyūr has a similar story: the Coḻa king was hunting in a forest when he came across another hunter; he pursued the man until he disappeared behind an anthill. The king shot an arrow at the anthill, and blood gushed forth; the king's men excavated the anthill and found a *liṅga* hidden inside.[52] Most of the Tamil anthill myths involve just such a violent sequence. Blood spurts from the anthill, thus revealing the divine presence. If I am right in suggesting that the anthill represents the sacrifice, and is in particular the locus of the seed/remnant produced by the sacrifice, then the Tamil myths would appear to have accentuated the element of violence necessary for the birth of the divine seed (the rebirth of the god in his son). The violent birth is an integral part of the *Brāhmaṇa* myths of sacrifice, as we have seen; but it is less apparent in classical versions of Skanda's birth from the union of Śiva and Pārvatī. There the notion of the creative sacrifice is almost totally submerged.[53] In the south Indian mythological tradition, however, blood is itself a form of seed, and seed is produced by piercing or wounding the god.

There is another major symbol related to the anthill myths. The *liṅga* rising from the anthill may be compared to the classic inhabitant of this site, the serpent. A five-headed serpent—Śiva as Sāmbaśivamūrti—rises from the anthill to drink the milk of the Kāmadhenu in the origin myth of the shrine at Velūr.[54] Let us look for a moment at the cult of Tiruvŏṟṟiyūr, which forms a close parallel to that of Tiruvārūr, the home of the anthill myth with which we began.[55] At Tiruvŏṟṟiyūr, too, the god of the anthill is the central object of worship, and here we find two myths of the snake: Vāsuki, the king of the Nāgas, is said to have worshiped at this shrine and to have been grasped by the god, Palakainātar ("lord of the plank") and made to rest at his feet; hence Śiva at Tiruvŏṟṟiyūr is also known as Paṭampakkar or Paṭampakkanātar, "having the hood (of the cobra) at his side."[56] Ādiśeṣa and Candra (the moon) are also said to have fought and to have been reconciled at this site.[57] Both of these myths are late attempts to deal with a fact explicitly recognized by the living folk tradition of Tiruvŏṟṟiyūr —that the god of the anthill is, as one might expect, a serpent. The priests of the shrine claim to have seen the serpent-god, who is believed to dwell in an underground passage connecting the anthill in the shrine to an *atti* tree outside.[58] If we pursue the analogy between the two shrines, the serpent of Tiruvŏṟṟiyūr would correspond to the *liṅga* implanted in the anthill at Tiruvārūr. Serpents are, in fact, said to emerge from the Hāṭakeśvara anthill there, as we have seen. There is, however, still a deeper association to be explored.

The origin of the anthill at Tiruvārūr is connected, as we saw at the beginning of our discussion, to the great sacrifice at Kurukṣetra. At this point we must raise the question of the serpent's symbolic role generally; indeed, it may be suggested that the sacrificial content of our myth is directly related to this very figure. For it is surely no accident that a serpent has come, as Ādiśeṣa, to embody the idea of the remainder. The serpent is a natural symbol of the goal of the sacrifice as rebirth: the serpent emerges from his own aged skin; he is the remainder of himself, an equivalent of the dangerous, fiery, yet fertile and productive seed. The serpent is the *vāstu*; it is, therefore, not surprising that the Vāstupuruṣa becomes a Vāstunāga,[59] or that the architectural handbooks prescribe the installation of a golden serpent—like the golden seed of creation—in connection with *vāstu* rites.[60] The serpent symbolizes the sacrifice and the result of the sacrifice. The earth is fixed on the remnant, the eternally reborn—Ananta-Ādiśeṣa, the serpent who has no end, no death, since he is reborn out of the very act of aging, as the sacrifice is slain and reborn as seed. Therefore the serpent knows the secret of the sacrifice, the means of conquering death, the way to restore the head of the sacrifice. Men and gods can but imitate the serpent: "Through this [rite] the serpents overcame death. Those who perform it overcome death. They crawl out of their old skin, for they have conquered death."[61]

This passage concludes the description of a snake-sacrifice which, if we may judge by the names of the participants, was the prototype for Janamejaya's famous sacrifice in the first book of the *MBh*. The story of Janamejaya's sacrifice frames the Mahābhārata story proper: Parikṣit, Janamejaya's father, was slain by the serpent Takṣaka; hence Janamejaya swore to destroy all the serpents in a sacrifice. Janamejaya is therefore known as *sarpasattrin*, the "serpent-sacrificer"; but his rite was interrupted when the snake-sage Āstīka was granted a boon, and asked that the sacrifice remain incomplete.[62] In the *Brāhmaṇa* text quoted above, however, the sacrifice is performed *by* the snakes; Janamejaya himself is mentioned as a snake, as are a Dhṛtarāṣṭra and others known to us from the Epic. By the time of the composition of the *Ādiparvan*, the sacrifice had been transformed into a human rite directed *against* serpents, although the archaic book of *Pauṣya* still records that the *purohita* of Janamejaya was the son of a snake-woman.[63] In the course of this transformation of the rite from a sacrifice by and for the snakes to a sacrifice to slaughter the snakes, the symbolism of the ritual has been lost. Or nearly so—for we may suggest that the setting of the *Bhārata* narration in the intervals of Janamejaya's serpent sacrifice is not, after all, a meaningless, inexplicable accident in the history of Indian tradition. Rather, it is the result of the innate power of the symbol, and a survival of the substratum of myth in the Epic. The story of the great battle-sacrifice of men—or are they gods, as the Epic itself insists, or indeed serpents, as so many of their names, attributes, and actions suggest[64]—is the story of the birth through violence of the rightful heir, the remnant, the dynastic father Parikṣit (killed in the womb by Aśvatthaman, the snake-man incarnation of Rudra; revived at birth by Kṛṣṇa; finally slain as king by the bite of the serpent Takṣaka).[65] The recitation of the *MBh* story in the course of the serpent sacrifice offers us a clue to the meaning of the myth hidden in the background. The great sacrifice is framed by the rite that, in its original form, epitomizes the ancient symbolism of the sacrifice.

Notwithstanding the distortion that the Epic account of Janamejaya's sacrifice causes to this earlier conception, another relic of the old serpent sacrifice can still be seen. Why does the *Ādiparvan* go to such lengths to describe the reasons for the *interruption* of the sacrifice? After all, the whole of the long book of Āstīka, which directly precedes the introductory genealogies, is devoted to explaining the background to the sacrifice and the birth of the snake-man Āstīka, who stops it. Moreover, there is in Hindu mythology a wider pattern of "interrupted sacrifices"; the Dakṣa myth, for example, exemplifies this theme. Or we may put the question differently: Why does Janamejaya rejoice when his sacrifice is stopped and the serpent-king Takṣaka saved from destruction?[66] Is the rite stopped or completed? The verb used is *sam-āp* and can have either meaning, although its basic sense is that of achieving, concluding, reaching the end. We are even told that the sacrifice was "concluded according to rite" (*samāpite tatas satre vidhivad*).[67] Has the notion of the remnant produced by the sacrifice survived in the motif of interrupting the rite? The serpents survive the sacrifice aimed at their destruction, although their activities are limited: they must not touch those who recite the story of the sacrifice (*dharmākhyāna*),[68] just as Yama is allowed only limited scope for slaughter after being revived by Śiva-Kālāntaka,[69] and the Rākṣasas survive the war with Rāma, but are reformed under the rule of the righteous king Vibhīṣaṇa. These may be seen as examples of the transformation of the idea of the *vāstu*, the remnant/germ that the old sacrifice aims at producing. The threatening aspects of the "seed" are eliminated through the act of sacrifice, and one is left with a violent force channeled into creative, necessary roles. In order to achieve this end, the ritual must be interrupted before the victim is totally destroyed.

So powerful is this theme in its relation to the serpent as sacrificial symbol that it appears twice more in the *Ādiparvan*: even before the serpent-sacrifice is begun and interrupted, Ādiśeṣa removes himself from the other snakes in order to survive, as Dharmadeva, bearing the earth on his head;[70] and at the end of the *Ādiparvan* we learn of the burning of the Khāṇḍava forest by Agni with the assistance of Arjuna and Kṛṣṇa.[71] The two heroes brutally exterminate the creatures of the forest, foremost among them clearly the Nāgas. But here again a remnant survives: four Śārṅgaka birds,[72] the demon Maya, and two serpents—Takṣaka, the same serpent-king who was saved at the last moment by Āstīka from death in the sacrifice of Janamejaya, and Takṣaka's son Aśvasena. Takṣaka survives because he is not in the forest at the time of the disaster; he is, in fact, at Kurukṣetra,[73] the archetypal site of the sacrifice! Aśvasena is swallowed by his mother and, when she is beheaded by Arjuna, Aśvasena crawls out of her and escapes.[74] The sacrificial nature of the burning of the forest is intimated by the story of Śvetaki, which is added by some manuscripts by way of explanation: Śvetaki, a king obsessed with sacrificing, persuaded Rudra (in his partial incarnation as Durvāsas) to serve as priest at a twelve-year sacrificial session; when the session ended, Agni, who was glutted with the offerings, lost his luster and appetite; to restore him to his normal state (as the receiver of offerings), Brahmā directed him to devour the Khāṇḍava forest.[75] But there is an even firmer link with the serpent sacrifice. According to *Baudhāyanaśrautasūtra* (17.18), the serpent sacrifice that we know from the *Tāṇḍyamahābrāhmaṇa*,[76] and that was ultimately made into the frame-story of the *MBh*, was performed by the kings and princes of the serpents in human form—in Khāṇḍavaprastha. The *Ādiparvan* thus begins and ends with a development of the idea of the serpent as the sacrifice.

If the interpretation I am suggesting is valid, then the presence of Ādiśeṣa in Tamil shrines becomes intelligible in the same terms. Ādiśeṣa comes up from the nether world to witness Śiva's dance at Citamparam, where the serpent is incarnate as Patañjali—this is perhaps the best-known example of Ādiśeṣa's association with a shrine.[77] But Ādiśeṣa is also the Nāganadī at Tiruppuṉavāyil,[78] and he is the tamarind tree under which Nammāḻvār sits in meditation;[79] Ādiśeṣa and the other Nāgas worship the *liṅga* at Śrīnāgeśakṣetra (Tiruppātāḷīccaram) to atone for Vāsuki's coughing up of poison that had to be swallowed by Śiva.[80] Undertones of the sacrifice are retained in the very widespread motif of Ādiśeṣa's contest with Vāyu, the wind: Vāyu attempts to dislodge Ādiśeṣa from Mount Meru, which the serpent is covering with his thousand hoods; Ādiśeṣa's head is blown off by the wind, and his blood drenches the shrine where a piece of the mountain falls.[81] The mountain peak that reaches the Tamil shrine in this way is thus a part of Meru, the cosmic mountain touching heaven; the blood of the serpent substitutes in these myths for the blood drawn from the deity or from his symbol, the *liṅga*. The serpent coiled around the mountain becomes the serpent encompassing the shrine; the serpent retraces the boundaries of Maturai after the universal flood.[82] Why does the serpent know the ancient boundaries? Is it not because serpent and shrine are one, the remnant of the sacrifice—the serpent surviving his own death, the shrine surviving the universal destruction of the *pralaya*?[83] Ādiśeṣa wishes to escape mortality; therefore he worships at Nĕllai (Tirunĕlveli), since that site is never destroyed; the shrine is his refuge during the destruction of the world.[84]

Let us go a step farther. Because the serpent retraces the boundaries at Maturai, that shrine is named Ālavāy, Sanskrit Hālāsya, "poison-mouth." But the tradition of Maturai undoubtedly regards Ālavāy as one of the *gods* of the city, worshiped in one of the four ancient temples (*māṭam*) that give the city its name Nāṉmāṭakkūṭal.[85] Ālavāy naturally becomes Śiva, who holds poison in his throat; as Nīlavāymaṇicerkaṇṭaṉ, "he whose neck is blue as sapphire," he is the god "who made Nāṉmāṭakkūṭal into Ālavāy," according to the verse introducing the boundary story in the *Tiruviḷai*.[86] We will turn to the circumstances that led to Śiva's blue throat in a moment. It would appear, however, that Ālavāy was originally a serpent, as the name itself suggests, and the local purāṇic account of the boundary myth confirms. An important development must therefore have taken place at Maturai: Śiva was at some point identified with the original serpent-deity there in a process activated by the coincidence in attributes—perhaps, in particular, through the relation to the sacrifice. That the serpent-god is

III. The serpent retraces the boundary of Maturai / Ālavāy after the flood.

ancient in Maturai may be deduced from other fragments of the tradition: *Paripāṭal*, in a hymn to Tirumāl in the Maturai area, refers to the "city/shrine of the Nāga who bears the world on his head" (*pū muṭi nākar nakar*).[87] And the folk epic develops this theme with respect to Arjuna—who is here a representative of the god of Maturai, while the Amazon Queen Alli is a form of Mīnākṣī, the goddess of this shrine:

> Arjuna took the form of an old wrinkled ascetic (*āṇṭi*) and forced his way into the palace of Alli on the pretext of seeking alms. Once inside, he spread his tiger skin and sat down, having placed before him a picture of Alli and her maidservant; he called out for Alli in love and in the pain of separation. When Alli heard his calls, she was furious: "No one speaks to me in this impertinent manner. Cut him to pieces!" Alli's servant persuaded her that it was dangerous to kill a Śaiva ascetic with her own hand. So they sought snakes to kill him; the wives of the snake charmers coaxed snakes from their anthills in the forest and brought them in boxes to Alli. Alli fed the snakes milk, fruit, and opium (*apiṉimaruntukaḷ*) until their eyes grew red. Then she sent them to kill the mendicant, whose words had made her body melt in rage.

The snakes hissed and crept toward the man; but seeing the mark of the fish on his back and other signs, they recognized him as the husband of the snake-woman Ulūpī (*nākakaṉṉi-maṇavāḷaṉ*), the younger brother of Yudhiṣṭhira and Bhīma, who had disguised himself as an ascetic in order to wed Alli. "Did Alli give us medicine in order to kill her husband?" they cried. Alli was enraged by these words: "This is the work of that Serpent Maiden (Ulūpī)!" And, as a five-headed serpent wound itself around Arjuna's shoulders, she said, "That evil man has bewitched the snakes with medicine, but he has no potion with which to bewilder me!" She called to her servants to beat the snakes with a whip; the snakes disappeared, calling as they went, "At the hour of your wedding to this man, we will come to make you a swing."

Alli then tried to have the ascetic killed by a wild elephant, but this attempt also failed. Finally the old man made his request; he wanted a piece of the queen's old petticoat in order to mend his bag, which had worn badly in his wanderings from Mallikārjuna to Maturai. Reluctantly, the queen gave him what he wanted, in order to be rid of him; as she put the cloth in his hand, he touched her hand with ash and revealed his shining teeth. Alli fell in a faint, and Arjuna departed like the wind.

Kṛṣṇa took the form of an aged snake charmer and, transforming Arjuna into a snake, took him in a box to the court. The snake drank all the milk brought in tribute to Alli by four thousand cowherdesses; the girls ran to Alli weeping, but when the queen heard them tell of a snake radiant as the sun and the moon, she summoned the charmer and asked to see it. Said Kṛṣṇa, "That snake was brought up by my younger sister. I will not take it from its box, for at the sight of a woman it becomes full of love." The queen begged for a sight of the snake. Kṛṣṇa let it out, and the snake crawled up on Alli's lap, embraced her breasts and shoulders, kissed her face, and rolled betel leaf for the queen. "Enough, let us go," said Kṛṣṇa, but Alli said, "Hear a friendly word. Let this snake remain here tonight, and tomorrow you can take it and go." "It is used to sleeping in my sister's soft bed," said the snake charmer. Alli promised to make good his loss in gold if any harm came to the snake, and Kṛṣṇa departed, after the serpent-Arjuna had signaled to him to stay away for at least eight days.

> When night fell, Alli's servants put her to bed. She locked and bolted the door and, putting the snake beside her, fell asleep. Arjuna prayed to Lord Rāma—now was the time to satisfy his desire. Kṛṣṇa made Mūtevi (the goddess of ill fortune) keep Alli soundly asleep for one watch of the night, and Arjuna put off his serpent form, took his own body again and embraced the queen. When dawn came, he became a serpent once more.
>
> Alli awoke from a troubled sleep. Her servants found her in complete disarray, her hair and garments disordered. "The serpent has sported quite a bit; it is truly used to intercourse with people (*maṉitaruṭaṉ kūṭiye maruviṉa pāmp' itu tāṉ*)," she said. She put the serpent back in the box, and Kṛṣṇa came and took it away.[88]

The Śaiva mendicant confronted by the serpents himself takes the form of a serpent to unite with his beloved. We need hardly comment on the universal phallic aspect of the serpent; what is more to the point here is the congruence between Arjuna's serpent form and the ophidian nature of Ālavāy-Śiva. Arjuna's disguise as a Śaiva ascetic complete with ash and tiger skin suits perfectly his mythic correspondence to Śiva himself; this identification, like that of Alli with Mīnākṣī, becomes clear when we compare the folk narratives to the purāṇic myths from Maturai. This problem will be taken up again later, along with many of the motifs that appear in the above story. For the moment, let us only say that Alli's attacks upon the ascetic belong to an entire series of attempted murders of the bridegroom, and that ultimately they derive from the slaying of Śiva by Mīnākṣī. Note that Alli also loves the suitor whom she wishes dead; she faints at the sight of his radiant teeth, and sends her maidservants to seek him, and she seems unconsciously to identify him and wish for his embrace when she learns of the radiant serpent. Eventually, Arjuna weds the queen, who is captured in a tiger's cage and thus subdued.[89] The episode described above thus constitutes, in effect, a survival of the ancient Tamil motif of *kaḷavu*, the premarital union of lovers;[90] only here the serpent-suitor embraces his bride after surviving several attempts on her part to kill him. Arjuna is not, in fact, the only object of Alli's murderous attention; earlier in the epic she kills the usurper Nīṉmukaṉ, "Blue-Face"—who is perhaps a multiform of Kṛṣṇa.[91] Like Arjuna, Nīṉmukaṉ is also related to the ancient god of Maturai; the blue-faced Nīṉmukaṉ may be directly linked to "Poison-Mouth"/Ālavāy, and by another stage to Śiva as the dark-throated Nīlakaṇṭha. Thus the series is complete. The folk tradition seems to have separated and elaborated upon the major elements of a single mythic event, in which the god as serpent is slain as he unites with the goddess.

Arjuna is saved from death by snakebite in this myth because the serpents recognize him as the husband of Ulūpī, the daughter of the serpents; but it is Ulūpī's son by Arjuna, Irāvat (Tam. Arāvāṉ), who personifies the old serpent sacrifice in the Tamil epic tradition:

> Kṛṣṇa learned that the Kauravas were going to sacrifice Arāvāṉ (to the goddess), and he hastened to Yudhiṣṭhira to recommend that he sacrifice first. "Sacrifice me," said Kṛṣṇa, but the five Pāṇḍava brothers said, "Better to die ourselves—we have no need of victory." Then Arāvāṉ, the son of the serpent (*aravamaintaṉ*), volunteered to be offered up in place of Kṛṣṇa, and Kṛṣṇa agreed, for Arāvāṉ was his only equal on earth; and he granted Arāvāṉ's request to live on after the sacrifice to see the defeat of his foes. So that night Arāvāṉ cut off all the limbs of his body and offered them to Kālī, and the Pāṇḍavas offered an elephant and other sacrifices according to the Śākta rite (*yāmaḷattiṉ paṭi*).[92]

Elephant and serpent are confused in the story of Irāvat; Irāvat, the son of the Nāginī, is offered together with an elephant—or, in other accounts, in order to counteract the Kauravas' sacrifice of a white elephant.[93] Airāvata is a patronymic of the serpent Dhṛtarāṣṭra, but it is also, of course, the name of Indra's white elephant, who is sometimes said to have bestowed Ulūpī on Arjuna.[94] Airāvata is also the rainbow, which rises, as we have seen, from the anthill, home of serpents.[95] The confusion of serpents and elephants is natural enough, in view of the resemblance of the serpent and the elephant's trunk; both serpents and elephants are referred to as Nāga; the Dinnāgas, the elephants of the quarters, support the world, as does the serpent Ādiśeṣa. Both groups are thought to dwell in the nether world; at Viruttācalam we find a shrine to the elephant-headed Āḻattuppiḷḷaiyār, "Gaṇeśa of the depths," sunk deep below the ground. Irāvat, however, is clearly a snake-man; in the *MBh* he simply dies in battle,[96] but in the Tamil tradition he is the sacrificed serpent. The agonistic rivalry for the sacrifice—an important feature of the early Vedic cult, reflected in the many myths of the struggle between gods and demons for the offering[97]—here takes a new form: both groups intend to sacrifice Arāvāṉ to the goddess, and the trick is to sacrifice first. In effect, Kṛṣṇa steals the sacrifice from Duryodhana, just as Śrī is won by the gods from the demons.[98] The goddess is here the recipient of the sacrifice; she will favor whichever side offers to her. Similarly, in the *Mayilirāvaṇaṉkatai*, a folk expansion of Rāma myths, the demon Mayilirāvaṇaṉ[99] steals Rāma and Lakṣmaṇa and brings them in a box to Pātālalaṅkā to offer them to Bhadrakālī; Hanūmat steals them back from out of the goddess's shrine; and when Mayilirāvaṇaṉ discovers that his intended victims have vanished, his immediate concern is to see if the goddess has gone with them. The image of the goddess in the shrine gives him a dejected, sour look (*pattirakāḷi akam nāṇi mukam koṇi vicaṉam aṭaintu*), and he knows that she has departed with Hanūmat.[100] Here, too, we have a serpent sacrifice: the Rākṣasas prepare a nine-cornered sacrificial pit and sprinkle it with the blood from the leg of a buffalo, poured in a skull; Mayilirāvaṇaṉ cuts up a serpent, dips the pieces in ghee, and offers them as oblations; from the fire that blazes up a huge Bhūta is born and sent to kill Hanūmat; Hanūmat fights with him, drags him back down to Pātāla, and destroys the sacrifice.[101] The Rākṣasa sacrifice is no doubt meant as a parody of the system, but the serpent-victim links the rite with the Arāvāṉ myth; in both, the serpent is simply slain at the sacrifice, as in the *Ādiparvan* of the *MBh*, yet the serpent still epitomizes the sacrificial ideal—it is not by chance that Duryodhana chooses the snake-man Irāvat as the most suitable victim, and Arāvāṉ lives as a folk-hero in Tamiḻnāṭu today because he embodies the ideal of self-sacrifice.[102]

One oral variant of the myth offers a different explanation of the need for the sacrifice:

> Aravāṉ (*sic*), the son of Bhīmasena and a serpent-princess, was very strong, indeed so strong that he could have slain all the Duryodhanas at once. This would have prevented the Bhārata war from taking place! And since the war was necessary, Kṛṣṇa decreed that a human sacrifice was needed before the fighting started, and picked Aravāṉ as the sacrificial victim. When they commenced the sacrifice, Aravāṉ asked that his head remain alive to witness the entire Bhārata war; this wish was granted. Hence he is still worshiped in the form of a head during the annual recitation of Villiputtūrar's *Pāratam* in the village shrine.[103]

Arāvāṉ's serpent origin is here derived from the story of Duryodhana's attempt to poison Bhīmasena, the strongest of the Pāṇḍava brothers, who was rescued by the Nāgas from Duryodhana's plot.[104] Arāvāṉ is sacrificed by Kṛṣṇa so that the greater sacrifice of the war can take place; like the *devāsura* struggle, the war between Pāṇḍavas and Kauravas is clearly recognized as necessary by the folk source. One wonders if this oral version retains an ancient strand of myth: the violence of the struggle is necessary not to restore the Pāṇḍavas to their kingdom—for could not Arāvāṉ have destroyed their enemies single-handed?—but for some deeper purpose to be fulfilled. Perhaps the Epic notion of the war as sacrifice, from which the king and heir is born, has left a trace on the village tradition. Arāvāṉ himself dies only in part; his head (the head of the sacrifice, the remainder, the seed) survives as a witness, like the head of the serpent Rāhu (cut off by Viṣṇu after the churning of the ocean), the elephant's head of Gaṇeśa, and the horse-head of Dadhyañc.[105]

There is yet another myth of a serpent-sacrifice at Maturai/Ālavāy:

> The Jains wished to kill the devout Śaiva king of Maturai. They held a sacrifice, and the demon that emerged from the fire advanced in the form of a serpent against the city. The king slew the serpent with an arrow with a tip shaped like the crescent moon, but in dying the serpent vomited forth poison that entered the city in a flood, like the flood of poison produced at the churning of the ocean. Śiva sprinkled a few drops of *amṛta* from the moon on his crest; the *amṛta* mixed with the poison as buttermilk is mingled with milk, and the city was rendered pure. (Hence it is known as Maturai, from *madhurā*, "sweet".)[106]

The serpent is born from a sacrifice; its death produces first poison and then, by a transformation effected by the god, the opposite, *amṛta*. The myth itself refers to the churning of the ocean, and may be seen as a partial multiform of that myth, in which Śiva drinks poison as if it were *amṛta* or transforms poison to *amṛta*.[107] The poison colors his throat and makes him Nīlakaṇṭha (or Śitikaṇṭha, Śrīkaṇṭha).[108] Such, in any case, is the usual explanation; but we also hear that Rudra is Śitikaṇṭha because Nārāyaṇa seized him by the throat at Dakṣa's sacrifice,[109] or that he is Nīlakaṇṭha because

(Kāvya) Uśanas tore a matted lock of hair from his head and threw it at the god (or into the fire)[110]—and from it serpents originated which bit the throat of the god.[111] Kāvya Uśanas is Śukra, who is elsewhere known as the creator of Vāstoṣpati, the microcosmic exemplar of the sacrifice upon whose body the temple is erected.[112] The fragment of myth preserved here seems, in fact, to point to an original sacrificial basis for the Nīlakaṇṭha image. The dark neck of Śiva divides his head from his body; the sacrifice supposedly severs and restores the head of the victim; the secret that Dadhyañc knows and can only teach after his own head has been replaced by that of a horse is how the head of the sacrifice is put back on. Śiva's throat becomes dark from the bites of serpents, born from the sacrifice, symbolizing the sacrifice. But, as we have seen, the god is himself the serpent; he marries a serpent-maiden;[113] like the serpent, he dies and is reborn. Through self-sacrifice he wins life, conquering his own death; his head is restored and—marked only by the scar that forever recalls the shattering of the original unity and its subsequent reintegration, the dark neck that bears witness to the necessary sacrifice—he lives on, as the horse head of Dadhyañc survives forever in the waters of Śaryaṇāvat, and as the serpent head of Rāhu eternally chases the sun and the moon. Nīlakaṇṭha thus becomes a symbol of the god triumphing over his own destruction.

This triumph is, it must be stressed, the effect of the sacrifice. Here the analogy that has been suggested between Nīlakaṇṭha-Śiva and the peacock[114] offers a new perspective. The peacock is itself tied to the nether world: the dark-necked *śitikaṇṭha* feeds upon the dead;[115] the demon Cūr is divided at his death into peacock and cock;[116] Rāma's enemy is Mayilirāvaṇaṉ, Peacock Rāvaṇa, who dwells in Pātāla under the earth.[117] Śikhaṇḍinī, the man-woman who causes Bhīṣma's death in the *MBh*, is associated by her name with this series.[118] Śiva himself becomes a peacock to dance for the goddess (as peahen) at Māyūram,[119] or to drink the poison produced by the churning of the ocean.[120] In the latter case, the poison remains in the throat of Śiva as the peacock, and thus the link between Nīlakaṇṭha and the peacock becomes explicit. But the peacock is the enemy of the serpent;[121] as peacock, Śiva destroys himself and the symbol of his sacrifice.

To summarize: The anthill myth of Tiruvārūr seems to describe the sacrifice and rebirth of Śiva, whose appearance in the anthill is connected to the birth of seed through violence. The anthill is the locus of the *vāstu*, the remnant of the sacrifice that produces new life. As Valmīkanātha, Śiva submits to death in order to gain more life, while as Hāṭakeśvara he is castrated in order to become fertile again. The *liṅga* in the anthill may also be a transformation of the serpent, who embodies the symbolism of the sacrifice as rebirth from death. The serpent dwelling in the anthill is the fiery seed of creation. Yet this level of symbolism is blurred in our myths. The serpent is devoured by the god as peacock; Ālavāy loses his ophidian attributes in the purāṇic myths of Maturai, although the folk tradition recalls his original nature; most significantly of all, Viṣṇu replaces Śiva as the divine victim at Tiruvārūr. This pattern raises what we may call the problem of the surrogate, which will concern us in the following pages.

## 4. The Surrogate: Enemies and Devotees

If, as I have suggested, the Tamil purāṇic myths reveal a consistent effort to remove the deity from the arena of sacrifice without relinquishing the fundamental symbolism of the sacrifice, the need to search for a surrogate victim becomes clear. The power rooted in violence and symbolized by the blood of the offering is by nature polluting; yet the Tamil purāṇas describe their god as *nirmala*, without taint. We may regard this idealized image of God as resulting from the attempt to dissociate oneself, and one's deity, from the contamination of power;[1] and we have seen here a coalescence with the Upaniṣadic ideals of purity and freedom from the chain of death and rebirth. Yet for the great majority of Tamil pilgrims, freedom and release are remote goals of little immediate interest or relevance; what the worshiper seeks is more life and a solution to pressing mundane concerns. And since vitality depends ultimately on a substratum of chaos that is expressed and to some extent manipulated in the ritual of sacrifice, the god's role in this scheme must devolve upon some other figure. The surrogate defuses—significantly, but never completely, as we shall see—the tension between the ideal of purity (*nirmalatva*) and the necessity of the sacrifice. The god is relieved of the burden of death and rebirth. Still, as in the case of Viṣṇu at Tiruvārūr, the relationship of the substitute victim and the original victim, the local deity, is never wholly obscured; if we but scratch the surface of the tradition, the identity of the god and the sacrifice becomes apparent. Moreover, I will attempt to show in the following chapters that the very figure of the surrogate often retains the basic ambivalence that we have discovered in the god.

Probably the most striking instance of the role given to the surrogate appears in the context of the myths of Śiva's marriage. Before turning to those myths, however, we may briefly note three types of substitution, which occur without reference to marriage, in myths such as those discussed in the preceding sections. In these myths the god is replaced as the object of violence by 1) his bull, Nandin; 2) his devotee; or 3) an enemy, human or demonic. In the first case the substitution is quite straightforward, like that of Viṣṇu in the anthill myth from Tiruvārūr: a divine being other than Śiva suffers in place of the god, who functions on a higher plane—either as the transcendent source of violence done to others, or as a being entirely absent from the scene of the sacrifice. The other two types are the two major facets of the evolution we are pursuing.

We begin with Nandin, Śiva's theriomorphic vehicle. The motif of the wounded bull was discussed earlier in connection with the soothing properties of milk: Basavanna, the bull-deity of the Badagas, both inflicts and suffers violence while animate; he must therefore be literally petrified by a libation of milk.[2] An analogous case is found at Tirupuvaṉam, where the bull Nandin is continually soaked in water. The wounded bull turns up in a considerable number of shrines: at Tañcāvūr the huge image of Nandin kept expanding until a nail was driven into his back.[3] The same motif of dangerous growth is applied to the Bṛhadīśvara-*liṅga* at Tañcāvūr; here the correspondence of the deity, Śiva, and his bull-vehicle is complete. At Tirupperūr Śiva himself is said to have wounded the bull:

> Śiva and Umā took the forms of a Paḷḷaṉ and Paḷḷi (members of a low peasant caste) and, accompanied by the gods in similar form, were working in the fields of Tirupperūr. When the poet Cuntaramūrtti arrived there, he went into the temple and found the god missing. He asked Nandin where Śiva had gone; the bull, who had been forbidden to reveal the secret, indicated the direction with his eyes. Cuntaramūrtti went and found the lord in the fields, and together they bathed in the river. When the lord came back to the shrine, he cut the bull with his spade. Nandin trembled and asked for forgiveness, and Śiva told him to dig a *tīrtha* with his horns and set up a *liṅga*.[4]

The god goes into hiding from his devotee: this universal theme may be seen as the reversal of the idea of god's pursuit of the soul, which the Tamil Śaiva tradition dramatizes in the myth of Murukaṉ's wooing of Vaḷḷi.[5] Still, Śiva disguised as the Paḷḷaṉ seems to welcome his discovery by Cuntarar; he bathes with him in the river and then returns to his shrine. The true devotee must penetrate the masks of his lord, including his incarnation in lowly or despised forms. To such persistence the god, unveiled, responds—yet Nandin, who has connived at the revelation, must still be punished. Note the symbolic importance of eyes: Nandin's glance points the way to the god, thus enabling the saint to *see* his beloved. Motifs of blindness and vision are particularly prominent in the myths of Cuntaramūrtti: Śiva blinds him for deserting his second wife Caṅkiliyār, incurs the reproaches of his sightless devotee for inflicting this punishment, and ultimately restores his vision upon his return to the home of his first wife in Tiruvārūr.[6]

We find another wounded Nandin at Tiruvĕṇkāṭu:

> Marutvāsura was born when Śukra churned the body of Jalandhara. He performed *tapas* and won from Brahmā the boon of ruling the universe. Marutva conquered the gods, who were driven from heaven to earth, where they grew weak and emaciated from a lack of sacrifices. Śiva granted them refuge at Śvetāraṇya (Tiruvĕṇkāṭu), and there Marutva sought them out to kill them. Nandin defeated Marutva in battle, and the demon then worshiped Śiva and won from him his spear. He rushed back to Śvetāraṇya and cast the spear at Nandin, wounding him in his horns, ears, tail, and hooves. With Nandin thus unable to fight, the demon molested the sages engaged in worshiping Śiva. From Śiva's eye Aghoramūrti took form; when Marutva saw Aghoramūrti, he collapsed and died. From his body a great light emerged and joined with the form of Aghoramūrti.[7]

This summary is taken from the *Śvetāraṇyamāhātmya*, one of the oldest Sanskrit *māhātmyas* attached to a Tamil shrine. In the Tamil version of this myth, Nandin passively accepts the wounds inflicted on him, since he knows the spear was given to the demon by Śiva. Here Nandin is the archetypal devotee who offers his body, and in effect his life, to the god or to the instruments of his will. But Marutvāsura is also a devotee of Śiva; by attacking the gods and sages who worship Śiva, he forces the god to kill him, but in his death he attains union with the object of his devotion. The enemy who merges into the deity is a well-known motif (compare, for example, the case of Śiśupāla);[8] its appearance here may be partially explained by Marutva's prehistory as a village god in this area.[9] Nevertheless, the demonic devotee belongs to a much wider pattern of crucial importance to an understanding of the Tamil tradition. The *bhakta* incorporates elements of the god's identity; but, unlike the god of the Tamil purāṇas, the demon—even a devoted demon—can be slain without serious cost. How this becomes possible will be discussed below; one rationalizing argument is cited by the Tamil version of our myth, which stresses that Marutva became arrogant after incapacitating Nandin. Arrogance, indeed any kind of egoism (*ahaṅkāra*), inevitably calls down punishment in the Tamil myths. In any case, both Marutva and Nandin may be seen as surrogates for Śiva at Tiruvĕṇkāṭu. Nandin, as always, survives the act of violence, although his image at this shrine still shows the wounds he received from Marutva.[10] Marutva is killed and his life force fuses with Aghoramūrti—the fearful emanation of Śiva enshrined at Tiruvĕṇkāṭu—but this sequence, too, becomes an acceptable model for the aspirations of Śiva's *human* devotees.

The myth from Tiruvĕṇkāṭu combines all our categories. We have the wounded Nandin, who is also a devotee; and Nandin confronts a demon-*bhakta* who is slain by the god. Other myths separate more clearly the enemy from the devotee, as in the following hagiography:

> A Brahmin boy guarded the cows of the Brahmins of Ceyñalūr; he used their milk to worship a *liṅga* on the bank of the river. When his father heard of this, he kicked over the pails of milk. The boy was maddened by this impiety and struck his father with his staff, which became the axe of Śiva and cut off the father's legs. Śiva appeared, revived the father, and took him with his son to heaven.[11]

This immensely popular story contains the standard conjunction of blood and milk, but here the blood comes not from the god but from his clear-cut enemy. Inevitably, this myth has been read as an expression of the Oedipal conflict. Note, however, that the aggression against the father is not allowed to stand alone; just as Śiva intervenes to nullify the sacrifice of Manunītikaṇṭacoḻaṉ's son, here he reverses the effect of the violence carried out by his devotee.[12]

*Bhakti* acquires the force of an absolute value, which may override traditional loyalties and cancel out other norms; yet the violent sacrifices that *bhakti* elicits in the Śaiva hagiographies are usually restored or translated to another plane of meaning in the end.

A final example, also drawn from the hagiographies, makes the substitution of the devotee for his god most explicit:

> Nākaṉ, a king of the Pŏttappināṭu, worshiped Murukaṉ together with his wife Tattai, and the god granted them a son, whom they named Tiṇṇaṉ. Like his father, Tiṇṇaṉ became a hunter, and, after sacrificing to the gods of the forest (*vaṉa-tĕyvaṅkaḷ*), hunted in the hills with his followers. One day after chasing a wild boar, Tiṇṇaṉ came upon a *liṅga* on the hill of Kāḷatti. The moment he saw the *liṅga* he was filled with love for the god. He embraced the *liṅga* and kissed it; then he hunted animals, cooked and chewed the meat, and, after spitting out whatever was without flavor, offered the rest to the god in a container of leaves. Tiṇṇaṉ remained at Kāḷatti to provide food and drink for the god and to protect him from the wild animals of the forest, while his men, believing him to be possessed by the forest deity, returned home in despair.
>
> A Brahmin named Civakocaṉ used to serve the *liṅga* in the forest according to proper rite. He was horrified when one day he found it polluted with meat and blood; he purified it and consecrated it anew, but each day he returned to find it once more rendered impure. For five days the Brahmin and the hunter worshiped the god by turns, each in his own manner, until the priest could bear it no more and cried to Śiva. Śiva appeared to him in a dream and said, "After the meat chewed and offered by Tiṇṇaṉ, the *amṛta* of the gods drunk in golden cups is like poison together with the bitter fruit of the neem." To prove the hunter's devotion, Śiva devised a test. While the Brahmin hid and watched, Tiṇṇaṉ arrived to find the image of the god bleeding from the right eye. To stop the flow of blood, the hunter tore out his own eye and placed it on the *liṅga*. But then the left eye of the god began to bleed. The hunter placed his foot on the bleeding eye so that he would be able to find the spot; then he began to scoop out his remaining eye as a gift to the god. Śiva stretched out his hand from the *liṅga* and stopped the devotee, who was ever after famous as Kaṇṇappar (from *kaṇ*, "eye").[13]

Both the god and his *bhakta* bleed, and blood is clearly included in the series of sacred fluids, with a rank seemingly higher than that of *amṛta*. The devotee seeks to suffer in place of his god. The story in its present form demonstrates a theme common to many devotional movements—the superiority of crude but sincere worship over more conventional, "orthodox" forms.[14] *Bhakti* makes acceptable even the anathema of offering food and water that has come into contact with saliva (*ĕccil*). Kaṇṇappar's offering is the reversal of the idea of *prasāda* as the gift of the deity:[15] the god grants the remainder of the offering, which in this context is sacred rather than impure, and which expresses a relationship of servant and lord between the worshiper (the recipient of *prasāda*) and the deity who grants it. In the Kaṇṇappar story, it is the simple devotee who offers impure food to the god, but the polluted is accepted and even preferred because it is offered in love.

The god's wound serves to elicit from Kaṇṇappar the sacrifice of an eye, which is made symbolically in the worship of Māriyammaṉ,[16] and which appears in many related myths. Recall the symbolism of eyes in the myth of the wounded Nandin at Tirupperūr cited above.[17] Thematically, the Kaṇṇappar story is related to the myth of Andhaka, born blind when Pārvatī hid the eyes of Śiva; Śiva purifies the blind Andhaka by burning him with his third eye, while Kaṇṇappar heals the blind god with the gift of his own vision.[18] As we shall see, the act of blinding the god is frequently the cause of Devī's exile from heaven in the Tamil myths. The god's blindness is the reversal—and sometimes the cause of the emergence—of his supernatural vision, which is symbolized in Śaiva mythology by Śiva's third eye. Vaiṣṇava myths also sometimes associate the god with eyes, as in the following instance, which probably depends on a pun on Kṛṣṇa's name in Tamil (Kaṇṇaṉ): Kṛṣṇa and Garuḍa were playing hide-and-seek; Kṛṣṇa hid himself in the eyes (*kaṇ*) of the bird, and to this day Garuḍa is searching for the god, crying "Kṛṣṇa! Kṛṣṇa!"[19]

The stories cited above may serve to outline the dynamics of substitution in the Tamil myths. Tamil Śaivism in particular is marked by themes of violence and passion, but the Tamil purāṇas assert the purity and unconditional freedom of the god. Śiva therefore gives up his place as victim to a surrogate—at times, a symbol close to him, such as his bull Nandin; very often, his devotee; most strikingly, his enemy. Both enemy and devotee are intimately related to the god. The demon Marutva merges into Śiva-Aghoramūrti; the rude devotee Kaṇṇappar offers his eyes to save the lord's. In one case, beatitude is attained through opposition, in the demon's war against the god or his servants. In the other, self-sacrifice is the dominant theme. In the remainder of this study, we will observe the convergence of these patterns in the figure of the demon-exemplar who takes the place of Śiva as husband and victim of the goddess.

CHAPTER IV

# The Divine Marriage

More than the man wants to marry a woman, the woman wants to wed.[1]

## 1. Introduction

The central structural element of the Tamil *talapurāṇam* is, in a majority of instances, the myth of Devī's marriage to the god. The marriage of the god and the goddess is one of the year's major rituals in the temples;[2] the myth provides the background to this celebration by explaining how the main gods worshiped in the shrine came to be present there. In a sense, the marriage myth is thus a kind of origin myth, and we shall see that the myths of marriage are linked in many ways to the complex of symbols and motifs analyzed earlier with reference to the myths of origin. But the marriage myths are also more than origin myths, for they describe in addition to the revelation of the god and goddess the essential nature of their relations to one another, to their worshipers, and to the sacred site. In these myths the most basic concepts of the cult are made clear. Here, too, myth may be closest to the society which produced it: the divine marriage is regarded as a paradigm for human marriage; the necessity for Śiva's marriage is, in fact, explained in terms of the need for the god to serve as a model for man. Underlying social attitudes and assumptions are expressed, often in extreme form, in the myths.

It is, in particular, the goddess who draws our attention in this corpus of myths. The Tamil shrine is often conceived of as the home of the goddess: thus Mīnākṣī is born in Maturai and rules there, while her husband Sundareśvara-Śiva has to be imported from the north. Even myths that assert that a sacred spot was marked from time immemorial by a *svayambhūliṅga* or other sign insist that Devī arrives there *before* Śiva can be induced to come for the wedding. In these myths Devī goes to worship at the shrine to expiate some fault, and her worship causes Śiva to appear and to agree to a second, terrestrial wedding (after their earlier wedding in heaven). This explanation would appear to be a late rationalization of the myth. Nevertheless, the sequence it describes is probably accurate. The god joins the goddess for the wedding at the shrine.

We saw earlier that the goddess is sometimes said to locate the god physically in the shrine: a major instance is that of Kāmākṣī, who holds the sand-*liṅga* in place at Kāñcipuram. The goddess thus provides the very foundation of worship, and in this way she is associated with the concept of *pratiṣṭhā*, the firm support upon which life rests, surrounded by disorder and chaos.[3] Life is rooted in the goddess as a repository of power and a focus of stability. Moreover, the goddess is earthbound, identified with the soil from which she creates the divine image. Her intimate connection with the soil is perhaps demonstrated by the frequent alliteration of place names with names of the local goddess: thus we have Mīnākṣī at Maturai, Kāmākṣī at Kāñcipuram, Nīlāyatākṣī at Nākapaṭṭiṉam, Akhilāṇḍeśvarī at (Tiruv-) Āṉaikkā, Apītakucā at (Tiruv-) Aṇṇāmalai, and so on.[4] Often the main shrine of a town will be called simply by the name of the goddess, although it houses her consort as well: the great shrine of Maturai is the "Mīnākṣī" Temple. The god may be drawn to the site by the goddess and be rooted there by marriage to her. In the same way, man, the devotee, seeks a secure foundation to his existence by imitating ritually the god's role in this marriage.

In her identification with the soil, the Tamil goddess is linked to concepts of both fertility and death. The dark soil is, in a manner attested from early times in Tamiḻnāṭu, as in many agricultural societies, the locus of the sacrifice of life. Death and decay, and indeed the violence that must accompany ploughing and reaping, are the substratum out of which new life is grown: recall the important analogy of war and the harvest in Caṅkam poetry.[5] The dark goddesses of India—Kālī, Draupadī / Kṛṣṇā, and others—are all forms of the dark chthonic goddess;[6] and although light and dark female images are found already in the Vedic literature,[7] the hypertrophy of goddess myths in medieval south India clearly reflects the deep-rooted contact with the soil of a settled agricultural society. The earth as an incarnate goddess, Bhūmi or Bhūdevī, is in classical purāṇic mythology linked specifically with Viṣṇu;[8] but the local goddesses of south India may claim with equal justice to represent the earth in its character of the universal womb from which life issues, and to which life returns, in violence. To unite with the goddess is thus to merge for a moment with the dark and life-giving soil.[9]

Yet this is but one aspect of the Tamil goddess. Devī epitomizes, in the variety of her local incarnations, the characteristics ascribed to woman. From earliest times the Tamils have seen in woman a concentration of dangerous power. As Hart observes:

> "From the moment she reaches puberty, a woman is thought to be filled with a force which, if controlled, can produce auspicious results, but which if not controlled is extremely dangerous. It is especially menacing when a woman is menstruous, when she has just given birth, and when she is a widow. During those periods, a woman must observe strong ascetic practices."[10]

The woman's violent power—sometimes called *aṇaṅku*, and often thought to be concentrated in her breasts[11]—is erotic in character; sexual desire (*kāma*) belongs, together with other dynamic elements (music, the dance, evil in its diversity of forms), in the creative realm of chaos and death.[12] Hence, like other manifestations of power,[13] the woman must be circumscribed and controlled. The major form of control is chastity (*kaṟpu*), one of the central values of south Indian culture. The chaste woman safeguards the life and prosperity of the male relatives to whom she is attached, and chastity itself comes to be thought of as imbued with a divine power.[14] It is important to realize that the power residing in the woman is considered vital to the safety of the men surrounding her, for this helps explain the attempt to preserve this power in its strongest, most pristine state—that is, in the woman's virginity. As we shall see, the myths express a strong preference for the virgin goddess, who, as the epitome of violent power, must be contained by the strongest bonds; this idea gives us the popular image of the goddess locked in a box. Young women in Tamiḻnāṭu are not, however, locked forever in boxes in order to preserve their virginity; they are given in marriage (often to their cross-cousins),[15] and the state of marriage becomes in itself a form of control and limitation. The chastity of a married woman expresses itself in total devotion to her husband, whose life is felt literally to depend upon the sacred power vested in his wife.

The view of marriage offered by the Tamil myths is, however, more complex than this. Myth takes our assumptions to their logical conclusion. Thus the image of the woman as a source of violent and menacing power is given full expression in the myths, while at the same time the insistence on virginity is in no way compromised—even in the context of Śiva's marriage. The virgin goddess is a focus of violent eroticism; she is, indeed, at her most powerful as long as her virginity is intact, so that in marrying her the god exposes himself to an intense, even lethal danger. Moreover, it is essential, for the good of her devotees, that the goddess remain powerful—or, in other words, that she remain a virgin. Faced with this demand, wedded to an incarnation of violent power, the god inevitably succumbs and dies in her embrace. The lustful virgin is a voracious killer. Such, in any case, is the predominant resolution at one level of the Tamil myths. But we also have myths that correspond more closely to the human ideal of marriage: here the ideas of subjugation and control are dominant. The power of the wife is channeled and limited by her divine husband. To accommodate both these images, the goddess is sometimes literally split in two, into dark and golden halves, or into male and female halves that are united in the androgyne.

This bifurcation in the goddess myths corresponds, it may be noted, to the two levels we have isolated in the myths of sacrifice. On one level, the god undergoes the sacrifice himself; on the other, the violence does not affect him, and a surrogate may be brought in to take his place. Given the lethal nature of the encounter with the virgin goddess, it is not surprising that a surrogate is sought for these myths, as well. And, just as the sacrificial symbolism is shattered against the uncompromising ideals of purity and detachment—just as the shrine, the site of the sacrifice, becomes an idealized refuge from the world of power and violence—so the marriage of Śiva comes to be idealized as nonviolent and even nonsexual.[16] Śiva simply marries the golden, submissive goddess, and takes up residence in her shrine. Nevertheless, it would seem that the poets' basic attitude was that Śiva's marriage—and marriage generally—is opposed to the ideal of release.[17] Marriage is the central element in the wholly terrestrial ideal of fertility and rebirth; and fertility, as we have seen, is inextricably tied up with power and pollution. It is this goal of vitality in the real world that the worshiper pursues, and, because life proceeds from dark and dangerous sources, it is the figure of the dark goddess who provides the basic focus of the marriage myths. Even when Śiva is safely married to the golden Gaurī, the violent Durgā or Kālī lurks in the corners of the myth, just as the dark virgin is usually given her own, separate shrine inside the temple complex. More often, in fact, the dangerous virgin has the central role in the myths of marriage.

The comparison with the myths of sacrifice is not, of course, fortuitous. The underlying reality of the marriage myths is one of violence and, indeed, of sacrifice; the ideology of sacrifice imparts meaning to the divine marriage. In view of the conception of the goddess as a locus of power homologized to the dark womb of the earth, the assimilation of marriage to the sacrifice is quite natural. Stated schematically, the myth describes the god's death at the hands of his wife and his subsequent rebirth from her womb. If our texts do not state this sequence explicitly, the reason lies in the existence of the two levels mentioned above. Nevertheless, the basic thrust of the myth is clear from a variety of recurrent images. The comparison of marriage to sacrifice is found in classical Sanskrit sources; the *BĀU* includes sexual union in a series of sacrificial metaphors:

> "Woman, verily, is a sacrificial fire, O Gautama. The sexual organ, in truth, is its fuel; the hairs, the smoke; the vulva, the flame; when one inserts, the coals; the feelings of pleasure, the sparks. In this oblation the gods offer semen. From this oblation a person (*puruṣa*) arises."[18]

The same metaphor is implied when, in the context of the Śunaḥśepa story, we are told: "The husband enters as an embryo his wife, [who becomes] his mother."[19] The husband is identified with the seed that he gives to his wife; the womb of the wife is then analogous to the sacrifice out of which the sacrificer is reborn. The Tamil myths work this concept out in all its richness, and, as we might expect from the discussion in the previous chapter, they concentrate in particular on the violence attendant on the sacrifice. The god seeks and attains a death-in-love in order to gain greater power in another birth.

The stages of this pattern and its associated motifs will be explored in the following pages. One recurrent element may be mentioned now. The local marriage is usually described as a "remarriage": Śiva and Devī repeat in the shrine an event already celebrated on Kailāsa. To explain the need for this second celebration, the myths often resort to the story of Agastya's exile to the south; forced to miss the ceremony on Kailāsa, the dwarf-sage demands a repeat performance closer to his new home.[20] Let us look at one characteristic example of this motif:

> All the gods and sages came to witness the wedding of Śiva and Umā on Kailāsa; hence the world became unbalanced, the

> northeast being weighted down with all the guests, and the south rising up. Śiva singled out Agastya, the first of the seven sages, who were ready to perform the ceremonies. "Go south," he said. Agastya could not understand: "Am I, who am no bigger than a thumb, to balance the world? Lord, you can accomplish anything simply by thinking in your heart. Why must I miss the wedding?"
>
> Śiva said, "You do not grasp your own greatness. You can balance the entire world when I, Umā, and all the rest are on the other side. You, the best disciple of Kumarakkaṭavuḷ (= Skanda / Murukaṉ)—who granted *me* instruction and is the best of devotees[21]—will be granted a special sight of the wedding, alone." So Agastya headed south, going backwards so as not to show his back to Śiva. He worshiped at all Śiva's shrines along the way until he reached the Tamaratta Forest. There he felt peace such as he had never known before. He wished to set up a *liṅga*, in the hope of achieving the vision of the wedding at that spot. A voice spoke to him: "Reveal us who dwell beneath the Tamaratta tree and worship us with its flowers; if you then go south, we will grant you your vision."
>
> Agastya immediately dug up a *liṅga* at the base of a great tree; he found water with which to purify the site. Śiva appeared from out of the *liṅga* and promised that the place would be called by the name of the sage, and that those who worshiped there would achieve their desires. Agastya still could not bear to leave; at last, at Akattiyaṉpaḷḷi a little to the south, he was granted a sight of Pārvatī in her wedding apparel.[22]

Agastya's exile from Kailāsa leads to the discovery of the *liṅga* beneath the Tamaratta tree and its consecration as a pilgrimage site. The Tamaratta (or Tamarattai, *Averrhoea carambola*)[23] has "blood red" flowers,[24] which the sage uses in worship; here the symbol of redness/blood/vitality is paired not with milk, but with purifying water. The discovery of the *liṅga* is followed by the vision that the sage seeks in compensation for his exile. It is perhaps significant that it is the goddess whom Agastya ultimately sees in her wedding costume; although the sage is promised a glimpse of the original ceremony on Kailāsa, what he sees is the local marriage, in which the goddess is at the center. Śiva's marriage to a local goddess has a multiform in Agastya's own marriage to the Kāviri,[25] and one Tamil purāṇa has Śiva send Agastya south with the explanation, "He [Agastya] is like us, and [his wife] Lopāmudrā is like Pārvatī."[26] Agastya thus enacts the second marriage himself. The myth from Paḻayaṅkuṭi makes the most of the irony of the dwarf who alone can balance all the other gods and sages. But there is another aspect to Agastya's appearance in this context: the sage who combines in his person the learning of Tamil and Sanskrit, and whose migration from the north is seen as the starting point of Tamil culture, is a fitting witness to the rite that unites the chthonic goddess to the god whom she attracts or creates, thus crystallizing the identities of the divine couple, and establishing the basis for their worship by men.

## 2. The Reluctant Bride

In classical Śaiva mythology, the goddess Pārvatī uses *tapas* as a means to win Śiva for her husband. The gods send Kāma to wound Śiva with arrows of passion, but the desire engendered by Kāma must find its proper object: the lord of yogis must be won by a woman whose powers of *tapas* match his own. Essentially, however, Pārvatī's *tapas* is but a method of seduction, and she remains in the myths closer to the *apsaras* than to the ascetic.[1] Her seductive *tapas* is celebrated during the Navarātri festival.[2] Many of the Tamil marriage myths adhere to this pattern, merely requiring the goddess to perform her *tapas* in a particular shrine instead of the Himālaya, her usual spot. And while the goddess is frequently sent to earth to perform *tapas* in order to expiate some fault, with the promise of marriage (or remarriage) no more than an additional incentive to exile, in some cases the erotic intent stands alone. At Tirupperūr, for example, where the marriage myth is doubled (to include Pārvatī and Śiva, Tĕyvayāṉai and Murukaṉ—the two versions obvious multiforms), the brides reach the shrine because of Nārada's advice: *tapas* there will produce results much more quickly than in the Himālaya.[3] The argument is utilitarian, and the marriages take place at Tirupperūr for reasons of convenience.

There are other myths, however, that suggest that a local goddess was reluctant to take the fatal step. One village goddess boldly announces, "I am a happy woman without a husband."[4] Occasionally the goddess succeeds in avoiding marriage altogether: Parāśakti performs *tapas* throughout the ages in Tiruvārūr so that all creatures may rejoice.[5] Sometimes the tension between erotic and antierotic goals splits the goddess in two: Śiva informs Devī, who is performing *tapas* at Tiruppātirippuliyūr, that a part (*kalai*) of her will remain there as Aruntavanāyaki, a maiden (*kaṉṉikai*) practicing austerities and granting boons; the rest of her will safeguard *dharma* as Pĕriyanāyaki / Umā (Śiva's wife).[6] Elsewhere the scheme of the *yugas* is used to postpone the wedding: Devī performs *tapas* as a virgin at Kaṉṉiyākumari until the end of the Kaliyuga when, during the cosmic flood, she is to be married to the lord of Ñāṉāraṇiyam (Cucīntiram).[7] It is clear in the latter case that the authors of the myth wished to avoid the terrestrial marriage altogether, for it can take place only at a time of universal destruction—a solution that also builds upon the association of eroticism and death. The whole point of Devī's appearance at the shrine of Kaṉṉiyākumari is that she is a virgin:

> Bāṇāsura performed *tapas*, and Brahmā granted his wish that he could not be killed except by a woman. He conquered the worlds and caused the gods distress. When he heard that the sage Mārkaṇḍeya was still sacrificing to the gods, he demanded a share, and Mārkaṇḍeya cursed him to be killed by a woman. Alarmed, Bāṇa sought the counsel of his guru, Śukra, who advised him, "Virgins are rare on the earth. Go and perform *tapas* again and ask that the boon be changed so that only a *virgin* can kill you." Bāṇa was puzzled: "Why do you say that virgins are rare?" To this Śukra replied, "Śiva and Śakti constitute the world; just as neither can exist without the other, so woman cannot exist without man. Virgins are only an abstraction. Do you know what a virgin is? A virgin is a woman who is always wondering what handsome man will come to give her bliss!"
>
> Bāṇa got his boon emended as Śukra had suggested. Śiva sent Pārvatī to deliver the gods from their troubles, and she took the form of a virgin and killed Bāṇa on the shore of the southern sea. There she dwells even now, awaiting the *pralaya*, when Śiva will appear and make her his bride.[8]

Śukra's cynicism is, as usual, short-sighted; if virginity is a sham, it is all the easier for the goddess to pretend to it, and she does so in other myths as well: in an Assamese version of the Manasā cycle, for example, Durgā magically restores her virginity in order to dupe her father after several days of love-making with Śiva in a garden.[9] Mādhavī, the daughter of Yayāti, has the useful gift of restoring her virginity after childbirth; she is thus able to wed four husbands in succession, appearing in each case as a virgin bride.[10] A myth from Kerala supports Sukra's suspicions: a girl who became a goddess was excommunicated by her caste for maintaining, while still a virgin, that sex was the highest pleasure.[11] The love of the virgin goddess for the god is described in another version of Devī's arrival in Kaṉṉiyākumari:

> Once Pārvatī (Tam. Imayamātu) took the form of a virgin named Puṣpahāsā (Tam. Puṭpakācai) and worshiped Śiva. The god appeared and asked what she desired, and she said, "I wish to be with you without cease." He said, "One day of Brahmā is made up of a thousand cycles of the four *yugas*; when ten Brahmās die, that constitutes one hour in the life of Viṣṇu; when twelve Viṣṇus die, that is a single instant (*nimiṭam*) in my life. When such an instant passes, I will take the name of Rudra and marry you. Until then you must perform *tapas* by the shore of the sea, and I will be a *brahmacārin* in the Pūraṇacapai (at Cucīntiram)."
>
> The goddess bowed and went at once to the spot mentioned by the god; hence the place is known as Kaṉṉikākettiram (the site of the maiden).[12]

Although the goddess goes to Kaṉṉiyākumari to achieve union with Śiva, once again the myth strives to delay this result, this time by establishing the relativity of time, a perspective sometimes used to put a presumptuous Indra in his place.[13] The goddess pining for Śiva is faced with a rather severe test of her emotion: now Śiva promises to marry her at the end not of one cosmic cycle but of millions, and until then he, too, is to remain chaste. Other shrines share the wish to keep the male deity chaste; Skanda is sometimes said to be an eternal *brahmacārin*, and as such he resides without his consorts in several shrines (Cuvāmimalai, Antaraṅkam, Mallikārjuna).[14]

In the myth just cited, Śiva volunteers to remain alone at Cucīntiram until the wedding, but he can hardly be said to suffer on this account—after all, in the dimension of time that Śiva describes as his own, the millions of earthly years that must pass will seem but a second. In other versions from Kaṉṉiyākumari, however, Śiva desires to marry the goddess without delay, and the gods conspire to prevent the wedding from taking place:

> The lord of Cucīntiram informed the gods that he wished to marry the virgin goddess Kaṉṉiyākumari. The gods were

> alarmed, for they wished the goddess to remain a virgin in order to retain her power to fight demons. Nārada requested Śiva to bring as presents on the day of the wedding coconuts without eyes, mangoes without seeds, betels without veins, and the like; somehow the god gathered all these gifts, and midnight was fixed as the auspicious time for the wedding.
>
> Śiva left Cucīntiram in a grand procession. Nārada took the form of a cock and announced the dawn prematurely, and the god, believing the auspicious hour had passed, turned back in disappointment. Kaṉṉiyākumari waited until dawn in her bridal clothes; when the sun rose and her lord had not come, she cursed the items assembled for the feast to turn into sea-shells and sand.[15]

In another version of this myth, the goddess loses patience and goes in search of her bridegroom, but she fails to find him before sunrise, and is therefore doomed to remain unwed.[16] The seductive virgin in her bridal clothes reigns, alone, today as the goddess of Kaṉṉiyākumari in her shrine at the edge of the sea. The test that Śiva must pass[17] consists of assembling a series of objects that seem to symbolize barrenness, and this symbolism is in line with the general reversal of the myth of Śiva's marriage to Pārvatī: there the gods induce Śiva to marry in order to create a son who will fight the demon Tāraka, while in the Tamil myth the gods seek to keep the goddess a virgin so that *she* can fight their enemies. It is precisely the goal to which Pārvatī aspires that is rejected by the Tamil myths. Yet Kaṉṉiyākumari no less than Pārvatī yearns for union with Śiva—hence her rage when the marriage is thwarted.[18] The myth acknowledges the seductive qualities of the virgin goddess, but seeks nevertheless to prevent the union from taking place. The *Kaṉṉiyākumarittalapurāṇam* completes the picture of frustration by extending the idea of the suitor's test to Bāṇāsura, who, like Mahiṣāsura and other demons,[19] lusts for the goddess who is soon to destroy him: the goddess asks him to bring her the flowers of the *atti* tree and the banyan, as well as other proverbially rare items.[20] Bāṇa creates by the power of *māyā* all that she asks for, but the goddess then makes the objects disappear by her own power. The demon-suitor, like the god, must be stopped from attaining his bride.

The point of this insistence on virginity is the power ascribed to the virgin. The gods oppose Devī's marriage because they need the powerful virgin to combat their demon-foes. The function of the virgin has been described by Dumézil as follows:

> "To be a virgin, to remain a virgin, is not simply to be chaste. Chastity is of the order of purity; virginity is something higher, of the order of plenitude. A woman who remains a virgin conserves in herself, unutilized but not destroyed, intact, and as if reinforced by her will, the creative power that is hers by nature."[21]

Here we may detect an intimation of paradox. Only the virgin has the power to create; but the act of sexual creation destroys the basis of that potential. As we shall see, some Tamil myths attempt to solve this problem by resorting to the concept of the virgin as mother. It is not, however, only the creative potential of the virgin that interests the authors of the Tamil myths—it is more a question of the virgin's power in general. Virginity is a kind of *tapas*, its loss equivalent to the squandering of accumulated energy. The virgin is invested with innate power (*aṇaṅku*) which, if properly controlled, can be used to great effect; thus in a number of Tamil folk stories a woman's brothers make efforts to keep her unmarried in order to benefit from her sacred power.[22] For the same reasons, the myths of Kaṉṉiyākumari elect to prevent the union of the goddess with her lord. This image of the goddess at Kaṉṉiyākumari must be very old; early sources attest the association of this site with the virgin goddess,[23] and there is no doubt a connection with the virgin as praised in the *Tai. Ār.*, the *MBh*, and the *Cilappatikāram*.[24]

The myths of Kaṉṉiyākumari explicitly sanctify the virgin, and rule out the possibility of her marriage on earth. In most Tamil shrines, however, the situation is much less clear-cut. Almost every shrine has a place for both the god and the goddess, who constitute a divine couple; their marriage is described in the local purāṇa; each night the image of the god is brought to the bedchamber (*paḷḷiyaṟai*) of the goddess. In these circumstances it clearly becomes difficult to insist on the virginity of Śiva's wife! The goddess of the shrine still embodies the ideal of *kaṟpu*, "chastity," but *kaṟpu* now seems to refer not to virginity but to a wife's devotion and faithfulness to her husband. Nevertheless, the myth does not give up its cherished notions so easily. In many cases the latter ideal (chastity as devotion to one's husband) has been modified in the temple myths in the direction of the former (chastity as virginity).[25] To illustrate this development—which I believe to be indicative of a general trend in the Tamil myths of marriage—I will discuss the myths of Cucīntiram, the nearest major shrine to Kaṉṉiyākumari, and the home of the virgin bride's chaste and disappointed bridegroom.

The major myth of the Cucīntiram tradition centers on the figure of Anasūyā, the wife of the sage Atri. Anasūyā appears in a number of Tamil purāṇas as an exemplar of the chaste wife;[26] in this role she recalls the conventional paragon of womanly devotion to a husband, Arundhatī (Vasiṣṭha's wife who, alone among the wives of the seven sages, is protected by her virtue from sexual implication in the birth of Skanda).[27] Arundhatī and Anasūyā are, in fact, closely associated in Sanskrit mythology.[28] Anasūyā is also closely linked to the Trimūrti (Brahmā, Viṣṇu, and Śiva); one widespread myth relates how Anasūyā gave birth to these three gods after winning a boon by the power of her chastity:

> A Brahmin was being carried by his devoted wife to a prostitute's house when he brushed against Māṇḍavya, an innocent man impaled on a stake. Māṇḍavya cursed him to die at sunrise. The Brahmin's wife then prevented the sun from rising, by the power of her chastity, and the gods were distressed. They appealed to Anasūyā, and she persuaded the lady to allow the sun to rise by promising to revive her husband. In gratitude the gods granted the wish of Anasūyā that Brahmā, Viṣṇu, and Śiva be born as her sons.
>
> Atri enjoyed Anasūyā mentally, and a wind impregnated her with Soma, the radiant form of Brahmā. Viṣṇu fathered in her Dattātreya, who, as Viṣṇu incarnate, sucked at her breast. A portion of Śiva was born from her as Durvāsas, whose irascible nature was the result of his resentment at being kept so long in a womb; he wandered the earth, devoted above all to his parents.[29]

Anasūyā is granted the privilege of giving birth to the divine children because she is famous for her chastity, in the sense of devotion to her husband; hence the gods have recourse to her to overcome a problem caused by another woman's similar devotion. The wife who, out of obedience to her husband, *carries* him to the house of a prostitute is a striking enough symbol of what is demanded of the ideal woman; the wife who is faithful to this ideal derives from her conduct a power great enough to stop the sun in its course. Anasūyā's power, which flows from the same source, enables her to revive the dead; elsewhere she is credited with causing the Ganges to flow after a drought, once again through the power of her chastity.[30] Note that in the myth just summarized Anasūyā conceives without being touched physically by her husband; Atri simply enjoys her mentally (*manasā bheje*), and this ethereal contact, together with the gods' readiness to be born from a woman, is enough to make Anasūyā pregnant. This element in the myth is a step in the direction of the virginal Anasūyā of the Tamil myths. Another Sanskrit purāṇa offers a much more dramatic instance of Anasūyā's avoidance of a sexual connection:

> One day Brahmā, Viṣṇu, and Śiva came to Atri, who was sunk in meditation, and offered him a boon. He made no reply, and the gods went to his wife Anasūyā. Śiva had his *liṅga* in his hand, Viṣṇu was full of desire, and Brahmā said to her, "Give me pleasure or I will die." Anasūyā was silent, and the gods, deluded by *māyā*, prepared to rape her. Then Anasūyā cursed them to become her sons, and she cursed Śiva to be worshiped as the *liṅga*, Brahmā to be worshiped in the form of a head, and Viṣṇu to be worshiped in the form of feet. The gods were stricken with terror and bowed to her, and she promised them contentment when they would become her sons. Brahmā was born as Candramas, Hari as Dattātreya, and Śiva as Durvāsas.[31]

Here Anasūyā narrowly escapes rape. Atri's presence is of little consequence—he is busy with his meditation; but the Trimūrti have explicit sexual designs on his wife. Anasūyā saves her chastity by transforming the gods into children. Sexual tension is often defused in the myths through this device of making one of the parties a child: thus Śiva takes the form of a baby when he is surprised by Vaiṣṇava parents-in-law in the house of a young bride,[32] and Lakṣmī, jealously pursuing her husband Viṣṇu after his marriage to a second wife, turns into an infant upon arriving at Viṣṇu's local home.[33] Note that Anasūyā's curse on the gods to be worshiped in various humiliating forms[34] preserves the spatial relationship of the *liṅgodbhava* myth, where Brahmā flies as a goose to the top of the fire-*liṅga*, and Viṣṇu as a boar digs down toward its base.[35] Another attempted rape of Anasūyā is described in a Tamil text: this time the perpetrators are not gods but demons who see her worshiping a *liṅga*; she burns them by the power of her chastity and her *tapas*, accumulated by worshiping Śiva.[36]

Let us turn now to the myth of Anasūyā at Cucīntiram, where once again we find her pitted against the Trimūrti:

> Atri left the Ñāṉāraṇiyam (Cucīntiram) for the world of Brahmā, who was conducting a sacrifice; he left his love and water from his feet (*pātacalam*) with his wife Anasūyā. Brahmā, Viṣṇu, and Śiva wished to test her chastity, so they sent down a drought, but she created water and sustained the sages as if she were Annapūrṇā, mother of all. The three gods then went there in the form of three emaciated old men, begging for food; she prepared food for them, but they demanded that she serve it to them while she was naked—otherwise they would refuse to eat and would die on the spot. Perceiving that this was a test (*coṭaṉai*), she said, "Let it be as you desire"; then she thought of her husband and wished that they might become infants (*ciṟār*), and when she sprinkled them with water, they did.
>
> She mixed ghee with milk and fed it to them, washed them, put ash on their foreheads, and sang lullabies to the three gods who are father and mother of all. Meanwhile, the three wives of the gods, learning from Nārada where their husbands had gone, became maidens (*kaṉṉiyar*) and came to the *āśrama* to beg Anasūyā to restore their lords. Anasūyā refused to help until her husband's return, so the goddesses (*tevimār*) went off to do *tapas* at the Ñāṉatīrttam.
>
> Nārada informed Atri that there were babies in his *āśrama*, and the sage hastened back to confront Anasūyā. She told him what had happened and, at his command, sprinkled the infants with water, whereupon they stood up with their old forms. They said, "There are no householders who can equal you, and there is no loosening the bond of your love. Choose a boon." Atri said he was satisfied with the vision granted him, but Anasūyā asked that her love for her husband might always grow, that the three gods be born as her children, and that the penance of the goddesses bear fruit. The gods agreed to be born to her as the moon (Nāṇmati = Candramas), Dattātreya, and Durvāsas, and to be present there always in a *liṅga* and an *aśvattha* tree.[37]

The sexual encounter between Anasūyā and the Trimūrti is masked in two ways in this myth: first, by explaining the entire situation as a trial (the gods wish to test the chastity of Anasūyā, just as Śiva is often said—particularly in later texts—to come to the Pine Forest in order to test the sages and their wives);[38] and the request for food served by the naked Anasūyā replaces the attempted rape of the *Bhaviṣyapurāṇa*.[39] Anasūyā again manages to remain pure by converting the gods into infants; while they are in this form, she is able to feed them without exposing her nakedness to their view.[40] Anasūyā's invulnerability is clearly meant to contrast with the erotic susceptibilities of the gods' own wives; the penance performed by the three goddesses at Cucīntiram is directed toward marriage. Eventually, after being restored to their true forms, the gods appear at sunrise in their wedding apparel (*maṇakkolam*) and marry the goddesses. Note that the three wives of the gods come to Cucīntiram as maidens (*kaṉṉiyar*),[41] and their penance is the prototype for the vow observed by young women at Cucīntiram today: the three goddesses exemplify the young virgin desirous of marriage. In another Tamil version of our myth, the virginal goddesses appear as the famous Seven Maidens (*kaṉṉimār*), but here the Maidens play a very different role from that of the three goddesses at Cucīntiram:

> Pārvatī wished to see a demonstration of the importance of chastity. Śiva, Viṣṇu, and Brahmā came down to earth as naked beggars. They danced upon the Kañcimalai, which cracked and started rolling toward the Toṇi River, where the seven Kaṉṉimār were bathing. The latter heaped up the saffron they had brought for their bathing, and their little mounds of saffron stopped the mountain. The Kaṉṉimār worshiped the gods.
>
> The three gods then went to the *āśrama* of Atri. Anasūyā, seeing them, was ashamed and asked them to wait outside until her husband's return from bathing. They said, "We are yogis who have awakened from *samādhi*, and we are famished," and they made gestures to show their hunger. Anasūyā was silent, and now they cried, "If we are not fed soon, we will die!" Still perplexed but unable to send a guest away hungry, Anasūyā prayed that if her chastity were true they become babies upon whom she could look without shame. So it happened, and she took them in her arms, caressed them, sang them lullabies, and fed them with the milk which spontaneously filled her breasts.
>
> Atri came home and was astonished at this sight. By concen-

> trating his mind he perceived the true identity of the infants, and he fell to the ground to beg forgiveness for his wife's action. He bathed the gods' feet with the water of the Toṇi and with his tears. The three consorts of the gods came to reclaim their husbands. They persuaded Anasūyā to pray that they resume their old forms; reluctantly she did this, and the gods left with their wives for home.[42]

Here the trial takes a different form—instead of demanding that Anasūyā reveal her nakedness, the gods compromise her by revealing theirs (just as Śiva dances naked and ithyphallic in the Pine Forest). Again, Anasūyā transforms the situation, trapping the gods in infants' bodies. This in itself is a bold and interesting resolution that raises the problem of the dynamics guiding the divine avatar; the gods are trapped on earth in human form, and can be freed only by the intervention of the chaste Anasūyā. The gods who come to earth in order to test their devotees end up chained in bodies, and utterly dependent on a human will. In any case, Anasūyā manages to preserve her chastity; moreover, she is clearly intended to remain chaste even *after* the trial. Unlike the myth of Śiva's temptation of Pārvatī, for example, the Tamil myths of Anasūyā preclude an erotic ending of any kind, on either the divine or the human level. In these myths, chastity is its own reward.

In marked contrast with the three *kaṉṉiyar* consorts of the Trimūrti at Cucīntiram, the Kaṉṉimār in the second myth (from Tirimūrttimalai) reinforce Anasūyā's character; while the three goddesses oppose their erotic penance to her chaste behavior, the Seven Maidens prefigure her restraining, antierotic role. The Maidens succeed in stopping the mountain impelled toward them by the ecstatic, uncontrolled dancing of the naked gods. In other words, the Seven Maidens counter the gods' wild sexuality with their own power, just as Anasūyā overcomes the improper sexual demands made by the gods. The entire episode of the Kaṉṉimār in this text seems intended to foreshadow the confrontation of Anasūyā and the Trimūrti; Anasūyā is implicitly compared to the Kaṉṉimār. The comparison is apt: although, like Anasūyā, the Seven Maidens are married,[43] they are also the embodiment of chastity and, at least in Tamil folk religion, symbolize virginity.[44] They are also mothers (*mātṛkās*)—again like Anasūyā, virgin mothers. For this seems to be the underlying basis of the Tamil Anasūyā cycle: Anasūyā is the mother of the Trimūrti, but she does not conceive them sexually; she transforms them miraculously, through the power of her chastity, into her babies; and, in the myth from Cucīntiram, she is promised that they will once again become her children to fulfil the wish that she has made. Nowhere in these texts is Atri said to be their father—except in the Sanskrit myths cited earlier, where he impregnates Anasūyā through mental effort. Anasūyā's feat of giving birth without the intervention of her husband is known already in the *MBh*, where Atri's wife (who is not named) leaves the sage in anger and takes refuge with Mahādeva, and the latter promises her a son (without her husband, *vinā bhartrā*, according to the Vulgate).[45] Atri thus becomes totally redundant, and the next step—taken by a popular south Indian version of the myth—is to ignore him altogether:

> "There was a certain virgin, named Anusooya, who was as much renowned for her inviolable chastity as for her devotion to the gods and for her tender compassion for the unfortunate. The divinities of the *Trimurti*, having heard of her, became so greatly enamoured that they resolved upon robbing her of her virginity, which she had till then treasured with so much care. To attain their object, the three seducers disguised themselves as religious mendicants, and under this guise went to ask alms of her. The virgin came to them, and with her wonted kindness showered gifts upon them. The sham beggars, after being loaded with her gifts, told her that they expected from her another favour, which was to strip herself naked before them and to satisfy their impure desires. Surprised and frightened by this shameful proposal, she repulsed them by pronouncing against them certain *mantrams*. These, together with some holy water which she poured upon them, had the effect of converting them into a calf. After they had been thus transformed, Anusooya took upon herself to bring up this calf by feeding it with her own milk. The *Trimurti* remained in this humiliating position till all the female deities combined together and, fearing lest some great misfortune might befall them in the absence of their three principal gods, after consulting one another, went in a body to Anusooya and begged her most humbly to give up the *Trimurti* and to restore them to their former state. It was with great difficulty that Anusooya was persuaded to yield to their prayers, and even then she imposed a condition that they should first of all be ravished (by whom

> the fable does not say). The female deities, convinced that they could not otherwise rescue the *Trimurti*, consented to undergo the penalty required of them, choosing rather to lose their honour than their gods. The conditions being fulfilled, Anusooya restored the *Trimurti* to their former state, and they returned to the place whence they came."[46]

Abbé Dubois, who records this myth, cites no source, but the story corresponds in its essentials to the purāṇic versions from Cucīntiram and Tirimūrttimalai. Like other oral variants of purāṇic myths, however, it makes explicit those elements that are veiled in the literary texts. Thus the designs of the Trimūrti are openly acknowledged; the lust of the goddesses is violently gratified (although here the goddesses are reluctant to be ravished, while in the purāṇas they long for union with their lords); most important of all, Anasūyā is explicitly said to be a virgin, and the myth says nothing of any husband. The attempt to rape the virgin fails, and the Trimūrti lose their independent power; here they become not infants but a calf, which Anasūyā nurses with milk from her breast.[47] Anasūyā appears here as the virgin mother without a husband. The idea of the chaste wife utterly devoted to her husband has given way to the image of the invulnerable virgin.[48]

The folk myth suggests an explanation of the Cucīntiram tradition. The Cucīntiram purāṇa lacks a conventional myth of Śiva's marriage to the goddess; instead, it begins with, and gives great prominence to, the story of Anasūyā. In this story Anasūyā demonstrates her inviolable chastity in a confrontation with the Trimūrti, and in contrast with their three consorts. Anasūyā's relationship with her husband, Atri, is relatively unimportant; and related myths suggest that she is, in fact, a virgin. Apparently, an earlier myth about the virgin goddess—like Kaṉṉiyākumari at her nearby shrine—has been transposed at Cucīntiram into the Anasūyā cycle. Anasūyā represents the virgin who is never deflowered. A final consideration lends support to this conclusion. The myth of Anasūyā and the Trimūrti may well be late at Cucīntiram. Although the god of Cucīntiram is known today as Tāṇumālaiyaṉ—that is, the Trimūrti, composed of Tāṇu (Sthāṇu = Śiva), Māl (Viṣṇu), and Aiyaṉ (Brahmā)—the earliest reference to the Trimūrti at this site seems to date from 1471;[49] earlier names of the god as found in inscriptions (*mahādeva*, *paramasvāmin*, *parameś-vara*, *civīntiraṉuṭaiya ĕmpĕrumāṉ*) make no suggestion of a triple nature. Modern popular tradition seems to have conserved the earlier position, for the god is still frequently referred to as Sthāṇunāthasvāmin or Sthāṇumūrti—a reference to the antierotic form of Śiva, and a fitting counterpart to the virgin goddess. Sthāṇunātha may have become Tāṇumālaiyaṉ through pressure from the Vaiṣṇava cult centered on the Tĕkkeṭam shrine inside the Cucīntiram temple; Viṣṇu has, together with Brahmā, merged with the god of the Śaiva sanctum (Vaṭakkeṭam), so that Sthāṇunātha turns into the Trimūrti. This process of combination is attested at other shrines, as well.[50] Śiva's absorption of Viṣṇu and Brahmā (the latter god being little more than an accomplice to this transformation) results in the need for a myth of the Trimūrti; and the Sanskrit tale of the Trimūrti's encounter with Anasūyā is therefore brought into the Cucīntiram tradition, and adapted to the local cult of the virgin goddess. Anasūyā, the chaste bride and mother of the gods, fits the requirements of the revised Cucīntiram tradition admirably. We have here an excellent example of how a Sanskrit myth can be used in a Tamil purāṇa to express—and at the same time to conceal in part—the underlying reality of the indigenous cult. Local ritual reveals a similar ambivalence while preserving, in essence, the original scheme. Thus Sthāṇunātha's marriage is celebrated each year at Cucīntiram, but the myth told in explanation of it has no relation to that of Anasūyā: a young girl who came to worship Sthāṇunātha together with her mother merged into the god.[51] As we shall see in a moment, this is an example of the hagiographic variant of the Reluctant Bride; the god remains chaste and antierotic. The bride, Aṟamvaḷarttammaṉ ("the lady who made *dharma* increase"), is considered to be an avatar of Kaṉṉiyākumari.

In short, the tradition of Cucīntiram suggests that the god (Sthāṇunātha) and the goddess (who has come to be represented by Anasūyā) never actually wed. Both nevertheless endure at this shrine in separate, chaste forms: the goddess in the major myth of the local purāṇa, and the god in the tradition of the bachelor (*brahmacārin*) waiting to marry the virgin Kaṉṉiyākumari. The two deities long for each other—the goddess performs *tapas* in her bridal costume in order to win her husband, and the male god of Cucīntiram attempts, as the Trimūrti, to rape Anasūyā (the virgin bride)—but the myths show that the divine union must be prevented at all costs.

So far we have seen two ideals of chastity at work, on the most literal level, in the myths of marriage: there is the virgin whose marriage is postponed in order to preserve her power, and there is the wife whose devotion to her husband is put to the test. The first ideal seems to lurk beneath the surface of the second in the myths from Cucīntiram. There are other examples of this tendency, which reflects the central importance of the virgin goddess in our myths. To cite but one more example: in popular versions of the *Cilappatikāram*, Kaṇṇaki's special powers derive from the fact that she was never touched by her husband.[52] This is what enables her to burn the city of Maturai. The *Cilappatikāram* itself, of course, knows nothing of this: Kovalaṉ and Kaṇṇaki, like Kāma and his wife, embrace like serpents intertwined.[53] In the epic, Kaṇṇaki exemplifies the chaste wife devoted to her husband; the folk versions, which identify her with the goddess, require her to remain a virgin.[54]

But there is a third kind of chastity encountered in Tamil Śaiva mythology, a kind that crops up frequently in local marriage myths—chastity as *bhakti*, as devotion to the god or to the principle of surrendering to him.[55] In these myths human eroticism is usually rejected in favor of union with the divine; the woman remains chaste with reference to her earthly, normative existence, while being ravished by the god. The woman here may represent the soul longing for God, and forced to seek him outside the bounds of convention and social life. Although, as I have stated earlier, Tamil devotional religion is oriented basically toward life in the world, the encounter with the deity is often expressed in metaphors of transgression and chaos. Just as in the ancient Tamil love poems the illicit, premarital love of the heroine for a stranger is seen as the supreme, most fulfilling state of love,[56] so the total love of man and god is enacted in a dimension of disorder, in which conventional limits are shattered or transcended.[57] The temple builds fences around a concentration of sacred power, which thus—through limitation—becomes accessible to man; but the *experience* of divine love contemns confinement and convention. Shame must be abandoned, worldly pride and possessiveness destroyed: the soul bares itself completely before the naked power of the divine. The moment of union is therefore one of danger and excess, and may require the loss of one's conditioned, socially defined identity. Many stories express this seemingly antinomian search for disorder; we need not regard them as prescriptive of normative behavior, but as idealized metaphors that give voice to the longing of man in society. The ideal is immediate surrender to God. Here again, as in the myths of Anasūyā at Cucīntiram, we find the motif of the guest (the deity) who comes to test his host (Man) with an outrageous demand:

> Iyaṟpakaiyār, a merchant of Pukār, was an enemy of the ways of the world and a devoted servant of Śiva. He gave without stint to the devotees of the god. One day Śiva took the form of a Brahmin whose body was covered with ash and came to the merchant's house. "What have I done to merit this visit?" asked the merchant, bowing at his feet. "I have come for nothing specific," said the guest. "Whatever is mine I will give you," said Iyaṟpakaiyār. "I have come for your wife," said the guest.
>
> The merchant was not at all shocked. He hastened to inform his wife that he was giving her to the stranger. Although she was distressed, she did not dissent. The Brahmin then asked that the merchant accompany them until they had passed the limits of the city; so, taking his sword and shield, Iyaṟpakaiyār followed them. Soon he was surrounded by a crowd of hostile relatives. "Whoever heard of giving one's wife freely to a lecher? The whole land will blame us. Our enemies will laugh at us," they cried. The Brahmin, seeing them armed and menacing, pretended to be alarmed, but the wife reassured him: "Fear not. My husband will conquer."
>
> Iyaṟpakaiyār became angry and attacked the crowd, killing them all. He then accompanied the stranger and his wife for some distance, until the stranger told him to go back. He thanked the Brahmin, bowed to him and left. When he had gone a short distance, he suddenly heard the stranger calling loudly for help. When he raced in his direction, he beheld Śiva and Umā on the bull in the sky. The god took Iyaṟpakaiyār and his wife and all the dead relatives to heaven.[58]

The stark nature of the stranger's demand becomes clear when we recall the ideal of chastity discussed at the start of this chapter. A wife's chastity is surety for her husband's survival; a husband who willingly makes a gift of his wife to a stranger undoubtedly merits the name Iyaṟpakaiyār ("the enemy of nature"). The story seems suited to an allegorical interpretation: the wife is the soul, reluctant to part from the ego; the limits of the city—the site of violence—may be the limits of the body;[59] the relatives who protest the gift and must be slain may represent the desires and conventional concerns of the conditioned, ego-ridden Self. Salvation is attained after the self-sacrifice is complete. I will return to this ideal of self-sacrifice in the final chapter. Here it is essential to observe that human eroticism—the love of a man and his wife—is superseded by Śiva's demand. The god takes for himself the wife of his devotee. Iyaṟpakaiyār passes this test without protest; he is a model of the *bhakta* who is totally committed to his god, and thus he contrasts markedly with the sages of the Pine Forest who attack Śiva for seducing their wives.[60] The sages of the Pine Forest must learn the lesson of self-abnegation and subservience to God. To teach them this ideal, Brahmā tells them a story that may be seen as a multiform of the Tamil hagiography:

> The householder Sudarśana vowed to conquer Death. He instructed his wife, "All guests are Śiva; you must always serve a guest, even by giving yourself to him." To test their devotion, Dharma took the form of a Brahmin and came to their house. The lady welcomed him, and the guest said, "I do not want food. Give yourself to me!" The lady hesitated, ashamed, but, remembering her husband's words, she complied with the request. Sudarśana came to the door and called for his wife. Dharma called to him, "I am making love to your wife." Replied Sudarśana, "Enjoy her as you please." Dharma, delighted, revealed himself and said, "I have not made love to this lady even in thought; I came here to test your devotion. By this act of *tapas*, you have conquered Death."
>
> Then Dharma went away. All guests should be worshiped in this way.[61]

Like the wife of Iyaṟpakaiyār, Sudarśana's wife hesitates, but then obeys her husband's strange command. All guests are a form of Śiva; in offering his wife to the god, the husband attains salvation (here, victory over death). Brahmā advises the sages to follow Sudarśana's example and treat all guests in this manner; perhaps the sages may take comfort in the assurance that the test is, in the end, illusory, and that Dharma never *really* touches the householder's wife.

The motif of the trial is basic to the two myths just cited; the god tests his devotee by demanding his wife. In the story of Kāraikkālammaiyār ("the lady of Kāraikkāl"), this motif is missing, and the husband gives up his wife not out of self-sacrifice but from terror:

One day the merchant Paramatattaṉ was given two mangoes as a gift. He handed them over to his wife Puṉitavatiyār, and she gave one of them to a devotee of Śiva who begged for food. She served the other to her husband during his meal, and he so liked the taste that he asked for the other. In desperation the wife appealed to Śiva, and another mango appeared in her hand. When she served this to her husband, he immediately detected the divine flavor and asked his wife where she had obtained the fruit. She told him the truth. "If that is how it happened, bring me yet another fruit," he said. She went away and prayed to the god, "If you do not give me another, my word will appear false," and immediately another mango appeared. She gave this to her husband, and as he took it, it vanished. In terror at this demonstration of sacred power, Paramatattaṉ fled across the seas to another land.

Eventually he returned to dwell in the Pāṇṭiya land. He took another wife and fathered a daughter, whom he named after his first wife. However, when relatives of his learned of his presence there, they brought Puṉitavatiyār to him in a litter. He fell at her feet and worshiped her. At this the relatives were shocked and ashamed. "Is it right for you to worship your own wife?" they cried. "She is not a woman but a goddess," answered the merchant. "As soon as I discovered this, I left her; now I have married a real woman and called my daughter by the name of my former wife, our family deity."

Hearing these words, Puṉitavatiyār prayed to Śiva, "Until now I have carried this bag of flesh for the sake of my husband. If this is how he feels, I no longer need it; give me the form of a demon (*pey vaṭivu*) who worships your feet." Śiva dried up her flesh, and she became a demoness roaming the forest of Ālaṅkāṭu.[62]

The mango, which at Kāñcipuram is associated with the wedding of Śiva and Pārvatī, here serves as the instrument for the transition from human to divine consort—for Puṉitavatiyār becomes a form of Devī and is worshiped as such by her former husband. The power of the woman—which is enough to frighten her husband into leaving her—apparently derives in this case from her simple faith and from her act of piety in giving the first mango to a beggar; as we have just seen, the beggar or guest is thought to be the god incarnate, but here the guest's demand is only the indirect cause of the separation of husband and wife. In the final apotheosis, the devoted wife sacrifices her body; the lady must die to the world in order to enter the hosts of Śiva's servants. As the demoness of Tiruvālaṅkāṭu, Kāraikkālammaiyār is a form of Nīli, the ancient goddess there whose marriage to Śiva forms the subject of an important myth.[63] Thus once again the god acquires a human bride at the expense of her original husband.

The above examples of our third category—chastity as *bhakti*—all describe the loss of a wife to the god, or the replacement of human sexuality by self-sacrifice aimed at union with the divine. Several stories reveal a more extreme tendency still, in which the opposition of human to divine love is complete. Just as the ideal of the chaste wife may conceal an underlying preference for virginity, so the motif of stealing the devotee's wife must be compared to the motif of the god's virginal, human bride. Thus we have the Vaiṣṇava saint Āṇṭāḷ, who chooses the god Viṣṇu over any earthly husband:

> Āṇṭāḷ, who was discovered by Pĕriyāḻvār while he was digging in his *tulasī* garden, used to wear the garlands intended for Viṣṇu; secretly she would put them on and observe her image in the water of a well, to see if she was a suitable bride for the god. One day her foster father discovered her doing this and chided her; he could not offer the defiled garland to the god that day. But the god appeared to him in a dream and informed him that henceforth he wanted only garlands that had first been worn by Āṇṭāḷ.
>
> When the girl reached puberty, Pĕriyāḻvār wished her to marry. She refused even to consider a human husband; instead, she asked her foster father to relate to her the deeds of Viṣṇu in his 108 sacred shrines. Listening to this recital, she fell in love with Raṅganātha (Viṣṇu at Śrīraṅkam) and determined to marry him. The god announced his consent in a dream, and Āṇṭāḷ was taken to Śrīraṅkam where, at the age of fourteen, she merged with the god.[64]

Note that Āṇṭāḷ, while rejecting human sexuality, uses a traditional erotic symbol—the garlanding of the chosen consort.[65] Āṇṭāḷ is worshiped in Śrīvaiṣṇava shrines as a bride (*nācciyār*) of the god.[66] This pattern of choosing the lord for one's lover is very common in the myths. We saw earlier how the young girl Aṟamvaḷarttammaṉ merged into the *liṅga* at Cucīntiram; this virgin bride is a form of Kaṉṉiyākumari.[67] A merchant's daughter who refuses human husbands weds Śiva-Koṅkaṇeśa at a shrine near Tañcāvūr.[68] The Vīraśaiva saint Mahādeviyakka sings songs of love to the lord Cĕnnamallikārjuna as she wanders naked through the world; here we have a reversal of the myth of Anasūyā, who hides her nakedness from the Trimūrti and thus saves her chastity.[69] Yet, like Anasūyā, Mahādeviyakka is chaste—divine love in these marriages is an antithesis to sexuality, even if it is couched in erotic terms. Śiva's virgin brides are, and remain, virgins. In one unusual variation on this theme, a king forces his reluctant, virginal bride upon an equally reluctant god:

When the Cōḻa king came to fight the Pāṇṭiyaṉ at Kāḷipuram, Bhadrakālī, at Śiva's command, reduced his fort of swords to dust; hence she is known as "the Lady who walked on swords" (*vāḷ mel naṭanta ammai*). The Pāṇṭiyaṉ imprisoned the Cōḻa king. After some time the Cōḻaṉ sent a messenger to his captor to say that he had come not to fight, but to behold the beauty of Kāḷipuram; moreover, he would happily bestow all his wealth and his daughter on the Pāṇṭiyaṉ. Varakuṇapāṇṭiyan freed him from prison and asked him to send for his daughter. When he saw her beauty, he agreed to wed her.

After the ceremony, in the bridal chamber, the king looked carefully at his bride and said, "You are as beautiful as Pārvatī; you seem to be no mortal woman but a goddess. Because of the natural fragrance of your hair, you are named Sugandhakeśī.[70] Therefore not I but Śiva is your husband: live happily with him." The bride said, "Surely you are jesting in order to test me. Is it right to speak like this to a bride? You are my husband, and I can think of no one else." Said the king, "Transfer the desire you feel for me to Śiva." "No," said the girl, "be he king of kings or god of gods, I will pay no attention to him. *You* are my lord."

The king then took his bride to the temple. The priests had already performed the night service and locked the five doors of the shrine. By his powers of devotion and truthful speech, the Pāṇṭiyaṉ made the doors open one by one and took Sugandhakeśī into the inner shrine. Pointing to the god, he said to her, "Behold your husband. Unite with him in bliss." She refused, saying, "*You* are my husband." At this the king grew

> angry and took his sword in his hand. The god appeared, smiling, and asked, "Why have you brought me this woman you have wed?" "I married her thinking of you," answered the king. "You took her hand in love; now take her home," said Śiva. "You must take her," demanded the king; "otherwise I will take my life." He laid his sword on his neck. Śiva quickly stretched forth his hands and embraced Sugandhakeśī, taking her into the *liṅga*. Her bracelets and anklets remained on the left side of the *liṅga*, and the natural fragrance of her hair still fills the nearby wood.[71]

Here the human bride, instead of forswearing human love, seeks it, and her husband must reject her in order to thrust her into the unwilling arms of the god. Śiva is blackmailed into using force against her, and even he does not escape unscathed: the marks of the bracelets and anklets on the left half of the *liṅga* correspond to the scars of Kāmākṣī's breasts and bracelets on the sand-*liṅga* at Kāñcipuram.[72] Sugandhakeśī pathetically insists on her devotion to her husband, but, unlike the wives of Sudarśana and Iyaṟpakaiyār, she will not obey him by offering herself to the god; chastity, for this woman, clearly does not mean the negation of human eroticism. So striking is the reversal of the usual pattern of the myths that one is tempted to regard this story as expressing a hidden hostility to the very idea of the woman who rejects the world in order to marry a god. Yet in another version of the myth, from Tiruviṭaimarutūr, the bride offers no resistance to her husband's plan to transfer her to Śiva. Here the emphasis is entirely on the self-abnegation of the husband, who reminds us of Iyaṟpakaiyār and other devotees who cheerfully offer their wives to the guest or the god. In the version from Tiruviṭaimarutūr, the bride is absorbed into the *liṅga* except for her right hand, and at this the king is perplexed:

> "Did you reject this hand because it was the one part of her body touched by your poor servant?" asked the king in sorrow. Replied Śiva, "We will accept this hand tomorrow, so that those who live in the world will know your love." The king left the shrine, and the doors closed behind him. The members of the royal household searched for the king and his bride; when they discovered the king alone, they asked, "Where is the Queen (*teviyār*)?" "She is with Mahāliṅgamūrti (= Śiva at Tiruviṭaimarutūr)," he answered. Amazed, they

went with the priests into the shrine, and there they beheld the hand resting on the crest of the *liṅga*. As they watched, Śiva took the hand inside. At this, the king rejoiced, the others felt fear and wonder, and the gods showered down flowers.[73]

The king has taken the hand of his bride in the marriage ceremony, but this act is then repeated by the god in a symbolic demonstration of the rejection of human marriage in favor of union with the deity. The woman's hand emerging from the *liṅga* has an iconic analogue in the *satī* stone, the stone erected in honor of a wife who dies with her husband. Sometimes these stones show an arm bedecked with bangles emerging from a pillar;[74] the bangles suggest a woman whose husband is still alive (a widow breaks and removes her ornaments).[75] The folk tradition values highly the woman who dies before her husband,[76] and even Kampaṉ makes Daśaratha exclaim, when his wife Kaikeyī demands that he banish Rāma, that a woman's glory is to die before her husband.[77] Usually, of course, the *satī* stone indicates that both husband and wife are dead, while in the myth under discussion the woman, in fact, has a living husband, or rather two, one human, one divine.

In effect, the myth from Kāḷaiyārkoyil (Kāṉapper) combines two contrasting themes—the goddess who must not marry the god, and the woman who will marry *only* the god. The resulting hybrid perplexes even the sages of the Naimiṣa Forest, who demand further explanation from the narrator. He says:

> Once Pārvatī asked Śiva to repeat a lesson in *yoga* which he was giving to sages. Since she had already heard the lesson once, by virtue of being inseparable from her lord, Śiva became angry and cursed her to be born as a woman. She became the daughter of the Coḻa king. When she came of age, he arranged a *svayaṃvara* for her, but she simply remained silent in the presence of her suitors. At last she announced that she would marry anyone who could defeat her father in battle. When the Coḻaṉ was defeated at Kāḷipuram, she agreed to marry the Pāṇṭiyaṉ who had overcome him; but the latter, ascribing his victory to the grace of Śiva, insisted that she become the bride of the lord.[78]

This explanation, which reflects the invariable apotheosis of the local (human) bride of the god, is not altogether satisfactory. Pārvatī's reluctance to reunite with her husband remains unexplained, while the Pāṇṭiya victory as described in the myth depended more on the aid of the goddess ("the Lady who walked on swords") than of her spouse. The marriage myth itself makes the Pāṇṭiya bridegroom the only real partisan of the divine marriage; both Śiva and his destined bride object. In the end, *bhakti* triumphs over conventional ideas of marriage, though not without a struggle. The human avatar of Pārvatī is forcibly returned to her lord.[79]

Vaiṣṇava myths make the most consistent use of the theme of the human consort of the god. We have already referred to Āṇṭāḷ, Viṣṇu's local bride. Viṣṇu's consort at Tiruvuḷḷūr is Kanakavallī, originally Vasumatī, the daughter of the king Dharmasena; when the god came to the shrine as an anonymous wayfarer, the maiden fell in love with him, and the king agreed to the wedding (according to some accounts, after the bridegroom promised to remain at that spot).[80] At Kumpakoṇam Viṣṇu weds the daughter of the sage Mārkaṇḍeya; the girl is an incarnation of Bhūdevī.[81] Other versions say the foster father is Bhṛgu, and the daughter a form of Śrī (Komalavallī[82] or Hemāmbujavallī[83]). The local marriage of Veṅkaṭeśvara will be discussed in another context. In these instances, when the bride is a form of one of Viṣṇu's divine consorts, the god himself is hardly concerned to preserve his wife's virginity; it is only on the human level, in the eyes of the devotees, that the woman's marriage to the god acquires an ideal force as a contrast to earthly love. But at Tiruvaṭantai (south of Madras) the marriage myth combines the motif of the eternal *brahmacārin* with the theme of the god's union with a local girl:

> The sage Gālava had 360 daughters, each of whom lived in a separate street in the village. Viṣṇu took the form of a *brahmacārin* and sought the hand of the eldest daughter. After the marriage, the couple visited the local temple to pay homage to the god and receive his blessings; once inside the shrine, they vanished. The next day another *brahmacārin* appeared and married the second daughter; they too went to the temple and disappeared inside. This went on for 360 days, until the last of the daughters had married and disappeared. When all his daughters were gone, Gālava entered the temple to ask the help of the god, and Viṣṇu appeared before him as the boar, with all 360 daughters on his lap. The boar embraced all the daughters with his left hand, pressing their souls into the single soul of Lakṣmī. Because the marriage of the god lasted 360

days, he is known as Nityakalyāṇasvāmin ("the lord of the perpetual marriage").[84]

The marriage is frozen in the cycle of the year, and the god and his brides remain chaste.[85] A similar artifice allows Mīnākṣī to remain a virgin bride: according to one source, each year during Mīnākṣī's marriage to Sundareśvara-Śiva someone sneezes before the ceremony is completed; at this inauspicious sign, the marriage is postponed until the following year.[86] Thus, ritual can accomplish the elusive synthesis of conflicting ideals; for while the goddess must have her consort, her powers can be preserved only by maintaining her virginity.

## 3. The Lustful Bride

Although the myths of many Tamil shrines show a persistent attempt to prevent the nuptials of the local goddess, the erotic component of Devī's nature is still stressed. The virgin goddess is the epitome of the seductive, desired bride. Kaṉṉiyākumari lusts for her husband, and flies into a rage when he fails to turn up for the wedding, just as Pārvatī longs for Śiva and performs *tapas* to seduce him. The lust of the virgin goddess, and the corresponding desire of her chosen bridegroom, the god, constitute one of the major thrusts of the myths; but this force runs aground on the need to preserve Devī's virginity, which holds the key to her power. The resulting tension sets the myths in motion between two poles, just as the myths of Śiva move from images of the ascetic yogi to those of the divine lover; but, as we shall see in the next section, the Tamil myths have their own way out of this impasse. For the moment we must concentrate on the eroticism that pervades the myths of marriage. In particular, we will explore the association of the goddess with Kāma, the god of desire.

Devī's link with Kāma is apparent in several local names for the goddess: Kāmākṣī at Kāñcipuram; Civakāmiyammai at Tirukkūvam, Citamparam, and Tiruppattūr; Kāmākhyā in Assam. Some forms of the goddess are iconographically connected with Kāma: like him, she carries a bow of sugar cane and arrows of flowers.[1] In her seductive form (as Lalitā or Tripurasundarī) Devī is celebrated throughout the most popular Śākta text of south India, the *Saundaryalaharī* ascribed to Śaṅkara; here Kāma is said to conquer by Devī's grace.[2] One Sanskrit purāṇa makes the identification still more definite: after Kāma was burned by Śiva, his essence entered into the limbs of the goddess.[3] The goddess thus embodies the concept of desire. In a folk myth from the coastal area north of Madras, the goddess fulfils Kāma's classic role:

> "Ammavaru then related how she herself had desired marriage and gone to Vishṇu, who sent her to Brahmā, who passed her on to Śiva. She danced before Śiva, who promised to grant her wish, if she would give him the three valuable things she possessed—a rug, some betel leaves and a third eye. She gave them all to Śiva, who at once opened the third eye and reduced her to ashes. Then, filled with regret at the rash act, which involved the destruction of all womankind, he collected the ashes and made them into the form of three women, who became the wives of Śiva, Vishṇu and Brahmā."[4]

Śiva burns the goddess as he burns Kāma, in order to escape marriage, but in the end the burning of the goddess brings about the very result he originally opposed—just as Kāma's reduction to ashes is the first step toward the marriage of Śiva and Pārvatī. Like Kāma's ashes, which are used by the goddess to create the demon Bhaṇḍāsura,[5] the ashes of Ammavaru are a creative medium; Śiva fashions wives for the Trimūrti (including his own wife Pārvatī) out of the ashes of the goddess. Śiva's third eye, with which he usually burns Kāma, is here a gift of the goddess.[6] This is an important motif: the third eye is a source of supernatural power (not only extraordinary vision), and may be related to the *liṅga*; in a variant of this same myth, a menacing goddess loses all her strength upon relinquishing her third eye to Śiva.[7] The loss of the eye thus symbolizes the taming of the goddess, who needs to be transformed into a more gentle, subdued creature. The three-eyed goddess who dances before Śiva is imbued with aggressive, dangerous sexuality; she must be robbed of the eye, burned to death, and then revived before she becomes an acceptable wife for the god. We will return to this pattern in the context of the dance myths. It is the goddess as the source of the third eye and the eroticism it symbolizes who interests us now. The erotic nature of the third eye is clear from many stories: when Pārvatī, naked and ashamed, hides Śiva's eyes on their wedding night, to her consternation the god's third eye gazes steadfastly at her.[8] Eyes in general have an erotic force in Indian symbolism. Like the *liṅga*, the eye can impregnate: Vaḷḷi is born from a deer made pregnant by the glance of the sage Śivamuni.[9]

The god Murukaṉ, Vaḷḷi's husband, is born from sparks from the eyes of Śiva.[10] The mountain Vaḷḷimalai is full of eyes to watch the union of Murukaṉ and Vaḷḷi.[11] Indra produces extra eyes to witness the dance of the *apsaras* Tilottamā;[12] in some versions of the Ahalyā story, in which Indra commits adultery with the wife of the sage Gautama, the thousand *yonis* that cover Indra's body as a result of Gautama's curse are transformed (in one text by Devī / Indrākṣī) into eyes.[13] Indra's thousand eyes are associated with the eyes on the peacock's tail: once when Rāvaṇa invaded heaven and the gods fled, Indra hid under the wings of a peacock; in gratitude for this protection, the god with a thousand eyes (*sahasrākṣa*) blessed the peacock to have a thousand eyes on its tail.[14] The peacock's "eyes" undoubtedly contribute to the bird's erotic associations in both Sanskrit and Tamil literature: Kāma rides the peacock;[15] the dance of the peacocks during the rains suggests the union of lovers; the peacock is a distinctive attribute (*karu*) of the *kuṟiñci* region associated with lovers' union.[16] Murukaṉ, the god of the *kuṟiñci* region, rides the peacock; Kṛṣṇa, another young and handsome lover of women, is adorned with peacock feathers.[17] The tail of the peacock is an emblem of the goddess,[18] and several Tamil shrines make the goddess incarnate in the peahen:

> When Śiva was expounding the meaning of sacred ash and the *pañcākṣara* to Umā on Kailāsa, she lost attention because of a beautiful peahen which happened to be there. "Please tell me again; I am so tired," she said. Śiva was angry and cursed her to be born as a peahen with beautiful eyes in its tail. He promised the curse would end if she worshiped in Kapālinakaram (Mayilai = Mylapore). The goddess went there and made all the waters of the world enter the Kapālitīrtha; she bathed there and worshiped the god. Śiva appeared on the bull and gave her back her divine form.[19]

The appearance of the goddess as a peahen at this shrine may foreshadow the birth there of her son Murukaṉ, the peacock rider, who resides at Mayilai (< *mayil*, "peacock") as Ciṅkāravelaṉ, "the handsome holder of the spear."[20] But the peahen incarnation of Devī seems, in the light of the above discussion, to be a deliberate attempt to underline the erotic nature of her *tapas*; one may note, too, the constant reference to the peacock's "eyes" in the Mayilai myth.[21] At the same time, we must recall the lethal nature of the peacock and its close link with the nether world;[22] Devī's incarnation in this form thus reveals once again the conjunction of eroticism and death.

The seductive attitude of the goddess is particularly prominent in the myths and cult of Kāñcipuram, where she is known as Kāmākṣī, "having eyes of desire"—note again the importance of eyes in this context. One important myth of Kāmākṣī has already been discussed: Kāmākṣī saves the sand-*liṅga* from the waters of the flood and is subsequently married to Śiva at this spot.[23] Several myths discuss the association of this goddess and Kāma; according to the *Brahmāṇḍapurāṇa*, the goddess of Kāñci (here referred to as Lalitā) revived Kāma after he had been burned by Śiva:

> After the death of the demon Bhaṇḍa, who was born from the ashes of Kāma, the gods said to Lalitā, "Ever since the death of Satī, Śiva has been performing *tapas* in the Sthāṇvāśrama. We sent Kāma to arouse his love for Pārvatī, but Śiva reduced him to ashes. We need a leader of the army against Tāraka. Please help us by reviving Kāma!" Rati, Kāma's widow, came before Lalitā, and, seeing her haggard, grief-stricken appearance, Devī felt compassion. By her grace, Kāma was reborn. Lalitā said to him, "You will be invisible, and Śiva will never again be able to burn you." Kāma went to the *āśrama* and wounded the meditating Śiva; the god abandoned his austerities and thought only of Pārvatī. When he was satisfied with her *tapas*, he married her and created Kumāra (to lead the gods against Tāraka).[24]

In several purāṇas Pārvatī intercedes with Śiva to secure the revival of Kāma,[25] but here the goddess revives him herself and bestows invisibility upon him. This boon is meant to protect Kāma from Śiva, against whom Devī herself wishes him to proceed. Śiva is occupied with *tapas* in the *āśrama* named after Sthāṇu—the antierotic form of Śiva familiar to us from the myths of Cucīntiram. But, as often in these myths, the invisible, resuscitated Kāma is more successful than before, and Śiva succumbs to his second assault. The result is the god's marriage to Pārvatī, which has a parallel in the restoration of Kāma, now invisible, to the widowed Rati.[26] Another, possibly later myth from Kāñcipuram takes up the themes of Kāma's multiple attacks on Śiva, and Devī's collusion with the god of desire:

> After being burned by Śiva, Manmatha (= Kāma) worshiped Kāmākṣī at the Kāmakoṣṭha.[27] She restored his body and agreed to help him against Śiva. Once again he shot his flower-arrows at the god, and Śiva tried to burn him with his glance, but this time the fire had no effect. No more successful were the trident and the Pāśupata weapon, which became ornaments of Kāma. Defeated, Śiva got up from his seat and went into the women's quarters, closing the doors behind him. Kāmākṣī, the goddess of Kāñcipuram, gathered all her forms together in herself, removing them from Kailāsa and all other shrines, in order to fulfill her boon to Manmatha and give him victory.
>
> Śiva sought her everywhere and at last reached Kāñci, where he found her in a bewitchingly beautiful form, performing *tapas*. "Who are you?" she asked. "What are you saying, dear?" said Śiva, eager for the play of love; "where is my wife, who delivers me from desire? Why have you left all my (favorite) places and come here? Tell me this, and then satisfy my desire!" "I am not Gaurī," replied the goddess; "you may attain Gaurī through *tapas* and ask her (your questions); otherwise, take refuge with Kāma!" Hearing this, Śiva thought, "She delights in offending me in order to help Manmatha"; his anger blazed forth, and he decided to take her by force. The goddess created a crore of Kāmas and sent them to fight Śiva; he in turn created a crore of Rudras, who reduced the Kāmas to ashes. Devī revived them, and the battle continued until the forces of Śiva were defeated. Seeing Śiva alone, his army destroyed, Kāma again shot his arrows at the god. Then he put a begging bowl into his hand and led him to Devī, saying "Ask for alms." Seeing him thus humiliated, the goddess said, "Today you have been conquered by Kāma. Now take refuge with my Manmathas and meditate on me always. I am happy with you; your wife is born and will satisfy your desire." She took the radiant form of Kāmākṣī, and Śiva bowed to her and went round the Kāmakoṭi. By Devī's command, Kāma became a star; he performs *tapas* in the sky.[28]

Usually it is Śiva who comes to impart lessons to others, undermining their pretensions and revealing hidden aspects of their nature; but here the god himself must be taught a lesson. It is not merely a question of the attempt by the goddess to seduce the ascetic god, in accordance with the classic pattern of these myths of Kāma and Śiva. Śiva must be forced to acknowledge his own erotic vulnerability. His temptress mocks him by advising him to perform *tapas* to win Gaurī—the reverse of the standard situation in which the goddess performs *tapas* to seduce the god! The point of the ironic reversal is then driven home by the additional suggestion that Śiva take refuge with Kāma. The traditional confrontation between Śiva and Kāma is magnified many times, so that a crore of Rudras burn a crore of Kāmas; Devī, Kāma's ally, revives and sustains his army, and in the end Kāma's victory over the god is complete. Like Śiva in the Pine Forest,[29] Kāma even turns the weapons of his adversary into personal ornaments. The Pine Forest myth provides a useful backdrop to this myth: Kāma seems to play on the image of the naked Śiva pretending to seek alms in the forest, when Kāma gives the god a begging bowl and leads him to the goddess.[30] Here, too, there is a measure of irony: the standard Tamil versions of the Pine Forest myth insist that Śiva comes not to seduce the wives of the sages but to teach a lesson; the women are infatuated by the sight of the naked beggar, and their husbands lose their self-control in the presence of Mohinī, or when they realize how they have been tricked by Śiva.[31] In the myth from Kāñcipuram, on the other hand, it is Śiva's pride that must be shattered, and Śiva is *truly* reduced to the point of seeking alms from the goddess, who will permit him to satisfy his desire only after he acknowledges defeat. The conquest of the god is commemorated by a new name for the city, "Śivajitkṣetra" ("the site where Śiva was overcome"),[32] and in a final reversal the conqueror of Śiva, Kāma, is sent to perform perpetual *tapas* in the heavens.

The Kāñcipuram tradition thus makes the inherited figure of Śiva-Kāmāntaka, the destroyer of Kāma, into Kāma's servant. The god is ruled by passion as he meditates on the goddess; he devotes himself entirely to desire; he embodies desire. Thus it is not surprising that Śiva is known at Kāñci as Kāmeśvara, "lord of desire/Kāma."[33] Kāma himself appears in a different form in yet another myth from Kāñci, this time from a Vaiṣṇava text:

> Śiva and Devī quarreled after a game of dice, and Śiva cursed Devī to be black, to have a terrifying form, and to have misshapen eyes (or three eyes: *virūpanayanā bhava*). She worshiped her brother Vāmana (Viṣṇu the Dwarf) at Kāñci, and he made her eyes beautiful and gave her the name Kāmākṣī. He also ad-

vised her to build a *liṅga* of sand and worship it, in order that Śiva might come to marry her.

While she was worshiping, Śiva came down to see her. He burned her with the fierce heat of the sun, and she called to Vāmana to help. Vāmana created a mango tree to shade her, but Śiva burned it and the goddess as well with his glance. Vāmana hastened to cool Devī with rays of nectar (*sudhā*) from his moon form (*pūrṇacandrākṛti*). He created a lake full of nectar and made her bathe in it to cool herself. The mango, although burned, grew and bore fruit because of that lake, and Devī created the sand-*liṅga* at its base and worshiped Śaṅkara.[34]

The mango tree is the tree of Kāma burned by Śiva,[35] who also burns the goddess herself, as in the folk myth of Ammavaru cited above. Here the tension between Śiva and Kāma is restored, although eventually Śiva marries the goddess at this site, after testing her *tapas* and devotion still further. Trial by fire precedes trial by water in this text, for the sequel to this myth is the well-known flood myth from Kāñci in which the goddess embraces the *liṅga* in order to save it from the raging waters (in this case, of the Ganges rather than the local river Kampai).[36] Vāmana-Viṣṇu has adopted attributes of Śiva: he has the Soma-glance that revives Kāma (the burned mango)[37] and the name Candrakhaṇḍa, "having a part of the moon"—here explained as "destroying (*khaṇḍayati*) [heat] by the moon." The epithet is, of course, better suited to Śiva, who wears the crescent moon. Candrakhaṇḍa-Viṣṇu, Tam. Nilāttuṇṭa-pperumāḷ, has a small shrine within the temple of Ekāmranātha-Śiva at Kāñci, to the northeast of the main sanctum and immediately adjoining the *liṅga* known as Kaḷḷakkampaṇ.[38] The two gods thus share a physical proximity. The confusion between them persists and is even made explicit in another version of the Kāñci flood myth:

Once the hosts of *śaktis* (the female servants of Pārvatī) came to Śiva and demanded to be allowed to sit on his seat, like Devī. "You are but parts of Devī," he said. "She is part of us," they replied. As an amusement, Śiva made their clothes fall from their bodies, to teach them humility. Devī covered his eyes with her hands to stop him from looking at them; immediately the world was plunged into the *pralaya*. Because she had caused this premature destruction, Devī's body grew black.

> To overcome this fault, she was born as a child in Badarikāś-rama and was adopted by the sage Kātyāyana. He gave her some sand from the bank of the Ganges, water from the river, and other items, and sent her south; at the spot where the sand became a *liṅga* and the Ganges water turned to milk, she stopped to perform *tapas*. Nārada taught her the *mantra* of the five arrows (of Kāma), and she repeated it for six months, until the fire it engendered heated Kailāsa. Śiva tried to cool the heat of desire by embracing troops of *yoginīs*, but this was no help; he bathed in the Ganges, but this also failed to cool him. He sent the Ganges to stop Devī from repeating the *mantra*, and the river came down as a mighty flood. The goddess screamed for help. One of her companions[39] held out a skull (*kapāla*) in her hand, and the river disappeared inside. Kāmeśvara (Śiva) liberated the flood from the skull; again Devī cried for help, and her brother Viṣṇu took a form reaching up to heaven and blocked the river's advance. Seeing the moon on his throat, Devī took her brother for her husband, but Viṣṇu corrected her: "This flood is the form of your lord. Embrace the sand-*liṅga*, and you will be saved from his test." Devī embraced the *liṅga*, leaving on it scars from her breasts and bracelets. Śiva took her on to his seat, and her skin became golden. Now that she had a new form, she wished to be married again, and Viṣṇu performed the ceremony at Śiva's order.[40]

Although the myth informs us that Śiva merely wanted to teach the *śakti* hosts a lesson, Pārvatī's jealousy appears to be well-founded, for Śiva embraces *yoginīs* and the Ganges (his second wife) before appearing in Kāñci. Yet Śiva's adultery is balanced by the implicit incestuous connection between the goddess and her brother, who stands in the path of the river, just as in a multiform of this myth he lies naked at the boundary of Kāñci to block the advance of the flooding Sarasvatī.[41] Pārvatī mistakes Viṣṇu for Śiva because of the moon, here said to be placed on his throat; Candrakhaṇḍa has become Candrakaṇṭha ("having the moon on his throat") through the mediation of Tam. Cantirakaṇṭaṉ. The misunderstanding is of less consequence than the fact that the two gods are confused, so that the goddess of Kāñci comes close to incest.[42] The sacred power of the site transforms water into milk and gives sand the shape of the *liṅga*; at these signs the goddess chooses this spot to perform *tapas*, with the effect of torturing Śiva-Kāmeśvara with desire. This is the second act of aggression by the goddess against Śiva; the first is the covering of his eyes, the impulse that causes her skin to become black. We will return to this motif. Two further clashes follow: Devī swallows the river that is identified with Śiva,[43] and she wounds the *liṅga* with her breasts and bracelets. The first motif appears in the myths of Viṣvaksena (Viṣṇu's doorkeeper), where Bhairava catches a river of blood in the skull he holds in his hand.[44] The second belongs in the category of myths in which the god or his image is wounded or scarred.

Although the myth ends with Devī's marriage in a golden form, the images suggest the underlying theme of a dangerous eroticism, which is embodied in the person of the dark goddess Kālī. The dark goddess is exiled to earth, where she strives to unite again with her husband; Kālī is thus the central female figure of the marriage myths—including the myths of Kāñci, where the goddess is most closely identified with Kāma, with desire. In other words, the dark and frightening Kālī is the lustful and enticing virgin around whom the marriage myths revolve. Devī becomes dark by hiding her husband's eyes, or, in the first version, because of Śiva's curse after the dice game; the latter curse also includes the anomalous, threatening eye, which we have also discovered in the seductive and menacing folk-goddess. The dark goddess may be born in other ways; sometimes Devī splits away from her darker nature, which is described as a sheath (*kośa*, hence the name Kauśikī).[45] In these cases the light or golden goddess who remains may happily remarry her husband Śiva. But in still another marriage myth from Kāñci, even the dark portion of the goddess ("Aṇaṅku, who emerged from a part of Gaurī") demands and is granted the right to be married to Śiva-Ekāmparar.[46] Śiva stations his dark bride, Aṇaṅku / Durgā, at Kāñci, where she remains a virgin (*kaṉṉi*), and as such gives her name to the city. It is this second, terrifying bride, whose very title expresses her identification with violent power (*aṇaṅku*), who most truly represents all that is implied by the name Kāmākṣī. Lust belongs with the dynamic forces of chaos. Sexuality is a dangerous, violent force, and woman an insatiable temptress who drains the male of vitality.[47] Ultimately, in bearing children, woman creates new life; but this life is produced from the violence of sexual union, which clearly is felt to wreak destruction upon the male. Śiva cannot lightly escape the consequences of his marriage to the dark goddess, even if she retains her virginity—for in wedding her, he brings himself within range of her dangerous power. Let us look at one more myth from Kāñcipuram, which crystallizes many of these themes, and which offers an instructive portrait of the goddess Kāmākṣī / Lalitā. This myth is told as the prelude to the revival of Kāma by Kāmākṣī:[48]

> Once Śiva smiled when Gaṅgā was referred to as his wife. Seeing this, Devī was furious and went away, saying, "Once I performed terrible *tapas* for Śiva on the Himālaya. Then Kāma (Tam. Māraṉ) fought to save me from loneliness and was burned to ashes by Śiva because of it. I suffered that in silence, but this is too much to bear." From the ashes of Kāma she created the demon Bhaṇḍāsura.
>
> The demon worshiped Śiva for ten crores of years, and Śiva at last granted him his wish—to enter the bodies of his enemies, the gods, and drink their seed and blood (*cukkila curoṇitaṅkaḷ*). The gods, Tryambaka and the rest, thus became impotent and had no taste for their wives. "Why is this?" they wondered, and worshiped Śiva to find out. Śiva said to them, "The demon has entered you and is feasting on your seed and your blood. He has the power to do this because he was created by Śakti. I can help you only if you are prepared to die—otherwise you cannot overcome this sorrow." Because of their grief, they agreed to do as he recommended.
>
> Śiva made a great sacrifice and (as a *dīkṣita* at his sacrifice) offered up all that moves and is still. He created Śaktis for each of the gods; the demon, afraid of the fire, went out (from the bodies of the gods). When all had been sacrificed, Tripurā appeared in the flame holding a bow of sugar cane, arrows made of flowers, and an elephant goad. "Why have you summoned me?" she asked. Śiva told her of the suffering caused to creatures by the demon, and told her to kill him. She slew him with a single arrow. Śiva told her to create Hara and the other gods, to unite them with their wives, and to give them their proper work. She created the gods of the Trimūrti, each motivated by his own egoism (*ahaṅkāra*), and Śiva taught them that there was no difference between himself and Rudra. Then Śiva created everything by means of Śakti. The demon joined the hosts of Śiva, for he had been slain by the goddess.[49]

We recognize at once the goddess armed with the sugar-cane bow and arrows of flowers—this is the seductive Kāmākṣī, who has assumed the attributes of Kāmā. But here the erotic goddess is a violent destroyer who, through an act of violence, restores vitality to the gods. There is no mistaking the association of eroticism and death, even if a goal beyond death is proclaimed. The sacrificial concepts buried in the cult of the Tamil goddess are transparently clear in this myth. The goddess, the source of life and power, is born from the sacrifice; in their death the gods achieve life. Śiva is unable to refuse the request of the demon devotee, even though it costs him his life—for Śiva and Rudra / Hara / Tryambaka (the destructive member of the Trimūrti) are one, as Śiva himself takes pains to teach the gods. Thus while Śiva ostensibly remains outside the sacrifice and can command the goddess at her birth, in reality he dies as well, and the boon he grants the demon is an extreme example of the god's self-abnegating generosity to his devotees. But the distinction between god and demon is misleading here; in fact, the two are one. The demon is fashioned from the ashes of Kāma; Śiva, as we know, is Kāmeśvara at this site.[50] Both god and demon die for the ravishing goddess. The god perishes with the other gods in the sacrifice in order to create Śakti; the demon is slain by her arrow, but survives as a member of the hosts of Śiva. The coincidence of god and demon is explored in a closely related myth from the same shrine: there the demon is slain while asleep on Śiva's mountain Kailāsa by the virgin goddess; Śiva emerges from the nether world through the cave of Kāma.[51] The cave is the womb of the goddess, the Kāmakkoṭṭam—the shrine of Kāmākṣī at Kāñci; this site is closely linked with the Kaccimayāṉam, the graveyard (*śmaśāna*) that appears to be one of the oldest cult centers at this spot. The *śmaśāna* is the site of the sacrifice.[52] Devī gives birth to the gods at the sacrifice, as she restores Kāma to life at this shrine after he has been burned by Śiva; love is reborn from death, but will no doubt seek death again, for desire—or the yearning for desire!—impels the gods toward the sacrifice; the burning ground is one with the womb.

## 4. The Murderous Bride

The two main aspects of the goddess that we have been exploring—the goddess as a virgin barred from union, and as a temptress hungry for union—meet in the dangerous Kālī or Durgā who comes to earth in order to find her husband, and who eventually succeeds in this quest. Śiva appears in the Tamil shrine and weds the local goddess, who, as we have seen, is closely connected to the black and fertile earth. We must now attempt to understand the logic that lies behind the combination of seemingly antithetical ideals in the person of the goddess. Virginity and sexual longing are not, of course, in themselves contradictory; as we saw in the myths of Kaṉṉiyākumari, the virgin goddess epitomizes the seductive ideal. The virgin holds within her a latent sexuality and, corresponding to this potential, a concentration of power. A problem arises only when the worshiper wishes to preserve the basis of this power without renouncing the ideal of union with the goddess as acted out by the divine exemplar, Śiva—in other words, when the virginity of the goddess must somehow be retained in the circumstances of her marriage.[1] Of course, one could always opt for paradox and proclaim the goddess simultaneously chaste and voluptuous, even after her marriage, just as Śiva in the classical Sanskrit tradition is both ascetic and libertine. Before we succumb to the mystery, however, there is a further possibility to be explored. The violent nature of the virgin temptress Kālī may hold the key to the resolution of conflicting ideals.

The violence embodied in the dark goddess most often finds its object in a demon enemy of the gods. The need for Devī to kill a demon is often used alongside other factors (her wish to expiate some fault, such as hiding Śiva's eyes; her jealousy of Śiva's paramours or of his second wife, the Ganges; her pique at being teased or insulted by her husband)[2] to explain the arrival of the goddess on earth. Thus Kaṉṉiyākumari comes to earth to slay Bāṇa, and Lalitā overcomes Bhaṇḍa.[3] The most important of all such confrontations—and the myth that has had the most profound influence on the Tamil myths of divine marriage—is the story of Devī's war against the buffalo-demon Mahiṣāsura. This myth is, in fact, the archetypal myth of the goddess in India. It has been popular in the Tamil area since at least Pallava times, if one may judge by the frequency and scale of its iconographic representations. There is, for example, the magnificent frieze at Mahābalipuram of the combat between the buffalo-demon and the goddess. Other depictions from the same site show the goddess standing on the severed head of the buffalo.[4] Even before turning to the myths, we may note that the closest iconographic analogues of these and similar images are the much later Tantric icons of Devī dancing on the corpse of her husband Śiva.[5] Is this analogy merely fortuitous, or is there some deeper correspondence to be discovered between the demon victim and the divine husband of the goddess? We saw in

IV. Mahiṣāsuramardinī: Durgā slays the buffalo demon.

the concluding myth of the previous section that Śiva at Kāñcipuram shares the fate of Bhaṇḍāsura, the demon slain by the goddess Kāmākṣī. D. D. Kosambi has shown that the buffalo god Mhasobā (Mhātobā) appears in some villages in Mahārāṣṭra as the victim of the goddess, while in others he is her consort.[6] Parallels to this pattern, Kosambi felt, should exist in other parts of India.[7] I will argue below that the Tamil myths of divine marriage offer, in fact, such a parallel.

We begin with the Mahiṣāsura myth as it appears in its *locus classicus*, the *Devīmāhātmya* incorporated into the *Mārkaṇḍeyapurāṇa*:

> When Mahiṣāsura the buffalo demon was lord of the demons and Indra lord of the gods, the gods were cast out from heaven by the demon host. From the energy (*śakti*) born from the anger of the gods, Devī became incarnate. The gods bestowed their divine weapons upon her and sent her to do battle with Mahiṣāsura. Riding on a lion, she fought with the demon, and finally placed her foot on his neck and pierced him with a spear; he half came forth from his own mouth, and the goddess cut off his head and killed him.[8]

In many of the Sanskrit accounts, the war is preceded by an episode in which Mahiṣa lusts for the goddess and tries to seduce her; she encourages his desire as a means of weakening him—a classic ploy in Hindu myths.[9] Sometimes the battle is described by Devī as a suitor's test: "Hear, O Daitya, the bride-price (*śulka*) in our family. . . . Whoever conquers a daughter of our family in battle becomes her husband."[10] As we shall see, trial by battle does indeed precede the marriage of Śiva and Devī in the myths of several Tamil shrines; but in the case of the classical Sanskrit accounts of the Mahiṣa myth, Devī uses the idea of a suitor's test simply to lure the demon to his doom.

Tamil mythology, however, carries further these hints of an erotic link between Devī and her victim:

Śiva and Devī quarreled, made up, then started a game of dice. Suddenly Devī covered the two eyes of her husband with her hands, and the universe was plunged into darkness. Śiva opened his third eye and drenched the worlds with light.

Because she had brought untimely disaster on the universe and interrupted the rites of sages and ascetics, the goddess was afflicted by evil. To expiate her fault she was sent to Kāñcipuram. There she made a *liṅga* of sand and worshiped it. To test her, Śiva sent a flood, and she embraced the *liṅga* to keep it from being washed away.

Śiva, pleased with the goddess, directed her to Aruṇācalam, where she continued her *tapas* in a hut in the forest. The gods found her there, and complained to her of the mischief caused by the demon Mahiṣa: "He takes hold of Ādiśeṣa by the head and tail and flings the sleeping Viṣṇu like a rock from a sling; he has stolen Agni's ram; he rides around on Airāvata. . . ." The goddess angrily instructed Durgā (Tam. Vintai) to kill Mahiṣa in battle. The war raged around the hut of the goddess at Aruṇācalam; Durgā, aided by Aruṇanāyakī, and four *śaktis*, the eight Bhairavas (Tam. Vaṭukar), and the Seven Mothers, defeated the demon armies and cut off the head of Mahiṣa. To her horror and amazement, upon the severed head of Mahiṣa she discovered a bright (or, according to the commentary, crystal) *liṅga*.

Durgā brought this *liṅga* back to the goddess, but when Devī took it it stuck to her hand. To expiate the evil of killing a devotee of Śiva, the goddess commanded Durgā to strike the mountain with her sword. Water gushed forth, and Devī bathed in it for a month. Finally the *liṅga* dropped from her hand. The goddess then circumambulated the holy mountain, and Śiva appeared and granted her request to become the left half of his body.[11]

This version makes several radical changes in the myth, transforming the characters of Mahiṣa and the goddess, and imparting new values to the mythic action. The killing of Mahiṣa has become a sin, indeed a sin of a particularly heinous kind. In one version, Devī is taught by the sage Gautama that it is wrong to harm any living being (*jīvahiṃsā na kartavyā*)[12]—an injunction that seems rather exotic in the context of a myth wholly devoted to the violent encounter between the goddess and the demon. The introduction of this strain into the Aruṇācalam myth recalls the Buddhist and Jain ethic of nonviolence (*ahiṃsā*); but we may be closer to the basis of this phenomenon if we recall the concern of the sacrificial system with the evil and dangerous consequences of slaughter.[13] A similar concern appears in the ancient Tamil sources, which indicate that any contact with violent power, and specifically with death, was polluting;[14] hence, as we have seen, the attempt to dissociate the deity from the center of violence. In the Aruṇācalam myth, the god—Śiva—is not, in fact, implicated in the destruction of the demon, at least not on the level of the text's literal meaning. It is the goddess who must rid herself of the evil produced by shedding blood. Yet Śiva is linked to the victim in a way that makes Devī's crime far more serious than even this antipathy to violence would indicate: the terrible nature of her action stems from the transformation of Mahiṣa into a devotee of Śiva, as shown by the *liṅga* on his neck.

At first glance, our version of the myth would seem to fall into the category of myths of *dveṣabhakti*, the "*bhakti* of hate"—the extension of the *bhakti* idea to include any violent emotion toward the god.[15] Thus Śiśupāla, because he so hated Kṛṣṇa that he could never keep him from his thoughts whether walking, sitting, eating, or sleeping, wins salvation when killed by the god.[16] Similarly, the ogress Pūtanā, who attempts to poison the infant Kṛṣṇa, attains heaven after Kṛṣṇa drains her of life;[17] and a host of other demons or enemies of the gods—Gajāsura, Tāraka, Rāvaṇa, Andhaka, Hiraṇyakaśipu, Pauṇḍraka, Śaṅkhacūḍa, and so on—are saved and blessed in their death. The Tamil myths are very fond of this pattern: recall Marutvāsura, who merges into Śiva-Aghoramūrti at Tiruvĕṇkāṭu.[18] Both hatred and love establish an intimate relationship with their object; when the latter is a god, the intimacy carries its own reward. Another Tamil purāṇa makes it clear that Mahiṣa benefits from his defeat and death: Devī stood on his head, which she had cut off with her sword; if one is touched by the feet of the Maiden (*kaṉṉi*), the Mother of the three worlds, can there be any doubt that *māyā* will be destroyed? If one but thinks of her feet in his heart, all impurity departs and the sorrow of everlasting rebirth comes to an end.[19] Mahiṣāsura thus achieves in death the goal to which all devotees aspire; like Marutvāsura, Mahiṣāsura may be a model for man. Elsewhere, the salvation of the demon remains implicit:

> The gods were winning in their war with the demons, so Diti sent her daughter to the forest to give birth to a champion of the demons. The girl took the form of a buffalo and seduced the sage Supārśva, and from their union a son with a buffalo's head was born. He conquered the worlds. Śiva, hearing of the distress of the gods, fashioned from the fire of his anger and the anger of the other gods a woman of terrifying splendor. They gave her weapons and a lion to ride, and sent her to fight Mahiṣa, the buffalo-headed demon, in the *pālai* forest. After a long battle, the goddess jumped on to the demon's head. At this the demon screamed and ran south as fast as he could, with Devī in hot pursuit on her lion. Seeing he could not escape, Mahiṣa hid in the Cakratīrtha at Irāmeccuram (Rāmeśvaram).
>
> Devī could not find the demon, try as she might; she was looking back over the path she had taken, facing north, when a voice said, "He is hiding in the tank." Immediately she jumped in with her lion, leaving Mahiṣa no room to hide. She put one foot on his body and one on his head, and then she cut off his head. With a cry the demon died. Her hosts feasted on his blood, and because her lion had dried up the tank, the goddess caused it to be filled with nectar (*cutai*).[20]

The sanctity of the tank is marked by both blood (of the demon) and the nectar (*sudhā*) of the gods; we recognize the symbolic pair from the origin myths. The drying up of the water recalls Agastya's drinking the ocean in order to deny the demons a refuge;[21] this part of the myth also recalls a ritual devoted to Māriyammaṉ in the Coimbatore region, at the end of which the goddess, represented by a small camphor flame, pursues her demon lover into a well.[22] Mahiṣāsura dies when the goddess discovers him in the tank; yet simply by entering this tank, Mahiṣa may be presumed to have gained what *anyone* who bathes there is promised—release from evil, the satisfaction of desires, freedom from the cycle of rebirth.[23] Seduction by a buffalo cow explains the birth of Mahiṣa in Sanskrit purāṇas, as well,[24] but other Tamil versions agree on a different explanation: Varamuni was cursed by other sages, angered by his lack of courtesy, to become a buffalo and to be freed by dying at the hands of the goddess. While wandering in the forest in the form of a buffalo, he once swallowed a sage who carried a *liṅga* in his hand; that *liṅga* remained attached to his neck.[25]

Death at the hands of his enemy is thus the condition for Mahiṣa's liberation. Yet this myth does not belong to the classic type of *dveṣabhakti* myths, for Mahiṣa is freed not because he obsessively hates the god or goddess, as in the cases of Pūtanā and Śiśupāla, but simply by virtue of being killed by Devī. If anything, Mahiṣa appears to feel devotion for Śiva, and the horror felt by Durgā/Vintai at the discovery of the *liṅga* stems from the sense of having killed not an enemy but an ally. In fact, this idea goes considerably deeper. Mahiṣa as bearer of the *liṅga* is said to partake of Śiva's own form (*iṟaiyuruvam*;[26] *aṉṉoṉ mĕyyum accivaṉ ṟaṉ rūpam*[27]), and it is the murder of Śiva himself that is implicitly attributed to Devī. This is perhaps the most suggestive strand of myth in the Tamil versions, and the one most closely linked with the religious prehistory of the area. Truly ancient material has been preserved in a more modern guise: the buffalo god has become a demon, while his essential identity with the male consort of the goddess is affirmed. Another Tamil purāṇa transfers Devī's attack on her husband to a later stage:

> Mahiṣa was granted a boon by Brahmā to the effect that no god could kill him. He destroyed the sacrifices of the sages, injured temples and tanks, and committed other misdeeds. King Cūriyavaṉṉi pleaded with Śiva to help, so Śiva looked at Devī and said: "Take the form of Durgā (Tam. Turkkai) and go down to earth with the Seven Maidens in order to destroy Mahiṣa."
>
> Devī went to Aruṇācalam and challenged the demon to a fight. He at first refused to fight a woman. "If you are a man, come and show your mettle," she said. After a long battle, she stood on his head and cut it off with her sword.
>
> After the death of the demon, the goddess was followed by Brahminicide. She worshiped Śiva at Ratnagiri (Tiruvāṭpokki), and Śiva gave her a sword with which to rid herself of the evil, but she did not know how to use it. "Split the moun-

> tain in two," said Śiva. She struck the mountain with the sword; it split in two, and her sin departed. The goddess lives there still as Khaḍgā (Tam. Kaṭkai, "The Sword").[28]

Although Mahiṣa is portrayed as wholly evil, he cannot be killed with impunity. Any act of slaughter requires an act of atonement; in this version, the need for expiation is particularly severe, because the victim is a Brahmin. A similar problem besets Indra after the killing of Vṛtra.[29] The water that washes away evil is missing in the myth from Tiruvāṭpokki, but the redemptive *act* remains the same as at Aruṇācalam—cleaving the mountain with a sword. Here the full force of this image is made clear: splitting the mountain unites the divine couple, for Devī is the sword (*khaḍgā*), and the mountain, as we are told throughout this purāṇa, is the body of Śiva.[30] Devī unites with the god through the act of killing him. Note the reversal of roles: usually it is Devī who must split in two before marriage, casting off her dark "sheath" (Kauśikī or Kālī) in order to emerge as the golden Gaurī;[31] here the god is divided, while the goddess rather than Śiva has the form of the phallic sword.

The split goddess is evident in the first version we have studied, from Tiruvaṇṇāmalai/Aruṇācalam, where Devī sends Durgā along with other forms of herself to perform the killing—although Devī must still pay the price of expiation herself. Devī's impure state and need for atonement are symbolized by the *liṅga* sticking to her hand, an image obviously derived from the story of Śiva's Brahminicide: Śiva cut off one of Brahmā's heads; the skull (*kapāla*) stuck to his hand as he wandered over the earth pursued by Brahminicide, until he reached the Kapālamocana shrine in Benares.[32] At Tiruvaṇṇāmalai Devī is released from the *liṅga* in order to marry Śiva, thus creating the androgyne; the conjunction of episodes is not accidental, for the goddess in fact marries twice—first, symbolically, the dead demon and then, officially, the living god. The myth has distributed aspects of a single event between two male protagonists. The underlying tendency is to suppress the murderous aspect of Devī's marriage; and in yet another version, the dark goddess remains chaste so that the golden goddess can wed:

> The goddess killed Durga[33] and was followed by evil. Śiva said to her: "It seems you do not realize that you have acquired a new form by killing the wicked demon. Go, Nīli, and perform *tapas*." Paiññīli went to Vimalāraṇiyam and worshiped Śiva in her fierce, dark form.

> Suddenly the river there rose like the sea and surged toward the mountain where Śiva dwells. The goddess blocked its path. She pressed her foot against the earth, and at her command the river entered the nether world at that spot. The gods and sages then complained that there was no river at this shrine. The goddess stood to the north of the golden shrine of Umā and shot an arrow; the arrow pierced the mountain, and a river, the Nīlivananadī, poured forth. The goddess created the town of Tiruppaiññīli with its ramparts and palaces, and with a shrine where Śiva and Umā could happily dwell.[34]

Like most other shrines in Tamiḻnāṭu, Tiruppaiññīli claims to have survived a flood; this time it is the dark goddess Paiññīli who holds back the water. Again we see the association of the goddess with *pratiṣṭhā*.[35] But the security that Paiññīli provides has its price. No sooner has the goddess saved the god by diverting the flood than she wounds him by piercing his mountain with an arrow, just as she cleaves the body of the god at Tiruvāṭpokki.[36] The sacred water of the river substitutes for the blood of the slain god, which other myths retain as the sanctifying blood of the demon. The *tapas* of Paiññīli creates a home for Śiva and Umā; the killing of Mahiṣa is thus the prerequisite for the local marriage of the peaceful aspect of the goddess.

That Śiva's marriage to the golden goddess is the only form of union *explicitly* allowed by our texts should not surprise us. We have here the same tensions we witnessed in the myths of sacrifice. The Tamil myths of Mahiṣāsura clearly describe a violent confrontation between the dark goddess and her husband, in the course of which the male is slain. But Śiva must not die or even become soiled by contact with violence; his claim to purity precludes his active participation in the drama of death and rebirth that is acted out in the arena of a fatal union. Therefore the texts supply a surrogate victim, and, when this useful figure is violently disposed of, Śiva is safely married to a less alarming maiden. Nevertheless, the dark goddess creates and renders secure the earthly home of the divine couple, and it is not unreasonable to assert that this security on earth depends upon an act of sacrifice—the death of Mahiṣāsura—just as the Vāstupuruṣa is slain in order to sustain the temple. A sacrifice is a common, dependable source of *pratiṣṭhā*.[37] Moreover, the basic aggression against the god breaks through all attempts to mask it. On the one hand, the goddess—identified as the phallic sword, and thus apparently regarded as in some sense bisexual—

cleaves the mountain that is the body of the god. The violent goddess is then absorbed in the androgyne, her double nature thus persisting in a new form. On the other hand, Mahiṣa's real identity is never really in doubt.

The identification of Śiva and Mahiṣa is at its most explicit in a myth from the *Kālikāpurāṇa* (from the region of Assam):

> Ugracaṇḍā killed Mahiṣāsura in one of his births, and Bhadrakālī killed him in a second. In his third birth as a buffalo, he had a dream in which he saw the goddess drinking his blood after cleaving his head with her sword. When he woke, he worshiped the goddess and told her of his dream, and he also told her that he had been cursed by Kātyāyana to be killed by a woman, because he had distracted a pupil of that sage with a beautiful image of a woman. Mahiṣa asked the goddess for two boons: a share of the sacrifice, and the joy of never departing from her feet. She said, "The sacrifice has already been divided among the gods, and there is no portion left; but I grant you your second wish." Then she struck him and cut off his head. When he beheld his own buffalo-body pierced by the trident and spurting forth blood, he was very frightened, and he cried to her, "If the portions of the sacrifice have already been assigned, let me be killed at another time, and may I never quarrel with the gods." She replied, "I granted your former wish, and now you must be killed. You will not quarrel with the gods, and since you have touched my feet, your body will not be shattered, and you will have a share of the sacrifice."[38]

The exclusion from the sacrifice and the struggle to obtain a share are classic Śaiva themes, the underlying basis of the Vāstoṣpati and Dakṣa myths (with the associated theme of punishment of incest). Mahiṣa seeks, and in death achieves, a portion of the sacrifice, just as Sthāṇu is granted his unique share in the epic Dakṣa myth,[39] and Viṣṇu, decapitated by the ants, wins the "end of the sacrifice."[40] But the *Kālikāpurāṇa* then proceeds to make the implicit correspondence of Śiva and Mahiṣāsura explicit, for the listener (Sagara) asks: Many demons have been killed by the goddess Māyā without receiving boons; why did this demon receive a boon? The narrator (Aurva) replies:

> Mahiṣa was granted his wish because he was Śiva. The demon Rambha propitiated Śiva, and the god promised that he would

> become his son in three births. Rambha saw a buffalo cow (*mahiṣī*) and made love to it; that buffalo cow was Śiva, who gave birth to himself as Mahiṣa. This happened in three separate births. Therefore the goddess accepted Mahiṣa, who was Mahādeva himself.[41]

Śiva as the buffalo is also said to have become the *vāhana* of the goddess, for Viṣṇu as a lion was incapable of carrying her.[42] Van Kooij rightly notes that the point of this statement is to stress the fierce character of the goddess, for the buffalo is usually the vehicle of Yama, who rules the dead.[43] For the same reason, the myth of Devī's killing of Mahiṣa has been interpreted as a Śākta parallel to Śiva's destruction of Death (Śiva as Mṛtyuñjaya, Kālāntaka).[44] This interpretation finds no real support in the texts, except in the sense that Mahiṣa, through dying, attains a higher, more permanent, or more powerful existence.

Such a notion would, of course, be suited to an exegesis of the myth in terms of sacrifice. I have already suggested that a sacrificial scheme is implicit in the Tamil myths of Śiva's marriage to the dark goddess; since Mahiṣa carries the burden of Śiva's role in many of the versions, we must now investigate the connection between the buffalo and the sacrifice. The ritual of buffalo sacrifice is undoubtedly an underlying force in the Mahiṣa myth; in south Indian villages, the buffalo is still a favored sacrificial victim. In the village sacrifices, a special role is reserved for the buffalo's head, which may be offered to the goddess, carried in procession, or used in connection with boundary rites;[45] in the Tamil myths, Devī stands on the demon's head as she decapitates him, and she discovers the crystal *liṅga* on his neck. Let us recall that in the *Devīmāhātmya* the demon is said to have been killed while half-emerging from his own mouth.[46] Both texts and rituals thus seem to affirm the crucial importance of the "head of the sacrifice,"[47] which we may connect to the "end of the sacrifice," the remainder (*vāstu*), the seed.[48] In this symbolic range, the crystal *liṅga* on Mahiṣa's neck has a natural place as a symbol of his seed and vital force, just as it suggests his true identity; similarly, in a myth from Andhra, Skanda is able to overcome Tāraka only by smashing the *liṅga* the demon wears upon his throat.[49] By taking the *liṅga*, Devī thus draws to herself the concentrated power and vitality of the buffalo. This transfer of power entails an interesting reversal in the traditional role of the goddess: we are accustomed to think of the goddess as providing the god with power (*śakti*); but, if our reading is correct, in the buffalo myth she *drains* the male of his strength. Surely this is the significance of the closely related (though later) icons that show Kālī treading on the corpse of Śiva, her tongue thrust out to receive his blood.[50] In the village rituals of the south, the blood of the sacrificial victim—often a buffalo—is drunk precisely in order to transfer its strength to the participants.

Why is the buffalo chosen for the sacrifice? In the earliest Tamil sources, the buffalo is clearly a symbol of power. Attached to the poetry of war we find the theme of *ĕrumaimaṟam*, Buffalo's Valor, exemplified by the hero who takes a bold stand in battle against a flood of enemies and weapons that threatens to overwhelm him.[51] The same sense of the buffalo's power underlies the sacred status of the buffalo in Toda myth and ritual,[52] and it is hard to escape the feeling that the Todas have preserved in this, as in other instances, an archaic feature of south Indian culture. As the very epitome of power, the buffalo thus fits admirably into a myth describing the transfer of power from the male to the goddess.

The Tamil myths of Mahiṣāsura and the related village rituals may thus retain the ancient image of the buffalo, which Brahminism has demoted in favor of the present focus on the cow and the bull. The male god in the villages of south India is still often a Buffalo King (Potu Rāja in the Telugu areas and parts of Tamiḻnāṭu). Sometimes he is the husband of the goddess.[53] In the sacrificial rituals a buffalo is married to the goddess, and after the sacrifice the wedding ceremony is repeated with a new buffalo, lest she be left a widow.[54] The sacrifice of the consort of the goddess then has to be explained by a myth:

> A Paṟaiyaṉ passed himself off as a Brahmin in a foreign village and was given the daughter of a blind *karṇam* (accountant) as his wife. The Brahmin wife discovered by chance that her husband was an outcaste, so she burned herself alive by setting fire to her house. After her death she appeared as a goddess to the villagers and instructed them to behead her husband, put one of his legs in his mouth, the fat of his stomach on his head, and a lighted lamp on top. After being sacrificed in this way, the husband was reborn as a buffalo, and therefore a buffalo is sacrificed to the village goddess at ceremonies in which the descendants of the couple play a part.[55]

Unlike the purāṇic accounts, this myth attaches sin not to the goddess—who burns herself to death, just as Satī enters the fire of her father's sacrifice—but to her husband-victim, whose murder is thereby rationalized. Note again the association of Brahmins and outcastes, the two groups that specialize—from different perspectives!—in the manipulation of sacred power;[56] both Brahmins and Paṟaiyaṉs are here linked to the buffalo sacrifice. The blindness which causes Devī's descent to earth in the first place in the Tamil Mahiṣa myths is here ascribed not to her husband but to her father.

This plot motif is the final element of the Mahiṣa myths that calls for comment in this context. It is by no means limited to these myths: in fact, the blinding of the deity is seemingly the most frequently encountered cause for Devī's descent to earth in Tamil texts.[57] There are several variations on this theme: Devī steals up behind Śiva and covers his eyes with her hands in sport (sometimes in retaliation for a similar prank played on her by her husband);[58] Devī hides the god's eyes to prevent him from seeing the naked *śaktis*[59] or Tilottamā;[60] she blinds him in order to test the truth of his claim to support the world by the light of his eyes;[61] on her wedding night, Pārvatī is ashamed and puts her hands over Śiva's eyes, but to her chagrin his third eye gazes at her.[62] The blinded god gives birth to the blind demon Andhaka, who is burned by Śiva's third eye because of his lust for Pārvatī; reduced to a skeleton, Andhaka receives the form of Śiva and joins his hosts.[63] Andhaka is punished for an excess of lust, while his other form, Bhṛngin, suffers the same fate for the opposite reason: Bhṛngin refused to worship Devī, so she withered his body, but Śiva gave him a third leg to support his weight.[64] The third leg, like Śiva's third eye (which Andhaka also comes to possess), has obvious erotic associations, and the Bhṛngin story is told to explain the origin of the androgyne.[65]

In the Andhaka myth, blindness is a metaphor for lust,[66] but it more often has an antierotic force in the myths. Given the phallic symbolism of eyes in Śaivism—especially of the third eye, which, as we shall see, is linked with the south Indian motif of the third breast—blindness may be regarded as substituting for castration in some of these stories.[67] The myth of Cyavana and Sukanyā lends support to this suggestion: Cyavana was performing *tapas* in an anthill; Sukanyā, the daughter of King Śaryāti, saw his eyes glowing from within the anthill and pierced them with a thorn. Cyavana cursed the soldiers of Śaryāti to be unable to urinate or defecate, and the king gave him Sukanyā as his wife; the Aśvins tried to make her leave her old, blind husband for one of them, but when

V. Ardhanārīśvara: a three-headed androgyne.

she stood fast by her husband they took him into the water, and he emerged young, his sight and his virility simultaneously restored.[68] Elsewhere blindness is linked with death: devotees of Bhagavatī walk to her temple in Kallil with their eyes shut tight, for they die if they see anything before they see the goddess.[69] More common is the reverse: all who beheld the carving of the goddess in the Kŏlli hills were certain to die.[70] It is death to see the Seven Maidens in their procession with horses and torches.[71] Another myth from Assam applies this motif to the head-sacrifice, which we have seen to be a characteristic feature of Devī myths:[72]

> At the time of the evening prayer, the goddess danced within the closed doors of her temple. A king desired to see her dance and asked the chief priest to help him. The priest made a hole in the wall, and the king peeped through. His eyes caught the eyes of the goddess, and she became furious and tore off the head of the priest. Ever since the king and his descendants never look even at the hill of the goddess; if they must pass by it, they cover themselves with umbrellas.[73]

The penalty is transferred from the king to the priest, but it retains its force as a threat to the king's offspring. The punishment of death is incurred by the king's attempt to *overcome* a form of blindness—his inability to see the goddess—and to achieve this he must destroy the wholeness of the goddess's protective enclosure.

Why does seeing the goddess entail punishment? The motif may be linked to the prohibition on witnessing the sexual act, a theme of considerable importance in Hindu mythology.[74] Thus Iḷa (Sudyumna) is transformed from a man into a woman—that is, castrated—for stepping into a grove in which Śiva had been making love to Pārvatī; the real cause of this transformation is put back in time and transferred to a group of sages: Sanaka and other sages came upon Śiva and Pārvatī while they were making love in that grove; Pārvatī was ashamed and hastily covered her nakedness, and Śiva promised that from then on any man who entered the grove would become a woman.[75] There are many variations on this theme. Śiva and Pārvatī die of shame when the gods and sages surprise them in the act of intercourse.[76] Arjuna leaves for pilgrimage when he violates the pact of the Pāṇḍava brothers and sees Yudhiṣṭhira with Draupadī.[77] Closely allied to the Iḷa myth just mentioned is the myth of Iḷa's son Purūravas, who is deserted by Urvaśī when she sees his nakedness.[78] In folk variants, the hero steals the clothes of Indra's daughter; she calls him to look back, and when he turns to see the naked goddess he is paralyzed.[79] Kubera is blinded in his left eye when he sees the goddess together with Śiva and asks who she is (or, in other versions, wonders what she has done to merit being united with the god).[80] The same pattern obtains in a late temple legend from Andhra:

> The treasurer of King Kṛṣṇadevarāya used the king's funds to construct a temple at Lepākṣi. While he was supervising the completion of the *kalyāṇamaṇḍapa* (where the divine marriage is performed), the king returned and found his treasury empty. The king ordered that the treasurer be blinded in punishment, and, being a loyal servant, the man dashed out his eyes on the spot. The stains from his eyes are still evident on the wall near the unfinished *kalyāṇamaṇḍapa*; hence the village is known as Lepākṣi ("eye of the staining").[81]

The appropriation of a king's treasures by a devotee of the god who uses them for a pious purpose is a common motif.[82] Yet it is hardly by chance that the treasurer is blinded while constructing the *kalyāṇamaṇḍapa*, the site of the wedding of the god and his consort. The union of the divine couple is not to be witnessed even by their devotees.[83]

But what of those instances where the goddess is alone? Here the forbidden vision itself may be tantamount to union. Let us take a popular example that elucidates this motif. While a sculptor was polishing an image of a queen of Tirumalai Nāyakkar in the Putumaṇṭapam at Maturai, a splinter of stone fell from the thigh of the image. Nīlakaṇṭhadīkṣitar, the minister of the king, suggested that the loss of the splinter was due to divine intervention aimed at reproducing a defect actually found on the queen's body; the king angrily ordered his minister blinded for this remark.[84] The image has become more than a symbol; it appears to be invested with life, and in this way to be wholly identified with the person or deity it represents.[85] To see the image is thus to behold the naked queen; and to behold the queen is to defile her. For the same reason it is forbidden to see the Seven Maidens in their nocturnal procession—the human vision will destroy their virginity, and union with the virgin goddess means death. The myth from Assam may be understood in the light of this interpretation: here the seductive goddess dances alone, without a consort, within the confines of her shrine; and, although our version of the myth fails to state this plainly, we may deduce that here, as at Kaṉṉiyākumari, the source of the goddess's attraction and power is her virginity, which must not be shattered even by sight. One way to safeguard her virginity and at the same time to circumscribe the terrible energy she derives from it is to lock her in an invulnerable enclosure. The bolted doors of the sanctuary may themselves symbolize virginity, as in the earliest Tamil love poetry, where the lover must break down the locked door of his beloved.[86] For it is the virgin goddess who is the true siren, seductive, powerful, and dangerous. The god who desires her must face the threat of death at her hands; in the end, either he dies—as in the myth of Mahiṣa and in several of the folk variants from other shrines—or he tames his fearful bride.[87]

The choice of the motif of blinding as the introduction to the Mahiṣa myth now seems more intelligible. There is no reason to believe its use here was an accident; in effect, the Tamil versions have prefixed a weakened multiform of the myth to a rendering characterized by the survival of archaic elements. Śiva's blindness adumbrates Mahiṣa's violent death. Blindness suggests the castration or immolation consequent upon union with the dark virgin. It remains for us now to outline the permutations of the components of the myth as isolated in our analysis. In particular, we will be concerned with the theme of the locked sanctuary of the goddess, which the folk tradition knows as the sealed shrine of the dangerous Kālī. This image provides an important clue to understanding the myths of the main goddess of Maturai, Mīnākṣī, who, as we shall see, may be directly linked with the murderess of Mahiṣa from Tiruvaṇṇāmalai.

## 5. The Sealed Shrine: Mīnākṣī of Maturai

The motif of the locked shrine brings us back to the basic idea of limits imposed on a concentration of power. We have seen this idea expressed in the structure of the south Indian temple: at the center of the temple lies a focus of violent power, which may be associated with the sacrifice at which death is traded for life; this power is circumscribed by the temple walls and located within a ritually ordered universe. The inner sanctum—the *garbhagṛha*, the "womb" where the deity is conceived anew—is not alone as a symbol of bounded power in the shrine; the tree with its roots sunk in the nether world, and the temple tank, which draws its water from the realm of primordial chaos, are part of the same pattern of chaos subdued by order. The strict limits applied to the sacred force detach the shrine from the surrounding, less ordered sphere, which is saturated with impurity and evil—in contrast with the pure, harmonious realm within the temple walls. Death exists on the outside, but has no power within the shrine. The idea of limitation is joined to the guiding principle of separation in this scheme; the sacred power is controlled, and in this way made auspicious and accessible to the pilgrim, while its separation from the outside world creates a zone of purity. The essential ambivalence of the shrine emerges clearly at this point: the shrine is power preserved intact and made useful through limitation; and the shrine is also the point at which power is finally deprived of its link with pollution, with evil, with death and rebirth, and at which an other-worldly, absolute ideal of purity is achieved.[1] The south Indian temple is thus both an intensified but bounded expression of the violent power manifest in the world as a whole, and a symbol of total independence and detachment, of eternity as opposed to degenerative time; again we are reminded of Turner's description of the pilgrimage site as a place and moment both "in and out of time."[2] If this ambivalence is never completely resolved in favor of one of the two poles—just as the tension between the goals of purity and power reflects a fundamental problem of the Hindu tradition generally[3]—it nevertheless behooves us to recall the overwhelmingly practical, this-worldly orientation of the south Indian pilgrims. For them, the sacred power at the heart of the shrine is the primary goal. The point which I wish to stress here is that the temple wall that delimits the boundaries of the sacred site serves both facets of the temple's nature: the wall is a symbol of limitation and control, and it is also the means of enforcing the separation that leads to purity.[4]

This fundamental importance of the enclosing wall was seen earlier in the myths of ramparts and the flood. It appears in an equally striking manner in the motif of the locked or sealed shrine. The locked doors of the shrine symbolize the integrity of the enclosure and the complete detachment of the bounded microcosm inside. There are many stories of locked temples, in addition to those associated with the goddess. For example, the poet-saint Appar is said to have opened the bolted doors of the shrine at Vetāraṇiyam (Tirumaṟaikkāṭu, "Forest of the Vedas") by singing a Tamil hymn to Śiva.[5] In this story the opening of the shrine suggests an opening up of divine knowledge; the Vedas are assimilated to the locked doors,[6] and the *bhakti* hymn thus makes the hitherto remote and esoteric wisdom the subject of an immediate revelation.[7] This result is in line with the *bhakti* poets' demand for an immediate, unqualified salvation in this life;[8] hence the reversal of the classical view of knowledge as something hidden away, like the deity hidden in the dark center of the shrine. At Vetāraṇiyam the isolation of the sacred site is impaired; but following Appar's success in opening the doors, Tiruñāṉacampantar is said to have made the doors close again by singing another hymn. Ever since then, the doors of the shrine there have opened and closed like those of other temples.[9] Most south Indian temples are locked up at certain times during the day (usually mid-day, and again at night);[10] anyone who has traveled to pilgrimage sites in this area knows the experience of arriving at a locked shrine and waiting for the local priests to arrive to open it. Village shrines are sometimes left locked for long periods because of rivalries between opposing factions, or in connection with legal disputes and the search for justice;[11] we shall see a famous example of this theme in a moment.

The motif of the sealed shrine is, however, most prominent in the mythology of the goddess. The locked doors of Devī's shrine represent her virginity, that is, the state in which her sacred power is intact and therefore strongest. The following discussion will deal primarily with two major themes connected to this motif—the terrible consequences of breaking into the locked sanctuary of the goddess; and (a theme that will be developed further in our next section) the possibility of excluding the violent goddess from her own shrine.

The image of the locked shrine may be traced back in Tamil to the classical epic, the *Cilappatikāram*: a Brahmin was unjustly thrown into prison in the Pāṇṭiya land, so the goddess Aiyai would not open the doors of her temple. The king investigated the matter and made amends, and the heavy doors of the shrine opened with a noise heard throughout the streets of ancient Kūṭal (Maturai).[12] As we shall see, the locked shrine is particularly important in the Maturai tradition. The closing of a shrine is also associated with a miscarriage of justice in the story of one of the most violent of all Tamil goddesses:

> A Brahmin squandered his wealth on a dancing girl in Kāñci, neglecting his wife. When he ran out of funds, he coveted the ornaments belonging to his wife; he coaxed her to come with him from her parents' home to Kāñci, and on the way he killed

her and the child in her womb by pushing her into a well. On his way to hide the jewels he had taken from her, a serpent bit him and he died.

The Brahmin was reborn as a merchant with a magic sword to protect him from all evil. Pārvatī took the form of Nīli, a demoness roaming the forest of Ālaṅkāṭu, in order to take revenge for the murder of his wife. Although advised never to go north, the merchant went to Paḻaiyaṉūr to buy jewelry, leaving his wife in the forest when she grew tired on the way. Nīli made his wife reveal the name of her husband and, armed with this information, appeared before a court of seventy Veḷāḷas in Paḻaiyaṉūr to lay claim to the man as her husband. She convinced them of her identity by uttering his name, but the merchant knew her for a demoness determined to take his life. "No wife of mine would thus utter my name," he cried in despair to the Veḷāḷas; and, since the sun was setting and no decision had yet been reached, they locked the couple up in the temple of Kālī for the night, having first made the merchant relinquish his magic sword to Nīli, and having signed a document giving their own lives as surety for his.

Nīli killed the merchant and escaped by way of the *gopura*. When the Veḷāḷas came to the temple in the morning, they were unable to open the door. They prayed to Kālī; suddenly the door opened, and inside they found the disembowelled body of the merchant. Nīli took the form of an old woman claiming to be the merchant's mother; the Veḷāḷas were forced to produce the document they had signed, and, true to their word, all seventy entered the fire.[13]

Nīli (< *nīla*, "dark blue"), a dark goddess like Paiññīli of the Mahiṣāsura myth, is locked in her temple by the community rather than locking herself in, although the Veḷāḷas are unable to open the door in the morning without the aid of the goddess (Kālī / Nīli). The stimulus is an act of injustice, and the closing of the doors brings revenge, at the distance of a generation from the crime. The revenge, in fact, leads to a still more gruesome sacrifice when the goddess, apparently unsatisfied with her primary victim, forces the seventy truthful Veḷāḷas into the fire. There is a link with the appearance of this theme—the locked shrine and the miscarriage of justice—in the *Cilappatikāram*, for mention there of the closing of the temple of Aiyai is immediately followed by the story of Nīli's curse: Nīli, the wife of a man unjustly killed in the presence of the king of Kaliṅga, cursed the perpetrator of the deed to suffer the same fate in a future birth.[14] Hence, according to this passage, the events narrated in the Tamil epic:

> Kovalaṉ was married to the beautiful Kaṇṇaki, but he spent all his wealth on the dancing-girl Mātavi. After a quarrel with Mātavi, Kovalaṉ returned penniless to his wife. Together they set out for Maturai, where Kovalaṉ hoped to sell Kaṇṇaki's anklet (*cilampu*). A goldsmith who had stolen a similar anklet belonging to the Pāṇṭiya queen accused Kovalaṉ of the theft; the Pāṇṭiya king believed his false testimony and ordered Kovalaṉ's execution. Kaṇṇaki, learning of his death, came to the court of the king and proved his innocence. The king died of grief at the injustice he had committed. Then the furious Kaṇṇaki tore off her left breast and hurled it at the ancient city of Maturai, and the city was destroyed by fire.[15]

Kovalaṉ is identified by the epic with the murderer of Caṅkamaṉ, the husband of Nīli, by whose curse he was forced to undergo the same punishment. There are other close similarities between the story of the epic and the myth of Paḻaiyaṉūr Nīli: both share the motif of a husband's impoverishment by a prostitute; in both the husband dies as he is disposing of his wife's jewelry, and false accusations are believed with fatal consequences.[16] There is also a Jain story about yet another Nīli, again in a south Indian source: here Nīli is a chaste wife falsely accused by her (Buddhist) husband; she proves her chastity with the help of a friendly deity, who closes the gates of the city and informs the king in a dream that only a chaste woman will be able to cause them to open; Nīli, alone among the women of the city, is able to pass through the gates.[17] The locking of the temple of the goddess is replaced in the Jain story by the sealing of the city gates.

Nīli, or Nīlakeci, was the ancient goddess of Paḻaiyaṉūr near Tiruvālaṅkāṭu.[18] Her name was apparently so closely linked with violence that the Jain author of the tenth-century work *Nīlakeci* chose her to represent an extreme example of successful conversion: when a Jain sage persuaded people to stop offering blood sacrifices to Kālī, that goddess called upon Nīlakeci of the south to act against him—but Nīlakeci was herself converted to nonviolence![19] The Jain polemical poet clearly wanted to present as striking a success story as possible. For our purposes here it is important to note that it is as the *wife* of the protagonist that Nīli claims his life in the final form of the major myth from Paḻaiyaṉūr. The merchant dies at the hands of the goddess upon being forced to enter her shrine; once again the goddess is the aggressive bearer of the sword, which in this case she acquires from her victim. To enter Kālī's temple is to die. In other myths from this site, the conflict is between Nīli and Śiva, who overcomes the dangerous, destructive goddess in a dance contest.[20] The fierce goddess of Paḻaiyaṉūr must be tamed by her husband.[21] In a hagiographic variant of this myth, the ancient demoness (*pey*) of this region is identified with Kāraikkālammaiyār who, as a withered, skeletal devotee of Śiva, is the eternal witness to his dance.[22] The woman devotee, or the tame wife, represent the second stage adopted by the Tamil myths, the stage in which the god's participation in violence is ruled out and the divine marriage takes a new, harmonious form. Entering the sanctuary—that is, union with the dark virgin—means castration or death for the male; if this result is to be avoided, the violent goddess must be brought under control.

The closing of Kālī's shrine is, of course, in itself a symbol of control and limitation. We have here a basic type of myth, in which the dangerous goddess or woman is shut into a container. Thus the goddess Kuḷumāyiyammaṉ committed such atrocities that her worshipers put her in a box and dropped her in the Kāviri.[23] Śaṅkara is said to have thrown the goddess of Tiruvŏṟṟiyūr into a well.[24] Durgā was set adrift on the river in an iron box that miraculously did not sink.[25] A Brahmin caused a Paṟaiya girl he was fated to marry to be shut in a box and floated down the river after having a nail driven into her head.[26] Alli, the Amazon queen of Maturai, was caught in a tiger's cage by Sahadeva during her war against the Pāṇḍavas; thus trapped, she was forced to become Arjuna's bride.[27] According to a Telugu folk version of the *Rāmāyaṇa*, Sītā was born in a lotus pond in Laṅkā and discovered by Rāvaṇa; the astrologers predicted that the city would be destroyed if Sītā remained there, so the child goddess was locked in a box and pushed into the sea.[28] A parallel use of the motif, this time with reference to male deities, occurs in the *Mayilirāvaṇaṉkatai*: here the demon Mayilirāvaṇaṉ locks up Rāma and Lakṣmaṇa in a box and carries them off to Pātālalaṅkā.[29] There is also the Tortoise Prince of Tamil folklore, who is hidden by his mother in a box;[30] and the sage Saptávadhri, whose enemies placed him in a box at night to keep him from his wife, and who was rescued by the Aśvins and united with his wife until, at dawn, he chose to return to the box.[31] Arjuna, a representative of the serpent-deity of Maturai, is brought by Kṛṣṇa in a box to the court of Alli.[32]

In all these myths, the box motif expresses an underlying concept of control. Power, especially the power located in the goddess or woman, is contained within strict, tangible limits, just as the sacred forces residing in the shrine are bounded by the walls. In the case of Alli, the queen of Maturai, incarceration in a tiger's cage makes her into an acceptable, passive bride[33]—here the idea of control is obvious. It may be significant that it is Sahadeva who traps Alli in the cage, for Sahadeva is, in the Sanskrit epic, a symbol of the Hindu home and family;[34] the confined queen may be implicitly compared to the chaste wife in her domestic, carefully limited state. As Brenda Beck and George Hart have noticed, Tamil sources often homologize woman to culture, while man is homologized to nature;[35] a woman, that is, must be removed from her natural state, in which she is dangerous, and bound to her domestic, cultured roles. The box or cage are adequate symbols of the control so desperately sought. But the goddess in the box is also a symbol of virginity and of violence preserved intact. Disaster befalls the man who dares to open the box.

Shutting the goddess in a container is thus an attempt to solve the problem of her dangerous energy. On the one hand, the goddess in the box is a classic image of one of the predominant concerns of Tamil culture, indeed of Hindu culture generally—the channeling and control of potentially dangerous forces. On the other hand, the limitation of power does not eradicate its basic nature, and the classical Hindu tradition proclaims the ideal of transcending power altogether in order to rid oneself of the contamination inevitably consequent upon the use of power. Insofar as the sacred site becomes a concrete symbol of the desired state of total purity and transcendence, its relationship with the goddess, the embodiment of power, must be transformed. Some Tamil myths therefore attempt to remove the goddess from her own home. Kālī's exile—not, this time, from heaven, but from her native, terrestrial zone of power—sometimes accompanies Śiva's marriage to the golden, passive Gaurī. We will return to this theme. Here we may observe the motif of Kālī's exclusion from her own shrine in a folktale from Ramnad District, which makes use of the marriage motifs studied earlier, but which reverses the image of the sealed shrine:

> The king of Tevai had a son named Subuddhi, and his minister had a son named Durbuddhi. The two boys were close friends, although the prince believed that "Virtue alone conquers," while the minister's son's motto was "Evil alone conquers." While they were still boys, Durbuddhi exacted a promise from his friend that if he ever married, Durbuddhi would have the right to spend a night with his wife. One day the lads followed a deer deep into the forest. There, by the side of a tank, Durbuddhi tore out his friend's eyes, filled the sockets with sand, and ran away.
>
> Subuddhi crawled to the far side of the tank, where he discovered by touch the entrance to a temple of Kālī. He entered the shrine and locked the door behind him. When Kālī returned to find herself locked out of her own temple, she threatened to kill the usurper. Subuddhi refused to allow her entrance until she restored his sight; having no choice, she finally agreed.
>
> After some months Kālī sent the prince to the kingdom of the Kāviri, whose princess she had stricken with smallpox and blinded because the king had lapsed in his devotion to the goddess. With Kālī's aid Subuddhi cured the princess and married her. Years later Durbuddhi happened to come to the Kāviri kingdom; the prince forgave him and made him his minister, but Durbuddhi once again plotted against him, slandering him to the old king. The king believed Durbuddhi and ordered the execution of his son-in-law and his daughter. Learning of this, Durbuddhi hastened to claim his right to spend a night with his friend's wife, before the opportunity passed forever; but the princess substituted her foster sister for herself, and by mistake the king's executioners killed Durbuddhi and the surrogate bride.[36]

Kālī is locked out of, rather than into, her shrine, but the opening of the doors still leads to the restoration of vision and the consummation of a marriage, as we would expect from our analysis of the box motif. Only the hero's direct encounter with violence is altered: if breaking into the shrine is equivalent to the forbidden vision of the virgin, and hence to a fatal union, here it is not the prince but his evil alter ego who experiences the *Liebestod*. Durbuddhi dies through satisfying his lust. Note the doubling of the blinding/restoration sequence, which applies to both Subuddhi and his bride. Smallpox and blindness are both associated with an excess of heat or violent power emanating from the dark goddess;[37] they are reversed here through the exclusion of Kālī from her shrine, that is, by establishing new limits for the exercise of her power. This new demarcation does not persist in the folktale—Kālī is allowed back into her shrine in exchange for her help; but in several myths she is relegated permanently to the periphery.[38] Kālī's power must be regulated and bound to its proper place. In another tale, a prince wins the Pomegranate Maiden by the same device used by Subuddhi: he enters Kālī's shrine by night, while the goddess is out wandering in the forests, and locks the door; when she returns at sunrise, she has to promise to help him before he will let her in.[39] The dark, virgin goddess is forced to provide her devotee with a bride.

In one crucial point, the folktale deviates from the myth—by failing to identify the dark goddess herself as the bride. This suggests an important distinction with reference to the structure of the tradition. The folktale abstracts elements of myth and uses them for its own purposes; the purāṇas, in giving local myths their final, "Sanskritized" forms, distort ancient images and blunt their force. Where, then, do the archaic strands of myth survive? Sometimes the hints retained in the purāṇic versions can be elucidated with the help of the remarkably conservative substratum of popular variants, the living folk versions of the myths. Let us look, for example, at one such version of the goddess myth from Maturai:

> Once the wicked, arrogant Pāṇṭiya king closed the temple of Mīṉāṭciyammaṉ, the local goddess. Enraged, the goddess took the form of a child wearing a bracelet exactly like one that belonged to the queen. The king found the child in the palace and wished to adopt her, but the astrologers warned that evil would result, so she was put in a basket and cast into the river. She was fished out by a merchant, who named her Kaṇṇaki and brought her up. Śiva became incarnate as a merchant from Kāvirippūmpaṭṭiṉam; hearing of the girl's mysterious origin, he married her. He became poor and, ignoring his wife's pleas, went to Maturai to sell her bracelet; some days before this, the queen had lost her bracelet, and the merchant was therefore accused of stealing it, brought before the king and executed. Kaṇṇaki learned of his fate and came to Maturai to take re-

> venge; assuming the form of Durgā, she killed the king. "Since then she has been worshipped by the people. The slaughter of the Pandian created in her a desire for bloodshed, and she is now a deity whom it is thought prudent to propitiate."[40]

The locked enclosure of the goddess appears twice, first as the closed temple of Mīnākṣī, then as the basket in which the infant is sent down the river; other versions substitute a golden box for the basket, possibly through the influence of the important motif of the golden seed in a pot.[41] The locking of the shrine has become a prelude to a truncated version of the *Cilappatikāram* story, and Mīnākṣī, the goddess of Maturai, is equated with the epic heroine Kaṇṇaki, who takes the form of Durgā.[42] The first victim of Mīnākṣī/Kaṇṇaki's plan of revenge is none other than Śiva, who has become Kaṇṇaki's earthly husband (Kovalaṉ). So, indirectly, the goddess kills her consort—but let us go a step at a time. The slaying of Kovalaṉ / Śiva is doubled in other folk versions: in addition to his execution for allegedly stealing the anklet (bracelet), there is a similar episode that serves to introduce the story:

> An oil merchant vowed to light a lamp for Kālī with a pot of oil if he managed to sell nine hundred ninety-nine pots of oil. He succeeded in selling the required number, but he discovered the Kālī temple locked by the king because his wife had been childless for twelve years. The doors were not to be opened, on pain of death. Because of his vow, the merchant went in anyway to light the lamp; consequently, both he and his wife were beheaded before the goddess by royal command. The king's wife then became pregnant; Kālī herself placed the seed in her womb. The oil merchant was reborn as Kovalaṉ, and his wife was born as Mātavi.[43]

Once again death (by beheading!) is the penalty for opening the shrine of the goddess and for lighting the lamp, that is, for overcoming blindness / darkness. The slain oil merchant is identified with Kovalaṉ, the next victim, whom these versions also associate with Śiva.[44] This episode, built around the pattern of the intrusion into the inviolable sanctuary, thus strengthens our suspicions that an older level of myth is involved. But this is not all. The king locks the goddess out for a reason other than simple pride or jealousy (which explains his action in Whitehead's account): Kālī has refused him offspring from his wife.[45] Although the king's act is ostensibly hostile to the goddess, in effect he overcomes the curse of barrenness by sacrificing the oil merchant to Kālī. There is a precedent for his action in the *uraipĕṟukaṭṭurai*, which was prefixed to the *Cilappatikāram* by an anonymous editor. There, sacrifice to Kaṇṇaki releases not seed but rain: the Pāṇṭiya kingdom was stricken by drought, famine, fever, and plague; King Vĕṟṟiveṟ-cĕḻiyaṉ pacified (*cānti cĕyya*) the Lady (*naṅkai*, that is, Kaṇṇaki) with the sacrifice of a thousand goldsmiths, and rain came.[46]

The Pāṇṭiya king is clearly a pivotal figure in the folk versions of the Maturai myth; it is by his orders that the oil merchant and Kovalaṉ are killed, while he himself remains the final and principal victim of the goddess's revenge. It is in this light that we must note the myth of Mīnākṣī's marriage as recorded in the "official" purāṇic accounts from Maturai:

> The king of Maturai had no children. He performed ninety-nine horse-sacrifices, and Indra, alarmed lest he be driven from heaven, advised the king to perform a sacrifice to obtain a son. The sacrifice was carefully executed according to the rules, but to the amazement of all a girl with three breasts appeared instead of the longed-for son. "What have I done wrong?" cried the king; "all my enemies will laugh when they hear of the third breast on this girl." A voice from heaven reassured him: "Perform all the ceremonies as if she were a son. Her breast will disappear when she finds her husband."
>
> The girl was brought up as if she were a boy and, when her father died, she ascended the throne, to the delight of the fierce goddess whose spear seeks the flesh of enemies. She set out to conquer the world. Having overcome several armies, she came with her troops to Kailāsa. The army of Śiva fought with her and began to lose. Śiva himself took the field of battle. As soon as she caught sight of him, her third breast disappeared, and, overcome with modesty, innocence, and shyness, she began to scrape the ground shyly with her toe. One of the attendants who remembered the voice from heaven that had spoken at her birth approached her and said, "Lady, this man is your bridegroom." The princess took Śiva to Maturai and married him there, and the god reigned as Cuntarapāṇṭiyaṉ.[47]

The goddess is emphatically said to have preceded the god in Maturai; indeed, she attracts him to the site, which is her home and kingdom. Here, as in the traditions of other Tamil shrines, the chthonic, ancient character of the goddess is proclaimed. It is significant that Mīnākṣī, the three-breasted goddess, discovers her husband in battle. By marriage she is transformed from a violent multiform of Kŏṟṟavai, the goddess of war, into a gentle wife, just as Nīli of Tiruvālaṅkāṭu is tamed by the dance.[48] And it is *as the Pāṇṭiya king* that Śiva is the husband of the goddess of Maturai.

Here, then, is the missing link with the folk versions of the myth, which have conflated Śiva's role as Pāṇṭiyaṉ with his identification with Kovalaṉ, the slain protagonist of the epic. Śiva as Pāṇṭiyaṉ dies for locking the sanctuary, while as oil merchant he dies for entering it. Again the male is split and his role distributed, as in the buffalo myth from Tiruvaṇṇāmalai, but here all suffer the same fate. Still we may ask why the folk variants never explicitly identify the king with Śiva, since, after all, the Pāṇṭiyaṉ remains the direct object of Kālī's wrath. Two partial answers may be suggested. In the first place, the purāṇic reworking of the myth may itself have affected the folk versions. The purāṇic myths of Mīnākṣī and Śiva-Cuntarapāṇṭiyaṉ, which supply Śiva's role as king of Maturai, always end with the defeat of the goddess by her divine spouse. In other words, the purāṇic accounts adopt the theme of "taming" the violent bride. There is little doubt that the folk versions prefer the older idea of slaying the god, as in the Mahiṣa cycle; but, in light of the standard presentation of the myth in the Maturai purāṇas, the identity of Śiva and the slain king must remain implicit. In addition, the popular accounts have drawn from the recorded tradition that Mīnākṣī was the anomalous daughter of the Pāṇṭiya king. However we may interpret the insertion of a local goddess into the royal lineage of Maturai, the result in the folk tradition is that Mīnākṣī murders her father, not her husband.[49]

One offshoot of the Mīnākṣī myth in fact describes the anomalous princess as threatening *both* father and husband:

> In Madhupura on the northern trade route, there was born to a king a daughter with three breasts. The Brahmins warned the king never to look at the child, lest he die an early death. The king avoided the sight of his daughter, and he offered one hundred thousand gold coins to anyone who would marry her and take her out of the country. A blind man and his friend, a hunchback, decided to take up the offer; the king married his daughter to the blind man on the river bank and sent the couple together with the hunchback down the river in a boat.

> The three set up house together in a foreign land, and after some time the princess began to deceive her husband with the hunchback. She asked her lover to find a means of poisoning her husband. One day the hunchback brought a dead black snake to the princess to cook and feed to the blind man. She cut it up, put it in a pot to cook, and asked her husband to stir it, telling him it was his favorite fish dish. As he was stirring it, the poisonous vapor caused the film over his eyes to peel away, and he regained his vision. Seeing a snake cooking in the pot, he became suspicious and hid his recovery from his wife. Soon the hunchback came and embraced the princess. At this, the husband took hold of the hunchback and threw him at the princess. From the force of the collision, the hunchback's body became straight, and the lady's third breast was forced in.[50]

The blindness of the husband is duplicated by the self-imposed blindness of the father, who knows death will follow a vision of the three-breasted princess. The bride coolly premeditates the murder of her husband, but her poison is transformed into medicine, and her restored husband restores his murderous wife to normalcy by an act of violence. Similarly, in the Mīnākṣī myth the goddess is subdued and her third breast made to vanish in the course of a war. The container that carries the dangerous goddess down the river in several of the folk versions has here become a ship (*yānapātra*) that takes the princess to exile with her sightless husband. Although the text places the story in the north (*uttarāpathe*), there can be little doubt that we have here a development of the Mīnākṣī myth from Maturai. The softened dental of the Tamil name is preserved in the name Madhupura, and we should recall the folk etymology that explains the name "Maturai" as deriving from *madhurā*, "sweet" —because serpent's poison was converted there to nectar, as it is, in a sense, in the *Pañcatantra* story.[51]

The correspondence of the *Pañcatantra* story with the myth of Mīnākṣī was first noticed by Theodore Benfey, who also suggested that the appearance of the hunchback in the story may be connected with the hunchbacked Kūṉpāṇṭiyaṉ known from another part of the *Tiruviḷai*.[52] Benfey also mentioned as belonging in this series a well-known Ceylonese story, in which instead of a princess with two lovers we find a hero with two wives. This is the story of the "first king" Vijaya[53] who, upon arriving in Ceylon, unites with the fierce *yakṣiṇī* Kuveṇī (Pali Kuvaṇṇā); like Mīnākṣī, Kuveṇī has three breasts, one of which is destined to disappear when she first sees her husband. The sight of Vijaya makes the third breast vanish. But Vijaya seeks a wife better suited for a king; when he marries a princess from Maturai (!), the jealous Kuveṇī takes the form of a tiger with a crystal tongue, darts through seven doors into the nuptial chamber, and is about to pierce the hearts of the royal couple when one of the king's attendants cuts off her crystal tongue. The tongue is hidden under a lamp; when the king discovers it next morning, the tiger attacks again, and is slain.[54] The connections between this story and the Maturai traditions are striking. The three-breasted *yakṣiṇī* is a dangerous, *local* bride who eventually tries to kill her husband; the safe, acceptable wife is here imported from Maturai. The motifs of the locked nuptial chamber and the lamp that hides the tiger's crystal tongue are familiar from the Tamil myths; the tongue of crystal recalls Paiññīli's arrow, or the sword of Durgā at Tiruvāṭpokki—all weapons used by a violent, murderous wife against her lord. As we shall see, the crystal tongue may also be related to the dangerous *yakṣiṇī*'s original third breast.

The three-breasted goddess also appears in the myths of Nākapaṭṭam:

> Ādiśeṣa, king of the serpents, desired a child. He was advised by Vasiṣṭha to worship the *liṅga* to attain his wish; he worshiped Śiva at four shrines,[55] and the god granted his request. When a daughter was born to him from his wife, the serpent king was overjoyed, but his joy became a sea of sorrow when he saw that the child had three breasts. A voice from heaven spoke: "If the girl worships Karuntaṭaṅkaṇṇi ('the lady of the long dark eyes' = Nīlāyatākṣī at Nākapaṭṭiṉam), one breast will disappear when she sees the king who is to wed her."
>
> The child grew to maturity, and one day her father told her the tale of her birth, and sent her to worship the goddess at Kāroṇam (Nākapaṭṭiṉam). One day as she was walking beside a tank, the girl (*aṇaṅku*) saw King Cālīcukaṉ, who was born in the midst of the sea, enter the sacred site and worship the god. As soon as she saw him, one breast disappeared and she fell in love. Seeing this, her companions said in amazement, "She is like Taṭātakai (= Mīnākṣī). We knew nothing of this state; this is the fruit of worshiping the goddess."
>
> The king, too, was overcome by love. Observing that the girl's garlands did not fade and that she did not blink or sweat, he concluded that she was not of the earth (*taraimakaḷ allaḷ*). As he was thinking this, she disappeared. The king of the sea was

grief-stricken; at dawn he entered the shrine of Kāroṇam and stood before the god who is joined to Karuntaṭaṅkaṇṇi. The god spoke to him: "Grieve not. Go to Cavuntararācappĕrumāḷ (Saundaryarāja, Viṣṇu at Nākapaṭṭiṉam)." The king went and worshiped Viṣṇu, who appeared and told him of a passage to Nāgaloka not far from his shrine. Following his command, the king entered the passage and arrived in the nether world. Since the girl had told her father of the loss of her breast at the sight of the king, Cālīcukaṉ was greeted on arrival, quickly proclaimed bridegroom, and married to his beloved.

Ādiśeṣa handed over the kingdom to his son-in-law and left the nether world for the home of Śiva. He worshiped the god, and Śiva granted his request that the shrine be known by his name (Nākai, Nākapaṭṭiṉam < *nāga*).[56]

This myth, an obvious multiform of the purāṇic myth of Mīnākṣī's birth and marriage, lacks the violent encounter between bride and groom; instead, the hero must follow his bride to the nether world, the realm of death and the serpent. The serpent maiden is explicitly compared to Taṭātakai-Mīnākṣī; the god of beauty (Saundaryarāja) is here Viṣṇu rather than Śiva (Sundareśvara, Cuntarapāṇṭiyaṉ).[57] The worship of Viṣṇu-Saundaryarāja is basic to other versions of the myth: a princess with three breasts saw Nāgarāja performing *tapas* near the shrine of Saundaryarāja; as soon as she saw him, her third breast disappeared, and she asked him to marry her; Nāgarāja replied that he was engaged in worshiping the god of the shrine, so she joined him in worship. In these versions, the bridegroom rather than the bride is a serpent—like Ālavāy, the serpent-god of Maturai.[58] But why does the first, the Śaiva myth from Nākapaṭṭiṉam declare that the husband of the three-breasted maiden is born from the sea? One thinks at once of Varuṇa, the lord of the sea in the classical pantheon, and a figure closely tied to serpents and the nether world.[59] But we may have here another strand common to both Maturai and Nākapaṭṭiṉam. Many explanations have been offered for the name "Mīnākṣī" ("having the eyes of a fish"): the name is said to mean nothing more than "having beautiful eyes," since the eyes of a woman are often compared to a fish, even in the earliest Tamil poetry, in the sense of being shiny, quickly moving, and large.[60] There is also the convention of painting fish-shaped eyes.[61] Norman Brown suggested a metaphysical explanation of the epithet: neither fish nor gods blink (hence the term *animiṣa* can refer to either); but Devī's eyes are the support of the worlds—were she to blink, the universe would be plunged into darkness.[62] This is ingenious but late. A conventional philosophical exegesis is based on the belief that the fish hatches its eggs by a glance; in the same way, Mīnākṣī releases her devotees from the state of bondage (*pāśa*) by her sight.[63] Jouveau-Dubreuil offers a "pretty story told and known but to a few. . . . As the mother fish swims in the river with her little ones who follow behind crying in their distress, she is not able to do anything for them. She turns her head and looks at them and they are comforted."[64] Divine helplessness is not an end to mercy.

No doubt all these explanations are genuine in the sense of being meaningful to worshipers of Mīnākṣī today, or in the past; yet if we wish to seek the origin of the name, it would appear to be wrong to ignore the ancient complex of sea and fish symbols associated with the Pāṇṭiya kingdom. The carp (*kayal*) was the Pāṇṭiya emblem, and the Pāṇṭiya king is known as *mīṉavaṉ*, "he of the fish (symbol)." The economic life of the ancient Pāṇṭiya kingdom was permeated by the life of the sea—international trade, pearl-diving, fishing.[65] Mīnākṣī is still worshiped as a village goddess by fishermen castes, and a second marriage myth preserved in the *Tiruviḷai.* and relating the birth of Aṅkayaṟkaṇṇammaiyār ("the lady of the beautiful carp-eyes" = Mīnākṣī) in a village on the seashore still lives in a variant form among the Paravaṉ fishermen of the southeast coast of Tamiḻnāṭu.[66] Note, too, that the goddess is sometimes called not Mīnākṣī but Mīṉāmpikai, "Fish-Maiden." Sometimes even late works preserve a sense of her watery associations: Mīṉāmpikai is the sister of "Māyaṉ the fish" (*mīṉ āṉa māyaṉ*, Viṣṇu in his fish avatar); her worshipers, drowning in a sea of sorrow, plead, "When fierce Death (*kālaṉ*) casts his net, do not give me over to him, O golden Mīṉāmpikai."[67] The image of death as a fisherman is conventional; but in the *kāṉalvari* of the epic, it is the eyes of the beloved, the daughter of the fishermen, which are the net of death.[68]

Maturai and Nākapaṭṭiṉam thus share a common tradition; a major myth at both sites describes a princess with three breasts[69] who loses one breast at the sight of her husband. The motif of the lost breast is shared with the story of Kaṇṇaki, who destroys Maturai with her wrenched-off left breast; the single-breasted Bhagavatī of Kōṭuṅkoḷūr on the west coast is also identified with Kaṇṇaki.[70] The oldest examples of the motif, in fact, say nothing of a third breast: in *Puṟanāṉūṟu* 278, a mother threatens to cut off her breasts if her son has shown cowardice in battle. *Naṟṟiṇai* 216.9 refers to *tirumāvuṇṇi*, who cut off one breast; this is probably a reference to Kaṇṇaki—or to her ancient prototype—since similar terms (*ŏrumāmaṇi, tirumāmaṇi*, and *tirumāpattiṉi*) are attached to her in the *Cilappatikāram*, usually in connection with the casting-off of her breast.[71] And these names bring us back to our first myth of the Murderous Bride—for the phrase *tirumāmaṇi* ("the great jewel") appears in the first verse of Tiruñāṉacampantar's first *patikam* on Tiruvaṇṇāmalai, the home of the Tamil buffalo myth, in which the fierce goddess is joined to Śiva in the androgyne after killing the demon. This verse begins with a reference to the androgyne, but then seems to stray from the usual image: "This is the mountain of the great lord, the One who, joined with Umā whose breasts have not been sucked, became wholly woman; the mountain where the Great Jewel (of chastity—*tirumāmaṇi*) is resplendent . . ." (*uṇṇāmulaiy umaiyāḷŏṭum uṭaṉ ākiya ŏruvaṉ/ pĕṇṇākiya pĕrumāṉ malai tirumāmaṇi tikaḻa* . . .).[72] Uṇṇāmulaiyammai (Sanskrit Apītakucā), "the lady whose breasts have not been sucked," is the name of the goddess at Tiruvaṇṇāmalai, the female half of the androgyne.[73] The commentator struggles vainly to explain how the androgyne can become "wholly woman." It seems clear that the one-breasted goddess—*tirumāmaṇi*, the aggressive woman who casts her breast, the seat of her sacred power,[74] at her enemy (her husband?)—has been assimilated to the *ardhanārī* form of Śiva together with his wife.

Of course, the text of Tiruñāṉacampantar's poem could be corrupt, and the appearance there of *tirumāmaṇi* a coincidence. There would still appear to be ample reason to infer that the androgyne at Tiruvaṇṇāmalai is another example of "iconotrophy"—the misreading of ancient pictures[75]—or of the "Sanskritization" of a purely local motif. The murderous goddess has been neutralized through the myth of the androgyne. The image of the destructive, single-breasted goddess survives at Tiruvaṇṇāmalai in a more acceptable iconic form as the single-breasted androgyne; the major myth of this shrine, having already substituted Mahiṣāsura for the original divine victim of the goddess, provides the background for the new icon by describing the androgynous marriage of Śiva and Devī at this spot. The god is removed from the arena of death; the dark and threatening goddess hides in the left half of his body. A myth of violent confrontation culminating in the death of the god has been replaced by Devī's war against a demon (who, nevertheless, retains elements of his original identity), and by the local marriage of the god and his purified, submissive bride. The key to this evolution lies in the use of the androgyne to absorb the violent goddess with one breast.

But how did the myths of Maturai and Nākapaṭṭiṉam arrive at the idea of a *third* breast, which the goddess loses at the sight of her husband? Precisely, I would suggest, through the same process, and because of the same wish to suppress the stark image of the Murderous Bride. First, one must note the relation of the third breast to the third eye. Eyes and breasts are often associated in myths: a crow drew blood from the breast of Sītā and was half-blinded by Rāma in punishment.[76] Viṣṇu worshiped Śiva with a thousand lotuses each day; when one was missing, he offered one of his eyes instead, and was given the discus Sudarśana as a reward (a pun on the name Sudarśana, "having beautiful vision," may be intended);[77] the same story is told of Lakṣmī, who offers not an eye but her breast, which becomes the *bilva* (wood-apple tree, *Aegle marmelos*).[78] The nipple is called *mulaikkaṇ* ("breast-eye") in Tamil.[79] The Mīnākṣī myth may even represent a development of part of the Śiśupāla story: Śiśupāla was born with three *eyes* and four arms; a voice announced that the third eye and two of the arms would vanish when he beheld the man who was destined to slay him; when Kṛṣṇa took the child Śiśupāla on his lap, the extra eye and arms disappeared.[80] Mīnākṣī loses her violent nature when she loses her breast at the sight of her spouse, just as the village goddess is drained of menacing energy when deprived of her third eye by Śiva.[81] Note that it is *seeing* her husband that causes Mīnākṣī's breast to disappear (*kaṇṭav ĕllaiyil ŏru mulai maṟaintatu*).[82]

Both the third eye and the third breast, however, may be related to the phallus.[83] We have seen that breast milk and the seed of the phallus are equated in many origin myths, and the myths frequently associate the *liṅga* with the breast (of the goddess or the Kāmadhenu). The Mīnākṣī myth has been interpreted in this light: the loss of the breast is said to represent castration, that is, the transformation from a man into a woman.[84] The same motif leads to a reversal of sex in a story from the *Divyāvadāna*: Rūpāvatī cut off her breasts in order to feed a woman reduced by starvation to the point of eating her own child; Rūpāvatī's breasts were restored, and Indra came to test her; "if it is true," she declared, "that I abandoned my breasts for the sake of the child, not to attain sovereignty, heaven, or pleasure or to become Indra, then let my female nature disappear and let me become a man"—and at once she became Prince Rūpāvata! The prince is eventually reborn as a child who lets a bird pluck out his eyes.[85] Rūpāvatī loses two breasts and becomes a man; Mīnākṣī loses the anomalous third breast and becomes a woman.[86] But the Mīnākṣī myth is more complex: Mīnākṣī begins not as a man but as a male-female hybrid, as we may also learn from the popular ballads on Arjuna's marriage to the queen of Maturai. The Southern Recension of the *MBh* tells us that Arjuna married Citrāṅgadā, the daughter of the king of "Maṇalūru" in the south; there is no mention of a third breast, but the girl is regarded by her father as a son (*putro mameyam iti me bhāvanā*), and it is through her that the dynasty must be perpetuated.[87] In the folk ballads from Maturai, Citrāṅgadā has become Alli, the Amazon queen:

> Cokkecar (Śiva at Maturai) withheld offspring from the Pāṇṭiyas for twelve years. Nīṉmukaṉ, the son of a slave girl, was crowned king; the Pāṇṭiyas paid him six thousand pots of milk in tribute each year. They did *tapas* to overcome the curse of barrenness, and the goddess had mercy on them; she tore a piece of flesh from her shoulder and threw it on to the leaf of a water-lily (*alli*) in a tank and then called to the Pāṇṭiyas: "There is a son on the leaf of the water-lily; it is a male and a female." They found a child in the tank and took it home, crying "The Pāṇṭiyas have given birth." The child grew into a girl, whom they named Alli. When she was seven, she noticed the pots of milk collected for Nīṉmukaṉ; she spilled the milk and had snakes put in the pots, which were then delivered to the king. Nīṉmukaṉ came with an army against her, but she fought with him and killed him, thus assuming the crown of Nīli and the throne of Maturai.[88]

The slaying of Nīṉmukaṉ, whose name ("Blue-Face") and history suggest that like Kovalaṉ (< Gopāla) he may be an allotrope of Kṛṣṇa, is but the start of Alli's career. The rest of the story is devoted to Arjuna's wooing of the queen, who tries several times to kill her suitor—by having him rolled in burning sand, hanged from a tree, sacrificed to Kālī, and so on. In the end she is captured in a tiger's cage and subdued.[89] Alli is regarded as an incarnation of Mīnākṣī, and her story expands much that is compressed in the Mīnākṣī cycle. In particular, the ballads of Alli dwell on the theme of the goddess's war with her consort. The link with Nīli, which is stated explicitly and frequently throughout these works, is significant: although Alli is sometimes said to be light except for her black hair, she is a multiform of Kaṇṇaki / Kālī and of Mīnākṣī, who today is usually painted green. From birth Alli is an Amazon, physically female but masculine in instinct and action; her double nature is clearly stated by Pārvatī at her birth. Here, then, is direct confirmation of Mīnākṣī's bisexual nature as symbolized by her three breasts. In the case of Alli, even marriage fails to suppress the masculine component of the androgyne: in the sequel to the *Alliy-aracāṇimālai*, *after* her marriage to Arjuna, we again find her setting out to slay her spouse.[90]

Thus the purāṇic myths of Tiruvaṇṇāmalai and Maturai represent nearly identical solutions to the problem of the Murderous Bride. Only the sequence is reversed: in Tiruvaṇṇāmalai the goddess joins the androgyne after slaying Mahiṣa / Śiva; at Maturai she *begins* as the androgyne and is made a woman in the course of the battle. The terrifying, one-breasted goddess is in one shrine assimilated to the single-breasted *ardhanārī* icon; in the other she goes down in defeat, and her husband survives. Let us note in conclusion the irony of this resolution; for it must be emphasized that the god, far from fleeing the deadly encounter, seeks a Death-in-Love at the hands of his bride.[91] Śiva knows the price of entering the sanctuary of the dark virgin; if the lover's sacrifice is averted, it is because the god's devotees refuse to allow him to die. Paradoxically, only as demon can the god achieve union and self-effacement. Small wonder, then, that later poets sing to the goddess of Śiva's jealousy: "Feet that Śiva longs for, these in your fear you have given to Mahiṣāsura."[92]

## 6. Excursus: Marriage and the Dance

We are now in a position to attack the problem posed at the beginning of section 4. Marriage to the virgin goddess need not destroy the power guaranteed by her virginity. This power is preserved intact; the inviolable state of the goddess is symbolized by the box in which she is hidden or the sealed shrine in which she reigns. The god's attempt to unite with his bride—the intrusion into the locked sanctuary, or the extraordinary vision of the virgin—ends in blindness, castration, or death. The dark bride equipped with a sword or a bow, a crystal tongue, even a third breast, is a focus of violence and aggression; as such she clashes with the ideal image of the controlled, submissive woman, and must be regarded as part male, a menacing androgyne (as opposed to the gentle androgyne into which she is absorbed at Tiruvaṇṇāmalai). For all that, she is also seductive, the very symbol of erotic fascination; she entices her husband to a violent, self-sacrificing death. This is not, of course, the end of the myth—we will study its conclusion in the next section—but it is quite enough to embarrass the devotees of a god who is believed to be pure and without birth or death. Śiva, as the *nirmala* deity of the mature tradition, is not allowed to die. But neither can he do without the goddess, the source of life and power for the devotees. Therefore, the nature of the divine marriage must be transformed. The lethal union with the dark goddess is now relegated to a demon. Then the goddess may be split into dark and golden parts, and Śiva marries the golden, nonviolent bride. When this pattern is not adopted, the violent goddess herself has to be transformed. If the god is to survive his marriage to the goddess, his bride must be subdued. Thus we have the many myths of "taming," in which the Amazon is reduced to a docile spouse.

These myths thus reflect the collision of two opposed paradigms. The underlying pattern, which comes to the surface in various ways—for example, in the sacrificial rituals to which the myths are attached—is that of the self-sacrifice of the god to his bride. In worshiping the goddess, men imitate the divine exemplar by offering their strength, or their very life,[1] to Devī. We will return to this pattern once more in discussing ritual castration and the myths of sex reversal. But once the slaying of the god became unacceptable, the marriage of Śiva and Devī was made to conform to the conventional ethic of south Indian society. The divine marriage is no longer a mythic model of the symbolism of sacrifice, but an epitome of the human institution of marriage: Śiva must marry in order to set an example for men; without this example, men would become *yogis* and reach heaven, and the order of life proclaimed by the sacred books would perish.[2] For this paradigm to be meaningful, the symbolism of the murderous marriage had to be buried. The wild and terrifying virgin had to be domesticated, controlled, and locked in her normative, socially acceptable role.

The myth of Devī's transformation bridges the two levels of the tradition. The goddess begins as the dark, destructive virgin, and ends up as a gentle, submissive wife. Of the varying types of the myth, the most widespread and significant is that of the dance contest between Śiva and the goddess. Śiva overcomes the violent goddess in the course of a dance, and Devī remains as the indispensable witness to her husband's dance in all shrines that glorify the dancing Śiva.[3] In this role she is entirely devoted to her husband, and longs for union with him; hence she is known as Civakāmiyammai, "the lady who desires (or is desired by) Śiva,"[4] but here the envisaged union is in no way violent or threatening. There is, however, another possible outcome of the contest—the exclusion of the violent goddess. As we shall see, this resolution has its own advantages. As mediating between these two patterns we have the complex image of the androgynous marriage.[5]

We will trace these patterns in the myths of several shrines. At the outset it may be noted that the choice of the dance contest to explain the domination of the goddess by Śiva is no accident. During the Coḻa period, which witnessed the formalization of so many elements of south Indian Hinduism, the shrine of Naṭarāja at Citamparam achieved a primacy it has never lost since. Citamparam may not be the oldest center of the dance cult,[6] but it has become the most important: worship of the dancing deity, which has roots in ancient levels of religious life in the south (such as the dance of Kŏṟṟavai and her hosts on the battlefield,[7] and the ecstatic dance associated with Murukaṉ[8]), has rightly been seen as the most dynamic element in Citamparam in the period in which the purāṇic traditions of this shrine were recorded.[9] Naṭarāja is a fitting symbol for the classical resolution of Tamil mythology, which has buried the sacrificial symbolism of an earlier level under a theology asserting the supremacy and eternal life of the god. Naṭarāja, the lord of the dance, is Śiva as unique creator and destroyer, never himself destroyed.[10] Citamparam, his home, is for Tamil Śaivas simply *koyil—the* temple. We may regard the cult of Naṭarāja as the culmination of a process by which the divine Dancer became preeminent, and Citamparam became recognized as his outstanding shrine.[11]

The story of the dance *contest*, however, seems rooted at another spot, Tiruvālaṅkāṭu, where it forms the central episode of the local purāṇa. Although in its present form the *Tiruvālaṅkāṭṭuppurāṇam* clearly reveals the influence of the Citamparam tradition, it is possible that the myth of the contest originated at Tiruvālaṅkāṭu, whence it was borrowed by the folk tradition of Citamparam, and then ultimately borrowed back in a secondary form by the redactors of the Tiruvālaṅkāṭu traditions. Already in Appar's *Tevāram* there is a reference to Devī's witnessing the dance at Tiruvālaṅkāṭu (*āṭiṉār kāḷi kāṇa*).[12] It is noteworthy that it is Kāḷī, the goddess in her fierce form, who witnesses the dance. In view of the uncertainty of the textual tradition, I will not suggest a date for this verse; the point is that the *Tevāram* hymn, which usually represents a crystallization of the local tradition, retains the link with Kālī (or Nīli, as the other myths of this shrine call the dark goddess).[13] Moreover, the fact that we have a hagiographic variant of the dance myth from Tiruvālaṅkāṭu—Kāraikkālammaiyār, identified with the demoness (*pey*) of this site, is the eternal witness of Śiva's dance[14]—is an additional argument for the antiquity of this theme at Tiruvālaṅkāṭu.

The *Tiruvālaṅkāṭṭuppurāṇam* tells the story thus:

> Nimpaṉ and Cumpaṉ[15] destroyed the worlds, and the gods wandered in distress from their thrones. To help the gods, Devī took woman's form and destroyed the demons with the aid of the Seven Mothers and Cāmuṇḍī. Raktabīja ("having blood as seed"), the son of the younger sister of Nimpaṉ and Cumpaṉ, was attacked by the Seven Mothers;[16] from his blood more demons were born. The Mothers prayed to Umā, and from her wrath appeared the black-faced Kālī. She drank the demon's blood in her skull without allowing a drop to touch the earth. Thus the demon's army was destroyed, the gods were restored to heaven, and Kālī rejoiced at the feast of blood and flesh.
>
> Pārvatī called her and promised her all the power possessed by men and women in the triple world. "If Śiva comes to Vaṭāraṇya (= Tiruvālaṅkāṭu) to perform his dance, live in joy by his side," she said and disappeared, like lightning in a cloud. Intoxicated by these boons and the blood of the demons, Kālī came to the forest and insatiably devoured living creatures.
>
> Nārada came to worship Śiva at Tiruvālaṅkāṭu. The serpent sage Kāṟkoṭaṉ told him of the suffering of the inhabitants of the forest because of the depredations of Kālī. Nārada comforted him: "Surely it will be difficult for her to harm anyone in this beautiful spot where Śiva dwells." But when he left to see Sunandamuni, Kālī caught sight of him and wished to devour him; perceiving her intention, the sage hastened away to Vaikuṇṭha to seek the help of Viṣṇu. Viṣṇu told him that only Śiva could overcome the egoism (*akantai*) of Kālī. Nārada then complained to Śiva: "Lord, you guard the world with mercy (*karuṇai*),[17] so what can be lacking? Still, I have something to

tell you. If you do not remove the pride of Kālī, who is in the banyan forest, she will murder the world. No one but you can oppose her."

"Good," said Śiva and departed for the forest surrounded by his demon hosts and voracious dogs, his ankles circled by bells, his hands grasping the skull and trident. The demon hosts of the angry Kālī came to oppose the intruder; blood flowed, mountains and trees were uprooted, the earth quaked and split—but at the sight of Cāttaṉ[18] on his elephant, the hosts of Kālī fled. Kālī herself came to kill this handsome youth, and Cāttaṉ ran to inform Śiva. Śiva came to fight. Kālī, remembering the words of Devī, abandoned thoughts of overcoming him in battle; instead, she thought of finding some other means to defeat him. So she said, "Who are you, madman, who have come here? It appears you have not heard the name of Kālī, for even Kālarudra would not dare to enter this forest where the fierce goddess (*cūraiyāḷ*) resides. Say what brought you here. Abandon silence, or you are as good as dead." So spoke the goddess, and Śiva smiled and suppressed his anger. In a deep, soft voice he said, "Lady, who are you? Why do you live here? You have destroyed this forest where my devotees reside. Go to some other forest together with these fierce creatures (*kŏṭiyor*)." Answered Kŏṟṟavai:[19] "If you wish to live, leave at once! Otherwise, fight me, if you have the strength."

Śiva accepted the challenge, and the goddess proposed a dance contest. "I agree to whatever you suggest," said the god, and mentioned as a possible site of the contest a place near the Muktitīrtha. The two sages of the forest (Kaṟkoṭaṉ and Sunanda) were made spectators, and the gods became arbiters of the contest. As Brahmā kept time and the heavenly musicians sang, Śiva danced according to the rules in the ancient book (*paḻamaṟaiparatanūl*).[20] Kālī imitated this dance. Noticing that Śiva grew tired, she was filled with glee. When the god suggested they try the fierce dance called *pāṇṭaraṅkam*, she willingly agreed, confident of victory. Śiva pressed one foot on the ground and lifted the other straight into the heavens. As he danced thus, the worlds shook, the constellations fell from place like scattered pearls, the elephants, serpents, and mountains that support the earth grew weak, and Kālī fell to the earth in a faint. Grasping the earth with her long arms, she regained her power (*pīṭu*) and her breath (*āvi*). She watched as

> Śiva whirled around, his body embracing the worlds. So that the universe might not perish, he moved his foot and danced on.
>
> Kālī acknowledged defeat; shyly (*nāṇiṉ mevi*) she worshiped the lord; she stood helplessly like a puppet, confused. The gods sought Umā's help in putting an end to the violent dance of the god. Then they worshiped Śiva. He said to Kālī, "Only I could compare with you in the performance of the dance. Live here by my side as Bhadrakālī, worshiped by all." Kālī sought the lord's forgiveness for her acts committed in ignorance, and Śiva reassured her by declaring that he had performed the dance not on her account, but to grant a vision to the sages in the forest.[21]

The two sages, one of them a serpent, clearly recall Patañjali and Vyāghrapāda from Citamparam; moreover, this entire story is said to have been recounted by Viṣṇu to Ādiśeṣa, like the story of the *ānandatāṇḍava* in the *Cidambaramāhātmya* and the *Koyiṟpurāṇam*. Just as the *ānandatāṇḍava*, Śiva's dance at Citamparam, is linked with the Pine Forest myth,[22] here it is Śiva as Bhairava-Kaṅkālamūrti, the form he takes in the Pine Forest, who dances in the banyan forest. The late, derivative nature of this version is also revealed by the rationalization of the myth: Śiva comes to Tiruvālaṅkāṭu in order to remove the *ahaṅkāra*—the egoism and pride—of the goddess. The dance is, on the one hand, a means of instruction (Kālī goes from ignorance and pride to knowledge of the truth), on the other simply a boon to the sages, who have been absorbed in *tapas* in the hope of achieving a vision of the dance. The underlying myth must, however, be much older than the version that has survived in this text. One wonders if Kālī's intoxication at Pārvatī's promise of life together with Śiva does not reflect the basic thrust of the myth; the dark goddess seeks a violent union with the god. The chthonic character of the goddess is affirmed: Kālī regains her power from contact with the earth. Let us note, too, that it is the violent Kālī who is restored by the touch of the earth, not the remote and wholly benign Umā. The goddess is first split into dark and benevolent forms; then the dark goddess, who yearns for union, is subdued by her lord.

Once again we have an ironic reversal of the goddess's usual role as the source of power for her husband. Kālī seeks to defeat Śiva by a trick, for she recognizes that she cannot win by a trial of strength.

She therefore plots to exhaust the god in the dance. Similarly, Devī drains Viṣṇu of his strength in the anthill myth from Tiruvārūr,[23] and Durgā draws to herself all the power of her buffalo lover.[24] At Tiruvālaṅkāṭu the point of this reversal is to demonstrate the god's superiority; Kālī's stratagem fails, Śiva dances without pause, and the goddess is forced to admit defeat. The divine power at work in this episode in fact goes beyond all the usual bounds, in a manner often associated with Śiva:[25] the god's dance evokes images of the *pralaya*, the destruction of the world—stars fall from place, the supports of the earth give way, and only Śiva's mercy prevents a complete cataclysm. The violence of the dance replaces the violence of Mahiṣa's encounter with the goddess, only here its source is the god who triumphs over Kālī. And, just as Viṣṇu intervenes to stop Śiva's wild and destructive dance with the corpse of Satī,[26] here the gods—with the help of Umā, the peaceful, "proper" wife—bring the fierce *pāṇṭaraṅkam* dance to an end. Viṣṇu cuts Satī's body into pieces, which fall to earth and become shrines; at Tiruvālaṅkāṭu the dark goddess is restrained and then enshrined in her permanent place. We may summarize this development as the creation of a new order—the ritual order of the shrine—out of a violent upheaval caused by the dance; and, since everything hinges on the role of the goddess, Devī is again connected with the notion of *pratiṣṭhā*. The new, secure order established after the dance depends upon the proper channeling and limitation of power. Analogous to the ritual order, in which the goddess is held to her designated place, is the traditional concept of marriage, in which the woman—the shy, meek creature into which Kālī is transformed—is fixed in unchanging roles, her native power carefully restricted to prescribed, useful courses.

Śiva thus seems deliberately to unleash a tempestuous force in order to arrive at a clear resolution based on his total domination of the goddess. Nevertheless, he undoubtedly recognizes the power vested in his rival—indeed, he wishes to use this power—and thus in other versions it is Śiva rather than Kālī who makes use of a trick. Śiva thrusts his foot into the air while he dances—and the goddess is too modest to imitate this position.[27] In the *Tiruvālaṅkāṭṭuppurāṇam*, Kālī attains modesty only in the wake of her defeat. In both cases, the authors of the myths were eager to portray Kālī's transformation into a bride graced by the prescribed attributes of woman, foremost of which is *nāṇ*, shyness. Mīnākṣī, too, is overcome by *nāṇ* at the sight of her future husband, Śiva;[28] this is the moment when the Amazon becomes a woman. One version of the dance myth gives an ironic twist to Kālī's challenge: she proudly informs Śiva that the dance is proper only to women, not men.[29] Śiva then vanquishes her in the dance; Kālī must learn the true proprieties.

Yet it is important to note that the myth of the dance contest at Tiruvālaṅkāṭu does not end in the marriage of Śiva and Kālī. Rather, the fierce goddess is subdued and given a place of her own inside Śiva's shrine. Today this shrine of the goddess stands immediately before the entrance into the main shrine: here she is Bhadrakālī, worshiped *before* entering the realm of Vaṭāraṇyeśvara ("the lord of the banyan forest") and his consort, Bhramarālakāmbikā (Tam. Vaṇṭārkuḻali, "she in whose tresses hum the bees"). Like Śani at Tirunaḷḷāṟu,[30] the ancient deity of the shrine has been allocated the position of doorkeeper; as such, Bhadrakālī still retains her claim to the first offerings of the worshipers. Marriage is, however, the concomitant of the dance in the Ratnasabhā, the supposed site of the dance contest in the Tiruvālaṅkāṭu shrine. Here the dancing Śiva with one leg thrust into the sky (the position of the *ūrdhvtāṇḍava*) is flanked by Civakāmiyammai and Kāraikkālammaiyār; the first is the divine consort of Naṭarāja at Citamparam, the second a multiform of the defeated Kālī from Tiruvālaṅkāṭu.

There is yet another shrine to Kālī at Tiruvālaṅkāṭu, outside the main shrine, at the edge of the Muktitīrtha (which, we may recall, is the venue of the dance contest according to the purāṇa). Here Kālī is worshiped alone.[31] The priests of the Śiva temple still refer to this shrine as the *mūlasthāna* of Tiruvālaṅkāṭu, the oldest cult center on this site. This, presumably, is the scene of the Nīli story with its theme of the slain husband and locked doors.[32] Here Kālī reigns unsubdued, powerful—her power not dissipated through a conventional marriage—still a fearsome goddess whose primacy is recalled in the tradition of the Śiva temple that has grown up beside her shrine. Beside her, not in her place: the goddess has been excluded through the creation of a new shrine, which in the course of time has become the main temple at Tiruvālaṅkāṭu.

The Citamparam tradition describes a different process. Here the goddess was excluded from her own shrine by a triumphant Śiva:

> Before the creation of the shrine of Naṭarāja, there was a shrine to Kālī in the Tillai forest. Śiva, moved by the worship of

> Vyāghrapāda and Patañjali, wished to show them his *ānanda-tāṇḍava*, the dance of bliss. Then Kālī was filled with pride (*cĕrukuṟṟu*) and challenged the lord to a dance contest. Śiva wished to suppress her pride, so he laid down the following terms of the contest: whoever won would become lord of Tillai; whoever lost must leave the bounds of that site. While the gods and sages watched, Kālī and Śiva began to dance. Kālī saw Śiva perform the *ūrdhvatāṇḍava* (with one foot thrust into the sky) and, ashamed that she could not perform that dance, bowed her head and acknowledged defeat. Therefore she was forced to leave her shrine in the heart of the Tillai forest and go to the boundary of the town.[33] Kālī, in order to remove her fault in challenging Śiva to a contest, bathed in the Śivapriyā tank and worshiped the god. Her fierce form departed and she received a tranquil form (*cānta uruvam*) as Tillaivaṉamuṭaiyaparamecuvari ("the great goddess who possesses the Tillai forest"). She dwells now in her shrine as Cāmuṇḍīśvarī and grants boons to those who worship her.[34]

The original shrine to Kālī in the heart of the Tillai forest is identified by at least one author with the present Nṛttasabhā inside the Śrī Naṭarāja shrine.[35] The Nṛttasabhā is held to be the site of the dance contest, and it holds an eight-armed image of Śiva performing the *ūrdhvatāṇḍava*; Kālī is placed below the god on the right. The Nṛttasabhā, the scene of the *ūrdhvatāṇḍava*, is to be distinguished from the Kanakasabhā, where Śiva performs the *ānanda-tāṇḍava* in the presence of his wife.[36] The vanquished Kālī is exiled to the boundary, where she is worshiped in both benign and fearsome forms. The eight-armed Tillaikkāḷi, facing east, armed with the trident and covered with *kuṅkuma* paste, is situated opposite the central image of the shrine, the pacified Brahmacāmuṇḍīśvarī. The goddess is cooled by worshiping the lord and bathing in the tank (which is named "the beloved of Śiva," a fitting name for the nonviolent bride), but even in her pacified state she remains apart. In contrast with Tiruvālaṅkāṭu, where the original shrine of the goddess remains in her control, while the cult of Śiva grows up in contiguity, the Citamparam tradition asserts that Devī was banished to the edge of the city and her own shrine taken over. The Tiruvālaṅkāṭu myth first splits the goddess into benevolent and violent forms, then describes the subjugation of the violent Kālī; but Kālī survives in her own shrine as a unitary, dark figure. At Citamparam, the goddess is split into fierce and benign forms even inside her shrine on the outskirts, and the benign goddess has become the central figure of the cult. The process of reinterpretation has thus been taken a step further in Citamparam.[37]

The oral tradition of Citamparam gives us a slightly different version of the myth:

> Once Devī covered Śiva's eyes in sport on Kailāsa. Because of this, the worlds became still. Seeing this demonstration of Śiva's power, the goddess felt jealousy (*kāḻppuṇarcci*). Therefore Śiva cursed her to remain black as Kālī.
>
> To win release from this curse, Kālī was sent to Tiruvālaṅkāṭu. In her fierce form, she destroyed everything there and all that was in her path as she proceeded southward toward Citamparam. There Śiva appeared in order to cool her. He suggested a dance contest; whoever lost was to leave the temple and go outside the city. The competition took place in the Nṛttasabhā, and Śiva won by dancing with his leg thrust high into the air.
>
> Furious at having lost by a trick, Kālī left for the Pūtakkeṇi ("pond of the spirits") in the burning ground to the north of the shrine. While she was sitting there in her anger, Brahmā came to cool her by reciting the Vedas. As he recited, each of the four Vedas became in turn one face of the goddess, who is known as Brahmacāmuṇḍīśvarī. Pacified, Devī began to perform penance in order to be reunited with Śiva.[38]

The oral version may, once again, be more conservative than written accounts. Note the admission of the link with Tiruvālaṅkāṭu, and the adherence to the classic pattern of the marriage myths beginning with the blinding (castration/slaying) of Śiva by his wife. The curse to become Kālī is a good example of a curse that heightens the effect of its cause: Kālī's jealousy is perpetuated and ultimately brought to a pitch in the dance contest.[39] Unlike the written version, which ignores the question of Devī's union with Śiva, the oral account acknowledges that Devī's penance subsequent to her pacification is aimed at marriage with the god. The dance contest fails to cool the goddess or to effect a change of her heart, as it does in the written account; here Brahmā's recitation of the Vedas works the change. The four-faced goddess shares an attribute of Brahmā; one text, in fact, refers to her as a part of him (*pitāmakaṉ pirivāy vaikum piramacāmuṇṭi*).[40] The four Vedas are brought in to account for the four faces.[41] In any case, this episode marks a departure from the myths of the murderous bride; Devī is subdued and excluded, first defeated by the dancing Śiva, then pacified by the sound of the Vedic chant. Her husband survives after usurping her shrine. Here the myth ends—but is the marriage consummated? Does the seductive *tapas* bear fruit? To this my informant would only say: "We have no clue." We may deduce that Kālī remains chaste, outside, longing for union but prevented from attaining it.

Inside the shrine, things are different. Here marriage is the rule, without any lethal consequences. As Civakāmiyammai, or as the left side of the androgyne,[42] the goddess realizes her desire. Civakāmi is the spectator of the *ānandatāṇḍava*: here the dance symbolizes subordination and union. There is, however, another dimension to this resolution. Civakāmi also has her own shrine within the third *prākāra* (enclosing wall), but beyond the confines of the two innermost *prākāras*. The Kāmakkoṭṭam, as such shrines to the goddess are called (after the famous shrine of Kāmākṣī at Kāñcipuram), appears to have developed in south Indian temple architecture in late Coḻa times.[43] It has been regarded as "a significant universalization of folk ritual."[44] It may, however, be suggested that the devotion of a separate shrine to the goddess, usually to the north of the main shrine, has a logic of its own to which the myth contains a key. At Tiruvārūr, for example, the shrine of Kamalāmpikai (the "lotus-lady") lies outside the two inner *prākāras*, in the northwest corner of the third *prākāra*—a situation very similar to that of Civakāmi at Citamparam. The present structure of the Kamalāmpikai shrine is very late (sixteenth century?),[45] but local tradition, supported by the ancient names for Tiruvārūr preserved in the purāṇas,[46] would suggest that a shrine to Kamalāmpikai was the oldest cult center on this site. In the myths of Tiruvārūr, Kamalāmpikai practices *tapas* as a virgin throughout the ages.[47] *Inside* the main compound, Devī shrines have multiplied: there are shrines to Somālakāmbikā (Tam. Alliyaṅkotaiyammai, "the lady of tresses adorned by the lily"), the consort of Valmīkanātha; to Nilotpalāmpāḷ ("lady of the blue lotus"), adjoining the Valmīkanātha shrine; to Durgā as Ĕriciṉakkŏṟṟavai ("Kŏṟṟavai of burning anger"), who grants husbands to women who worship her during *rāhukāla* on Fridays.[48] At Tiruvŏṟṟiyūr, which provides a close parallel to Tiruvārūr in structure and myth, the virgin goddess Vaṭivuṭaiyammaṉ ("the lady of beautiful form") remains as a primary focus of the cult in her shrine outside the main compound. Inside we find the consort of the god and the shrine to Durgā/Kaṇṇaki, Vaṭṭapāṟainācciyār ("the bride of the large round stone").[49]

What is the significance of this division? The goddess is on the one hand excluded, apparently in the interest of preserving her virginity and, hence, her power; on the other hand, she gains ground inside the shrine through a process of bifurcation and multiplication. Outside, her shrine retains its primacy. In a situation in which, historically, the final crystallization of the cult takes the form of divine marriage along conventional lines, only the separation of the goddess can satisfy the requirements of the devotees. If one seeks strength from the goddess, then *her* strength must be guarded and preserved. Only outside the shrine, removed from her husband, can Devī remain virginal, powerful, and supreme. Note in addition that the cult has transferred to the goddess qualities originally associated with Rudra-Śiva, particularly those of marginality and violence.[50] The sacrificial butcher—and, as we have seen, Kālī undoubtedly merits this title—is a necessary but nevertheless horrifying figure, polluted and polluting by virtue of the violence he performs; hence the constant attempts to exclude him once he has accomplished his unpleasant task.[51] Kālī, who shares this identification with polluting power and violence, is similarly pushed to the edges of the sacred arena—either excluded from her own shrine, as at Citamparam and in the folktale from Ramnad District,[52] or made marginal by the consecration of a new shrine, a new center, at a spot not far removed from her own enclosure. In the course of a process by which the god is located, stabilized in the center, purified of evil, allotted his consort and given his share of the offerings, the chthonic goddess remains virginal, imbued with sacred power, and confined to the geographical periphery.

Thus we observe again a division of space corresponding to the fundamental split in the tradition. The center of the shrine—in its essence and origin a place of violent, contaminating power, especially the power at work in the destruction and reintegration of the blood-sacrifice—becomes pure, isolated, idealized as a realm of harmony and peace. Unlimited power, evil, death, rebirth, desire—all are relegated to the impure zone beyond the borders of the shrine. This zone belongs to the violent goddess, the epitome of power. Yet both realms are sacred, even if the purāṇic texts, true to the Upaniṣadic legacy and the Brahminical ideal of purity, assert the superiority of the isolated, other-worldly shrine. Power, or the goddess, can never be dispensed with completely, unless life itself is finally negated. Tamil *bhakti* religion will not take this step; it is too much in love with life, and with the world in which God is revealed. Both goals—purity and power—persist in the *bhakti* tradition; the ordering of the shrine, with the virgin goddess separate and the god with his "tame" wife located in the center, reflects the continuing conflict between the two vital religious ideals.

The story of the dance is used to explain both aspects of this situation—the conclusion of a conventional marriage, and the manner in which marriage is precluded. Inside the shrine, Devī is now the witness to her husband's cosmic dance.[53] The dance is a form of marriage, the male-dominating marriage which Śiva must accept in his role of exemplar to his devotees. But outside sits the dread Kālī, perhaps yearning for a union of violence and sacrifice, perhaps content forever to perform *tapas* alone, her powers assured by her freedom and her exclusion. Here, too, the dance explains her situation; because of Śiva's victory in the contest, she survives in solitude at the edges of the sacred ground, or at the doorstep of Śiva's temple. Like other doorkeepers, she is, in the development of the myth, absorbed and ostensibly subdued; but like them she retains by the nature of her position and by virtue of the power believed to reside in her, first hold on the minds of the worshipers. Here the devotees, who wish to benefit from her power in their own lives, seek her out with their offerings. Through mastery of the dance, the god transforms his bride and claims the center as his own; but the life that he, and his devotees, desire remains outside, with the goddess, in the twilight region of the boundary.

## 7. Rebirth: The Bride as Mother

> Is motherhood then a mere word of the lips? Bringing forth does not make a mother, unless she can understand the griefs of her child.[1]

As the source of life and of life-sustaining milk, the goddess worshiped in Tamil shrines has attributes of the mother.[2] So far we have concentrated on the role of the goddess as the bride of the deity—especially as the destructive, virginal bride who slays her husband as he attempts to unite with her. We have seen the efforts made to extricate the god from this violent confrontation: the dark virgin is offered a demon in place of the god, or else she is subdued by her husband, or divided into two parts (the benign, golden bride, and the aggressive, dark killer). These attempts are all characteristic of a second level in the myths, a level in which the underlying, motivating conception of the god's violent death has been overruled in favor of the belief in his total purity and freedom. We must now return to the sacrifice, which supplies meaning to the underlying conception of Śiva's death at the hands of his bride. I have argued that the divine marriage partakes of the symbolism of sacrifice;[3] the god's death is not, then, an end in itself but only a stage—admittedly, the most dramatic stage in the myths of marriage—on the road to rebirth. Out of the disintegration and chaos of the sacrifice, new life emerges; similarly, the god's death is but the means to his more secure, more powerful existence. What distinguishes the Tamil tradition from the religion of the *Brāhmaṇas* is the clear identification of the goddess with the whole complex of sacrificial ideas. The Tamil goddess is the focal point of violence to the victim, and she is also the source of the new life he is promised. The god, who exemplifies the process of death and rebirth through the sacrifice, offers himself to his bride and is then reborn from her womb. The symbolism of the sacrificial ritual is acted out from beginning to end in the relations of Śiva and his local consort.

That this symbolism comes through to us in a fractured, fragmented manner must be attributed to our authors' desire to escape from this pattern entirely. The sacrifice is inseparable from power, and power pollutes and destroys; the deity, far from undergoing a symbolic *Liebestod* in order to acquire greater power from the source hidden in the goddess, must be isolated from any contact with the rituals of death and rebirth. Nevertheless, many myths still reveal the complete sequence we are studying. Recall, for example, the myth of the Kāmakkoṭṭam at Kāñcipuram:[4] there all the gods, including the male protagonist in his two forms (Śiva, the consort of Devī, and his impersonator Bhaṇḍāsura), offer themselves in a great sacrifice, and are then created anew by the seductive, murderous goddess Lalitā. Śiva emerges from the cave that opens up in Devī's shrine; in this new birth—the god himself compares his journey to rebirth from the womb of a golden cow[5]—his manhood, which he had lost through the curse of the Pine Forest sages, is restored.[6] We may interpret this as meaning that Śiva is reborn with renewed power (*śakti*) out of the womb of the goddess Kāmākṣī. Yet Śiva dwells in this shrine as Kāmākṣī's husband. In another version from this site, Kāmākṣī gives birth to Śiva from her right side, and to a form of herself from her forehead-eye, and the two are married by the gods.[7] Evidently, the marriage myth thus requires a kind of incest: the male is sacrificed, or sacrifices himself, in violent marriage to his virgin bride, and is rewarded with rebirth from her womb; the strength that the goddess has drawn from him in his death will be restored to him in his new form, while the goddess remains virgin, bride, and mother. In the second myth from Kāñci just cited, the sexual relationship is still more complicated, since Kāmākṣī appears as mother, consort, and also sister of the god.

The Tamil myths in their present form offer us all the elements and episodes of the sacrificial sequence, but usually fail to connect them in their natural order. Rather, they tend to appear as discrete mythic images—and even as such, cut off from any unifying context or interpretation, their true force is often blunted or distorted, as we have seen. Nevertheless, such a context, which binds together these *disjecta membra* of an old and deeply rooted mythology and gives meaning to an otherwise bewildering mass of images, does exist. If the interpretation suggested here is correct, we could expect to find the following elements in the Tamil myths: first, an ambivalent portrayal of the goddess as mother—since this is a mother who has just destroyed her victim before giving birth to him once more; second, a myth of incestuous marriage (not the father-daughter incest of the Vedic creation myth,[8] but a union of a son and his mother, or in some cases of a brother and sister); finally, an insistence upon the virginity of the mother, who has slain her husband/child in order to maintain her virtue. All of these elements do appear in the Tamil purāṇas, and will be discussed below.

At this point another problem must be touched upon. The role of the mother in our sources is clearly, in light of the above, complex and multifaceted. Not only do we find distinct episodes of the myth that have merged in the retelling, but we must also deal with the tendency to break away from the sacrificial symbolism altogether. The importance of the idea of the split goddess becomes clear from this situation. Dichotomy becomes a major technique for handling ambivalence and contradiction. Myth, we are sometimes told, responds to oppositions and conflict through the elaboration of multivalent symbols; the tension that generates the myth endures in the opposing strands of mythological images, and the myth, by absorbing and fusing the extremes, becomes a creature of paradox.[9] Many Hindu myths, however, prefer a different approach; instead of resting content with the paradox, they divide the symbol into parts among which opposing forces can be distributed. This pattern is particularly prominent in Tamil mythology in its present form, for the Tamil authors delight in breaking down the basic symbols of the myths and in rationalizing their import. Moreover, this tendency to rationalize and explain goes along with the persistent attempt to do away with violence, at least in relation to the god. The technique of bifurcation is very useful here: we have seen how the dark goddess is made to shed her violent aspect (Kālī, Kauśikī) in order to unite, as the golden Gaurī, with Śiva. But the dark goddess may also be wedded to the god, sometimes peacefully,[10] at other times in a lethal manner. Śiva thus acquires two wives, one dark and virginal, the second golden and submissive. We will return to this pattern in our next section. In connection with Devī's maternal aspect, we observe a similar approach to the inherent ambiguities involved. The different components of the divine mother may be combined in a single figure—usually the life-giving but also murderous cow—or they may be separated and assigned to distinct carriers. The complex, unitary figure probably represents the more original conception, in which both aspects of the sacrifice—the violent death and the rebirth—are present and appear in association with the goddess. The split image and the accompanying separation of opposing strands reflect the attempt to accommodate a less violent ideology; just as the splitting away of Kālī allows the god to marry the more conventional Gaurī, the separation of the terrifying aspect of the mother allows a more idealized image of the goddess as mother to become dominant.

Why is the goddess so susceptible to this sort of surgery, while the god, instead of being cut in two, is usually removed altogether from the scene of violence, or provided with a surrogate to play his part? The answer seems to lie in the close identification of the goddess (or the woman) with power. If the god can finally govern power so that he comes to represent a state of utmost purity and separation, the goddess can never wholly abandon her native state. A part of her at least will always be tied to the earth—the dark soil that absorbs life into itself in order to give forth new life—and to the realm of violent power and creative chaos generally. And since Tamil *bhakti* religion can never completely dispense with power in any case, and tends rather to regard it as a manifestation of the sacred, the goddess, the natural source of power, can only be "purified" up to a point. She is needed, as the dark and potent virgin, to answer the prayers of the devotees. Insofar as our texts wish to draw harmonious portraits of the deities, male and female, the best they can do is to divide the goddess into benign and threatening parts, and then exclude the latter—as in the case of Kālī exiled through the dance.[11] The myths of the violent mother offer repeated examples of this solution.

One should not, however, regard the idea of split or multiple mothers as a recent, south Indian invention. The exigencies of the Tamil myths make this pattern very frequent in the Tamil purāṇas; but we find similar notions in the Vedic literature and in the classical Sanskrit purāṇas. Already in the *RV* Agni is described as *dvimātā́*, "having two mothers":[12] the commentators explain the two mothers as the fire-sticks, or earth and heaven, or night and day.[13] Night and day seek Agni as their calf[14]—note the image of the cow as mother and the doubling, one dark mother and one light one. Agni may also have three[15] or seven[16] mothers; Soma, too, has more than one,[17] sometimes also seven (who are sisters)—perhaps the seven rivers.[18] The much later tradition of the Seven Mothers, who in the folk tradition are sometimes said to be sisters, is thus adumbrated by the most ancient literary sources. We will discuss these seven goddesses below. The opposition between the good and evil aspects of the mother may be expressed in Vedic myth in the contrast between Aditi (or Anumati) and Nirṛti;[19] similarly, the common representation of this opposition in terms of a good natural mother and an evil stepmother—a universal folklore motif[20]—can be discovered in the *RV*.[21] But perhaps the most famous Vedic myth of multiple mothers has been lost. The lexicons and Sanskrit purāṇas explain Rudra's epithet "Tryambaka" as "having three eyes," although the Epic refers it to Śiva's worship of the three goddesses of the sky, earth, and water.[22] Sāyaṇa reverses the archaic image: Tryambaka is mother and father of the Trimūrti.[23] Only the late *Kālikāpurāṇa* follows the natural meaning ("having three mothers"): Śiva was born to the three queens of King Pauṣya in three sections that united to form a single child; hence he is known as Tryambaka.[24] This myth probably represents an unconscious reversion influenced by the examples of Jantu, born to one hundred mothers,[25] and Jarāsandha, born in two pieces to the wives of a king and united by the ambivalent Rākṣasī Jarā.[26] Skanda, too, is born in pieces in some accounts; in others the six-headed single child splits and reunites.[27] Although the motif of the "birth in pieces" is thus fairly widespread, its source seems to be the concept of the multiple mothers attached to a single child.[28]

A plurality of mothers is not an easy notion to accept. One text resorts to the theory of adoption to explain the title "Dvaimātura," "having two mothers," which is here applied to Gaṇeśa: when Gaṇeśa was born on earth, his parents were horrified at his elephant's head with its long trunk, his weapons carried in his four arms, and his fat belly; they abandoned the child near a pool, where he was found and adopted by a sage and his wife.[29] This myth reverses the usual values by making the natural mother abandon her child, while the foster mother—usually a more negative figure—nourishes him; attempting to explain the existence of two mothers, the myth gratuitously provides two fathers as well![30] A further development dispenses with the natural mother altogether: Cuṭalaimāṭacuvāmi (a folk deity popular in the Tirunĕlveli region) is given two foster mothers by Śiva when he is banished from Kailāsa; Peycci, who stands on his left in representations, eats infants and corpses, and Brahmarākṣasī, who stands on his right, "has similar tastes."[31] Although neither mother seems truly benign, a division in terms of rank may be intended: a Brahmarākṣasī may be presumed to be of higher status than an ordinary demoness, and she stands on the auspicious right. In India as in the West, the sinister is the left; Kaṇṇaki casts her left breast at the city of Maturai.[32] Other myths of Cuṭalaimāṭacuvāmi regard his natural mother Pārvatī as a symbol of the less positive aspects of the mother: the god himself is said to have taken to eating corpses because he was unsatisfied by his mother's milk.[33] Perhaps the ultimate step in the direction of the two mothers is taken by a myth about the birth of Bhagīratha: the two widowed queens of King Dilīpa asked Vasiṣṭha how the royal line could be continued; Vasiṣṭha performed a sacrifice and gave one of the queens an oblation (*caru*) to eat; he advised them to unite sexually, the second queen taking the part of the male (*anyā puruṣabhāvena maithunāya pravartatām*). In this manner, without seed, the elder queen gave birth to a boneless mass of flesh, which was named Bhagīratha (from *bhaga*, the female organ). Bhagīratha was eventually transformed into a man as radiant as Kāma by the intervention of the sage Aṣṭāvakra.[34] Here the father is eliminated altogether, but the unnatural birth without seed results in a boneless child—and a male sage has to be provided to restore Bhagīratha to normal human shape.

In essence, the conception of a plurality of mothers aims at expressing the ambivalence or multivalence of the mother figure, and it is at this point that our discussion of the Tamil purāṇic myths of the mother must begin. In particular, our concern is with the darker side of the mother. The wicked mother or stepmother is, of course, a universal figure; the Indian representatives of this type have been discussed at length by O'Flaherty with reference to the problem of evil generally, and in the light of modern psychological theories.[35] Here we will deal with the evil mother in the context of the divine marriage, and the sacrificial symbolism that permeates this myth. The goddess gives birth to her consort after murdering him or castrating him, and it is in this sense—as the source of life won from violence—that Devī acquires a maternal character in the Tamil shrines. As we have seen, some myths (notably those of Kāñcipuram) directly attribute the birth of the god to the local goddess. More often, the violent mother appears in the Tamil purāṇic myths as the ambivalent wishing-cow, the Kāmadhenu. In surveying the symbolism of blood and milk in the Tamil shrines, we discovered a tendency to associate both fluids with the Kāmadhenu; the cow both wounds the god, thus causing the flow of blood, and nourishes him with her milk. As the source of both life and dangerous violence, the cow recalls the role of the breast in Tamil symbolism generally.[36] Throughout India the cow serves as a natural symbol for motherhood. Aditi[37] and Pṛthivī[38] are identified with the cow in the *RV*; Rudra is the father of the Maruts through the cow Pṛśni.[39] Early Tamil literature contains a famous example of the cow as mother: Āputtiraṉ, abandoned at birth by his mother, was nursed for seven days by a cow before being found and adopted by a Brahmin. When he had become a boy, he once saved a cow from being sacrificed in the village; the Brahmins found him with the cow and beat him for freeing it, and the cow then attacked the sacrificer and wounded him. Āputtiraṉ was reborn as the son of the same cow that had nursed him, itself reborn as a cow with golden horns and hoofs and plentiful milk.[40] The cow's wounding of the sacrificer shows us again the association of blood and milk; but here the cow is essentially positive and life-giving, and in this way contrasts with Āputtiraṉ's natural mother, who abandons him.

The depiction of the cow as violent and even murderous is common throughout the Tamil purāṇic corpus. One striking example appears in another myth about Dadhīci (Dadhyañc), whom we have met in connection with the anthill sacrifice:[41]

> Indra shot arrows at the Rākṣasas with his bow. In anger, the Rākṣasas seized the bow, broke it, and swallowed the arrows. Indra fled in fear. The seven sages advised turning to Viṣṇu for help, and Viṣṇu suggested they take the adamantine bones of Dadhīci as a weapon. Indra asked the Kāmadhenu to bring the bones of this sage, who was performing *tapas*, vowed to silence. The cow hesitated, faced with the same dilemma as Kāma when asked to disturb the meditation of Śiva;[42] at length, under pressure from the gods and sages, the cow agreed.
>
> She approached the sage, who was lost in meditation.[43] First she sniffed his body, then she licked him with her tongue. The sage felt this and thought, "The divine cow is freeing me from evil." Then she caught hold of his spine with her teeth and pulled. The sage remained silent, thinking, "The cow is very hungry. It will be good if she eats." Those who have attained knowledge of Śiva do not reckon their body to have any reality.
>
> As the cow bit and pulled out his backbone, the sage did not budge. But when she began to walk away with his spine, he cried, "Return! Why have you come here?" She explained to him the cause of her action, and he cursed her to be troubled by Brahminicide because she had listened to the gods; he also cursed Viṣṇu to lose an arm in his incarnation as Vyāsa,[44] the sages to lose the fruit of their sacrifice, Indra to lose his strength and become confused, and the weapon made from his backbone to lose its luster. Sadly, the cow went to the gods and gave them the bones. They had Maya forge the weapon, and Indra worshiped it. Dadhīci succeeded in making his body grow back by meditation; a proficient sage can recreate the entire universe in a straw! But because of his curse, the divine weapon lost its splendor, until Indra worshiped the god of Paiññīli.
>
> The cow, afflicted by Brahminicide, devoured creatures and blood like a famished tiger, but her hunger was never assuaged. After afflicting the inhabitants of heaven, she began to prey on the world of men. But when she arrived at Paiññīli,

> she returned to her former state; she watered the *liṅga* there with urine and milk, and in cleaning it with her tongue and her tail she bruised it with her feet. The god, marked by her hoofs, melted in happiness; he granted her release from the curse and from the evil of killing creatures in hunger.[45]

This version of Dadhīci's self-sacrifice differs from most others, and from the *MBh* account from which they appear to have been drawn, by regarding the removal of Dadhīci's spine as evil, a form of murder.[46] In some texts Pippalāda, Dadhīci's son, wishes to take revenge on the gods for their murder of his father;[47] usually, however, Dadhīci joyfully offers to fulfil the gods' request for his spine. That this act of self-sacrifice should have terrible consequences in the Tamil version accords well with the complex attitude toward the cow, whose actions undoubtedly entangle her in evil. In the Tamil text, Dadhīci feels no sympathy for the gods, but appears to derive a masochistic joy from being devoured by the cow/mother. The joy of surrender recalls the longing of Śiva (or Mahiṣa) for annihilation at the hands of the goddess; indeed, the analogy with the marriage myths is borne out by the sequel, when Dadhīci's role as victim is transferred to the *liṅga*—the symbol of Śiva, the consort of the goddess in her various local forms (including her maternal aspect as the Kāmadhenu). Dadhīci's surrender to the mother is repeated with respect to the *liṅga*, which is scarred by the cow's hoofs, yet melts (*uṭal kuḻaintār*) in joy at this wound—just as the sand-*liṅga* at Kāñcipuram melts in the embrace of the goddess and is marked by her breasts. The same verb—*meṉi kuḻaintu*—is used in the Kāñci myth, which is perhaps the most famous Tamil example of the mother who wounds the god.[48] The watering of the *liṅga* at Paiññīli with cow's urine (*gojala*) is, of course, regarded positively by the text, *gojala* being one of the five sacred products of the cow; this, and the milk which is poured over the *liṅga*, represent the wholly munificent aspect of the mother. The Kāmadhenu at first reluctantly acts as a murderess; then, because of her victim's curse, she becomes "like a famished tiger" (again we see a curse that aggravates its cause); finally, while ostensibly transformed back to her pacific state, she manages to inflict several wounds on the god. A possible antecedent for this description of the Kāmadhenu is the statement in the *Padmapurāṇa* that the wishing-cow Surabhi licked Dadhīci's corpse clean of flesh so that the gods could take the bones for their weapon.[49] In any case, the violent, destructive side of the cow is no less clear than the positive, sustaining side of her character; again we are reminded of the cow-turned-tiger at Cikkal, and of the aggressive Kāmadhenu of Tiruvāṉmiyūr.[50]

Another murderous cow is known from the *Tiruviḷaiyāṭaṟpurāṇam*: the Jains produced a demon (*tāṉavaṉ*) in the form of a cow from a sacrificial pit and sent it to destroy Maturai, believing no one would resist because of the shame of harming a cow. Śiva sent his bull Nandin to stop it; Nandin caught the cow on his horns and threw it on to its back, and then he revealed all his beauty (*āriya viṭai taṉ māṇṭav aḻakiṉai kkāṭṭa*) without causing the cow harm. The cow was overcome with desire and, losing its life and its strength, turned into a mountain.[51] Lust is fatal to the demon-cow, which is here pitted against its natural consort, the bull; paralysis and turning upside down recur in association with the violent bull.[52] Milk is attached here to the bull rather than the cow: Nandin approaches the cow like a moving silver mountain, his horn—like a milk-white sliver of the moon—splitting open the pregnant abdomen of the cloud.[53] If the bull can thus claim the symbolism of milk and seductive beauty, the cow appears as the violent aggressor; we are not far here from the pattern of sex reversal that is discussed at the end of this chapter. A masculine nature is imputed to the dangerous goddess, who may appear either as wholly male or as a male-female hybrid, the androgyne.[54] Color symbolism is useful here as a means of expressing the ambivalent nature of the mother; in the myth just cited, Nandin's horn is white as milk, and the demonic cow is also usually depicted as white;[55] frequently, however, a violent cow is said to be black, or both black and white. In a myth from the *Śivapurāṇa*, a white cow, angered when a Brahmin strikes her calf, kills the Brahmin's son with her horn; she immediately becomes black, but regains her white color and expiates her crime by bathing in a *tīrtha*.[56] A myth from Āndhra relates that a black cow trampled by mistake an anthill in which the child Kṛṣṇa was dwelling, and over which she had previously poured her milk; the hoof was imprinted in the moist clay, and Śiva ordered that the anthill cool down and become a *liṅga*.[57] The black color of the cow is here shared by the *liṅga* that replaces the wounded deity residing in the anthill. At Velūr, another anthill shrine, the cow who nourishes the serpent-deity has an even more striking appearance:

> A cow (*kārāmpacu*) with black body, mouth white as the conch, and coral-red horns, ears, hoofs, and tail, with five

dugs as if made of sugar cane, gave birth to a calf to which it gave no milk. The calf did not cling to its mother and was never hungry, weary, or thirsty. One day the master noticed that when the cow came home in the evening from the fields, its udders were empty. He followed the cow one day as it went toward the forest, crossed over to an island, and stood over an anthill there. A five-headed serpent emerged from the anthill to suck the milk from each of the five udders of the cow.

The cow's master was overcome with joy. He slept there that night, and the lord appeared to him in a dream, saying, "I am Sāmbaśivamūrtti. I created the black cow, and I drink her milk and am content." The devotee built the god a shrine at that spot.[58]

The five-faced god (Pañcavaktra-Śiva) in the form of a serpent drinks the milk of the multicolored cow. According to the dictionaries, the *kārāmpacu* is a black cow with black tongue and udder, but it is also a form of the Kāmadhenu: the *kārāmpacu* lives in the world of Indra and has the face of a woman and the wings of a bird.[59] Yet the combination of black and white in the Velūr cow suggests an essentially ambivalent nature. Note that the cow's preference for the god means that she deprives her own child of milk, although the calf is expressly said not to suffer on this account in this text. More to the point is another myth from this shrine, which makes the aggression against the child explicit:

"There was a Raja named Dharma Raja. He had a son who was noted for his unrivalled beauty. He had a step-mother who became hopelessly fond of him. She once called him to her and tried by every means to make him make love to her. Sarangadram hereupon left his stepmother in great disdain. With a view now to ruin him, she told her husband Dharma Raja that his son had attempted to take improper liberties with her. The Raja was consequently so much enraged against him that he instantly ordered his hands and feet to be cut off, and his maimed body to be cast on the hill [from which the rocks used in building a shrine were later taken]. . . . Sarangadram did not take this undeserved cruelty to heart, but spent all his solitary hours in devotion to the god. Consequently his hands and feet were replaced, and the hill was also benefited by his meritorious sufferings, in that any extent of stones extracted from it was in no time replaced."[60]

The hill on which the stepson is thrown provides the rocks for the shrine of the five-headed serpent in the anthill, as described in the previous text. The virtuous son, slandered by his stepmother for rejecting her advances as Hippolytus is slandered by Phaedra, suffers unjustly at the hands of his father; the injustice is made still more bitter by the king's name, "king of *dharma*." The pattern of paternal aggression against a son is very pronounced in Tamil sources, so much so that A. K. Ramanujan has suggested that the Western Oedipal theme is inverted in India, so that violence is directed from father to son rather than *vice versa*;[61] there are, however, many instances of the "classical" Oedipal theme of the son's attack upon the father as well.[62] Our concern for the moment is with the aggressive mother or stepmother: in the above myth, nothing is said of the boy's true mother, while the stepmother has become the locus of violence directed against the son. The evil stepmother is, as I have mentioned, a universal figure well represented in Indian literature: one thinks of Chāyā, the sun's shadowy second wife, who curses her stepson Yama to lose a leg;[63] or Suruci, whose behavior drives her rival's son Dhruva to perform austerities in order to achieve a station higher than that of his stepbrothers—until ultimately he becomes the Pole Star.[64] But the evil stepmother is frequently no more than a representative of the dark component of the real mother. This seems to be the case at Velūr—not only is "Sarangadram's" natural mother completely absent, but the myth of the lustful stepmother fills the lacuna of the first myth from this shrine and explains the portrayal of the cow as partially black. The multicolored cow expresses the contrasting aspects of the goddess as mother.

The Velūr tradition, with its sexually aggressive but frustrated stepmother, thus brings us to our second theme—the question of incest. If the violent goddess does, in fact, give birth to her consort, an incestuous relationship is inevitable—even if, as we by now expect, the union is never completely consummated. We shall study several Tamil examples of this theme, which is also associated with the cow-incarnation of the goddess. First, let us note that the theme of mother-son incest is at least as ancient as the father-daughter incest that serves as the metaphor for creation. Pūṣan is the wooer of his mother and the lover of his sister.[65] *Nirukta* 10.46 suggests that Purūravas unites with his mother (Vāc).[66] A later myth that plays on the same theme is the story of Rati, who brings up Pradyumna as a son, then falls in love with him and marries him.[67] In the classical Śaiva purāṇas, however, incestuous desire for the mother is either restricted to the demons, as in the outstanding instance of Andhaka (who, however, becomes a form of Śiva), or allowed to surface—often only by implication—in myths about the children of Śiva and Pārvatī, especially Gaṇeśa. Vighneśvara (Gaṇeśa) wants a woman as beautiful as his mother, "and such a one he has not found, though he has every opportunity of beholding the damsels of the country, seeing that he stands at the most conspicuous places in the towns and villages, and at the threshold of innumerable temples."[68] We are also told that during his battle with Śūrapadma, each time Gaṇeśa overcame a demon his (Gaṇeśa's) mother gave birth to another; he therefore closed her *yoni* with his trunk to prevent her from giving birth.[69] This ingenious explanation of the popular Vallabhagaṇapati icon, an obvious sexual image, identifies the partner of the god as his mother. The Gaṇeśa myths bring out clearly the rivalry between the son and the husband for the mother's love; Śiva beheads the young Gaṇeśa (or breaks off one of his tusks in a symbolic act of castration) out of jealousy at Pārvatī's love for this child.[70] Hart notes that the competition between husband and son for the sacred power embodied in the mother underlies the separation of the father from his wife during and immediately after childbirth; in this period the father constitutes a danger for the child, and the child for the father, for both look to the same source of power for sustenance.[71] In the myths of Gaṇeśa, this rivalry remains constant. Skanda (Murukaṉ), the younger son of Śiva and Pārvatī, never to my knowledge competes with Śiva in this manner; in the Tamil tradition, Murukaṉ's eroticism is focused almost entirely on Vaḷḷi, his local bride,[72] while in the northern tradition Skanda—although married to Devasenā, the Army of the Gods, as befits a divine warrior—is often a symbol of chastity, an eternal *brahmacārin*, who presents no threat, sexual or otherwise, to his father.[73] In one myth Skanda is cured of lust when his mother Pārvatī takes the form of whatever woman he is about to seduce;[74] here we have no incestuous desires but simply a conventional antierotic argument. Only rarely does one encounter Śiva himself as a child of the goddess in northern sources: in the *MBh* he is said to have appeared on Pārvatī's lap as a child; Indra tried to strike the child with his thunderbolt, but the infant paralyzed Indra's arm.[75] In the *Liṅgapurāṇa*, Śiva takes the form of a baby to suck the anger from the breasts of the goddess after she has slain the demon Dāruka.[76]

The Tamil myths, however, offer many examples of the theme of incestuous love between Śiva and the goddess of a shrine. The context of this love, which never attains its object, is the local marriage of the divine couple. We turn first to Tiruvāvaṭuturai, where the marriage to the cow-goddess takes two forms:

> "Sometime before this, the goddess had cherished a desire that all souls in the world should obtain deliverance and that the celestial women (*dēvarambaiyar*) should have their desires satisfied. To achieve this object, she told the god that she did not have all the rituals in her marriage, which took place when she was only a child in the Himālaya mountains, and that she would like their marriage to be celebrated once again with all its attendant ceremonies. Śiva said that she could have her wish satisfied in due time; and meanwhile asked her to play dice with him. They played dice having Viṣṇu as the umpire. In the course of the play, the goddess, it is said, spoke disobediently to her lord, and the god cursed her to be born as a *paśu* (cow) and said, 'you shall worship me at Nandimānagar and get rid of this curse when we shall accept you again and marry you as you desired.' The god then sent his spouse to work out her curse along with Gaṇapati and others, and asked Viṣṇu to be the cowherd when the goddess would take birth as a cow. But the pang of separation was much even for Śiva to bear; he transformed the Bījākṣara of the goddess into seven seeds and sowed them in seven places beginning with Tiruvālangāḍu. When the goddess had passed through the ordeal, she made a plunge in the Gomukti tīrtha and was accepted again by the god under the name of Oppilāmulai ['(the lady of) the incomparable breast']. Then their marriage was celebrated."[77]

The identification of Devī and the cow is here explicit. The exile of the goddess leads to the appearance on earth of the divine seed, the *bījākṣara*; as in the flood myth from Cīkāḻi,[78] the reference is to a "seed-*mantra*," or to sound as a creative medium. The *mantra* of the goddess, which no doubt leads to the deliverance of those who know it (in accordance with Devī's wish *before* her descent to earth), is produced in connection with Devī's terrestrial marriage and distributed by Śiva among seven shrines. Śiva separates the divine seed, as in several versions of the birth of Skanda[79] and as in the myth of the Maruts, divided into seven while still in the womb of Diti by Indra;[80] the latter myth may even have contributed to the Tamil myth, and we should remember that the Maruts were earlier known as the children of a cow (*gómātaraḥ*).[81] Two marriages are recognized by the Tamil text, the first, unsatisfactory one with the child-bride in the Himālayas, the second in the shrine; the latter event is, of course, the primary concern of the Tamil myth. Yet there is an implicit doubling even of this second, localized marriage. The central figure of the shrine of Tiruvāvaṭuturai, the setting of this myth, is the bull Nandin;[82] Śiva himself refers to this site as Nandimānagar, "the great city of Nandin," when he sends the goddess off to work out her curse. The cow thus joins Nandin, her proper consort, in his shrine; only later is she remarried to Śiva, this time in her maternal form ("the lady of the incomparable breast," an epithet derived from the image of the cow and its milk). Another version of the myth makes this duplication clearer:

> Once, on Kailāsa, Devī asked Śiva to tell her a story. He told her of her birth as the daughter of Dakṣa, her suicide at her father's sacrifice, her rebirth as Pārvatī and her marriage to him. Umā bowed and said, "It has been such a long time since our wedding; it is like a dream seen by a mute. Marry me again." Śiva agreed to marry her once more in the coming era (*brahmakalpa*). Because he refused to marry her immediately, the goddess was sad and called to her companions to go out with her to the garden. Thus she was disrespectful to her husband in her mind, and Śiva cursed her to become a cow (*pacu*) on earth. Devī wept in grief and sought forgiveness. Śiva comforted her: to match her cow's form, he would become a bull and appear before her.
>
> The goddess went to earth in the form of a cow; the gods accompanied her as cowherds, while the goddesses became cows. Śiva followed her as a bull. The cow found a *liṅga* in a forest of *aracu* trees. She poured milk over it and won the name Ŏppilāmulaiyāḷ. She also watered a *liṅga* in a nearby banyan forest. When three years had passed thus, Śiva disappeared. The cow was stricken with sorrow at the separation. The god called to her from heaven, "We have rejoiced in your milk. Now bathe in the holy tank."
>
> The cow did so and gained back her divine form; hence that tank is known as Gomuktitīrtha ("the tank of the cow's release"). Śiva came to embrace the goddess; therefore he is

> named Aṇaintĕḻuntār ("he who rose to embrace"). He sent the gods back to heaven, promising to call them back for his wedding to Ŏppilāmulaiyammai, and he remained in Tiruvāvaṭutuṟai, holding the goddess in his embrace.[83]

Devī's exile is made easy to bear because her husband follows her in a form matching hers. The bull accompanies Devī to earth; its disappearance is the catalyst to the "human" marriage of Śiva and the goddess. Note that although the cow finds the *liṅgas* indicative of a divine presence in the shrine, she attracts the bull—the major deity of this site—to the spot, and then causes Śiva to remain there as Aṇaintĕḻuntār; in other words, the local goddess attracts and establishes the male divinity in the shrine. Release from the form of a cow (*paśu*) may refer to the concept of Śiva's grace in releasing souls (*paśu*) from bonds (*pāśa*);[84] the goddess would thus exemplify, in her exile and restoration, the process of deliverance that she is said to desire for all souls (according to the first version of the Tiruvāvaṭutuṟai myth). The god's grace is often personified by the goddess (*aruṭcatti*), but if the myth under discussion is in fact a Śaiva Siddhāntin allegory, the goddess would be in this case the *object* of the longed-for grace; like other souls, she achieves salvation by devotion on earth. One Sanskrit purāṇa suggests a somewhat similar idea: the gods became *paśus* in order to overcome the demons of the Triple City; they performed the *pāśupata* rite to rid themselves of this state.[85] Yet this kind of allegory is surely later than the basic myth of Śiva's marriage at Tiruvāvaṭutuṟai; a Siddhāntin exegesis cannot dispose of the essential images of the myth. In her appearance at the shrine as a cow, and in watering the *liṅga* with her milk, the goddess is seen as a mother. Śiva marries the cow-goddess after she is freed from this form, but his bride's name, Ŏppilāmulaiyammai, continues to evoke the incest theme. If such, indeed, is the underlying force of the second marriage, it is obscured by the presence of the bull, the proper mate for the cow-goddess. In other words, the maternal aspect of the goddess is separated from her erotic role, as it is in the myths of Skanda's birth examined below. Moreover, it is important to note that neither of the two marriages at Tiruvāvaṭutuṟai is actually celebrated in the myth; the first, between cow and bull, is entirely implicit, the second promised but seemingly postponed, although Śiva embraces Ŏppilāmulaiyammai even without a ritual celebration.

The tradition of Tiruvāvaṭutuṟai thus reveals two major

strands—Śiva marries the goddess as mother, but the incestuous union is not fully achieved. The maternal consort remains a virgin. Such a conclusion accords well with the most basic elements of the marriage myths as defined in our discussion so far; the myths of Ŏppilāmulaiyammai are unusual only in their boldness and clarity. Only in tribal myths is the incest motif more explicit.[86] In other Tamil shrines, the incestuous marriage is largely veiled, but Śiva retains a claim on the offspring of the cow-goddess:

> One day a bull forced himself on the cows of Indra's heaven, including the Kāmadhenu, and the sweat from their union poured like a waterfall on to the *liṅga* at Tiruvarañcai. The sages there were angered by this defilement, and the cows grew lean and discolored and sick. Indra was alarmed, and Brahmā came to tell him that the cause was the anger of Śiva. Brahmā advised the cows, "Even though Śiva will not regard evil committed unintentionally as a fault, still it will be difficult for you to rid yourselves of the disease, no matter how long you perform *tapas* or how many magical powers (*siddhis*) you attain. Only worship of Śiva with your milk together with pure water, ghee, and flowers will bring you purity of body." The cows hastened to Tiruvarañcai and bathed the *liṅga* in their milk (*tuyyav amutakkaṭal*) and created, by ploughing the earth with their faces, a river of pure water—the Gomukhī ("cow's face"). After one hundred years Śiva appeared on the bull and forgave them. They asked that their sons, born in joy, become the *vāhana* of the god, and that these sons flourish like Murukaṉ and Gaṇapati. Because they were granted their wish (*varam*), that shrine is known as Varañcai, where Paśupati-Śiva rejoiced upon the bull.[87]

An unintentional offense causes sickness and emaciation, just as Indra's necessary killing of Vṛtra causes him to become weak and lusterless;[88] and just as Indra restores his strength by drinking milk or Soma,[89] so the cows are healed by the gift of their milk/*amṛta*. The offense is positive in effect, producing sons born in joy and a holy river to offset the waterfall of defiling sweat; moreover, the sons are promised the status of the children of the goddess Pārvatī when Śiva (as Paśupati, lord of beasts—or cows!) reveals himself riding upon their father, the bull. Thus Śiva is both polluted by the sin and rewarded (with adopted children and a *vāhana*) by its atonement through the milk of the goddess. The association of the children of the cows with Murukaṉ and Gaṇeśa would seem to implicate the god himself—through his vehicle, the bull—in the rape that initiates the mythic action; this splitting of the god's symbols completely masks the motif of union with the cow-mother, just as the appearance of the bull at Tiruvāvaṭutuṟai obscures the incestuous relationship between Śiva and the goddess.

In a similar myth from the *Kālikāpurāṇa*, Śiva's mount is not his son but his grandson: Vetāla, the son of Śiva, desired the Kāmadhenu, and she, following the *dharma* of animals,[90] came to him of her own accord. From their union was born a bull named Śṛṅga; he worshiped Śiva, and Śiva made him his *vāhana*.[91] Elsewhere, the *vāhana* of Śiva is not the offspring but the husband of the cow:

> The Kāmadhenu, wife of Mārttāṇḍa the bull, came to Nāgeśakṣetra and worshiped the god, who stretched forth his tongue and drank the milk of her four teats. After four years the god said, "Enough! I am satisfied and can no longer drink your milk." He showed her his five faces, and she saw that her teats had left an impression on each of them. Śiva then appeared to her and granted her request for offspring, saying, "You will have three kinds of children—goats, cows, and buffaloes, all of which will have a part in the sacrifice. Your four daughters Nandinī, Kapilā, Rohiṇī, and Surabhi will reside in the four quarters together with their guardians, and your husband will serve as my *vāhana*."[92]

Again, worship of the god produces offspring; here the aggression is not in the rape of the cow-goddess but in the mother's wounding the faces of the god. The cow scars the god's image even as she nourishes him, just as Kāmākṣī wounds the *liṅga* during the Kāñci flood. Mārttāṇḍa (*sic*), who appears as a stallion in a famous myth of two mothers (Saṃjñā and her surrogate Chāyā),[93] is here the bull, husband of the cow; in Vedic mythology he is the eighth son of Aditi, rejected by his mother so that he dies and is born again—a classic expression of the murderous mother.[94] In the purāṇas Aditi, impregnated by a ray of the sun, performs terrible austerities until her husband Kaśyapa accuses her of killing the embryo; angered, Aditi gives birth on the spot to a son called Mārttaṇḍa, after Kaśyapa's fears that the egg had been destroyed (*māritam aṇḍam*).[95] The cow-mother at Nāgeśakṣetra is thus married to the epitome of the murdered child; her wounding of the god preserves this relationship in a different form, although nothing is said of any marriage between Śiva and the cow.

All the myths just discussed—from Tiruvāvaṭuturai, Tiruvarañcai, and Nāgeśakṣetra—show a common tendency to soften the impact of the incest motif, and even to do away with it entirely. This struggle to break away from an underlying pattern is, as we have seen, characteristic of the Tamil purāṇic tradition as a whole. South Indian village myths are less concerned with the proprieties; here the idea of incestuous lust is stated in plain terms. Nevertheless, the village myths share with the purāṇic tradition the refusal to allow the incestuous act to take place. Let us look at one striking example of a popular myth of the goddess as mother:

> "Ellamma is the Ādiśakti, without father or mother or husband, born out of the earth, a virgin. Before her was Ādijambuvu, a great muni, who was born six months before the Kaliyugam. . . . He by his mantras caused Ellamma to be born out of the earth. Nine hours after she was born, she attained to maturity and was like a twelve years' old girl. [She put on grand clothes and went to greet the sage; she tried to seduce him, but he refused her and gave her instead a root to plant in the ground. From this root a cock sprang up; the goddess became a hen and laid three eggs, one of which fell to the world of the Nāgas and gave birth to Ādiśeṣa, while the second went bad and produced the Brahmarākṣasī in the city of Bali, and the third was hatched by the goddess. From it Brahmā, Viṣṇu, and Śiva were born, and after their birth the goddess became a woman again. She asked them to satisfy her desire, but they replied:] 'Mother we came from your womb, how can we do this?' She answered, 'I am not your mother, but only your grandmother, as you were born from an egg, so you need not hesitate.' They fled from her in fear from place to place, and at length rushed into the presence of Ādijambuvu to tell him, who they were, and why they had fled from the Ādiśakti. He turned to Śiva and said, 'It is you she seeks and not the others. When she presses you to comply with her wishes promise to do so on the condition that she gives you her third eye. She will agree to give you her eye, and with it I shall take away her strength, so that her robe will become a burden to her.' Śiva

> did according to these directions, and the Ādiśakti's strength and vigour disappeared. He asked if she still wished him to comply with her request, and she replied that her robe had become a burden to her. The Trimurtulu left her, and after receiving instruction from Ādijambuvu, she returned to Matangagiri hill. Nine hours later the Kaliyuga began and the people came in multitudes to worship her."[96]

In a variant of this myth, Māriyammaṉ hatches the Trimūrti from the black speck of an egg; after rearing them until the age of twelve, she gives each of them a chariot and a trident and tries to seduce them. Brahmā and Śiva refuse on the grounds that she is their mother; Viṣṇu procrastinates, but when she returns the next day he takes from her the fairest of her thousand eggs, a weapon, and a forehead ornament; she loses her strength and her desire, becoming like a woman one hundred years old.[97]

This myth recalls at once the pattern of taming or transforming a dangerous goddess. Ĕllamma is the virgin mother, born from the earth, who lusts for her sons and must be restrained. Unlike the myths of the dance contest, however, the outcome of the village myth is not a conventional marriage but the final separation of the tamed virgin. The process of overcoming the menacing goddess is symbolized here first by the theft of the third eye, and then by the bizarre motif of the cumbersome robe. The third eye and its multiform, the forehead ornament, may be related to the third breast of Mīnākṣī—hence also to the weapon, probably the phallic trident, that Viṣṇu must steal in the second myth. First the goddess must be made a woman by the birth of her sons;[98] then, since she is still far from the conventional ideal of a woman, her lust and excessive vigor must be drained before she becomes fit for worship, and real time can begin—for in the village myths, the Kaliyuga is the one, primeval age. Māriyammaṉ is formed from light in the midst of the waters, light that takes the form of a woman in order to bring forth the Kaliyuga.[99]

The loss of power described here seems, at first glance, to clash with the recurring idea of *preserving* the power of the virgin goddess intact—as when Kālī is exiled to the boundary of the shrine in order to avoid the dissipation of energy consequent upon marriage. On closer inspection, however, the village myth is no exception to this pattern. Ĕllamma remains a virgin set apart in her shrine, and the transformation she undergoes simply reflects the necessary limitation of her native powers. Specifically, it is her dangerous lust for her children that must be neutralized. The village myth's total rejection of incest is most striking, and contrasts starkly with Sanskrit creation myths in which incest is the necessary first step. The Sanskrit pattern of the father pursuing his daughter is inverted in the village myth, and the daughter is made to attempt to seduce her creator, the sage Ādijambu(vu). She fails, and her failure adumbrates her rejection by her sons, especially Śiva, who profits from the advice of the sage. The father is at no time a threatening figure in this myth; the aggression toward the child takes the form of the mother's violent lust. The sons flee from their passionate, devouring mother, whose incestuous desires must be frustrated in order to preserve her chastity and power, and thus give meaning to her worship. In the village, the goddess remains both a virgin and a mother. If the androgynous Mīnākṣī becomes a woman in order to marry, the village goddess loses her unnatural powers—the third eye, the symbol of her aggression against the gods—in order to *block* the fulfilment of her desire. No union can take place between the gods and the dark virgin;[100] the virgin mother reigns alone in her shrine on the hill.

## *Sixes and Sevens: The Mothers of Skanda*

The three main themes we have been exploring—the dark or threatening mother, the incestuous relationship between husband and bride, and the mother as a virgin—all appear in one of the most important myths of multiple mothers, the Skanda birth myth with its many folk variants. In this myth—perhaps we should regard it as a many-colored spectrum of related myths—the technique of division is used to striking effect. We find here benign and malevolent mothers, seductive but infertile foster mothers, antierotic but fertile virgins, mothers who murder their beloved children, and a host of similarly anomalous heroines. The south Indian folk tradition is linked (perhaps indirectly) to the Skanda myth through the popular series of the Seven Mothers (*saptamātṛkās*) or Seven Maidens (*kaṉṉimār*). We will survey here a rather narrow selection of these myths, concentrating on the south Indian variants that shed light on the major themes of this chapter.[101] We begin with classical versions of the Skanda myth, in Sanskrit and in Tamil, where the distribution of contrasting roles is already clear:

Agni desired the wives of the Seven Sages but, ashamed of his desire, he entered the household fire in order to see them and touch them; then he went into the forest. Svāhā, the daughter of Dakṣa, was full of desire for Agni; she took the form of each of the sages' wives, and made love six times with Agni in the forest—only she was unable to take the form of Arundhatī, the seventh, because of the latter's chastity. Six times Svāhā took the form of a Garuḍī bird and deposited the seed of Agni in a golden pot on a white mountain covered with reeds. From that seed Skanda was born, with six heads and one body.

When the Seven Sages heard of the birth of the boy, they abandoned their wives, except for Arundhatī. Some time later the six wives came to Skanda and said, "We have been abandoned without just cause by our husbands on the grounds that you are our son; be, then, our son, and may we be (a constellation) in heaven." Skanda granted their request.[102] The gods advised Indra to kill Skanda at once, lest he usurp his position. Indra, believing he could not kill the boy, sent the mothers of the world (*lokasya mātaraḥ*) to do so. But when the mothers approached him and saw his might, they lost heart and took refuge with him, saying, "You are our son; we support the world. Our breasts are flowing with milk." Skanda worshiped them, for he wished to drink the milk of their breasts, and he worshiped Agni, his father, who remained in the midst of the mothers. Skanda's wet-nurse (*dhātrī*) was the Mother born in anger, daughter of the ocean of blood, a drinker of blood.

Indra cast his thunderbolt at Skanda, splitting open his side; a man, Viśākha, came forth from the open side. Indra then took refuge with Skanda. From the blow of the thunderbolt were also produced young men and maidens, who snatch away children.[103]

In this version—perhaps the earliest complete narrative of Skanda's birth—Agni rather than Śiva is the father of the child; Agni's wife, Svāhā, wins the divine seed by impersonating six of the Kṛttikās, the wives of the Seven Sages. The Kṛttikās become mothers by proxy of the newborn god; they have no actual erotic connection with Agni, who lusts for them, but only the seventh—Arundhatī—is possessed of sufficient virtue to be saved from implication in the birth of the child. We will return to the anomalous seventh goddess in a moment. The maternal role ascribed to the six Kṛttikās is characterized by the basic ambivalence that we have observed in the Tamil myths of the mother. Although the Kṛttikās are not explicitly identified with the mothers who come to kill Skanda, their identity may be inferred: Svāhā refers to the wives of the sages as "the mothers"; Agni takes up his place in the midst of the mothers who come to murder his son, just as earlier he unites with Svāhā masquerading as the wives of the sages; the sages and mothers are mentioned together in the assembly that comes to welcome Skanda; and the mothers fulfil the essential role ascribed to the Kṛttikās in later versions of the myth, that of nursing Skanda with their milk.[104] That Skanda's wet-nurse is the bloodthirsty Kālī is particularly significant; as we shall see, the Seven Mothers are often associated with blood and killing in both purāṇic and village sources. In the myths of the slaying of Raktabīja, Śumbha-Niśumbha, Mahiṣa, and Andhaka,[105] the Mothers—now paired with the various male gods, although the lists vary[106]—participate in the battle, their main function being to drink the demon's blood. In some versions, the blood intoxicates them, and they have to be subdued by another set of Mothers sent by Viṣṇu—an obvious sectarian element introduced into the Śaiva-Śākta myth.[107] The Epic, in a postscript to the Skanda birth story, describes the troops of Mothers linked with Skanda: they ask to be given control over creatures now allotted to another set of Mothers;[108] Skanda hesitates, preferring them to protect creatures instead of devouring them, but in the end he gives them his own terrifying (*raudra*) form and the right to afflict creatures to the age of sixteen.[109] The *mātṛkās* are therefore considered demons that seize children and make them ill;[110] sometimes they are invoked to protect little children as if they were their real mothers.[111]

The anomalous seventh goddess plays a pivotal role in the Epic and most subsequent versions of the Skanda myth. The role is presumably occasioned here, as in Greek mythology, by the faintness of the seventh star in the constellation of the Pleiades.[112] Arundhatī is thus usually excluded from the episode of Skanda's birth, her chastity being yet more pure than that of the other six Kṛttikās. In purāṇic versions of the myth, the Kṛttikās as a group oppose Pārvatī, Śiva's wife, as antierotic yet fertile mothers who contrast with the barren but seductive wife of the yogi Śiva; a yogi, having renounced the world, is a most improper father of new children, and thus Pārvatī is forced to adopt the son she cannot carry in her womb.[113] In these myths, the complete purity of Arundhatī simply exaggerates a quality common to the Kṛttikās as a whole; the anomalous seventh represents an extreme expression of a general feature of the group. In other cases, however, the seventh goddess is in opposition to her six companions. The seven sages are said to have loved a single woman,[114] and in one late purāṇa Skanda is adopted by a single Kṛttikā.[115] Arundhatī, the exemplar of devotion to the husband, became a star that is barely visible and not very beautiful because she distrusted her husband Vasiṣṭha.[116] Sometimes, in folk or tribal myths, Arundhatī's role is completely reversed: instead of being a paragon of chastity who has no connection with the child's birth, the seventh (or eighth) woman is fertile and gives birth to a son, while her six cowives (or sisters) remain barren and jealous.[117] Another pattern of opposition involves the relegation of the violent or murderous aspect of the mother to the extra goddess, who is separated from the benign, gentle mothers. Already in the *Cilappatikāram* we find a passage suggestive of this pattern: the watchman of the Pāṇṭiyaṉ, announcing Kaṇṇaki's arrival at the gate of the palace, includes among the fierce goddesses with whom she might be compared "the youngest woman of the seven" (*aṟuvarkk' iḷaiya naṅkai*), who may be identical with the woman who made Śiva dance (or witnessed his dance—*iṟaivaṉai āṭal kaṇṭ' aruḷiya aṇaṅku*), Kālī who loves the terrible forest, the killer of Dāruka, and so on.[118] All are forms of the violent goddess. We will observe other instances of this distribution in the folk myths of the Seven Mothers.

Arundhatī is altogether missing from the standard Tamil version of the Skanda myth, which also drastically reduces the entire theme of aggression toward the divine infant:

> The gods sent Vāyu to find out what was happening in Śiva's abode, for they desperately needed a son from the god to save them from Śūrapadma. Vāyu was stopped by Nandin from entering. Then all the gods came to see Śiva, whom they found seated on his throne with Umā. They asked him for a son. Śiva sprouted six heads, and from the eye in the forehead of each of them a spark flew out; from their heat the worlds and the sea dried up, and Umā fled in terror, smashing her anklets in the process. Śiva told Agni and Vāyu to take the sparks and deliver them to the Ganges; Vāyu handed them to Agni, who threw them into the river. Dessicated by the fierce heat, the Ganges carried them on her head to Caravaṇam.

> From that pond Murukaṉ arose with one body, six heads, and twelve arms, floating on a lotus, in the form of an infant. The gods called the Kṛttikās (*kārttikaittĕrivaimār*) to nurse the child and, as they entered the water, they beheld six children instead of one; each took one to nurse.
>
> Śiva and Umā went to the pond; at Śiva's command, Umā embraced the six infants at the edge of the water, and they merged into one child with six heads and twelve arms. Milk flowed from the breasts of the goddess, and she collected it in a golden cup and fed it to her son. The milk from Umā's breasts flowed into the pond and transformed the six sons of Parāśara into men instead of fish, a form they had taken because of a curse.[119]

This version is much closer to the purāṇic accounts than to the Epic myth just summarized; the mothers of Skanda by now include Pārvatī (Umā), who nurses the restored single child by the side of the Caravaṇam pond,[120] and the Ganges, who carries the divine seed/sparks. Nevertheless, the Tamil version softens the force of the Sanskrit myths in several ways: sparks of light substitute for the divine seed; Śiva and Umā are simply sitting on their throne when the gods enter, not making love; there is no apparent tension between Pārvatī and the Kṛttikās (or between eroticism and fertility)—Skanda's birth is wholly unnatural, asexual, and diffuse. The wind, Vāyu—a form sometimes taken by Kāma to enter Śiva's presence[121]—here fails to get past the gatekeeper; but his function as the carrier of the intoxicating, aphrodisiac odors of spring is in any case superfluous, for Śiva no longer needs to be seduced in order to produce a son. Skanda is born as an act of grace by Śiva, who responds at once to the prayers of his supplicants, the gods. None of the mothers of Skanda threaten him in this version. Representatives of the violent goddess are, however, present in this text as well: as Umā flees the burning sparks of light, she breaks her anklets; from her reflections in the shattered jewels of her anklets, nine *śaktis* are born. They bow to Śiva and become pregnant at the mere sight of him, "like the wives of the sages" (of the Pine Forest).[122] Just as sparks from Śiva's eyes engender the divine infant, the sight of the god is enough to impregnate the nine *śaktis*.[123] In addition to cursing the wives of the gods to be barren, the jealous Umā then curses the pregnant *śaktis* to endure a long pregnancy—thus transferring the motif of violence from the infant to the embryo in the womb, who must suffer as do Durvāsas and Koccĕṅkaṇ.[124] The fierce children who are born join the hosts of Murukaṉ.

In the version just quoted, the six sons of the sage Parāśara replace the husbands of the Kṛttikās; their form as fish in the Caravaṇam pond recalls one account of the birth of the Maruts:

> Seven sons of a king were performing *tapas* to attain Indra's position. Indra, alarmed, sent the *apsaras* Pūtanā to disturb them. As soon as they saw her bathing in a river, they shed their seed; their *tapas* being ruined, they then returned home. The seed was drunk by a female water-demon swimming in the river; after some time she was caught by a fisherman. The seven sons of the king brought her to the palace, and there she gave birth to seven sons, the Maruts, and died. The infants cried for milk, and Brahmā came and comforted them.[125]

This myth belongs to a series of seven that relate the births of the Maruts and are closely tied to the myth of Skanda. The *apsaras* sent by Indra is Pūtanā, who appears in the troops of Mothers in the Skanda birth myth,[126] but who is best known as the demoness who tried to kill the infant Kṛṣṇa with a poison breast.[127] Pūtanā is thus another classical symbol of the evil mother. Here Pūtanā releases the seed, but neither she nor the demon mother nurses the infants who cry for milk.

The better-known myth of the Maruts' birth—after Indra cuts the embryo in the womb of Aditi into seven pieces—may have influenced the oldest complete Tamil version of Skanda's birth (which, as François Gros has noticed,[128] is also one of the oldest versions altogether):

> "When the green-eyed god who had devoured his share in the sacrifice of the immortal gods joined Umā in unbearable union on the day of their nuptials, the lord of the celestials' sacrifice begged a boon from him of the unblinking forehead-eye—'Desist!'[129] Still he [Śiva] did not retract that [promise] he had given to him who is adorned with shining gems [Indra], on the grounds that it was difficult [to accomplish], for he is the Truthful One. He took a hatchet blazing with fire and changed his [that is, the child's] form to confuse the seven worlds. Those who received the embryo, the Seven Sages in their rare wisdom, clearly recognized the expelled body of Ce [= Murukan]. They said, 'If the wives of the sages rich in *tapas*

> cook [and eat] the pieces of flesh, they will lose their virtue. Let the fire bear them.' They cast them into the fire together with the offering, and the three-fold fire in its pit cherished them. Aside from the divine star Cāliṉi, six of the seven women who shine in the north ate what was left [of the embryo from the fire]. Without straying from virtue, the wives of the sages of flawless chastity became pregnant from it. It is said that they gave birth to you, O great Murukaṉ, on a bed of lotuses in a spring with blue lotuses in the towering Himālayas. On the day you were born, the lord of the immortals whose glory it is difficult to attain took his fiery thunderbolt and angrily came and hurled it [at you]; the six separate pieces united into One—praise to you, Victorious Cey!"[130]

The Kṛttikās conceive not by bathing in water that carries the seed or by warming themselves before the fire, but by swallowing the ashes of the body of the embryonic Skanda, burned by Agni; the remnant of the offering is, as we have seen, an equivalent of the divine seed born from the sacrifice. Agni's role here is close to his disguise in the first Epic account, when he hides in the household fire in order to be near the Kṛttikās; in the Tamil text, the fire is interposed between the mutilated child and the Kṛttikās, who eat the ashes of Murukaṉ rather than his cooked flesh. The Seven Sages play a more active part than in most Sanskrit accounts of the birth; they receive the embryo and, aware of the threat to their wives' virtue, decide to cast it into the fire. This device is successful: the text takes pains to stress that the wives suffer no loss of virtue, although Arundhatī (Cāliṉi)[131] still excels. As in those versions where the divine seed enters and pours out from the bodies of the Kṛttikās,[132] the six wives here actually give birth to the child (instead of simply adopting and nursing him, as in the account of the *Kantapurāṇam* cited above); in this case Murukaṉ is born (in six pieces) on a bed of lotuses in a spring of water instead of in the forest of reeds. It is Indra's attempt to kill the child rather than Pārvatī's maternal affection that unites the separate pieces. According to the commentator Nacciṉārkkiṉiyar, who cites an unknown purāṇa (*purāṇam kūṟiṟṟu*) before referring to the *Paripāṭal* account, Indra himself receives the *undivided* embryo from Śiva, and the sages take it from him and cast it into the fire; but Indra is later said to have forgotten this episode when he hurls his thunderbolt and causes the six forms to unite.[133] Indra's aggression against the child follows upon the violence done to the embryo by the sages, who cast it into the fire, and their wives, who consume its ashes; and all these actions conform to the precedent set by Śiva, who chops up the embryo with a hatchet—seemingly while it is still in the womb. This element, which is perhaps the most striking feature of the *Paripāṭal* version, may owe something to the myth of Indra's attack upon the Maruts while they lay in the womb of Aditi. Although Śiva's action is said to be "for the confusion of the seven worlds," and Śiva will still not change his promise (to grant a leader of the army of the gods, or, according to Gros, simply to desist from intercourse),[134] the episode appears to be an extreme instance of the father's violence to his son. It is also noteworthy that Śiva is first described here as having devoured his share of the sacrifice; not only does this text explicitly connect the birth of the divine seed to the violence of the sacrifice, but the Tamil myth may also retain the sense of Śiva's primary role in this rite—in contrast with that strand of the Dakṣa myth that concentrates on the exclusion of the god.[135]

In the texts of the Skanda myth discussed so far, the Kṛttikās appear as chaste mothers, their chastity sometimes contrasting with the voluptuous nature of Svāhā or Pārvatī. One Tamil myth defines the relationship between the Kṛttikās and the goddess more carefully: the Kṛttikās are said to have won Skanda as their son by worshiping Aruntavanāyaki at Pātirippuliyūr.[136] Aruntavanāyaki is the chaste, ascetic form of the goddess who is split from the erotic consort of the god (Pĕriyanāyaki). The Tamil folk tradition goes a step further, and insists that the seven wives of the sages are virgins. Sometimes these folk goddesses have no individual consorts at all, although they are still depicted with a child in their arms.[137] Often their presence is symbolized by a pot (*kumbha*, *karakam*)—another indication of their maternal character.[138] The pot is the womb that carries the sacred seed. The Seven Mothers are fertile virgins (*kaṉṉimār*) untouched by any husband; unmarried virgins are compared to the seven *kaṉṉimār* and, if they die before marriage, are thought to merge with them.[139]

For all this, the antierotic role attached to the Kṛttikās in the Skanda myth is not necessarily suited to the folk virgin goddesses. As we have seen, virginity need not imply the negation of eroticism. The virgin is the epitome of the seductive woman, whose potential for intense eroticism is at its peak. This potential may, indeed, have a disastrous effect upon any male who comes within its range. The seductive virgin may kill the man who unleashes her native power. Hence, as we have noted, it is forbidden even to behold the Seven Virgins in their nocturnal procession around the village. The seven goddesses represent a dangerous, possibly lethal eroticism, the hunger and power of the virgin, a menacing sexuality waiting to break out of its bounds. The aggressive love of the Seven Virgins may be turned against their child (or children), unnaturally conceived and born—as in the case of Skanda's murderous mothers. Or their power may be brought under control by the male—as when Śiva turns the six Kṛttikās (*iyakkamātar*, that is, *yakṣīs*) into rocks because they failed to worship Umā.[140] The Seven Mothers are, in fact, worshiped in the form of stones in most Tamil villages.[141] One Tamil purāṇa, perhaps translating the village cult into an acceptable myth for a Brahminical shrine, portrays the seven goddesses as seductive nymphs:

> Karikāṟcoḻaṉ while hunting shot an arrow at a pig that had come to drink water from a pool. The pig turned out to be a Brahmin who had taken this form in order to get away from his wife and relatives who were following him into the forest. He told the king he would not leave him alone, and Karikāl was therefore haunted by a ghost. He went on pilgrimage to Tiruvāṉaikkā, where he met seven girls born on earth because of a curse by Umā: they had been late in bringing flowers for her worship because they were making love with a Gandharva in the forest. The king and the seven girls went to Tirupperūr and were released from the consequences of evil; they sacrificed and set up a *liṅga*.[142]

Here all seven women (*ĕḻuvar mātar*, v. 45) are lustful and suffer punishment, while murder attaches to the single man instead of to the Mothers or to Indra. The king has acquired the role of the single male who appears in association with the seven women in most local versions, sometimes as the son (Skanda), sometimes as husband or brother, or both, of one or of all seven maidens. The eroticism ascribed to the seven women here reverses the character of the Kṛttikās in most purāṇic versions of the Skanda myth, although some classical sources lend support for this reversal by associating the Kṛttikās with sexuality in *other* contexts: in one purāṇa they lead Rati, the wife of Kāma, to Śiva,[143] and sometimes they are implicitly identified with the wives of the sages tested by Śiva in the Pine Forest.[144] On the whole, we may say that Sanskrit versions of the Skanda myth tend to exclude any erotic role for the seven goddesses, who appear as chaste, antierotic mothers; but in the Tamil popular tradition, the seven goddesses are *virgin* mothers, and as such are possessed of the latent eroticism and dangerous power of the virgin. Thus when Rati is said to worship at the tank of the Seven Maidens at Tiruccĕṅkoṭu in order to recreate the body of her husband Kāma, she is appealing to the virgin goddesses as symbols of sexual power, and as partaking of the dynamic but dangerous character of Kāma himself.[145]

Unlike Rati, the Seven Maidens are often unmarried, their link with the Kṛttikās thus being obscured through the emphasis on their virginity. When the seven goddesses *are* given a husband in village myths, he is frequently their brother (and they themselves are said to be sisters):

> In the land of the West, on the bank of the Pŏṉṉi River, lived Cāstirivarmā and his wife Vijayavati. They performed *tapas* together, and Śiva granted them a son and seven daughters. When they were grown, the parents entrusted the girls to the care of their elder brother and went away to Kāśī.
>
> One day the girls wanted to play in the forest; not wishing them to be alone, the brother came and played with them. As they were preparing to return, a snake bit him and he died. The girls cried to the Trimūrti in grief, and Nārada came and taught them a vow that brought the brother back to life. They then asked Viṣṇu for a place to live as householders. He sent them to the *kaṭampa* forest near Nākapaṭṭaṇam (*sic*), where he had earlier stationed Durgā (*Turkkai*) to guard a pot of *amṛta* that had fallen there during the churning of the ocean. There they dwell to this day together with their brother.[146]

The seven sisters are known collectively as Pattiṉiyammaṉ (from *pattiṉi*, Skt. *patnī*, a wife, especially the chaste or even virginal wife).[147] The seven are connected to a shrine near Nākapaṭṭiṉam where, we must assume, they are represented together with their brother—the single male—and with Durgā. The association of seven goddesses with Durgā is widespread in south India; sometimes they are said to be the daughters of Māriyammaṉ, who is often equated with Durgā.[148] Elsewhere Māriyammaṉ holds herself aloof from the seven sisters; they are kind and indulgent, while she is vindictive, evil-tempered, and more powerful than they.[149] In either case, Durgā-Māriyammaṉ is the anomalous extra goddess who serves to oppose or contrast with the rest, an allotrope of

Arundhatī in the Skanda birth story. Thus Māriyammaṉ either attracts the violent aspects of the mother goddess to herself, leaving the sisters benign and gentle—another example of the splitting of functions; or she epitomizes and exaggerates a characteristic shared by them all, just as Arundhatī's inviolability may symbolize the basic purity of all the Kṛttikās.

In the myth of Pattiṉiyammaṉ from Nākapaṭṭiṉam, Durgā's presence serves an additional purpose. This is a myth about brothers and sisters, and about incest, and the incest theme is strengthened by the appearance of Durgā—who in the south Indian tradition is the sister of Viṣṇu. Viṣṇu usually gains his wife, Lakṣmī, from the churning of the ocean; here he sends his sister to guard the *amṛta* produced from the same event. The incestuous love between the elder brother and his seven sisters is thinly veiled by the motif of playing in the forest. In addition, one has his death by the bite of the phallic serpent and his resuscitation by his sisters/wives—an echo of the well-known tale of Tiruñāṉacampantar's revival of a bridegroom killed by a snake after eloping with his cross-cousin, the seventh of seven daughters who were promised him in turn by their father, but never given to him in fulfilment of the promise.[150] Moreover, the seven sisters in the folk myth from Nākapaṭṭiṉam are granted a place to dwell *as householders* with their brother, although they collectively embody the ideal of chastity. The *kummi* folk song that accompanies this myth, clearly troubled by the implications of the story, admits that all is not well with the communal marriage: the seven women (*catta mātar*) have to go to Kāśī to rid themselves of the evil of living as householders with their brother.[151] Still, we may doubt that the Pattiṉiyammaṉ sisters ever really lose their chastity. If the pattern observed in the myths of Śiva's incestuous marriage to the cow / mother could be applied to this situation as well—and there is no reason to assume otherwise—we may deduce that the incestuous union of brother and sisters is never consummated. The evil that Pattiṉiyammaṉ must expiate in Kāśī derives from the juxtaposition of the unmarried sisters and their brother in the house, in a manner that allows the latent sexuality of the women to be expressed entirely in incestuous desires for the brother. One may recall the important folk motif of the brothers who keep their sister or sisters unmarried in order to profit from the power vested in the virgin.[152] This power is rooted in the erotic potential of the woman, in her threatening and enticing sexuality. The incest motif, especially in its appearance in folk myths in connection with the love of brothers and sisters, expresses clearly the idea of a dangerous eroticism, of sexuality gone awry, of the power that lurks in the virgin and that seeks an outlet in violent, potentially destructive and even forbidden behavior. The appearance of Durgā, the dark and terrifying virgin, sister of Viṣṇu, seductive bride of the Mahiṣāsura myths, serves to underline the attributes of power, virginity, and latent eroticism embodied in the seven sisters at Nākapaṭṭiṉam.

Although the names vary, the pattern recurs. The buffalo king Poturāja is often the husband of the seven goddesses of the village; he is also their brother.[153] In Mysore "all the seven sisters are regarded vaguely as wives or sisters of Śiva"[154]—or, more probably, as both. It is important to remember that the seven sisters/virgins are also Seven Mothers; the virgin, incestuously tied to her brother (later to her son), possesses the power to create new life. Brother-sister incest is often the impetus to creation in tribal myths,[155] and Bengali folk tradition ascribes the creation of living beings to the impregnation of a female bird by her brother's seed.[156] The primordial act of procreation is seen as incestuous by many cultures; the single creator gives birth to a daughter, with whom he unites, or divides himself into male and female halves (brother and sister united in an androgynous embrace). The androgynous creator appears in some Tamil myths as the "male" goddess, that is, the virgin who creates alone, possessed of male and female components within her own nature; we will return to this figure in section 9. However, it should be stressed that in contrast to the incestuous creation as described in many traditions, the Tamil myths of brothers and sisters tend to preclude the act of incest itself. Creation here is a function of the virgin's latent powers, the fearful, disturbing aspect of which is displayed in her association with her brother and/or husband. The incestuous union remains a latent, dangerous desire. The same unsatisfying conclusion is found, we should remember, in the most famous Vedic example of the incestuous love between a brother and a sister—Yamī's pathetic, ultimately frustrated solicitation of her brother Yama.[157]

It should be noted that in the folk myths the incestuous relationship is multiple: a single male confronts the seven goddesses Pattiṉiyammaṉ. To understand the symbolism involved, we would do well to look at a Vedic parallel: the son of the waters, *apā́ṃ nápāt*, is surrounded by the female waters; he drinks the milk of the goddesses, he enters them and engenders an embryo in them.[158] Dhātṛ also enters the goddesses who surround him.[159] These images express a form of number symbolism that is widespread throughout India: the single male united to the goddesses is the extra, additional element that both embraces the totality of the series to which it is attached and, as the leftover remnant, is the seed of the new birth from that series.[160] We have observed the importance of the remnant in the ideology of sacrifice, and, bearing in mind the sacrificial background of many Tamil myths, the identification of the lone god with the seed/remnant produced through the agency of the seven goddesses is entirely natural. The child of the goddesses is the divine seed won through violence—the violence that flows from these murderous mothers. Because of the tendency to split the ambivalent mother and redistribute her roles, the village myths often include more than a single "extra" figure; the male contrasts with seven or more goddesses, and often the seventh (or eighth, or ninth) goddess opposes the rest, as Arundhatī stands apart from the other wives of the sages in the myth of Skanda's birth. The male is thus juxtaposed not with a single, composite figure or with a homogeneous series, but with a complex, internally divided group of goddesses.

Sometimes there are seven brothers alongside the seven wives. In some versions of the Gond Lingo cycle, Lingo is the youngest of seven brothers; he withstands the temptations of his brothers' wives and the attacks of his brothers; eventually he marries his cross-cousin and, when she is carried away by a demon and delivered of a child, he kills her and marries seven wives.[161] In other accounts he marries seven wives, drives away six of them, kills the seventh (who was stolen by another warrior) and cuts her body into seven pieces.[162] Lingo's brothers try to kill him when they suspect his involvement with their wives; they fail, but Lingo himself successfully murders his bride—the anomalous seventh thus epitomizing the nature of the other six. The reversal is more complete in those south Indian village shrines in which a single goddess (often Kaṉṉiyammaṉ, the Maiden) is connected with seven brothers, of whom the youngest is dominant.[163] The female thus joins seven males, including one who is anomalous or "extra." At Tirumullaivāyil the goddess Paccaimalaiyammaṉ, who performed *tapas* to become the left half of the androgyne, faces the lone figure of the sage Gautama; to her right sit six more sages[164] in a group; a little beyond this group one finds the huge, separate image of Muṉīcuvaraṉ / Vāḻumuṉi. Śiva as Maṉṉātīcuvarar has a small shrine near the goddess's shrine; inside there is an image of Śiva, with Piḷḷaiyār (Gaṇeśa) on his right, and the goddess and Naṭarāja on his left; behind him there is a painting of Maturaivīraṉ with a single bride.[165] The goddess here is thus associated with nine males, of whom three—Gautama, Muṉīcuvaraṉ, and Śiva—are separated from the rest.

Often the lone goddess is a form of the fierce Kālī, the dark and threatening virgin. The Amazon Queen Alli, whom we have seen to be a representative of the violent, dark goddess, plots with seven carpenters to build a magic ladder to take revenge on Duryodhana; when the eldest carpenter mounts the ladder as a trial and is wounded, Alli heals him and grants him wealth.[166] In another popular folk ballad, the violent goddess appears together with seven children and with an evil sister-in-law:

> Rāmaliṅgarāja did *tapas* in the forest, and Śiva, at the urging of Pārvatī, granted him two children, a boy and a girl. They went to school together, studied Tamil and Telugu, archery, horsemanship, and other subjects. When he came of age, the boy was married to Mūḷi ("Defective"), daughter of the king of the Kuṇḍala land. Soon after the wedding, the queen and king died. The boy, Nallatampi ("good younger brother") gave his sister Nallataṅkāḷ ("good younger sister") to the king of Kāśī, together with a handsome dowry. When the wedding celebration was over, Nallatampi said to his sister, "Enter this palankeen, dear sister (to go to your husband's house)." At this she became enraged, wept and tore off her ornaments; he soothed her and she went off with her husband to Maturai.
>
> In seven years Nallataṅkāḷ bore seven children. Then a drought afflicted the city of Maturai; after selling all her valuables for food, Nallataṅkāḷ determined to go and seek help from her brother, against her husband's wishes. She lost her way in the forest and sat down to weep with her children under a tree, and there she was found by Nallatampi while out hunting. He told her to proceed ahead of him to his home. She was reluctant: "If Mother were alive, she would herself have invited me; but would your wife invite me? I will not go without you." He convinced her to go, saying, "Is not your brother your foster mother?"
>
> When her sister-in-law saw her coming, she quickly hid all her valuables and bolted the doors to her house. When Nalla-

taṅkāḷ arrived, Mūḷi pretended to be asleep and would not even answer her cries. At last Nallataṅkāḷ opened the doors by the power of her chastity. She went straight to the kitchen, but all the food was hidden away; in her sister-in-law's room her children found unripe fruit, but Mūḷi tore even these fruits from their hands and cooked for them instead a niggardly broth. "We could do better begging," cried Nallataṅkāḷ, and left with her children for the forest.

Learning from some shepherds of an abandoned well, Nallataṅkāḷ went there and tore off her wedding-chain (*tāli*) and an ornament given her by her brother (*paṭṭai*); by her power they became a tall rock. She climbed the rock and threw six of her children, five boys and one girl, into the well. The eldest son fled, pleading for his life: "Let us two live; those who have gone are gone." "They will laugh at us as motherless children," said Nallataṅkāḷ. She called to the shepherds to catch him; they returned the boy to her, and she threw him into the well and jumped in after him.

When Nallatampi returned home, his wife lied to him, claiming to have met his sister with great hospitality. Hearing the truth from the neighbors, Nallatampi hastened in the path of his sister. He found the bodies in the well and burned them; the fire caught hold when he promised to avenge their deaths. He went home and made arrangements for his son's wedding. At the ceremony he denounced his wife to their son as a murderess (*attaiyai kkŏṉṟavaḷ tāṉ arum pāvi uṉ tāyār*), and then engineered her death and that of her relatives. When the husband of Nallataṅkāḷ arrived the next day, seeking his wife, the king told him the story, and both committed suicide.

Śiva and Pārvatī revived the dead brother and sister as well as her husband and seven children. Nallataṅkāḷ asked that the image of her sister-in-law be carved in stone for travelers to deride. She had a temple and tank constructed for her in Kāśī. Her children became *vaṉṉi* trees, while the brothers-in-law, happy at seeing her revived, went to Kailāsa.[167]

Here there are seven children—six boys and a girl—instead of seven mothers; the single goddess, Nallataṅkāḷ, is the mother of these children, but she is also linked to her brother, her husband, and her brother's wife, the latter figure serving as a foil for the complex character of the heroine. The sister-in-law appears wholly villainous; Nallataṅkāḷ shows us the conflicting strands of the mother image, an amalgam of sustenance, virtue, and violence. Nallataṅkāḷ is both a chaste wife (*pattiṉi*, like Kaṇṇaki and Pattiṉiyammaṉ) and a virgin (*kaṉṉi, kumāri, kaṉṉikaḻiyā pĕṇ*).[168] Again we find traces of an incestuous love between sister and brother; this relationship is most clearly suggested by the scene at the wedding of Nallataṅkāḷ, when she refuses to go to her husband's home and even tears off her ornaments in grief. The mutual jealousy of the sisters-in-law thus is rooted in rivalry for the love of Nallatampi. Nallatampi himself is hardly indifferent to his sister; although he arranges her wedding, and later refers to himself as a "foster-mother" for his sister, his true attitude is revealed by his actions subsequent to her death. Nallatampi embraces his sister's corpse as Śiva embraces the body of Satī; he then plots the death of his wife and kills himself in mourning for his sister and her children. Another version states the connection between the brother and sister in terms of a transparently sexual metaphor: "Nallannan and his sister Nallatankal worked together while they were young and unmarried. They raised crops and planted trees."[169] Later, when Nallataṅkāḷ is insulted by Mūḷi, she leaves because she realizes that all her labor over the years was for nothing—her sister-in-law's children would inherit the family wealth![170] But the incest theme is here closely linked to the figure of the murderous mother. There are, in fact, two murderous mothers: Nallataṅkāḷ, who throws her children into a well (just as the Ganges, another mother of Skanda, drowns her first seven children by Śantanu),[171] and Mūḷi, who bears the ultimate responsibility for the disaster and who is revealed as a murderess at the wedding of her son. The latter incident, which is otherwise superfluous, seems to have been added precisely because of the influence of this theme. The two mothers then become two violent goddesses, one represented by a stone image, the other in a shrine. The wicked sister-in-law has attracted the motif of the violent goddess locked in a house/box/shrine (while Nallataṅkāḷ, like Kālī in the folk myth, is locked *out* of the shrine); moreover, Mūḷi's house (*koyil*) is said to be guarded by a black cow—as we have seen, a classic symbol of the dark or evil mother. Barren black cows are offered to Nirṛti, the goddess of bad luck,[172] and throughout the *Nallataṅkāḷ katai* the evil sister-in-law is equated to Mūtevi-Jyeṣṭhā, who brings ill fortune (the formula that recurs in the poem is *mūḷiyalaṅkāri mūtevi cāṇṭāli*, the latter epithet indicating that she is also a demoness or of low caste). Like Skanda, then, who as Ṣaṣṭhīpriya is married to the goddess of bad luck (identified with Devasenā),[173] Nallatampi is the husband of a dangerous, wicked goddess; but unlike Skanda, whose second wife Vaḷḷi is gentle and benign, Nallatampi is erotically tied to a second woman, his sister, who, although virtuous, is no less violent and destructive. There is thus a degree of irony in Nallataṅkāḷ's repeated nostalgia for *her* mother, while for her eldest son the threat of being laughed at as "motherless" seems considerably less menacing than the fate reserved for him by his own grim mother.

Although the text states that the children of Nallataṅkāḷ become *vaṉṉi* trees,[174] they are worshiped along with their mother as stones (one big stone and seven small ones) in Ramnad District.[175] The representation is, of course, identical with that of the Seven Mothers, and the large stone fittingly represents the anomalous "extra" goddess, in this case the destroyer of seven children. In the narrative this figure of the devouring mother confronts another, no less appalling figure, so that the septad is joined by two "extra" goddesses as well as by the two males—the brother, who is essential to the plot, and the rather shadowy husband of Nallataṅkāḷ. We find a similar arrangement in another Tamil folktale, but here the distribution of attributes is more complete, and the component strands of the mother image more strictly separated:

> Prince Kāntarūpaṉ married Princess Kāntarūpi, and the young couple lived happily in a seven-storied palace built for them by Kĕntesvaraṉ, the father of the bride, to keep them from the evil eye (*kaṇtiruṣṭi*). They used to sleep on a terrace (*upparikai*). One night when the moon was full, the Seven Maidens (*kaṉṉikaikaḷ*) were coming from the world of the gods when they saw the terrace and the young lovers. They were so enamored of the beauty of the prince that they took him away to the world of the gods.
>
> Kāntarūpi awoke to find her husband missing. In alarm she sent for her father; he was grieved, but so that she would not stray from the law of devotion to a husband, he had her kept under guard in that terrace, with the servants and companions she had enjoyed before. So Kāntarūpi continued to live in the palace, while the Seven Maidens took turns amusing themselves with the prince. One day the Maidens thought, "That wife of the prince is a woman like us. She is greatly devoted to her husband; because of the pain she is suffering, great evil will

befall us." So they decided to bring her husband to her every eighth day, first bewitching her senses so that she knew nothing; then, after the prince had been with her, they would take him back to heaven.

After some time the princess became pregnant. Her servants were startled to discover this, but, though they tried to see if she had a secret lover, they could find no evidence of any fault. When at last they informed her father, he consulted his ministers and, according to their advice based on the rules of Manu, had his daughter taken out at night and abandoned in a forest.

The delicate princess had never before set foot outside, and she suffered greatly from thorns, although the wild beasts of the forest fled from her in fear, knowing her to be a woman true to her husband (*makāpativiratai*). Suddenly she saw a light: it came from a fire in which a prostitute (*tāci*) was burning the body of her daughter, who had died giving birth to a still-born child. The princess determined to end her life by entering the flames, but the old lady caught her hand; she asked her to take the place of the daughter she had just lost. Kāntarūpi went with her to her house.

When her time came near, the prostitute, Cauntaravalli, called a midwife and said, "If it is a boy, kill him; if a girl, let her live." The midwife bound the eyes of the princess with cloth. She gave birth to a boy as radiant as the sun. Cauntaravalli took a wooden doll and showed it to Kāntarūpi, saying, "See what you brought forth." Kāntarūpi was silent.

The midwife, instructed to slay the child, instead took it to the forest and left it by the side of an anthill where lived a five-headed snake, near a shrine to the goddess (*ammaṉkoyil*). The serpent lifted the child on its hoods and deposited him in front of Kālī's shrine. Kĕntesvaraṉ, the father of the princess, came there to worship and heard the child crying; overjoyed at the gift of a child from the goddess, he took him home, raised him, and had him educated. One day, when the boy was out riding through the town in his chariot, he passed through the street of the prostitutes and saw Kāntarūpi at the door of one of the houses. He fell in love with the beautiful woman and sent a messenger to arrange a meeting. Cauntaravalli accepted the gold the messenger brought and sent word that the prince should come that night.

When the prince arrived after dark, by mistake he stepped

over a calf asleep by its mother's side in the courtyard. The calf cried out, "Ammā! Did you see him step over me?" The mother replied, "Hush! What can you expect of someone who is going to embrace his own mother?" Now the prince understood the language of animals; greatly perplexed and despondent at these words, he entered the house. Cauntaravalli had him sit in the bedroom while she went to harangue Kāntarūpi—who had so far preserved her purity—to go to the prince. Finally she took the girl by the hand and brought her to the room. Kāntarūpi clutched the leg of the bed. The prince looked at her face—and since he had never tasted the *amṛta* of his mother, all that *amṛta* gathered together and burst from her breasts on to his face. He hastened away, determined to find out from his father the truth of his birth.

Confronted by the prince, the king confessed that he had found him in the shrine of the goddess. He summoned Cauntaravalli and Kāntarūpi; the first told of how she had found the princess in the forest and taken her home, and how she had ordered the midwife to kill the male child. The midwife was brought to the court and revealed that she had left the child on the anthill. But was the abandoned infant the same one found by the king? They went to the shrine of Kālī and sought her help, and Kālī appeared and informed them that the child was indeed the son of the chaste Kāntarūpi, whose husband had been stolen by the Seven Maidens. At the advice of Kālī, Kāntarūpi fasted, performed *tapas* on the terrace where she had lived with her husband, and worshiped the Seven Maidens, and the Seven Maidens had compassion on her and restored Kāntarūpaṉ to his wife and son.[176]

The major elements of the myths that portray the divine mother—chastity, fertility, eroticism, violence, sustenance—have been parceled out among the female characters of this story. The Seven Maidens are erotic but barren—the exact reversal of the role of the Kṛttikās in the myth of Skanda's birth. The fertile wife is first deprived of her husband,[177] then blinded (!) and robbed of her child by the prostitute Cauntaravalli, who here acquires the part of the violent "extra" member of the series of seven or eight. Two women thus contrast with the septad, Kāntarūpi by her fertility, Cauntaravalli by her murderous nature. But the prostitute shares with the Maidens the attribute of eroticism without fruit; her professional hostility to fertility is illustrated not only by her attempt to murder the new-born infant of the princess, but also by the death in childbirth of her own daughter, whose infant dies in the womb. As a symbol of barren eroticism, Cauntaravalli thus epitomizes the major characteristic of the septad (the anomalous goddess giving an extreme expression to a feature shared by all members of the group); moreover, the prostitute's infertility leads directly to her depiction as murderous, for the barren woman is regarded by the folk tradition as the most terrible and terrifying female form, a destroyer rather than the creator of new life.[178] If the Seven Maidens and Cauntaravalli thus embody the elements of eroticism and violence to the child, the notions of fertility, chastity, and sustenance are exemplified by the two remaining female figures. The fertile princess remains chaste; she conceives without even being aware of the embraces of her endlessly accommodating husband, and her purity is symbolized by the conventional motif of the locked and guarded palace (its seven stories replacing the seven pots that often represent the Seven Mothers). The chastity of the princess is then threatened by the schemes of her murderous stepmother-prostitute (here the contrast between the virtuous Kāntarūpi and the representatives of a barren eroticism is most marked) and saved by the sight of her son—for the revelation of maternity is the classical antidote to lust in these stories, as when Skanda is cured of desire when every woman appears to him as his mother. Unconscious incest is the danger here, underlined by the presence of the cow, the prime symbol of maternity; the prince's offense against the calf and the consequent remark by the mother-cow provide the first intimation of the real identity of the princess. The son's lust for his mother leads ultimately to the restoration of the father, Kāntarūpaṉ—another case of the reversed Oedipal pattern. This dénouement is rendered possible by the role of the foster mother, who in the version of the *Mataṉakāmarājaṉkatai* is none other than the fierce Kālī: when the midwife deposits the child near the shrine of the goddess, Kālī takes the form of a serpent to shade him from the sun and feeds him with honey from a honeycomb (*teṉkūṇṭu*) on a shrub she creates nearby.[179] In the *Vikkiramātittaṉkatai*, Kālī is foster mother only indirectly: the king takes the child from her shrine—adjacent to the anthill, which, as we have seen, is the locus of the divine seed—and regards it as a gift from the goddess. In any case, the image of the dark Kālī as a benevolent foster mother, which we recognize from the appearance of Kālī in the Epic Skanda myth, contrasts with that of the evil stepmother Cauntaravalli. Kālī, the dark yet sustaining virgin, thus joins the series as yet another anomalous, "extra" goddess, just as Durgā / Māriyamman̲ is linked to the Seven Mothers in village shrines; but here Kālī is gentle and benign, while the Seven Maidens have isolated the latent eroticism of the Mothers from their creative potential. The creative virgin is represented by Kāntarūpi, supported by the virgin Kālī: only the chaste goddess can have a son, and only the chaste and violent mother can sustain him.

The folktale, with its clear-cut division of roles, thus offers the following pattern: the septad is juxtaposed with three additional female figures, one of whom (Cauntaravalli) exaggerates a basic attribute of the seven, while the other two (Kāntarūpi and Kālī) contrast with them; this entire series confronts three male characters—the father, husband, and son of Kāntarūpi—like the three "extra" male gods at Tirumullaivāyil. Many of the outstanding themes and motifs of the Skanda myth, and of the related sacrificial scheme in which the divine seed is produced through violence, appear in the Tamil folktale; note in particular the transformed but still obvious motif of the birth in darkness or blindness (Kāntarūpi blindfolded by the prostitute). The importance of blindness in the myth of the god's death and rebirth at the hands of his bride has been studied above. We may look at one last variant of the Skanda myth, this time from Bengal (with another version from the Punjab), in which the motif of the blind mother is combined in a striking manner with the theme of the barren and violent "extra" goddess:

> A king had seven wives, all of whom were barren. At the advice of a mendicant, the king gave each of them a mango to eat, and they all conceived. One day while hunting the king encountered a beautiful Rākṣasī, whom he married and took home. As proof of his love she demanded that he blind and kill the seven queens. The king had their eyes plucked from their sockets and handed them to the executioner, but he hid them in a cave. Eventually, the eldest gave birth to a child; she killed him and gave her companions a part of the body to eat. Six ate their portion, but the youngest queen kept her share instead of eating it. So it happened when the other queens gave birth: they killed the child and shared its flesh. But the seventh was determined to nurse her child rather than kill it, and when she

gave birth she gave her companions the portions of flesh she had saved from their children. Noticing they were dry, they questioned her, but when she told them of her resolve to nurse the child, they were glad and helped her to nurse him. Thus he was suckled by seven mothers, and he became the hardiest and strongest boy that ever lived.

Meanwhile, the Rākṣasī was eating up the members of the royal household to satisfy her hunger. The boy came to the court and volunteered to protect the king. The Rākṣasī-queen sent him across the ocean to her mother with a letter asking her to devour him, but the boy tore up the letter before departing. He won the heart of the old Rākṣasī who, believing he was her grandson, revealed to him that the queen's life was hidden in a bird in a cage. The boy stole the bird and returned to the kingdom. There he revealed the wicked nature of the queen and killed her by dismembering the bird. The seven mothers were reinstated and their eyesight restored.[180]

Only one of the seven queens is wholly good; the eighth, the Rākṣasī, is entirely evil, and the other six are ambivalent—devourers of their children who yet nurse the seventh son. The double nature of the Mothers/Kṛttikās in the Skanda myth is thus explicitly combined in the role of the six queens, while the seventh and eighth each acquire a distinct part of this role—the seventh, fertility, and the eighth, aggression. The goddess exists in integrated and split forms in the same story. The evil Rākṣasī also exemplifies the idea of a dangerous, destructive eroticism; out of love for her the king commands the blinding and execution of his seven wives. The single fertile goddess who protects her child reverses the role of Arundhatī in the Skanda myth; as in that myth, the single child is here nursed by many mothers. This son survives the dangers surrounding his birth as well as the machinations of his evil stepmother, the Rākṣasī, whom he eventually manages to kill.

The son's attack upon his stepmother in this story brings to mind the most famous south Indian myth of split mothers, which must at least be mentioned here. This is the myth of Paraśurāma's matricide, which appears in the *MBh* (3.116.1-18), but which is known throughout south India in the following variant form:

Māriyammaṉ, the mother of Paraśurāma and the wife of the sage Jamadagni, was so chaste that she could carry water in a

> ball without any container. One day she admired the reflection of a Gandharva (a celestial musician) as he flew over the water she was carrying; because of this lapse in her virtue, she lost her power and the water flowed away. Jamadagni, seeing her wet and without the ball of water, made her confess to her fault; then he ordered Paraśurāma to cut off her head. Paraśurāma took his mother into the wilderness; there she met a Paṟaiya woman and, longing for sympathy, embraced her. Paraśurāma cut off both their heads together and returned to his father. In return for his obedience, his father promised to fulfil any wish, and Paraśurāma asked that his mother be revived. The father sent Paraśurāma to accomplish this by sprinkling water on his mother and striking her with a cane. In his haste he put his mother's head on the body of the Paṟaiya woman and *vice versa*, and brought them both back to life. The woman with the Brahmin head and Paṟaiya body was worshiped as Māriyammaṉ, while the woman with Paṟaiya head and Brahmin body became the goddess Ĕllammaṉ ("Yellamma"). "To Yellamma buffaloes are sacrificed; but to Mariyamma goats and cocks, but not buffaloes."[181]

Paraśurāma, the obedient son who executes his mother, acquires a new mother with a double nature. The transposed heads, a well-known motif,[182] serves to explain the hierarchy of goddesses; in the process the buffalo-sacrifice is provided with some legitimacy. Both Māriyammaṉ and Ĕllammaṉ are familiar to us from other myths, the former in her association with the Seven Mothers, Ĕllammaṉ as the lustful virgin pursuing her sons. Both appear here as composite figures uniting Brahmin and outcaste elements.[183] The mother is split and reunited, slain and revived; as in the case of other sacrificial figures, the head of the sacrifice has a crucial importance. The confusion of the heads of the goddesses allows the expression of a complex view of the deity. Māriyammaṉ is given a double nature by her son, who by mistake forces her to absorb a lower element; the benign mother—an exemplar of chastity, whose moral lapse is surely no greater than that of the six Kṛttikās implicated in the birth of Skanda—is made ambivalent by the violence of her son. It has been shown that the idea of aggression against the mother is relatively undeveloped and unimportant in the Epic version and in the Sanskrit tradition generally; what matters is the son's total subservience to his father's wish.[184] In the folk myth, too, no sin attaches to the matricide—in striking contrast to the fear of killing a woman (*strīvadha*) that troubles Viṣṇu[185] and Rāma.[186] Paraśurāma is the instrument of a necessary division of the goddess. The splitting of the goddess into "higher" and "lower" forms recurs in many myths of the double bride of the god; this pattern will be taken up again in our next section.

Let us summarize the conception of the goddess as mother. The mother is by nature ambiguous, benign and threatening, nourishing and destructive. In the context of the marriage myths, she is both erotically tied to her son, yet precluded from sexual contact with him; the goddess as mother remains virginal and powerful, her power being used in both creative and destructive ways. Her innate eroticism is carefully limited by isolation—or, in other cases, by dividing her into parts and splitting away her erotic and menacing components. Tamil folk myths bring into sharp focus the ambivalence and oppositions already implicit in classical versions of the Skanda birth myth: there Pārvatī, whose role is generally positive, cannot nurse her son;[187] the Ganges drowns seven of her sons but allows the eighth to live; the Kṛttikās combine maternal love with aggression toward the child. Skanda's wet-nurse is the gruesome Kālī, who nourishes the infant yet remains a source of violence and death for the man, as the dark earth sustains and yet reclaims our life, and as the Murderous Bride destroys and also restores life to her consort. The folk myths of the *saptamātṛkās/kaṉṉimār* maintain both aspects of the mother, sometimes distributing them among the goddesses. The seventh goddess is cast in varying roles, sometimes fertile and benign and in this way opposed to the other six, sometimes the focus of aggression and destruction. As a group, the seven goddesses relate to the single male as multiple mothers—or, in some cases, as sisters incestuously tied to their brother; in both cases they retain the power and creative potential of the virgin. The virgin mother is aggressive, seductive, permeated by strong incestuous desires that are inevitably frustrated. In the perspective offered by the accompanying sacrificial concepts, the ambivalence of the mother reflects successive stages in the ritual; the goddess, who is identified with the sacrifice as the source of death and new life, gives birth to her consort after slaying him as the dark virgin. Devī thus becomes a murderous mother married to her victim/son in chaste embrace. Her symbol in the myths of many shrines is the black and white cow, the violent Kāmadhenu who gives milk to the deity and yet draws forth his blood. The god offers up his life to the devouring goddess in the expectation of winning through this sacrifice a new existence, an existence made secure by association with his powerful bride; the seed transferred in violence issues from the womb of the chaste goddess, the maternal, fertile consort in her terrestrial home.

## 8. The Double Bride

It is not only the maternal aspect of the goddess that is split into contrasting elements. As we have seen, Śiva's bride is often divided into two—a dark, destructive "sheath" (Kauśikī, Kālī) and a golden, gentle wife (Umā, Gaurī). Śiva's union with the dark Kālī lies at the heart of the Tamil myths of marriage; but the god's wedding to the benign goddess is most frequently celebrated in temple rituals today. Some myths, such as those of the dance contest, describe the transformation of the violent goddess into an acceptable, submissive wife who is allowed to take her place beside her lord in the central shrine; other myths relegate the violent virgin to the periphery, while the golden goddess is joined in harmonious union with the god. But at Kāñcipuram, Śiva weds both the pacified golden consort and the dark Aṇaṅku / Durgā, who "emerged from a part of Gaurī."[1] The god thus acquires two brides, both completely tied to the local shrine. As the husband of two wives, the deity of the shrine offers a local, south Indian example of a very widespread pattern: the conflict between gods and demons, basic to Hindu myth generally, is a war between the descendants of the two wives of Kaśyapa (Diti, mother of the demons, and Aditi, mother of the gods). Indeed, in one Tamil text the gods and demons are said to fight in imitation of their mothers who, though sisters and wives of the same man, were always at odds.[2] This text states plainly the fundamental tension between the two wives—a recurring theme in the myths that will concern us here. In classical Sanskrit purāṇas, Śiva's household is pervaded by this very tension, for the god is married to two wives—Pārvatī (Umā) and the Ganges.[3] The two relate to one another as jealous rivals: Pārvatī is aided by her son Gaṇeśa in removing Gaṅgā from Śiva's presence,[4] and for her part, Gaṅgā attempts to drown Pārvatī.[5] Śiva's love for Gaṅgā is an excuse for Pārvatī to desert her husband and a constant reproach in their quarrels.[6] Pārvatī is usually considered the most important of Śiva's brides, the mother of his children; but in Bengal Gaṅgā has pride of place.[7]

The two wives in the Tamil shrines thus recall the classical Śaiva pattern. Still, it is the local brides who interest us here. The shrine is the site of a double marriage: either the bride is split in two and both fragments are connected to the god; or the deity may take a local, Tamil bride in addition to his usual consort in the classical Hindu pantheon. Moreover, let us recall that the local marriage is in any case considered to be a second marriage, a repeat performance of Śiva's wedding in the Himālayas: thus Devī becomes Ŏppilāmulaiyammai at Tiruvāvaṭuturai because she wishes to reenact her first wedding, which she can no longer remember;[8] and the marriage ceremony in the shrine is often said to be a repetition for the benefit of Agastya, who was forced to miss the original ceremony in the Himālayas.[9] The idea of the second marriage thus occurs throughout the Tamil purāṇic corpus, both as a means of explaining the relation between the local marriage and the classical, Sanskritic system, and as an expression of the complexities rooted in the nature of the goddess.

In one Tamil myth, from Kāṉapper (Kāḷaiyārkoyil), the complex nature of Śiva's bride is revealed by a series of bifurcations:

> While Śiva was wandering in the Cotivaṉam, Umā asked him about his forms and functions, and he said, "When my eyes are open, the worlds appear; when they are shut, the worlds are destroyed." Umā wished to test this proposition, so, just like a woman, she crept up behind him and covered his eyes with her hands. The worlds were plunged into darkness, and Śiva was angered. He cursed her to have a fierce, dark form as Kālī because of the sin she had committed in causing confusion to the rites of the Brahmins and in putting the workings of *karma* in doubt. The goddess begged for forgiveness, and Śiva said, "When you have destroyed the demons who plunder the world, you will be released from the curse." He disappeared, and she began to perform *tapas* in the Marutavaṉam nearby.
>
> The gods were troubled by the demon Caṇḍa, and Śiva sent them to ask Bhadrakālī for help. She fought with the demon and killed him by destroying the five serpents that were his life. Then she stood facing the Seven Mothers, who were drunk on the blood of demons, and provided them with delicious curries; hence she is known as Annapūrṇā (Tam. Aṉṉapūraṇi, "she who is full of food").
>
> Kālī returned to the Cotivaṉam and prayed that the undivided god (*akaṇṭam*) become manifest in two *liṅgas*, a *sthūlaliṅga* and a *sūkṣmaliṅga*. The *liṅgas* appeared. She worshiped them and became golden, so the gods named her Suvarṇavallī

> ("golden creeper"), and they named the *sūkṣmaliṅga* Kālīśa ("lord of Kālī"). The goddess still reigns outside the shrine as Bhadrakālī. Inside, however, she split into two: Umā, who, by the grace of Śiva, merged with the *sthūlaliṅga* (which was renamed Someśvara);[10] and Gaurī, who demanded that Śiva marry her so that they might never be parted again. Śiva took half of the golden Gaurī into the *sūkṣmaliṅga*; hence that *liṅga* is black on the right side and golden on the left. The other half of Suvarṇavallī-Gaurī entered the *vīraśaktipīṭha* to the north of that *liṅga*.[11]

The goddess who, by hiding Śiva's eyes, brings premature disaster to the universe and thus imperils the operation of the usual laws of cause and effect is redeemed by saving the universe twice—first, from the demon Caṇḍa, and then from the Mothers who have become wild from his blood. The bloodthirsty nature of the Mothers is familiar to us from the myths of the previous section; here Kālī provides them with food in order to keep them from devouring others, just as Prajāpati is said to have given Svāhā to Agni so as not to be devoured himself by the fire.[12] Although the goddess is said to have become wholly golden by worshiping the two *liṅgas* (one "gross," *sthūla*, and the other "subtle," *sūkṣma*), she leaves her black aspect outside the shrine, where the dark Bhadrakālī continues to dwell. This is the first split, a conventional one, and the black goddess remains chaste, unmarried, and excluded. Then, however, two further splits occur within the golden goddess. We might represent the divisions as follows:

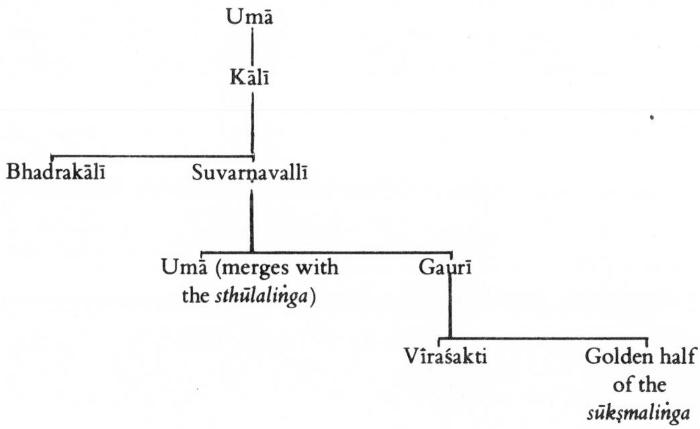

The myth makes an important distinction between *merging* with the god and *marrying* the god: Umā merges into the *sthūlaliṅga* and loses her identity, except for a late etymological explanation of the name of the *liṅga*, Someśvara; Gaurī insists on marriage, which implies the preservation of separate identity—hence the golden left half of the *sūkṣmaliṅga*, which imitates the androgyne. The distinction may hold good in historical terms: compare, for example, the assimilation of animal cults (the god as bull, lion, elephant, monkey, and so on) by means of theriomorphic representations of the deity, with the compromise solution of divine marriage, with all its tensions. Although the androgyne might be seen as a merger, the myth carefully distinguishes it from Umā's absorption by the *liṅga*; Gaurī's demand to be married to Śiva "so that they might never be parted again" implies their continued distinct identity, for only that which is already differentiated or divided can be truly separated. As we have seen, other shrines also regard the androgyne as simply a form of marriage,[13] despite—or because of?—the unsatisfying nature of a union that makes conventional sexual activity impossible.[14] The androgynous marriage absorbs and perpetuates the underlying conflicts between the partners; note that the "subtle" (*sūkṣma*) symbol, which incorporates the god and his bride in the two contrasting halves, is also the more complex. Yet even here only half of the golden Gaurī unites with the god, and the other half, the power-giving *śakti*, must be kept chaste. There are thus two chaste forms of the goddess at Kāḷaiyārkoyil, one black and one golden, and two distinct patterns in which the golden goddess joins the god.

The idea of Śiva's union with a fissiparous goddess is sometimes used to explain his double marriage to Pārvatī and the Ganges. Devī divides herself into water (the Ganges) and woman (Pārvatī).[15] The combination is repeated in the Tamil myths of the Kāviri River, which is regarded as a personified divinity, just as the Ganges is seen as Śiva's wife. In the *kāṉalvari* of the *Cilappatikāram*, the Kāviri (Kāveri, with fish-eyes, *kayaṟkaṇṇāy*)[16] is described metaphorically as the first bride in a double (or triple) marriage; she is advised not to quarrel with her "husband," the Coḻa king, if he unites with the Ganges, or with the Virgin (*kaṉṉi* = Kaṉṉiyākumari), that is, if he conquers the territories of the north and the far south.[17] In the myths, however, Kāviri herself is divided into two parts, both of which are connected to the sage Agastya, just as Devī marries Śiva in her two forms as Pārvatī and the Ganges: Kāviri performed *tapas* in order to win a learned *brahma-*

*cārin* for her husband. Agastya persuaded her to marry him, although he was her brother; half of her then entered the water-pot of the sage and overflowed on to the earth as a river, and her other half became his wife Lopāmudrā.[18] Agastya's marriage to the Kāviri in her two forms is described as the incestuous union of a brother and a sister, but this theme is neither stressed nor developed further in this myth. Other versions, not content with so simple a division of the bride, describe multiple marriages for both the river and the sage:

> King Kavera performed *tapas* for a thousand years in the Himālaya. Brahmā appeared and promised him that his daughter, Viṣṇumāyā, would be born as Kavera's daughter. A daughter was born to the king; when she came of age, she began to practise *tapas* in order to become a river that would purify evil. Viṣṇu promised her that she would have her wish, that she would be greater than the Ganges, and that she would flow from Viṣṇu's lap.
>
> Viṣṇu appeared to Agastya in the south and told him he should take a wife. "Why should I fall into the hell of family cares?" asked the sage; but Viṣṇu overcame his objections and sent him to the Himālaya, where he found Kāviri at her *tapas*. She divided her nature, half of her entering his pot and the other half marrying the sage in a wedding as splendid as that of Pārvatī. The couple went south after the wedding. When they reached the mountain of Brahmā, Agastya left the pot and went to bathe in the Suvarṇamukhī River. When after some time he failed to return, Kāviri wished to leave the pot; Brahmā came and bathed a tree, which was a form of Viṣṇu, with water from the pot, and Kāviri then left the pot of Brahmā and flowed over the feet of Viṣṇu. Agastya returned and found the pot overturned. He pursued the fleeing Kāviri, but she cried to him that she had left in accordance with his will. Agastya was appeased. Brahmā appeared and gave his daughter in marriage to Samudra (the ocean) at Śvetavana (= Tiruvĕṇkāṭu, Śvetāraṇya).[19]

The courtship of Kāviri and Agastya imitates the prelude to the myth of Skanda's birth, the courtship of Śiva and Pārvatī; here too the result is the release of a golden seed (the river carried in the pot).[20] Kāviri performs *tapas*, as does Pārvatī, and Agastya attracts the antierotic role and arguments usually given to Śiva. Their wedding is actually compared to that of Śiva and Pārvatī. Kāviri divides herself into river and woman, but this double bride is not enough for her husband; Agastya, who in the *KP* takes the Kāviri south with him in order to have water for his ritual ablutions, here abandons her for yet another golden river, the Suvarṇamukhī ("gold-faced"). As a result, Kāviri herself acquires two more husbands through Brahmā's intervention (a return to the motif of Prajāpati's seed in a golden pot): first she is united with Viṣṇu in the form of a tree, as is appropriate for an incarnation of Viṣṇumāyā, the cosmic "illusion" associated with Viṣṇu; and finally, she is married at Tiruvĕṇkāṭu to the ocean, the conventional husband of the rivers.

The marriage to the ocean appears in another important myth of multiple marriages, this time concerning Brahmā and his wife Sarasvatī:

> Sarasvatī and Lakṣmī quarreled over the question of which of them was superior. They took their case to Indra, who pronounced in favor of Lakṣmī, Mother of the worlds, the source of prosperity for creatures. Sarasvatī cursed him to become an elephant. At the urging of Lakṣmī, Indra learned from Prahlāda the *mantra* of the Man-Lion (Narasiṃha)[21] and, reciting it, entered Kāñcipuram. Emerging from out of his heart, the Man-Lion split open the elephant form. (The elephant became the hill Hastigiri, while the heart from which the Man-Lion emerged became a cave in which Viṣṇu dwells as Narasiṃha.)
>
> Sarasvatī and Lakṣmī then took their quarrel to Brahmā; he too decided in favor of Lakṣmī. In anger Sarasvatī robbed him of his staff of creation (*sṛṣṭidaṇḍa*), which had been given to him by Viṣṇu.
>
> In order to regain his powers of creation, Brahmā was advised by Viṣṇu to start an *aśvamedha* sacrifice at Kāñci. Sarasvatī was enraged at not being invited. She sent fire, demons, and the skull-weapon (*kāpālāstra*) to destroy the sacrifice, but Viṣṇu took the fire in his hand, drank the blood of the demons and, now red as coral, took the form of the Man-Lion to destroy the skull-weapon. Sarasvatī sent Kālī to fight, but Viṣṇu threw her to the ground and sat on her head. Then Sarasvatī became a flood raging toward the sacrificial pit. Viṣṇu lay naked in her path to destroy her pride (*mānabhaṅgāya*).
>
> Dishonored thus by Viṣṇu, Sarasvatī became very sad and, without looking in his face, went to hide in a cave. Brahmā

> then completed the sacrifice and was rewarded with his staff. Sarasvatī in her shame meditated on Viṣṇu. "I have lost my chastity and offended against my husband by seeing your *liṅga*," she said; "please restore my honor and make my husband fond of me again." Viṣṇu told her she could regain her purity by joining the Payoṣṇī River in its flow to the sea. She did this, and when Brahmā beheld her union with the sea he rejoiced and took her back to his world.[22]

A popular myth of double marriages has been superimposed on an origin myth based on the flood motif, as a variant in the *Kāñcippurāṇam* makes clear: there the flooding Sarasvatī-Vegavatī is stopped not by Viṣṇu but by his serpent Ādiśeṣa, who circles the sacrificial site with his body and thus delineates the boundaries of the shrine.[23] The story is an obvious analogue to the Hālāsya / Ālavāy myth, in which a serpent, this time belonging to Śiva, retraces the boundaries of the city of Maturai after the cosmic flood.[24] The symbolism of serpents and boundaries has been discussed above, but one may note again the association of the serpent with the flood and, hence, with a new creation and demarcation of the limits of the shrine. Sarasvatī's attempt to destroy the sacrificial fire by a flood is also a multiform of the best-known myth from Kāñcipuram, that of the sand-*liṅga*, which Pārvatī preserves from the flooding river (the Ganges or the Kampai); in both cases the ancient flood motif has attached itself to a marriage myth. As in the Vaiṣṇava accounts of the sand-*liṅga*,[25] Viṣṇu here appears to have substituted for Śiva: it is Śiva who slays an elephant, holds fire in his palm, and is red as coral; Śiva in the Pine Forest makes his enemies' weapons into ornaments; and it is far more likely that Śiva would fight with Kālī than that Viṣṇu would—indeed, we have seen that this struggle is a major theme of the marriage myths. Probably an old layer of Śaiva myth has been attached to Viṣṇu in the versions before us. Note, too, that the exclusion of Sarasvatī from Brahmā's sacrifice at Kāñci arouses resonances of the Dakṣa myth, in which Śiva is not invited to a sacrifice; but unlike Śiva, Sarasvatī fails to destroy the sacrificial rite.

That Sarasvatī should take the form of a river is, of course, most fitting, for this is her most ancient form. Yet the myth as it stands describes a curious chain of events: Brahmā's loss of the *sṛṣṭidaṇḍa* because of his wife's curse may be a metaphor for castration; Sarasvatī then loses her chastity by the implicit adultery with Viṣṇu (note again the equation of the forbidden vision of the naked deity with sexual union), but she purifies herself and regains her husband by a second marriage—with the sea! The final image is a reversal of the river's fate in a story from the *MBh*: Varuṇa stole Bhadrā, the daugher of Soma, from Utathya, and Utathya in anger drank up the waters of the ocean and of six hundred thousand lakes, causing a wasteland (*iriṇa*) to appear where water had been, so that the Sarasvatī River lost herself in a desert (*maru*) and could not reach the sea.[26] In this story rape leads to the dessication of the ocean and the river; at Kāñci, Sarasvatī's sexual offense is expiated by union with the purifying waters of the sea. Water as a medium of purification is, of course, found in every shrine (in the form of a tank, a pool, a river, or the sea). We may understand the theme of marrying the ocean in this light, that is, as a ritual purification rather than an actual second marriage; and it therefore becomes clear why Brahmā is prepared to accept Sarasvatī as his wife once more. In addition, the myth from Kāñcipuram has conflated two popular and contextually related stories: Sarasvatī's carrying the doomsday fire (*vaḍavānala*) to the sea,[27] and Brahmā's famous sacrifice at Puṣkara.[28] The former has supplied major elements to the southern myths: Sarasvatī receives the golden (*śātakaumbhastha*) fire from Viṣṇu, who has taken the form of a tree, just as the golden Kāviri flows from Brahmā's pot over the roots of Viṣṇu standing as a tree; and before reaching the sea Sarasvatī inundates the sacrificial pits at Puṣkara.[29] Moreover, the myth from Puṣkara divides Brahmā's consort in a classic instance of the double marriage:

> Brahmā went with the gods and sages to Puṣkara to perform a sacrifice. The *adhvaryu* priest went to summon Sāvitrī, but, just like a woman, she was unprepared: "I still have to wash the vessels at home and put on my ornaments; and besides, none of the other goddesses has yet arrived!" Brahmā was angry and ordered Indra to bring him some other woman, paying no heed to her social class (*varṇa*), in order that the sacrifice could be held before the proper moment passed. Indra abducted a beautiful cowherdess, Gāyatrī, and Brahmā married her in the *gāndharva* rite.[30] Sāvitrī arrived to find her husband in the wedding booth with Gāyatrī; she cursed her husband and the other gods, but at length she was appeased and became reconciled to the idea of having a cowife.[31]

Sometimes Gāyatrī is said to have been purified before the wedding by being passed through the stomach of the Kāmadhenu.[32] In the myth from Kāñcipuram, the jealousy of Sāvitrī over the choice of another wife has been transformed into a quarrel between Lakṣmī and Sarasvatī. In other versions there are three distinct wives: Brahmā wanted to perform a Soma sacrifice at Kāñci; Sarasvatī, being late, hid in the trees (and hence is said to be present in musical instruments made from wood); Brahmā started the rite with only Gāyatrī and Sāvitrī present, and this so infuriated Sarasvatī that she tried to destroy the sacrifice by a flood.[33] After celebrating ten *aśvamedhas*, Brahmā went to bathe in Kāśī with his three wives; Sarasvatī, charmed by the singing of one of the women of heaven, tarried; when she saw that Brahmā had already bathed with Gāyatrī and Sāvitrī, she was angry, and for her temper Brahmā cursed her to be born in part as the poets of the Caṅkam.[34] At Irāmeccuram, Sarasvatī and Gāyatrī perform *tapas* to revive Brahmā, slain by Śiva for pursuing Vāc.[35]

In its account of the marriage at Puṣkara, the *Padmapurāṇa* lavishes attention on the figure of Gāyatrī, the *gopakanyā* with her load of fresh butter, thick soured milk, and buttermilk to sell, who suddenly finds herself elevated to the status of wife of the Creator. Unlike Sāvitrī, the senior wife, Gāyatrī is thoroughly located in the site; her kinsmen come to seek their stolen child, and in an exchange of much humor and beauty she tries to explain to them her joy at being married to the elegant stranger.[36] The whole force of the passage suggests that Gāyatrī is rather more important and possesses greater prestige than her prim, orthodox rival, despite the humble origins of the *parvenue*. Here *bhakti*, with its preference for the unconventional, the socially inferior, the inversion of values, intrudes upon the scheme of the double marriage.

Precisely the same pattern obtains in the most important of all Tamil myths of the second marriage, the story of Murukaṉ's courtship and union with the daughter of the hunters, Vaḷḷi. In the Sanskrit tradition, Skanda is either an eternal *brahmacārin* or the husband of the Army of the Gods, Devasenā.[37] But in Tamil the earliest reference to a bride of Murukaṉ is to Vaḷḷi,[38] and there can be no doubt that Vaḷḷi is the more popular and important of Murukaṉ's two brides in the Tamil area today.[39] The story of the wooing of Vaḷḷi ranks among the most intricate and beautiful passages of the entire Tamil purāṇic literature. It also contains some of the oldest indigenous fragments of myth to survive. We begin with the standard account of the *KP*:

(Two daughters of Viṣṇu performed *tapas* near Caravaṇappŏykai to be wed to Murukaṉ. By the grace of Murukaṉ, one of them was born as the daughter of Indra and raised by his white elephant; hence she was named Tĕyvayāṉai.[40] After the war in which Murukaṉ defeated Śūrapadma, Indra gave his daughter in marriage to Murukaṉ at Tirupparaṅkuṉṟam).[41]

The second daughter was born to a deer impregnated by the lustful glance of the sage Śivamuni, who was performing *tapas* on Vaḷḷimalai. Seeing that the girl, who was born with bangles of fine workmanship on her arms, was not of her own kind, the deer abandoned her in the pit in which she had given birth, and there she was found by the lord of the Kuṟavar hunters, Nampi, who longed for a daughter. The hunter chief adopted her and named her Vaḷḷi, since she was born in a pit from which old men scrape the roots of the *vaḷḷi*.[42]

When Vaḷḷi reached the age of twelve, she was sent to guard the ripening millet from a raised platform (*itaṇam*); she frightened away birds and beasts with a sling-shot and the cry of "*ālolam*." To grant her grace, Murukaṉ came from Kantavarai to Taṇikai. There he was met by Nārada, who sang the praises of Vaḷḷi. Murukaṉ sent Nārada away and placed within himself the grievous disease of love.

Taking the form of a hunter, the love-sick god went to the millet fields and there beheld Vaḷḷi. He said to her, "Lady, hear me—did Brahmā fail to provide those barbarians with knowledge, that they have made you sit here guarding the millet? Tell me your name; or, if you will not say, tell me the name of your village; or, if you will not tell me even that, then show me the way thither." As he was pleading, her father suddenly arrived with his retinue of hunters, and Murukaṉ transformed himself into a *veṅkai* tree. Nampi gave his daughter some *vaḷḷi* roots, mangoes, honey, and the milk of a wild cow. Then the hunters noticed the new tree. "This tree was never here before; no good will come of it," they said, and made preparations to cut it down and dig up its roots. Nampi stopped them. "How did this tree come to be here?" he asked, scrutinizing the face of his daughter. Alarmed, Vaḷḷi said, "I do not know how it came; it appeared, I think, like magic (*māyam*). I have been trembling at the thought that something that was not here before has sprung up so suddenly."

"Be not afraid; the tree came here to be a sweet companion for you," said the hunter, and left with his men. Murukaṉ resumed human form and said, "Daughter of the Kuṟavar, I shall never leave you. How could anyone depart from you, who are like life to a body? My life is in your hands. Watching the fields is low, demeaning work; come with me, and the very women of heaven will worship you, and I will give you perfect gifts."

The daughter of the hunters understood. "I am but a humble girl who guards the fields of millet," she said, ashamed. "You are a leader who rules the whole world. Is it not wrong (*paḻi*) for you even to speak of embracing me?"

Suddenly the drums of the hunters were heard. Vaḷḷi urged Murukaṉ to flee; instead he transformed himself into an old ascetic. He bowed to Nampi, and the hunters' lord asked what he desired. "I have come to rid myself of age and my heart of its delusion; I wish to bathe in the Kumari (spring) of this, your mountain," replied the god. Said Nampi, "Father, bathe in that *tīrtha* and be a companion to our daughter, who is all alone." He gave Vaḷḷi fresh fruits and millet and departed.

The old man asked Vaḷḷi for food, and, when she had given him from her honey and fruits, he complained of thirst. She told him of a spring on the mountain, on the other side of seven hills; he asked her to show him the way there. He drank from the spring as if parched by the heat; then he asked her to satisfy his desire. "You are saying things which must not be said; if the hunters knew, they would cause you harm. Are you mad, that you speak without understanding?" Saying this, Vaḷḷi hastened away. Murukaṉ, watching her go, thought of his elephant-headed brother Gaṇeśa. Gaṇeśa took the form of a wild elephant in Vaḷḷi's path. She fled back to the arms of the old man: "Save me and I will do as you wish!" Murukaṉ embraced her and revealed to her his true form.

Vaḷḷi returned to the millet fields. Her companion noticed the change in her manner. Murukaṉ appeared again as a hunter and asked the companion if she had seen a wild elephant go past. Guessing he was really seeking Vaḷḷi, she told him to leave, lest the fierce hunters take his life. He threatened to mount the *maṭal* hobby-horse[43] and ride through the streets of the village if he were not allowed to meet Vaḷḷi; succumbing to this threat, the companion became an accomplice to their secret union.

When the millet was ripe, the hunters, preparing for the harvest, sent Vaḷḷi back to the village. She pined for her lover, and her foster mother (*cĕvili*) and mother noticed that she was not well. They locked her in the house and consulted women (skilled in divination). "She is possessed by the spirit (*cūr*) of these mountain slopes," they said, not knowing her to be possessed by the enemy of Cūr.[44] The hunters therefore held a ceremony of ecstatic dance (*vĕriyāṭṭu*) for Murukaṉ. During the dance, the god descended upon the wild dancer (*vĕriyāṭṭāḷaṉ*) and indicated by signs that he had taken possession of Vaḷḷi while she was out in the fields, but that her sickness would depart if he were worshiped. No sooner was this uttered than Vaḷḷi arose restored; her foster mother and mother praised Murukaṉ.

Not finding Vaḷḷi in the fields, Murukaṉ lamented and wandered over the mountain. At midnight he stood outside the hut of Nampi. Vaḷḷi's companion saw him there and urged him to elope with his beloved; with her help the couple were united and fled the village.

In the morning they were pursued by the angry Kuṟavar, who found them in a grove. They showered arrows at Murukaṉ, but at the crow of his cock they all fell dead. Vaḷḷi mourned her relatives and, at Nārada's urging, Murukaṉ revived them and agreed to their request that he return to the village and marry Vaḷḷi in a proper ceremony.[45]

The myth is replete with ancient elements: the clandestine, premarital union of lovers (*kaḷavu*) on the slopes of the mountains in the *kuṟiñci* region, sacred to Murukaṉ; the cast of characters, which includes the heroine who drives away birds from the millet fields, her companion, and her foster mother, and the hunter with his spear who becomes her lover; the *kuṟiñci* attributes of honey, millet, hill-ponds, *tŏṇṭakam* drums, the elephant, small village (*ciṟṟūr*), and so on; Murukaṉ's threat to ride the *maṭal* hobby-horse; the maid locked in her house; the attempt to exorcise the spirit that is thought to possess her; the nocturnal elopement.[46] The ancient *akam* conventions relating to the union of lovers have been used in a deliberate, comprehensive manner—so much so that Kacciyappamuṉivar added to his version of this myth several hundred verses in imitation of the Caṅkam love poems, using the traditional cast of characters and applying the conventions in a rather studied, scholastic way.[47] The eighteenth-century scholar's attempt to imitate the achievements of the classical bards may pale in comparison with the original, but the power and life of the myth itself remain. For the myth bends the conventions to its own purposes through a rich use of irony and *double entendre*. Thus the Caṅkam poems poke fun at the relatives of the love-sick girl who, believing her to be possessed, sacrifice and offer garlands to Murukaṉ so that she will be released, when in reality she is sick with love and the effects of separation from the beloved; here, however, Vaḷḷi is truly possessed by Murukaṉ and longs only for him, as the Caṅkam heroine longs for her beloved, and as the soul longs to overcome its separation from the divine. This ironic inversion of the *akam* motif is itself reversed in another version of the myth:

> While Vaḷḷi was guarding the millet fields, Murukaṉ appeared to her on his peacock in the sky. The two gazed at each other and were overcome by love. "Lady, if you are still a maiden, you must put the (marriage) garland on me," said the god. "I am the daughter of the hunters' chief and his wife, and I am unmarried," she replied. "Then marry me at once!" "Do not deviate from *dharma*, O my one and only lord. It is the custom (*marapu*) for a girl to be given by her parents. If you ask mine, they will surely give me to you. I come of good family and my reputation is unblemished."
>
> Murukaṉ agreed and went to see her parents. He asked her father for her hand, and the hunters' lord was angry. "I will give her to none other than Murukaṉ who protects our mountain. I would refuse even the Trimūti—let alone you! Be off!" he said.[48]

This time possession by the god is not a sickness to be avoided but a goal to be sought, yet the ironic note is sustained—for the rejected suitor is none other than the god to whom Nampi wishes to offer Vaḷḷi. The hunters' chief fails to identify the god who stands before him. Throughout the myth of Vaḷḷi, the Kuṟavar are depicted as devout worshipers of Murukaṉ, the god of their tribe and of the region in which they dwell; the power of the myth derives in part from their inability to recognize the god when he manifests himself among them. Hence the irony of their words and actions, and the recurrent use of *śleṣa* (paronomasia) in the text: for example, Murukaṉ (as the aged ascetic) tells Nampi he has come "to rid myself of age and my heart of its delusion; I wish to bathe in the Kumari (lit. 'Maiden') of this, your mountain."[49] Nampi understands "Kumari" as a reference to a hill-pond; the reader or listener knows that Vaḷḷi is intended. The delusion (*maruḷ*) which Murukaṉ wants to destroy is the confused state of the lovelorn; and the recovery of youth, apart from being a motif basic to the myths of the lust of the ascetic,[50] probably hints at the meaning of Murukaṉ's name (and hence his true identity)—the Tender One, Young One.[51] The words of nearly all the participants in the myth come to be loaded with double meanings. Vaḷḷi wonders at something that was not there before but that sprang up suddenly—ostensibly the *veṅkai* tree, but actually her love for the hunter; in this case it is not even certain that Vaḷḷi is herself aware of the hidden meaning of her words, for in subsequent episodes she seems to forget the identity of her lover. The god is hidden even from his chosen bride! Nampi innocently suggests that first the tree and then the aged ascetic might be a companion (*tuṇai*, cf. *tuṇaivaṉ*, "husband") for Vaḷḷi. Murukaṉ promises Vaḷḷi that she will be praised by the women of heaven; Vaḷḷi understands this as simple hyperbole, although it is meant as simple truth. In one modern version of the myth, the hunter god tells Vaḷḷi: "If you refuse to show me love, know for a fact that evil (*pāvam*) and disgrace (*paḻi*) will be yours."[52] Again the two levels, human and divine, are ironically joined.

Even Murukaṉ's threat to ride the *maṭal* hobby-horse is more complex than it might seem. Ostensibly this fits perfectly the role of the suitor who must threaten the girl's companions and guardians in order to gain access to his beloved. Yet the threat to mount the *maṭal* hobby-horse is primarily a weapon in the hands of the man to shame his beloved into responding to his love, and this sense gave birth to the metaphoric usage of the early *bhakti* poets, who threaten to shame their god into responding to their yearning. There the usual picture of the soul as feminine and the god as masculine is reversed, and the god appears as a hard-hearted woman.[53] In the myth of Vaḷḷi, which is, after all, a myth of *bhakti*, the roles are again reversed; the god is male, and he uses the threat of the *maṭal* hobby-horse to achieve union with the devotee. This is the famous theme of God in pursuit of the soul.

In addition to the conventions of the old *akam* love poetry, the myth is suffused with more general erotic symbols—the ripening millet, the food that Vaḷḷi gives Murukaṉ and the water to which she leads him to quench his thirst, the *veṅkai* tree that the god becomes in order to hide from the hunters. In one version the erotic symbolism of the tree is made even more obvious: after her father departs, Vaḷḷi climbs the tree, plucks its flowers to put in her hair and its leaves to cover her *mons veneris* (the *ta<u>l</u>ai* leaf-dress is a common symbol of the love relationship given by the man to the woman in the *akam* poems),[54] and embraces the tree with her arms and breasts, like a creeper coiled around the trunk.[55] The image of creeper and tree representing the union of lovers is conventional, and in the myths women sometimes embrace trees as a means of conceiving a child.[56] The meaning of the erotic imagery is clear in the light of the *bhakti* spirit that informs the myth: Vaḷḷi represents the immediate, spontaneous, ecstatic union of the soul with the divine. And just as *kaḷavu*, premarital union, is the most passionate and joyful of the states of love according to the classical canons, so the love of the humble hunters' daughter is more highly celebrated than that of Tĕyvayāṉai, the daughter of Indra and a symbol of orthodoxy, authority, and hierarchy.[57] Of course, Vaḷḷi ultimately celebrates a "proper" wedding in the village, *after* the initial *kaḷavu* episodes, just as Pārvatī sometimes demands that Śiva undergo a conventional wedding celebration for her sake.[58] But it is the *kaḷavu* union that is the emotional focus of the Vaḷḷi myth: the clandestine, premarital union, with all its dangers and its conflict with prescribed norms of behavior, symbolizes that state of disorder and unlimited power in which man most directly experiences the divine.[59] In one text Vaḷḷi herself is made to express the untrammeled, unconventional nature of her love: "Just as there is no *mukti* unless the three forms of evil (*mala* = *āṇava*, *māyā*, and *karma*[60]) are destroyed, so there is no union of lovers if innocence, timidity, and modesty (*maṭam*, *accam*, *nāṇ*, the three attributes of a woman) are not dispensed with. Is there anything lower than to be born a woman? Yet we do not seek to destroy that birth by *tapas* in this world full of goodness."[61] It is precisely the humble, the despised, which responds most readily to the divine, while the love of god for man gives positive meaning to life in the world. Let us recall that for the Śaiva Siddhāntins creation is not a caprice or an amusement of the deity, but an act imbued with meaning and mercy.[62]

There is yet another dimension to Vaḷḷi's prominence in the Tamil myths of Murukaṉ. Unlike Tĕyvayāṉai, who is imported from the world of Indra to the Tamil land, Vaḷḷi is indigenous, a child of the soil, born in a pit in the ground—just as Sītā, another representative of the earth goddess, is found in a furrow.[63] Vaḷḷi's connections with the soil are reinforced at points throughout the myth: she sits on a raised platform in the millet fields, guarding the ripening crop; her food is all in its natural state, fresh and uncooked—honey, fruits, millet, the milk of a wild cow, and the *vaḷḷi* root from which she derives her name.[64] One senses throughout that Vaḷḷi is drawn as the classical Tamil heroine of the mountains, the daughter not of the gods but of a real, historical group grounded in the Tamil area, the Kuṟavar hunters. Vaḷḷi thus epitomizes the idea of a local, Tamil bride, in contrast with the usual, "proper" consort according to the northern purāṇic tradition.

Vaḷḷi's role as the local bride as opposed to the "imported" first wife survived even the transfer of the cult to another tradition: the Sinhalese belief is that of the two wives of Kataragama (who is a form of Skanda/Murukaṉ), Tēvānī (< Tĕyvayāṉai) is the Tamil wife brought over from India, while Vallī Ammā is a Sinhalese or Vädda wife the god met in the Kataragama area.[65] Vaḷḷi remains the bride whom the worshiper recognizes as native to his region, and with whom he most easily identifies. Note that Vaḷḷi usually stands on the prestigious right of her husband.[66] That Tĕyvayāṉai, the symbol of orthodoxy and authority, should thus be relegated to the "sinister" left is a striking indication of the symbolic importance of the humble, local bride. According to Śaiva Siddhānta, Tĕyvayāṉai symbolizes the *kriyāśakti* (Tam. *kiriyācatti*, the power of works or motivation), while Vaḷḷi embodies the *icchāśakti* (Tam. *iccācatti*, the power of desire).[67] Even on the level of abstract symbolism, Vaḷḷi is connected with the human experience of desire (*icchā*).[68]

In the *KP*'s account of Vaḷḷi's birth, the goddess who grows up in the house of the humble Kuṟavar is compared to Kṛṣṇa, the incarnation of Viṣṇu who was raised in the midst of the cowherds.[69] Vaḷḷi is also linked with Kṛṣṇa by the golden peacock feathers that decorate her crib;[70] the peacock feathers are associated with Kṛṣṇa, as we have seen, as they are with Vaḷḷi's lord Murukaṉ. One Tamil purāṇa connects Vaḷḷi's birth with the famous myth of rivalry between two of Kṛṣṇa's wives:

> Nārada brought a flower of the *pārijāta* tree to Kṛṣṇa in Dvārakā. Kṛṣṇa gave the flower to Rukmiṇī. At this, his second wife Satyabhāmā became angry, so Kṛṣṇa promised to bring her the entire tree. He went to the city of Indra, and there he was seen and desired by a woman named Vibudhā. From their union a girl was born.
>
> The girl was brought up by the relatives of Vibudhā. One day, while swinging in a golden swing, she heard her companions sing of Murukaṉ, and she fell in love with the god.

> She performed *tapas* for twelve years by the side of Caravaṇappŏykai. Murukaṉ appeared to her and told her that he had promised Devasenā not to make love to any other woman in all the three worlds; he therefore advised her to give up her present life and be born as the daughter of a deer.
>
> The girl was born as the child of a deer impregnated by a sage. Seeing the beauty of the child, the deer felt she could not be of its own kind and therefore abandoned her. The child was found by the Kuṟavar, who named her Vaḷḷi and brought her up.[71]

Kṛṣṇa and Murukaṉ, so closely allied in other ways as to seem allotropes,[72] are here linked by the goddess: Murukaṉ's bride is the daughter of Kṛṣṇa, a specific incarnation of her usual father Viṣṇu-Tirumāl. Moreover, Vaḷḷi is born because of the jealousy of Satyabhāmā, a theme that is already known to the *Harivaṃśa*[73] and which has an exact parallel in the relations of the two wives of Murukaṉ. In this myth, Murukaṉ conspires with Vaḷḷi to circumvent his promise to the jealous Devasenā; perhaps the daughter of a deer is not, technically speaking, a woman. In the south Indian iconographic tradition, Rukmiṇī and Satyabhāmā appear as the consorts of Kṛṣṇa, who thus also has two main wives, although his alliances with over sixteen thousand other women are also remembered in southern myths.[74] Like Vaḷḷi, Satyabhāmā, the beloved second wife, is closely associated with the earth.[75] It would appear that the south Indian tradition of two wives has prevailed over the inherited myth of Kṛṣṇa's multiple marriages, both in the iconography and in the emphasis in the mythology on the theme of the rivalry and jealousy between Rukmiṇī and Satyabhāmā. The story of the theft of the *pārijāta* tree by Kṛṣṇa in order to appease the jealous Satyabhāmā became the subject of popular versions in Tamil and especially Telugu;[76] these popular myths belong in the series of folk depictions of the double marriage, in which the tensions and even open enmity between the two wives are stressed.[77]

In another version of Vaḷḷi's birth, it is the rivalry between Vaḷḷi and Tĕyvayāṉai rather than the jealousy between Rukmiṇī and Satyabhāmā that causes the *avatāra*:

> Murukaṉ was happily married to two women, Amutavalli (Tĕyvayāṉai) and Cuntaravalli (Vaḷḷi), who were born from the eyes of Viṣṇu; but Cuntaravalli became proud since she felt Murukaṉ loved her better. "The daughter of Indra is no equal

> of mine," she said. She scolded Amutavalli, and the latter bore it in silence. Murukaṉ came to know of this, so he cursed Cuntaravalli to be born on earth from the womb of a deer and to be brought up by hunters in expiation of her fault.[78]

This version is unique in pushing back the rivalry between Vaḷḷi and Tĕyvayāṉai to a time *before* Vaḷḷi's appearance on earth. Here the entire myth of Vaḷḷi derives from a situation of tension between the two wives of the god. Although not supported by the *KP*, which insists that the relations between Vaḷḷi and Tĕyvayāṉai are always harmonious,[79] the myth just quoted from Tiruccĕntūr is, together with the above myth of Rukmiṇī and Satyabhāmā, firmly within the popular tradition of *ecal*, "abuse"—the mutual denunciation and exchange of insults between two wives. The application of the *ecal* theme to the two wives of Murukaṉ is adumbrated in *Paripāṭal*, where the rain over Paraṅkuṉṟam is compared to the tears shed by Tĕyvayāṉai on the day that Murukaṉ secretly married Vaḷḷi.[80] Later the term *ecal* is applied to a class of popular compositions that share many features with oral traditions, such as the folk drama or the extempore verse of local bards.[81] The following passage may be cited as typical of these works:

> Tĕyvayāṉai: What village do you live in, *aṭi*? Do not hang your head, girl—look at me! Tell me, what trick did you employ to catch my Velaṉ? Who are you to kiss my husband, my own lord?
>
> Vaḷḷi: He of the great spear belongs to me (*ĕṉakku ccŏntam*). I play with him all the time. Bliss is mine, O Lady. Now if you only knew the ways of women. . . .
>
> Tĕyvayāṉai: So I do not know the ways of women! Say that again and I will kick you, girl. . . . Many know that *I* am the wife of Kantaṉ (Skanda, Murukaṉ); I wear the wedding-chain on my neck.
>
> Vaḷḷi: Yes, Indra forced you on my lord. What sort of trick was that?[82]

They proceed to revile each other's family: Vaḷḷi is attacked for being of low caste, and the Kuṟavar are maligned as eaters of meat, drunkards who fornicate in the marketplace, and so on. Vaḷḷi indignantly denies these accusations, and retorts that her rival has little cause for pride in being the daughter of the immoral Indra, who seduced Ahalyā. Eventually Murukaṉ makes peace between them.

The *Vaḷḷiyammaṉvilācam*, a popular drama on the subject of Murukaṉ's wooing of Vaḷḷi, devotes its last pages to the *ecal* theme. When Vaḷḷi comes to ask Murukaṉ to visit her, the god is alarmed: "If Indra's daughter sees you here arguing with me, I do not know what sorrow will result! Leave this place at once lest she catch a glimpse of you." But Tĕyvayāṉai learns from her companions that Vaḷḷi is in heaven and hastens to confront her, again charging her with trying to steal her husband: "You had the whole world to choose, but still you came here—is that the proper thing to do?" They insult each other and nearly come to blows before they are pacified, this time by their father-in-law, Śiva.[83]

Another variation concentrates on the trouble Murukaṉ encounters because of his wives' mutual jealousy. Tĕyvayāṉai locks herself in her house and refuses to let her husband in (recall the motif of the goddess locked in her shrine/box). He promises to give her gifts and to abandon Vaḷḷi if she but open the door: "If you embrace me now, I will never leave you, and let all the world know it!" "Enough of these polite words," she replies, adamant. Finally he opens the door himself with the aid of the *pañcākṣara*.[84] In another composition, Vaḷḷi is angered when her husband asks permission to return to Tĕyvayāṉai; a quarrel (*ūṭal*) develops in which husband and wife insult each other and each other's family;[85] but when Murukaṉ succeeds in leaving her home, he finds Tĕyvayāṉai no less jealous and angry.[86]

The *ecal* theme is by no means limited to Murukaṉ and his wives. A famous example from the *MBh* is the strife between Devayānī and Śarmiṣṭhā, the two wives of Yayāti (one the daughter of the Brahmin priest Śukra, the other the daughter of the demon king Vṛṣaparvan).[87] We have seen that Śiva's wives Pārvatī and Gaṅgā are often at odds; their rivalry sometimes figures in the myths that seek to explain Pārvatī's preference for a terrestrial rather than a celestial home. There are exact Vaiṣṇava parallels in the relations between Śrī and Bhūdevī,[88] or between Raṅganāyakī at Śrīraṅkam and the "upstart" local bride (*nācciyār*) Āṇṭāḷ.[89]

The *Cilappatikāram* and the Vaiṣṇava poet saints, the Āḻvārs, refer to a consort of Viṣṇu-Māyavaṉ called Nappiṉṉai (Piṉṉai, Piññai),[90] a cowherdess (*āymakaḷ*) who appears in conjunction with the theme of the suitor who must master a bull. This theme, associated with Kṛṣṇa,[91] is ancient in Tamil, and has endured in the villages while being transferred to another heroic youthful god, Aiyaṉār.[92] Is Nappiṉṉai then a Vaiṣṇava parallel to Vaḷḷi, the adored local bride? In the tradition of the commentators, she is identified with

Nīlā,[93] but her name may mean "Beautiful Younger One"[94] and therefore refer to Lakṣmī as opposed to her older sister Alakṣmī/Jyeṣṭhā (Mūtevi). Āṇṭāḷ, indeed, identifies Śrī and Nappiṉṉai.[95] However, Filliozat's conclusion—"Il semble que la personne divine de Lakṣmī (ou Mahālakṣmī) n'ait pas encore été divisée en Śrī et Nīlā a l'époque d'Āṇṭāḷ ou qu'elle l'ait été dans une tradition différent de celle qu'elle suivait"[96]—implies a break between the tradition of Āṇṭāḷ and the *Cilappatikāram*, where Mātari is made to ask: "Is our Piṉṉai of bangled arms [the cause of] the inattention paid by the One who measured the world to Śrī [who resides] in his own breast?"[97] This verse appears firmly in the tradition of the two wives, one senior and orthodox, one local and better loved. The *Bhāgavatapuraṇa* mentions a favorite cowherdess (*gopī*) of Kṛṣṇa's without naming her;[98] the later tradition, especially in Bengal, developed this hint into the rich mythology and cult of Rādhā, a symbol of immediate, ecstatic, unconventional union with the divine; and it has been suggested that Rādhā's southern analogue and predecessor was Nappiṉṉai, whose role the compiler of the *Bhāgavata* deliberately diminished.[99] This view considerably outpaces the evidence. Certainly the final form of southern Vaiṣṇava mythology gives little enough scope to Nappiṉṉai.

Nevertheless, the pattern of the second marriage to a beloved local wife has been adopted by the myths of many Vaiṣṇava shrines.[100] One of the most striking instances, in which close ties to the Murukaṉ-Vaḷḷi myth are apparent, is the tale of Viṣṇu's marriage at the great shrine of Tirupati:

> Brahmā feared that men on earth would become evil in Viṣṇu's absence, so he sent Nārada to bring the god to earth. Nārada asked the sages to whom they were sacrificing; they could not answer, and Nārada suggested that they give the sacrifice to whichever of the Trimūrti had the attribute of "goodness" (*sattvaguṇa*). They sent Bhṛgu to determine which this was; Brahmā and Śiva failed his test, but Viṣṇu was not moved to anger even when Bhṛgu kicked him on the chest—he merely inquired if the sage had not hurt his foot.
>
> Lakṣmī, however, who dwells on Viṣṇu's breast, was moved to fury when Viṣṇu failed to punish the sage. She left for Kŏllāpuram on earth. Viṣṇu came to search for her and stayed in an anthill at Veṅkaṭācalam.[101] One day he left the anthill to hunt. He chased an elephant a long distance; on his way back he caught sight of Padmāvatī, the daughter of

Ākāśarāja, king of Nārāyaṇapuram. He fell in love and asked her to marry him, but she became angry and pelted him with rocks. The god fled back to the anthill, where he lost himself in lovesickness.

He sent his maidservant Bakulamālikā to Nārāyaṇapuram to plead his cause, but fearing she would fail in her mission, he took the form of a *kuṟatti* soothsayer and went ahead into the town. When the queen heard that a fortune-teller was in town, she had the old woman brought to her, for she was worried about her daughter: since seeing Viṣṇu, Padmāvatī had been sick with love, and had not touched food or drink. The false *kuṟatti* said to the queen, "You are concerned about your daughter. She is sick because of her love for Hari. Marry her to him and great joy will result." He announced that a woman would soon come about this very matter, and then the false *kuṟatti* returned to Veṅkaṭamalai.

Bakulamālikā arrived during the ceremony of Rudrābhiṣeka, which the king was performing for his sick daughter according to the advice of the Brahmins. She had little difficulty in arranging the match; a letter was quickly despatched to Hari, who joyfully accepted the proposal. But because he was deserted by Lakṣmī, Hari had no money to cover the expenses of a wedding. He was forced to ask Kubera for a loan; according to the contract, witnessed by Brahmā and Rudra, the principal of the loan is due at the end of the Kali Age, and each year the god must pay interest. Hence the god of Veṅkaṭam is known as Vaṭṭipaṇampĕrumāḷ ("Viṣṇu [who pays] interest on money").[102]

Kubera, who is associated with Śrī in some sources,[103] here provides Viṣṇu with the means of marrying her rival! Devotees who come to Tirupati gain merit by helping the god make his interest payments on the loan; this shrine has accordingly been able to play a very significant role in the economic life of the area.[104] Tirupati may well be the most richly endowed of all south Indian temples. Not that the god really needs this help from his devotees: Lakṣmī is ultimately mollified and agrees to repay the loan, but Viṣṇu asks her to wait until the end of the Kali Age so that his devotees would have a way of winning merit.[105] There are varying versions of Viṣṇu's reconciliation with Lakṣmī: in one, Viṣṇu searches for her, and she hides in the nether world in the *āśrama* of Kapila; he then performs *tapas*, meditating on a thousand-petaled golden lotus brought to him from heaven by Vāyu. Indra sends *apsarases* to disturb him, but he creates the goddess Viśvamohinī ("she who bewitches all"), who puts them to shame; Lakṣmī, instructed by Kapila in the meaning of Bhṛgu's original test, comes up the stalk of the lotus and resumes her place on Hari's breast at an auspicious moment celebrated ever since.[106] In another version, the meddling Nārada (who engineers Viṣṇu's descent to earth in the first myth from Tirupati) succeeds in effecting the reunion:

> Nārada told Lakṣmī about her husband's marriage to Padmāvatī, and Lakṣmī was infuriated. Then Nārada told Viṣṇu (*pĕrumāḷ*) that Lakṣmī was coming to Tirupati in great anger, and the god, pretending to be afraid of his angry spouse, left a form of himself with Padmāvatī and ran to hide in Kumpakoṇam. Lakṣmī happened to catch a glimpse of him while he was running; she followed on his heels, but as soon as she entered the sacred site of Kumpakoṇam, her wrath disappeared. She became a child lying on the thousand-petaled lotus in the Pŏṟṟāmarai ("Golden Lotus") Tank; after she had performed *tapas* for many years in that tank, the god appeared and married her again.[107]

Viṣṇu's first wife must be restored to her position, for she is no less necessary than the local bride; indeed, the attraction of the local bride, the symbol of direct union with the god, exists only in the context of the proper, ritually appropriate senior wife.[108] Note how sexual tension is resolved through the transformation of the goddess into a child; in the Anasūyā myths, the goddess frees herself from a sexual threat by turning the male gods into infants—a similar resolution in which the sexual roles of the Tirupati/Kumpakoṇam myth are reversed.[109] In many ways the courtship of Padmāvatī recalls that of Vaḷḷi: there is the premarital encounter with the consequent love relationship; the wild elephant who brings this encounter about (this is the form taken by Gaṇeśa in the Murukaṉ and Vaḷḷi myth); the apparent wavering and confusion in the heart of the girl, who first pelts the god with stones and then longs for him as lover, just as Vaḷḷi responds to Murukaṉ's advances but then forgets his identity and flees from his embrace; the lovesickness which is wrongly diagnosed and treated at first by completely misguided measures. The *kuṟatti* fortuneteller is a stock figure in the folk literature that describes a heroine's love, often for the local god; she is essential, for example, in the *kuṟavañci* poems, a late genre that has inherited the *kuṟatti* soothsayer from the *akavaṉmakaḷ* of the earliest Tamil love poetry.[110] As in the Murukaṉ and Vaḷḷi myth, there is an ironic reversal: while the companion of the lovesick heroine mocks the *akavaṉmakaḷ* in the early poems ("Sing a song, soothsayer, sing another song—sing a song about *his* tall hill!"),[111] in the myth of the wooing of Padmāvatī the suitor-god is himself the soothsayer, who disguises himself and pretends to read the signs in order to achieve union with his beloved. In the classical *akam* texts, the soothsayer must be wrong, mistaking lovesickness for possession by the god; in the myths of the local bride, the soothsayer is entirely right—either by ironic coincidence, as in the Vaḷḷi myth, or by deliberate masquerading, as in the myth of Padmāvatī. The two myths, both structured around ancient Tamil motifs, are undoubted multiforms. In the folk tradition of the *MBh* episodes centered on Maturai, Kṛṣṇa takes the form of a *kuṟatti* in the course of Arjuna's wooing of Alli.[112] These examples may also be seen as an extension of the motif of the suitor who dresses as a woman.[113]

Unlike the mythology of Murukaṉ, the Vaiṣṇava myths of the second, local bride often felt it necessary to provide an explanation for the newcomer in terms of the classical pantheon. Thus Padmāvatī is said to have participated, in a former birth, in the story of Rāma:

> When Rāvaṇa was carrying Sītā to Laṅkā, Agni appeared to him and said, "*Aṭā*! The woman you are taking is not the real Sītā. Rāma gave *me* the real Sītā." The demon believed him, and was gratified when Agni gave him another woman, Vedavatī, instead of the woman he had captured in the forest. Vedavatī went with the demon to Laṅkā. After the war and the death of Rāvaṇa, Rāma returned to Ayodhyā and made the woman he had recaptured enter the fire. Suddenly he beheld in the fire two Sītās. He asked Jānakī (= Sītā) for an explanation. She explained that she had been with Agni the entire time, and that Rāvaṇa had been duped into taking a false Sītā, whose real name was Vedavatī; and she asked him to marry Vedavatī, who had gone through so much for his sake in captivity. But Rāma had vowed to have only one wife, so he promised to wed Vedavatī in the Kali Age, when he would come down to Veṅkaṭācalam.

> Therefore Vedavatī was born to Ākāśarāja; he discovered her as an infant on a thousand-petaled lotus while ploughing the earth for a sacrifice.[114]

Padmāvatī's birth in a furrow exactly imitates that of Sītā; to underline the point, her mother, the wife of Ākāśarāja, is named Dharaṇī ("Earth"). Thus the autochthonic nature of the second bride of the god is affirmed, as in the cases of Vaḷḷi and Satyabhāmā. The thousand-petaled lotus appears again in the local "birth" of Lakṣmī, as we have seen. But the existence of a second, local bride is now supported by the tradition that there were two Sītās, a real and a false (*māyāmayī* or *chāyā*) Sītā—a fairly widespread development of the Rāma story, the point of which is to spare the divine consort the humiliation and future consequences of captivity in the land of the demon. According to the *Kūrmapurāṇa*, the real Sītā entered the fire *before* Rāvaṇa could abduct her; Agni committed her to the care of Bhavānī, and replaced her with a false Sītā whom Rāvaṇa captured; after the war the false Sītā entered the fire and was burned to ashes, and the fire then revealed the true Sītā to Rāma.[115] In the *Devībhāgavatapurāṇa*, this operation takes place with the collusion of Rāma, who nonetheless keeps the vital information from everyone else, even Lakṣmaṇa, throughout the search for "Sītā" and the lethal fight to recover her. The Chāyā-Sītā for whose sake all this takes place was in a former birth Vedavatī; while performing *tapas* at Puṣkara she was seen by Rāvaṇa, who tried to rape her; she cursed him to be killed one day on her account, and then abandoned her body. During the trial by fire of the woman regained from Laṅkā, Agni reveals the real Sītā again; the Chāyā-Sītā is sent off to perform *tapas* once more at Puṣkara. In a later birth she becomes, appropriately, the fire-woman Draupadī.[116] The *uttarakāṇḍa* of the *Rām*. knows Vedavatī as a former incarnation of the *real* Sītā;[117] later myths have divided the goddess into the true Sītā and her proxy, who undergoes the tribulations of captivity in her stead. In the Tamil myth, this Chāyā-Sītā is identified with the second bride of Veṅkaṭeśvara (Viṣṇu at Tirupati / Veṅkaṭam), who is himself divided into two forms—the "real" Viṣṇu who runs away to Kumpakoṇam, and the part (*aṃśa*) or image (*bimba*) of himself, which he leaves behind with the shadow goddess Padmāvatī at Veṅkaṭācalam.[118]

Hindu mythology knows several other shadow brides. Sūrya, the sun, is married to both Saṃjñā and Chāyā, the "Shadow" that

Saṃjñā leaves behind to take her place when she flees from the unendurable splendor of the sun.[119] The marriage of the Sun and the Shadow has, indeed, a measure of logic, and this tradition endures in a Tamil shrine: at Cūriyaṉārkoyil in Tañcāvūr District, Sūrya has two brides, Uṣā (Dawn) and Chāyā (Shadow).[120] In one late variant of the Dakṣa myth, Satī substitutes a shadow for herself at the time of her father's sacrifice; it is this shadow, and not the real Satī / Umā, who enters the sacrificial fire, and whose corpse is later carried by the grief-stricken Śiva.[121] This myth, which relieves the real goddess of the necessity of dying in the fire, may reflect the splitting off of the violent Bhadrakālī, who in some versions joins Vīrabhadra in destroying the sacrifice;[122] just as only the dark goddess is allowed to take part in the act of destruction, here only a shadow is permitted to die. Another shadow goddess appears in the myth of Pradyumna and Rati, who was captured by the demon Śambara, but saved from rape in his palace by the substitution of Māyādevī or Māyāvatī, a "shadow" cast in the exact image of the chaste Rati.[123]

The contrast between a light or golden bride and a dark, shadowy second wife is thus a recurrent feature of the marriage myths; we have already noticed this pattern in relation to Śiva's double marriage (to the dark Kālī or Kauśikī and the golden, submissive Gaurī). The myth of Veṅkaṭeśvara and Padmāvatī underlines the importance of the darker bride: Padmāvatī is the Shadow Sītā born from the earth; the dark goddess is the second, *local* consort of the god. It is the dark, local bride who claims the attention of the devotees in the myths of marriage; the prim and passive "northern" consort—the wife inherited from classical purāṇic sources—definitely takes second place in the affections of the Tamil pilgrims, who seek the help of the dark, earthbound, powerful goddess in her native home. Similarly, the black Kālī rather than the golden Gaurī is the true heroine of the Tamil marriage myths, and, as we have seen, it is the "murderous" rather than the peaceful union of the divine couple that is the underlying, active concern of the authors. The contrast in color is carried through in other cases: Tĕyvayāṉai is gold or red, Vaḷḷi dark (black, brown, or purple).[124] Bhūdevī is dark[125] or light green, while Lakṣmī is usually golden or white.[126] Kṛṣṇa's first wife is Rukmiṇī, "the Golden"; her rival, Satyabhāmā, is a form of the earth and therefore, presumably, dark. Of the two wives of Khaṇḍobā in Mahārāṣṭra, one is fair and the other dark.[127] The local goddess in many Tamil shrines (such as

Mīnākṣī at Maturai and Akhilāṇḍeśvarī at Tiruvāṉaikkā) is usually painted green—a color strongly associated with fertility and vegetation, and hence with the earth; green in these cases may reflect the basically dark, chthonic aspect of the local goddess. As we have seen, the green Mīnākṣī is directly linked with the "dark-blue" Nīli (or Paiññīli).[128] Apītakucā (Tam. Uṇṇāmulaiyammai), the goddess at Tiruvaṇṇāmalai—where the violent virgin slays Mahiṣa / Śiva before being absorbed into the androgyne—is pictured as dark blue on the colorful printed sheets sold to pilgrims. The wives of Aiyaṉār (Pūraṇā and Puṣkalā, or Madanā and Varṇanī) are both said to be yellow;[129] but at least one set of terra-cotta images in North Arcot District shows one wife as white and the second, on the right of the god, as red.[130] I have no information on the colors of the two wives of other folk deities in the Tamil area, such as Maturaivīraṉ, "often accompanied by his two wives and servants,"[131] or the demon Kāttāṉ, with his mistresses Pārppātti and Cĕṭṭippĕṇ.[132] In the case of the latter, one may at least observe that the principle of hierarchy still obtains: Kāttāṉ's first wife is a Brahmin, his second a merchant's daughter. This pattern, as we have seen, is entirely predictable; Vaḷḷi is of much lower social standing than her rival, Tĕyvayāṉai, as is Gāyatrī in relation to Brahmā's first wife, Sāvitrī. Dumont notes that the royal custom of having two wives prescribed that one be of her husband's rank, the second below it.[133] In the myths of the goddess, it is the second, local bride, who is dark and socially inferior, who attracts the interest and love of the worshipers.

Sometimes the two brides of the god are contrasted in different terms: at Viruttācalam Śiva has two wives, Vṛddhāmbā ("the old goddess") and Bālāmbā ("the young goddess"). Only the first, as Pĕriyanāyakiyār, merits a verse in the *pāyiram* of the purāṇa, and it is probable that she alone was the original goddess of the shrine (note the alliteration of her name, Vṛddhāmbā, with the name of the shrine). A story is told to explain the arrival of the second, younger bride:

> "When Sundara, the poet-saint, came to the place he wearied of its ancient air; everything in it was called 'old'—the town, the hill,[134] the god, and the goddess—and he went away without singing any of his usual hymns in praise of the shrine. He had not gone far when the god, in the shape of a man of the Védan caste, stopped him and robbed him of all he possessed.

> He returned to the town and on his arrival found that the god had just then moved a certain pious individual to set up an image of Bálámbá. Repentant, he chanted verses in praise of the place and its deity and went his way."[135]

The deity who robs his devotee is a prominent motif in the Tamil hagiographies (cf. the devotee who robs others out of devotion to his god).[136] Theft carried out by or for the god appears to be of a different order than ordinary stealing; these motifs reflect what might be called the "totalitarian" nature of the demands made on the Tamil *bhakta*, at least in the realm of the popular hagiographies.[137] It should be noted that the poet Cuntarar himself is said to have had two wives, Paravai of Tiruvārūr and Caṅkili of Tiruvŏṟṟiyūr; his desertion of Caṅkili in order to return to Tiruvārūr, in violation of a promise exacted at the time of the wedding, brings down punishment in the form of blindness.[138] In Cuntarar's case, the tension is not only between the two women, who are in any case separated by a great distance, but also between human eroticism *per se* and the passionate, uncompromising love of man for his god.

To summarize: the concept of the double marriage is widely applied to both Brahminical or "purāṇic" deities[139] and folk gods in the Tamil area. The goddess is divided into two brides, who oppose each other in several ways: the senior wife may be "imported" from the northern, classical pantheon, while the second bride is purely local, a child of the Tamil land, born from the soil; one wife is light or golden, the second dark or black; one is orthodox, of high status, a ritually proper wife for the deity, while the second is of humble, socially inferior origin.[140] Tamil *bhakti*, even while affirming the social order and the conventional scheme of mundane existence, extols the devotion of the humble and the despised; the myth of Vaḷḷi and Murukaṉ illustrates the divine love between the lowly believer (the soul in its exile) and God. Man identifies himself with the earthbound, local bride, who is also closest to the terrestrial sources of power and life. It is thus hardly surprising that the myths focus their attention on the second, Tamil bride, just as the dark and blood-stained Kālī rather than the golden, pure Gaurī is the dominant figure in the marriage myths. Indeed, Kālī in the Tamil myths epitomizes the local conception of woman no less than the mythic exemplars of the indigenous bride (Vaḷḷi, Padmāvatī). But the Kālī of the Tamil myths is herself ambivalent; as we saw in the previous section, she is the sustaining, life-giving mother of the divine child as well as a focus of danger and violence. The double marriage is an attempt to come to terms with these opposing aspects. We thus find two consorts who are fundamentally at odds, their quarrels even recorded in a special genre of folk literature, the *ecal* poems. The tension between the two wives thus reflects an ambivalence rooted in the personality of the goddess, indeed in the Tamil conception of woman generally as a locus of power that is potentially both dangerous and creative. It now remains for us to observe how the ambivalent wife and mother appears as a sexually ambiguous goddess, whose contrasting aspects alternate in time, just as destruction and creation are locked in causal, sequential association in the related rituals of sacrifice and rebirth.

## 9. Sex-reversal: The Male as Goddess and Mother

> O Mother, Mother of the universe,
> art thou male or female?
> Who can say?[1]

> The cow is a wonderful animal,
> also he is quadruped and because
> he is female he gives milk but
> he will do so only when he has
> got child.[2]

The split goddess represents an attempt to resolve the complexities of Devī's nature through dichotomy. The god will have two wives, a high and a low, a white and a black; the divine child will have two or more mothers, beneficent and destructive. The myths of Maturai and Tiruvaṇṇāmalai suggest another form of division: the goddess is male and female, the unitary icon of the androgyne. We have seen how this image absorbs the tension of the Murderous Bride: the single-breasted Kaṇṇaki / Kālī, slayer of her husband, becomes at Tiruvaṇṇāmalai the single-breasted androgyne; at Maturai she is the three-breasted Mīnākṣī, the Amazon made woman by her spouse. The inherently ambivalent goddess has developed into the sexually ambivalent icon, which the authors of our texts clearly understand as symbolizing a form of marriage. Nevertheless, there is good reason to regard the Tamil goddess as already in some sense bisexual even before her marriage to Śiva: the goddess is undoubtedly female, but the aggressive, violent side of her nature is easily seen as masculine. Certainly, her menacing, martial behavior clashes with the idealized picture of the submissive, devoted wife—especially insofar as this behavior is directed against her future husband! In other words, the androgynous marriage of the local goddess and Śiva in a Tamil shrine, while possessed of a powerful symbolism of its own,[3] may well have developed in some cases from an original conception of the goddess as a male-female hybrid. In this section we will probe this concept further, concentrating on two particular facets—the androgyne as a symbol for the principle of exchange that operates in the sacrifice; and a mythology of sex-reversals that express the bisexuality attributed to the goddess in terms of a sequence or a cycle of alternating sexual roles. Both of these facets are useful in explaining the creative potential of the goddess, who gives birth to the divine child without losing her virginity.

The androgyne appears frequently in classical Hindu mythology as a form of the creator, usually Brahmā or Śiva. The creator who divides himself into male and female halves that unite incestuously to produce creatures is, by definition, a primeval androgyne.[4] The androgyne is a symbol of the wholeness and autonomy that characterize the First Creator;[5] deities that are essentially either male or female may thus naturally be described as androgynous. Such is the case with the Tamil goddess, and with the purāṇic Brahmā and Śiva. But in one Tamil shrine, Brahmā, the androgynous creator, is said to have undergone a complete change of sex:

> In the beginning, Brahmā thought, "There is no-one on earth who has a pure nature except me." He created the worlds, including a lovely woman with whom he was infatuated because of the *māyā* of Śiva. He made love to her shamelessly, and because of that great evil all his creatures became short-lived (*alpāyus*), and he became afraid and lost his power to create. Like a madman (*unmatta*) he wandered the earth, worshiping at shrines of Śiva and bathing in holy waters, until he reached Gajāraṇya (= Tiruvāṉaikkā) and received knowledge. He performed *tapas* there, and Śiva was pleased with him.
>
> Śiva said to the goddess, "O beautiful one, Brahmā is performing *tapas*. I must go there together with you. Give me your form." He took the form of the goddess and gave her his

> form, and together they went to see Brahmā. Śiva appeared to Brahmā as Śakti and said, "You are the creator. I am pleased with your *tapas* and have come to grant you a boon." Brahmā was amazed; he worshiped the god, and Śiva gave him the power to create (*sṛṣṭiśakti*) and disappeared together with the goddess. Brahmā, taking the same form of Śakti in which Śiva had granted him his boon, celebrated a festival to him whose form is *amṛta*; then he returned, satisfied, to Brahmaloka. Those who see Śiva in that *śakti* form during the festival go to the highest station.[6]

This myth concludes the Sanskrit *māhātmya* from Tiruvāṉaikkā; the Tamil purāṇa from this shrine merely hints at the story by stating that Brahmā received the power to create *as a woman* (*ciruṭṭiyum ĕytiṉaṉ mātarāy*).[7] The creation myth has been doubled: first, we have the conventional incest motif, here used to explain the origin of evil (and thus this myth belongs to the corpus of creation myths that regard sexual union as the first link in the chain of evil,[8] although here the evil of pride appears to exist even before the act of creation); then, Brahmā is granted the power to create by the female Śiva. Brahmā's own need to take female form reflects on one level a consciousness of the anomaly of a male creator who gives birth to the world; if Brahmā is to have the role of Mother, he must become, at least in part, a woman. In a sense, the two parts of the androgyne have been split and separated in the myth: Brahmā is first male, the incestuous father; then, in the course of expiating his fault, he becomes female. Birth from the male, who is both mother and father, is not uncommon in Hindu mythology;[9] but the myth from Tiruvāṉaikkā strives to clarify the anomaly. Thus the female component of the primeval androgyne must be given tangible form, and the same impulse affects the second male, Śiva—who historically has inherited Brahmā's role as creator, and who mediates between Brahmā and the goddess in this myth by exchanging genders with his wife.

There is, however, another facet to these reversals. The Tiruvāṉaikkā myth implies that the power of creation is truly proper only to Devī. Only the goddess, as Śakti and Mother, or as the locus of intense creative power, can transfer the ability to create to Brahmā. Why then, we may ask, is Śiva needed in this myth? Devī at Tiruvāṉaikkā is known as Akhilāṇḍeśvarī, or Akhilāṇḍanāyakī, the creative "mistress of the universe" who forms the *liṅga* at this shrine from the waters of the *tīrtha*, that is, creates and locates the presence of the god.[10] It is therefore not surprising that Brahmā is said elsewhere in this purāṇa to have worshiped by meditation and to have installed the image of Devī (*akilāṇṭanimalaiy uruvam*) along with those of her two sons and the other gods (*pulavar*).[11] This, we may suspect, is the basic myth of Brahmā's worship: the male creator worships the powerful local goddess of Tiruvāṉaikkā, from whom, we must assume, he derives his creative energies.[12] The Sanskrit *māhātmya* adds to this essential pattern the important information that Brahmā acquired a female form in this shrine in imitation of Śiva; the latter god serves as the vehicle for the transfer of power. Ritual practice at the shrine still mimics the mythic sex-reversal: each day the priest of the goddess shrine at Tiruvāṉaikkā dresses as a woman and worships the god.[13] Note that although the god, Śiva, is the object of this transvestite worship, it is the ritual servant of the goddess who performs the rite.

The ritual transvestism enacted at Tiruvāṉaikkā is undoubtedly linked to the myths of Brahmā's worship at this spot; similar rites are, however, common in the village religion of the Tamil region.[14] In attempting to understand this practice, one may distinguish at the start between two main varieties, one centered on the goddess, the other on the god. Both types are linked by a series of shared motifs and ideas. The most common explanation of the rite[15] as expressing identification with the goddess is, as we shall see, most suited to the second type (the worship of the god); only in a limited sense can it be applied to the worship of the goddess. The myth from Tiruvāṉaikkā seems to describe a close tie between Brahmā, the male god in female form, and the local goddess; but is this tie an indication of the identification of the two? Here the puzzling, seemingly superfluous role of Śiva may offer a clue to the transvestite motif. Śiva communicates Devī's creative power to Brahmā after exchanging personae with the goddess. This idea of exchange brings us back to the dynamics of the sacrificial rituals associated with the goddess: just as the sacrifice produces new life from the destruction of the victim's vital force, the Tamil goddess in her shrine gives birth to the god after draining him of life and power. We have seen how the male offers his life to his virgin bride in order to be reborn from her womb; the goddess is the source first of death, then of a new flow of vitality. This process operates through the exchange of power between the victim and his bride. The life drained away in the first instance is restored to the male in a new form. Of course, as we have seen, the virgin goddess is thought to be possessed of an inherent power in her own right; she may not need the influx of power from the sacrificed male in order to create life anew. Nevertheless, the old agonistic model of the sacrifice, in which two parties transfer back and forth the material and intangible fruits of the ritual,[16] appears to have survived in the Tamil marriage myths with their underlying sacrificial symbolism. Let us recall that the goddess who slays Mahiṣa at Tiruvaṇṇāmalai acquires the crystal *liṅga*—that is, the power and vitality—of the demon and loses it only the moment before her androgynous marriage to Śiva. As we have seen, this marriage hides the terrifying, bisexual nature of the lone goddess; it might also be said to mark the transition from her warlike to her peaceful, beneficent state.

The notion of an agonistic exchange occurring in the course of a murderous marriage suggests another meaning for the Tamil androgyne icon. I have interpreted the androgynous *goddess* as a combination of aggressive and pacific elements, or as a woman who violates the feminine ideal by realizing her potential for violence (for example, by casting her breast at her victim, like the single-breasted Kaṇṇaki / Tirumāmaṇi). We might also see the androgynous goddess as embodying the principle of exchange: she absorbs the masculinity of her victim or devotee, while he, for his part, offers up his power and is left castrated or slain. It is in this sense that we may speak of an identification of the worshiper with the goddess through the reversal of sex: through the exchange of vital power, both the devotee and the goddess become sexually ambiguous; the male loses his manhood to the goddess. Ritual castration creates a woman-like male (recall Arjuna's disguise as the long-haired eunuch Bṛhannaḍā in *MBh* 4.2.21-27), while Devī becomes, for a moment, partially male. But the offering of the fullness of man's power and sexuality may easily be regarded as the sacrifice of life itself; in this case the donor is totally identified with his gift, and we have the recurring theme of death and rebirth through the agency of the woman. The two interpretations of the androgynous goddess suggested here are, it should be noted, entirely compatible; both point to the myth of the god's death-in-love and consequent rebirth from the womb of his bride.

Ritual transvestism is a symbolic enactment of this series of sacrificial acts;[17] the devotee who dresses as a woman in order to worship the goddess is presenting her with his power, his seed, perhaps his very life. That the transvestite rituals may express the idea of self-sacrifice to the goddess is clear from the folk myths of Pāvāṭairāyaṉ ("King of the Long Skirt"), an attendant of the goddess who wears the lower garment of a girl: Pāvāṭairāyaṉ once shot an arrow into an anthill by mistake. He took a pickaxe and dug it out, thus unintentionally wounding the goddess who dwelt there. He wished to atone; the goddess asked for food, so he disembowelled himself with his pickaxe and offered her his vitals. The goddess (Aṅkāḷammaṉ) was pleased and ordered him to remain near her always.[18] The transvestite Pāvāṭairāyaṉ stands to this day outside the shrines of Aṅkāḷammaṉ; his act of self-sacrifice, obviously symbolized by his woman's attire, has won him eternal life as an attendant of the goddess. The equation of death and castration, both reduced to the transvestite image of the devotee, is clear from this myth. In the marriage myths studied earlier, death or castration follow union with the dark virgin or the penetration of her locked enclosure; the blinding of the male may precede this union, and adumbrates the fate in store for the god. The motifs of blindness and the locked shrine also occur in connection with the theme of castration—and with its opposite, as in the following myth from Tirukkaḷar:

> A Brahmin priest (*kurukkaḷ*) was rewarded with a girl after worshiping Śiva for many days, sinking his mind and his eyes in the body of the god. One night he forgot his daughter in the shrine of the goddess while she was asleep; he remembered only after reaching home after the midnight service. Unable to open the locked doors of the shrine, he meditated on the goddess all night. Next morning, when the doors were opened for the morning service, all beheld the grace of the goddess: the child had become a boy.[19]

The sex-reversal in this myth follows upon the intrusion into the sanctuary of the goddess; the enclosure remains intact throughout the night, and a male child emerges when the doors are opened in the morning. If we apply to this myth the interpretation followed in other myths of the locked sanctuary, we find a multiform of the myths of rebirth, the second stage in the sequence of the divine marriage—the stage in which the castrated or slain divinity is revived and transformed into a fit consort for the inviolate goddess. The child locked in the shrine (or womb) of the goddess is born as a male by the goddess's grace; similarly, the castrated Śiva has his manhood restored when he emerges from the cave of the goddess.[20] Castration is the concomitant of union with the goddess, or of the extraordinary vision that is a form of that union (the penetration of the sealed shrine); but castration in this context is also the prelude to rebirth. At Tirukkaḷar the original female birth takes the place of the castration / slaughter in the marriage myths; the daughter granted by the male Śiva is then "reborn" as a son through the intervention of the goddess in her virginal, "bounded" state.

In the myth from Tirukkaḷar, the element of blindness is wholly implicit: the goddess is hidden from sight in her inviolable enclosure. But blindness is also associated with the prohibition of witnessing the sexual act, as in the myth of Iḷa and in many south Indian stories,[21] and another series of myths connects this idea with the theme of sex-reversal:

> Once Nārada came upon Viṣṇu while he was making love to Lakṣmī. Lakṣmī hastily left the room, and Nārada asked Viṣṇu why she had done so—for was he not an ascetic in control of his senses, a master of *māyā*? "You should not claim to have conquered *māyā*," said Viṣṇu; "I have not done so, nor has Śiva, or Brahmā, or the sages. No one can conquer *māyā*; you yourself are bewitched by the music you play on your *vīṇā*." Viṣṇu took Nārada to a tank and told him to enter the water; the sage emerged as a woman, and Viṣṇu took away his *vīṇā* and deerskin and returned to his abode.
>
> King Tāladhvaja ("having a palmyra standard") saw the beautiful woman and married her; the couple had many sons and grandsons, and the wife of the king was happy. But one day all her sons and grandsons were killed in battle. As she was weeping on the battlefield, Viṣṇu appeared as an old Brahmin and led the old woman to another tank. She entered the water and emerged as Nārada, in his old form. Viṣṇu comforted the old king Tāladhvaja, thus deprived of his wife, and expounded the meaning of *māyā*.[22]

Nārada's lesson in the meaning of *māyā* is initiated by his witnessing the union of Viṣṇu and Lakṣmī. The pedagogic framework of the story is secondary, perhaps influenced by the well-known myth of Nārada and Parvata and the daughter of Ambarīṣa;[23] the heart of the story is Nārada's change of sex. Here an important connection has to be noticed: Nārada becomes the wife of Tāladhvaja, "he who has the palmyra as his standard"—a common epithet in the Epic for Bhīṣma. Now Bhīṣma is intimately tied to a famous story of sex-reversal, that of Śikhaṇḍin, born a woman but transformed into a man by the *yakṣa* Sthūṇa; Śikhaṇḍin is the direct cause of Bhīṣma's death in battle. That Bhīṣma should be killed by a male-female hybrid is a matter of first importance for an understanding of the mythic element connected to the Epic; the explanation offered by the *MBh* itself is that Śikhaṇḍin was a reincarnation of Ambā, the princess of the king of the Kāśīs stolen together with her sisters Ambikā and Ambālikā by Bhīṣma as brides for Vicitravīrya. Ambā, however, was secretly betrothed to the king of the Śālvas; Bhīṣma released her when she told him of this, but her betrothed rejected her, and she consequently vowed revenge on her abductor, Bhīṣma.[24] Although a detailed investigation of this story is beyond the scope of the present chapter,[25] one cannot but wonder whether Nārada in the purāṇic myth just cited is not identified with Śikhaṇḍinī / Ambā. Our suspicion that such is, indeed, the case is strengthened by another version of the myth, where Nārada is said to have become the daughter of the king of Kāśī by bathing in the tank.[26] The purāṇas appear to have retained and developed an archaic strand nearly lost to the epic, that is, the tradition that Śikhaṇḍinī was Bhīṣma's bride as well as his destroyer. Perhaps it is not, after all, by chance that the stories of Śikhaṇḍinī / Ambā are built around the recurrent theme of the bride contest and suitor's test.[27] If our suggestion is correct, Bhīṣma dies at the hand of his androgyne-bride, just as Mahiṣa/Śiva is slain in the Tamil shrines by the violent, bisexual Tirumāmaṇi.

Bhīṣma's title of "Tāladhvaja" also recalls the ancient Tamil theme of riding the *maṭal* hobby-horse, which a rejected suitor would fashion, it is said, out of the leaves of the palmyra (*paṉai*, Skt. *tāla*).[28] One use of the *maṭal* theme in the context of divine worship was discussed earlier, with reference to the myth of Murukaṉ and Vaḷḷi;[29] here we may note that the rider of the hobby-horse (the devotee in love with the remote and hard-hearted deity, in the standard usage by the *bhakti*-poets; the god Murukaṉ, in the Vaḷḷi myth) performs an act of self-sacrifice. In view of the existence of spines on each side of the palmyra branch, the ride on the hobby-horse may well have represented a ritual castration. George Hart has suggested that in addition to shaming the beloved into responding, the rider of the hobby-horse wished to establish a sacramental relationship with her "by shedding his own blood in a perversion of the sexual act."[30] The palmyra palm may thus be associated both in the myths of Bhīṣma and the ancient Tamil motif of the *maṭal* hobby-horse with the theme of sex-reversal or castration.

The Epic also informs us that Bhīṣma's slayer Śikhaṇḍin was a Rākṣasa reborn,[31] and this element is developed in a multiform of the myth that is added to an expanded south Indian version of the *Pañcatantra*:

> A king was childless for many years. At last, because of the vows and sacrifices he performed, his wife began to bear him children; but all the children were girls. The king was on the point of divorcing his wife when his minister persuaded him to wait to see what the child she was then carrying would be. When the queen once again gave birth to a girl, the minister hid the child and sent an astrologer to tell the king that a son had been born—but at an inauspicious moment, so inauspicious, in fact, that the father must not see the child for sixteen years. After fifteen years had passed, it was necessary to arrange a match for the "prince;" the minister asked to be given an army for this purpose, and besieged the city of another king, asking for the king's daughter as a condition of lifting the siege. The other king gladly agreed.
>
> At this time a Brahmarākṣasa who had seen and fallen in love with the young hidden princess asked the minister for help in attaining his desire. The minister told him the story of the princess and asked the Rākṣasa to change sex with the princess for six days. The Rākṣasa agreed, and the minister was thus able to arrange the wedding. But when it was time for the "prince" to return the loan to the Rākṣasa, the latter begged to be allowed to remain female—for in the meantime someone had fallen in love with her and made her pregnant! So the prince remained a man, and the kingdom had an heir.[32]

There are clear parallels between this tale and the Mīnākṣī myths, including the *Pañcatantra* "Mīnākṣī" variant, discussed above:[33] again we find a childless king who performs sacrifices in order to obtain a child, and who is disappointed when the result is female rather than male offspring, as in the standard descriptions of Mīnākṣī's birth; and once more there is a daughter who must be hidden from the sight of her father. Both the "demonic" associations of the sex-reversal (which is dependent upon the aid of the Brahmarākṣasa) and the blinding / hiding complex suggest that we are dealing with a series of stories related to the myths of the Murderous Bride. Mīnākṣī, the Amazon Queen of Maturai, epitomizes the bisexual goddess imbued with violent power; Śikhaṇḍinī, in both the Epic and the folk myths of the androgynous bride, is no less violent and threatening. In a Marathi version of the *Pañcatantra* story just summarized, the Rākṣasa who exchanges sex with the princess is far from happy at the permanent loss of his masculinity, unlike the Brahmarākṣasa of Dubois's version; he comes to the prince's palace to demand the return of his manhood, and when this demand is refused, he (or rather, "she," now condemned to remain a demoness) kills thirty-five million male demons and tries to attach their genitals to her body; she fails, but becomes pregnant in the process.[34] One could hardly ask for a more dramatic illustration of the motif of the castrating, bisexual goddess and mother! A Gujarati variant reverses the sex-change along with other elements of the story: here the princess, returning from slaying a tiger, rides on a mare into a pool; when she sees her mare transformed into a stallion, she bathes herself and becomes a man.[35] The horse changed from male to female is a prominent feature of the Iḷa myth, and sometimes Iḷa himself becomes a Kiṃpuruṣa, half-man and half-horse.[36] In the Gujarati variant, the direction of the change is reversed; the hybrid nature of the princess—first a tiger-slaying Amazon, then a full-blooded male—remains clear.

The *Pañcatantra* variants replace the *yakṣa* (Sthūṇa) of the Epic with various kinds of demons (Brahmarākṣasa and Rākṣasa); and, while Sthūṇa is forced to remain female after the loan of his sex because his master Kubera, is amused by the change, the Brahmarākṣasa in the version of Dubois *asks* to remain a woman. Perhaps this story has been influenced by the closely related myth of Bhaṅgāśvana:

> The royal sage (*rājarṣi*) Bhaṅgāśvana performed the *agniṣṭut* rite[37] to gain offspring, and was granted one hundred sons. Indra, jealous (at not being named in the rite), made Bhaṅgāśvana enter a lake, from which he emerged as a woman. In this form he had another one hundred sons by an ascetic; they went to share the kingdom with their brothers, but Indra created division among them and they killed one another. The god then appeared to the grieving mother; when she learned his identity, she fell at his feet, and Indra was moved to offer to revive one set of her children. She chose to have back her sons born to

> her as a woman, for a woman's love is stronger than a man's. Then Indra offered to change her back to a man, but she elected to stay a woman, for a woman has greater pleasure in sexual union than a man.[38]

Like Nārada, Bhaṅgāśvana bears children only to lose them in war; but while Nārada learns the nature of *māyā* from this experience and ultimately reverts to his original sex, here the sex-reversal is permanent (as with Śikhaṇḍinī and the *Pañcatantra* variants).[39] Nārada and Bhaṅgāśvana both belong in the series of male mothers, or, to be more precise, of men transformed into women who then become mothers of children. This association of sex-reversal and maternity is an important element in the Tamil myths; we may observe one more example, which also shows again the link between castration and the forbidden vision:

> Aruṇa ("Dawn"), the charioteer of the Sun, heard the music of Urvaśī's dance; taking the form of a woman, he stole into the vicinity of Urvaśī and witnessed the dance. Indra saw the new woman by the side of Urvaśī and fell in love with her; from their union, Vālin was born. Aruṇa returned to the Sun and told him of these events. The Sun then wished to see Aruṇa's female form; he, too, united with the female Aruṇa and produced a son, Sugrīva. To free himself of the evil of having taken woman's form, Aruṇa set up a *liṅga* near Vedapuri.[40]

Aruṇa's change of sex may owe something to the ambiguous sexuality of the solar deity in early Indian myths.[41] Aruṇa offends in devising a manner of seeing the heavenly dance; sight is again the root cause of transformation, as in the myth from Assam in which a king strives to catch a forbidden glimpse of the dancing goddess, and the priest who aids him pays with his head.[42] Sex-reversal (castration) takes the place of the head-sacrifice in that myth, and the interdiction of vision is here transferred to the loss of sex, the act that enables Aruṇa to see. Hence Aruṇa's need to expiate at the Tamil shrine. Elsewhere, as we have seen, the prohibited vision of the goddess is tantamount to union, and therefore leads to the castration consequent upon this union; here the reversal of sex *precedes* the vision of Urvaśī. Urvaśī is also linked to the motif of sex-reversal through her lover Purūravas, the son of the sexual hybrid Iḷa.[43] Other Tamil texts also affirm the birth of Vālin and Sugrīva from a male (usually a monkey) made into a woman.[44]

The connection between sex-reversal and motherhood in the Tamil myths derives its logic from the basic myth of the androgynous goddess. Bisexuality is in any case a convenient symbol of wholeness and independence; a bisexual being should be capable of producing offspring, and thus we have the many myths of the androgynous creator. The sex-reversal simply spreads out over time the two facets united in the androgyne. The goddess who is both male and female, either simultaneously or at separate moments in time, is the creative, virginal mother. In addition, the maternal role of the androgynous goddess proceeds naturally from the principle of exchange studied earlier: the male devotee/victim offers his power to the goddess, who returns the gift in the form of a new child; both donor and recipient undergo a sexual transformation through the process of exchange. The castrated male confronts the sexually ambiguous goddess at this juncture. Whether we explain the maternal androgyne as a symbol of autonomy, virginity, and perfectly preserved power, or as a symbol of a dynamic ritual of exchange, we can understand the importance of the change in sex as the background and prelude to the divine birth: the goddess absorbs a male element before giving birth, or—the more usual type of story—the male becomes a woman or a goddess and subsequently conceives. The idea of the pregnant male thus recurs throughout these stories, and, just as the concept of multiple mothers called forth prosaic attempts at explanation and rationalization, the notion of the male mother could be challenged and even parodied:

> In the Cetu kingdom lived a learned Vidyādhara (a class of celestial beings attendant upon Indra). His wife, who was pregnant, asked him one day to bear the embryo in her stead while she went to the temple to participate in a festival. The Vidyādhara agreed and took the embryo from his wife. But when his wife arrived at the temple and saw the actresses who sang and danced during the festivities there, she thought it better to stay in their company and enjoy herself than to return home to bear the child. Meanwhile, the embryo developed in the belly of the Vidyādhara; since it could not come out, he died.[45]

In this playful story, from another southern version of the *Pañcatantra*, the concerns and assumptions of the myth are shattered by common sense. This is a luxury we cannot yet afford; we will return to the male mother in a moment, in the myths of Mohinī.

Let us sum up our results so far. The sex-reversals in the myths discussed above revolve around the worship of the goddess, who demands the sacrifice of her lovers.[46] Both the goddess and her devotees are implicated in this process: the male castrates himself in the service of the inherently ambivalent goddess, the violent Amazon possessed of both male and female natures. The male becomes woman to worship the goddess. Sometimes this idea is stated explicitly by the myths: Śiva came to earth as a Kāpālika, leaving Pārvatī in the care of Viṣṇu, who took the form of a woman to serve her (as did the other gods, as well).[47] The gods became maidservants of Devī to hide from Andhaka; they dressed as women and spoke women's dialects.[48] But to serve the goddess is not necessarily to identify with her. Identification with the goddess is, however, a definite feature in the second type of ritual transvestism, that which is centered on the god: "I saw the haughty Master/ for whom men, all men/ are but women, wives."[49] The gods wish to become women when they behold the beauty of Śiva as a bridegroom at Tirutturutti. The transvestite worship of Śiva at Tiruvāṉaikkā, as distinct from the myth of Brahmā's worship of Devī and consequent sex-reversal, reveals the same idea.[50] In yearning for God, the soul pictures itself as a woman longing for her lover. The worship of the village god Kūttāṇṭavar illustrates the ritual expression of this idea; diverse traditions explain the ritual in which men dress as women, cut the wedding chain, and mourn the slain god Kūttāṇṭavar. The god is identified with Arāvāṉ (Irāvat), Arjuna's son who, according to the southern tradition, was sacrificed on the field of Kurukṣetra to ensure the Pāṇḍavas' victory.[51] On the day of his sacrifice, Viṣṇu (Māyaṉ) had mercy on the young man and, taking the form of Mohinī (Mokiṉiyāḷ), wed him and then went away; after his sacrifice, Mohinī burned the wedding garland.[52] Another myth takes this idea further: Kūttāṇṭavar was destined to die on the day of his marriage, so no one would give him a bride; Kṛṣṇa at last had mercy and, taking the form of Mohinī, married him, whereupon Kūttāṇṭavar withered away except for his head.[53] The god is worshiped in the form of a huge head, sometimes placed in the shrine of the village goddess Draupadī, and thus he may be related to the demon Rāhu, who stole some of the *amṛta* by disguising himself as a god; the sun and the moon discovered him, and Viṣṇu, who had saved the *amṛta* for the gods by bewitching the demons with the female form of Mohinī, cut off his head. Because the *amṛta* had reached his throat, Rāhu's head was immortal.[54] Mohinī links the two myths of gods worshiped in the form of a head; moreover, both Rāhu and Arāvāṉ, who is often equated with Kūttāṇṭavar, are serpents.[55] The men who dress as women to weep for Kūttāṇṭavar are acting the role of the widowed goddess Mohinī. But here the focus is on the *god*, and this worship is thus directly analogous to the "literary transvestism" discussed by Piatigorsky—the use of the ancient conventions of *akam* love poetry in the literature of devotion to Śiva or Viṣṇu.[56] There, too, the poet imagines himself as a bride of the god, or as a woman pining for her beloved. We have seen this symbolic usage in those myths of the Reluctant Bride in which a young virgin rejects human eroticism out of love for the god; the devotee who reads or hears these stories undoubtedly identifies himself with the earthly bride who seeks union with the divine. By the same token, the transvestite worshiper of the god may be assimilated to the goddess who is married, or yearns to be married, to this deity.

Nevertheless, the myths of Kūttāṇṭavar reflect the same complex of ideas as the goddess myths discussed above, in particular the theme of the death-in-love. Kṛṣṇa's act of mercy is, to say the least, ambiguous: Kūttāṇṭavar gains a bride, but in marrying him Mohinī causes his death. The major distinction in the cult is that the worshipers here direct their rites to the victim rather than to the Bride who claims his life. The folk literature recognizes that Kūttāṇṭavar is sacrificed to the goddess (*ammaṉ*);[57] this god is clearly seen as an exemplar of the sacrifice, a model for human worship of the violent bride and mother, a symbol of the dangers of sexuality and marriage. The god's ophidian identity confirms this range of associations.

The transvestism of the worshipers of Kūttāṇṭavar has a fitting parallel in the fact that the goddess they imitate, Mohinī, is herself a form of the male god Viṣṇu. Mohinī appears in the lists of village goddesses in the South,[58] but that her sex is ambiguous is clear from the popular belief that her son Aiyaṉār stands at crossroads in order to learn from wayfarers the identity of his mother: Viṣṇu can hardly be his mother because he is male, and Pārvatī (the wife of his father, Śiva) is not his mother since she did not give him birth.[59] Mohinī first appears in connection with the churning of the ocean, when she fascinates the demons and steals from them the *amṛta*.[60] Sometimes the birth of Aiyaṉār (usually Śāstṛ in Sanskrit) is added on to this episode,[61] but later myths connect it with the Pine Forest[62] or with the myth of Bhasmāsura:

A demon worshiped Śiva and was given the power to turn anything to ashes with the touch of his hand. He tried to turn Śiva himself to ashes; the god fled from him, and Viṣṇu took the form of Mohinī and bewitched the demon into imitating the hand movements of her dance. Mohinī put her hand on her head, and the demon followed suit—and turned himself to ash. Śiva made love to Mohinī, and their son, Aiyaṉār, was born.[63]

VI. The Pine Forest: Bhikṣāṭana-Śiva (white with ash) seeks alms together with Viṣṇu as Mohinī.

Aiyaṉār is not the only son of Viṣṇu-Mohinī. One text substitutes Hanūmat for Aiyaṉār as the son produced when Śiva released his seed at the sight of Mohinī,[64] and the *KP* applies the story to the birth of Brahmā: after Brahmā died, Śiva united in joy with Viṣṇu, who became a mother by giving birth to Brahmā from his navel.[65] There is a general, widely distributed insistence on Viṣṇu's female capabilities: Śiva deposits his seed in the womb of Viṣṇu,[66] and Viṣṇu takes the form of the *yoni* to receive the fiery *liṅga* of Śiva.[67] One purāṇa identifies Bhagavatī at Kaṉṉiyākumari as a form of Viṣṇu, who has many female forms—the Maiden, Durgā, Mātaṅgī the slayer of Mahiṣa, and so on.[68] So conventional has this idea become that one Tamil text invokes Viṣṇu as the female half of the androgyne: Śiva has "sea-colored Viṣṇu who has Śrī (on his body) as half of himself" (*tiru ttaṉ mā kkaṭaṉ meṉiyuñ cĕmmalār aruttaṉ*).[69] In another verse Viṣṇu proudly claims to be one of the four *śaktis* (along with Aiyai, Kālī, and Gaurī);[70] but in another passage in the same text, Śiva has some difficulty in convincing Viṣṇu that he is a *śakti* of Śiva.[71] Perhaps an element of sectarian sarcasm is present in the latter verse; it has also been suggested that the prominence given by the Citamparam tradition to Viṣṇu's role as Mohinī in the Pine Forest reflects a desire on the part of the Śaiva cult to supersede or assimilate the local Viṣṇu shrine of Tiruccittirakūṭam.[72] On the other hand, the worship of Aiyaṉār / Śāstṛ (also known as Hariharaputra, "the son of Viṣṇu [that is, Mohinī] and Śiva") is often seen as expressing syncretistic or harmonizing tendencies between the two cults of Śiva and Viṣṇu.[73]

Mohinī first appears in the Pine Forest myth in the *Kūrmapurāṇa*:

> The sages of the Pine Forest sacrificed and performed *tapas* with their minds still set on life in the world (*pravṛtti*). To teach them the meaning of withdrawal (*nivṛtti*), Śiva went to the forest together with Viṣṇu, who took the form of a beautiful woman. The wives of the sages were stricken with love for Śiva, and the sons of the sages were tormented by passion for Viṣṇu. Śiva performed the dance, followed by Viṣṇu. Seeing all this, the sages became angry and cursed Śiva, thus losing their powers accumulated through *tapas*. "Who are you?" they asked Śiva. "I have come here to perform *tapas* with my wife, together with you," he answered. "Then put on your clothes and abandon your wife first," they said. "How can you ask me to abandon my wife when you are intent on keeping yours?" asked Śiva. When he refused to cast off Mohinī, the sages told him to go away. He went to the *āśrama* of Vasiṣṭha, where he was welcomed by Arundhatī; but when he left, the Brahmins beat him with sticks and cursed him to have his *liṅga* fall. Śiva made his *liṅga* fall and disappeared, and terrible portents occurred. Anasūyā learned from a dream that it was Śiva who had visited them; she told the sages, and they sought the advice of Brahmā. He told them to worship the *liṅga* together with their wives and sons. Śiva was pleased and came back to the forest with Pārvatī to enlighten them.[74]

This myth is concerned with the tension between life in the world and renunciation / release; ultimately *bhakti* (the worship of the *liṅga*) resolves the conflict, at a point closer to the "this-worldly" pole of *pravṛtti*: for although Śiva is said to go to the forest in order to teach the meaning of *nivṛtti*, in the end the sages keep their wives and sons. Such a resolution is in line with the mainstream *bhakti* attitude toward life in the world.[75] Śiva demonstrates the imperfect nature of the sages' striving for release; the lesson centers on the sages' continued attachment to their wives, an attachment revealed and ultimately sustained and consecrated by Śiva's appearance in the forest together with his women. Mohinī serves as a foil to Śiva during the initial part of the lesson; but Pārvatī accompanies Śiva on his second, final trip to the forest. Oddly, Pārvatī is said in this episode to have come to the Pine Forest "as before" (*pūrvavad*);[76] this version of the myth may represent a conflation of different accounts. Sometimes Śiva's journey to the Pine Forest is undertaken to prove a point to Pārvatī;[77] at other times he enters the forest because of his grief at being separated from Satī.[78] An apparently unique version can be derived from a verse in Cuntaramūrtti's *Tevāram*: the women of the forest refuse to give him alms because he has come as the androgyne, with Umā occupying half his body.[79] Here the myth has nearly frozen into icon. Other verses of Cuntaramūrtti suggest that Śiva comes alone; why, ask the sages' wives, need he seek alms from them when the home of his wife, the Kāmakkoṭṭam, is near?[80] Most of the versions of the Tamil purāṇas, however, insist that it was Mohinī who accompanied Śiva to the Pine Forest,[81] and in one myth this becomes an accusation made by Devī:

> Śiva went to the Pine Forest (*tārukāvaṉam*) with Mohinī. He seduced the wives of the sages, and they gave birth to forty-eight thousand sons. Śiva sent the sons to perform *tapas*. Mohinī diverted the sages from their asceticism; they made a magical sacrifice (*apicāraveḷvi*) to kill Śiva, but Śiva mastered their devices and went back to Kailāsa with Viṣṇu.
>
> When he arrived, Pārvatī said to him, "I was right here and yet you took Viṣṇu as your *śakti* to the forest!" She went off angrily. Śiva thought for a moment, then quoted a verse to the effect that the single *śakti* was Bhavānī in pleasure, Viṣṇu in male form, Kālī in anger, and Durgā on the battlefield. This saying appeased the goddess a little, and she asked to see the dance Śiva had performed in the main street of the sages' settlement. Śiva danced as he had done in the forest, adorned with the ornaments from the sacrifice of the sages, and Pārvatī

was overcome with joy and returned to her place in the women's quarters.[82]

Pārvatī's jealousy of Mohinī recalls the rivalry between the two consorts of the deity in the myths of the double marriage; as we shall see, one Tamil shrine does in fact make Mohinī into a consort of Śiva, although in the northern tradition she is not, strictly speaking, a wife of the god. Śiva overcomes Pārvatī's jealousy by a repetition of the dance, just as elsewhere he repeats his dance in a new site in order to illustrate his powers of specific revelation[83] or to prove the equation of the site with the navel of the universe—the dance that nearly fails in the Pine Forest is always proper in Citamparam.[84] Dance, however, is also one of the weapons of Mohinī, as in the Bhasmāsura myth quoted above, and this association is preserved in the dance style from Kerala known as Mohinī-āṭṭam.[85] The birth of sons of Śiva from the wives of the sages appears to be a south Indian innovation in the Pine Forest myth; although the *KP* says simply that "all the women entered the state of pregnancy"[86] without explaining how, elsewhere this is said to have been the result of seeing the god[87]—another instance in which vision and sexual union are interchanged. The dancing-girls of Tiruccĕṅkoṭu are said to be descended from the wives of the sages, who fell in love with the god and came to serve him with music and dance at his shrine.[88]

One Tamil purāṇa connects the birth of Śiva's sons from the wives of the sages with the birth of his son from Mohinī:

> The sages of the Pine Forest of the south performed rites without worshiping Śiva. To teach them, Śiva went there with Mohinī. He seduced their wives, who gave birth to forty-eight thousand sons; the children worshiped Śiva, while their mothers still surrounded the god. The sages were in turn deluded by Viṣṇu, but when they saw their wives following Śiva, they cried, "We have been misled by that fool Śiva, and this woman is Viṣṇu, following his orders no doubt. It is no fault of Viṣṇu's; he has destroyed our *tapas*, but we can restore it by much labor. But Śiva has ruined the chastity of our wives, and that is a reproach which will endure as long as the sun and the moon exist." Śiva turned to them and said, "This is my wife Mohinī, great in chastity. Many have died longing for her. I am without like or dislike; you have been living in a place of power (*cittitāṉam*), and I have come to give you power

> (*citti* = Skt. *siddhi*)." Nevertheless, they tried to kill him with a sacrifice; but when their efforts failed, he enlightened them and taught them to worship the *liṅga*.
>
> Afterwards Viṣṇu resumed his old form. Śiva asked him what he wanted as a reward for his help, and Viṣṇu replied, "I fell in love with you while playing that part; now I want you to embrace me." Śiva promised that he would do so at the time of the churning of the ocean, when their son Hariharaputra would be born.[89]

Viṣṇu's participation in the Pine Forest myth is here made to foreshadow his older, inherited role as Mohinī in the Epic myth of the churning of the ocean. Mohinī's passion for Śiva may be an extension of the devotion that Viṣṇu-Mohinī feels for Śiva in the *Cidambaramāhātmya*, which offers a version of this myth.[90] The passion of the wives of the sages and the anger of their husbands contrast with the devotion of the forty-eight thousand sons born from the encounter; here the sons worship Śiva, while in the version of the *Kūrmapurāṇa* cited earlier[91] the sons of the sages are infatuated with Mohinī. The Pine Forest itself is now located in the shrine, and the lesson that Śiva imparts to the sages in the course of the episode includes a recognition of the benefits of worship in the shrine, the site that grants *siddhi* to those who feel proper devotion. Śiva introduces Mohinī to the sages in terms that suggest the background of a Mohinī cult: she is the wife of the god, and many have died longing for her. The worship of Mohinī in the villages may explain this statement, including the element of death-in-love. Mohinī's identity with the goddess is carefully articulated in the myths of another shrine:

> Śiva related to Devī the story of the Pine Forest: The sages there had left the path of the Vedas; each of them believed himself to be *brahman*. Śiva went there in the form of a Kāpālika, followed by Viṣṇu as Mohinī. Seeing the beautiful woman following him, Śiva felt desire for her, but Mohinī said, "You will embrace me after destroying the chastity of the wives of the sages and the sages' conceit." Śiva went from street to street begging alms with his skull-bowl, and the women, seeing him, lost all shame. "Come into our houses, our husbands are away," they said; "do not ask for useless alms; will you not seek the alms of sexual delight?" Meanwhile Mohinī went deeper into the forest, the site of evil-doing (*tīt' ā<u>rr</u>a<u>r</u>k'*

> *iṭam*). The sages devoured her with their eyes and thus lost their *tapas*. Perceiving what had happened, they cursed Śiva; when their curses had no effect, they made a sacrifice against him, but Śiva took the weapons sent against him and made them ornaments.
>
> Afterwards, Mohinī said to Śiva, "Be my husband, and I shall be your Devī." Since this was already true, Śiva granted the request, promising soon to marry Mohinī. "And so it happens," said Śiva to Devī, "that Viṣṇu is you, Devī, residing in half my body. One part of you is Māl, who gives birth to Brahmā and supports the world." Śiva sent Devī to the *koṅku* forest to perform *tapas* before their wedding there.[92]

Mohinī is the incarnation of Devī at Paḻani; thus Pārvatī has no cause to feel jealousy, and the anomaly of the male who is goddess and mother is resolved in the same manner as in the Tiruvāṉaikkā creation myth. Viṣṇu can create because he is part of the goddess; the text states this plainly with reference to Brahmā's birth from Viṣṇu, and the explanation will hold for the birth of Aiyaṉār, who, although not mentioned in the myth, is later said to have come to witness the wedding of Śiva and Umā at Paḻani.[93] The Pine Forest Myth thus supplies the background to the marriage myth at this shrine. Moreover, Paḻani is primarily a Murukaṉ shrine, and it is perhaps significant that the shrine that equates Mohinī with the consort of Śiva is essentially devoted to the worship of the Śaiva child god, Skanda / Murukaṉ. Although Mohinī is never said to have given birth to Skanda, her son Aiyaṉār could well be regarded as an allotrope of the southern Murukaṉ.[94] We may also note in passing that, since Paḻani (associated with the ancient Tiru Āviṉaṉkuṭi) is so closely tied to Murukaṉ, the identification of the goddess there with Viṣṇu constitutes another illustration of the pairing of Murukaṉ and Viṣṇu / Māl in Tamil cult centers.

In the Paḻani Pine Forest myth, Śiva desires Mohinī *before* she falls in love with him. Several versions of the birth of Aiyaṉār support this idea: in one, for example, Viṣṇu warns Śiva to restrain himself at the sight of Viṣṇu's female form, but Śiva is ravished and lets his seed fall, to the annoyance of Mohinī.[95] Yet the myth from Paḻani, like the variant from Tirunĕlveli, is essentially a myth of devotion for the god; thus it is not surprising that Mohinī eventually asks to be united with the god, and the identification of the male Viṣṇu with Devī falls naturally into our category of transvestite worship revolving around the male. The devotee who hears this story will no doubt see himself in the role of Mohinī; the soul of man is the temptress beckoning to God, who responds with yearning to match the longing of the embodied soul. Note, too, the scorn with which the Tamil text treats the Upaniṣadic concept of individual identification with *brahman*: the sages' pursuit of such a goal in the absence of *bhakti* has here become a serious offense tantamount almost to heresy. The sages have strayed from the Vedic path, and the Pine Forest has become quite explicitly a place of evil. Love of God is the only acceptable religious ideal in this version; and, as in other Tamil myths, the passionate tie between the deity and his devotees is to be realized on earth, in the shrine in which the divine marriage serves as a symbol of this love.

The myths of sex-reversal draw together many of the most prominent strands of the marriage myths. Here we see clearly the ambivalent goddess, who castrates her devotees; we have the theme of self-sacrifice, directed either at the god or the goddess; and, with striking regularity, we observe the culmination of the myth in the divine birth (or rebirth) from the fertile, virginal androgyne. The portrait of the "male" goddess expresses as a sequence or progression the union of genders synchronically combined in the androgyne; the maternal powers of the "converted" goddess follow naturally from this combination. Like the split mother, the bisexual goddess embraces a diversity of parts that grant her independence and allow her to preserve her powers intact; but the androgyne, as a symbol of the murderous marriage, may also express an important principle of exchange operating between the god and his devouring bride. In any case, the goddess appears as a complex concentration of conflicting attributes. At Paḻani, the local goddess is a male transformed; other shrines present a comparable idea by attributing to the god of the site female powers and forms. It remains for us to mention in illustration of this latter type the outstanding Tamil example of Śiva as a mother—the major myth of Tiruccirāppaḷḷi, where Śiva is known as Mātṛbhūteśvara / Tāyumāṉavar, "he who became even a mother":

> A merchant of Pukār worshiped Śiva to win offspring; lacking the grace of the god, he begot a daughter. When she came of age, he married her to a merchant of Tiricirāmalai (Tiruccirāppaḷḷi); soon afterwards he died, and the girl was comforted by her husband.

The girl became pregnant. Because the Kāviri was in flood at that time, her mother was unable to cross it to come and help her daughter through her pregnancy and birth. The girl knew nothing of this, and each day she thought, "Surely she will come tomorrow, or even today, bringing all the necessary items—I am sure she will have thought of everything. How I long to embrace her!"

Śiva (Cirāmalaināṭar) took the form of an old woman like her mother—his back bent like the crescent moon, his hair white as moonlight, a bamboo staff in his hand—and came to the house, slowly moving forward, sighing and panting for breath. Umā and Gaṅgā had been sent ahead as servants with the bundles. The girl was overjoyed to see her mother. "I have brought new saris, jewels and ornaments, and *kāyam* stimulants for after the birth," said the old woman. The next day labor began, and the old mother performed all the services of a midwife. A boy was born, and the girl's mother placed him in a cradle and cared for him as if he were Murukaveḷ.[96]

When the floods abated, the real mother approached the house. As she entered, Śiva began to move away. Seeing the two women, the husband and wife were amazed: "Which is my mother?" cried the girl from the door. As she watched, Śiva disappeared into the sky like lightning and, praised by the gods, entered his shrine.[97]

Śiva merely disguises himself as a mother, and the myth concludes with the usual epiphany; still, one should note that as mother and midwife Śiva assists at the birth of a son, whom the god loves as if he were his own son Skanda. At the moment of revelation, the young bride possesses two mothers—her real mother, and the masquerading god who is mother and father of all. Śiva's maternal character is revealed in other shrines as well; at Maturai, Śiva becomes a sow in order to nurse with milk twelve orphaned baby pigs. Again the god is called mother (*tāy*),[98] and here the chthonic associations of the pig[99] are tied to the male. In the buffalo myth from Assam, Śiva is said to have taken the form of a buffalo cow and to have given birth to himself as Mahiṣāsura.[100] One version of the birth of Agastya makes Śiva both mother and father of the sage:

Agastya renounced the world and lived in caves. His *guru* told him to jump into a jar in which he had lit a sacrificial fire.

> Agastya did so, and was consumed and reborn from the jar, which was changed into the form of a woman. "Verily that jar was a form of Maheswara, and the Brahmin (*guru*), of Mahadewa, who were my (Agastya's) parents."[101]

Agastya is *kumbhayoni*, born from a pot. Here the pot, symbolizing the womb, is a form of Śiva, the androgynous creator who is made responsible for the second birth of the sage (after the first birth, presumably from the seed of Mitra and Varuṇa, as in the oldest accounts). Agastya offers himself into the fire and is reborn, thus undergoing the classical progression of the sacrifice; the bisexual deity, like the ambivalent goddess of many Tamil shrines, creates new life for the devotee prepared to burn away his former existence. In the following chapter, I will attempt to bring into sharper focus the different meanings attached to this pervasive pattern of self-immolation.

# CHAPTER V
# The Demon Devotee

ONE important problem remains to be discussed. In the previous chapters we have seen how the divine marriage in south India may be interpreted in the light of the creative sacrifice. We have studied the concept of woman as a focus of dangerous power and as the natural ground of the sacrifice, and we have seen how ritual requires the devotee to imitate the sacrifice of the god by offering his power and life to the goddess. This is the most ancient layer of the myth, in which the deity functions clearly as a model for man. But, as we have seen, this layer is obscured by a more recent attempt to eliminate the death of the god in sacrifice in the interests of establishing his total purity. Śiva can no longer be slain or castrated; he gives life without sacrificing his own, indeed without coming into any contact at all with the pollution attendant upon death and rebirth. In his place—since the sacrifice is still needed as a metaphor for union with the goddess and as a symbol of the creative processes of the universe—the Tamil myths introduce the ambiguous and powerfully attractive figure of the demon devotee. The demon (often Mahiṣāsura) dies at the hands of the goddess, and in this way achieves salvation; his death requires an act of expiation on the part of his slayer, but precipitates no theological crisis. There is no need to keep the demon pure from contamination; he epitomizes the dangerous, polluting forces at work in the world. How, then, are we to explain the great popularity of the demon, both on the level of village religion and within the Tamil purāṇic tradition, which we have seen to be preoccupied with the ideal of purity? In the remaining pages of this study, we will explore the religious significance of the devoted demon.

As in the preceding chapters, we shall find here a coalescence of several layers of meaning. The demon clearly means one thing to the devotee who sees him as a model, and another to the author of the Brahminized purāṇic text, where his death and salvation are rationalized or given allegorical interpretations. Nevertheless, there can be no doubt that the authors of the Tamil purāṇas were fascinated by the devoted demon; again and again we find the demons worshiping Śiva alongside the gods, even rivaling the gods in the intensity of their devotion. Yet the demons must die, and the gods survive: the Tamil myths, however different their own perspective may be, can hardly demolish the inherited guidelines of classical Hindu myths. The Tamil authors must therefore explain how such ardent worshipers of Śiva can and must be killed. This is by no means a simple matter: *bhakti*, which functions as an absolute touchstone in these myths, has shattered the old agonistic framework of Hindu mythology. The wars of the gods and the demons—the constant theme of the classical Sanskrit purāṇas—have become largely anachronistic through the elevation of *bhakti* to the position of the one criterion of salvation; deprived of its original connection with the agonistic rite of sacrifice,[1] the struggle between the two camps has no inherent rationale, and there is no reason for man to ally himself with the gods rather than with their demon enemies.[2] All is now subordinate to the supreme ideal of devotion, and the demons appear to be no less devoted to Śiva than the gods. In other words, the old distinctions have become irrelevant to a mythology that is yet unable to reform its essential plots and structure. Having inherited the decree that the demons must ultimately be defeated, the Tamil myths must search for a new explanation of this defeat.

There is still another side to this problem. In south Indian village religion, the worship of demons and evil spirits is in many ways more prominent than the worship of Brahminical, "purāṇic" deities. Men propitiate, often through blood sacrifices, the dangerous and potentially malevolent spirits that dwell in the village.[3] One might, then, regard the important role of the devoted demon in the Tamil purāṇic tradition as reflecting an attempt to assimilate the folk deities to a a Brahminized cult. There are, in fact, numerous examples of just such a process.[4] Yet the significance of the demon devotee certainly goes far beyond this point. As I have already hinted,[5] the Tamil pilgrim or devotee can hardly help identifying himself with the demon enemies described in the myths; the demon's fate—immediate salvation at the hands of the god or goddess—is sufficient proof of this identification. How are we to understand the relationship of man to the devoted enemy slain by the god he worships? Three possibilities of interpretation suggest themselves here: 1) as a polluted and polluting figure, the demon joins the ranks of the humble, despised devotees promised salvation by Tamil *bhakti* religion. As we saw in the myth of Vaḷḷi, *bhakti* often prefers the lowly, the socially inferior, the unconventional as symbols of devotion and the rewards devotion brings. *Bhakti* promises salvation for all, including the outcastes and the impure. Of course, the sincerity of one's devotion is important here; although some texts proclaim the *automatic* efficacy of certain devotional acts (such as reciting the name of the god), the Tamil purāṇic tradition is, on the whole, very concerned with the actual *content* of devotion. As we shall see, this point is crucial to the case of the demon devotee; imperfect or self-centered *bhakti* helps explain the demon's death. But one may also see in the demon's ultimate fate another major facet of *bhakti* religion—the affirmation of the social order with its prescribed hierarchy of relations.[6] *Bhakti* in general sustains the social fabric instead of undermining it (as is sometimes claimed); the impure demon suffers a violent death, which, however, may bring him salvation. Put slightly differently, we may say that the impure devotee is a fitting candidate for the pollution attached to death at the hands of the deity, in particular the ritual death of the sacrifice. This leads us to our second point: 2) the demon-victim relieves the god of the need to be polluted through the sacrifice; by the same token, he achieves the power that is to be won from the sacrifice. To the extent that the old sacrificial ideology survives—and we have seen how it keeps breaking through the surface of the myths—it is carried along by the demon-surrogate for the god. The demon is a symbol of power, the innate power that justifies his worship in the villages, and the power that he attains by undergoing death in the sacrifice. Considering the predominant Tamil view of power as sacred, it is hardly surprising that the demon maintains a hold over the believers. But there is a further element here: the devoted demon also derives power from his devotion. *Bhakti* must produce a divine response, in the view of the Tamil *bhaktas*; the demon uses this path to achieve greater power, more life, the satisfaction of his desires, and so on. The demon devotee becomes the prime example of earthly rewards won through devotion. 3) At this point the rationalizing, moralistic element in the Tamil tradition steps in and makes a striking contribution. The identification of the demon with material success and with naked power, even when this power is attained through *bhakti*, provides meaning to the demon's death. The salvation achieved by the death of the devoted demon comes to represent the ideal state in which all forms of egoism and possessiveness are suppressed; it is in this state, when the ego is finally overcome, that the devotee perceives his identity with the god hidden within him and in this way finds freedom. The demon, in other words, symbolizes the evil within man (preoccupation with a false "selfhood," the lust for power, opposition to the divine ideals); this evil must be destroyed before redemption becomes possible—indeed, redemption is directly consequent upon the destruction of egoism and wrong desires. For the human devotee, this process need not culminate in actual death (as it does on the symbolic level for the demon devotee); it does, however, require a form of self-sacrifice. The *bhakta* loses himself in the god, who replaces the transcendent goal of *mokṣa*.[7] Throughout the Tamil purāṇic corpus, the greatest mistake the devotee can make is *ahaṅkāra*, "egoism" (< *aham*, "I"); *ahaṅkāra*, which manifests itself in diverse ways but most significantly in the striving for power, is the major stumbling block on the way to salvation. It is *ahaṅkāra*, taken in its broadest sense as the factor motivating man's opposition to the ideals of purity and freedom, that underlies the constant sense of personal unworthiness expressed in the major works of the Tamil *bhakti* tradition.[8] The demon exemplifies the evil of *ahaṅkāra*; his slaughter points the way to redemption. Thus the demon remains, even at this level of the tradition, a mythic model for man; his death, however unwilling, at the hands of the god is a recommendation for self-sacrifice, for the loss of self that accompanies the recognition of an inner identity with the god. An inner sacrifice has replaced the actual sacrifice of blood.[9] The myth has given way to allegory; clearly, our texts now possess a means of explaining why the devoted demon has to die.

The demon devotee is obviously an ambivalent figure; in his ambivalence lies the secret of his immense popularity. The demon expresses the ambivalence in the heart of man, the war between the obsession with self and the yearning for God. Moreover, we may observe in the demon *bhakta* the general division in the Indian tradition between the goals of power and purity: as the exemplar of the sacrifice, the demon embodies the old ritual goals of rebirth, of life and power won from death, indeed of the ritual conquest of death; but as a symbol of *ahaṅkāra* destroyed by the god, the demon demonstrates the recommended process of self-purification and, ultimately, self-extinction. We might describe this double role in different terms, for example as the conflict between sacrifice and *self*-sacrifice: the sacrificial ritual produces more life and more power, while self-sacrifice leads to purity and salvation. Both ideas take shape in the myths of the demon devotee; indeed, the demon's devotion may lead him to either goal, although the texts subordinate the first goal (power) to the ideal of purity and self-sacrifice. Whether the Tamil devotees prefer this ideal is less certain; I suspect that the identification with the demon is motivated above all by the devotee's sense of his own *opposition* to this ideal, that is, by his basic, persistent lust for vitality and power.[10] Man finds himself trapped by his ego; like the misguided demon, he seeks earthly power through devotion; insofar as he remains cognizant of a supposedly higher ideal, he can only picture his salvation in terms of a violent negation of his "self." Put somewhat harshly, we have a conflict between the "real" goal of power or rebirth and the "ideal" goal of self-sacrifice. Faced with such variance between a remote yet compelling ideal and the reality of his needs, the devotee can hardly help feeling that he is evil, an ego-ridden creature at odds with his god; like the demon, he is devoted yet bound by his delusion; he seeks power and yet is comforted by the demon's salvation through violence. Small wonder that the ideas of cleansing and expiation take so large a part of the Tamil pilgrimage literature!

The demon's death thus holds two symbolic meanings: he offers himself (in place of the god) in order to be reborn through the sacrifice; and he dies in *opposition* to the god, and in this way gains his salvation. Both senses allow the demon to serve as a model for human emulation. The devotee immolates himself in a sacrifice—either in imitation of the mythic sacrificial victim, whose death transfers to the deity (usually the goddess) the power that motivates the act of creation and that will ultimately be restored to this same victim; or in imitation of the demon who, while still seeking more power, is destroyed in his own better interests. The fact that the demon is himself a *bhakta* sustains his role as a model; love of god and the self-seeking lust for power coexist within man; *bhakti* can lead both to power and to the rejection of power, but, while the devotee will strive for the first goal, the Tamil purāṇas, obsessed with the *content* of one's devotion, recommend the second. We must now see how these ideas are worked out in the myths. The first pattern—the sacrificial death and rebirth—has been explored in detail in the preceding chapters; our major concern here will be with the second complex of ideas (the identification of the demon with *ahaṅkāra* and misguided devotion, and the salvation that he wins in being slaughtered). This second pattern is characteristic of the most mature level of Tamil devotional religion, in which inherited myths have been reinterpreted in the light of rational theological concerns. These myths show us the Tamil Śaiva tradition in its final, literary, rather idealized form. Several demon devotees—Mahiṣa, Marutvāsura, Bhaṇḍāsura, and so on—have been studied earlier; here we will encounter three more figures in this series, Rāvaṇa, Bali, and Dakṣa. The last of these, Dakṣa, is not, of course, a bona fide demon; he is, however, an enemy of Śiva, and the Tamil version of his story provides an excellent example of the major themes outlined above.

## *Rāvaṇa and the Upside-down Tree*

Rāvaṇa, the enemy of Rāma in the *Rāmāyaṇa*, is in many ways the most complex and striking figure in the gallery of demon devotees. The *uttarakāṇḍa* of the *Rāmāyaṇa* states that Rāvaṇa won his great powers through sacrificing his heads into the fire; after nine of his ten heads had gone in this way, Brahmā appeared and granted his request that none among the gods, demons, or various other creatures would be able to overcome him.[11] The later tradition makes Rāvaṇa seek his boons from Śiva,[12] and Rāvaṇa becomes famed as a devotee of Śiva—so much so that Devī can reproach Śiva for helping Rāma, an enemy of his servant,[13] just as elsewhere she incites Rāvaṇa to carry off the fickle (*aticañcalā*) wife of Rāma (Sītā).[14] In the Tamil myths, Devī has a special relationship with Rāvaṇa, as we shall see in a moment. One Tamil tradition states that Appar in a former birth advised Rāvaṇa to sing praises to Śiva; for this reason, it is said, Appar refers to Rāvaṇa in each of his *patikams*.[15] In fairness it should be noted that Tiruñāṉacampantar also refers to Rāvaṇa in practically all his *patikams*; in neither case are the allusions necessarily favorable. The tradition of Rāvaṇa's songs of praise may, however, be related to the belief that Rāvaṇa was the originator of music.[16] Rāvaṇa's positive side is also evident in his role as a great doctor.[17] The demon king of Laṅkā has undoubtedly long been a popular figure; he is often portrayed with sympathy and admiration by Vālmīki,[18] and Kampaṉ has been accused of preferring Rāvaṇa to Rāma.[19] The folk myths follow suit, and it is hard not to feel some sympathy for the demon when, at the eleventh hour, he calls for help from his counterpart Mayilirāvaṇaṉ and explains to him his history: "Once the two brothers (Rāma and Lakṣmaṇa) harmed my sister Śūrpaṇakhā; then I took Sītā; then sorrow came to Laṅkā."[20]

Still, Rāvaṇa is a Rākṣasa who must be defeated. His impure nature is made clear in the myths of several shrines,[21] and the gods naturally fear that the boons he wins from Śiva will be used for dangerous ends; Nārada is therefore sent to persuade him not to rely on the promises of the unpredictable Śiva, and Rāvaṇa demonstrates his arrogance and lack of understanding by carrying out Nārada's suggestion to lift up Kailāsa.[22] The myths of one Tamil shrine go to much greater lengths to demonstrate the flaws in Rāvaṇa's character and discrimination:

Rāvaṇa tried to uproot Kailāsa; Śiva pressed him into Pātāla with his toenail. Rāvaṇa tore off one of his heads and made a *vīṇā*, using the tendons of his forearm for strings, and the music he sang appeased Śiva. When Rāvaṇa asked for a *liṅga* to take back to Laṅkā, Śiva gave him a *liṅga* so heavy it had to be carried in both hands. The gods, alarmed that Laṅkā would become great and that they would have to hide, sent Vināyaka in the form of a Brahmin to intercept Rāvaṇa. The demon handed the *liṅga* to the false Brahmin while he went off to worship;[23] Vināyaka set the *liṅga* down, and it struck roots as deep as Pātāla. Rāvaṇa returned to find he could no longer move the *liṅga*; after repeated efforts he succeeded only in bending it into the shape of a cow's ear (*kokarṇam*, Skt. *gokarṇa*). That place is known today as Gokarṇa.[24]

Rāvaṇa went to Kailāsa. Nandin[25] (the doorkeeper) ordered him out of his aerial chariot (*vimāna*), for the place was inhabited by devotees of Śiva. "How dare someone like you with a monkey's face try to stop me!" cried Rāvaṇa, whereupon Nandin cursed him to die because of monkeys.[26] Rāvaṇa meditated on Śiva, and Nandin then let him enter. For a thousand years, the demon sang the Sāmaveda and performed *tapas*. Śiva appeared and said, "Who can compare with you? We will give you whatever you ask." Rāvaṇa thought for a moment: "Śiva owes his greatness to being united with Śakti. I will ask for her." So he said, "I want Umā who is your left side."

Śiva said, "I promised you whatever you wished; take her—but if you forsake her (even for a moment), all your gains will be lost." Śiva looked at the goddess and said, "Those who perform *tapas* must be granted their desire. You must go with him." "How can I go away with a Rākṣasa who does not know the rules of conduct (*virak' aṟiyāṉ*)?" asked Devī. "Listen," said Śiva, "you remember you wished me to tell you

> about sacred ash? I will instruct you at Varañcai, and I grant you the further boon of never being separated from me there." Umā felt better at this, and thought of her brother Viṣṇu; he appeared and, hearing her story, said, "It is only right to give those who perform *tapas* their desire." But he took the form of a Brahmin and said to Rāvaṇa, "You received three and a half crores of lifetimes; if you win another half-crore, you will see what happens to the Trimūrti and the novel state of the sea at the end of the *yuga*." Rāvaṇa hastened to return to his *tapas*, and Śiva laughed and said to Umā, "This is the work of Viṣṇu." He granted the request, and Rāvaṇa, satisfied, put Umā in his chariot and headed south.[27]

Rāvaṇa escapes not with Sītā but with Pārvatī / Umā; this unusual development of the Rāvaṇa cycle is also the subject of a Kucipudi dance drama, the *Maṇḍūkaśabdam*, in which Rāvaṇa willingly abandons Pārvatī when he catches sight of Mandodarī (transformed from a frog into a woman at the sight of her future lord).[28] Rāvaṇa's devotion to Śiva is first elicited by the demon's defeat at Kailāsa; thrust down into the nether world, Rāvaṇa invents the *vīṇā* and thus wins a *liṅga* (in other accounts, this *liṅga* is usually known as the *ātmaliṅga*). The gods conspire to prevent this powerful shrine from reaching Laṅkā, and we therefore discover another example of the immovable shrine (the *liṅga* at Gokarṇa).[29] Rāvaṇa then wins two further boons from Śiva—the goddess (Śakti, Pārvatī/Umā) and, at the instigation of the crafty Viṣṇu, a multitude of lives. Both Śiva and Viṣṇu declare that *tapas* (that is, *bhakti*, either by itself or accompanied by the performance of austerities) must bring its proper reward—even if the beneficiary is a demon, and the reward entails disastrous consequences for the universe. Śiva *must* answer the prayers of his devotees; *bhakti* always produces results. Here, however, the situation is still more complex: for what Rāvaṇa has done, in effect, is to reverse the test that Śiva classically springs on his devotees. Śiva demands the devotee's wife as a test of devotion, usually appearing to make his request in the guise of a Śaiva mendicant;[30] here the devotee, Rāvaṇa, makes the same claim on his god, and Śiva is in no position to refuse. All he can do is to lay down conditions for his compliance, justifying himself to Devī by a promise of better circumstances in the future. Śiva is effectively "trapped" by his devotee, whose request he is bound not to refuse; this motif of the "trap" set for God by a demon or an evil devotee is one of the standard attempts to explain the deity's implication in evil.[31] Rāvaṇa's bold demand for the goddess is motivated by unworthy goals, especially a lust for power (*śakti*), and the myth concentrates on this side of the demon's nature in describing how Śiva manages to extricate himself from this situation:

As Rāvaṇa was taking Umā south to Laṅkā, Viṣṇu went and stood in their path. As soon as he caught sight of Umā's wedding-chain (*maṅkalanāṇ*), he created a site for the performance of *tapas* on the north bank of the Mayūranadī, and there he stood in the form of a sage by the side of a grove of *muḷḷi* shrubs that were growing upside down, their roots in the air, bearing ripe fruit. Rāvaṇa observed this strange phenomenon and brought the chariot down to ask the sage what it meant. "Who are you, and who is this lady?" asked the sage. "The fact is that she is the wife of Śiva, and I have won her through *tapas*," said Rāvaṇa. The sage replied, "To those who die after a life of following *dharma*, Yama appears as a just king; but to the wicked, he has a hideous appearance. Similarly, Śiva gave you Māyā and told you she was his wife. This *muḷḷi* grove is the first sign you have had of how you were deceived."

Rāvaṇa was disheartened by these words. Getting down from the chariot, he said, "Please watch the woman. I will go and perform my vows (*niyamam*) and receive the real reward (the true Umā)." He went off to the river. Viṣṇu at once put off his sage's garb and took the form of a two-footed horse. He helped the goddess get down from the chariot, and the two raced to Varañcai, Viṣṇu stepping with his horse's feet on the footprints left by the goddess. There Devī took her place surrounded by a wall of sacred ash, while Viṣṇu, leaving Garuḍa to guard her, stood to the left of Śiva.

Rāvaṇa meanwhile came back from the river and was astonished to find the sage and the goddess missing. He searched everywhere in a panic: "The *liṅga* given me by Śiva penetrated the earth, and now the goddess has disappeared into the air," he said in sorrow. Suddenly he noticed the hoofprints and began to follow them. He reached Varañcai and thought, "This is a place suitable for Śaṅkarī (Devī)," but though he looked everywhere, he could not find her, for she was made invisible by the wall of sacred ash. Instead he found a *liṅga* that he worshiped, complaining, "Instead of giving me the wish I chose, you deceived me by giving me Māyā. Now that I have lost her, how can I go on? I will again perform *tapas*." He put his neck in an iron grate (*arikaṇṭam*), which he fastened to the *liṅga*, bending it and covering it with his blood. Śiva appeared in the sky and asked him what he wanted. Rāvaṇa asked for all his previous boons, including a sword and a spear. "You agreed that if you abandoned the goddess, all your glory would depart. You may have the sword and spear and the Māyāśakti," said Śiva.

At this, Rāvaṇa's grief grew lighter, and he asked that in addition to these gifts the eight forms of Śrī would flourish in Laṅkā, and that the *liṅga* would always bear the scar of his iron grate. Śiva agreed and disappeared into the *liṅga*.

Rāvaṇa, thinking that all was now right (commentary: that he now had the real Śakti), put Māyā in his chariot and went toward Laṅkā. On the way he noticed the *muḷḷi* he had seen before, but now it was right side up. He asked the sage, who was once again performing *tapas* there, where he had gone while Rāvaṇa was at the river—and where the woman was. The sage replied, "Because you had not received a superior boon (*pīṭu kŏṇṭa varaṅ kŏḷāmaiyiṉāl*), you came to grief; I disappeared from your sight, and this *muḷḷi* appeared upside down. All this was *māyā*. Now that you have mortified your body in *tapas*, you have received a real boon of a beautiful woman. There is no doubt of that—the sign is that the shrub now appears right side up." Rāvaṇa was content and went to Laṅkā with the sword, spear, Māyāśakti, and many life spans. Viṣṇu, now known as Aśvapādavilāsa ("he who sports with horse's feet"), dwells in Varañcai on the left of the lord.[32]

Again Rāvaṇa forces the god to appear to him by performing *tapas*, and the blood of the demon here replaces that of the god or his symbol—although the *liṅga*, too, is scarred. But Rāvaṇa's *tapas* is of little avail, for the boon he achieves by it only serves to demonstrate and reinforce the delusion under which he suffers. The nature of his delusion is clear from the moment he first catches sight of the upside-down tree—a classic Indian symbol for the reality that underlies and is hidden by life in the world, with its false goals and misleading perceptions.[33] The inverted tree is truth, the essential nature of creation, but to Rāvaṇa it appears as no more than an aberration, an inexplicable anomaly, nature stood on its head.

Rāvaṇa is unable to understand the truth: thus he is easily persuaded by Viṣṇu, the master of *māyā*, that Pārvatī is not the goddess but an illusion, and he foolishly abandons the real goddess in order to seek another. When he ultimately obtains a replacement, she is of course truly an illusion, the Māyāśakti—as Śiva actually announces to his devotee. Śiva's candor is no use: Rāvaṇa in his blindness is satisfied that he now has the real Pārvatī, and thus he goes off to Laṅkā with Māyā, just as in other myths he takes a Māyā- or Chāyā-Sītā instead of the real Sītā.[34] To drive home the point of Rāvaṇa's blindness, the myth makes him fail to see the true goddess at Varañcai, although the sacred ash that makes her invisible is no doubt also a symbol of her inviolability.[35] Finally, Rāvaṇa's utter confusion is made clear by the fact that while smugly returning home with the false goddess he now sees the *muḷḷi* growing normally, roots below and branches above.

In contrast with Śiva, Viṣṇu appears throughout to be intent on taking advantage of Rāvaṇa's inability to see the truth. To save his sister Pārvatī, Viṣṇu employs his own powers of illusion: one short version of the myth tells us that he stands watering the inverted *muḷḷi* shrub with a watering can without a bottom.[36] The horse form that Viṣṇu adopts in this myth is unusual: perhaps the two-footed horse is a development from the horse-headed Hayagrīva, a popular form of Viṣṇu located in the Tamil region at Tiruvahīntirapuram (which, like Varañcai / Tiruvarañcaram, is situated in South Arcot District).[37] Viṣṇu hides all trace of the goddess by covering her footprints with the hoofprints of the horse, just as earlier he hides the truth from Rāvaṇa by claiming Devī was Māyā. Rāvaṇa, accepting the claim, sees the real as false;[38] and we may assume that this basic misapprehension, expressed in the use of *bhakti* to gain material success and power and an endless, self-perpetuating string of lives, is seen as explaining Rāvaṇa's eventual defeat in the war with Rāma. Even Śiva's devotee may be defeated and slain, if his devotion is not filled with the proper content; the boons won through misguided, self-seeking *bhakti* evaporate without warning. In abandoning the true goddess, Rāvaṇa—in accordance with the conditions laid down by Śiva—loses all his glory; his subsequent bargaining with the god for another goddess, and for the eight forms of Śrī (a survival of the ancient theme of rivalry between the gods and the demons for prosperity, *śrī*, the fruits of the sacrifice)[39] is meaningless because of the demon's self-deception. Only truth, that is, the correct perception of the universe in relation to the god who creates, sustains, and destroys it, can bring security and salvation to the devotee.

The problem of the demon's understanding of the truth appears in a different light in the Tamil myths of Bali, to which we now turn.

### *Bali and the Dwarf in the Irāmāvatāram*

The myth of Bali, the over-generous king of the demons, and Viṣṇu's avatar as the dwarf (*vāmana*) who deprives him of his throne, has absorbed the ancient myth of Viṣṇu's three steps, which express the upward movement of the god who "spreads out" or measures the universe in an act of creation.[40] We will not attempt to follow the tangled history of this myth from its sources in the Vedas to the purāṇic accounts of the avatar; our concern here is with Bali's role as a devotee.[41] Bali is the grandson of Prahlāda, the impassioned devotee of Viṣṇu;[42] and, in late versions of the myth, Bali has clearly inherited some of Prahlāda's positive characteristics, including the love of truth and faithfulness.[43] Bali performs sacrifices and rules Indra's city, from which all evil, arrogant, and lustful individuals are excluded.[44] Such righteousness on the part of the demons is in itself problematic, for it violates the natural duty (*svadharma*) of the demons (that is, murder, rape, stealing, and so on); in other myths, it is precisely this transgression against *svadharma* that allows the pious and virtuous demons to be defeated.[45] But Bali's defeat by Viṣṇu is explained in different terms by the Tamil texts; and here, once again, the question of the content of devotion plays an important part. For Bali is also a devotee; as we shall see, he worships Viṣṇu as the supreme deity; and in the standard Tamil Śaiva accounts, he is an accidental *bhakta* of Śiva:

> A rat (*kaḷimam*) once trimmed a lamp in the shrine of Vetāraṇiyam (or: in the shrine of Śiva on Kailāsa) by nibbling at the ghee that had soaked through the wick. Because of this unconscious act of devotion, he was born as the great king of the demons, Bali (Tam. Māvali). He defeated the gods in battle and, in his joy at victory, announced that he would give to anyone whatever was asked of him. Viṣṇu came in the form of a dwarf and asked for the space he could cover in three steps. As the king was about to pour water from a pot in token of his agreement to this request, Śukra (his *guru*) warned him: "This

> dwarf is Viṣṇu, who devoured the whole world. What do you have in your poor mind to do?" Bali just laughed, and Śukra, desperately trying to save his king from ruin, took the form of a fly and blocked the opening of the water-pot. Viṣṇu stuck a blade of *darbha* grass into the opening, blinding Śukra in one eye. Thus the gods destroy those who attempt to stop the granting of a gift.
>
> Śukra went to Mayilai and worshiped Śiva, and Śiva restored his sight.[46]

Śukra, the demon *guru* who is known as a devotee of Śiva,[47] sees the truth behind Viṣṇu's disguise, just as he teaches the demons to free themselves from the false teachings of Viṣṇu as the Buddha in other myths.[48] But the myth cannot allow truth to remain with the demons: Bali is deceived, and Śukra pays for his perspicacity by losing his sight in one eye. Śukra's punishment is explained by his moral lapse in attempting to stop the offering of a gift; we shall see in a moment how Kampaṉ deals with this deceptively simple theme. As in other versions of the myth, Bali's generosity is his undoing;[49] no real justification is offered for Bali's defeat by the dwarf, which follows immediately upon the events narrated above. One wonders, however, if Bali's ruin is more easily acceptable simply because the devotion that brings him kingship is so hollow—no more than an accidental, self-seeking act (for the rat trims the lamp in the process of appeasing its hunger). A version of this myth from the shrine where it is celebrated (Vĕḷḷīsvararkoyil, to the south of the great Mylapore shrine in Madras) states explicitly that the rat was unconscious of its good deed.[50] Although even this unconscious act of *bhakti* brings its reward, the Tamil myths remain hostile to the idea of automatic, mechanical effects of worship. *Bhakti* must be informed by the proper spirit and by true understanding; when this is not the case, the deluded devotee may well find himself in collision with his god.

In the myth just cited, Bali fails to recognize the dwarf as Viṣṇu, despite Śukra's explicit warning; the demon king simply laughs and proceeds to grant the dwarf's request. In the version of this myth in Kampaṉ's *Irāmāvatāram* (*Pālakāṇṭam* 428-49), the confrontation of Bali and the dwarf is portrayed with far greater subtlety; Bali realizes at an early point that it is Viṣṇu who stands before him, and the final revelation of the god in his three steps is used to teach a deeper lesson. Bali is brought to recognize his identity with the supreme god; his defeat, as we might expect, is a form of salvation. Let us see how Kampaṉ skillfully leads the demon—and with him the reader, as well as the incarnate god Rāma himself, who hears this story from the sage Viśvāmitra—to this conclusion.

Already in the first verse of the story (428), the cosmic imagery of the original Vedic myth is joined to the moral concerns of the Tamil text: Viśvāmitra has brought Rāma and Lakṣmaṇa to the spot where Viṣṇu, "whose name is recited on earth and in heaven in order to become free of attachment" (*pāriṉ pāl vicumpiṉ pālum paṟṟ' aṟa ppaṭippat' aṉṉāṉ per ĕṉpāṉ*), performed *tapas* for one hundred cosmic ages. The dwarf's ascent from earth to the limit of the heavens is foreshadowed by the very first words of the narrative; Viṣṇu, and devotion to Viṣṇu, embrace both the terrestrial and celestial worlds; characteristically, the poet begins with the earth (*pār*), the scene of the divine revelation.[51] *Bhakti* delivers the devotee from attachment to the wrong goals;[52] already we have an intimation of the lesson that Bali will learn. For Bali is eager for power and worldly glory:

> While He (Viṣṇu) was dwelling here,
> Bali, strong as the One Boar
> whose tusk held the entire, flawless world,
> seized heaven and earth. (429)

Again, heaven and earth are joined—under the rule of the demon king; note that this time heaven is mentioned first (*vāṉamum*, at the start of the fourth line—the point of greatest poetic tension in a Tamil verse). The movement implied is *downward*, the reverse of Viṣṇu's creative manifestation. Already Viṣṇu and Bali have been implicitly compared and contrasted; both unite heaven and earth, but in ways that are symbolically opposed. Even more striking is the explicit comparison of Bali to Viṣṇu's boar avatar. This image is surely deliberately chosen: the point is the suggestion of a hidden identity between Viṣṇu and Bali, a suggestion that becomes more definite at the myth's climax.[53] The boar is a symbol of terrestrial power, even of aggressive sexuality;[54] these associations are undoubtedly meant to apply to Bali as well, but the force of the image depends on the relation of the demon to a popular form of the god.

Now that Bali has acquired the earth, he is free to dispose of it as he pleases:

He whose mind was free of doubt,
intent on completing a sacrifice
beyond the power even of the gods,
decided to bestow the earth and all its fullness
upon the Brahmins. (430)
When the gods learned of this,
they came before Viṣṇu, bowed, and begged:
"Remove the harsh acts of the evil one."
The Lord, full of love, agreed. (431)

Bali has no doubts (*aiyam il cintaiyan̲*)—in his own power, in his ability to complete the sacrifice, in his goals; he is confident of himself, of his identity as the all-powerful king. To whom, then, does he sacrifice? Surely not to his enemies, the gods? The problem of the demon-sacrificer has been discussed by a number of texts;[55] the solution seems to lie in the conception of the sacrifice as having an automatic efficacy, no matter who performs it or to whom it is directed. But the commentary of Kopālakiruṣṇamācāryar suggests that Bali was sacrificing to Viṣṇu—for he had no doubt as to which of the three chief gods was supreme.[56] This interpretation would make Bali a devotee of Viṣṇu at the very start of his career; it also raises the question of the nature of his devotion. If Bali is sacrificing to Viṣṇu, we would be justified in wondering if his motives are purely utilitarian. At this stage Viṣṇu intervenes—ostensibly at the request of the gods, but, we might suspect, with Bali's redemption in mind, as well. The avatar is clearly seen as an act of love and divine mercy; the verb *naya* (*nāyakan̲um . . . nayantān̲*) used to describe Viṣṇu's response to the gods carries these connotations.

Viṣṇu is born as the son of Aditi and Kāśyapa, who is possessed of true knowledge (*vāl ar̲ivu*); note the emphasis on knowledge, which becomes the leitmotif of the following verses. The god is born as a dwarf, "like a seed which contains an entire banyan tree" (*or āl amar vittin̲ arun̊ kur̲aḷ ān̲ān̲*, 432). Adorned with the triple thread, a belt of *muñja* grass, a ring of *darbha* grass, his tongue chanting *mantras*—like an embodiment of Divine Knowledge (*cir̲patam ŏppat' or mĕy*) he goes to the court of Bali (433). The king is filled with wonder at this sight:

The conqueror of the entire world
knew he had come.
Amazed, he came forward to welcome him:

"O You who are full (of virtues),
no Brahmin can equal you;
and who is more blessed than I?" (434)

This verse begins a dialogue suffused with irony and *double entendre*. Bali knows (*aṟintu*) the dwarf has come—but this knowledge is still incomplete; he has still not perceived the divine identity of the dwarf. The compliments Bali pays his guest derive their power for the reader from this situation of ignorance: Bali utters them as mere formalities, as the polite duty of the host; but for the devotees of Viṣṇu, they are literally true. No one can equal the god; and Bali, to whose court Viṣṇu has come, is truly blessed. Indeed, Bali stands on the threshold of salvation, as Viṣṇu hints in the following verses:

On hearing these words of the manly king,
He who knows all replied:
"O you, whose hand is stretched forth
to give yet more than is desired
by those who seek your gift—
illustrious are they who come to you,
and those who have not come
lack greatness." (435)

Rejoicing, Bali said:
"What now can I do?"
"If you have mercy, O powerful one,
give me three steps of land"—
before the Brahmin had finished these words,
the reply came: "I have given them." (436)

The recipient of the gift must praise the donor; but here it is literally true that the *beggar* is illustrious. Viṣṇu, who has the true knowledge (*aṟiṇtoṉ*) that is the subject matter of this myth, plays on Bali's ignorance: he flatters the king by saying that those who seek his gifts achieve greatness through the king's largesse; but in reality he is describing the relation of the god to the demon, and foreshadowing the reversal in status that is about to take place in the epiphany. What, then, is the desire (*veṭkai*) of the suppliants (*veṇṭiṉar*) mentioned by Viṣṇu in 435? The god is, indeed, filled with ardent longing for something that Bali can give him—not, of course, the area covered by his three strides. Viṣṇu seeks the gift of love from his enemy. God pursues the soul passionately; he takes form on earth in order to win the love of man,[57] or of the demon king. And Bali will, ultimately, give him this love, although at first he fails to realize the inner significance of his actions. The dwarf makes his request politely ("if you have mercy," lit. "if there is grace," *aruḷ uṇṭ'el*)—Bali imagines the grace is his own, but the god is, of course, referring to the redemptive nature of the transaction. In granting the request, Bali is making an offering to the god who possesses everything; one can give to the lord only what is already his, yet the gift still brings its reward. So far Bali is unaware of this problem; he accedes to the dwarf's wish without penetrating his disguise, and he thus fails to understand the deeper meaning of the gift. But now Śukra interferes (*vĕḷḷi taṭuttāṉ*, end of 436) and enlightens him:

> Fraudulent is this form you see, my lord:
> this is no dwarf with the color of a rain-cloud;
> know this is he who once long ago
> devoured this universe and all it contains. (437)

Śukra recognizes the dwarf as Viṣṇu, who, at the time of the *pralaya*, reabsorbs the created universe into himself;[58] ironically, Śukra accuses Viṣṇu of Bali's own action of seizing the worlds (see verse 429 above). Again the god and demon are implicitly compared; but while Bali's control of the universe is a threat to order and the proper workings of creation, Viṣṇu in swallowing the worlds performs a necessary act, a stage in the cosmic process. The antagonism of the god and the demon suddenly looms clearly in the consciousness of all the mythic characters, and of the audience following the story; but, to Śukra's surprise, Bali makes no effort to retract his gift:

> "You do not understand!
> If it is, as you say, the hand
> of the flawless one dark as a cloud
> which is stretched out below mine (to receive a gift),
> in a manner that does not befit him—
> then what could be better for me?" (438)

This verse begins a long lecture on the dynamics of giving and receiving gifts. Bali now knows the true identity of the dwarf, and he believes that giving him a gift will bring him, Bali, a reward—indeed, as Kopālakiruṣṇamācāryar suggests, Bali is prepared to risk losing everything he possesses in order to enjoy the privilege of giving Viṣṇu a gift. In other versions, Bali's refusal to go back on his word is seen as motivated by a sense of honor and self-sacrifice; as Bali himself remarks to the less scrupulous Śukra, "there is no evil greater than falsehood" (or "unfaithfulness": *na hy asatyāt paro 'dharma*).[59] Traces of this concern with righteous action appear in Kampaṉ's version as well: Bali reproves Śukra for attempting to prevent the meritorious action of offering a gift (442); a gift brings the donor praise (*icai*; commentary: in this world) and the fruits of pious action (*aṟaṉ*; commentary: in the next life); greed is a destructive enemy hidden in the heart (*uṭ ṭeṟu vĕm pakaiy āvat' ulopam*, 443); one should give without examining the fitness of the recipient (439). But there is another element here, suggested by Bali's glee at Viṣṇu's appearance as a beggar, "in a manner that does not befit him" (*taṉakk' iyalā vakai*, 438). Bali believes that Viṣṇu has provided him with an opportunity to humiliate his rival, the supreme god, by establishing the relationship of dependence that follows the transfer of a gift. The gift brings with it evident dangers; it creates a link between the donor and the beneficiary that may implicate the latter in the sins of the former, and it expresses a difference in rank between the two parties.[60] The aversion to accepting gifts is one of the salient features in the Brahmin move toward separation and independence from the sacrificial cult, in which the patron's presents to the priests were accompanied by the demand that the priests shoulder the burden of the victims' death. That the gift has a double meaning—positive for the donor, dangerous and even shameful for the recipient—is clear from Bali's speech, as well: "taking is evil, giving is good" (*kŏḷḷutal tītu kŏṭuppatu naṉṟu*, 440). One can hardly regard this statement as abstract praise for the virtue of generosity; both sides of the transaction are important here, and Bali is clearly overjoyed at seeing Viṣṇu in the role of a client. The same attitude is apparent in verse 441:

> The dead are not as dead as those
> who, while alive, stretch out their hands to beg;
> and who is as alive as he who, though now dead,
> once gave a gift?

In presenting Viṣṇu with a gift, Bali expects to win lasting fame, while his enemy will be burdened with shame.[61] To make this point even more forcefully, Bali turns with a sarcastic taunt to Śukra at the end of his lecture: is it right for Śukra, asks Bali, to try to prevent the giving of a gift? The families of the cruel men (*kŏṭiyor*; variant reading: *your*, that is, Śukra's family) will perish, having neither clothes to wear nor food to eat (444). Power argues for itself; Bali is reminding Śukra that, as the domestic priest (*purohita*) of the demon king, Śukra is himself caught in a classic situation of dependence. The *purohita* lives on the gifts of the king; hence the ambiguous, not to say despised, status of the *purohita* in the perspective of the law books.[62]

Let us briefly recapitulate the stages Bali has traveled so far. Kampaṉ begins by implying an intimate link between Bali and Viṣṇu; but Bali has as yet no inkling of this relationship. He seizes the worlds and offers sacrifice—perhaps to Viṣṇu, although this offering can hardly have other than a mechanical, uninspired quality. He then fails to recognize the god incarnate in the dwarf, until Śukra reveals the disguise; and, once aware of Viṣṇu's presence in his court, he insists on completing his gift to the god, but with motives that are, at the very least, mixed. A sense of opposition between the king and the dwarf is maintained throughout, although as Bali pours out the water in an act symbolizing the granting of the request, and orders the dwarf to take his three steps, he is said to disbelieve Śukra's warning that the dwarf is a cruel enemy (*kŏṭiyoṉ*, 445). Perhaps by now, even in his antagonism, Bali senses the happy fate that awaits him. For this is the moment in which all pride and all delusion must give way before the sudden revelation:

As soon as that sweet water from a spring touched his hand,
the dwarf, scorned even by his parents,
rose up to heaven
like the reward of a gift given to the great—
and all who were watching were seized by wonder,
then by fear. (446)

One foot covered the earth, and then,
since the earth was small,
could go no farther;
another foot conquered the heavens,
uniting in one step the upper worlds,
and returned, having nowhere to go. (447)

If, having enclosed all the worlds within his steps,
the One Lord crowned with bright *tulasī*
had no place to put his foot except
the body of his beloved—
O You whose arms bend back the bow,
was He not small indeed?[63] (448)

Antagonism has dissolved into identity. Bali, now explicitly a devotee (*anpaṉ*), is saved: Viṣṇu rests his foot upon Bali's head, thus giving life to an archetypal Vaiṣṇava image of salvation. In Vaiṣṇava shrines today, the pilgrim is rewarded when the *caṭakopam*, a metal bell-shaped object surmounted by a representation of the deity's feet, is placed on his head. Again cosmic imagery is suited to the internal, spiritual development described by the myth: Viṣṇu rises up to embrace the entire created universe, and this cosmic unity achieved within the god is mirrored by the unity of the god and his devotee. The text stresses in this moment of climax the idea of "oneness" (thus *ŏṉṟa . . . ŏṭukki*, 447; *eka nāyakaṉ*, 448); the latter phrase ("the One Lord") harks back to 431, where the Lord (*nāyakaṉ*) agrees to come down to earth. This concept of unity is the lesson the god comes to teach in his avatar; the body (*mĕy*, 433) he takes on earth is used to demonstrate the essential unity of the embodied soul with God. The *mĕy* of verse 433 leads to the *mĕy* of 448—Bali's *body* on which Viṣṇu places his foot. The metonymy of "body" for "head"—in all other known versions, Viṣṇu places his foot on Bali's head—is no doubt intentional; Kampaṉ, exercising his usual care and subtlety, wishes to direct our attention to the dynamics of embodiment. The soul, even while trapped in matter, is divine in nature; God takes a body to make this idea clear. Viṣṇu, who holds the entire universe within himself, makes himself truly small! He incarnates himself on earth in order to bring redemption to incarnate souls.[64] The identity of the god and the demon, which is hinted at already in the first verse of the myth, is more palpably demonstrated at its conclusion. Moreover, just as Bali is brought from the level of opposition and pride in his ability to give the god a gift to a recognition of his inner identity with the god, so Rāma, who hears the story from the lips of Viśvāmitra, is taught the same lesson. Why does Kampaṉ interject at the very climax of the revelation, the beginning of the fourth line in the final verse, the vocative addressed to Rāma (*cilai kulān toḷiṉāy*, "O You whose arms bend back the bow")? Why this sudden turn from the drama of Bali's salvation to the young Rāma, who plays no part in the myth being narrated? Surely Viśvāmitra has no need to fear that his listener has lost interest or let his attention wander—for this is the supreme moment of the myth, and the entire epiphany has just been sung in three breathless verses that seem to imitate in their very language the explosive ascent of the god. Once again, the poet is suggesting a deeper level of the myth. The vocative in 448 follows a string of vocatives (in the dialogue between Bali and the dwarf, and between Bali and Śukra), all leading up to this moment of revelation; moreover, the invocation of Rāma here is exactly parallel to the description of Viṣṇu in the preceding line ("the One Lord crowned with bright *tulasī*"). Here, in this conjunction, at the moment of greatest tension, Rāma learns of *his* identity with Viṣṇu, just as Bali has learned of his. The incarnate god is revealed to himself.[65] And this is what all men must come to understand: God is within us; the sense of an independent ego is false; redemption comes through the loss of self, through the recognition of man's inner divinity. It is this gift, the gift of the self, that brings a reward reaching up to heaven (446); Bali's self-sacrifice is the secret of his salvation.

The revelation thus takes place on several levels, as is typical of Kampaṉ. There is the simple, literal level of the story: the dwarf reveals himself as Viṣṇu. Then there is the element of self-recognition in the demon: Bali is at first, in preparation for the conclusion, compared to Viṣṇu the boar; in the course of his confrontation with the dwarf, he recognizes his close relationship with his rival and becomes a devotee, *aṉpaṉ*. Bali is prepared to give his very life in order to sustain his honor (440); instead he receives life, beatification, and divine love. The agonistic battle is resolved through the fusion of the two parties; the false knowledge of the demon, who is said with gentle irony to have no doubts in his mind, becomes true knowledge and *bhakti*. The process of self-understanding is repeated on a different level at the climax of the myth, when Rāma is, by implication, confronted with his own divine identity. The devotee who hears the story may choose his model; his promised salvation is seen to lie in the total surrender of the self.

### *Dakṣa and His Daughter*

Nowhere is the distance between the Tamil myths and their Sanskrit counterparts more evident than in the different versions of the myth of Dakṣa's sacrifice. Some of the major elements of the classical Dakṣa myth have been discussed in another context;[66] in the Sanskrit purāṇas, Śiva and Dakṣa are rivals both for the love of the goddess Umā (Dakṣa's daughter) and for the position of supreme god and creator. The Tamil tradition refuses to take this rivalry seriously; Śiva can hardly be compared to Dakṣa, who is reduced to the status of but another foolish enemy of the one great god, like the ego-driven demons of which the Tamil myths are so fond. In fact, the Dakṣa myth shows with great clarity how the old agonistic conflict between gods and demons has been finally superseded in the Tamil tradition: in one text the gods are joined at Dakṣa's sacrifice by demons, Rākṣasas, devils (*kaṭi*), and others of their erstwhile opponents; the gods killed by Vīrabhadra at the site of Dakṣa's sacrifice become demons (*pey ākiye*), or are reborn as evil spirits (Bhūtas and Vetālas), and thus enter Śiva's hosts.[67] The distinction between gods and demons is deliberately blurred by this text; one is either *with* Śiva or *against* him—the god's enemies form a single undifferentiated camp. True *bhakti* is now the only valid criterion of virtue: the social affiliation of the mythic characters is no longer of any consequence; all that matters is the nature of one's relation to Śiva. Dakṣa's sacrifice, from which Śiva has been excluded because of Dakṣa's arrogance and ignorance, becomes a symbol of misguided opposition to the divine. The *KP*, which gives us the main Tamil version of the myth, uses Dakṣa's sacrifice to explain the sufferings of the gods, who are subjugated by the devoted demon Śūrapadma; the gods' state of slavery is a deserved punishment for their opposition to Śiva at the sacrifice. But, as we might expect, the demon's devotion to Śiva is itself riddled with error and the lust for power—hence Śūrapadma is eventually punished by being slain by Murukaṉ. The *KP*, in effect, equates the sins of the gods with the mistakes of the demons; the betrayal of Śiva by the gods is the precise equivalent of the demons' error, and in both cases punishment justly and inevitably follows. The Tamil text applies the same moral standard to all.[68]

Given this concern with the right attitude toward the divinity, it is not surprising that Dakṣa, like the Tamil demons, turns out to be another deluded and self-seeking devotee of Śiva:

> Dakṣa, the wisest and most learned of all the sons of Brahmā, learned from his father that Śiva was lord of the universe. Brahmā advised him to seek release by worshiping Śiva in his shrines, but Dakṣa wanted wealth (*vaḷam*) instead of release (*vīṭu*). Impelled by fate (*ūḻi*), he asked his father to recommend a place for the performance ot *tapas*, and Brahmā sent him to Maṇippĕruntaṭam.[69]
>
> When Śiva appeared in response to his *tapas*, Dakṣa asked to become supreme in the universe except for Śiva, to be served by the gods and demons, to have Parāparā (Devī) born as his

daughter, and to bestow her on Śiva as his bride. Śiva promised him all this if he would but follow the right path (*naṉṉĕṟi*).

When Brahmā learned of Dakṣa's boons, he smiled and sighed. "I spoke of Śiva as the Truth; my son, who could have won freedom by his worship, chose instead a material reward (*paricu*). What can one do—the neem, even if dipped every day in *amṛta* from the sea, will not lose its bitterness. He has received from Śiva only rebirth and everlasting sorrow. Who can overcome fate?"[70]

Reluctantly, Brahmā went to see his foolish son (*mai vaḷar tīya punti maintaṉ*) and agreed to create for him a golden city. The *guru* of the gods informed Indra of the boons Dakṣa had won from Śiva, and Indra and the other gods sadly went to offer their submission. The demons learned from their *guru* of the new ruler of the universe and, happy that they no longer had anything to fear, also paid homage to Dakṣa.

Because Umā in her pride had claimed to be all the forms of Śiva in her character as his grace (*aruḷ*), the goddess was sent to atone by becoming incarnate in a *valampuri* conch in the Kāḷinti River. There she was found by Dakṣa; when he picked up the conch, it became a baby girl in his hand. He adopted her and brought her up. When she was six years old, she announced her intention of performing *tapas* for Śiva. Her mother was shocked, but Dakṣa, explaining to her the nature of the boons he had received from Śiva, constructed a golden pavilion for her penance. To test her, after she had performed *tapas* for six years, Śiva came to her in the form of a Brahmin ascetic and told her he wished to marry her. Angrily she announced that she would wed none but Śiva himself—and at this Śiva revealed himself to her. As she fell at his feet and sought pardon, Dakṣa began making preparations for the wedding.

Dakṣa invited all the gods to the ceremony, which he wished to celebrate with great pomp. But just at the moment Dakṣa placed his daughter's hand in Śiva's, Śiva made himself disappear. Not seeing her bridegroom, Devī was plunged into sorrow; weeping in the presence of Śrī and others, she cried, "My lord has disappeared, like a thief (*kaḷvaṉ*), there in the hall where Indra, Viṣṇu, and the other gods were all standing. Perhaps my *tapas* was not sufficient; could I even imagine that such a one as my lord is a cheat (*kaitavaṉ*)?"

Her mother, Vedavallī, said, "Do not lose heart. The way to

win your husband is by *tapas*; return to your penance." Śrī and Sarasvatī also comforted Umā: "Is there a way to hide your husband, who is always present in everything?" Devī dismissed them and went back to her *tapas*.

But Viṣṇu and the other gods were amazed and confused: "Where is the lord? Is this a trick (*māyam*)? Why should he have hidden from this maiden?" Dakṣa put his finger on his nose and said bitterly, "This is quite a wedding we have celebrated with such splendor! He came and asked to marry my daughter in front of all the gods, according to rite, and I agreed; what fault did he see in me that made him vanish into thin air? He has no consideration for me or for the scandal he is causing. Today I have learned the nature of that Śiva." To Viṣṇu and the others he said, "Go home"; and he thought and thought about Śiva's trick.

While Devī was performing *tapas* as before, Śiva again appeared to her, first as a devotee of Śiva, then as himself on the bull, without her. She bowed in joy and said, "Why did you leave me behind? Are you now abandoning such meanness (*puṉmai*)?" He took her on to the bull.

When Dakṣa heard the news, he said to all present in his court, "Not only did Śiva dishonor me and my family by disappearing at the wedding I arranged—now that Kāpālika with matted locks has made off with my daughter. Is it right to take a wife like that? Who but Śiva would do such a thing, disgracing our family and transgressing my command? Śiva has long been known as a beggar (*irantaṉaṉ*); now the whole world will know he is also a thief (*karantaṉaṉ*)."[71]

The gods, fearing the consequences of the quarrel between Dakṣa and Śiva—would not Dakṣa be killed, and with him the gods, his servants?—persuaded Dakṣa to talk to Śiva on Kailāsa. But the gatekeepers would not let him in unless he first agreed to worship the god. Dakṣa was insulted: "I will never worship your lord. Do you not know that he is my son-in-law, and I am Dakṣa, worshiped by the whole world? I have no intention of worshiping your madman (*pittaṉ*)." Returning home, he ordered the gods to withhold all worship and respect from Śiva and Umā.

Brahmā wished to hold a sacrifice and, despite Dakṣa's orders, to offer the first portion to Śiva. Dakṣa came to stop the offering of an oblation to Śiva. Śiva sent Nandin to take his portion, and when Brahmā welcomed Nandin and gave him a seat, Dakṣa stood up and said, "If you were not my father, I would cut off your head! Listen to me, you ignoramus: do not give the oblation as formerly to the madman who dances in the burning-ground, surrounded by demons, wearing bones and snakes and a garland of skulls. He is certainly unfit to receive the sacrifice. Previously he was given his share because people thought such was the custom and did not investigate the matter further (*maṟaiyŏḻukk' ĕṉa niṉainti yāvatum orāmal*); should that be regarded as ancient usage? Give the portions to Viṣṇu and the other gods, and cast aside the Vedas (*māmaraic-curutikaḷ*) which declare the long-haired, three-eyed god to be the highest."

Nandin closed his ears with his hands so as not to hear these blasphemies. Then he cursed Dakṣa and the gods: the sacrificer would lose his head, Dakṣa would have his head replaced with another one more base and would lose all his glory (*tiru*), the gods would die and be revived only to serve the demon Śūrapadma for endless ages. Then Nandin departed.

Dakṣa determined to offer a sacrifice from which Śiva would be excluded. First the sage Dadhīci tried to dissuade him; then his daughter Umā came, after Dakṣa had already begun to feed the gods oblations that were as bitter as poison. Dakṣa upbraided his daughter; she grew angry, defended her husband and the merciful nature of all his actions, and returned to Kailāsa. She asked Śiva to destroy her father's sacrifice. The merciful god at first pretended not to hear her. "Destroy the sacrifice for my sake, O my husband," she asked. From his eye on his forehead, Śiva created Vīrabhadra and sent him to destroy the sacrifice.[72]

As in the ancient sacrificial myths,[73] Śiva is here the indispensable lord of the sacrifice; even Dakṣa admits that he is customarily offered a share, and that the Vedas proclaim Śiva the highest god. This admission leads Dakṣa to advise rejecting the Vedas, an act certainly meant to be seen as utterly heretical (for overt rejection of the Vedas is the one seemingly infallible touchstone of heresy in India); thus the Tamil myth has reversed the usual charge of heresy made by Dakṣa against Śiva.[74] Dakṣa's statement that Śiva normally receives his share, and the implicit assumption that Dakṣa is deliberately departing from tradition by denying him one, should be contrasted with one description of the sacrifice from the *MBh*: the Prajāpati Dakṣa begins a sacrifice according to the ancient rule (*pūrvoktena vidhānena*); and even Śiva agrees that he is excluded in accordance with *dharma* (*na me surāḥ prayacchanti bhāgaṃ yajñasya dharmataḥ*).[75] The versions of the Epic and the Sanskrit purāṇas are characterized by an ambivalent view of Śiva's role: Śiva, excluded from the sacrifice, asserts his primacy by destroying it and then claiming the share that has been denied him; at the same time he in effect completes the sacrifice by fulfilling the altogether crucial task of the sacrificial butcher.[76] The Tamil version returns to a situation, which seems to be implicit in the earlier *Brāhmaṇa* myths of sacrifice, in which Śiva, for reasons inherent in the ritual, can claim not only a share but, as we have seen, his peculiar, primary share. There is nothing ambivalent about Śiva's position; a sacrifice not directed to Śiva is useless, even evil. Hence the statement in the *KP* that the gods' portions of Dakṣa's offering tasted like poison: the swallowing of poison through the sacrifice "usually refers to the accepting of food and presents from, and the officiating at the sacrifices of, an unqualified patron."[77] Dakṣa's pretensions to power are denied in the Tamil myth even the limited credence they may arouse in the Epic, where at least Dakṣa presents something of a challenge to Śiva; in the *KP* he is no more than a famous, but obviously foolish, sacrificial patron (*veḷvi cĕykiṉṟavar*).[78]

Let us now look more closely at the nature of Dakṣa's offense. Dakṣa begins as a devotee of Śiva. In itself, this idea resolves some of the tension that lies at the heart of earlier versions;[79] Dakṣa's hatred of Śiva has therefore to be explained by several episodes, of which the most important is the innovating description of events at the wedding of Umā. However, Dakṣa's mistakes go back to the very beginning of the story, for even as a devotee of Śiva, Dakṣa makes a wrong choice by preferring material rewards to release (*vīṭu*). Like Bali, Dakṣa wishes to give the deity a gift (in this case, his daughter); he fails to see the absurdity of giving Śiva something that is already Śiva's, and he takes offense when the god reclaims his wife in a manner that destroys Dakṣa's pride in the offering. All of Dakṣa's aims are clearly motivated by a sense of his own importance, accompanied by an appetite for power. Brahmā, Dakṣa's father and teacher, is aware of his son's mistaken attitude, and grieves over it; and this initial difference of opinion between Brahmā and Dakṣa is carried over to a later episode, when Brahmā defies his son and tries to sacrifice to Śiva, and is threatened by

Dakṣa on this account ("If you were not my father, I would cut off your head"—a surprising reappearance here of the theme of the son's aggression against the father, as in the myth of Śiva's Brahminicide, a close multiform of the Dakṣa cycle).[80] What we see in the depiction of Dakṣa at the first stage of the story, when he solicits boons from Śiva, is the now familiar attempt to make distinctions between different types of *bhakti*. It is no longer enough that someone—god, man, or demon—worship the god; the author of the myth is now concerned with the *content* of the devotion. Of course Dakṣa at first wins his boons from Śiva—the god is still almost compelled to respond to the requests of his worshipers—but because Dakṣa's worship is impure, dominated throughout by his own ulterior motives, self-serving rather than self-sacrificing, it will not save him from punishment. Indeed, it *demands* punishment: for Dakṣa is propelled by his egoism, his *ahaṅkāra*, into a confrontation with the very god from whom he originally solicits boons.

The *KP* Dakṣa myth is a good illustration of just how thorough the Tamil attempt to reinterpret the great myths of Hinduism can be. It also reveals the rather exotic tone the Tamil myths have in comparison with other versions. Specifically, we see here a strong didactic, rationalizing tendency that transforms the values of the mythic actions without destroying the inherited narrative structure. For example, the incest theme, which is still a powerful crux in the Sanskrit versions of the myth, has been replaced by an elaborate episode very much in the tradition of Śiva's arguments with his in-laws—in this case with his father-in-law, who deduces from the events at the wedding that Śiva is far from an ideal son-in-law! The violent climax to Dakṣa's rivalry with Śiva for Umā—the self-immolation of the goddess at the sacrifice—is completely missing from our version; the goddess reproaches Dakṣa and then simply goes home. The myth masks the sexual antagonism, but still uses Umā's love for Śiva as a means of clarifying the opposition between Śiva and Dakṣa. It then converts Dakṣa into a devotee of Śiva and then, by specifying the flaw in his devotion, lays down an entirely new basis for his punishment. It is not merely lack of devotion for Śiva that starts Dakṣa on his wrong course, as in many of the Sanskrit versions—it is lack of the proper kind of devotion. It is hard to escape the feeling that an ideological revolution has taken place.

The Tamil myth then proceeds to achieve much of its effect and power by playing on Dakṣa's insensitivity, his inability to perceive the truth even when it is so clearly brought home to him. We thus find here the same use of irony and *double entendre* that we saw in the myth of Murukaṉ's wooing of Vaḷḷi.[81] Indeed, the Tamil Dakṣa myth shares with that myth the theme of elopement and premarital love, and, like Murukaṉ, Śiva is accused of stealing his bride. In both cases the accusation is entirely justified. Both myths use the idea of premarital love to symbolize ecstatic union with god, just as *kaḷavu* is the state of love celebrated as supreme by the Caṅkam poets; the Murukaṉ myth applies the old conventions to an entire episode of courtship and escape, while in the Dakṣa myth Śiva disappears at the last possible moment, before the ceremony can be completed—only to return to steal his bride when she is alone. The point, no doubt, is the reality and power of Śiva's love for Umā, or indeed for the soul of man. In his first *patikam*, Tiruñāṉacampantar adopts this image in worshiping Śiva as "the thief who steals my heart" (*eṉṉ uḷḷaṅ kavar kaḷvaṉ*).[82] Nothing could so clearly demonstrate Dakṣa's blindness than the fact that he calls Śiva a thief (*kaḷvaṉ*, *karantaṉaṉ*)—and means it literally. Umā, on the other hand, considers this possibility (that Śiva is a thief) and rejects it in order to return to her worship; her reward is to be stolen.

Dakṣa's failure to understand Śiva's action at Umā's wedding thus becomes a symbol of the self-glorification that leads to his sacrifice, and one Tamil text ironically connects these two events: when Dadhīci asks Dakṣa, "Who will give you the fruit of the sacrifice, if not Śiva?" Dakṣa replies, "the effort alone will produce the fruit." Dadhīci's response—his final advice to Dakṣa before leaving the site of the sacrifice—is to state, "to have a sacrifice without Śiva is like dressing up a bride for a wedding without a bridegroom."[83] Dakṣa's belief in the automatic efficacy of the ritual is totally antithetical to the spirit of a myth dedicated to proving the superiority of content over form; and of course Dakṣa knows well the experience of holding a wedding without a bridegroom. Knows and yet does not know—here lies the power of the words.

Very similar is the play on Śiva's madness. To Dakṣa, Śiva has acted incomprehensibly; hence he is mad (*pittaṉ*). But this same epithet is familiar from another story about a wedding:

> When Nampi Ārūrar (Cuntaramūrtti) came of age, his parents arranged a match for him. At the wedding ceremony, an old Brahmin suddenly appeared and put a halt to the rite by claiming Ārūrar as his slave. Ārūrar abused the old man and called

> him a madman (*piṭṭaṉ*). The old Brahmin produced a document signed by Ārūrar's grandfather and witnessed by others of his generation; the document proved the claim was valid, as the assembly of Brahmins in the village had to admit. So the old man walked off with Ārūrar following until he disappeared into his shrine. Then Ārūrar understood that the old Brahmin was Śiva, and that he was truly his slave, and Śiva commanded him to sing his praises, beginning with the very term of abuse he had used earlier. (Thus Nampi Ārūrar sang his first *patikam*, which begins with the word "Madman!"—*pittā*.)[84]

Śiva steals the bridegroom rather than the bride in this story, but the symbolism is the same; Devī in the Dakṣa myth represents the soul of the devotee ravished by his god. Once again, human eroticism (the marriage of Cuntarar and his bride) is rejected in favor of union with the divine, as in many myths of the Reluctant Bride.[85] Cuntarar will then refer to Śiva as *pittaṉ* as a sign of his submission; Dakṣa calls him by the same title and sees no further than the literal meaning, just as Rāvaṇa sees the inverted tree as no more than a violation of nature's norm. It is thus altogether fitting that Dakṣa is said to have become afflicted himself with madness (*paittiyam*) because of the destruction of his sacrifice. He is released from madness by worshiping Śiva at Tirukkaṇṭiyūr.[86] Dakṣa, who never sees beyond the surface of events, who is concerned about etiquette, his reputation, and his success in the world, who seeks only worldly wealth when truth is within his grasp—he, in the eyes of the myth, is truly mad.

To summarize: Rāvaṇa, Bali, and Dakṣa are all symbols of false understanding, cupidity, egoism, and utilitarian devotion. Their death or defeat by the deity signifies their purification, the transition to true knowledge and salvation through the loss of self. The demons' salvation in the Tamil myths does not fit the classical pattern of *dveṣabhakti*, "the devotion of hate," that is, the realization of an obsessive, intimate relationship with the god through hatred and violent antagonism; rather, the Tamil demons are saved when opposition is overcome by self-sacrifice. The old agonistic structure of Hindu myth is superseded here; the Tamil texts show concern only for the right knowledge that leads to freedom. The eradication of all forms of egoism is the prerequisite for redemption. This recommendation is superimposed upon the concept of sacrifice as leading to rebirth and greater power; the demon who exemplifies in his death the latter concept is made to act out a new drama of *self*-sacrifice and salvation. The convergence of two very different goals in the common pattern of self-immolation reflects the union of conflicting aspirations within the human devotee. Self-sacrifice leads to power won from death, most often through the agency of the goddess; it may also lead to an ideal state of purity and union with the god.

# CHAPTER VI
# Conclusion

Two themes have persistently engaged our attention in our progress through the myths of the Tamil shrines—the search for power and all that power can bring; and the attempt to make this search subservient to an ideal of purity. Power is believed to be derived from forces that are, in their very essence, contaminating; these forces belong to the violent substratum of chaos out of which the world has emerged, and which is represented in the shrine by tangible symbols (the tree and the sacred tank). In Tamil myth, as in Hindu thought generally, the creative processes of the universe are bound up with evil. Evil in its variety of forms (including death, dirt, unlimited violence) is dynamic and life-giving. Life is won only out of the darkness and violence of chaos. The outstanding symbolic expression of these beliefs is the cluster of themes and motifs surrounding the sacrifice, at which life is traded for life. The sacrifice produces new life—the divine seed—from the disintegration of a previous existence; more specifically, it is the impure remainder of the sacrifice, the *vāstu* portion sacred to Rudra, that gives birth to the new life produced from death. This symbolism is applied to cosmic processes of destruction and regeneration as well as to the individual level of the sacrificial rites; and the shrine partakes of this cosmic symbolism through its survival of the universal flood and subsequent role as the site of the new creation. The shrine is the symbolic correlative of the *vāstu*, which remains after the violent destruction of the sacrifice. The serpent that traces the ancient boundaries of the sacred site after the flood sustains the identification of the shrine with the sacrifice, for the serpent is an archaic symbol of the fiery seed, the remainder.

All of these notions are given life and immediate relevance for the pilgrim by the role of the main god of the shrine, who must originally have acted out the part of the sacrificial victim as a model for his devotees. This mythic self-sacrifice may take place with or without reference to the goddess of the shrine; it survives in the myths of origin in the inevitable wounding of the god or his symbol, and in the conjunction of blood and milk—both connected to the divine seed—in the discovery of the sacred site. Nevertheless, the most striking expression of the god's sacrificial role is found in most Tamil shrines in the myth of divine marriage. Marriage is regarded as a sacrifice, in which the god is slain and revived by his bride, the local goddess. Just as the sacrifice is connected with the creative realm of death and darkness, the goddess identified with the sacrificial process is the black, seductive, terrifying Kālī. This dark bride is a focus of inherent power, potentially dangerous as well as creative; her womb is the dark earth to which she is closely tied, and in which she locates forever the presence of the god.

In all these myths, the underlying goal is sacred power, the power that can give life and material prosperity. But this power, in order to be useful to man, must be limited and channeled into proper courses. Limited in this way, power becomes auspicious and accessible. The ritual ordering of the shrine is one form of limitation; an idealized universe of water, rock, and tree holds in check the forces welling up from the nether world to find a permanent, circumscribed dwelling in the shrine. A major symbol of this limitation is the temple wall, which marks the boundary between the outer world of chaos and the inner realm of peace; evil, death, the corruption of the Kali Age, the raging waters of the *pralaya*—all are excluded from the shrine by the *prākāra* wall. This concept of bounded power is, as we would expect, particularly applicable to the goddess, who is so intimately linked with power; hence we find the recurrent image of Devī's sealed shrine.

I have spoken of a fundamental split in the tradition, of a clash between the longing for power and the ideal of purity. This clash is very evident in the final stages of the tradition, when the demon devotee is made an example of the dangers that await the power-hungry. But is this perspective strictly necessary? Could we not see in the principle of limitation a solution to the conflict of purity and power? Is not the regulation of power a sufficient guarantee of purity? Yes and no. It is true that power, properly contained, fulfils a necessary and auspicious role in a creative process regarded by the Tamil tradition as essentially positive and redeeming. Yet this process cannot but be characterized by impurity in certain basic ways. Impurity breaks into every life at the most crucial moments—birth and death; for a woman, puberty and childbirth. No amount of control or limitation can rule out such moments of impurity, of contact with the violent and creative forces of darkness, just as no wall, however high, can keep the real world from impinging on the idealized microcosm of the shrine. At the center of the shrine lies the site of the god's death and rebirth in the sacrifice; and the myths' constant, never fully successful attempts to remove the god from this forum testify to the inherent impurity attached to his role. Impurity is dynamic, purity ultimately static; in affirming the sacred character of creation, the Tamil myths are unable to avoid implicating man, and the deity he worships, in impurity—even if, as in Śaiva Siddhānta, the goal of the creative process is a transcendent state of freedom from evil. All that one can do is to isolate the source of impurity, either temporarily (as in the case of the woman at puberty) or permanently (as in the case of the evils excluded from the shrine). The idea of isolation, in fact, goes further than the principle of limitation; perhaps if power could be isolated to the point of total independence, a zone of complete purity could be established, while impurity would be relegated to the area beyond the borders. This is the aim of the Brahmin who performs the *prāṇāgnihotra* and thus cuts himself off from the surrounding realm of relations and impurity. Like the isolated sacrificer, the shrine may become an idealized island of independence. The difficulty here is that isolation can never really be carried far enough. Life constantly compromises the ideal of final independence from evil. The ideal of purity is not relative, but rather an absolute ultimately removed from the world—hence the relentless need to expiate the manifold kinds of pollution that constantly encroach upon the purity of the individual. Purity is, in other words, an ever-receding goal so long as life on earth is eagerly desired.

The limits of limitation emerge clearly from the myths of the virgin goddess. The virgin is, after puberty, a locus of power; she is also pure, her chastity preserved from physical contact. The state of virginity is, indeed, an archetypal image of power sealed within limits; the virgin goddess reigns alone in her locked and guarded shrine. But the myths of Kaṉṉiyākumari and other virgins depict the goddess as virtually exploding with pent-up erotic power: the virgin, for all her purity, is the epitome of the seductive, menacing force that calls the god to the sacrifice. So long as this force is totally contained and isolated, the danger remains latent; but as soon as the male comes into contact with the virgin—for example, by entering her shrine, thus shattering the wholeness of her enclosure, or simply by seeing her in her splendid isolation—he unleashes the full force of her power against himself. In some shrines (Kaṉṉiyākumari, Cucīntiram) this point is never reached, and the goddess remains isolated forever, or until the end of the present age of time. Most shrines, however, insist on celebrating the marriage between the goddess and the god; in the course of this rite, Śiva accepts the violent consequences of union. The god dies or is castrated, only to be reborn from the womb of his virgin bride. Even if the myth manages to achieve this result without actually destroying the virginity of the goddess—the death of the god is her salvation, as it is, in another sense, his—the separation of the goddess is irreparably damaged. The virgin belongs to this world; her power is needed by her devotees as well as by her mythic victim. Her implication in the web of relations is revealed by the process of exchange through the sacrifice: the god/devotee offers her his seed, his power, his very life, believing they will be restored to him in a better, more secure form. The security (*pratiṣṭhā*) that the goddess provides is inextricably bound up with the sacrifice, which anchors god and man in the earth of her shrine. Devī's marriage is a means to this goal, just as it is a necessary prototype for human marriage, in which the male is felt to deplete himself in the act of procreation. The point is that this act is, on both the divine and the human levels, a necessary, sacred stage in a redemptive process that takes place on earth, in the flesh, notwithstanding the claims of purity.

But the ideal of purity is not relinquished so easily. If marriage to the virgin entails a violent sequence of death and rebirth, another possibility must be sought for the god who is declared pure. The virgin goddess may be "reformed," her terrible powers brought under control—hence the many myths of taming the bride, most often by means of the dance contest. The state of virginity appears to be one of containment and control, but the myths recognize that the virgin's power must eventually be let loose. Another form of control is therefore established by chaining the goddess in the idealized domestic role of the Hindu wife. If the dark Kālī refuses to be ruled in this way, she is exiled to the impure realm beyond the borders of the shrine, where her power can act without threatening the harmony within the walls. This harmony is now symbolized by Śiva's marriage to the golden, submissive Gaurī. The goddess is, in other words, split into two parts, one dark and still virginal, the other golden and meek. It should be obvious that it is the dark goddess who is a focus of erotic attraction, while the golden goddess is much closer to the ideal of purity.

At Kāñcipuram Śiva is married to both the black and the golden goddesses, and we have seen that the idea of a double marriage is very widespread in the Tamil shrines. On a more abstract level, we might see this double marriage as symbolizing the basic ambivalence of the deity, who is wed both to power, with its intractable impurity, and to purity, which seems antierotic and detached. Of course the two brides may also simply represent the different elements of Devī's nature, for the goddess is inherently complex, an amalgam of destructive and creative forces, of benevolence and violence, order and chaos. The myths divide her into parts in an effort to deal with these conflicting attributes. It must be stressed that in this case this conflict within the goddess is not a clash between two contradictory forces, but rather a union of separate stages in a single creative process: life is fashioned out of death and chaos, and the goddess is identified with both parts of the cycle. Perhaps the most important symbol of her double nature is the androgyne, which plays a major role in Tamil mythology. We have discovered a number of very different uses for this symbol. First, the virgin goddess is regarded as androgynous because she violates the ideal of womanly submission; as a source of violence and aggression, especially of an aggressive sexuality, she cannot be wholly woman. This is the virgin who throws her breast at her victim; she may also be equipped with a sword, a bow, a crystal tongue, or another symbol of masculinity. As a diachronic equivalent of her bisexuality, we have the reversal of sex in the myths of marriage: the goddess is first male, then female. In the course of her confrontation with the male god—a moment that we have seen to reflect a crucial stage in the sacrifice—she also acquires the power and masculinity of her victim; at this point her bisexuality becomes far more explicit, while the male is left castrated, woman-like, awaiting the return of his gift. But the single-breasted goddess is absorbed in some shrines, notably Tiruvaṇṇāmalai, by the single-breasted *ardhanārī* form of Śiva; the myth, struggling to free itself from the entire sacrificial scheme, describes an androgynous marriage between Śiva and the local goddess. As the androgynous creator, Śiva-Ardhanārī is a symbol of wholeness and autonomy; he holds the power of the woman in inseparable union. This androgynous union merely masks the underlying tension between the two partners, but it is, at the same time, a striking symbol of limitation: the androgyne is that form of union in which conventional sexual activity is impossible, and the goddess locked in this embrace retains her virginity and her power.

The attempt to empty the divine marriage of its inherent violence is characteristic of a stage in the development of the myth in which the god's role in the sacrifice is no longer possible. The deity is pure, *nirmala*, just as the shrine in which he dwells has become devoid of evil. Śiva neither dies nor is reborn; nor, obviously, can he be described in the familiar terms of the northern Śaiva tradition, where Śiva epitomizes the extremes of antithesis to social life (the god is an outcaste, unclean, a mad dancer in the cremation ground, a seducer of women, a gambler who cheats his opponents, a murderer of a Brahmin). The Tamil myths attempt to exonerate the deity from all such embarrassing charges. Śiva becomes a very different kind of outsider, in the ideal view of the Tamil purāṇas; he is no longer affected by the dynamic processes of change. Yet we have just seen how susceptible this ideal is to the onslaught of reality in the form of a love for life and a readiness to accept the burden of creation. The Tamil Śaiva tradition clearly leans in the direction of life in this world; violence, death, blood-sacrifice, and impurity thus remain as integral elements in the ecstatic worship of Śiva. The devotee achieves salvation on earth, not by renunciation but by undergoing the process of sacrifice. Two developments are important here. A demon *bhakta* takes the place of the god as the exemplar of the sacrifice. The demon is the natural prey of the goddess, who slays him in a revised version of the divine marriage; but in his death the demon achieves all that the sacrifice can offer. The demon is a focus of power and, as such, an attractive model for men; moreover, the Tamil myths do not really obscure his essential identity with the god, the consort of the goddess. But—this is the second development—the purāṇic texts explain the demon's death in different terms. Idealism reasserts itself with the demand that the sacrifice aimed at power and rebirth become a self-sacrifice aimed at union with the deity. The ancient symbolism of the sacrifice is reinterpreted in the light of an ideal of salvation, in which the identity of the embodied soul with god is perceived through the loss of egoism. What must be stressed is that this salvation, no less than the concrete goals of power and vitality, is won on earth; it is proclaimed in the hagiographies of the Śaiva saints and in the myths that describe the deities in their terrestrial home. God is present in man's life; he is rooted forever in the very soil of the Tamil land. The localization of the divine presence in the Tamil shrine guarantees the rewards open to the pilgrim in this life.

# APPENDIX. MAJOR AUTHORS AND THEIR DATES

| *Century* | *Author* | *Works* |
|---|---|---|
| 12th | Pĕrumpaṟṟappuliyūr-nampi | Tiruvālavāyuṭaiyār tiru-viḷaiyāṭaṟpurāṇam |
| 14th | Umāpaticivācāriyar | Koyiṟpurāṇam |
| 16th | Purāṇa Tirumalainātaṉ | Citamparapurāṇam (c. 1508) |
| 16th | Citamparam Maṟaiñāṉa-tecikar | Aruṇakiripurāṇam (1555) |
| 16th | Ĕllappanayiṉār | Aruṇācalapurāṇam<br>Tiruviriñcaippurāṇam |
| 16th | Kamalai Ñāṉappira-kācar | Tirumaḻuvāṭippurāṇam |
| 16th | Tiruvŏṟṟiyūr Ñāṉa-ppirākācar | Tiruvŏṟṟiyūrpurāṇam (c. 1580) |
| 16th | Nirampavaḻakiyateci-kar | Cetupurāṇam<br>Tirupparaṅkiripurāṇam |
| 16th | Campantamuṉivar | Tiruvārūrppurāṇam (1597) |
| 16th | Ñāṉakkūttar | Tiruvaiyāṟṟuppurāṇam (Cĕppecapurāṇam)<br>Viruttācalapurāṇam |
| 17th | Parañcotimuṉivar? | Tiruviḷaiyāṭaṟpurāṇam |
| 17th | Kaḷantaikkumaraṉ | Tiruvāñciyattalapurāṇam (1616) |
| 17th | Cekarācacekaraṉ | Taṭcinakailāyapurāṇam |
| 17th | Kantacāmippulavar | Tiruvāppaṉūrppurāṇam<br>Tiruppūvaṇappurāṇam (1621) |
| 17th | Pālacuppiramaṇiya kkavirāyar | Paḻanittalapurāṇam (1628) |
| 17th | Antakakkavivīrarākava Mutaliyār | Tirukkaḻukkuṉṟappurāṇam |

Note: The names are given in approximate chronological order. For exact references, see the Bibliography. For a discussion of the textual history and sources of many of these works, see Shulman (1976-a), pp. 19–41.

| *Century* | *Author* | *Works* |
|---|---|---|
| 17th | Akoratevaṉ | Vetāraṇiyappurāṇam<br>Tirukkāṉapperppurāṇam<br>Kumpakoṇappurāṇam |
| 17th | Vĕṉṟimālaikkavirācar | Tiruccĕntūrppurāṇam |
| 17th | Tuṟaimaṅkalam Civa-ppirakācacuvāmikaḷ | Tirukkūvappurāṇam |
| 17th | Caiva Ĕllappanāvalar | Cĕvvantippurāṇam<br>Tiruvĕṇkāṭṭuppurāṇam<br>Tīrttakiripurāṇam<br>Tiruccĕṅkāṭṭāṅkuṭi-ppurāṇam |
| 17th | Iḷaiyāṉ kavirāyar | Avinācittalapurāṇam |
| 17th | Cŏkkappappulavar | Kumpakoṇappurāṇam |
| 18th | Velaiyacuvāmi (with his brothers Civa-ppirakācacuvāmikaḷ and Karuṇaippira-kācacuvāmi) | Cīkāḷattippurāṇam |
| | (with Umāpākatevar) | Vīraciṅkātaṉapurāṇam |
| 18th | Tirikūṭarācappaṉ | Tirukkuṟṟālattala-purāṇam (c. 1718) |
| 18th | Civañāṉayoki | Kāñcippurāṇam |
| 18th | Kacciyappamuṉivar | Kāñcippurāṇam (2)<br>Taṇikaippurāṇam<br>Tiruvāṉaikkāppurāṇam<br>Tirupperūrppurāṇam<br>Pūvāḷūrppurāṇam<br>Vināyakapurāṇam |
| 18th | Ilakkaṇam Citampara-nātamuṉivar | Tiruppātirippuliyūr-purāṇam |
| 18th | Aruṇācalakkavirāyar | Cīkāḻittalapurāṇam |
| 19th | Mīṉāṭcicuntaram Piḷḷai | Tirunākaikkāroṇappurāṇam<br>Tirukkuṭantaippurāṇam<br>Tirutturuttippurāṇam, etc.<br>(See I.3 at nn. 50-52.) |

# NOTES

## I.1. Tamil Mythology and the Indian Tradition

1. Tiruviḷai., *tirunāṭṭu ccirappu* 60. The three gods are, according to the first two lines of this verse, Devī (the goddess), Śiva, and their son Murukan̲.

2. See Marr (1958) and Hart (1975). On the Caṅkam legend itself, see below, II.2.

3. Kiruṣṇacāmi, p. 123, lists thirty-six different names for this type of composition.

4. These may be said to include the Agni, Bhāgavata, Bhaviṣya, Brahma, Brahmāṇḍa, Brahmavaivarta, Bṛhannāradīya, Devībhāgavata, Garuḍa, Kālikā, Kūrma, Liṅga, Mārkaṇḍeya, Matsya, Padma, Saura, Śiva, Skanda, Vāmana, Varāha, Vāyu, and Viṣṇu purāṇas. (Hereafter these texts will be cited in the notes by the first part of their title alone: thus, Brahma = Brahmapurāṇa.) The traditional lists try to reach a standard number of eighteen major purāṇas and therefore omit several of the above works (not always the same ones!); and there are, of course, other important Sanskrit purāṇas, such as the Bṛhaddharma, Devī, Kalki, Mahābhāgavata, Narasiṃha, and Sāmba purāṇas. Many local *māhātmyas*, some of southern origin, are found in the *mahāpurāṇas* (the Skanda is outstanding in this respect), but most of the classical myths of the *mahāpurāṇas* are not at all tied to a specific place—in contrast to the myths of the Tamil *sthalapurāṇas*.

5. In Telugu as in Sanskrit, Āṇṭāḷ is usually called Godā: see Marr (1969), p. 594. Even the Telugu tradition, however, localizes Godā in Villiputtūr in the Pāṇṭiya land. The stories of the Tamil Śaiva saints (*nāyan̲mār*) have been similarly borrowed by the Kannada tradition: see Meenakshisundaran (1970), pp. 137-43.

6. See the well-known descriptions by Whitehead, Elmore, and Oppert, *passim*.

7. On the circumstances of his migration to the south, see below, IV.1.

8. Commentary to IA, aphorism 1. For the Agastya corpus in Tamil, see Nilakanta Sastri (1966), pp. 75-77; Zvelebil (1973-b), pp. 136-37; Sivaraja Pillai, *passim*.

9. See Tiruviḷai. 52-55. For a critical evaluation of the story, see Marr (1958), pp. 3-17; Zvelebil (1973-b), pp. 45-49.

10. Meenakshisundaran (1965), pp. 166-67.

11. MBh 3.102.1-14; Rām. 3.10.53-64; cf. KP 2.20, 22-26.

12. This is a reference to the location of two hills at Paḻani: see below, II.1 n. 58.

13. Paḻani 21.1-18, 28-54.

14. On the commentators' view that the Kumari River was the old, an-

tediluvian southern boundary of a greatly expanded Tamil land, see S. B. Bharati, *passim*; below, II.2.

15. Cf. Kāñci 13.1-42; Skanda 4.1.95.28-74.

16. KP 2.28.1-19; Tirukkuṟṟālam 2.3.33-171.

17. On Murukaṉ and Tamil, see Paripāṭal 9.23-26; Tiruviḷai. 55.1-14; Zvelebil (1973), pp. 109-33. This association may be part of the conception of Murukaṉ/Skanda as a teacher (*guruguha*) generally: in KSS 1.2.30-83 and 1.7.4-14, this god appears as a teacher of the sciences, especially grammar. See below, IV.1 n. 21.

18. Heesterman (1975).

19. Some scholars have tried to describe the dynamics of the south Indian cultural synthesis in terms of Robert Redfield's distinction between "great" and "little" traditions: see Singer (1960); Ramanujan (1973), pp. 22-37; Kulke (and cf. the review by J. R. Marr, 1972-a); Srinivas (1952). Hart (1975), pp. 132-33, has leveled some cogent criticisms of this model. In practice, the great/little dichotomy requires one to postulate the existence of an almost infinite series of intermediate stages in the tradition, into which the actual texts can be fitted; Redfield himself (p. 57) seems to have recognized this problem. Although we must, of course, remain aware of different levels in the tradition—village worship, for example, contrasts in many ways with "purāṇic" or Brahminized cults—I have avoided Redfield's terms and tried instead to explain the evolution of the tradition by its own internal logic.

20. Hart (1975), pp. 132-33.

21. See Heesterman (1964) and (1975).

22. See Graves and Patai, pp. 11-19.

23. See n. 6 above; information on folk religion in south India can also be found in Thurston (1912); Diehl; Beck (1969), (1974), (1975-a), and (1975).

24. The Aṇṇaṉmār katai: Beck (1975).

25. For example, the Tiruppūvaṇanātarulā of Kantacāmippulavar; Tiruviṭaimarutūr mummaṇikkovai of Paṭṭiṉattuppiḷḷaiyār; Caṅkaranayiṉārkoyiṟ caṅkaraliṅka ulā, etc.

26. See the critical study by Kandiah; and cf. Piatigorsky (1962); Zvelebil (1973-b), pp. 185-206.

27. See Dorai Rangaswamy, 1:19-22, following the Tirumuṟaikaṇṭa purāṇam.

28. See below, IV.5 nn. 18-22.

29. On the problem of Kampaṉ's date, see Zvelebil (1975), pp. 181-84. I would lean toward a date in the first half of the twelfth century.

30. See below, III.2.

31. See below, IV.4.

32. There is also a stylistic barrier to translation; see section 3 below. In Chapter V I have, however, translated a passage from Kampaṉ's

Irāmāvatāram into English verse; these verses may suggest something of the flavor of medieval Tamil poetry, although the purāṇas are, on the whole, more ornate and less careful than Kampaṉ.

33. A note on transliteration is in order here. I have used the system of the Tamil Lexicon, except for marking short ĕ and ŏ, in order to preserve the correspondence of long e and o with Sanskrit equivalents. Gemination in compounds is marked at the beginning of the second member.

34. As the title indicates, I have limited myself for the most part to the Śaiva *talapurāṇam* literature. There exists a corresponding Vaiṣṇava literature in Tamil, similar in many respects to the Śaiva purāṇas, and certainly deserving of a separate study; I have drawn upon a number of select representatives of this literature for purposes of comparison. The composition of purāṇas in Tamil was by no means limited to Hindus: the Jains were active in this field, while the Christians can claim a Yoceppuppurāṇam (by Kūḻaṅkaittampirāṉ) and the Muslims the well-known Cīṟāpurāṇam of Umaṟuppulavar on the life of the prophet, as well as a number of *talapurāṇam* on Muslim sites of pilgrimage in the Tamil area.

## I.2. The Ritual of Pilgrimage

1. For example, Āṉantakkūttar of Vīrainakar (Vīravanallūr) in the Pāṇṭiya country produced the Tirukkāḷattippurāṇam in the course of a pilgrimage to Kāḷatti. See the introduction by U. Ve. Cāminātaiyar to his edition of the text.

2. MBh 3.80-153. See the analysis of this section in Bhardwaj, pp. 29-57. For an earlier example of a localized myth, see Bṛhaddevatā 6.20-24; and see below, II.1 at n. 54.

3. Vīraciṅkātaṉam 1.12-32; Kaṉṉiyākumari 18.31-37; Vaittīsvaraṉkoyil 5; Thurston (1909), 6:121-23; Carr, p. 182.

4. Hemingway (1915), p. 276.

5. See Aghenanda Bharati, pp. 160-61.

6. Dasgupta, p. 2.

7. South Indian Hinduism is not, however, overly confident of the merits of actual mortification except in special cases (for instance, the widow who must practice asceticism in order to contain her dangerous power—see Hart, 1975, pp. 102-107). In the philosophical school of Śaiva Siddhānta, *tapas* is defined simply as devotion for Śiva; and many of the Tamil purāṇas state bluntly that worship at a shrine is a superior—and easier!—path to the truth than *sannyāsa*, renunciation. See n. 11.

8. This is the case in Brahminical shrines. In the case of non-Brahminical deities (such as the village gods), the worshiper purifies himself *after* contact, just as in ancient times contact with the memorial stone (*naṭukal*) required subsequent purification (Hart, 1975, pp. 42, 126).

9. See van Buitenen (1971), pp. 35-36. See below, I.3 at n. 49.

10. See Kramrisch (1946), 1:161-76, esp. p. 163.

11. See Kāñci 6.49-54. Turner (1974), p. 203, sees pilgrimage in many traditions as dissolving the antithesis between "solitude and society." While this is largely true of the Tamil tradition as well, we shall see that the shrine retains in part the symbolism of solitude and separation.

12. Viruttācalam 6.1-24.

13. See the discussion by O'Flaherty (1976), pp. 248-71.

14. This problem is stated very clearly in the myth of Somanātha: by seeing the god there, all people went to heaven, which became so crowded that everyone had to stand with his arms held over his head; hell became empty, and the lord of death was silenced. Pārvatī created Gaṇeśa to keep pilgrims away from this shrine, and thus a proper balance was restored. Skanda 7.1.38.9-34; cf. Kennedy, pp. 354-56; O'Flaherty (1976), pp. 253-54.

15. Tiruviḷai. 40.29.

16. *Ibid.* 40.68. See also Tiruppūvaṇanātarulā 87.

17. Tiruvŏṟṟiyūr 2.36; Mattiyārccuṉam, p. 216.

18. See Shulman (1978); Zvelebil (1973-b), pp. 193-94, distinguishing between the *vaṉtŏṇṭar*, the devotees who reject society, and the *mĕṉtŏṇṭar*, who do not. Extreme movements, such as that of the early Vīraśaivas, did show hostility to the world—but even Vīraśaivism lost this early characteristic in the process of becoming institutionalized.

19. Irāmāvatāram 2.2065.

20. Commentary to this verse in the edition of the U. Ve. Cāminātaiyar Library.

21. Dēvara Dāsimayya 98, in Ramanujan (1973), p. 105.

22. See O'Flaherty (1976), pp. 232-37; Tirupperūr 25.1-22; Tiruvāṉmiyūr 10 (pp. 33-35); Tiruvāñciyakṣettirapurāṇam 38 (pp. 146-50). Yama is himself slain by Śiva at the Tamil shrine of Tirukkaṭavūr when he tries to kill Śiva's servant Mārkaṇḍeya there: Tirukkaṭavūrpurāṇam 9-14 (pp. 52-84); Tirukkaṭavūr kṣettirapurāṇam 3-5 (pp. 19-47).

23. Tiruvāñciyakṣettirapurāṇam 39 (pp. 151-53); cf. Tiruveṟkāṭu 14.23-34; Tiruvārūr 109.1-75; Tiruvŏṟṟiyūr 15.5-6.

24. Tiruvāñciyakṣettirapurāṇam 38 (pp. 146-50). John Marr has noted that the tall *gopuras* of the temple are suited to the purpose of excluding the impure (the outcastes): see his review of Barrett in BSOAS 39 (1976), p. 672. The symbolic importance of the gatekeeper may also be seen in the light of Victor Turner's observation that the pilgrimage site is itself a limen, a "threshold," a place and moment both "in and out of time": Turner (1974), p. 197. The gatekeeper guards the transition to a spot which is, in itself, a gateway. See below, III.3 and IV.5-6.

25. Skanda 6.13.32-39.

26. See O'Flaherty (1976), pp. 174-211.

27. Kūrma 2.31.3-109; Vāmana 2.20-55, 3.1-51; Skanda 5.1.2. 1-65,

5.1.3.1-33; Kāñci 34.1-38. Bhairava is himself a doorkeeper: Cūtavaṉam 12.143-57. Bhairava and Viṣvaksena are worshiped side by side at Aḻakarkoyil: see Vṛṣabhādrimāhātmya, introduction, pp. 172-74.

28. See Tirunaḷḷāṟu canippĕyarcci makimai, p. 4.

29. Field notes, Tiruviṭaimarutūr. According to the Maddhyārjunamāhātmya 62.28-9, this figure is blinded by good deeds.

30. Tiruviḷai. 40.1-25; Mattiyārccuṉam, pp. 226-27; cf. Maddhyārjunamāhātmya 61-62.

31. Tiruvāṉaikkā 16.5-52.

32. Indra distributes his sin among various scapegoats: Agni, Trita Āptya, the earth, waters, trees, women, and so on. See O'Flaherty (1976), pp. 146-60; Dumézil (1969), *passim*; TS 2.5.1.2-4; Rām. 7.86; Tiruviḷai. 1.12-13.

33. But cf. the motif of "saving" the sin as well as the sinner, as in one myth of Śiva's Brahminicide, where the personified evil following the god becomes his servant, who is purifying herself under the pretext of haunting him: Śiva 3.9.44. And cf. Śrīkṛṣṇakṣetramāhātmya 4.3-33, where Viṣṇu saves Indra's evil of Brahminicide from destruction by distributing it among various carriers, as in the myths quoted in n. 32.

34. See Falk, *passim*.

35. I am indebted to the works of Heesterman cited in the bibliography for this description of the process by which the ideals of release and renunciation were crystallized.

36. See the end of the preceding section. However, as we have just seen, *mokṣa* (in the sense of release from the world) is not a primary goal of Tamil devotional religion. The Tamil tradition has absorbed the symbolism of purity and release without succumbing to the world-negating attitude of the renouncer.

37. See above; and see II.1 after n. 81.

38. On this tension within Hinduism—which is hardly alone in this conflict—see Heesterman (1973).

39. This idea, which has been noted by George Hart and Brenda Beck, is discussed again below: IV.2 nn. 55-57.

40. RV 5.62.1. See Kuiper (1964), p. 120; Kramrisch (1962-1963), p. 272.

## I.3. The Tamil Purāṇas: Types and Prototypes

1. Commentary on IA, aphorism 1.

2. For details see Zvelebil (1973), pp. 130-31.

3. Hazra (1940), pp. 8-26. An earlier form of the Matsya may have been complete by the fourth century; *ibid.*, p. 32.

4. Kiruṣṇacāmi, p. 12; Aruṇācalam, fifteenth century, p. 124; Zvelebil (1975), p. 220. The genre persisted in the Jain tradition of Tamiḻnāṭu, for we have the well-known Śrīpurāṇam, a fifteenth-century work in *maṇi-*

*pravāḷa* based on the Sanskrit Mahāpurāṇa (ed. Venkatarajulu Reddiyar, 1946). See Zvelebil (1975), p. 213.

5. *Ibid.*, p. 220; Kiruṣṇacāmi, p. 12; Veṅkaṭacāmi, pp. 147-48.

6. See Zvelebil (1974), p. 170; Kiruṣṇacāmi, pp. 3-4.

7. Zvelebil (1974), p. 170.

8. *Ibid.*, p. 191. The text, edited by U. Ve. Cāminātaiyar, was printed in 1952 by the Tirupati *devasthānam*. At least two other Tamil versions of the Bhāgavata are known, one by Varatarāca Aiyaṅkār (Aruḷāḷa Tācar, 1543), the other by Āriyappapulavar in the eighteenth century.

9. Zvelebil (1975), p. 228.

10. *Ibid.*, p. 229. These and similar works have been studied by V. Raghavan (1960) for their importance in tracing the history of the text of the Sanskrit *mahāpurāṇas*.

11. See Hart (1976), p. 343.

12. The prototype seems to have been the Gaṇeśapurāṇa (or *upapurāṇa*) mentioned by Wilson in his introduction to Viṣṇu, pp. lv-lvi.

13. Zvelebil (1973-a), p. 131.

14. KP, *pāyiram* 56.

15. See Eggeling, 6: nos. 3671-72 (pp. 1362-65); Keith, 2: nos. 6900-6903 (pp. 1027-29); Haraprasada Shastri, 5:3864A (pp. 525-39). The text was published under the title Śrīskāndamahāpurāṇa (Celam, n.d.), with a Tamil translation by S. Aṉantarāma Tīkṣitar. The printed text may be slightly longer than the manuscripts; for example, the Upadeśakāṇḍa in the printed version has ninety-one *adhyāyas*, compared to eighty-five in the manuscripts listed by Eggeling and Haraprasada Shastri. The text refers to itself as the Śivarahasyakhaṇḍa of the Śaṅkarasaṃhitā of the Skandapurāṇa. It is not found in printed versions of the Skanda, but may indeed have belonged to the lost Southern Recension of the Skanda (see n. 34 below). I refer to it as ŚRKh. That Śivarahasyakhaṇḍa was the original title is supported by a Tamil prose summary of this work entitled Civarakaciyakaṇṭam, published by the Tiruviṭaimarutūr *devasthānam* in 1969.

16. Filliozat, introduction to Dessigane et Pattabiramin (1967), p. ii; cf. Zvelebil (1975), p. 222.

17. Space prohibits a full discussion of this point, but I may at least outline my conclusions after having studied both texts. The ŚRKh appears to be composed of three parts: a text setting out in a reasonably coherent fashion the myths of the south Indian Skanda/Murukaṉ (Kāṇḍas 1-5); the Dakṣakāṇḍa, which was attached to the latter with the help of an interpolation in 5.3.1-18 (the episode of Jayanta and Bṛhaspati); and the Upadeśakāṇḍa, which may or may not have been part of the original Dakṣakāṇḍa (and which was certainly adapted into Tamil sometime *after* Kacciyappar had created the KP on the basis of the combined Murukaṉ text and the Dakṣakāṇḍa). For a more detailed discussion, see Shulman (1976-a), pp. 22-28.

18. See IV.8 below. Another instance of Kacciyappar's reworking of his material is the transposition of the Mucukunda-Tyāgarāja myth from the end of *kāṇḍa* 5, where it concluded the original Sanskrit text, to 6.23, where it serves to introduce the myth of Vaḷḷi. On the Mucukunda myth, see Shulman (1978-a).

19. See IV.8 below.

20. Aruṇācalam, fourteenth century, pp. 73-88. For the impossible early date, see Chitty, p. 31.

21. Zvelebil (1975), p. 223.

22. *Ibid.*, n. 126. See Nilakanta Sastri (1966), p. 387.

23. The parallelism between the two works has been shown by Cetup-piḷḷai (1962).

24. Aruṇācalam, fourteenth century, p. 88; cf. Zvelebil (1975), p. 225.

25. The Tamiḻnāvalarcaritai (191)—hardly an unimpeachable source—connects him with Kāḷamekappulavar, who is easily datable in the mid-fifteenth century. Ñāṉavarotayar also refers to Murukaṉ's teaching *ĕn tai* in Vayalūr (Upatecakāṇṭam, kaṭavuḷvāḻttu 6). This has been understood as a reference to Aruṇakirinātar (fifteenth century?), but could also refer simply to Śiva (thus Cĕṅkalvarāya Piḷḷai in his comment on this verse). See Aruṇācalam, fifteenth century, p. 141.

26. His work is quoted by Vĕḷḷiyampalavāṇattampirāṉ at the start of the eighteenth century: Aruṇācalam, fifteenth century, p. 147.

27. See Zvelebil (1975), p. 225.

28. *Ibid.*, p. 223.

29. This work, like so many Tamil classics, was rescued from oblivion and edited by U. Ve. Cāminātaiyar (Madras, 1906, reprinted 1972). The consensus on the date of this author would place him in the twelfth century. See the editor's introduction, especially pp. 15-16; Catāciva Paṇṭārattār, p. 6; Irākavaiyaṅkār (1961), pp. 127-28; Aravamuthan (1932), pp. 95-97, 103-104; Zvelebil (1975), p. 220.

30. As an example of the continuing process, see Śrī tevikarumāriyammaṉpurāṇam of Tevikarumāritācar (1969).

31. The Cidambaramāhātmya, for example, may belong to the eleventh or twelfth century (Kulke, pp. 146-48); the Hāṭakeśvaramāhātmya on Tiruvārūr (the sixth *khaṇḍa* of the Skandapurāṇa) may even be pre-Coḻa, and in any case offers a very early version of the Tiruvārūr mythology. In discussion, R. Nagaswamy cited the Śvetāraṇyapurāṇa on Tiruvĕṇkāṭu as another early work of this class.

32. On the mutts—the religious "colleges" or "academies" of Tamiḻnāṭu—see Baker and Washbrook, pp. 28, 36-38, 73-76. For a biography of the founder of the Tarumapuram mutt, see the short work by M. Arunachalam.

33. See, for example, the invocations in Cetu (11) and Tiruviḷai. (22). On Caṇṭecurar see below, III.4 at n. 11.

34. Such ascriptions are generally regarded as spurious, since the printed editions of the Skanda have no trace of most of these works. However, considering how little we know of the textual history of the Skanda, we might be better advised to keep an open mind. The southern manuscripts seem to describe a Skanda quite different from the printed text; this lost southern text was, according to the manuscripts, divided into *saṃhitās* (of which six, the Sūta, Śaṅkara, Saura, Sanatkumāra, Brāhma, and Vaiṣṇava, are most frequently listed). See Eggeling, pp. 1320, 1362-64; Keith (1935), pp. 1027-29; Burnell, pp. 194-96; P.P.S. Sastri, 15:6966-67. The Sūtasaṃhitā is extant and has been printed. The northern, printed Skanda is divided into *khaṇḍas*, all of which claim to be part of an *Ekāśitisahasrī saṃhitā*; this would seem to support Hazra's conclusion (p. 163) that the *saṃhitā* division was the original and that the *khaṇḍas* of the printed text were once part of "one or other of the *saṃhitās*." Note, however, that the Viṣṇu- and Brahma- *khaṇḍas* of the printed text may bear some relation to the Vaiṣṇava- and Brāhma- *saṃhitās* of the lost southern Skanda. It is not by chance that Dessigane, Pattabiramin, and Filliozat were unable to procure the Grantha edition of the Skanda (1960, p. iii n. 2)—no such edition exists. The southern Skanda is known only from the colophons of manuscripts. At present the best hope of solving the mystery of the Skanda's earlier history would seem to lie in the recovery of this southern recension on the basis of the manuscripts available in the collections of London, Madras, and especially Tañcāvūr.

35. The terms may, of course, vary: see Kiruṣṇacāmi, pp. 30-33, for a discussion of the common format of the *talapurāṇam*.

36. See, for example, Tirukkaḻukkuṉṟam 1 (pp. 12-13).

37. Tiruviḷai., *purāṇavaralāṟu*. 1-25.

38. See below, IV.8.

39. A similar case is the preoccupation of the sages of the Talmud with Midrash and Aggadah.

40. Kiruṣṇacāmi, pp. 130-202.

41. Zvelebil (1975), p. 248 n. 68.

42. As in other south Indian shrines, a myth explains the origin of the local Brahmin priests as well as their peculiar name and characteristics: Tiruccĕntūr 10.

43. An epithet of Murukaṉ.

44. A Sanskrit purāṇa on Tiruccĕntūr does indeed exist, and has been published under the title Śrī jayantīpuramāhātmya (Triplicane, 1915). It closely resembles the Tamil text.

45. This is a reference to Tiruñāṉacampantar's contest with the Jains at Maturai: the Śaiva saint and the Jains threw palm leaves inscribed with verses into the Vaikai River; the verses of the Jains were carried away, but Tiruñāṉacampantar's verse floated safely against the current. See Tiruviḷai. 63.50-52.

46. Zvelebil (1975), p. 230.

47. See below, III.4 at n. 13.

48. Zvelebil (1973-b), pp. 239-40.

49. See van Buitenen (1971), p. 35. The same theme appears in the Siddha myths of Matsyendranātha, who learns the secret doctrine of Śiva while hiding in the waters in the form of a fish: Eliade (1958), pp. 308-309; cf. Nāradapurāṇa, pp. 28-29, and Briggs, p. 182. For another Tamil instance of this theme—the recovery of the *potanūl* from the sea—see Tiruviḷai. 57. And cf. Tukārāma's poems cast into the river: Ranade, pp. 273-74.

50. See Cāminātaiyar (1965), pp. 66-72, 93, 118-61. Cāminātaiyar was instrumental in preserving many of these compositions.

51. There follows a description of several well-known dignitaries who used to participate in the *araṅkeṟṟam*. This is followed by a notice of the verses composed by Mīṉāṭicicuntaram Piḷḷai in honor of Komalavallittāyār (Śrī, the consort of Viṣṇu, at Kumpakoṇam).

52. Cāminātaiyar (1965), pp. 130-34. I have added the information in brackets in order to clarify the narrative.

53. On the medieval poetic ideal in Tamil, see Shulman (1978).

## II.1. The Shrine as Center

1. Narayan, p. 17.

2. This is a reference to Śiva's dance in the Pine Forest: KP 6.13.30-127; below, IV.9.

3. Commentary: "because it is not the center of the world."

4. Koyil 3.68, 70-71.

5. Zvelebil (1973-a), p. 41; Eliade (1958), pp. 236-41.

6. Zvelebil (1973-a), p. 42. Thus Tiruvārūr 5.17; Nāgeśakṣetra 1.4-6; Cīkāḻi 2.31.

7. Citamparapurāṇam 7.103-104; Citamparamakātmiyam, p. 7; U. Ve. Cāminātaiyar (1949-a), p. 1.

8. Cf. for example BĀU 2.1.17-18.

9. See the discussion by Kulke, pp. 136-45.

10. Bṛhadīśvaramāhātmya 10.17-19, 14.21ff. (fol. 15a and 20a). Note again the stress on the "subtle" (*sūkṣma*) image, which maintains an invisible link to infinity.

11. *Ibid.* 15.55-58.

12. Tirunĕlveli 60.86.106.

13. Field notes, Tiruvŏṟṟiyūr, December 1, 1975.

14. Aruṇācalam 2.1-88; Skanda 1.3.1.1.23-72, 1.3.1.2.1-63; Śiva, *Dharmasaṃ.*, 10.1-25; Kathāsaritsāgara 1.1.27-32.

15. Tiruccĕṅkoṭu 1.2.2-6.

16. Mattiyārccuṉam, p. 216.

17. Cīkāḷatti 2.57-64.
18. Tiruvaiyāṟu 3.18-19.
19. Aruṇācalam 5.42, commentary; Das, p. 48.
20. Cf. Buddhist *vajrāsana*, and the folk belief that rock crystals are born from lightning: Gonda (1954), p. 82.
21. Tiruppuṉavāyil, pp. 2 and 21.
22. See BĀU 1.2; Long (1975), *passim*; below, chapter III.
23. Rosu, p. 36.
24. Skanda 6.2.1.
25. Vaṭāraṇya 11.12.
26. For the subterranean source of the shrine's water, see Tiruppaiññīli 4.7-9; Tañjāpuri 1 (fol. 1); Tirukkaṇṭiyūr 7 (p. 21); Kanyākṣetramāhātmya 6.
27. Śvetāraṇya 7.68.
28. Koyil 3.75-76, 81-84.
29. Tiruvārūr 7.19-41. Cf. Skanda 6.70.4-68, 6.71.1-44.
30. See above, I.2 nn. 12-17.
31. See O'Flaherty (1976), pp. 248-60; ŚB 1.6.2.1-4; MBh 13.40.5-12.
32. KP 4.13.392-499. See the discussion in Shulman (1979).
33. Brown (1942); Ogibenin, pp. 81-83.
34. Dowson, p. 126.
35. Skanda 6.71.32. The four goddesses are said to hold the mountain down with the point of the spear (*śūlāgra*); in return they are worshiped by Brahmins (verse 35). Cf. Tiruvārūr 7.39.
36. Tiruvārūr 7.38 plays on the two meanings: *cattika' ṇālvaroṭu caṇmukappĕrumāṉ cĕṅkail ccatti tāṉ aṉṟu tŏṭṭu ttaṉi ppĕruṅ kāval pūṇṭu*. . . .
37. Whitehead, p. 40. For the immovable spear of Skanda, see also MBh 12.314.7-17.
38. The motif is still alive in tribal myths: see Elwin (1949), pp. 11-14, 34, 40. Viṣṇu's avatar as the tortoise is linked to this theme: cf. Gonda (1954), pp. 126-28; Kramrisch (1946), 1:111. And cf. Irāmāvatāram 4.7.143 (the *diggajas* nailed in place).
39. Above, I.2 n. 34.
40. Tiruvāṉaikkā 11-12.
41. Skanda 1.2.29.86-87; Matsya 158.35-37; Saura 62.1-18; Kāñci 25.43. On the Skanda myth, see below, IV.7, after n. 103.
42. Skanda 5.1.45.61-66.
43. Matsya 158.47-48; Padma 5.41.126-39.
44. MBh 12.278.6-38; Śiva 2.5.74.10-11, 2.5.48.1-48; Vāmana 43.25-44. The swallowing of Śukra by Śiva may be derived from the myth of Śukra's swallowing of Kaca: MBh 1.71.5-58.
45. Matsya 154.506-12.
46. KP 6.24.65-81; Tiruccĕntūr 8.11.
47. MBh 13.17.107.

48. Macdonell (1897), pp. 13-14; Bosch (1960), *passim*; cf. BĀU 3.9.28.
49. Veṅkaṭācalam, pp. 4-5; Rām. 7.35.19-24.
50. Frere, pp. 250-52; Mataṉakāmarājaṉkatai 4 (pp. 50-51).
51. MBh 1.38-39; cf. Frere, p. 250.
52. Przyluski, pp. 60, 64-65.
53. Renou (1953), pp. 33-34.
54. For example, Maṇimekalai 6.105-205; Cil. 11.35-56, 91-140; 24, pāṭṭumaṭai 7. Cf. the remarks of Kandiah, pp. 104-11, on Paripāṭal and Tirumurukāṟṟuppaṭai. The sanctity of the localized shrine is, of course, implicit in the hymns of the *Tevāram* and the *Nālāyirativiyappirapantam*.
55. Hart, pp. 21-27.
56. Kramrisch (1946), p. 359; Beck (1975-c), p. 9.
57. For the importance of the *liṅga*'s self-manifestation, see Tiruvāppaṉūr 6.1-81.
58. Paḻani 19-20 (condensed).
59. MBh 3.186-87; Matsya 167.13-67; cf. Zimmer (1946), pp. 35-53; Shulman (1979).
60. Jagadisa Ayyar, p. 81.
61. Śrīraṅgamāhātmya 3.24; 7.3-75; 8.1-61; 9.1-56. Cf. Irāmāvataram 6.38.17-20.
62. Śiva 4.28.1-22; Civarāttiripurāṇam 6.55-71; Oppert, pp. 375-76 n. 115; Gupte, pp. 15-16; Wilkins, p. 43; see below, V nn. 11-39.
63. See below at n. 81; I.2 n. 12.
64. Skanda 6.13.1-27; Tiruvārūr 19.1-18.
65. Skanda 3.1.44.82-117, 3.1.45.1-90, 3.1.46.1-79; Cetu 40 (Irāmaṉ aruccaṉai ccarukkam). 77-243 (on Irāmeccuram/Rāmeśvaram).
66. The *liṅga* in the Ekāmbareśvara shrine at Kāñci is usually referred to as the *pṛthivīliṅga* and belongs in the set of five *liṅgas* representing each of the five elements (see below, II.3 n. 12). However, texts of the shrine's major myth often refer to the *liṅga* as *saikata*, "made of sand" (e.g., Kāmākṣīvilāsa 8.30 and 33). According to the priests of the shrine, both terms refer to the sandy soil in which the mango tree there is rooted.
67. See below, II.2 n. 33.
68. We will pursue this theme in Chapter IV.
69. Gonda (1966), pp. 31-32.
70. Kāñci 62.117-21.
71. Cāyāvaṉam 2.1-60, 3.1-9, 4.1-31, 5.1-77, 7.1-39. See also Tiruccāykkāṭu talavaralāṟu, p. 32.
72. Rām. 7.16.7-46.
73. This festival recalls the *intiraviḻavu* at the nearby Kāvirippūmpaṭṭiṉam described in Cil. 5.
74. Perhaps the most famous example is from the sun temple at Konarak, but there are also fine representatives of the type at Citamparam (the *nṛttasabhā*), Tārācuram, and Tirupuvaṉam.

75. Thurston (1909), 6:25-28.

76. Told to me by R. N. Natarajarathina Deekshitar of Citamparam on January 5, 1976.

77. See Gayāmāhātmya 2.1-76; Kālikā 64.1-48. Here too belong the myths of Śiva's dance with the corpse of Satī (to stop the dance Viṣṇu cuts off the limbs of the dead goddess, and they fall to earth to become shrines) and Kālī's dance on the corpse of Śiva (Bṛhaddharma 1.23.6-8).

78. For a Śaiva Siddhāntin exegesis of the motif of the arrested chariot, see Nallaswami Pillai (1913), pp. 146-48.

79. Meghadūta 36; see Dorai Rangaswamy, 1:343-51. The frequent *Tevāram* references to this myth stress Devī's alarm, e.g., Cuntarar 17.10.

80. Vāmana, saromāhātmya, 23.16-34.

81. Told to me by Gurukkaḷ Balasubrahmanian, Tiruccāykkāṭu, on January 18, 1976.

82. See I.2 nn. 12-17, and the myth from Śrīraṅkam cited above n. 61 (where men are preferred to demons).

83. Gupte, p. 13.

84. PP 3.4.23-28; Tiruppaṉantāḷ 18.1-48.

85. See, for example, the carving of this scene in the *nāyaṉmār* series at Tārācuram.

86. See above, I.2 nn. 12-14, 25-26.

87. Jagadisa Ayyar, p. 234. The drop of *amṛta* falling from heaven recalls the single feather released by Garuḍa after stealing the *amṛta* and being struck by Indra: MBh 1.29.17-21; Cūtavaṉam 4.2-78.

## II.2. Surviving the Flood

1. Iṟaiyaṉār akappŏruḷ, aphorism 1, commentary. See Zvelebil (1973).

2. The commentators always define the southern boundary as the Kumari *river*; see, for example, the ancient commentary on Puṟam 6.1-2; 17.1; 67.6. Cf. Thiagarajah, pp. 8-9, 12-13, 81-82; S. B. Bharati, *passim*. This tradition conflicts with Iḷaṅko's description of the southern border as *tŏṭiyoḷ pauvam*, "the sea of the maiden" (*Cil.* 8.1-2); hence Aṭiyārkkunallār's lengthy gloss, which explains that the great flood that devastated the old Pāṇṭiya land happened long before Iḷanko's time, so that it was natural for the poet to describe the present, postdiluvian border. This ingenious explanation conveniently fits all references to the sea as the southern border, and leaves intact the story of the old capitals swallowed by the flood.

3. Aṭiyārkkunallār's description of the forty-nine lost provinces (*nāṭu*) of the old Pāṇṭiya land shows the weak points of the tradition. The provinces are listed in groups of seven, which appear to reflect a formalization akin to the conventional division of the Tamil land in *akam* poetry: there were seven coconut provinces, seven Maturai provinces, two groups of seven

*pālai* provinces, seven hill provinces, seven *kārai* provinces of the east, and seven *kuṟumpaṉai* provinces. (The last group appears in Perāciriyar's commentary to Tŏl.Pŏruḷ. 649 [p. 482] as "palmyra province.") With the exception of the "Maturai provinces," the only names that look like authentic place names in Aṭiyār.'s description of the lost homeland follow immediately on the above list: "Kumari, Kŏllam, and many other mountain provinces, forests, rivers, and towns." It is noteworthy that the first of these names is shared by the *historical* southern boundary of the Tamil land, while Kŏllam exists today as Quilon. That the present-day Kŏllam was not unrelated to the "lost" Kŏllam was recognized by the commentators: see Dorai Rangaswamy, 1:131. Note also that the number of provinces in Aṭiyār.'s list—forty-nine—is a formulaic number that appears again in the Caṅkam story: forty-eight of the fifty-one characters that make up the body of Sarasvatī became the poets of the Caṅkam; their number was completed when they were joined by Śiva, who inheres in the world as the vowel *a* inheres in syllables (Tiruviḷai. 51.1-39). All this casts doubt on the account of Aṭiyār.

4. See Joseph, pp. 3-4.

5. Maṇimekalai 24.27-74, 25.178-200.

6. On the question of a historical Caṅkam, see Marr (1958), pp. 2-15; Zvelebil (1973-b), pp. 45-49; Hart (1975), pp. 9-10; Nilakanta Sastri (1966), pp. 115-16.

7. ŚB 1.8.1-10.

8. See Suryakanta Shastri, *passim*; Regnaud, pp. 59-151; Oppert, pp. 311-28. In Iran the flood theme and the survival of man attaches to Yima—whose Indian counterpart is in this case not Yama but his half-brother Manu! Dumézil is oddly silent on this point, surely relevant to the comparison of Yima and Yama: see Dumézil (1968-1973), 2:246-49; *idem* (1965), *passim*.

9. O'Flaherty (1975), pp. 179-81; and cf. RV 7.88.3; Kuiper (1970), p. 104.

10. Matsya 1.11-12.

11. Bhāgavata 8.24.13.

12. Elwin (1949), pp. 20-26, 30-32, 37, 41, 46-48.

13. See Defourny.

14. See Chapter III.

15. MBh 3.185.29-30, 34.

16. Matsya 2.10-12.

17. Cīkāḻi 2.15-41. See Figure I.

18. See above, section 1 after n. 4.

19. This idea is said to be symbolized by the drum (*ḍamaru*) carried by Naṭarāja-Śiva in his upper right hand. See Zimmer (1946), p. 152.

20. KP 6.13.364-70.

21. Kāñci 58.37; cf. Tiruviḷai. 13.4.

22. Cil. 15.6; Tirukkūvam 2.53.
23. Paḻani 13.48; cf. Tiruccĕṅkoṭu 1.1.2.
24. Tiruvŏṟṟiyūr 2.37.
25. Tiruviḷai. 56.27.
26. Jagadisa Ayyar, p. 75. Elsewhere Nandin has this function: Tiruppĕṇṇākaṭa varalāṟu, p. 21.
27. Dorai Rangaswamy, 1:6; cf. Cuntarar, Tev. 96.
28. Tiruccĕṅkoṭu 1.2.6.
29. Tiruvāñciyakṣettirapurāṇam 14 (p. 55).
30. Vedāraṇyamāhātmya 2.65-67.
31. Tiruttĕṅkūr 2.1-13.
32. Bereshit Rabbah 33.6.
33. PP 4.5.62-70; Kāñci 63.364-401. See Shulman, 1979.
34. Skanda 1.3.1.4.21-36.
35. Cil. 21.6-10.
36. Ramachandra Dikshitar (1939), p. 251 n. 4.
37. PP 4.5.67. For the motif of *bhakti* melting stone, see Tiruvaiyāṟu 3.18-19.
38. Kāmākṣīvilāsa 8.55-70. See below, IV. 3 at n. 40.
39. Kanyākṣetramāhātmya 6. Cf. Cĕvvanti 4.1-18.
40. Harivaṃśa 2.133.12-68. Cf. Gonda (1954), p. 155. In this, as in other ways, Kṛṣṇa is strongly reminiscent of Skanda/Murukaṉ: see below, IV. 8 at n. 72.
41. Harivaṃśa 2.59.31-38; cf. Viṣṇu 5.23.13. We will return to the motif of the city reclaimed from the sea. On Dvārakā as the gate to the nether world, cf. Kuiper (1964), p. 113.
42. MBh 16.8.40-41.
43. Viṣṇu 5.38.8-10.
44. Bhāgavata 11.31.23-24.
45. Wilson (1972), p. 482 n. 4.
46. See Vyāsa's speech to Arjuna in the sequel to the myth: MBh 16.9.25-36. And cf. O'Flaherty (1976), pp. 260-71.
47. Maṇimekalai 24.27-74, 25.178-200.
48. Ions (1970), pp. 77-83.
49. Chambers, pp. 13-15. See summary and discussion in O'Flaherty (1976), pp. 270-71.
50. O'Flaherty (1973), pp. 87-89. At Mahābalipuram the king falls in love with an *apsaras*, who smuggles him into heaven; upon returning to earth, he constructs his city in imitation of the splendors of heaven; this excites Indra's jealousy, and leads to the city's destruction.
51. Nacciṉārkkiṉiyar on Pĕrumpāṇāṟṟuppaṭai 30-37.
52. Oppert, pp. 250-52; cf. Tiruvŏṟṟiyūr 12.2. One wonders if the famous relief of "Arjuna's penance" at Mahābalipuram, with the serpent figures issuing from its central crevice, is not in part connected to this story

of dynastic origins (*tŏṇṭai* presumably giving us the Sanskrit dynastic title "Pallava").

53. MBh 1.16. Recall the birth of Aphrodite from the sea: Graves (1955), 1:49.

54. Tiruvŏṟṟiyūr 2.1-36. Cf. Bhāgavata 3.8.10-33.

55. This is also the view of Śaiva Siddhānta: see *ciṟṟurai* of Civañāṉacuvāmikaḷ on CÑP, cū. 1, 1 (pp. 8-10).

56. Kumpakoṇam kṣettirapurāṇam, pp. 35-38; cf. Kumpakoṇam makāmakam, pp. 3-4; Kumpakoṇappurāṇam, verse 106; Kumbhaghoṇamāhātmya 1.70-77; Tirukkuṭantai 7-8.

57. KB 6.1-2.

58. AB 3.33. Cf. Matsya 158.35-38.

59. Saura 59.54-55.

60. See Kosambi (1962), pp. 72-74. For other examples of the motif, see Meyer (1930), 1:262-63. For a *tīrtha* formed from the water in Brahmā's pot, see Tiruvaiyāṟu 7.1.

61. Pal, p. 48.

62. Bṛhaddevatā 5.148-53.

63. Jagadisa Ayyar, p. 103.

64. KP 2.23.17-28, 2.27.9-66, 2.29.1-27. For other versions of the descent of the Kāviri, see Tulākāverimāṉmiyam 5-6; Kāverippurāṇam 4.1-49; Tiruvaiyāṟu 4.1-25; Kāveri uṟpattiyum kalyāṇa vaipavamum aṭaṅkiya carittiram, *passim*; Srinivas (1952), pp. 244-45; Rice, pp. 153-61; below, IV.8.

65. Rām. 1.42-44.

66. MBh 3.102.16-23, 3.103.1-29. The story of Jahnu appears in verses added by some mss. after Rām. 1.42.24 of the Baroda edition.

67. KP 2.27.37. See above, n. 33.

68. Maṇimekalai, *patikam* 1-31.

69. MBh 3.214.12; Skanda 1.2.29.106; Śiva, *Dharmasaṃ.*, 11.30.

70. MBh 13.84.52-54; Rām. 1.36.12-17; Vāyu 72.28-31; Skanda 1.2.29.88; Brahmāṇḍa 2.3.10.30-34; Viṣṇudharmottara 1.228.8.

71. KP 1.11.89-91; Kāñci 25.44; cf. Matsya 158.28.

72. Skanda 1.2.29.104-106; 6.70.65; Vāyu 72.32-33.

73. Cf. ŚB 6.3.1.26 and 31; MBh 5.16.11.

74. KP 2.27.29.

75. Fabricius, s.v. *pŏṉ*.

76. MBh 13.84.68; Rām. 1.36.18; Vāmana 31.9-10; Liṅga 1.20.80-82.

77. See note 69.

78. Śiva 2.4.2.39; MBh 9.43.14; Skanda 1.1.27.63; Saura 62.19; Viṣṇudharmottara 1.228.9.

79. Matsya 158.28-29; Padma 5.41.118-42; MBh 9.43.18; Vāmana 31.15-19; Skanda 3.3.29.23.

80. Brahma 128.24-27.

81. KP 1.13.23 and 31; cf. Raghuvaṃśa 2.36; PP 6.1.68.

82. Rām. 1.36.21-22, and the line added by many mss. after v. 22; MBh 13.84.70.

83. KP 2.29.12.

84. See III.2 below, and O'Flaherty (1973), pp. 277-78.

85. *Ibid.*, p. 277.

86. See, for example, MBh 1.57.39-46; Manasākāvya of Manakar, cited Maity, p. 120. For another instance of the crow upsetting a pot (which is in this case filled with milk, another multiform of seed), see Tiruvāṭpokki 12.1-17.

87. Brahma 128.16-23; Matsya 158.24-26.

88. Skanda 1.2.29.83.

89. Vāmana 28.41.

90. Brahma 38.1-5.

91. MBh 3.213-14; Skanda 1.2.29.104.

92. Brahmavaivarta 3.8.17-43, 83-89, 3.9.1-37.

93. Tiruviḷai. 13, 18-19; Tiruvāl. 21, 12.

94. Tiruviḷai. 49; Tiruvāl. 47.

95. Tiruviḷai. 16; Tiruvāl. 64.

96. Tiruviḷai. 9; Tiruvāl. 8.

97. Tiruviḷai. 56; Tiruvāl. 20.

98. Tiruviḷai. 61; Tiruvāl. 30.

99. Tiruviḷai. 14, 15, and 31; Tiruvāl. 44, 61, 40.

100. Tiruvāl. 12.

101. Kalittŏkai 92.65; Cil. 21.39; Paripāṭal, fragment 1.3 and fragment 7.4.

102. Tiruvāl., tirunakaraccir̲appu 12-15. On the name "Nān̲māṭak-kūṭal" for Maturai, see Gros (1968), pp. xxvii-xxviii; and cf. Campantar, Tev. 7.5 and commentary. "Kūṭal," "junction," may well be the original title.

103. Śiva 2.2.20.21-24.

104. Tiruviḷai. 14.41; Tiruvāl. 44.36-37; Cil. 11.26-29. The same motif of imprisoning the clouds is used in the battle between Śūrapadma and Vīrabāhu in KP 4.6.52-67; cf. Taylor (1862), p. 111, and note the connection between the Maturai flood myths and the Murukan̲ cycle.

105. Viṣṇu 5.11.1-25.

106. Tiruviḷai. 18.1-9, 19.1-26.

107. For the myth of churning the ocean, see MBh 1.15-17; Rām. 1.45; Long (1975). For another link with the myth of churning in the Maturai tradition, see Tiruviḷai. 28.1-23; below, III.3 at n. 106.

108. For example, the case of Appar: PP 5.1.49-71.

109. Tiruvāl. 21.1-9.

110. Aravamuthan (1932), pp. 291-92.

111. See the note by Cāminātaiyar on Tiruvāl. 21.9; the possibility that the Ganges is actually intended can be ruled out.

112. Tiruviḷai. 13.1-20; cf. Cuntarapāṇṭiyam 3.6.11-12. Compare Indra's theft of the sacrificial horse of Sagara (sometimes by a wave of the ocean) in the myth of the descent of the Ganges and the filling of the sea: MBh 3.104-108; O'Flaherty (1971), pp. 19-20.

113. MBh 3.102.16-23, 3.103.1-28.

114. *Ibid*. 3.116.29; 14.29.1-7.

115. *Ibid*. 3.214.31.

116. *Ibid*. 1.94.23-24.

117. Nilakanta Sastri (1966), pp. 73-74; Padmanabha Menon, 1:17-20; Raghuvaṃśa 4.53, 58; Keraḷateca varalāṟu, pp. 33, 41; Kaṉṉiyākumari 18.66-75; PP 2.6.1; Skanda 6.68.6-16; for the version of the Keralotpatti, see Thiagarajah, pp. 120-21.

118. MBh 12.49.53-60; on Śūrpāraka see Pargiter's note on Mārkaṇḍeya 5.49 (translation, p. 338); Kuiper (1964), p. 113. Elsewhere Paraśurāma is said to have retreated to Mount Mahendra. Cf. MBh 3.117.14; Wilson, p. 323 n. 21.

119. Nilakanta Sastri (1966), p. 74; Saletore, pp. 9-38. In Assam, Paraśurāma creates not land but a flood by cutting a channel for the Brahmaputrā River: Kālikā 84-86.

120. See above at nn. 40 and 41.

121. Skanda 3.1.2.54-96; Cetu 5.27-41.

122. See Tiruviḷai. 11.19, which plays on this identification.

123. Cil. 24, pāṭṭumaṭai 6. Cf. Tirumurukāṟṟuppaṭai 45-46, 59-61; Kalittŏkai 104.13-14. The battle with the sea and the casting of the spear against Krauñca combine in a myth about the worship of the spear: Iḷaiyaṉār velūrppurāṇam 6.2-8.

124. See Shulman (1979).

125. Patiṟṟuppattu, fifth decade, 46.11-13; cf. 42.21-23; 48.3-4; Akam. 127.3-5; 347.3-5; 212.15-20.

126. Marr (1958), p. 308.

127. Aravamuthan (1931), pp. 203-205.

128. *Ibid*., pp. 209-14; (1932), pp. 97-103.

129. Hālāsyamāhātmya 17.46-47.

130. Kalittŏkai 104.1-4.

131. Cil. 11.17-22.

132. Aṭiyār. on Cil. 11.17-22.

133. For example, Campantar, Tev., 1.7.2; cf. Zvelebil (1973-b), p. 45 n. 1.

134. This seems to have been recognized by Filliozat, Dessigane, and Pattabiramin in their introduction to the Tiruviḷai. (1960), p. xi. They note that the flood at Maturai was the *pralaya*, not a "cataclysme local." Was the

expansion of the story assisted by the existence of the name "Southern Maturai" (*tĕṉmaturai*, as in Tiruvāl., kaṭavuḷ vāḻttu 14; or *dakṣiṇā mathurā*, as in Bhāgavata 10.79.15), presumably to distinguish the present city of Maturai from the northern town of Mathurā? Cf. *vaṭamaturai* for Mathurā: Tiruppāvai 5.1.

135. See, for example, Kāñci 58.37.

136. See Ramachandra Dikshitar (1939), p. 22; Kaliṅkattupparaṇi 197; Aravamuthan (1925), pp. 1-14, 60-76; Venkata Ramanayya (1929), *passim*. In Cil. 21.10-15, the daughter of Karikālvaḷavaṉ is said to have followed the flood that carried away her husband until the sea returned him to her.

137. Tiruvāṇaikkā 24.1-23.

138. MBh 3.102.2-13; KP 2.25.1-13.

139. See Viruttācalam 4.13-21; Rice, p. 150.

140. Tiruviḷai. 61.1-57; Tiruvātavūraṭikaḷ purāṇam 4.1-95; cf. Alliyaracāṇimālai, pp. 16-21.

## II.3. The Specialization of the Divine

1. RV 4.30.20; cf. 2.19.6; 4.26.3; 6.26.5; 6.31.4; 9.61.1-2.

2. MBh 13.31.26-28.

3. *Ibid.* 12.97.20.

4. Brahmāṇḍa 2.3.67.28-64; Vāyu 2.30.25-55; Harivaṃśa 1.29.29-68.

5. Brahmāṇḍa 2.3.67.63-64; Harivaṃśa 1.29.67-68.

6. Skanda 4.1.39, 43-46; 4.2.52-58, *passim*; Kennedy, pp. 423-31; Skanda 5.1.2.74.1-65.

7. Vināyaka 81.109-67.

8. Skanda 4.1.44.22-24.

9. *Ibid.* 4.1.44.27.

10. See ŚB 6.1.3.8-18; Gonda (1970), pp. 35-42; Nallaswami Pillai (1911), pp. 93-103, 228-29.

11. Text of the verse in Tirukkaṇṭiyūr, p. x, and in Kandiah, who devotes a critical discussion to the *vīraṭṭāṉam* in the Tevāram: pp. 277-92. Cf. Cuntarar, Tev. 38.1-10; other references in Dorai Rangaswamy, 1:180-81.

12. Hemingway (1907), p. 323; Pate, p. 414. For the five elements, see Basham, pp. 498-99; Campantar, Tev. 11.4; Ait. Ār. 2.3.1-2.

13. Eliot, 2:208; Walker, 2:350.

14. For example, the Saundaryalaharī, Subrahmaṇyabhujaṅga, etc.

15. See Cucīntiram 11; Mahalingam (1949), p. 47; Jagadisa Ayyar, p. 112.

16. Hart (1975), pp. 130-33. In Hart's view, the power inhering in sacred objects or places was considered to be polluting and could be controlled only by specialized low groups of people; the attempt by Brahmins and other groups to dissociate themselves from this contaminating, immanent power led to the insistence on the purity of deities they worshiped.

Note that in this respect—the emphasis on purity—there is a convergence with the Upaniṣadic ideal of freedom from the world of relations, power, and the cycles of death and rebirth. See above, I.1.

17. See Chapter III; Shulman (1978). On the indigenous Tamil deities as frightful beings linked to concentrations of dangerous power, see Hart (1975), pp. 21-27.

18. The inherent ambivalence of the shrine can also be described in terms derived from the sacrificial ritual. I will argue in Chapter III that the shrine—like the "renouncer" who separates himself from the world and thus achieves both total purity and the fullness of power, that is, the power to create the universe anew—is homologous to the excluded remnant of the sacrifice. The shrine is the separate, independent microcosm, that part of creation that is "left over," the sole survivor of the deluge, removed from all other categories—hence inevitably impure, like remnants generally in India and elsewhere. See the discussion by Mary Douglas of the impurity that attaches to all that stands outside the society's classificatory system: Douglas, pp. 48-53. Nevertheless, by the logic of independence, the shrine is also totally free from evil. Hence the double nature of this symbol: the shrine is impure as the remainder carrying the whole potential for creation, but pure as a universe set apart from the existing realm of the created, with all its evils.

19. Tiruvŏṟṟiyūr 2.25.

20. Śiva 2.4.19.4-55, 2.4.20.1-37.

21. Tāṇḍya 25.13.3.

22. Gopinatha Rao (1914) 1:61-62; Wilkins, p. 341; Leach (1962).

23. Cf. Tiruvaruṭpayaṉ 1.5.

24. Paḻani 13.27-73. Note that although the spelling Paḻaṉi does occur, the correct form is Paḻani, as the etymology suggested by the myth explains.

25. In this respect, Tamil Śaivism differs from the more staid Śrīvaiṣṇava tradition. See Hart (1975), pp. 71-72, where Kampaṉ's Irāmāvatāram is rightly excluded from this generalization.

26. Śiva 2.4.20.31-35.

27. See below, IV.6; Kulke, pp. 94-154; Sivaramamurti (1974), *passim*.

28. Tirukkaḻukkuṉṟam 17 (pp. 126-35); cf. Tiruviḷai. 6.1-28; Kāñci 63.151-82.

29. Sivaramamurti (1955), pp. 28-29.

30. The dances are, in addition to the *ānandatāṇḍava* at Citamparam: the *sandhyātāṇḍava* in the Rajatasabhā at Maturai; the *gaurītāṇḍava* in the Citsabhā at Tirupputtūr; the *tripuratāṇḍava* in the Citrasabhā at Tirukkuṟṟālam; the *kālikātāṇḍava* (or *ūrdhvatāṇḍava*) in the Ratnasabhā at Tiruvālaṅkāṭu; and the *munitāṇḍava* in the Tāmrasabhā at Tirunĕlveli. The seventh dance, the *saṃhāratāṇḍava* or Dance of Destruction, is said to take place in the whole universe, not only in the Tamil land. See Dorai Rangaswamy, 1:441-42,

citing Tirupputtūrppurāṇam; and cf. Tiruvŏṟṟiyūr kṣettirattiṉ makimaiyum mahāṉkaḷiṉ stutiyum, p. 12.

31. Tiruccir̲r̲ampalam is the name of the "small hall" in Citamparam (the Citsabhā) where Śiva dances. See Sivaramamurti (1974), p. 383.

32. Pirutiviyampalam is a cult site in Kāñcipuram.

33. Cāminātaiyar (1940), pp. 44-46; Ci. Aruṇaivaṭivelu, introduction to Kāñcippurāṇam, p. 34.

34. See Tiruvaruṭpayaṉ 1.1; Shivapadasundaram, pp. 55-59.

35. *Ibid.*, p. 58. Compare the Śrīvaiṣṇava attempt to deal with this problem through the concept of the *arcāvatāra*: Hardy, *passim*.

36. PP 7.4.41-44.

37. Tiruviḷai. 56.11-20; Alliyaracāṇimālai, pp. 22-23.

38. Varadachari, pp. 30-31; Hardy, p. 144.

39. See, for example, Akam 167; Hart (1975), p. 137.

40. Pfaffenberger, p. 24.

## III.1. Introduction

1. BĀU 1.2.

2. AB 7.13-15 (the story of Śunaḥśepa). The same motif—the gift of the son who must be sacrificed—occurs in the Tamil myths of Mārkaṇḍeya and Yama (Tirukkaṭavūrpurāṇam 9-14; Tirukkaṭavūrkṣettirapurāṇam 3-5), and Ciṟuttŏṇṭar (PP 7.3); in these myths, however, the sacrifice is ultimately reversed and eliminated, just as Śunaḥśepa escapes death by invoking various deities. See the discussion below, III.2 after n. 38.

3. ŚB 1.7.3.1-7; cf. TS 3.1.9; AB 3.33-34.

4. See Heesterman (1957), p. 19; Gonda (1954), p. 152; Kramrisch (1946), 1:44-45; Long (1975).

5. See ŚB 1.7.4.1-3; Heesterman (1962), pp. 27-28.

6. See Kramrisch (1946), 1:75-76 (citing Īśānaśivagurudevapaddhati); Beck (1975-c); Marr (1972), pp. 71-76; O'Flaherty (1976), pp. 275-76.

7. See Keith (1925), 2:354-56.

8. The Ciṉṉatampikatai, for example, tells of the sacrifice of an unmarried youth so that treasure can be excavated from the earth: see Vanamalai (1968), p. 192. The sage Heraṇḍa dies to bring the Kāviri River to the earth's surface; his sacrifice creates the shrine of Tiruvalañcuḻi: Tiruvalañcuḻikoyilvaralāṟu, summarized by Mahalingam (1972), p. 257. A sacrifice often accompanies the building of walls and ramparts: Karikālaṉ destroys the third eye of Trilocana Pallava, who failed to come help build embankments for the Kāviri. See Kaliṅkattupparaṇi 197, and the discussion by Venkata Ramanayya (1929), *passim*; Aravamuthan (1925). And see above, II.1 at n. 75.

9. Singaravelu, p. 118.

10. Hart (1975), pp. 31-40.

11. *Ibid.*, p. 40.

12. See, for example, Kuṟ. 362 (Murukaṉ); Puṟam 50 (the drum); Akam 35 (the *naṭukal*). On the *naṭukal*, see Hart (1975), pp. 25-26; Kailasapathy, pp. 235-37.

13. Elmore, pp. 135-36; Whitehead, pp. 49, 85, 87-88, 94-100. On the role of blood in south Indian rituals, see also Beck (1969), pp. 558-59, 563.

14. See Manusmṛti 5.123, 135.

15. On the intriguing connections between Brahmins and outcastes, see Hart (1975), p. 123 (and pp. 119-33 for the role of Paṟaiyaṉs and others in controlling sacred power); Dumont (1966), pp. 92-98; Pfaffenberger, pp. 20-23. For the Brahmin role in the Vedic sacrifice, see Heesterman (1964).

16. Heesterman has analyzed this development in detail: (1964); (1967).

## III.2. Milk, Blood, and Seed

1. Pillay, p. 91 n. 8. A similar origin myth from a nearby shrine is Tirunělveli 60.1-145.

2. Frere, pp. 262-63; cf. Cil. 17-18.

3. Elwin (1949), p. 40.

4. Srinivas (1942), pp. 92-93.

5. Kurup, p. 78.

6. JB 1.44; cf. ŚB 11.6.1.7, 12-13.

7. Fowler, *passim*; cf. ŚB 12.7.3.1-4.

8. Beck (1969), *passim*. Compare the symbolism of red and white in the Ndembu rituals of sacrifice: Turner (1977), pp. 192-201.

9. Personal communication from George Hart; Beck (1969), pp. 561-62.

10. Whitehead, pp. 124-25.

11. Liṅga 1.106.13-23. See also Jātaka 513.

12. Field notes, December 29, 1975.

13. Beck (1969), pp. 564-65.

14. Tiruvāṉmiyūr 9 (pp. 29-33).

15. Tiruvāṭāṉai 9.3-39, 10.1-26.

16. MBh 1.165.31-40; Rām. 1.53.17-23. 1.54.1-4.

17. See below, IV.4. On breast symbolism in early Tamil literature, see Hart (1975), pp. 98-107.

18. Cil. 21.43.

19. Das, p. 164.

20. This is the name used by the Skandapurāṇa in its version of the myth. The meaning of the name is perhaps relevant to the symbolism of milk and seed: see below, after n. 38; above, II.2 after n. 56.

21. Tiruvārūr 21.4-51; Skanda 6.49-51.

22. The cow's argument with the tiger is an instance of the motif of "promising to return"—see Tawney and Penzer, 7:203. Cf. the variant from Tirukkuṟuṅkuṭi in Martin, p. 370.

23. Śrīcurapistalapurāṇam 1.43-104. Cf. Bhojarājīyamu of Anantāmatya, summarized by Aiyer (1975), pp. 139-48.

24. Padma 5.18.252-454.

25. Skanda 6.10.1-24; Tiruvārūr 18.1-60.

26. This correspondence was stated explicitly in an oral version of this myth related to me by Śrī Mu. Irattiṉa Tecikaṉ of Tiruvārūr.

27. Compare the case of Pāṇḍu, cursed by a deer (sage) slain by Pāṇḍu while it was mating in the forest: MBh 1.109.5-31.

28. Maturaimāṉmiyam of Citamparacuvāmi, p. 71 (a 65th *tiruviḷaiyāṭal*). This myth is a multiform of the well-known myth from Maturai in which Śiva himself becomes a sow to nurse twelve motherless pigs: Tiruviḷai. 45.1-63. Cf. Śiva as a mother (Tāyumāṉavar) at Tiruccirāppaḷḷi: Cĕvvanti 10.1-47; below, IV.9.

29. Manasāvijaya of Vipradāsa, cited by Maity, pp. 81-82.

30. Tirupperūr 8.1-85, 9.1-112.

31. Elwin (1939), p. 326.

32. See n. 4 above; Beck (1969), pp. 564-65.

33. On this title, see Shulman (1978-a).

34. PP 1.3.1-50. This story is depicted in stone in a small courtyard to the northeast of the Tiruvārūr temple complex; here the cow is shown standing over her fallen calf and the chariot of the king is being driven over his son. See Figure II.

35. The Kovalaṉkatai (pp. 3-4) makes the events of the Cil.—specifically the death of the hero Kovalaṉ—proceed from a similar act of aggression against a calf.

36. Viṣṇu 4.1.14; Śiva 5.36.53-60.

37. See Kaliṅkattupparaṇi 187. The story was known much earlier in Tamil: Cil. 20.53-56. The Mahāvaṃsa (21.13-18) seems to have borrowed the story from the Tamil tradition: see Ramachandra Dikshitar (1933-1934), p. 218.

38. Raghuvaṃśa 1.12-95, 2.1-67; cf. Kaliṅkattupparaṇi 193 with commentary.

39. Compare the case of Ciṟuttŏṇṭar, who offers Śiva his son, but is then given the child once more: PP 7.3.

40. MBh 1.16.32-37; Rām. 1.44.17-24; Appendix I, no. 8; Viṣṇu 1.13.87-93; Bhāgavata. 4.18.12-13. On the important transformation of milk into liquor or mead, see n. 75 below.

41. MBh 13.76.21-33. For milk as *amṛta*, see also KP 1.11.117; Śrīcurapistalapurāṇam 1.72.

42. AV 9.4.4 (Whitney's translation); see also verse 7.

43. ŚB 1.8.1.7.

44. MBh 13.85.11.

45. *Ibid*. 13.76.31.

46. Tiruviḷai. 11.15. One of the five *tīrthas* at Tiruvaiyāṟu is formed

from *amṛta* diffused by the rays of the moon, another from the milk of Pārvatī's breasts: see Tiruvaiyāṟu, commentary to kaṭavuḷvāḻttu 16.

47. Saundaryalaharī 75.

48. PP 6.1.66-68.

49. Saundaryalaharī 72-73.

50. Das, p. 164. For milk identified with seed in popular symbolism, see Carstairs, pp. 84, 166-67; Spratt, pp. 78, 176, 197, 261. For the motif of the cream-filled tank, see Frere, pp. 5-6.

51. See above, n. 14.

52. Tirukkūvappurāṇavacaṉam, introduction, p. 2. On rain as seed, see O'Flaherty (1973), pp. 42-52 and examples listed under motif 15c in the index. Of the many south Indian examples of this equation, we may cite the myth of Śukra and the goddess: when Śukra ("seed") stays with the goddess more than six months, drought ensues. Thurston (1909), 6:85. Rain is also *amṛta*, as in the famous *kṛti* of Muttusvāmidīkṣitar beginning *ānandāmṛtakarṣiṇī* (in *amṛtavarṣiṇī-rāga*), sung according to the tradition in order to produce rain during a drought. See Sambamoorthy, p. 135. At Tirukkūvam rain is associated with white, but rain may also be linked with green, the color of fertility. See Beck (1969), pp. 558 and 561.

53. Vāmana 30.24-26; Tevīparākkiramam, pp. 191-92.

54. Matsya 179.2-40.

55. Tirukkūvam 7.231.

56. Vāmana 2.43-48.

57. KSS 1.2.10.

58. Temple, p. 419. The role of blood as sacred food occurs in the story of Paraśurāma, who supports the *pitṛs* with oblations of blood: MBh 3.81.22-32.

59. Elwin (1949), p. 420.

60. *Ibid.*, p. 133; see also p. 142.

61. Elmore, pp. 86-87.

62. See Hart (1975), pp. 93-96 and references cited there. The impurity is greatest during the *puṉiṟu* period after childbirth. See Puṟam 68, where the Kāviri is compared to a breast overflowing with milk after *puṉiṟu* (and cf. the equation of the Kāviri with seed, a symbolic coordinate of milk: above, II.2 after n. 64).

63. See Akam 26.

64. Yalman, p. 340; Beck (1969), pp. 558-59, 563-65; O'Flaherty (1976), pp. 336-46. Milk becomes poison during the churning of the ocean, and in the myth of Pūtanā, who "nurses" Kṛṣṇa with breasts smeared with poison (Bhāgavata 10.6.1-44).

65. Keith (1925), 1:273; Heesterman (1957), p. 97.

66. Bhāgavata 6.13.10-12.

67. MBh 9.41.11-36; Skanda 6.172-73. On pollution from blood in the Tamil tradition, see n. 76 below.

68. Carstairs, p. 83.

69. O'Flaherty (1973), p. 271.

70. Zimmer (1951), p. 209.

71. O'Flaherty (1976), p. 340; Eliade (1958), p. 239; Eliade (1971).

72. MBh 3.81.97-115; 9.37.34-50; Padma 5.18.132-42; KSS 1.5.132-39.

73. Vasudeva Agrawala, p. 72.

74. O'Flaherty (1973), pp. 245-46.

75. The sap of plants is equated with *madhu*—mead, liquor, another form of seed—in Tirupporūr, pp. 76-77, 81-82.

76. See I.2 above. Note that the blood of menses—and especially its first appearance at the onset of puberty—brings about a state of pollution requiring seclusion (*tīṭṭu*), yet this blood is a highly sacred indicator of future fertility: see Subramaniam, pp. 50-51 n. 6, and Hart (1975), pp. 93-94.

77. Tiruppātirippuliyūr 13.1-66; cf. Tiruvārūr 23.4-14.

78. Tiruppātirippuliyūr 14.1-10.

79. One wonders if this myth, and the related story from Velūr (Velaimānakarcaritai, p. 26) are connected with the demon Muyalakaṉ (< *muyal*, "hare"), upon whose back Śiva performs the cosmic dance.

80. Koyil 2.24-25; cf. Tiruvārūr 103.1-2. The story is based on MBh 13.14.75-84, 189-95; cf. Liṅga 107.1-64.

81. Koyil 2.1-25. Kulke, pp. 34-36, regards the appearance of Upamanyu at Citamparam as the link between a local hagiography and the "great tradition," which knows a Vyāghrapāda as the father of Upamanyu. I prefer to regard the two figures as representing the standard elements attached to the origin myths.

82. Cāminātaiyar (1953), p. 136.

83. Cf. the story of Śiva struck by the Pāṇṭiyaṉ: above, II.2 at n. 140.

84. Cāminātaiyar (1953), pp. 135-36. The prototype of this myth of the Kirāta-Śiva is MBh 3.40.1-62.

85. Blood as a symbol of the sacred is not, of course, limited to Indian religion: see James, pp. 30-31, 302-305, 335-36. For milk imagery in Christianity, see *ibid*., p. 33 n. 1; and cf. Psalms 131.2.

86. Veṅkaṭācalam, pp. 12-14.

87. The story is told in a notice printed by the Tirumullaivāyil temple (Tiruppaṇi veṇṭukoḷ, n.d.); see also Das, p. 257; Oppert, pp. 246-48; Taylor (1862), 3:41-42.

88. Skt. *mālati* (Jasminum grandiflorum); according to the notice cited in n. 87, this site is also known as *mālativaṉam*.

89. As an additional substitute for milk, there are the temple pillars made from the *ĕrukku* plant, which has milky leaves; Das, p. 257. Note that the combination of blood, white jasmine, and the hidden black *liṅga* provides us with the complete series of red, white, and black (the latter often hidden or unknown) regarded by Victor Turner as a basic, universal triad.

See Turner (1967), pp. 85-90; and Hiltebeitel (1976), pp. 71-74, for the application of this series to the MBh.

90. There is an interesting parallel here with the idea of the avatar, or birth on earth, as actualizing a latent presence. Kampaṉ plays with subtlety on this idea in his description of the conception and birth of Rāma: Irāmāvatāram 1.265-83. I hope to discuss the problem of the avatar in a separate study.

91. Tiruvāṭpokki 11.1-270.

92. See above, II.2.

93. See below, III.4 at n. 13.

### III.3. Serpents and Anthills

1. Tiruvārūr 6.1-112. Cf. Kāñci 33.1-19.

2. Near the *mūlasthāna* is the shrine housing the processional image (of Śiva-Somāskanda) known as Tyāgarāja, who has given his name to the Tiruvārūr temple as a whole. See Shulman (1978-a).

3. See Heesterman (1967), pp. 24-27.

4. ŚB 14.1.1.1-15.

5. Tāṇḍya 7.5.6; Mai. Saṃ. 4.5.9.

6. Tai. Ār. 5.1.1-7.

7. *Ibid.* 1.5.1-2; Sāyaṇa on RV 10.171.2. For a discussion of the myth and its variants, see Oliphant; Gonda (1954), pp. 167-71. A striking parallel to the basic image of our myth occurs in Muslim traditions about the death of Solomon: Solomon was doomed to die before his *jinn* slaves had completed the building of the Temple; so that they would not cease work upon the death of their master, the Angel of Death took Solomon's soul while he was leaning on his staff. His lifeless body remained supported by the staff before the eyes of the *jinn* for an entire year. When the temple was completed, a white ant gnawed through the staff, and Solomon's body fell to the ground. See *Qur'ān* 34.14; al-Kisā'ī, p. 295. One wonders if this tradition does not preserve a vestige of the ancient notion of the builder's sacrifice, as in the myths of the Vāstupuruṣa (and see above, III.1 at notes 7 and 8). The ants play an equally pivotal role in the death of Og in Midrashic sources: see Bamidbar Rabbah 19.32.

8. Tai. Ār. 1.5.1-2.

9. *Ibid.*, 5.1.7.

10. ŚB 14.1.1.18-26; Bṛhaddevatā 3.18-24.

11. *Ibid.*; Sāyaṇa on RV 1.84.15.

12. Devībhāgavata 1.5.1-112.

13. See MBh 12.335.21-65; Viṣṇu 5.17.11. On Viṣṇu as Hayagrīva, see Mahalingam (1965).

14. Bhāgavata 8.24.7-57.

15. MBh 12.Appendix 1, no. 28; 12.274.2-58; Kūrma 1.14; Liṅga 1.35-36, 99-100; Vāyu 1.30; Bhāgavata 4.2-7; Skanda 1.1.1-5.

16. Bṛhaddharma 2.40.18-54; Kālikā 18.1-117; Devībhāgavata 7.30.40-50.

17. See above, II.2 at note 58.

18. Dakṣa's incestuous love for Satī is perhaps most clearly stated in Devībhāgavata 7.30.1-37.

19. Takkayākapparaṇi 323-34.

20. Tiruvārūr 13.1-53; Skanda 6.8.34-131; cf. Tiruviḷai. 1.28-36.

21. RV 1.84.13-15. See Bosch (1961), pp. 137-52.

22. Meghadūta 15; cf. Vogel (1926), p. 29. Liṅga 1.100.31; Takkayākapparaṇi 725-26. It is noteworthy that in the latter text Dakṣa's sacrifice turns into the sacrifice of Viṣṇu. This idea seems, in the light of the above myths, to be more than a mere sectarian development. Note that the bow that Śiva uses against the gods at Dakṣa's sacrifice is the same bow broken by Rāma to win Sītā: Rām. 1.65.7-17.

23. MBh 13.145.5-29.

24. *Ibid.* 10.18.1-26. It is the position of this version of the Dakṣa myth at the end of the *sauptikaparvan* that serves Hiltebeitel so well in his analysis of the relations between myth and epic in the MBh. See Hiltebeitel (1976), pp. 312-35. The conclusions arrived at there accord well with the interpretation developed below of the sacrificial significance of the anthill/serpent complex and its relation to the Epic.

25. Thus for *avaṣṭabhya dhanuṣkoṭim*, cf. *sa dhanuḥ pratiṣkabhyātiṣṭhat* (Tai. Ār. 5.1.5); *sa dhanuḥ pratiṣṭabhya* . . . (Tāṇḍya 7.5.6); *sa dhanurārtnyā śira upastabhya* . . . (ŚB 14.1.1.7); *sa dhanvārtiṃ pratiṣkabhyātiṣṭhat* (Mai. Sāṃ. 4.5.9). Similarly for *viṣphurad dhanuḥ*: *dhanurārtnyau viṣphurantyau* . . . (ŚB 14.1.4.9), and so on.

26. Sāyaṇa on Tai. Ār. 1.5.2.

27. ŚB 6.4.2.3.

28. See the discussion in O'Flaherty (1971).

29. Śiva 2.3.20.2-23.

30. KB 6.1-2; ŚB 1.7.3.8.

31. *Ibid.* 1.7.4.1-9; Gopathabrāhmaṇa 2.1.2. See section 1 above.

32. MBh 10.18.23.

33. AB 3.33-34.

34. MBh 10.17.1-26. On Sthāṇu—the antierotic form of Śiva—see O'Flaherty (1976), pp. 224-28; below, IV.2.

35. See Tirukkaṭavūrpurāṇam 9-14 (pp. 52-84); Tirukkaṭavūrkṣettirapurāṇam 3-5 (pp. 19-47); Tiruvāṇmiyūr 10 (pp. 33-35). Śiva emerges from the *liṅga* encircled by Yama's noose, and kills Yama with his foot. See the analysis in Shulman (1976-a), pp. 386-400.

36. MBh 1.33.10-28. On this serpent-sacrifice, see below.

37. See Bolle (1965), pp. 32-33; Heesterman (1957), p. 19. Worship of

the anthill is a well-known feature of village religion in south India. Cf. Elmore, pp. 82, 100; Whitehead, p. 82.

38. For demons and the anthill, see AV 2.3.3; snakes and the anthill: Vogel (1926), pp. 28-30; below, after n. 54. The anthill leads to the subterranean waters, and the ants are thought to be able to find water even in the desert (see above at n. 4).

39. Crooke, 2:256; cf. Mārkaṇḍeya 10.64-66.

40. TB 3.7.2.1; cf. ŚB 2.6.2.1-19.

41. TB 3.7.2.1; TS 5.1.2.5; cf. Heesterman (1957), p. 19.

42. Kāṭhakasaṃhitā 20.8; TS 5.1.8.1; cf. Heesterman (1967), p. 39.

43. For seed from the anthill, cf. Nanjundayya and Ananthakrishna Iyer, 4:84: Nāgāmbikā ("Snake-woman") conceives by swallowing a seed that her brother saw brought out of the earth by an ant. And cf. Matan̲akāmarājan̲katai 5 (pp. 84-85).

44. Śiva 2.5.1-10; Kāñci 30.2-42. Cf. O'Flaherty (1976), pp. 180-89. It is also possible that a layer of Vaiṣṇava myth has been absorbed by the classical mythology of Tiruvārūr.

45. Nar̲r̲iṇai 125.1-3; 325.1-6; 336.8-11.

46. Skanda 6.1.4-68. As noted earlier, the sixth *khaṇḍa* of the printed editions of the Skanda is the Hāṭakeśvaramāhātmya, which is largely devoted to Tiruvārūr. The association of the Hāṭakeśvara shrine there with the Pine Forest myth persists in Muttusvāmidīkṣitar's *kṛti* beginning "Hāṭakeśvara": Raṅkarāmānuja Ayyaṅkār, 5:356-59.

47. Tiruvārūr 6.16; see above at the beginning of this section.

48. Skanda 6.2.1.

49. *Ibid*. 6.8.21-23.

50. MBh 10.17.24. See also Śiva, *Dharmasaṃ*., 10.12.

51. Elmore, p. 94.

52. Ceyūr ttala varalār̲u, p. 31; Das, p. 214. For other examples of this type, see Tirupperūr 8.1-85, 9.1-112; Ramesan, pp. 52-53; Oppert, p. 474 (note).

53. There are, however, remnants of this pattern in the Skanda myth—the piercing of Śiva by Kāma, and Kāma's death by fire; the violent, dangerous intercourse of Śiva and Pārvatī, which is interrupted by Agni, just as the sacrifices of Dakṣa and Janamejaya are interrupted (see below); the fiery nature of the seed, which dries up the Ganges and bursts through the stomachs of the Kṛttikās or the womb of Pārvatī (see II.1 at nn. 42-43). Violence accompanies—indeed, seems necessary to—Skanda's birth. See also Paripāṭal 5.26-54, where the sacrificial overtones of the Skanda myth are very clear; below, IV. 7 at n. 130.

54. Velaimānakar caritai, pp. 12-21.

55. In addition to the central anthill deity, Tiruvŏr̲r̲iyūr also has an adjoining shrine to "Tyāgarāja," the processional image; the virgin goddess Vaṭivuṭaiyamman̲ is analogous to Kamalāmpikai of Tiruvārūr; inside the

main shrine, we find Durgā as Vaṭṭapāṟaiyammaṉ, like Ěriciṉakkŏṟṟavai of Tiruvārūr, and the consort of the god, Tarppanāyaki, like Alliyaṅkotaiyammai at Tiruvārūr.

56. Tiruvŏṟṟiyūr 8.1-39.

57. *Ibid.* 9.1-37. For the enmity between the moon, the abode of Soma/*amṛta*, and the poisonous serpent, cf. Makāpāratam of Villiputtūrāḻvār 1.3.

58. Field notes, Tiruvŏṟṟiyūr, December 1, 1975. The connection with the *atti* tree is part of a general association of serpents with fig trees, although usually it is another species of fig, the *aśvattha*, that is the home of serpents—perhaps because it is latexiferous, and serpents are thought to be drawn to milk. See Gonda (1970), p. 112; Kalyanasundaram Aiyar, p. 425. The milky appearance of the serpent before it sloughs its skin may explain this association.

59. Kramrisch (1946), 1:85.

60. *Ibid.* Vāstu becomes a brother of the serpent Rāhu: *ibid.*, p. 94.

61. Tāṇḍya 25.15.4.

62. MBh 1.13-53. This story provides the setting for the narration of the epic proper: Vaiśampāyana relates the MBh tale during the intervals of Janamejaya's serpent-sacrifice (1.53.27-34).

63. *Ibid.* 1.3.11-18.

64. For example, the blind Dhṛtarāṣṭra (cf. Bosch, 1960, p. 86 n. 34); Kauravya is a name for a clan of serpents (MBh 1.206.14); Hastināpura (the Kaurava capital) = Nāgāhva according to the lexicons (and for the association of elephants and serpents, see below), and so on.

65. See the view of Hiltebeitel (1976), especially pp. 312-53. Recall that Kurukṣetra, the scene of the Bhārata war, is in the Brāhmaṇas the sacrificial site *par excellence*.

66. MBh 1.53.9-15.

67. MBh (S) 1.48.10 (after 1.53.10 of the Poona edition).

68. MBh 1.53.20. Cf. Skanda 6.31.1-34, where the serpents of good conduct (*śuddhasamācāra*) are allowed to worship at Hāṭakeśvara on condition that they not bite people who come there free of faults.

69. Tirukkaṭavūr 18 (pp. 99-111); cf. Ziegenbalg (1869), p. 92. Yama is ordered to limit his activities to punishing the wicked.

70. MBh 1.32.1-25.

71. *Ibid.* 1.214-19. On this myth see Hiltebeitel (1975), *passim*; Karve, pp. 94-106; Biardeau (1971-1972-a), pp. 139-47.

72. On the significance of the name Śārṅgaka, "horned," see Defourny.

73. MBh 1.218.4.

74. *Ibid.* 1.218.5-10.

75. MBh (S) 1.214.29-98; Poona ed. 1.App. I.118-21.

76. See n. 61.

77. Koyil 3.1-97; cf. Kalyanasundaram Aiyar, p. 425.

78. Tiruppuṉavāyil 17.

79. Govindâchârya, p. 197.

80. Śrīnāgeśakṣetra 1.1-6.

81. Tiruccĕṅkoṭu 1.2.1-34; Paḻani 9.6-13; Cīkāḻi 19.11-30; Tirupparaṅkuṉṟam 3 (pp. 22-23); cf. Paripāṭal, Fragment I. 72-73. This myth may also be seen as a descendant of the ancient image of the cosmic serpent coiled around the mountain, an image represented in the Vedic myth of Vṛtra: see Kuiper (1970), p. 108. In Indra's slaying of Vṛtra we may detect an act of sacrifice linked to the process of creation: see Ogibenin, pp. 122-23.

82. Tiruviḷai. 49.13-26. See Figure III.

83. See section II.2 above. The serpent as guardian of the boundary also belongs in the series of terrifying gatekeepers: see above, I.2.

84. Tirunĕlveli 93.1-26.

85. See above, II.2 at nn. 100-102.

86. Tiruviḷai. 49.3.

87. Paripāṭal, Fragment 1.59.

88. Alliyaracāṇimālai, pp. 78-108 (condensed).

89. See below, IV.5 at notes 27 and 33.

90. The text in fact compares the union of Alli and Arjuna to that of Murukaṉ and Vaḷḷi, the mythic exemplars of the *kaḷavu* theme. See below, IV.8.

91. See below, IV.5 at note 88.

92. Makāpāratam of Villiputtūrāḻvār, 5.7.1-8. On the birth of Irāvat from the Nāginī, see 1.7.8-9. For the Śākta *yāmaḷam*: Takkayakāpparaṇi 136, commentary.

93. See Francis (1906-a), pp. 375-76; Thurston (1909), 6:11; Oppert, p. 97; Gros and Nagaswamy, p. 122. For the elephant-sacrifice to Kālī, cf. Vikkiramātittaṉkatai 7 (pp. 364-65).

94. MBh 6.86.6-7; cf. 1.206.12-34.

95. Zimmer (1946), p. 104.

96. MBh 6.86.68-71.

97. See Heesterman (1964), pp. 1-10; O'Flaherty (1976), pp. 57-93.

98. MBh 12.218.1-30; cf. Gonda (1954), pp. 222-25; Shulman (1978).

99. In Sanskrit this demon is Mahīrāvaṇa, "Rāvaṇa of the Earth": see Śiva 3.20.34.

100. Mayilirāvaṇaṉkatai, pp. 61-68.

101. *Ibid.*, pp. 85-90.

102. This is the conclusion of Irāmacāmippulavar, who gives another version of the Arāvāṉ myth in Meṟkoḷviḷakka kkatai akaravaricai, 1:40-41 (citing the "Pāratam").

103. Village tradition of Nĕppattūr, Tanjore District, recorded January 19, 1976.

104. MBh 1.Appendix I, 73 (especially lines 32-85), added after 1.119.

105. Cf. also Bhīṣma's refusal to die while the Bhārata war raged. On Rāhu see MBh 1.17.4-8; KP 2.32.25; Jagadisa Ayyar, p. 68; Hart (1975),

pp. 76-77. For the beheading and subsequent revival of Gaṇeśa, see Brahmavaivarta 3.12, where it is the gaze of Śani—perhaps himself another serpent—that burns the head of the god and causes the substitution of an elephant's head.

106. Tiruviḷai. 28.1-23. Cf. Paripāṭal, Fragment 1.4. The folk etymology may obscure an historical link between Maturai and the northern Mathurā.

107. See, for example, Tiruvācakam 6.32. Recall that in the Tiruvārūr anthill myth the gods flee from Viṣṇu "as once before they had fled from the poison produced from the churning of the ocean" (see above).

108. See Gonda (1954), pp. 209-10. For Śitikaṇṭha in the Dakṣa myth of MBh 10.18, see above at note 24.

109. MBh 12.329.15; 12.330.47; Harivaṃśa 3.32.47.

110. MBh (S) 12.330.50.

111. MBh 12.329.15.

112. See above, section 1; Kramrisch (1946) 1:75-76.

113. At Tiruvāñciyam (Tanjore District): see Tiruvācakam 2.79-80 (with commentary); Venkataraman, p. 32.

114. Long (1970), p. 276.

115. MBh 1.85.6. See Kosambi (1962), pp. 75-76.

116. KP 4.13.492-99. The cock is also associated with death; cocks are born from the body of the serpent-demon Vṛtra; Yama, lord of the dead, is given a cock by his father to pick the worms from his festering foot (Matsya 11).

117. But see n. 99 above.

118. See Kosambi (1962), p. 60; below, IV.9.

119. Māyūram 6-11.

120. Skanda 5.2.14.1-9.

121. This opposition is often depicted iconographically, as in the case of Skanda's peacock, which is shown devouring serpents (see, for example, the painting of Skanda in the Tiruviḷai. series on the *prākāra* wall at Tañcāvūr).

## III.4. The Surrogate

1. Note the contrast with the Śiva of the classical purāṇic tradition, where Śiva epitomizes the unclean—he is an outcaste, a murderer (of a Brahmin—the god Brahmā!), a gambler, a mad dancer in the cremation ground, and so on. The Tamil tradition goes to great lengths to explain away these traits. For example, Śiva beheads Brahmā to punish a sin of *Brahmā*'s—and Śiva has no need to expiate this action. This is the exact reverse of the northern myth, in which Śiva atones for Brahminicide by wandering over the earth and begging for alms with Brahmā's skull in his hand. See, for example, Kūrma 2.31.3-109; and cf. Kāñci 34.1-38;

Tirumayilai 10.2-25; Tirukkaṇṭiyūr 6 (pp. 17-19); Paḻayaṅkuṭi talavaralāṟu, pp. 9-12.

2. See above, section 2 at n. 10.
3. Bṛhadīśvaramāhātmya 15.55-58. See above, II.1 at nn. 10-11.
4. Tirupperūr 19.23-44.
5. See below, IV.8.
6. See the summary in Dorai Rangaswamy, 1:79-83. This entire story, with the *Tevāram* hymns around which it has been woven, constitutes an essay in religious symbolism: Cuntarar's blindness is a sign of two kinds of desire, his lust for the dancing girl Caṅkiliyār ("the Chain") as well as his thirst for the god, for whose sake he leaves Caṅkiliyār and is consequently blinded. The quarrel of the blind saint and his god is a lovers' fight (*ūṭal*), the gift of renewed vision a surrender and revelation by the deity.
7. Śvetāraṇya 41-47; cf. Tiruvĕṇkāṭu 15.1-106.
8. MBh 2.42.21-23. See below, IV.4 at and after n. 15.
9. A village near Tiruviṭaimarutūr is still called by his name (Maruttuvakkuṭi); cf. Śvetāraṇya, Tamil prose summary, p. 13. Note that "Maroti" is a widely diffused village deity: Maury, p. 75.
10. See Das, plate XIV. Nandin's wounds here may be compared with the "stigmata of valor" that Dumézil sees in the piece of whetstone in the head of Thorr and the flint fixed by a nail in the head of the Lapp god Hora galles: Dumézil (1969), pp. 161-64.
11. PP 4.6.1-60 (Caṇṭecuranāyaṉār).
12. Spratt, p. 333. See above, section 2 at n. 34.
13. Cīkāḷatti 6.1-178; PP 3.3.1-186; Tirukkāḷatti, Kaṇṇappar civakocāriyar muttiyaṭainta attiyāyam, 1-88 (appendix to the edition of U. Ve. Cāminātaiyar).
14. For a comparable example, see Buber, pp. 69-70.
15. See above, II.1, the discussion following n. 40.
16. Oppert, p. 479.
17. See note 4.
18. Śiva 2.5.42.14-22; Matsya 179.2-40.
19. Presumably *kaṇṇā!* in the original. Rice, p. 214. Cf. the myth of Viṣṇu's eye-sacrifice: Śiva 4.34.5-32; Liṅga 1.98.159-77; Mahimnastava 19; Kāñci 44.1-13; KP 6.13.297; Carapapurāṇam 6 (especially v. 24). We will return to the symbolism of eyes and vision in sections 3 to 5 of the following chapter.

## IV.1. Introduction

1. Talmud Bavli, Gittin 49b.
2. Diehl, pp. 165-66; Beck (1974), pp. 17-19.
3. See above, II.1 at notes 68-69; Gonda (1966), pp. 31-32.
4. The god's names also alliterate in some places (e.g., Puṣpavananātha

at Tiruppūnturutti), but on the whole the alliteration of the goddess's names is more striking.

5. See above, III.1 at nn. 10-11.
6. For the earth as dark, see Biardeau (1971-1972), pp. 40-41; Hiltebeitel (1976), pp. 67-68.
7. See below, IV.7.
8. See below, IV.8.
9. See Gonda (1954), pp. 133-34, on the connection between agricultural and sexual imagery.
10. Hart (1974), p. 32.
11. Hart (1975), p. 98f.
12. See O'Flaherty (1976), pp. 46-56. In JB 2.69-70, Death's weapons are song accompanied by the lute and the dance. Cf. Heesterman (1964), pp. 12-14.
13. See above, I.2 and II.1.
14. See Beck (1974), pp. 7-8; Subrahmanian, pp. 286-88; Hart (1975), pp. 93-119.
15. On cross-cousin marriage as a means of maintaining stricter control over the woman's power, see Hart (1974).
16. See Biardeau (1972), p. 182. Note that the androgyne, an important symbol for the divine marriage and an attempt to resolve its tensions, is precisely that form of union in which conventional sexual activity is impossible!
17. See for example Tiruvācakam 12.9 and 13.
18. BĀU 6.2.13 (Hume's translation).
19. AB 7.13. Śakuntalā echoes these words in MBh 1.68.36.
20. Kāñci 63.250-88, 422-27; Tirunĕlveli 15-20; Tiruvŏṟṟyūr 11.1-25; Tiruppuṉavāyil 13; Tirukkaḻukkuṉram 17 (p. 126).
21. Skanda/Murukaṉ became the teacher of his father Śiva at Cuvāmimalai (hence Murukaṉ there is known as Guruguha or Svāminātha): Śrī svāmimalaikṣetramāhātmya 1.37-48; Satyagirimāhātmya 1.10-99; Das, p. 127; cf. Śiva 6.11.10-55. For Murukaṉ as the teacher of Agastya, see above, I.1; Tiruviḷai., *purāṇavaralāṟu* 1-25.
22. Paḻayaṅkuṭi talavaralāṟu, pp. 4-8.
23. DED 2507.
24. Paḻayaṅkuṭi talavaralāṟu, p. 4.
25. See above, II.2 at n. 64 and references cited there.
26. Tiruviḷai. 54.10. See also the old commentary on Takkayākapparaṇi 40.

## IV.2. The Reluctant Bride

1. O'Flaherty (1973), pp. 151-54.
2. See Kane, V, 1:155-87; Patmanāpaṉ, p. 4; Marr (1967), p. 421.

3. Tirupperūr 29.1-116, 30.1-134.
4. Whitehead, p. 132.
5. Tiruvārūr 16.2; *kaṭavuḷvāḻttu* 5.
6. Tiruppātirippuliyūr 10.41-49; 11.24.
7. Kanyākṣetramāhātmya 4 and 22; Kaṉṉiyākumari 14-17; Tevīparākkiramam, pp. 277-88.
8. Kanyākṣetramāhātmya 2-5, *passim*.
9. Manasākāvya of Manakar, cited by Maity, pp. 120-21.
10. MBh 5.104-18. See also Meyer (1930), 1:39-45.
11. Kurup, p. 48.
12. Cucīntiram 17.1-10; Kaṉṉiyākumari 14.1-47.
13. Brahmavaivarta 4.47.81-154; cf. Zimmer (1946), pp. 3-11.
14. See Bṛhaddharma 2.60.107-108; Śiva 2.4.20.23-37; Katiraiveṟ Piḷḷai, pp. 308-10.
15. Das, pp. 1-2; Patmanāpaṉ, p. 3.
16. Dave, 2:59.
17. This motif of the suitor's test recurs in other myths of the thwarted marriage. In Assam, the goddess Kāmākhyā agreed to marry Naraka on condition that in one night he construct a temple, a tank, and a road; Naraka had nearly completed this task when, inspired by the goddess, a cock crew prematurely. See Kakati (1948), p. 46. The Pāṇḍavas attempted to make a reproduction of Kāśī in a single night; the goddess Jogāī (of Mahārāṣṭra) took the form of a cock and put a stop to their work by crowing before dawn: Kosambi, p. 142. Note the motif of the false announcement of dawn in both these myths, as in the Kaṉṉiyākumari tradition. The same device of the premature crowing of the cock is used by Indra to ensure Gautama's absence from his house in some versions of the seduction of Ahalyā; there the motif is the prelude to erotic adventure rather than a means of precluding it. See Irāmāvatāram 1.9.75 (commentary); Narayan, p. 21; Dowson, p. 9. For other examples of the suitor's test, see Tevīparākkiramam, pp. 273-74; Mataṉakāmarājaṉkatai 5 (pp. 84-86).
18. This point was strongly emphasized in a version of the myth used in the Tamil film Tevikaṉṉiyākumari (1975). Compare the myth of the unicorn, which can be captured only by a virgin: van Buitenen, introduction to MBh III, 118-93. This myth, with its obvious sexual imagery, may go back to the cycle of Ṛśyaśṛṅga.
19. See below, section 4; Devībhāgavata 5.9-11; Vāmana 20.1-36; Kaṉṉiyākumari 12-13.
20. Kaṉṉiyākumari 17.56-62; cf. Percival, p. 23 (nos. 198, 200-201).
21. Dumézil (1973), p. 123 (1968-1973, 2:368).
22. See Hart (1974), p. 32, citing stories collected by Brenda Beck.
23. Cil. 8.1; Nilakanta Sastri (1939), p. 59; cf. Bhāgavata 10.79.17.
24. Tai. Ār. 10.1.7; MBh, verses added after 4.5.29 (App. I.4.D.11 and 16); Cil. 12.67 and 73; cf. Mazumdar, *passim*; Devībhāgavata 3.26.38-62.

25. Another solution is for the virgin to coexist with the married goddess in the same temple, each in her own subshrine. This arrangement is discussed in section 6 below.

26. See Tirimūrttimalai 5 (pp. 25-34); Pillay, p. 82 n. 2.

27. Early Tamil tradition also knew Arundhatī (*vaṭa mīṉ*) in this light: see Paripāṭal 5.44; Pĕrumpāṇ. 302-303; Akam 16.17-18; Hart (1975), p. 59. The star identified as Arundhatī is pointed out to a newly married couple as a symbol of the chaste conduct they are to emulate. See Dubois, p. 228.

28. See O'Flaherty (1973), pp. 102-103; Vāmana 6.61-62.

29. Mārkaṇḍeya 16.14-90, 17.1-25; cf. Skanda 5.3.103.1-109; Tirunĕlveli 28.1-3; Śiva 3.19.1-28.

30. Rām. 2.109.8-11; cf. Śiva 4.3.7-39, 4.4.1-61; Tirimūrttimalai 3 (pp. 10-14). Hindu myths stress the direct correlation between chastity and rain; see, for example, the story of Ṛśyaśṛṅga: O'Flaherty (1973), pp. 42-52; Irāmāvatāram 1.215-35, where the chaste ascetic brings rain to the drought-stricken land. Cf. Cil. 15.145-48; Tirukkuṟaḷ 55; Cucīntiram 1.9; Thurston (1909), 6:85.

31. Bhaviṣya 3.4.17.67-78.

32. Tiruviḷai. 23.1-33.

33. Tirukkuṭantai aruḷ miku cārṅkapāṇi cuvāmi ālaya talavaralāṟu, pp. 33, 31; cf. Das, p. 138; below, section 8.

34. This case belongs among a series of such explanations of the divine symbols. Cf. Bhṛgu's curse that Śiva be worshiped in the form of a *liṅga* because the god was too busy with his wife to receive him: Padma 6.282.8-52; Veṅkaṭācalam, pp. 10-20. Brahmā is worshiped in the form of a head because he was beheaded by Śiva: Oppert, p. 300f.; Thurston (1909), 6:357-58; Whitehead, p. 133; Kūrma 2.31.3-109.

35. See above, II.1 at n. 14. In the Anasūyā myth from Cucīntiram, however, the foot (of the *aśvattha* tree) is associated with Śiva, the middle with Viṣṇu, and the top, again, with Brahmā: Cucīntiram 7.18.

36. Tirimūrttimalai 3 (pp. 10-11).

37. Cucīntiram 2.1-21, 3.1-30, 4.1-31, 6.1-23, 7.1-26. See the sculptures of Anasūyā and the disguised gods from the "Dark Maṇḍapa" at Maturai: Shenoy, pp. 41-42. It is said that in the Kali Age the *aśvattha* tree at Cucīntiram becomes a *kŏṉṟai*, the present *sthalavṛkṣa* there.

38. O'Flaherty (1973), pp. 178-203; below, section 9. For another trial of Anasūyā, see Tirimūrttimalai 5 (pp. 25-34); Pillay, p. 82 n. 2.

39. See n. 31. For food as a symbol of or surrogate for eroticism, see O'Flaherty (1973), pp. 279-82.

40. A vision of her nakedness would be tantamount to sexual union: see the discussion of this theme in section 4 below.

41. Cucīntiram 7.6.

42. Tirimūrttimalai 6-7 (pp. 35-57).

43. This text gives their names as Apirāmi, Mākecuvari, Kaumāri, Kāḷi,

Varāki, Ayirāṇi, and Intirāṇi—thus revealing their connection to the male divinities.

44. See Beck (1974), p. 8; below, section 7.

45. MBh 13.14.65-67, including the line inserted by many mss. after 67[ab].

46. Dubois, pp. 543-44.

47. This picture of the "human" mother nursing a calf reverses the common motif of the child-god sucking at the teats of a cow (usually the Kāmadhenu): see section 7.

48. In another folk version of the Anasūyā myth, Anasūyā (here called Nāgāvalī) is originally married not to Atri but to Bhṛgu; after being disfigured by the Trimūrti, she is driven away by her husband. See Whitehead, p. 115. Here, too, the heroine is ultimately independent, separated finally from any husband. She becomes the fierce goddess Māriyammaṉ, who is also famous for her chastity and, like Anasūyā, for her ability to bring rain (see Arokiaswami, *passim*). Cf. the fine discussion by Brubaker.

49. Thus Pillay, p. 55 n. 1, on the basis of an inscription given in TAS IV, 94. Pillay reads *tāṇumālaiyappĕrumāḷ* for *tāṇuvālaiya* . . . as given by the editor. There seems to be no reason to support Pillay's emendation other than the irregular spelling of *ālaya*, shrine.

50. For example, at Caṅkaranārāyaṇakoyil, originally Caṅkaranayiṉārkoyil. At Tiruvahīntirapuram (Tiruventipuram), the god, Devanātha, is known as Mūvar ākiya ŏruvaṉ, "the One who is the Three," and is represented with attributes of Śiva as well as those of Viṣṇu (he has three eyes, matted locks, a conch, discus, lotus, and so on). In this case Viṣṇu seems to have absorbed Śiva—the reverse of Cucīntiram. See Tiruvahīntirapuram . . . mahā samprokṣaṇam, p. 1; Śrī cĕṉṉai mallīcurar . . . varalāṟu, p. ix; Krishnaswami, pp. 15-16.

51. Pillay, p. 72f.; field notes, February 9, 1976; Pirasaṉṉā, p. 6.

52. See Beck (1972), p. 25; Aiyappan, pp. 291-92, especially n. 1 on p. 291.

53. Cil. 2, *vĕṇpā*.

54. See section 5 below.

55. See the remarks of Hocart, p. 139.

56. See the myth of Murukaṉ and Vaḷḷi, below, section 8; Zvelebil (1973-b), pp. 91-93.

57. Similarly, in Bengali Vaiṣṇavism the adulterous love of the *parakiyā* for her lover is the prevalent metaphor for the love of man and God. See Dimock (1967), pp. 78-79; Hart (1974), pp. 48-51.

58. PP 2.3.1-36; Cāyāvaṉam 8.1-49.

59. Cf. Allama Prabhu 431, cited by Ramanujan (1973), p. 157.

60. See section 9 below.

61. Liṅga 1.29.46-64; cf. Śiva 3.27.1-69; Tirunĕlveli 57.268-85; O'Flaherty (1973), pp. 197-99. The myth has an earlier form in MBh 13.2.36-85.

62. PP 5.4.1-50.

63. See section 5 below at n. 13; section 6 n. 21.

64. Govindâchârya, pp. 41-58; Das, pp. 51-54; Filliozat (1972), pp. vii-viii.

65. As in the wedding ceremony. At the *svayaṃvara* the woman supposedly chose her husband by throwing a garland over his neck (as in the story of Nala and Damayantī); here Āṇṭāl garlands herself to see if she is a fit bride for the god.

66. Nilakanta Sastri (1963), p. 67.

67. See above at n. 51.

68. Bṛhadīśvaramāhātmya 21.1-20 (f. 33b-34a).

69. Ramanujan (1973), pp. 111-14; other examples in Jacob, p. 120; Tadhkirat al-Awliyā', 1:59-73.

70. Tam. Cukantakeci, fr. Skt. *sugandha*, "fragrant," + *keśa* (*keśī*), "hair."

71. Kāḷaiyārkoyil 16.2-39, 17.2-42.

72. See above, II.2 at n. 33.

73. Mattiyārccuṉam, p. 227, Cf. Tiruviṭaimarutūr mummaṇikkovai 28.54-55.

74. A good example is the stone from Pĕnukŏṇḍa, Anantapur District, in the Madras Government Museum.

75. See Cil. 23.181 (Kaṇṇaki breaks her bangles in the shrine of Kŏṟṟavai).

76. Elmore, p. 31.

77. Irāmāvatāram 2.3.37.

78. Kāḷaiyārkoyil 17.36-42.

79. The influence of the Mīnākṣī myth from nearby Maturai may be reflected here in the motif of finding a husband through battle—although here not the bride but her father is defeated. See below, section 5 n. 47. The Kāṉapper bride, Sughandakeśī, is linked by her name to Ñāṉappūṅkotai, Śiva's consort at Kāḷatti, and, more spectacularly, to the famous story of Tarumi and his (or Śiva's) poem about the naturally fragrant tresses of the Maturai queen: Tiruviḷai. 52.1-107 (see verses 103-105 for Ñāṉappūṅkotai); and cf. Marr (1958), pp. 10-11, and Kuṟ. 2 (the poem mentioned in this story).

80. Vīkṣāraṇyakṣetramāhātmya 3.1-49; Das, pp. 260-61.

81. Kumbhaghoṇamāhātmya 4.34-65, 5.1-49.

82. Tirukkuṭantai . . . cārṅkapāṇi cuvāmi talavaralāṟu, pp. 31-32.

83. Tiruvahīntirapuram śrī tevanāta svāmi tirukkoyil mahā samprokṣaṇam, pp. 2-3.

84. Das, pp. 238-39; Tirupporūr, p. 9.

85. Gālava, here the father of the bride, is associated with the theme of virginity in the myth of Mādhavī—Yayāti's daughter matched by Gālava with four different husbands, each time as a virgin. See MBh 5.104-18.

86. Elmore, p. 80. I am informed by Dennis Hudson and Christopher Fuller that this well-known tradition is not reflected in present-day rituals in the Maturai shrine. Carol Breckenridge has reported witnessing a similar ritual sneeze in a shrine in Tirunělveli.

## IV.3. The Lustful Bride

1. Tirumantiram 1025; Saundaryalaharī 7; Krishna Sastri, p. 220.
2. Saundaryalaharī 5 and 6; 19.
3. Bṛhaddharma 2.53.44.
4. Whitehead, pp. 133-34.
5. Cf. Brahmāṇḍa 3.4.11.24-31; below, after n. 48.
6. Cf. Elmore, pp. 89-90; Oppert, pp. 465-66 n. 253.
7. *Ibid*. See section 7 at n. 96.
8. Kumārasambhava 8.7.
9. KP 6.24.20-24.
10. *Ibid*. 1.11.44-45. And cf. Eliade (1971) for the symbolism of light and seed.
11. KP 6.24.10.
12. MBh 1.203.26.
13. Padma 5.51.7-50; Irāmāvatāram 1.9.81.
14. S. C. Mitra, pp. 145-47. The myth is based on Rām. 7.18.5, 22-24, where Indra *becomes* a peacock to hide from Rāvaṇa.
15. See the south Indian wood carving in Ions (1967), p. 86.
16. Iḷampūraṇar on Tŏl. Pŏruḷ. Akattiṇai. 20; Nampiyakappŏruḷ 20; see for example Kuṟ. 249; cf. Subhāṣitaratnakoṣa 215, 222, 225, 236.
17. Thankappan Nair, p. 163.
18. MBh 4.5 (App. I.4.D.14 and 26); Hopkins (1915), p. 224; Long (1970), p. 359.
19. Tirumayilai 6.20-80, 7.1-68. Cf. Māyūram 6-11; Tirumayilāṭuturai ttalavaralāṟu, p. 4; Das, p. 180.
20. Murukaṉ is Ciṅkāravelaṉ at Cikkal as well. Mayilai has its own version of the birth of Murukaṉ: Tirumayilai 9.45-54. On the peacock vehicle of the god, see Mayil viruttam attributed to Aruṇakirinātar.
21. Tirumayilai 6.39, 7.45, etc.
22. See above, III.3 nn. 114-21.
23. See above, II.2 at n. 33.
24. Brahmāṇḍa 3.4.30.33-95.
25. Saura 54.1-19; Skanda 1.1.35.3-18; KSS 3.6.60-71.
26. See the eponymous myth from Kāmakkūr (Kāmanakar): Kāmakkūr 5. Cf. Tirumayilai 9.1-43. Rati's mourning for her burned husband, before his restoration, becomes an important folk theme: see, for example, Irati pulampal.

27. Also called the Kāmakkoṭṭam or Kāmakoṭi, the shrine of Kāmākṣī at Kāñcipuram. On these names, see Dessigane et al. (1964), pp. i-vi.

28. Kāmākṣīvilāsa 14.9-66. The story may be an elaboration of Brahmāṇḍa 3.4.30.59. The Kāmākṣīvilāsa, of uncertain date, offers perhaps the most complete and most mature versions of the myths of Kāmākṣī.

29. KP 6.13.99-115; Koyil 3.29-36. See below, section 9.

30. In the Kāmākṣilīlāpirapāvam, which gives a version of this myth (14, pp. 88-95), Kāma refers explicitly to the Pine Forest when he advises Śiva to seek alms from Devī.

31. See section 9 below.

32. Kāmākṣīvilāsa 14.75.

33. Brahmāṇḍa 3.4.39.50.

34. Kāñcīmāhātmya 23.3-35, 24.1-56.

35. Meyer (1937), 1:98-100, 106-32, 204-206; O'Flaherty (1973), pp. 158-62; Shulman (1979).

36. Kāñcīmāhātmya 25.1-24.

37. See Śiva 2.3.51.13-14.

38. Kāñci 57.1-9 offers an explanation of the name Nilāttuṇṭappĕrumāḷ. On Kaḷḷakkampaṉ and the associated two *liṅgas* see Cuntarar, Tev. 61.10; Ramanatha Ayyar, *passim*; Shulman (1979).

39. Durgā-Mahākāḷī, according to the Sanskrit version (Kāmākṣīvilāsa 8.67-70).

40. Kāmākṣilīlāpirapāvam 8 (pp. 47-57); Kāmākṣīvilāsa 8.13-133; cf. Kāñcīmāhātmya 23-25; Kāñci 53.1-55.

41. Kāmākṣīvilāsa 4.44-49. See below, IV.8.

42. The motif of brother-sister incest hinted at here appears in full force in Tamil folk myths: see below, section 7 after n. 146.

43. For the equation of the god with a river, cf. Tīrttakiri 5.1-14 (Śiva melts to water in the embrace of the goddess).

44. Kūrma 2.31.89-91; Vāmana 2.43-48.

45. Tiruviriñcai 2.95-97; Tiruppuṉavāyil 11; Śiva 7.1.24-25; Devībhāgavata 5.23.1-5; Skanda 1.2.29.45-52.

46. Kāñci 64.79-80.

47. This appears to be a general view of woman and sexuality in India: see Carstairs, pp. 84, 156-59, 163, 165-66; Koestler, p. 230. For a striking example of the motif of the woman who drains the male of seed, see the myth of Śukra: Thurston (1909), 6:85; Diehl, pp. 165-66. Sexual union threatens the life of the male: recall Pāṇḍu, who dies in embracing his wife (because he had once killed a sage uniting with his wife in the form of a deer)—MBh 1.109.5-30. The village god Kūttāṇṭavar is cursed to die on the day he marries: Whitehead, p. 27; below, section 9. For a modern example of this theme, see Rāmāmirtam, pp. 32-34.

48. See above, n. 24.

49. Upatecakāṇṭam of Koṉeriyappanāvalar, 30.1-72; ŚRKh 7.74.1-60. I have combined the two versions in the description of the sacrifice. Cf. Kāñci 61.1-23; Kāmākṣīvilāsa 12.17-47; Kāmākṣilīlāpirapāvam 12 (pp. 74-82).

50. See above, nn. 33 and 40. The Brahmāṇḍa, which offers another version of this myth, gives us this identification.

51. Kāmākṣīvilāsa 12.17-47; Kāmākṣilīlāpirapāvam 12 (pp. 74-82).

52. Kāñci 61.23. Cf. Ramanatha Ayyar, p. 160.

## IV.4. The Murderous Bride

1. See section 2 above, the myths of the virgin bride. One specific aspect of this problem—the attempt to preserve the virginity of the mother—will be discussed in section 7.

2. See the examples in the previous section at nn. 40, 49, 19; further instances will be cited below.

3. See above, section 2 n. 8; section 3 n. 49.

4. See, for example, Rowland, p. 304 plate 237. See also Figure IV.

5. See Zimmer (1946), plates 66-69; Archer, figs. 13 and 45; Rawson, p. 132 and plates 89, 110-11. For the textual support for this icon, see Bṛhaddharma 1.23.6-8.

6. Kosambi (1962), pp. 2-3, 85-91.

7. *Ibid.*, p. 85.

8. Mārkaṇḍeya 82.1-68, 83.1-41.

9. Devībhāgavata 5.9-11; Brahmavaivarta 2.16-20; Vāmana 20.1-36; Devīpurāṇa 13, cited Hazra (1963), p. 45.

10. Vāmana 20.34.

11. Aruṇācalam 4.1-77, 5.1-67; cf. Skanda 1.3.1.3, 1.3.1.10-13; Aruṇakiripurāṇam 5.

12. Skanda 1.3.1.11.69.

13. See above, III.1.

14. Hart (1975), pp. 122-25.

15. See Bhāgavata 7.1.29.

16. MBh 2.42.21-23; Viṣṇu 4.14.50-53, 4.15.1-17; Bhāgavata 7.10.38; 11.5.48.

17. Bhāgavata 10.6.30-40, 10.14.34. One modern version of this myth (Śrītās, *passim*) insists that Pūtanā actually loved Kṛṣṇa; as soon as she saw his beauty, she fell in love with the god. The account of the Bhāgavata does not support this view.

18. See above, III.4 after n. 7.

19. Tirunĕlveli 52.110.

20. Cetu 11 (*tevipuraccarukkam*).1-78; Skanda 3.1.6.8-77, 3.1.7.1-48.

21. MBh 3.102.16-23, 3.103.1-3.

22. Personal communication from Brenda Beck; cf. Beck (1969), pp. 560-61 and n. 21.

23. Cetu 11.82; Skanda 3.1.7.47-48, 63-64.

24. Vāmana 18.41-74; Devībhāgavata 5.2.17-50; Kālikā 62.136-57.

25. Aruṇācalam 5.46-49; Tirunĕlveli 52.112-16.

26. Aruṇācalam 5.49.

27. Tirunĕlveli 52.116.

28. Tiruvāṭpokki 10.1-45.

29. Vṛtra is also considered a Brahmin: see MBh 5.9-10, 5.13; ŚB 11.1.5.7-8, 9.5.2.4. In some versions of the Vṛtra myth, Vṛtra is a devotee of Viṣṇu or of Śiva, and thus Indra's need to expiate is intensified—as is the problem of atoning for the slaughter of the demon-devotee Mahiṣa in the Tamil accounts. See MBh 12.274.55-58; Bhāgavata 6.11.21-27, 6.12.19-22; Tiruvārūr 13.1-53; Skanda 6.8.34-131.

30. See, for example, the summary of *carukkam* 11: above, III.2 at n. 91. Similarly, the Aruṇācala mountain struck by the sword of Durgā is equated with the *liṅga*, the manifestation of Śiva: see above, II.1 at n. 14.

31. See above, IV.3 at and following n. 45.

32. Kūrma 2.31.1-111; O'Flaherty (1973), pp. 123-27.

33. The anonymous commentator identifies this demon with Mahiṣa. He is, of course, to be distinguished from the goddess Durgā.

34. Tiruppaiññīli 4.1-23.

35. See above, II.2, nn. 33-39.

36. Recall the goddess armed with arrows at Kāñcipuram: above, section 3 n. 49.

37. For *pratiṣṭhā* achieved through a sacrifice, see Viruttācalam 1.12-39.

38. Kālikā 62.84-164.

39. See above, III.3 after n. 24.

40. See above, III.3 n. 4.

41. Kālikā 62.136-57.

42. *Ibid*. 62.153.

43. Van Kooij, p. 33.

44. Bhattarcharji, p. 166; cf. Biardeau (1972), pp. 183-84.

45. Whitehead, pp. 44, 50-54, 72-76, 93-94, 106-109; Elmore, pp. 19, 22, 38-39, 118-26; Dumont (1957), p. 378.

46. Mārkaṇḍeya 83.37-39; cf. Cil. 12.65-66.

47. See above, III.3 n. 3, and the discussion of Śitikaṇṭha/Nīlakaṇṭha (after n. 108 of that section). In the Aṇṇaṉmār katai (Beck, 1975), Viṣṇu deprives the brothers of the head of the sacrificed boar (which is also, as one would expect, the "remainder" of the sacrifice). In the story of Ciṟuttŏṇṭar, Śiva demands in particular the head of the saint's sacrificed son: PP 7.3.65, 72-75; cf. Ciṟuttŏṇṭapattaṉkatai, pp. 33-34. Recall that the secret known to Dadhyañc is how to complete the sacrifice by restoring the head (ŚB 14.1.1.18-26).

48. Cf. the identification of the anthill with the head of the sacrificial victim, and with the *vāstu*/seed: above, III.3 nn. 40-43.

49. Ramesan, pp. 91-92. For the motif of the life vested in an external object, see below, section 7 n. 180, and the Mayilirāvaṇaṉkatai (the demon's life guarded by five bees in five caves).

50. This feature has often been euphemistically misinterpreted: see, for example, Thompson and Spencer, p. 36 n. 2; Jogendra Natha Bhattacarya, p. 322. And cf. the fate of Viṣṇu in the anthill myth, above, III.3.

51. See Puṟappŏruḷ vĕṇpāmālai 139 (*tumpaippaṭalam* 13); Puṟam 80, 274, 275.

52. See Emeneau (1971), pp. xxxix-xlv; 14-23.

53. Whitehead, p. 18; Oppert, pp. 460-61.

54. Whitehead, pp. 72-73; Elmore, pp. 129-30; Thurston (1909), 3:375.

55. Whitehead, pp. 117-19; cf. pp. 84-85.

56. See above, III.1 n. 15.

57. Aruṇācalam 4.2-9; Kāñci 63.20-46; Kāñcippurāṇam of Kacciyappamuṉivar 1.263-80; Tiruppātirippuliyūr 2.1-90; Tirunĕlveli 51.36-39; Kāḷaiyārkoyil 6.2-13; Tiruccĕṅkoṭu 4.1-40; Tirukkovalūrppurāṇavacaṉam 1 (pp. 1-4).

58. MBh 13.127.26-38; Tirunĕlveli 51.36-39.

59. Kāmākṣililāpirapāvam 7 (pp. 43-44); see above, section 3 n. 40.

60. Skanda 6.153.2-20.

61. Kāḷaiyārkoyil 6.2-13 (below, section 8 n. 11); for a Śākta variant on this type, see Brown (1947).

62. Kumārasambhava 8.7.

63. Matsya 179.2-40; Kūrma 1.15.89-90, 125-38, 168-218; Śiva 2.5.42-46.

64. Gopinatha Rao, II, 1, pp. 322-23.

65. *Ibid*.; cf. Arddhagirimāhātmya 2.9-183; Krishnaswami, pp. 12-13.

66. Compare the blind Cupid of Western tradition: Panofsky, pp. 95-128. The Lurianic Kabbalah pictures the Shechinah as blind.

67. On the symbolism of eyes, see above, section 3 after n. 8. The link between blindness and castration may be carried out over several stages in time: if the extraordinary vision leads to death (see below), the loss of vision may be compensated by sexual contact with the goddess, which in turn leads to castration and/or death. Although this sequence is possible in the light of the Tamil Mahiṣa myths, I prefer to regard blindness, castration, and death as symbolically equal in these myths. Any one of the three may prefigure or substitute for the others.

68. MBh 3.122.1-27, 3.123.1-23; Devībhāgavata 7.2.30-65, 7.3.1-64, 7.4.1-56, 7.5.1-57. Cyavana's anthill home suggests a connection with the serpent, a connection sustained in the cases of other members of Cyavana's family (Dadhīca, Pippalāda). I hope to deal with this point in a separate study.

69. Wariar.

70. Kuṟ. 89 and 100, commentary of U. Ve. Cāminātaiyar.

71. Whitehead, p. 26.

72. Above, after n. 45; cf. Vogel (1931); Rose; Cil. 5.76-88, 12.20.

73. Kakati (1948), pp. 46-47.

74. See Gonda (1965), p. 32.

75. Bhāgavata 9.1.13-35; Devībhāgavata 1.12.16-22; see the discussion of these and other variants in O'Flaherty (1973), pp. 302-10.

76. Dubois, pp. 629-30.

77. MBh 1.205.1-30; Alliyaracāṇimālai, pp. 47-49.

78. RV 10.95; ŚB 11.5.1.1-17; cf. Kosambi (1962), pp. 42-81; Wright (1967), pp. 526-47.

79. Mataṉakāmarājaṉkatai 5 (p. 68).

80. Rām. 7.13.22-31; Tevīparākkiramam, pp. 30-34.

81. Ramesan, pp. 40-41.

82. Cf. Tiruviḷai. 30.1-41; 58.1-86; 59.1-127; 60.1-45.

83. The motif is reversed but the punishment remains the same in a gloss in the Talmud (Niddah 31A) on Numbrs 24:3: Bil'am is blinded (*shᵉtum ha'ayin*) for asking how the Holy One, who awaits the birth of the righteous from the seed of Israel, can watch their intercourse. Here physical blindness punishes and reflects the failure to perceive the sanctity of union (of men and women rather than of gods); the reversal of human and divine in the Hebrew myth is also illustrated by Bil'am's attempt to project blindness on to God.

84. Filliozat (1968), 1:9. Another version of the story has it that the king himself maimed the queen when she compared the Putumaṇṭapam to her father's stables at Tañcāvūr (*ibid.*).

85. Note that this identification may depend on putting in the *eyes* of the image. See Gombrich (1966), pp. 23-36.

86. Kuṟ. 244; Akam 102.13; 311.1-5. Cf. the crystal palace (*paḷikk'aṟai-maṇṭapam*) in which Maṇimekalai hides from the prince: Maṇimekalai 4.86-88. And cf. Song of Songs 4:12.

87. Note that Kāmākhya, the goddess who dances within the closed doors of her shrine in Assam, is pictured standing on the corpse of Śiva when it is time for love (*kāma*): Kālikā 60.58.

## IV.5. The Sealed Shrine

1. See above, I.2 and II.3 at n. 16. The principle of separation underlies the Brahmin claim to purity, and is directly linked to the goal of *sannyāsa*. See Heesterman (1964).

2. Turner (1974), p. 197. See the myths of the gatekeeper: above, I.2.

3. Heesterman (1973).

4. See the rampart myths, above, II.2. In the light of this discussion, the role of the gatekeeper as guardian of the wall becomes even more striking.

5. PP 6.1.578-82.

6. See verses 580 and 589.

7. On the esoteric nature of knowledge, see above, I.3 at n. 49, and I.2 at n. 9.

8. See I.2. For an instance of the demand for immediate salvation, see Tiruviriñcai 7.1-38. The impatient longing for divine joy is apparent in Kāraikkālammaiyār's desire to know "what day" her suffering will be over (*eññāṉṟu tīrppat' iṭar*)—*Aṟputa ttiruvantāti* 1.

9. PP 6.1.587-90.

10. See the story of Varakuṇapāṇṭiyaṉ: above, section 2 n. 71.

11. Personal communication from Brenda Beck.

12. Cil. 23.99-125.

13. PP 4.5.3; Cekkiḻārpurāṇam, verse 15; Campantar, Tev. 1.45.1 (with commentary); Tamiḻnāvalarcaritai 139-41; cf. the modern retellings by Ekāmpara Mutaliyār; Rāmanātaṉ, pp. 5-50; Irākavaiyaṅkār (1955), pp. 38-45. A multiform of the story can be found in Wilson (1828), 2:54-56.

14. Cil. 23.138-69; cf. Maṇimekalai 26.5-34.

15. Cil., *kāṇṭam* 1-2. The third *kāṇṭam*, which I believe to be an integral part of the work, describes the establishment of the worship of Kaṇṇaki/Pattiṉi. On folk versions of the epic, see Beck (1972); Zvelebil (1973-b), p. 173.

16. For a discussion of the parallels between the two stories, see Hameed, *passim*.

17. Ratnakaraṇḍakaśrāvakācāra of Samantabhadra, cited by A. Chakravarti in his introduction to Nīlakeci, pp. 15-18.

18. See below, section 6 after n. 11. For Nīli as a name for the fierce goddess generally, see Cil. 12, *palikkōṭai* 1.3; Takkayākapparaṇi 359; Tiruviḷai. 3.43; Oppert, p. 494.

19. Nīlakeci 1.27-65.

20. See section 6.

21. It is thus fitting that Sri Saila, the Tamil translator of Shakespeare's *Taming of the Shrew*, called his book Nīlivacīkaram.

22. PP 5.4.1-50; see above, section 2 n. 62.

23. Puttūr kuḷumāyiyammaṉ cintu, pp. 4-5.

24. Mahalingam (1949), p. 47; cf. Kovalaṉkatai, pp. 103-104.

25. Manasākāvya of Manakar, cited by Maity, p. 120.

26. Thurston (1909), 6:120-21.

27. Alliyaracāṇimālai, pp. 143-46.

28. Sarma, pp. 52-53.

29. Mayilirāvaṇaṉkatai, pp. 23-25.

30. Mataṉakāmarājaṉkatai 4 (pp. 50-65). A close parallel, substituting a snake for the tortoise, is Pañcatantra (Pūrṇabhadra) 1.23. The snake is married to a Brahmin girl; when he emerges from his box in radiant, human form, the girl's father burns the serpent's skin left in the box.

31. Sāyaṇa on RV 5.78.5.

32. See above, III.3 n. 88.

33. She must, however, still be convinced by Draupadī and Arjuna's other wives of the merits of marriage.

34. See Hiltebeitel (1976), p. 222 and n. 51.

35. Hart (1975), pp. 110-12.

36. Natesa Sastri (1884), 1:63-83; retold by Ions (1970), pp. 151-55.

37. Beck (1969), p. 561.

38. See section 6.

39. Tevakuñcariyammāḷ, pp. 5-22. For an Oriya variant of this motif, see Lakṣmīpurāṇa of Balarāma Dāsa, cited Mansinha, pp. 229-31: Jagannātha locks Lakṣmī out of the shrine. See also Nallataṅkāḷ katai, pp. 21-25 (below, section 7 n. 167).

40. Whitehead, pp. 112-13 (my summary).

41. Frere, pp. 252-53; Beck (1972), pp. 26-27. For the image of the seed in a pot, see above, II.2 after n. 56.

42. Kaṇṇaki is identified with Durgā already in Arumpatavurai on Cil. 12.47-48 (referring to her description as *kŏṅka ccĕlvi*).

43. Beck (1972), pp. 26-27; Kovalaṉkatai, pp. 4-7.

44. Specifically with Cŏkkecar, Śiva as worshiped at Maturai, the husband of Mīnākṣī: Kovalaṉkatai, pp. 7-8; Beck (1972), pp. 26-27.

45. See the destruction of the shrine of Gaṇeśa for the same reason by Divodāsa: above, II.3 n. 4.

46. Cil., *uraipĕṟukaṭṭurai* 1; cf. 27.127-30. On the equation of seed and rain, see above, III.2 at n. 52.

47. Tiruviḷai. 4.1-42, 5.1-44.

48. The process of transformation from violent goddess to docile wife is attested at many other shrines, as well; sometimes the goddess is known as Śāntanāyakī or Śāntaguṇanāyakī ("the lady of calm character"—as at Tiruveṭṭakkuṭi, Tirumayilāṭutuṟai, etc.). The change may be effected by adorning her with golden earrings (Tiruvāṇaikkā), drawing the *śrīcakra* at her feet (Kāñci), or, perhaps most frequently, by the dance. See section 6.

49. Although Megasthenes, the Greek ambassador to the court of Candragupta Maurya, is an unreliable source, one must at least mention his description of the incestuous union of "Pandaia" (= the Pāṇṭiya queen) with her father "Herakles." This account makes father and husband identical! See McCrindle, p. 207.

50. Pañcatantra (Pūrṇabhadra), 5.10 (pp. 285-89). The story is first found in the Jain recensions of the Pañcatantra (Pūrṇabhadra and the Vulgate) but is missing from Southern Recension, the Kashmiri version, and even the late, much-contaminated southern "Amplior." See Hertel (1914), pp. 301-303. Did the ancient Jain community of Maturai preserve the story and transmit it to the Jains of western India? The nineteenth-century Tamil version of Tāṇṭavarāya Mutaliyār (*Pañcatantiram*, pp. 176-79) substitutes a

third eye for the third breast; we will return to this association in a moment.

51. *Tiruviḷai*. 28.1-23; above, III.3 at n. 106.

52. Benfey, 1:511-12. Kūṉpāṇṭiyaṉ appears in Tiruvilai. 62.1-68. The theme of the hunchback lover and rival is, however, very widespread: Draupadī, for example, is said in Jātaka 536 (V, p. 426) to have taken a hunchback as lover in addition to her five Pāṇḍava husbands. Cf. Kalittŏkai 94.

53. On Vijaya as a "first king," and for the earlier part of the story, see Hiltebeitel (1976), pp. 181-85.

54. Davy, pp. 293-95. Cf. Mahāvaṃsa 7, where, however, no mention is made of a third breast.

55. Nākecuram (Kumpakoṇam), Caṇpakāraṇiyam (Tirunākecuram), Tiruppāmpuram, and (Nākaik)kāroṇam.

56. Tirunākaikkāroṇappurāṇam 19.1-147.

57. A Vaiṣṇava form of the handsome god also exists in the Maturai region—Aḻakar of Tirumāliruñcolai.

58. Chockalingam, pp. 368-69; Das, p. 166. See above, III.3 after n. 84.

59. On Varuṇa as a serpent, see Kuiper (1964), pp. 107-108; Monier-Williams, s.v. *varuṇa*. The name Cālīcukaṉ (Śāliśūka?) unfortunately offers no clue to the bridegroom's identity.

60. Kingsbury and Phillips, p. 31; cf. Cil. 7.25.2.

61. Cil. 7.11.1.

62. Brown (1947), pp. 209-14. See the application of this motif to Śiva: above, section 4 at n. 61. For a Kabbalistic parallel to this aspect of fish symbolism, see *Sefer Taamei Haminhagim*, p. 96. I am grateful to Rabbi Joseph Green for this reference.

63. See Civañāṉacittiyār, *cupakkam*, 327. I am indebted to His Holiness Śrī Mahāliṅkattampirāṉ for suggesting this explanation of the name.

64. Jouveau-Dubreuil, p. 35 n. 2.

65. Singaravelu, pp. 64-69; Subrahmanian, pp. 235-44.

66. Tiruviḷai. 57.1-64; cf. Tiruvāl. 22; Thurston (1909), 6:141-42; Whitehead, pp. 24-25.

67. Mīṉāmpikai tottiram, verses 5 and 8.

68. Cil. 7.17-18. This metaphor fits the Mīnākṣī myths, with their dominant theme of a dangerous eroticism, quite well. Recall, too, that the fish is a symbol of violence in Hindu culture: *matsyanyāya*, the law of the fish, is a common term for anarchy (the larger fish devouring the smaller). Graves (1948), pp. 349-63, regards the fish as a symbol of chastity; this notion, which I have not encountered in explicit form in Tamil sources, would nonetheless be suited to the image of Mīnākṣī as the dark and threatening virgin.

69. Multiple-breasted goddesses appear elsewhere as well: Artemis at Ephesus has "a multitude of protruding breasts"—Frazer, 1:37. The Mexi-

can goddess Coatlicue, who is both benign and fierce, the nourishing earth mother who slays her lovers, has four hundred breasts. Cf. Spence, pp. 14, 16, 183-87. I am indebted to John Marr for this information.

70. Aiyappan; Zvelebil (1973-b), p. 173 n. 4. For a story associating Bhagavatī here with the motif of the sealed shrine, see Francis Day, p. 11.

71. Cil. *patikam* 5; 12.49-50; 15.93; 23.14; 27.129.

72. Campantar, Tev. 1.10.1, lines 1-2.

73. There is a considerable mythology capable of explaining why Pārvatī, the wife of the yogi Śiva, should be considered unwilling or incapable of nursing her children: see O'Flaherty (1973), pp. 265-70; to the examples cited there may be added the folk myths about Cuṭalaimāṭaṉ, the son of Pārvatī who took to eating corpses because he was unsatisfied by his mother's milk: Cuṭalaimāṭacuvāmivilpāṭṭu, pp. 1-6. Nevertheless, Uṇṇāmulai as a head-rhyme with Aṇṇāmalai seems too good to be true, and one cannot help feeling that metrical considerations were crucial to the choice of this name for the local goddess in her benign form.

74. See above, section 1 at n. 11.

75. Graves (1955), 1:21.

76. Rām. 5.36.12-32; cf. Rice, pp. 211-12; Caṅkaranārāyaṇacāmikoyil 11.8-9; Bhūkailāsamāhātmya 22.6-11. Note again the association of blood with the breast, as in the myths of the Kāmadhenu (above, III.2).

77. Śiva 4.34.4-32; Kāñci 44.1-13. Skt. *darśana* = vision, eye.

78. Bṛhaddharma 1.10.38-65.

79. For example, Tiruvācakam 29.5.

80. MBh 2.40.

81. Oppert, pp. 464-71; Whitehead, p. 133. See above, section 3 following n. 4, and below, section 7 n. 96.

82. Tiruviḷai. 5.43.

83. For the third eye, see above, section 3 at n. 8; on the correspondence of breast and phallus in India, see O'Flaherty (1976), pp. 331-46.

84. Spratt, p. 268.

85. Divyāvadāna 32 (pp. 470-76).

86. When the bride becomes dangerous again, the third breast may reappear in a new form—recall the crystal tongue of Kuveṇī.

87. MBh (S) 1.203.15-30. The Poona edition adopts the southern reading (*Maṇalūra*) in 1.207.14-23 but, with better judgment, rejects it in favor of the northern Maṇipura in 14.78-82 (the story of Babhrūvāhana, the son of this union, who slays his father in battle). The southern tradition appears to have conflated two separate stories. See also Makāpāratam of Villiputtūrāḻvār 1.7.21-43. "Maṇalūra" is the Maṇavūr of Tiruviḷai. 3.2.

88. Alliyaracāṇimālai, pp. 20-47 (condensed).

89. *Ibid.*, pp. 47-164; see the discussion above at n. 33, and the episode summarized in III.3 at n. 88.

90. Pavaḷakkōṭimālai, *passim*. In the light of the Tamil myths, the

etymologizing myth of the Amazons who cut off one breast "in order to shoot better" may seem less fantastic; so is the tradition that it was the Amazons who set up the image of the many-breasted Artemis at Ephesus—Graves (1955), 1:355 and 2:125, 130-31.

91. We will return to this point in section 9 below.

92. Rāmprasād Sen, cited by Thompson and Spencer, p. 34.

### IV.6. Marriage and the Dance

1. Recall the head-sacrifice to the goddess: above, section 4 at n. 72.

2. Tiruvācakam 12.9 and 13. In later times this argument becomes the *only* rationale for Śiva's wedding, since the Śaiva Siddhāntins are reluctant to admit the possibility (developed in earlier Śaiva myth) of true eroticism in the god. Śiva is chaste and without desire, but marries in order to preserve the world. See Muttukumāracuvāmi ttampirāṉ, pp. 114-15. Note, too, the "this-worldly" orientation—the hostility to release (*vīṭu*) and to the winning of heaven—in the Tiruvācakam verse just cited.

3. See Tiruvŏṟṟiyūr 3.12; Tirukkuṟṟālam 2.9.1-40; Kāñci 20.1-3; Śvetāraṇya 4; Dorai Rangaswamy, 1:442-47. On Citamparam, see below.

4. Civakāmiyammai is the goddess inside the main shrine at Citamparam (as distinct from Tillaikkāḷiyammaṉ, who is completely excluded; her shrine today is about a quarter of a mile to the north of the Śrī Naṭarāja temple complex). An image of Civakāmiyammai nearly always appears in Naṭarāja shrines in temples throughout Tamiḻnāṭu.

5. See the first paragraph above. The entire series may be represented at the old shrine to Śiva at the southern end of the hill at Tirupparaṅkuṉṟam (not the Murukaṉ shrine): here we find Śiva dancing in competition with Kālī in the central shrine, Subrahmaṇya with his two wives (the conventional marriage) to the east, and a shrine to Ardhanārīśvara to the west. See Francis (1906), p. 280.

6. It is striking that the main shrine of the eighth-century Kailāsanātha temple at Kāñci is flanked on both sides by subshrines depicting the *ūrdhvatāṇḍava* of Śiva (the dance he adopts during his competition with the goddess), with Devī as witness. Clearly, the story of the dance contest was popular already in Pallava times.

7. On the *tuṇaṅkai* dance of the demons, see Tirumuru. 56 and the commentary of U. Ve. Cāminātaiyar on Kuṟ. 31.

8. See Kuṟ. 214; Tirumuru. 222.

9. Kulke, p. 43.

10. On the symbolism of Naṭarāja, see Coomaraswamy, pp. 56-66; Zimmer (1946), pp. 151-75; Sivaramamurti (1974), pp. 23-41. We will be concerned in this section only with those parts of the Naṭarāja myths relating to divine marriage.

11. On other shrines of the dancing Śiva, and the forms of the dance proper to them, see above, II.3 following n. 26.

12. Appar Tev. 666 (*patikam* 68.8). Note that this verse begins with a reference to the androgyne. Tiruvācakam 12.14 is usually taken to refer to the story of the dance contest: if Śiva had not performed his dance, the entire earth would have become food for Kālī.

13. On Nīli, see above, section 5 at note 13.

14. See above, section 2 n. 62. It is unclear how Kāraikkāl came to be linked with Tiruvālaṅkāṭu and the dance story in this manner. Kāraikkālammaiyār is worshiped today in a separate shrine at Kāraikkāl, but the Śaiva tradition firmly connects her with Tiruvālaṅkāṭu.

15. These names are probably derived from Niśumbha and Śumbha of the Sanskrit tradition.

16. On Raktabīja, see above, III.2 at n. 53.

17. Commentary: *aruṭcatti*, i.e., the goddess.

18. Cāttaṉ = Śāstṛ (nom. Śāstā), Aiyaṉār, the son of Śiva and Viṣṇu-Mohinī. For his myths, see section 9 below.

19. Kŏṟṟavai is here a synonym for Kālī. In the Caṅkam poems, Kŏṟṟavai is the Tamil name for the fierce goddess of war, identified from early times with Durgā.

20. Commentary: *cāmavetam*, the Sāmaveda.

21. Tiruvālaṅkāṭṭuppurāṇam 10.1-77, 11.1-32, 12.1-61, 13.1-35, 14.1-55.

22. Koyil 3.29-46; see above, II.1 n. 4. For the Pine Forest myth, see below, section 9.

23. See above, III.3.

24. See above, section 4.

25. Hiltebeitel (1976), pp. 81-85; Biardeau (1971-1972), p. 38. On the *pralaya*, see above, II.2.

26. See above, III.3 n. 16.

27. Naidu et al., pp. 7-8; Sivaramamurti (1974), p. 379; Tirukkūvam 7.270-74. The latter text makes explicit the iconographic analogy between this figure of the *ūrdhvatāṇḍava* and the pose of Trivikrama-Viṣṇu (verse 270).

28. Tiruviḷai. 5.43.

29. Cīkāḻi 6.5.

30. See above, I.2 n. 28.

31. See the note in Kârâvelane, p. 44. This author states that Kālī, subdued, is married to Śiva at Tiruvālaṅkāṭu.

32. See above, section 5 at and following n. 13.

33. Hence the proverb *tillaikkāḷi ĕllaikk'appāl*, "Tillaikkāḷi is beyond the pale."

34. Naṭarācaṉ, pp. 4-5.

35. Somasundaram Pillai, p. 72.

36. To be precise, the Kanaksabhā leads to the Citsabhā, which is considered to be the site of the dance: Sivaramamurti (1974), p. 383.

37. Note in this connection that the Tillaikkāḷi shrine is under the care of the Dīkṣitar Brahmin community, like the Śrī Naṭarāja shrine. The version of the myth published by the *devasthānam* may have been influenced by Brahmin concerns for purity and the suppression of violence.

38. Told to me by R. N. Natarajarathina Deeskhitar, one of the priests of the Tillaikkāḷi shrine, on January 5, 1976.

39. The folk etymology confusing ḷ and ḻ is attested at Cīkāḻi as well: Cīkāḻi 6. See also Mahalingam (1972), p. 1.

40. Citamparapurāṇam 8.23.

41. For other examples of the common motif of the Vedas' presence in a shrine, see Tirukkaḻukkuṉṟam 5 (pp. 27-31); Kāñci 62.3, 65-81; Vedāraṇyamāhātmya 2.65-67; Tiruvŏṟṟiyūr 5.1-28; Tirumayilai 8.1-26; Tiruvāṉmiyūr 8 (pp. 26-29).

42. In Cil. 6.39-43, elucidated by 28.67-75, Śiva as *ardhanārī* performs the dance in the burning-ground where Kālī (Pārati) dances. See also Sivaramamurti (1974), p. 130.

43. See Sarkar, p. 52; Srinivasan, pp. 50-56.

44. Stein (1973), p. 75.

45. Ponnusamy, p. 76.

46. For example, Śrīnakaram, Kamalālayam, Cattipuram. See Tiruvārūr 5.5-6.

47. *Ibid*. 16.2. Here the goddess is *parācatti* (*parāśakti*), while in canto 10 Kamalāmpikai is associated with Lakṣmī/Padmā, who wins a husband at Tiruvārūr. Yet the original Kamalāmpikai must have been the goddess who performs *tapas* alone, without marrying: see *pāyiram* 5.

48. According to the modern inscription on the wall of the shrine.

49. The stone (*vaṭṭapāṟai*) was, according to the tradition there, originally the site of blood offerings to the goddess.

50. See above, III.1.

51. Cf. the Dakṣa myths and their antecedents, the Rudra-Prajāpati cycle, in which the gods seek to deprive Rudra-Śiva of his share: above, III.3; O'Flaherty (1976), pp. 272-77.

52. Above, section 5 n. 36.

53. For earlier attempts to remove her from even this forum, according to one reading of the *Cidambaramāhātmya*, see Kulke, pp. 146-47.

## IV.7. The Bride as Mother

1. Rāmprasād Sen, in Thompson and Spencer, p. 30.

2. It has become something of a convention to describe some (if not all) forms of Devī as representatives of a supposedly original Mother Goddess (see, for example, Kosambi, 1962, pp. 42-109; Dikshit, *passim*). I shall en-

deavor here to isolate those aspects of the Tamil goddess myths that are in fact capable of being linked with maternity.

3. See section 1 above.

4. Above, section 3 n. 49.

5. Kāmākṣīvilāsa 11.18-43; Kāmākṣilīlāpirapāvam, p. 72. See also the following story (Kāmākṣīvilāsa 11.46-55), in which worship at the Kāmakoṭibila is compared to the gift of the womb of a golden cow.

6. *Ibid*. 11.36. For the castration in the Pine Forest, see above, III.3 n. 46.

7. Brahmāṇḍa 3.4.39.50-54.

8. See above, II.2 n. 58; O'Flaherty (1975), pp. 28-31.

9. Lévi-Strauss, pp. 226-27; Piatigorsky (1974).

10. See above, section 3 n. 46.

11. See section 6.

12. RV 1.31.2; 3.55.6-7; 1.112.4; cf. 3.25.1; 1.140.2-3, 10; 7.2.5.

13. Cf. 1.142.7 (night and dawn).

14. *Ibid*. 1.95.1; 1.96.5.

15. *Ibid*. 3.56.5; 1.164.10.

16. *Ibid*. 1.141.2; cf. 3.1.6.

17. *Ibid*. 9.100.7; 9.111.2.

18. *Ibid*. 9.86.36; cf. 1.34.8; 1.158.5; 9.10.7; 9.8.4; 9.102.4.

19. See Heesterman (1957), pp. 17-18, 22.

20. Stith Thompson, motifs S12 and S31.

21. RV 5.2.1-2. The commentators connect these verses with the story of the Piśācī wife of Tryaruṇa: Bṛhaddevatā 5.14-22. Both Sāyaṇa and Mādhava gloss *péṣī* (v. 2) as *piśācikā* (Geldner: "Stiefmutter").

22. MBh 7.173.89. Cf. the explanation offered by ŚB 2.6.2.9; and for the problem of Tryambaka, see Keith (1925), 1:143 and 149; Venkataramanayya (1941), pp. 29, 49, 56. See also Wright (1966).

23. Sāyaṇa on RV 7.59.12 (and see the note by Max Müller, p. 14).

24. Kālikā 49.26-64.

25. MBh 3.127.2-21, 3.128.1-7; KSS 2.5.57-65.

26. MBh 2.16.12-51, 2.17.1-5.

27. See the discussion below.

28. On the split child, see O'Flaherty (1976), pp. 353-57.

29. Vināyaka 71.43-75. The Śabdakalpadruma quotes from a probable Sanskrit original for this story under *dvaimātura*. Cf. Amarakoṣa (Benares) 1.1.38; Tanjore ed., 1.1.44.

30. Compare in this connection the tradition of Draupadī as *dvepitikā*, having two fathers—her real father and the king of Benares, who kills him and adopts his daughter. Jātaka 536 (V, 424).

31. Pate, pp. 115-16. On the nature of the Brahmarākṣasa, see Oppert, p. 298; Natesa Sastri (1888), pp. 214-20; Tirukkaṇṭiyūr 2-3. The Cuṭalaimāṭacuvāmivilpāṭṭu makes no mention of the foster mothers, but

describes a single wife of the god, Cuṭalaimāṭātti, created by Śiva for his son when he refuses to leave Kailāsa alone.

32. Cil. 21.43. On the symbolism of left and right, see Beck (1975-c), pp. 22-23.

33. Cuṭalaimāṭacuvāmivilpāṭṭu, pp. 1-6; see section 5 n. 73.

34. Padma, *svargakhaṇḍa* 16.2.21.

35. O'Flaherty (1976), pp. 321-69.

36. See above, III.2, especially the myths from Tiruvāṉmiyūr and Cikkal (nn. 14 and 19); on breast symbolism, see above, sections 4-5.

37. RV 1.153.3; cf. 10.11.1; 9.96.15.

38. *Ibid*. 1.160.3.

39. *Ibid*. 5.52.16; 1.23.10; 1.85.3.

40. Maṇimekalai 13 and 15.

41. Above, III.3 nn. 10-11.

42. See section 3. In some texts (KP 1.4; Campantar, Tev. 3.7 comm.) Kāma prefers to die at Śiva's hands, rather than to live on in the company of such evil creatures as the gods, who would send him to disturb Śiva's meditation.

43. To be precise, in *nirvikalpasamādhi* (8.8).

44. See Kāñci 13.1.42; Skanda 4.1.95.28-74; above, I.1. n. 15.

45. Tiruppaiññīli 8.1-24, 9.1-20.

46. See MBh 3.98.1-24; 12.329.26; Tiruviḷai. 1.28-36; Tīrttakiri 8.1-3. Ultimately this myth goes back to a Vedic myth: Indra slays ninety-nine Vṛtras with the bones of Dadhyañc. See RV 1.84.13-15.

47. Skanda 7.1.32-33; Brahma 110.85-86.

48. PP 4.5.64. See above, II.2 n. 33.

49. Padma 6.148.25-27.

50. Above, III.2 nn. 14 and 19.

51. Tiruviḷai. 29.1-23.

52. See above, III.2 n. 10.

53. Tiruviḷai. 29.18.

54. See the introduction to section 6.

55. As in the paintings of this myth in the Tiruviḷai. series in both Maturai and Tañcāvūr (on the *prākāra* wall).

56. Śiva 4.5-6.

57. Ramesan, pp. 52-53.

58. Velaimānakar caritai, pp. 12-21 (and see the engraving on p. 17). In the multicolored cow we see again the triad of red, white, and black (see III.2 n. 89).

59. See Winslow and Tamil Lexicon, under *kārāmpacu*; also Aṇṇaṉmār katai (Beck, 1975, pp. 7-9). In my experience, however, processional images and paintings of the Kāmadhenu are invariably white or gold.

60. Taleyarkan, p. 174.

61. Ramanujan (1972).

62. In addition to the classic instance of Śiva's beheading of Brahmā, and the possibility of Indra's slaying Tvaṣṭṛ (see O'Flaherty, 1976, pp. 102-103), there is the story of Babhrūvāhana, who slays his father Arjuna in battle (MBh 14.78-82); Hanūmat is defeated by his son Matsyakalpa but then evens the score by striking his son down (Mayilirāvaṇaṉkatai, pp. 29-36); Murukaṉ humiliates his father Śiva, who has to seek instruction from his son at Cuvāmimalai (Śrī svāmimalaikṣetramāhātmya 1.37-48; Das, p. 127; Śrī satyagirimāhātmya 1.10-99; Śiva 6.11.10-55).

63. Mārkaṇḍeya 106 and 108.

64. Viṣṇu 1.11-12. See also Jātakas 510 and 513.

65. RV 6.55.5. Compare the description of Sūrya in RV 1.115.2; Macdonell (1917), p. 92.

66. On the symbolism of the Vedic incest myth, see Wright (1967), pp. 526-47; Kosambi (1951).

67. Harivaṃśa 2.106.1-64; 2.110.1-35; Bhāgavata 10.55.1-40; Tiruccĕṅkoṭṭumāṉmiyam, pp. 200-204.

68. Ziegenbalg, p. 60 note. See also O'Flaherty (1975), pp. 261-62; Leach; Beck (1974), pp. 11-12.

69. Pillay, pp. 76-77.

70. See the sources cited in n. 68.

71. Hart (1974), pp. 36-39. Note that the woman is impure during the *puṉiṟu* period after childbirth: above, III.2 nn. 62-63.

72. See section 8 below; Beck (1974), p. 42.

73. See Chatterjee, pp. 102-103; Bṛhaddharma 2.60.106-108. Skanda is the patron of prostitutes—because they can never marry? Women are banned from the grove sacred to Skanda: see Vikramorvaśīya, Act IV, pp. 89-90.

74. Brahma 81.1-6. Similarly Joseph, tempted by Potiphar's wife, sees the image of his mother before him and desists: Bereshit Rabbah (Albeck), p. 1072.

75. MBh 7.173.59-63, following Southern Recension; see also the 16 lines inserted by northern mss. after verse 60. And cf. *Liṅga* 1.102.28-41. Indra's aggression against the child mirrors the conclusion of the Skanda birth myth (see below).

76. Liṅga 1.106.21-23.

77. Tiruvāvaṭuturai kovil katai, summarized by Mahalingam (1972), pp. 250-51.

78. Above, II.2 n. 17.

79. Matsya 158.38-48; Padma 5.41.121-26; Paripāṭal 5 (see below).

80. Rām. 1.45.1-22.

81. RV 1.85.3.

82. Mattiyārccuṉam, p. 215; Tiruvāvaṭuturai ttaricaṉam, p. 5; T. N. Arunachalam, pp. 10 and 14.

83. Tirutturutti 5.10-25; 10.25-27; 12.1-23. I have omitted the adventures of the cow goddess on her way to Tiruvāvaṭuturai.

84. Tiruvaruṭpayaṉ 1.2-3; 10.8.

85. Liṅga 1.80.44-57.

86. See, for example, Elwin (1939), p. 325: "Mahadeo was the son of Amardevi. . . . When he grew up, he desired his mother, and married her, changing her name to Parvati."

87. Tiruvarañcaram 2.5-72.

88. Mārkaṇḍeya 5.8-11; Bhāgavata 6.13.15.

89. TS 2.5.3.1-6; JB 2.157.

90. A pun on *paśudharma*, "intercourse."

91. Kālikā 93.1-15.

92. Śrīnāgeśakṣetramāhātmya 5.

93. Mārkaṇḍeya 106 and 108.

94. RV 10.72.8-9. Śiva is Mārttāṇṭavayiravamūrttam in Vairavaṉkoyil, *mūrttiviceṭam*.

95. Mārkaṇḍeya 105.1-19.

96. Oppert, pp. 465-66 n. 253.

97. *Ibid.*, pp. 472-73 n. 265.

98. Cf. the motif of the goddess pacified by the sight of her sons: above, III.2 nn. 11-12.

99. Oppert, pp. 472-73 n. 265.

100. Cf. the Anasūyā myths from Cucīntiram (above, section 2), where the frustrated sexual aggression is attributed to the three gods.

101. For a fuller treatment, including tribal and northern variants, see Shulman (1976-a), pp. 239-64; and see the extensive discussion of the Skanda myth by O'Flaherty (1973), pp. 93-110.

102. The wives of the sages, the Kṛttikās, are the Pleiades (Tam. *aṟumīṉ*).

103. MBh 3.213-18 (condensed).

104. *Ibid.* 3.216.1; 3.214.6; 3.215.18-23, including the line interpolated after 18; 9.43.10-12.

105. Mārkaṇḍeya 88.11-21, 38-61; Matsya 179.2-90; Varāha 27.1-39; Kūrma 1.15.170-75, 219-36; cf. Gopinatha Rao, I, 2, pp. 379-83; Aruṇācalam 4.27; above, section 6 n. 16.

106. The Varāha (27.1-39) lists eight: Yogeśvarī, Māheśvarī, Vaiṣṇavī, Brāhmaṇī, Kaumārī, Indrāṇī, Yāmī, and Varāhī. Kulke (pp. 53-57) believes this version conflates two myths—hence, eight *śaktis* instead of seven, with two of them (Yogeśvarī and Māheśvarī) associated with Śiva.

107. Matsya 179.2-90; Varāha 27.1-39; see Gonda (1970), p. 104.

108. According to Nīlakaṇṭha (on 3.230.16 of the Vulgate), these are the *śaktis* of the gods: Brāhmī, Māheśvarī, and so on. Van Buitenen (1975), p. 834, note on 3.219.15, suggests that they are the real mothers of the infants preyed upon by the Mothers of Skanda.

109. MBh 3.219.14-58; cf. 9.45.1-40. Cf. also the Seven Mothers listed in 3.217.9.

110. Filliozat (1937), pp. 67-82.

111. Getty, p. 11. It is not hard to imagine how sick children may be thought to be preyed upon by invisible mothers hungry for offspring of their own.

112. See Graves (1955), 1:152-54.

113. O'Flaherty (1973), pp. 255-313.

114. MBh 1.188.14.

115. Kālikā 48.12-96.

116. MBh 1.224.27-29.

117. See Elwin (1939), p. 328; *idem* (1944), pp. 202-204; Frere, pp. 50-65; Parker, 3:152-54.

118. Cil. 20.37-40.

119. KP 1.11.1-127; 1.13.1-34. Cf. Taṇikai 10.17-31; Tirumayilai 9.45-54; Kāñci 25.1-45.

120. The clump of reeds (*śaravaṇa*) in which Skanda is born (related to Śaryaṇāvat at Kurukṣetra?) is always, like Śaryaṇāvat, a pond or tank in Tamil sources. For an early reference, see Cil. 11.94.

121. Skanda 3.3.13.33; and compare the role of Vāyu in Skanda 6.70-71.

122. KP 1.12.6-10. The reference to the Pine Forest is made clear in KP 6.13.44-85; see below, section 9 following n. 82.

123. On the erotic significance of eyes and visions, see above, sections 3 and 4.

124. Mārkaṇḍeya 17.9-10 (above, section 2 n. 29); for Koccĕṅkaṇ, see Tiruvāṉaikkā 21. Another child who suffers in the womb is Dīrghatamas: MBh 1.98.6-16.

125. Vāmana 46.24-41; see also 46.71-75.

126. MBh 3.219.26; 9.45.16.

127. Bhāgavata 10.6.1-44.

128. Gros (1968), p. xxxviii.

129. Parimelaḻakar elaborates: "Please destroy the embryo conceived through this embrace." However, Nacciṉārkkiṉiyar in his commentary on Tirumuru. 58 takes it as I have translated (*nī puṇarcci tavira veṇṭum ĕṉṟu*). This is surely better for *vilaṅk' ĕṉa* (line 31).

130. Paripāṭal 5.26-54. I have added the bracketed identifications for the sake of clarity.

131. On Cāliṉi see also Cil. 12.7.

132. See above, II.1 at n. 42.

133. Nacciṉārkkiṉiyar on Tirumuru. 58.

134. Gros (1968), p. 26; cf. xxxviii-xxxix.

135. See above, III.3 n. 15; below, V, final section.

136. Tiruppātirippuliyūr 11.17. And cf. Tiruviḷai. 33.1-29, where the

six Iyakkamātar are cursed by Śiva to become stones because they forgot to worship Umā.

137. Jouveau-Dubreuil, p. 38 n. 2; Krishna Sastri, p. 229.

138. See above, II.2 n. 60.

139. Beck (1974), p. 8.

140. Tiruviḷai. 33.1-29. The Kṛttikās here suffer the same fate as Ahalyā, cursed by her husband Gautama to become a rock because of her adultery with Indra.

141. Whitehead, p. 26; Diehl, p. 260.

142. Tirupperūr 18.1-62.

143. Matsya 154.449-50.

144. Kūrma 2.37.1-45; Śiva, *Dharmasaṃ*. 10.79-207; see section 9 below.

145. Tiruccĕṅkoṭṭumāṉmiyam, pp. 200-204.

146. Pattiṉiyammaṉ varalāṟu carittiramum kummiyum.

147. Thus Kaṇṇaki, the chaste wife (and in folk myths, the virgin goddess) is known as Pattiṉi.

148. Oppert, p. 484.

149. Whitehead, p. 32.

150. PP 6.1.473-83.

151. Verse 23 of Pattiṉiyammaṉ . . . kummi (see n. 146).

152. Above, section 2 at n. 22.

153. Whitehead, pp. 40, 24.

154. *Ibid*., p. 29.

155. Elwin (1949), pp. 30-35, 41-48.

156. Manasākāvya of Manakar, cited by Maity, p. 120.

157. RV 10.10. But the last day of Dīpāvali celebrates Yama's dining with his sister Yamunā: Underhill, p. 63. For other Vedic examples of brother-sister incest, see n. 65; RV 1.115.2 (Sūrya); Vāj. Saṃ. 3.57 and TB 1.6.10.4 (Rudra following his sister Ambikā). Cf. the Kāñci tradition cited above, section 3 nn. 34-42; Jagannātha and Subhadrā at Puri are a well-known incestuous pair (Dowson, p. 305; Mishra, pp. 216-18).

158. RV 2.35.3-5, 15; cf. Macdonell (1897), pp. 69-70; Keith (1925), 1:135-36; Heesterman (1957), pp. 86-88.

159. *Ibid*., pp. 43-44.

160. *Ibid*., pp. 13-14, 34-37, 51-52.

161. Elwin (1947), pp. 240-43.

162. *Ibid*., pp. 247-48.

163. Whitehead, p. 32. Cf. Jouveau-Dubreuil, p. 116.

164. The inscriptions under the figures identify each one twice: from left to right, they are Parācar-Jaṭāmuṉi, Viyākkiramar-Lāṭamuṉi, Viyāsar-Muttumuṉi, Nāratar-Vetamuṉi, Vicuvāmittirar-Karimuṉi, and Vaciṣṭar-Cĕmmuṉi.

165. Field notes, Tirumullaivāyil, December 29, 1975.
166. Eṇiyeṟṟam, pp. 39-50.
167. Nallataṅkāḷ katai, *passim*.
168. *Ibid.*, p. 15.
169. Vanamalai (1969), pp. 119-20.
170. *Ibid.*
171. MBh 1.91-92.
172. ŚB 5.3.1.13.
173. Devībhāgavata 9.46.25-26; MBh 3.218.47; cf. Kosambi (1962), p. 88; Neogi, p. 131.
174. For the *vaṉṉi* tree in Śaiva myth, see Tiruviḷai. 64.1-55 (Cil. 21.5-6). The *vaṉṉi* is the *sthalavṛkṣa* at Viruttācalam.
175. Vanamalai (1969), pp. 119-20.
176. Vikkiramātittaṉkatai 3 (pp. 132-62); Mataṉakāmarājaṉkatai 3 (pp. 42-50).
177. In KSS 18.4.204-47, the *mātṛkās* also steal a bridegroom while he is asleep beside his bride.
178. I am indebted to Brenda Beck for this observation.
179. Mataṉakāmarājaṉkatai, p. 46.
180. Lal Behari Day, pp. 339-42; cf. the version of Steel, pp. 64-71. For other variants of this pattern, see Elwin (1944), pp. 197-202.
181. Whitehead, pp. 116-17; cf. Elmore, pp. 95-96; Oppert, pp. 466-67; Thurston (1909), 4:300-303; Brubaker.
182. KSS 12.80 (Vetālapañcaviṃśatika 6); see also Mann.
183. On the relations between Brahmins and outcastes, see above, III.1 at n. 15, and section 4 at n. 55.
184. See the discussion by Goldman, pp. 80, 86; Biardeau (1968), pp. 569-72.
185. Rām. 7.51.2-24; Matsya 47.101-107; cf. Civañāṉacittiyār, *parapakkam*, 6.29.
186. Rām. 1.24.3-19, 1.25.1-14. However, Kāñci 45.4-62 suggests that Paraśurāma commits a crime in slaying his mother.
187. Cf. Apītakucā at Tiruvaṇṇāmalai: above, section 5 n. 73.

## IV.8. The Double Bride

1. See section 3 at n. 46.
2. Tiruvārūr 25.22-36. But the two wives of the single god need not always be opposed: in Vāj. Saṃ. 31.22, Puruṣa (Prajāpati) has Śrī and Lakṣmī as his consorts.
3. He is also erotically linked with Sandhyā, Mohinī, Anasūyā and other women: see O'Flaherty (1973), pp. 226-33. For Mohinī, see section 9 below.
4. Brahma 74-75.

5. Manasākāvya of Manakar, cited Maity, p. 120; Kāñcīmāhātmya 25-26.
6. Tiruviriñcai 2.26-82. See above, section 3 after n. 48.
7. Bṛhaddharma 2.41-43.
8. See above, section 7 at nn. 77-83.
9. See above, section 1 at nn. 20-22.
10. The text derives this name from *sa* + *umā*. Tantric Śaiva cults similarly derive the idea of union with the goddess from the epithets Someśvara, Somanātha, and so on, using the same false etymology: see Lorenzen, pp. 82-83, 90.
11. Kāḷaiyārkoyil 6.1-43, 7-8 (condensed), 9.2-32, 10.2-45.
12. ŚB 2.2.4.1-8.
13. Aruṇācalam 5.64; Tiruccĕṅkoṭu 1.4-5.
14. See Subhāṣitaratnakoṣa 82; O'Flaherty (1973), pp. 257-58.
15. Bṛhaddharma 2.41.106-108; O'Flaherty (1973), p. 232.
16. For this epithet, see the myths of Mīnākṣī/Aṅkayaṟkaṇṇammai, above, section 5.
17. Cil. 7.2-3.
18. Tulākkāverimāṉmiyam 5-6; Kāverippurāṇam 4.1-49; Tiruvaiyāṟu 4.1-25; Srinivas (1952), pp. 244-45; see above, section 1 nn. 25-26, and II.2 n. 64.
19. Rice, pp. 153-61 (after an unnamed Sanskrit source).
20. See above, II.2 following n. 64.
21. Prahlāda is, of course, familiar with the Man-Lion, for Viṣṇu takes the form of the Man-Lion to save Prahlāda from his father Hiraṇyakaśipu.
22. Kāmākṣīvilāsa 3.7-28, 4.10-58; 5.11-30; Kāmākṣilīlāpirapāvam 3-5 (pp. 21-33). The identification of Hastigiri (Attikiri) in the first paragraph is taken from the Tamil source. For the origin of the name Hastigiri (ultimately from *atti*, Ficus glomerata), see Raman, pp. 5-7. For another version of the myth, see Hardy, p. 145. The story has also been attached by popular etymology to Paḷḷikŏṇṭa in North Arcot: see Cox, 2:424.
23. Kāñci 11.1-49; 16.1-6.
24. See above, III.3 n. 82 and Figure III.
25. See above, section 3 nn. 34-40.
26. MBh 13.139.9-30.
27. Padma 5.18.159-99.
28. *Ibid*. 5.16-17.
29. *Ibid*. 5.18.198-99.
30. The *gāndharva* marriage by mutual consent could be celebrated simply by pledging one's love. Clandestine or irregular unions often fall into this category: see Basham, p. 169.
31. Padma 5.16.112-90, 5.17.1-337. Cf. Skanda 6.181.
32. Oppert, pp. 289-92; Tiruvārūr 50.1-23. There is an associated folk etymology of the name Gāyatrī (from *go*).

33. Kāñci 11.10-22. Cf. the old myth of Vāc hiding in wood: Tāṇḍya 6.5.10-13.

34. Tiruviḷai. 51.1-10.

35. Skanda 3.1.40-41; Cetu 41 (Kāyattiri caracuvati tīrtta ccarukkam), 1-37. This is, of course, a descendant of the myth of Rudra's attack on Prajāpati in punishment for incest.

36. Padma 5.16.130-90, 5.17.1-31.

37. See above, section 7 nn. 72-74.

38. Naṟṟiṇai 82.4.

39. In addition to the evidence of the mythology, this preference is sometimes stated explicitly: Vaḷḷi is the preferred wife (*muntiya tāram*) of Murukaṉ—Tiruccĕntūr 6.18. On the historical prominence of Vaḷḷi, see Zvelebil (1977), *passim*.

40. This is a folk etymology based on *yāṉai*, "elephant"; in reality Tam. Tĕyvayāṉai is undoubtedly derived from Devasenā. The folk etymology leads to such names as Tevakuñcari, Kajavalli (Diehl, p. 135), etc.

41. KP 1.18.1-11; 5.2.1-268; ŚRKh 5.1.35-87, 5.2.1-66. For the marriage of Tĕyvayāṉai see also Tiruccĕṅkoṭu 2.7.1-12; Tirupperūr 30.1-134; Iḷaiyaṉār velūr 10 (pp. 87-88).

42. Convolvulus batatas.

43. According to the *akam* conventions, a rejected suitor might ride a hobby-horse fashioned from the leaves of the palmyra palm in a public place in order to shame the beloved into accepting him. See Nacc. on Tŏl. Pŏruḷ. 50-51; Kuṟ. 17; Kalittŏkai 139; Marr (1958), pp. 30-35; below, section 9 nn. 28-30.

44. Cūr (Skt. Śūrapadma) is in the Tamil tradition the major enemy of Murukaṉ.

45. KP 6.24.1-200; ŚRKh 5.3.19-86, 5.4.1-58, 5.5.1-23.

46. For the relevant conventions see Nampiyakappŏruḷ 20, 54; Ramanujan (1967), pp. 103-14; Zvelebil (1973-b), pp. 97-98. For the heroine guarding the millet fields, see, for example, Kuṟ. 142; 214; 217; 223; Tirumuru. 242. For exorcism: Kuṟ. 214; 263. For *maṭal*: Kuṟ. 14; 17; 32. For the maiden locked in the house: above, section 4 n. 86.

47. Taṇikai 16.1-643; see esp. vv. 57-104, and the verses interspersed with the narrative, 150-620.

48. Tiruccĕntūr 7.1-24, 8.1-6.

49. KP 6.24.97.

50. As in the myths of Cyavana: see O'Flaherty (1973), pp. 57-64.

51. DED 4081. This name for the god (*muruku*) appears already in Naṟṟiṇai 82.4, where Vaḷḷi is also mentioned.

52. Tiruttaṇikai kṣettira mahātmiyam . . . , p. 126.

53. Perhaps the outstanding Śaiva example of this very striking reversal is Tirukkovaiyār (esp. chapter 10). Cf. Hart (1974), pp. 50-51.

54. Kuṟ. 214; see Hart (1973), pp. 244-45.

55. Taṇikai 16.116-18.

56. MBh 3.115.23-24; Elmore, pp. 81-82. The Tamil myth may suggest an implicit gloss on *valli*, "creeper."

57. See Beck (1975-a), pp. 108-11.

58. Kālikā 46.1-5.

59. See above, section 2 after n. 55.

60. For the three kinds of evil according to Śaiva Siddhānta, see Dhavamony, pp. 177-78, 276-81.

61. Taṇikai 16.97.

62. See *ciṟṟurai* on CÑP 1; Dhavamony, p. 346.

63. Rām. 1.65.14; see Gonda (1954), p. 125. Note, however, that Sītā is identified with Śrī rather than with Bhūdevī, Viṣṇu's "chthonic" consort. Vaḷḷi, too, presents an analogy with Śrī as the dominant wife of the god; see n. 66 below, and Zvelebil (1977), pp. 230-32. But for reasons that will become clear, I cannot agree with Professor Zvelebil's conclusion that there is no parallelism whatsoever between Vaḷḷi and Bhūdevī (p. 231).

64. Beck (1975-a), pp. 110-11, notes the interesting link here with Lévi-Strauss's distinction between the raw and the cooked.

65. Gombrich (1971), pp. 172-73. In Tamiḻnāṭu the Vaḷḷi myth is usually located at Taṇikai, although other shrines do claim the goddess as their own: see Tiruvalañcuḻi ĕṉum naṟppatiyil vaḷḷittiṉaippuṉam kārkkum uccavakummi.

66. Diehl, p. 135; Beck (1975-a), p. 95.

67. Kandiah, p. 95.

68. See Sivaraman, p. 99.

69. KP 6.24.44.

70. *Ibid*. 6.24.41.

71. Tiruccĕṅkoṭu 2.9.1-30.

72. In the myths of both we find the unnatural birth, the hero who enters the ocean to destroy a demon, the association with the peacock and the *kadamba* tree, the image of the youthful erotic god alongside that of the divine child, the double marriage, and so on. In addition, one must note the striking association of Murukaṉ and Tirumāl-Viṣṇu on the ground, in the location of Tamil shrines: there is still discussion about which of the two is the deity of Tirupati (Sitapati, pp. 21-29); the Cil. locates a *puṇṇiya caravaṇam* (the birthplace of Skanda) at Tirumāliruñcolai (11.94); the two gods are connected with Tirukkuṟṟālam, Paḻani, and other sites.

73. Harivaṃśa 2.67.4-55, 2.68.1-55, 2.69.1-36. Cf. Sarasvati, pp. 266-68.

74. See Gravely and Ramachandran, pp. 92-94 and plates X and XI; for the manifold marriages of Kṛṣṇa, see Vaṭāraṇya 2.1-52.

75. Gonda (1954), p. 125.

76. On the Telugu Pārijātāpaharamu of Timmanna, see Marr (1969), pp. 595-96. Cf. Pārijātapuṣpāpaharaṇa carittiram. The most famous of the Kucipudi dance dramas is about this story; every Brahmin in Kucipudi village is expected to take the role of Satyabhāmā at least once during his lifetime, as an offering to Kṛṣṇa for preserving the tradition of dance. See Gargi, p. 190.

77. Another folk treatment of this theme occurs in the late genre of *paḷḷu*, which is built around the rivalry between an elder and younger wife of a Paḷḷaṉ agriculturist; the two wives are also conventionally divided along sectarian lines. The best example of this type of composition is the Mukkūṭaṟpaḷḷu. See Zvelebil (1975), pp. 257-59; *idem* (1974), pp. 226-27. Folk sources tend to depict one wife as good, the second as evil: thus the Kovalaṉkatai reinterprets the story of the Cil. in such a way as to stress Kaṇṇaki's loyalty and virtue while making Mātavi an evil temptress and a murderess by intention (see pp. 40-50). This polarization may be connected with the theme of the evil foster mother; the child of the rival brings out the latent evil in the bad wife. See for example Śiva 4.32-33; also Tiruviḷai. 64.1-55.

78. Tiruccĕntūr 6.17-28.

79. KP 6.24.232-59.

80. Paripāṭal 9.8-11; cf. 19.1-7. On the two wives of Murukaṉ in Paripāṭal, see Kandiah, pp. 90-95.

81. Beck (1975-a), pp. 96-97.

82. Jayanakaram vaḷḷi tĕyvayāṉai ecal, verses 1-4.

83. Vaḷḷiyammaṉvilācam, pp. 79-86.

84. Rĕṭṭikuṭiyecal, esp. vv. 3-17.

85. Cf. the insults traded by Śiva and Pārvatī: Subhāṣitaratnakoṣa 35; Padma 5.41.4-10; O'Flaherty (1973), pp. 224-26.

86. Beck (1975-a), pp. 97-107.

87. MBh 1.73 and 78. The Tamil Tĕyvayāṉai (< Devasenā) is not, however, related to Devayānī. Note the difference in status between the two wives, just as Murukaṉ's two wives belong to different social strata.

88. Tiruvāñciyakṣettirapurāṇam 4. In parallel passages of Devībhāgavata 9.6.17-54 and Brahmavaivarta 2.6.16-56, three wives of Viṣṇu quarrel; as a result, Sarasvatī is given to Brahmā, Gaṅgā to Śiva, and Lakṣmī is cursed to become, as Tulasī, the wife of the demon Śaṅkhacūḍa. In addition, all three become rivers. The conclusion of the text is: "He who has one wife is not happy—how much less happy is he who has many wives!" (Brahmavaivarta 2.6.44).

89. See Raṅkanāyakikkum nācciyārukkum camvātam. For the story of Āṇṭāḷ, see section 2 n. 64. The term *ecal* is also applied to the mutual abuse of Lakṣmī and Pārvatī, each of whom lampoons her rival's lord: Śrīmakālaṭcumikkum pārvatikkum vākkuvātam.

90. Piññai in Cil. 17, *karuppam*, apparently overlooked by Filliozat: Tiruppāvai, p. xvi n. 3.

91. Bhāgavata 10.58.32-47; for further references in the literature, particularly about Nīlā, see Filliozat, Tiruppāvai, pp. xvii-xix; Edholm and Suneson; Govindacharya Svamin; Oppert, pp. 363-64.

92. Dumont (1959), p. 80.

93. As in the *taṉiyam* of Parāśarabhaṭṭa, cited in Filliozat, Tiruppāvai, p. xviii; and the commentary to Tiruppāvai by Śrīraṅgarāmānujasvāmin, *ibid.*, pp. 57-67.

94. So Zvelebil (1974), p. 103 n. 32. The TL derives the name from *piṉṉu*, to plait, braid, etc.; hence, "she of the beautiful tresses"; see Irāmāvatāram 1.399. But cf. *nam piṉṉai*, Cil. 17, *ĕṭuttu kkāṭṭu*.

95. Tiruppāvai 20.6.

96. Filliozat, Tiruppāvai, p. xvi.

97. Cil. 17, *ĕṭuttu kkāṭṭu*.

98. Bhāgavata 10.30.35-38.

99. Vaudeville (1962).

100. See above, end of section 2.

101. I delete the lengthy anthill episode: see above, III.2 n. 86.

102. Veṅkaṭācalam, pp. 10-20; cf. Skanda 2.1.3-8; Tiruveṅkaṭa talapurāṇam 37-41.

103. Gonda (1954), pp. 195, 202, 223; Hopkins, p. 146; Bolle (1965), pp. 29-30; cf. MBh 2.10.18.

104. Stein (1960).

105. Veṅkaṭācalam, p. 26.

106. *Ibid.*, pp. 21-25.

107. Tirukkuṭantai aruḷ miku cārṅkapāṇi cuvāmi ālaya talavaralāṟu, pp. 33, 31; Das, p. 138.

108. Beck (1975-a), p. 111.

109. See section 2 nn. 37-48.

110. See the commentary of U. Ve. Cāminātaiyar on Kuṟ. 23; Zvelebil (1974), pp. 224-26. Note that the *kuṟatti* is linked to the Kuṟavar of the Vaḷḷi myth.

111. Kuṟ. 23.

112. Alliyaracāṇimālai, pp. 61-64.

113. Daśakumāracarita 5; Vikkiramātittaṉkatai 4 (p. 115).

114. Veṅkaṭācalam, p. 15.

115. Kūrma 2.33.113-41.

116. Devībhāgavata 9.16.28-54. For another permutation of the double Sītā, see below, V nn. 27-39. For the false Sītā in the Adhyātmarāmāyaṇa and in Tulsī Dās, see Vaudeville (1955), pp. 191, 259.

117. Rām. 7.17.1-38.

118. Tirukkuṭantai . . . cārṅkapāṇi cuvāmi, p. 33.

119. Mārkaṇḍeya 106 and 108; cf. Bṛhaddevatā 6.162-63, 7.1-6.

120. Tam. Uḻai and Cāyai, according to the priests of this shrine.

121. Mahābhāgavata 9-11, cited Hazra (1963), pp. 264-65.

122. Devībhāgavata 7.30.40-50; Skanda 1.1.3.49-52; Takkayākapparaṇi 328-34, 351, 429-33, 728, 794-96; cf. MBh 12.274, Appendix I, no. 28, lines 69-75.

123. Harivaṃśa 2.110; Bhāgavata 10.55; Tiruccĕṅkoṭṭumāṉiyam, pp. 200-204. Cf. the *māyā* forms of the *gopīs* which, according to the Bengal commentators, had consummated their marriages with their husbands, leaving the "real" *gopīs* pure for Kṛṣṇa's love: Dimock (1971), p. 56.

124. Gopinatha Rao, II, 2, p. 445; Beck (1975-a), p. 111; Ziegenbalg, p. 68.

125. Sarasvati, p. 265.

126. Gopinatha Rao, I, 2, p. 375; but the Viṣṇudharmottara says Lakṣmī should be dark (*ibid*.).

127. Gupte, p. xi; Kosambi (1962), p. 121.

128. See IV.5 at the end; on the symbolism of the color green in south India, see Beck (1969), p. 559.

129. Ziegenbalg, p. 133; cf. Gopinatha Rao, II, 2, pp. 488-89.

130. Field notes, December 5, 1975.

131. Jouveau-Dubreuil, p. 116.

132. *Ibid*., p. 115; cf. Oppert, pp. 482-83.

133. Dumont (1959), p. 87.

134. Viruttācalam = Vṛddhācala, "ancient hill."

135. Francis (1906-a), p. 398; cf. Krishnaswami, p. 10.

136. See above, section 4 at n. 81. Cuntarar is robbed by *bhūtas*, at the instigation of Śiva, near Tirumurukaṉpūṇṭi—to teach him that all wealth comes only from God. See PP 7.4.164-68. The Vaiṣṇava saint Tirumaṅkaiyāḻvār is said to have been a thief who robbed Viṣṇu himself. See Govindâcârya, p. 164ff.; Nilakanta Sastri (1966), p. 426.

137. We have noted earlier that there is a divergence between the ideals proclaimed by the stories and the normative rules of conduct—as in the case of the devotee who offers his wife to the god: above, section 2 after n. 57.

138. See above, III.4 n. 6.

139. Even Gaṇeśa, who is often thought of as a bachelor—perhaps because of his lust for his mother and the castrating influence of his father Śiva—is granted two wives, Siddhi and Buddhi, in a well-known myth: above, II.3 n. 19. The names of the brides sometimes vary: thus Vāṇī and Kamalī are the consorts of Śvetavināyaka at Tiruvalañcuḻi. See Jagadisa Ayyar, p. 81 and fig. 50. Gaṇeśa's wedding to two brides is depicted at Kovilūr, where he is worshiped as Kuḻantaināyakar: Bazou, p. 384. If Gaṇeśa is to be married at all, it had better be twice!

140. The two wives may also be polarized into "good" and "evil": see n. 77 above.

## IV.9. The Male as Goddess and Mother

1. Nīlakaṇṭha Mukhopādhyāya, cited by Thompson and Spencer, p. 78.
2. From a B.A. honors examination in English, Delhi.
3. See section 8 nn. 11-14.
4. O'Flaherty (1976), pp. 352-53.
5. Eliade (1960), pp. 176-77.
6. Gajāraṇyamāhātmya 26.5-27; cf. Tiruvāṉaikkāvalmāhātmiyam 26.
7. Tiruvāṉaikkā 8.34.
8. O'Flaherty (1976), pp. 27-29.
9. Thus Iḷa is both mother and father to Purūravas: MBh 1.70.13-20. Yuvanāśva gives birth to Māndhātṛ, who is nursed by Indra: MBh 3.126.5-29. The myth of Pṛthu and Vena may follow this pattern; see O'Flaherty (1976), pp. 321-69.
10. Tiruvāṉaikkā 12.88-89.
11. *Ibid.* 15.3.
12. In the Tamil purāṇas, it is usually Devī who worships the god at a shrine, not vice versa, even though the goddess is often definitely said to precede the god at the site. Another instance of the reversed pattern, as at Tiruvāṉaikkā, may be the myth of Śiva's worship at Tiruviṭaimarutūr "to show his devotees how to worship;" in fact, he is devoted to his bride, the local goddess. Mattiyārccuṉam, pp. 216-17, 231-32. It is noteworthy that it is Māndhātṛ, born from the male, who conducts the marriage festival of Śiva and Pārvatī at this site (*ibid.*, p. 232).
13. Das, p. 106.
14. Venkataramanayya (1941), pp. 59-60; Whitehead, pp. 27, 53, 58-59; Elmore, pp. 11, 18, 44, 30, 37. Cf. RV 8.33.19.
15. Kakati (1948), p. 46; Spratt, p. 248.
16. See Heesterman (1964) and (1975).
17. Blindness should probably be added to the series as a symbolic correlative of death and castration: see IV.4.
18. Oppert, p. 485; Francis (1906-a), p. 364.
19. Tirukkaḷar cāracaṅkirakam, pp. 46-47; Tirukkaḷarppurāṇam, *teviyār tiruviḷaiyāṭal*, p. 111.
20. Kāmākṣīvilāsa 11.18-43.
21. See IV.4 nn. 74-83.
22. Devībhāgavata 6.28.1-54, 6.29.1-66, 6.30.1-53. Nārada also experiences a reversal of sex in Padma 4.75.25-46.

23. MBh 12.30.4-41; Śiva 2.1.2.1-55; Devībhāgavata 6.26-27; Liṅga 2.5.52-154.

24. MBh 5.170-93.

25. Kosambi (1962), pp. 59-61, 77, discusses Bhīṣma, whom he sees as the victim of a river goddess Ambā. He notes the association of Nārada and Śikhaṇḍinī in the Anukramaṇī on RV 9.104, but fails to perceive the relation in the myth under discussion.

26. Zimmer (1946), p. 30. I have not been able to locate the text on which this version is based.

27. Note also Nārada's appearance in the myth of Bhīṣma's fight with Paraśurāma, who demands that Bhīṣma take Ambā as a wife!—MBh 5.186.2-23. Southern Recension (5.175-76) slightly expands Nārada's role.

28. Marr (1958), pp. 30-35; Nacc. on Tŏl. Pŏruḷ. 50-51; Paṉṉiru pāṭṭ'iyal 146-47. Cf. Kuṟ. 17; above, section 8 after n. 52.

29. See section 8 at nn. 43 and 53.

30. Hart (1973), pp. 244-45. Note that in Kalittŏkai 139, cited by Nacc. as illustrating *pĕruntiṇai* (see n. 28), the rejected lover complains that he has lost his manliness (*āṇ*).

31. MBh 1.61.87.

32. Dubois, Pañcatantra, pp. 15-24. Dubois's source was closely allied to the late and expanded Southern "amplior," which also has this story: cf. Hertel (1907), pp. 18-19; *idem* (1914), pp. 303-304, and Renou's introduction to the reprint of the Lancereau translation (1965), p. 16 n. 2. The story is missing from the Jain "vulgate" versions and their derivative southern works, but is found in altered form in the old Marathi and old Gujarati texts of the Pañcatantra: see Hertel (1914), pp. 148-49, 281-82.

33. See section 5, esp. n. 50.

34. Hertel (1914), pp. 281-82.

35. *Ibid.*, pp. 148-49; Brown (1927), pp. 11-12.

36. Matsya 11.43-66, 12.11; Liṅga 1.65.19-23; cf. Rām. 7.87-88.

37. On the *agniṣṭut* and the parallel myth of Ṛtuparṇa, see Caland, pp. 20-21.

38. MBh 13.12.2-49.

39. Note the male hostility to sexuality evident in Bhaṅgāśvana's final statement. This accords well with the general attitude discussed at the end of section 3.

40. Vetapuri sthalapurāṇam, Mackenzie Ms. T.D.1119 in the Government Oriental Manuscript Library, Madras, leaves 49-51 (cf. the summary by Mahalingam [1972]), p. 256.

41. See Macdonell (1897), pp. 30-54; Bhattacharji, pp. 224-25; Hopkins, pp. 84-89.

42. See section 4 n. 73.

43. MBh 1.70.13-20; ŚB 11.5.1.1-7.

44. Tiruvāṉmiyūr 2 (p. 8); Vaṭāraṇya 3.19-25 (7.5-45 of this purāṇa establishes another link with Nārada); Tiruvarañcaram 4.1-68; Wilson (1828), 2:51-54; Irāmāvatāram 1.5.26, commentary. Other versions of the birth of Vālin and Sugrīva say nothing of a reversal of sex: Rām. 1.15.1-7, and lines added after v. 8; Brahmāṇḍa 2.3.7.209-15.

45. Venkatasubbiah, pp. 113-14; cf. Artola, p. 36.

46. It is important to distinguish true sex-reversals from the common literary motif of the suitor who dresses as a woman: Daśakumāracarita 5; Kāmasūtra 5.6; KSS 1.7.77-82 (cf. Tawney and Penzer, 7:222-23); Vikkiramātittaṉkatai 4 (pp. 175-77); cf. the appearance of Kṛṣṇa as a *kuṟatti* in Alliyaracāṇimālai, pp. 61-64 (above, section 8 n. 112). Indra may also belong here: see Oertel, pp. 176-88; Brown (1927), p. 3. Hiding one's identity may require sexual transformation: Arjuna disguises himself as the long-haired eunuch (*ṣaṇḍhaka*) Bṛhannaḍā in MBh 4.2.21-27, 4.10.8-11. Arjuna is thus in any case akin to his Amazon bride Alli, a sexual hybrid who claims him as her victim. For the long-haired *keśava* as eunuch, neither man nor woman, see ŚB 5.1.2.14; the eunuch is confused with the sex-reversal, for example in Kŏvvākam kūttāṇṭavar cittirai tiruviḻā vicittira cintu, p. 5. For the diffusion of the motif of sex-reversal, see Brown (1927); Kalipada Mitra; Benfey, 1:41-52.

47. Kūrma 1.15.120-23.

48. ŚRKh 7.73.1-20. One of the signs by which a god is recognized is his impeccable Sanskrit: see Filliozat (1937), p. 120.

49. Mahādēviyakka 68, in Ramanujan (1973), p. 120. Cf. Irāmāvatāram 1.380.

50. Tirutturutti 18.23. See n. 13 above. It seems likely that this transvestite worship of Śiva at Tiruvāṉaikkā is a secondary development from the cult of the goddess.

51. See above, III.3 nn. 92-103; Kŏttiṭṭai kūttāṇṭavar utsavakkummi, *passim*.

52. Kŏvvākam kūttāṇṭavar . . . cintu, *passim*, esp. p. 4.

53. Whitehead, p. 27.

54. MBh 1.17.4-8.

55. For another explanation of Arāvāṉ's worship in this form, see III.3 n. 103.

56. Piatigorsky (1962), pp. 157-59.

57. Kŏvvākam kūttāṇṭavar . . . cintu, p. 4. See also the Arāvāṉ myths in III.3, esp. n. 92.

58. Oppert, p. 455.

59. *Ibid.*, p. 509. Cf. Kāmākṣilīlāpirapāvam, p. 67; Adiceam, p. 19.

60. MBh 1.16.38-40; cf. Skanda 1.1.12.14-59.

61. Brahmāṇḍa 3.4.10.27-77.

62. KP 2.32.27-40.

63. Keraḷatecavaralāṟu, pp. 29-30; Adiceam, p. 20; Dumont (1957), p. 401; Vināyaka 81.1-13; de Zoete, pp. 56-57; cf. the story of Vṛkāsura in Bhāgavata 10.88.13-36.

64. Śiva 3.20.3-7. Again a monkey, like Vālin and Sugrīva, is born from a "male" mother.

65. KP 2.32.36. Cf. Beck (1974), p. 14.

66. Liṅga 2.54.24-26; cf. Vāyu 24.72-73.

67. Sonnerat, p. 179. Cf. Jouveau-Dubreuil, pp. 11-12.

68. Kaṉṉiyākumari 10.5-7.

69. Tiruvāppaṉūr, *kāppu*. The commentator, Pa. Vacavaliṅka Paurāṇikar, makes clear the point of the invocation: Viṣṇu is addressed thus because he is one of Śiva's *aruṭcattimārkaḷ*, while Śrī (Tiru) is mentioned because it is wise to begin a book with this word.

70. KP 6.20.134.

71. *Ibid*. 2.32.27-40. See also KSS 1.1.32.

72. Kulke, p. 94. But the suggestion that the Mohinī myth is originally an anti-Vaiṣṇava thrust (*ibid*., p. 75 n. 136) is unlikely, considering its appearance in the MBh myth of churning the ocean.

73. See Beck (1974), p. 17; Bolle (1969), pp. 134-37.

74. Kūrma 2.37.1-162. See also Saura 69.37-54, which Kulke (p. 91) believes to be earlier.

75. See above, I.2.

76. Kūrma 2.37.103. Some mss. replace this phrase with other readings, thus obviating the problem of a previous visit to the forest by Pārvatī.

77. Darpadalana of Kṣemendra, 7; KSS 3.6.131-33.

78. Skanda 6.1.4-68; see above, III.3 n. 46.

79. Cuntarar, Tev. 36.5. See Shulman (1978).

80. Cuntarar, Tev. 5.6.

81. The prototype for these versions may well be the Cidambaramāhātmya, with the associated dance theme (but note the dance motif in the Kūrma version cited above, n. 74). Kulke (pp. 84-87) believes the version of the ŚRKh 6.13-14 to be older, but there is no firm evidence of this.

82. Tevīparākkiramam 9 (pp. 51-53).

83. See above, II.3 n. 27.

84. Koyil 3.68, 70-71; II.1 nn. 2-4.

85. Bhavnani, p. 77; Singha and Massey, pp. 114-16. Another seductive dance by a male who hides his manhood may be the *peṭiyāṭal* of Kāma mentioned in Cil. 6.56-57 and Maṇimekalai 3.116-25.

86. KP 6.13.83.

87. *Ibid*. 1.12.6-10; see above, IV.7 nn. 119-23.

88. Tiruccĕṅkoṭṭumāṉmiyam, p. 18, note.

89. Tirunĕlveli 57.77-260, 297-354 (condensed).

90. See Kulke, pp. 88-90, for a discussion of this version.

91. Kūrma 2.37.15; above, n. 74.

92. Paḻani 8.37-67.

93. *Ibid*. 11.16.

94. Shared features are obvious in the names of the gods: Aiyaṉār, like Murukaṉ, is Kumāraṉ ("the youth"); Koḻikkŏṭiyoṉ ("having the cock as his banner"); Śāstṛ (a teacher, like Guruguha, Gurumūrti). As Vĕḷḷaiyāṉaiyūrti, Aiyaṉār is the rider of the white elephant, like Murukaṉ in the oldest Tamil references. On the white elephant Piṇimukam of Murukaṉ, see Paripāṭal 5.2 (and the commentary of Gros on this verse, p. 192); Tirumuru. 247. The white elephant of Murukaṉ still survives outside the shrines of Tiruttaṇi and Cuvāmimalai, where it is ascribed a different mythical history: Śrī svāmimalaikṣetramāhātmya 4.1-35. Murukaṉ rides a white elephant in procession on the fifth day of the Māci festival at Tiruccĕntūr. Aiyaṉār has preserved the elephant vehicle of the ancient youthful warrior god. Both Aiyaṉār and Murukaṉ are young heroes; both have two wives; both are sometimes hunters; both are sons of Śiva, and Śāstṛ is sometimes nursed by Devī: Kāmākṣilīlāpirapāvam, p. 67. Cf. Oppert, pp. 504-13.

95. Dumont (1957), p. 401.

96. A name for Murukaṉ/Skanda.

97. Cĕvvanti 10.1-47.

98. Tiruviḷai. 45.1-63, esp. v. 1 and 60.

99. See Gonda (1954), pp. 129-45.

100. Kālikā 62.138-57; above, IV.4 n. 41.

101. Wilson (1828), 1.228-29.

## V. The Demon Devotee

1. See Heesterman (1964) and (1975).

2. For the stages leading up to this development, see O'Flaherty (1976), pp. 57-93. Some myths celebrate the breaking down of the barriers: see below, n. 67.

3. Whitehead, *passim*. Cf. the ancient worship of the *naṭukal*, in which the spirit of the dead hero was thought to reside: Hart (1975), pp. 25-26, 42-43.

4. For example, the worship of the folk deity Maturaivīraṉ at Tirumāliruñcolai; the purāṇic myths of Aiyaṉār/Hariharaputra, and so on. Many of the main deities of the Tamil shrines may be assumed to have derived essential features from local non-Brahmin cults.

5. Above, III.4.

6. I am indebted to George Hart for this suggestion of a link between the demon and the low-caste devotee. On the social attitude of *bhakti*, see above, I.2 at n. 18.

7. See Shulman (1978). Note that the identification of the demon with

evil is an innovation in the Hindu tradition. See O'Flaherty (1976), pp. 57-138.

8. Many scholars have seen this persistent theme of inadequacy as one of the outstanding features of Tamil *bhakti* religion. See, for example, Basham, p. 333; Hart (1976), p. 343.

9. Just as the internalized *prāṇāgnihotra* replaces the blood-sacrifices of the classical Brahminical cult.

10. The close affinities between men and the devoted demons are apparent in folk icons; human heroes, such as Tecinkurājaṉ or Maturaivīraṉ, are portrayed in a manner that makes them almost indistinguishable from the demon kings (Bali, Mayilirāvaṇaṉ, etc.).

11. Rām. 7.10.10-26. In his pride, Rāvaṇa neglects to include men among those who cannot conquer him; hence Viṣṇu's incarnation as Rāma.

12. Already in Rām. 7.16.8-46, Rāvaṇa's *bhakti* for Śiva results from the episode of lifting up Kailāsa, after which he receives the sword Candrahāsa from Śiva. Cf. Śiva 4.28.1-10; Tiruvāṉaikkā 23.2-3.

13. Wilkins, p. 272.

14. Arkaprakāśa, cited in Filliozat (1937), pp. 172-76.

15. Dorai Rangaswamy, 1:296.

16. See below, and Campantar, Tev. I.7.8.

17. See Filliozat (1937), *passim*, esp. pp. 159-70.

18. See, for example, Vibhīṣaṇa's eulogy: Appendix I no. 67, lines 27-94, inserted after 6.97 of the Baroda edition.

19. See Zvelebil (1974), pp. 148-49; Aiyar, pp. 211-53. Both Aiyar and Zvelebil note the parallel with Milton's descriptions of Satan. The modern, politically motivated attempts to "rehabilitate" Rāvaṇa may thus have deep roots: cf. Zvelebil (1973), p. 212 note.

20. Mayilirāvaṇaṉkatai, pp. 9-10.

21. Ātipuram 4.1-47; Tiruvāṉaikkā 23.1-16; Oppert, pp. 375-76, n. 115.

22. Śiva 4.28.1-76.

23. Other versions say Rāvaṇa went off to urinate, for Varuṇa had filled his bladder with all the waters of the sea: Gupte, pp. 15-26; Wilkins, p. 43; cf. Śiva 4.28.1-76; Oppert, pp. 375-76, n. 115; Civarāttiripurāṇam 6.55-71. A similar story is told of Vibhīṣaṇa, Rāvaṇa's pious brother: Śrīraṅgamāhātmya 7-9; above, II.1 n. 61.

24. For another version of the Gokarṇa myth, see Gupte, pp. 13-15. Gupte cites as his source the third chapter of the Śivalīlāmṛta, which he ascribes to the *Brahmottarakhaṇḍa* of the Skandapurāṇa. Printed editions of the Skanda seem not to have this part, but there is a reference to Rāvaṇa at Gokarṇa in the *Brahmottarakhaṇḍa*: Skanda 3.4.2.111-13. See also Thomas, pp. 83-84.

25. = Nandikeśvara. This episode is taken from Rām. 7.16.7-21.

26. The reference is to Rāma's army of monkeys who fight against Rāvaṇa.

27. Tiruvarañcaram 5.1-38 (condensed).

28. Personal communication from Anne-Marie Gaston (Añjali), who performed the Maṇḍūkaśabdam in London in June 1975.

29. On this motif see above, II.1, especially the myth of Tiruccāykkāṭu (n. 71), which is closely related to the Rāvaṇa cycle.

30. See above, IV.2 nn. 55-63.

31. Usually it is the threat of suicide that, at the last moment, brings about the god's acceptance of the devotee's wish: thus Triśiras cuts off two of his three heads and is on the point of cutting off the third when Śiva appears and grants his wish that a city bear his name (Tiricirāmalai, Tirucciráppaḷḷi)—Cĕvvanti 6.2-17. Cf. the cases of Śūrapadma and his brothers (KP 2.8.84-116, 2.9.1-28) and Citraśarman (Skanda 6.107.1-77); and see the continuation of the Rāvaṇa myth from Tiruvarañcaram.

32. Tiruvarañcaram 6.3-48, 7.3-39.

33. On the inverted tree, see Bosch (1960), pp. 73-74; Arapura; Kuiper (1964), pp. 116-18; *idem* (1972), pp. 151-52; Ogibenin, pp. 43-44; Emeneau (1949); cf. Kaṭhopaniṣad 6.1; Bhagavadgītā 15.1-4.

34. See above, IV.8 nn. 114-18.

35. For sacred ash as an instrument of invisibility, see also Aṇṇaṉmārkatai (Beck, 1975, p. 14).

36. Francis (1906-a), p. 344.

37. See Mahalingam (1965).

38. In a variant of this myth, he similarly mistakes beauty for ugliness: the goddess given him by Śiva appears to him as a hideous hag, and he abandons her at Gokarṇa. See n. 24.

39. See Hiltebeitel (1976), pp. 143-91; Shulman (1978).

40. See Gonda (1954), pp. 55-72; O'Flaherty (1975), pp. 175-79; Hiltebeitel (1976), pp. 128-39.

41. For a full discussion of the myth's development, see Tripathi, *passim*. Hiltebeitel (1976), pp. 128-39, follows Dumézil in seeing an Indo-European background to the myth of the three steps.

42. On Prahlāda see Hacker, *passim*; O'Flaherty (1976), pp. 131-36.

43. See Bhāgavata 8.20.1-11 and 8.22.12-17 (where Prahlāda comes to visit his grandson bound with the bonds of Varuṇa).

44. *Ibid*. 8.15.22, 33-36.

45. Vāmana 11-16; cf. O'Flaherty (1976), pp. 129-30.

46. Tirumayilai 11.1-25; Vedāraṇyamāhātmya 95.58-62; Vetāraṇiyam (2) 12.3-12; Vetāraṇiyam (1) 21.3-12. The latter text plays on the name of the king: *avvĕli . . . māvaliy ākave* (v. 12). Is this a clue to the origin of the link between Bali and the rat?

47. See Viruttācalam 9.13; KP 2.10.24-50. In the latter text, Śukra instructs the demon Śūrapadma in devotion to Śiva—but, as in the case of Rāvaṇa and other Tamil demons, Śukra's devotion is motivated by selfishness and materialistic aims, and his preaching to Śūrapadma drives the

demon to ruin. For a discussion of the intriguing and ambivalent figure of the demons' *guru*, see O'Flaherty (1976), pp. 118-22, 124-27; Dumézil (1968-1973), 2:160.

48. Padma 5.13.421. Cf. O'Flaherty (1975), pp. 289-300.

49. See Tripathi, pp. 52-57, 124, 142; O'Flaherty (1976), pp. 131-32.

50. Śrī vĕḷḷīsvararkoyilvaralāṟu, p. 2.

51. On Kampaṉ's positive attitude toward life on earth, see above, I.2 at nn. 19-20.

52. Commentary: *ulaka pparrukkaḷ nīṅkum pŏruṭṭu*, "(his name is recited) so that earthly attachments depart."

53. The Bhāgavata achieves a similar effect in 8.19.5-10, when the dwarf (his true identity still veiled) tells Bali about the slaying of Hiraṇyākṣa by Viṣṇu *as the boar*; when Hiraṇyakaśipu then sought revenge on the god, Viṣṇu hid inside the demon (Bali's own great-grandfather).

54. These associations are prominent in the myths of Śrīmuṣṇam, where Viṣṇu rested after rescuing the earth in his boar avatar; see Ramanujachariar, pp. 2, 5, 11-12, 15-16; Francis (1906-a), pp. 290-91; Tirukkūṭalaiyāṟṟūr stalapurāṇavacaṉam 10 (pp. 68-73). And cf. Kālikā 30-31.

55. O'Flaherty (1976), pp. 99-100.

56. See the commentary on v. 436 of the Kopālakiruṣṇamācāryar edition (p. 324).

57. See the discussion of the myth of Murukaṉ's wooing of Vaḷḷi: above, IV.8 after n. 53.

58. Cf. Kāñci 58.26-35, where this trait of Viṣṇu's inspires Mārkaṇḍeya with distrust; and cf. Matsya 167.13-67; MBh 3. 186-87.

59. Bhāgavata 8.20.4 (see also vv. 11-13).

60. See Heesterman (1964), pp. 19-21.

61. Cf. Tirukkuṟaḷ 222, 1061-70, and the verses cited by the commentators on Kampaṉ 1.441.

62. See Manusmṛti 3.64, 153; 12.46; Heesterman (1964), pp. 20-21.

63. In the final verse, "You" refers to Rāma, who hears the story from Viśvāmitra. The "beloved" (*aṉpaṉ*) is Bali; *aṉpaṉ* might be translated as devotee, *bhakta*, if we wished to stress the devotee's side of what is clearly a two-sided relationship. "Body" is a metonymy for "head" (Viṣṇu places his foot on the head of the demon).

64. In Śaiva Siddhānta, too, the state of material embodiment is part of the process of salvation.

65. For a similar revelation of the divinity to himself, see Rām. 6.103-106; O'Flaherty (1975), pp. 197-98.

66. Above, III.3 following n. 16.

67. Takkayākapparaṇi 437-72; 559-60; 565-66; 780-93.

68. See KP 5.5.1-66; ŚRKh 5.3.1-17.

69. Commentary: Mānasasarovana.

70. Fate = *viti*, a pun on *viti*, "Brahmā."

71. A pun: *karantaṉaṉ* also means "he who disappeared."

72. KP 6.1-2, 5-11, 16-20 (condensed); Tirukkuṟṟālam 1.13.1-134; Tiruvārūr 51.1-24.

73. See above, III.1.

74. See Renou (1965). The Takkayākapparaṇi also makes Dakṣa a heretic who is sacrificing according to "some other tradition" (*maṟṟ' ŏru keḷvi*) than the Vedas, which proclaim Śiva lord of the sacrifice (v. 246). See O'Flaherty (1976), pp. 272-77.

75. MBh 12.274.18, 26.

76. See the discussion by O'Flaherty (1976), pp. 272-77, and Hiltebeitel (1976), pp. 312-60.

77. Heesterman (1962), p. 9; cf. Dorai Rangaswamy, 1:334. The contrast with Śiva, whom Dakṣa quite rightly accuses of eating poison (at the time of the churning of the ocean), is here most pointed: Śiva swallows poison, saves the world, and survives; the gods swallow *amṛta* (the sacrificial portions, KP 6.17.8-9), and it is poison to them—they die at the sacrifice.

78. KP 6.10.24. Hence the identification of Dakṣa as the sacrificial *victim*, which we have seen (above, III.3) to be important in the classical accounts, is at its weakest in the Tamil version. There is no need for Śiva and Dakṣa to vie for this privilege here.

79. Dakṣa worships Devī in Śiva 2.2.12.5-37; Devībhāgavata 7.29-30.

80. On the relations between these two myths, see O'Flaherty (1973), pp. 111-40; Shulman (1976-a), pp. 406-26.

81. See above, IV.8 nn. 45-62.

82. Tiruñāṉacampantar, Tev. 1.1-10.

83. Tirukkuṟṟālam 1.13.112-15.

84. PP 1.4.1-74. Cf. Piatigorsky (1962), pp. 147-53.

85. See above, IV.2 after n. 55.

86. Tirukkaṇṭiyūr 14. It is noteworthy that this site is associated with Śiva's decapitation of Brahmā—a multiform of the Dakṣa myth.

# BIBLIOGRAPHY

## Tamil Texts, by Title

Note: Abbreviations used in the footnotes appear before the title.

*Akanāṉūṟu*. With commentary by Na. Mu. Veṅkaṭacāmi Nāṭṭār. Madras, SISS, 1965.

*Alliyaracāṇimālai*. Madras, 1973.

Aruṇācalam. *Aruṇācalapurāṇam* of Ĕllappanayiṉār. With commentary by Maḻavai Makāliṅkaiyar. Madras, 1907.

*Aruṇakiripurāṇam* of Citamparam Maṟaiñāṉatecikar. Ed. Vāmateva Murukapaṭṭar. Madras, 1880.

Ātipuram. *Ĕyiṉaṉūr, cantāṉapuri ĕṉṟu vaḻaṅkum ātipuratalapurāṇam* of Ta. Ka. Cupparāyacĕṭṭiyār. With *vacaṉam* by Citamparam A. Cāmināta Piḷḷai. Madras, 1896.

*Avinācittalapurāṇam* of Iḷaiyāṉ kavirāyar. With commentary by Ta. Ci. Mīṉāṭcicuntarampiḷḷai and Kuḻantaiveṟpiḷḷai. Kumpakoṇam, 1955.

Caṅkaranārāyaṇacāmikoyil. *Caṅkaranārāyaṇacāmikoyiṟpuraṇam* of Cīvalamāṟapāṇṭiyaṉ and P. Muttuvīrakkavirāyar. With commentary by Mu. Rā. Aruṇācalakkavirāyar. Maturai, 1909.

*Caṅkaranayiṉārkoyiṟ caṅkaraliṅka ulā*. Ed. U. Ve. Cāminātaiyar. Paḻavāṉkuṭi, 1933.

*Carapapurāṇam*. Ed. Vī. Cŏkkaliṅkam. Tanjore, 1972.

Cāyāvaṉam. *Tiruccāykkāṭ' ĕṉṉum Cāyāvaṉapurāṇam* of Kavirājanāyakam Piḷḷai. Ed. Tĕ. Ci. Tuṟaicāmi Piḷḷai. Citamparam, 1909.

*Cekkiḻārpurāṇam* of Umāpaticivācāriyar. In the same volume as *Pĕriyapurāṇam*.

*Śrī Cĕṉṉai mallīcurar śrī cĕṉṉai kecavappĕrumāḷ tirukoyilkaḷiṉ varalāṟu* of Kukaśrī Rasapati. Madras, 1958.

Cetu. *Cetupurāṇam* of Nirampavaḻakiyatecikar. Ed. Āṟumukanāvalar. Madras, 1932.

Cĕvvanti. *Cĕvvantippurāṇam* of Caiva Ĕllappanāvalar. With commentary by Tiricirapuram Comacuntara Mutaliyār. Tiruccirāppaḷḷi, 1927.

*Ceyūrttalavaralāṟu* of Cĕyyūr Muttaiya Mutaliyār. Madras, 1944.

Cīkāḻi. *Cīkāḻittalapurāṇam* of Aruṇācala kkavirāyar. Madras, 1887.

Cīkāḷatti. *Cīkāḷattippurāṇam* of Karuṇaippirakācacuvāmikaḷ, Civappirakācacuvāmi, and Velaiyacuvāmi. Ed. with commentary by Rāmāṉanta Yoki. Madras, 1913-1915.

*Cilappatikāram* of Iḷaṅkovaṭikaḷ. With Arumpatavurai and the commentary of Aṭiyārkkunallār. Ed. by U. Ve. Cāminātaiyar. Madras, 1927.

———. Trans. V. R. Ramachandra Dikshitar. *The Śilappadikāram*. Madras, 1939.

*Ciṟuttŏṇṭapattaṉkatai*. Madras, 1975.
*Citamparapurāṇam*. With commentary by Pe. Irāmaliṅkapiḷḷai. Madras, 1906.
*Civañāṉacittiyār* of Aruṇanti. *Cupakkam*. Tarumapuram, 1962.
———. *Parapakkam*. See *Mĕykaṇṭacāttiram*.
———. Trans. J. M. Nallaswami Pillai. *Śivajñana Siddhiyār of Aruṇandi Śivāchārya*. Madras, 1913.
*Civañāṉapotam* of Mĕykaṇṭatevar. With *ciṟṟurai* of Civañāṉacuvāmikaḷ. Aṇṇāmalainakar, 1953.
*Civarāttiripurāṇam* of Varatarācakavirācar (Varatapaṇṭitar). With commentary by Kumāracūriyappiḷḷai. Jaffna, 1970.
*Coḻarājentirapuram ĕṉṉum iḷaiyaṉār velūrppurāṇa mūlamum vacaṉamum*. *Vacaṉam* by Vā. Makāteva Mutaliyār. Madras, 1921.
Cucīntiram. *Cucīntirastalapurāṇam* of Muttamiḻkkavirāyar. Ed. Ti. Māvaṭi Citamparam Piḷḷai. Tirunĕlveli, 1894.
*Cuntarapāṇṭiyam* of Aṉatāri. Ed. T. Chandrasekharan. Madras Government Oriental Manuscripts Series no. 41, Madras, 1955.
*Curuḷi ĕṉṟa pĕyar vaḻaṅkukiṉṟa śrīcurapistalapurāṇam* of Śrīnivāsayyaṅkār. Tevāramānakar, 1915.
*Cuṭalaimāṭacuvāmivilpāṭṭu* of Melakaram Muttucāmi Piḷḷai. Maturai, n.d.
Cūtavaṉam. *Tiruvucāttāṉam ākiya cūtavaṉapurāṇam* of Cŏkkaliṅkaccĕṭṭiyār. Maturai, 1905.
*Eṇiyeṟṟam*. Ed. S. Pavāṉantam Piḷḷai. Madras, 1914.
*Iḷaiyaṉār velūrppurāṇam*. *See Coḻarājentirapuram . . .*
*Irāmāvatāram* of Kampaṉ. Ed. U. Ve. Cāminātaiyar Library. Tiruvāṉmiyūr, 1967.
———. With commentary of Vai. Mu. Kopālakiruṣṇamācāryar. 5th ed. Madras, 1953-1955.
———. *Ayottiyā kāṇṭam*. Ed. Aṇṇāmalai University, Madras, 1960.
*Iratitevi pulampal* of Citamparam Nārāyaṇa Piḷḷai. Madras, 1927.
*Jayanakaram vaḷḷi tĕyvayāṉai ecal*. Pattukkoṭṭai, 1927.
Kāḷaiyārkoyil. *See* Tirukkāṉapper.
*Kaḷaviyal ĕṉṟa iṟaiyaṉār akappŏruḷ*. With the commentary ascribed to Nakkīraṉār. Madras, SISS, 1953.
*Kaliṅkattupparaṇi* of Cayaṅkŏṇṭār. With commentary of A. Vī. Kaṉṉaiya Nāyuṭu. Madras, 1944.
*Kalittŏkai*. With commentary of Nacciṉārkkiṉiyar. Madras, SISS, 1938.
Kāmakkūr. *Kāmakkūr ĕṉa vaḻaṅkum kāmanakarppurāṇavacaṉam*. Ed. Kāmakkūr Maṅkalakkavirāyar Kantapiḷḷai. Velūr, 1909.
*Kāmākṣilīlāpirapāvam* of Ka. E. Ālālacuntaram Piḷḷai. Madras, 1906.
Kāñci. *Kāñcippurāṇam* of Civañāṉayokikaḷ. Ed. C. Aruṇai Vaṭivelu Mutaliyār. Kāñcipuram, 1937.
———. Trans. R. Dessigane, P. Z. Pattabiramin, and Jean Filliozat. *Les légendes çivaïtes de Kāñcipuram*. Pondicherry, 1964.

*Kāñcippurāṇam* of Kacciyappamuṉivar. In *Kāñcippurāṇam*, ed. Kāñci Nākaliṅka Mutaliyār. Madras, 1910.

Kaṉṉiyākumari. *Kaṉṉiyākumarittalapurāṇam* of Caṅkaranāvalar. With *vacaṉam* by Mu. Rā. Aruṇācalakkavirāyar. Maturai, n.d.

*Kantapurāṇam* of Kacciyappacivācāriyar. With commentary by Ma. Ti. Pāṉukavi. 2 vols. Madras, 1907.

———. Trans. R. Dessigane and P. Z. Pattabiramin. *La Légende de Skanda selon le Kandapurāṇam tamoul et l'iconographie*. Pondicherry, 1967.

Kāraikkālammaiyār. *See Patiṉorāṉ tirumuṟai*.

Katirkāmam. *Katirkāmapurāṇavacaṉam* of C. Tāmotaram Piḷḷai. Cuṉṉākam, 1937.

*Kāverippurāṇam* of Tirucciṟṟampalamuṉivar. Ed. P. Cuppaiyatecikar. Madras, 1871.

*Kāveri uṟpattiyum kalyāṇa vaipavamum aṭaṅkiya carittiram* of Ti. Lakṣimi Ammāḷ. Tiruppātirippuliyūr, 1916.

*Keraḷatecavaralāṟu*. Ed. T. Chandrasekharan. Madras Government Oriental Manuscript Series no. 56. Madras, 1960.

*Kŏttiṭṭai kūttāṇṭavar utsavakummi* of Ko. Āṟumukacĕṭṭiyar. Citamparam, 1915.

*Kovalaṉkatai*. Madras, 1975.

*Kŏvvākam kūttāṇṭavar cittirai tiruviḻā vicittira cintu* of Kuppucāmicĕṭṭiyār. Viḻuppuram, 1926.

Koyil. *Koyiṟpurāṇam* of Umāpaticivācāriyar. Ed. Kāñcipuram Capāpati Mutaliyār. Madras, 1867.

Kumpakoṇam. *Kumpakoṇappurāṇam* of Cŏkkappappulavar. Ed. Mu. Caṭakoparāmāṉujam Piḷḷai. Tanjore, 1971.

*Kumpakoṇam kṣettirapurāṇam*. Kumpakoṇam, 1933.

*Kumpakoṇam makāmakam*. Madras, 1933.

*Kuṟuntŏkai*. Ed. U. Ve. Cāminātaiyar. 2nd ed., Madras, 1947.

*Makāpāratam* of Villiputtūrāḻvār. Ed. Citamparam Naṭarājappiḷḷai. Madras, 1914.

*Maṇimekalai* of Cīttalai ccāttaṉār. Ed. Na. Mu. Veṅkaṭacāmi Nāṭṭār and Auvai. Cu. Tuṟaicāmippiḷḷai. 2nd ed. Madras, SISS, 1951.

*Mataṉakāmarājaṉkatai ĕṉṉum paṉṉiraṇṭu katai*. Ed. Kumpakoṇam Kumpaliṅkacuvāmi. Madras, 1888.

———. Trans. V.A.K. Ayer. *Stories of King Madana Kama*. Bombay, 1972.

———. Trans. S. M. Natesa Sastri. *Dravidian Nights Entertainment, being a translation of the Madanakamarajankadai*. Madras, 1886.

Mattiyārccuṉam. *Srīmattiyārccuṉamāṉmiyam* of U. Ve. Cāminātaiyar, in *Tiruviṭaimarutūr kkumpāpiṣeka malar*. Tiruviṭaimarutūr, 1973, pp. 215-232.

*Maturaimāṉmiyam* of Citamparacuvāmi. Ed. A. Cuntaranātapiḷḷai. Maturai, 1908.

*Mayilirāvaṇaṉkatai*. Maturai, 1922.

*Mayilviruttam* ascribed to Aruṇakirinātar. With commentary by Va. Cu. Cĕṅkalvarāya Piḷḷai. Madras, SISS, 1971.

Māyūram. *Māyūrappurāṇam* of Tiricirapuram Mīṉāṭcicuntaram Piḷḷai. Ed. Cupparāya Cĕṭṭiyār. Madras, 1868.

*Meṟkoḷviḷakka kkatai akaravaricai* of Cu. A. Irāmacāmippulavar. 2 vols. Madras, SISS, 1963.

*Mĕykaṇṭacāttiram (cittānta cāttiram)*. Madras, 1942.

*Mīṉāmpikai tottiram*. In *Katirkāmamālai* of Ĕs. Ayyācāmi Piḷḷai. Maturai, 1914.

*Nālāyirativyaprapantam*. Ed. Citrakūṭam Kantāṭai Tiruveṅkaṭācāryar. Madras, 1898.

*Nallataṅkāḷ katai*. Ed. Kuppucāmināyuṭu. Madras, 1904.

*Nampiyakappŏruḷ* of Nāṟkavirācanampi. With an old commentary. Ed. Kā. Ra. Kovintarāca Mutaliyār. Madras, SISS, 1956.

*Naṟṟiṇai nāṉūṟu*. With commentary by A. Nārāyaṇacāmi Aiyar. Madras, SISS, 1956.

*Nīlakeci*. Ed. A. Chakravarti. N.p., 1936.

*Nīlikatai* of Cĕñci Ekāmpara Mutaliyār. Madras, 1922.

*Nīlivacīkaram*. An adaptation by Sri Saila of Shakespeare's *Taming of the Shrew*. Madras, 1912.

Paḻani. *Paḻanittalapurāṇam* of Pāla Cuppiramaṇiya kkavirāyar. With commentary by Na. Katiraiveṟpiḷḷai. Madras, 1903.

*Paḻayaṅkuṭi talavaralāṟu* of Pa. Irāmanāta Piḷḷai. Paḻayaṅkuṭi, 1943.

*Pañcatantiram* of Tāṇṭavarāya Mutaliyār. 3rd ed. Madras, 1862.

*Paṉṉiru pāṭṭ'iyal*. Ed. Kā. Ra. Kovintarāca Mutaliyār. 2nd ed. Madras, SISS, 1949.

*Pārijātapuṣpāpaharaṇa carittiram* of Maturai Kantacāmi Piḷḷai. Madras, 1905.

*Paripāṭal*. With commentary of Parimelaḻakar. Ed. U. Ve. Cāminātaiyar. 3rd ed. Madras, 1948.

———. Trans. François Gros. *Le Paripāṭal*. Pondicherry, 1968.

*Patiṉorān tirumuṟai*. Śrīvaikuṇṭam, 1963.

———. Kârâvêlane. *Kâreikkâlammeiyâr, oeuvres éditées et traduites*. Pondicherry, 1956.

*Patiṟṟuppattu*. With the old commentary. Ed. U. Ve. Cāminātaiyar. 6th ed. Madras, 1957.

*Pattiṉiyammaṉ varalāṟu carittiramum kummiyum* of A. Ki. Aṉantanārāyaṇacāmi Upāttiyāyar. Nagapattinam, 1915.

*Pattuppāṭṭu*. Ed. U. Ve. Cāminātaiyar. Madras, 1918.

———. Jean Filliozat. *Un Texte de la religion Kaumara: Le Tirumurukāṟṟuppaṭai*. Pondicherry, 1973.

*Pavaḷakkŏṭimālai*. Madras, 1914.

———. Trans. T. B. Krishnaswami. *The Queen of the Coral-Reefs: Old Time Wreaths of Romance from the Coast of Coromandel*. Madras, 1916.

*Pĕriyapurāṇam ĕṉṟu vaḻaṅkukiṉṟa tiruttŏṇṭarpurāṇam* of Cekkiḻār. Ed. Āṟumukanāvalar. 5th ed. Madras, 1916.

*Puṟanāṉūṟu*. Ed. U. Ve. Cāminātaiyar. 6th ed. Madras, 1963.

*Puṟappŏruḷ vĕṇpāmālai* of Aiyaṉāritaṉār. With commentary by Pŏ. Ve. Comacuntaraṉār. Madras, SISS, 1955.

*Puttūr kuḷumāyiyammaṉ cintu* of Maturakavi Murukatās. Maturai, 1912.

*Raṅkanāyakikkum nācciyārukkum camvātam*. Ed. Namacivāyanāyakar. Kottūr, n.d.

*Rĕṭṭikuṭiyecal*. Ed. Tiruvĕṉkāṭu Āṟumukacuvāmi. Tiruvŏṟṟiyūr, 1878.

*Śrīcurapistalapurāṇam*. *See Curuḷi* . . .

*Śrīpurāṇam*. Ed. Venkatarajulu Reddiyar. Madras, 1946.

*Śrī makālaṭcumikkum pārvatikkum vākkuvātam*. Ed. Kokulāpuram Aruṇācala Mutaliyār. Madras, 1876.

*Takkayākapparaṇi* of Ŏṭṭakkūttar. With old commentary. Ed. U. Ve. Cāminātaiyar. Madras, 1945.

Takṣiṇakailācam. *Takṣiṇakailācapurāṇam* of Ci. Nākaliṅka Piḷḷai. Vatiri (Jaffna), 1928.

*Tamiḻnāvalarcaritai*. Ed. Cāmi. Tillainaṭeca Cĕṭṭiyār. Madras, 1916.

Taṇikai. *Taṇikaippurāṇam* of Kacciyappamuṉivar. 2 vols. Madras, SISS, 1965.

*Tevāram*. 7 vols. Tarumapuram, 1953.

*Śrītevikarumāriyammaṉpurāṇam* of Śrītevikarumāritācar. Madras, 1969.

Tevīparākkiramam. *Aṣṭāṣṭalīlaiy ĕṉṉum tevīparākkiramam* of Īkkāṭu Irattiṉavelu Mutaliyār. 2nd ed. Madras, 1923.

Tirimūrttimalai. *Tirimūrttimalaippurāṇavacaṉam* of Aruṇācala Kavuṇṭar. Madras, 1936.

Tīrttakiri. *Tīrttakiripurāṇam* of Caiva Ĕllappanāvalar. Ed. with commentary by Putuvai Ka. Cupparāya Mutaliyār. Madras, 1870.

*Tiruccāykkāṭu talavaralāṟu* of Ji. Kaliyāṇam. Kumpakoṇam, 1971.

*Tiruccĕṅkoṭṭumāṉmiyam* of A. Muttucāmikkoṉār. Tiruccĕṅkoṭu, 1938.

Tiruccĕṅkoṭu. *Tiruccĕṅkoṭṭuppurāṇam* of Tĕṉkāci Kavirājapaṇṭitar. With commentary by Ciṟṟampalakkavirāyar. Tiruccĕṅkoṭu, 1932.

Tiruccĕntūr. *Tiruccĕnturttalapurāṇam* of Vĕṉṟimālaikkavirāyar. With commentary by Kukaśrī Rasapati. Tiruccĕntūr, 1963.

*Tirukkaḷar cāracaṅkirakam* of Ti. Mu. Cuvāmināta Upāttiyāyar. Tiruvārūr, 1910.

*Tirukkaḷarppurāṇam* of Kaḷantai Ātiyappaṉār. Ed. A. Nārāyaṇacāmi Aiyar. Madras, 1912.

*Tirukkāḷattippurāṇam* of Vīrainakar Āṉantakkūttar. Ed. U. Ve. Cāminātaiyar. Madras, 1912.

Tirukkaḻukkuṉṟam. *Tirukkaḻukkuṉṟam ĕṉṉum uruttirakoṭi ttalamāṉmiyam* of S. R. Namacivāya Rājayoki. Madras, 1924.

*Tirukkāṉapper ĕṉṉum kāḷaiyārkoyiṟpurāṇam* of Cuppiramaṇiya Ayar. Madras, 1899.

Tirukkaṇṭiyūr. *Tirukkaṇṭiyūrppurāṇam*. Ed. Va. Cu. Caṇmukam Piḷḷai. Tiruppātirippuliyur, 1939.

*Tirukkaṭavūrpurāṇam* of Pālakiruṣṇa Tīkṣitar. Madras, 1905.

*Tirukkaṭavūrkṣettirapurāṇam* of Pa. Pañcāpakeca Cāstiri. Kumpakoṇam, 1925.

*Tirukkovaiyār* of Māṇikkavācakar. Ed. Rā. Vicuvanātayyar. Tañcāvūr, 1955.

Tirukkovalūr. *Teyvīkarājapuram ĕṉṉum tirukkovalūrppurāṇavacaṉam* of Ti. Vai. Catācivappaṇṭārattār. Ed. A. Pālacuppiramaṇiya Piḷḷai. Kumpakoṇam, 1918.

*Tirukkuṟaḷ* of Tiruvaḷḷuvar. Madras, SISS, 1972.

Tirukkuṟṟālam. *Tirukkuṟṟālattalapurāṇam* of Tirikūṭarācappaṉ kavirācamūrttikaḷ. Maturai, 1910.

*Tirukkūṭalaiyāṟṟūrstalapurāṇavacaṉam*. Ed. Vāmateva Māṇikkapaṭṭār. Citamparam, 1883.

Tirukkuṭantai. *Tirukkuṭantaippurāṇam* of Tiricirapuram Mīṉāṭcicuntaram Piḷḷai. Madras, 1883.

*Tirukkuṭantai aruḷ miku cārṅkapāṇi cuvāmi ālaya talavaralāṟu* of Ĕṉ. Ĕs. Tātācāriyar. Kumpakoṇam, 1973.

Tirukkūvam. *Tirukkūvappurāṇam* of Tuṟaimaṅkalam Civappirakācacuvāmikaḷ. Ed. Ka. Va. Tiruveṅkaṭa Nayuṭu. 2nd ed. Madras, 1908.

*Tirukkūvappurāṇavacaṉam* of Tiruvicainallūr Ciṉṉayanāyakar. Madras, 1910.

Tirumāliruñcolai. *See Vṛṣabhādrimāhātmya*.

*Tirumaḻuvāṭippurāṇam* of Kamalai Ñāṉappirakācatecikar. Ed. Tañcai Ulakanāta Piḷḷai. Tanjore, 1908.

*Tirumantiram* of Tirumūlar. With commentary by Pa. Irāmanāta Piḷḷai. 2nd ed. Madras, SISS, 1957.

Tirumayilai. *Tirumayilaittalapurāṇam* of Amurtaliṅkattampirāṉ. With commentary by Kāñcipuram Capāpati Mutaliyār. Ed. Puracai-Aṣṭāvatāṉam Capāpati Mutaliyār. Madras, 1893.

*Tirumayilāṭuturai ttalavaralāṟu* of Cī. Irāmaliṅkam Piḷḷai. Māyūram, 1949.

*Tirumullaivāyiṟpurāṇam* of Vaṭukanātatecikar. Cīkāḻi, 1927.

*Tirumurukāṟṟuppaṭai*. *See Pattuppāṭṭu*.

*Tirunākaikkāroṇappurāṇam* of Tiricirapuram Mīṉāṭcicuntaram Piḷḷai. Tiruvāvaṭuturai, 1970.

Tirunaḷḷāṟu. *Tirunaḷḷāṟṟuppurāṇam*. Kumpakoṇam, 1935.

*Tirunaḷḷāṟu canippĕyarcci makimai*. Kāraikkāl, n.d.

Tirunĕlveli. *Tirunĕlvelittalapurāṇam* of Nĕllaiyappa Piḷḷai. Ed. Cālivāṭīcura Otuvāmūrtti. Tirunĕlveli, 1869.

Tiruppaiññīli. *Tiruppaiññīlipurāṇam*. Ed. A. Cuppiramaṇiya Pāratiyār. Madras, 1927.

Tirupparaṅkuṉṟam. *Tirupparaṅkirippurāṇavacaṉam* of Mu. Rā. Aruṇācalakkavirāyar (based on the purāṇa of Nirampavaḻakiyatecikar). Madras, 1899. *See also Satyagirimāhātmya*.

Tiruppātirippuliyūr. *Tiruppātirippuliyūrpurāṇam* of Ilakkaṇam Citam-

paranātamuṉivar. Ed. Civacaṇmuka Mĕyññāṉacivācāriyacuvāmi. Madras, 1896.
*Tiruppāvai* of Āṇṭāl. Ed. Jean Filliozat, *Un text tamoul de dévotion vishnouite*. Pondicherry, 1972.
*Tiruppĕṇṇākaṭa varalāṟu* of Kaṭantai Ĕḻilaṉ. Pĕṇṇākaṭam, 1970.
Tirupperūr. *Tirupperūrppurāṇam* of Kacciyappamuṉivar. Madras, 1930.
Tirupporūr. *Tirupporūr ttalapurāṇa carittira ccurukkam, śrī citamparacuvāmikaḷ paramparai ccurukkam mutaliyaṉa* of Puracai Aṣṭāvatāṉam Capāpati Mutaliyār. 2nd ed. Tirupporūr, 1934.
Tiruppuṉavāyil. *Tiruppuṉavāyiṟpurāṇavacaṉam* of Pŏ. Muttaiya Piḷḷai (based on the purāṇa of Tiruvārūr Tiyākarācakavirājatecikar). Tevakoṭṭai, 1928.
*Tiruppūvaṇanātarulā* of Kantacāmippulavar. Ed. with commentary by Vai. Irattiṉacapāpati and Ayaṉ Pĕrumāḷ Koṉār. Madras, 1957.
*Tiruttaṇikai kṣettira mahātmiyam* (sic) *ĕṉṉum taṇikaipurāṇa vacaṉam* of Ta. Pū. Murukeca Nāyakar. Madras, 1925.
Tiruttenkūr. *Tiruttenkūr talapurāṇam*. Ed. Vitvāṉ Caṇmukaccuvāmi. Cīkāḻi, 1914.
Tirutturutti. *Tirutturuttippurāṇam* of Tiricirapuram Mīṉāṭcicuntaram Piḷḷai. Kumpakoṇam and Madras, 1933.
Tiruttuṭicai. *Tiruttuṭicaippurāṇam*. Madras, 1913.
*Tiruvācakam* of Māṇikkavācakar. With commentary by Ka. Cu. Navanīta Kiruṣṇa Pāratiyār. Māviṭṭapuram (Jaffna), 1954.
———. Trans. G. U. Pope. *The Tiruvāçagam*. 1900, reprinted Madras, 1970.
*Tiruvahīntirapuram śrī tevanātasvāmi tirukkoyil mahāsamprokṣaṇam*. Tiruvahīntirapuram, 1972.
*Tiruvaiyāṟu śrī pañcanatīcuvaracuvāmi tirukoyil makākumpāpiṣeka viḻāmalar*. Tarumapuram, 1971.
Tiruvaiyāṟu. *Tiruvaiyāṟṟuppurāṇam* of Ñāṉakkūttar. Ed. Mu. Rā. Aruṇācalakkavirāyar and A. Muttuttāṇṭavarāya Piḷḷai. Madras, 1930.
*Tiruvalañcuḻi ĕṉum narpatiyil vaḷḷittiṉaippuṉam kārkkum uccavakummi* of Cŏkkalinkatāsaṉ. Ed. S. Namacivāya Cĕṭṭiyār. Kumpakoṇam, 1914.
*Tiruvālankāṭṭuppurāṇam*. Madras, 1864.
*Tiruvālavāyuṭaiyār tiruviḷaiyāṭaṟpurāṇam* of Pĕrumpaṟṟappuliyūrnampi. Ed. U. Ve. Cāminātaiyar. Madras, 1906.
Tiruvāṉaikkā. *Tiruvāṉaikkāppurāṇam* of Kacciyappamuṉivar. Ed. T. K. Balasubrahmanya Aiyar. Śrīrankam, 1909.
*Tiruvāṉaikkāval māhātmiyam* of Pa. Pañcāpakeca Cāstiri (*vacaṉam* based on the *Gajāraṇyamāhātmya*). Śrīrankam, 1932.
Tiruvāñciyam. *Tiruvāñciyattalapurāṇam* of Kaḷantaikkumaraṉ. Madras, 1959.
*Śrī tiruvāñciyakṣettirapurāṇam* (based on an unknown Sanskrit source). Kumpakoṇam, 1939.

Tiruvāṉmiyūr. *Tiruvāṉmiyūr stalapurāṇavacaṉam* of Rā. Vicuvanātaṉ. Madras, 1966.

Tiruvāppaṉūr. *Tiruvāppaṉūrppurāṇam* of Tiruppūvaṇam Kantacāmippulavar. With commentary by Pa. Vacavaliṅka Paurāṇikar. Maturai, 1909.

Tiruvarañcaram. *Tiruvarañcarattalapurāṇam* of Aruṇācalakkavirāyar. Ed. with commentary by Ti. Vaṭivelu Mutaliyār. Tirukkovalūr, 1925.

Tiruvārūr. *Tiruvārūrppurāṇam* of Aḻakai Campantamuṉivar. Ed. Cu. Cuvāminātatecikar. Madras, 1894.

*Tiruvaruṭpayaṉ* of Umāpaticivācāriyar. Madras, 1958.

Tiruvāṭāṉai. *Tiruvāṭāṉaippurāṇam* of Tiruvārūr Cāminātatecikar. Madras, 1929.

*Tiruvātavūraṭikaḷ purāṇam* of Kaṭavuṇmāmuṉivar. Ed. with commentary by Ma. Ka. Veṟpiḷḷai. Jaffna, 1915.

Tiruvāṭpokki. *Irattiṉakiri ĕṉṉum tiruvāṭpokkippurāṇam* of Kamalainakar Vaittiṉātatecikar. Ed. A. Civāṉantacākara Yokīcuvarar. Madras, 1911.

*Tiruvāvaṭuturaittaricaṉam* of V. Kandasami Pillai. Madras, 1921.

*Tiruveṅkaṭatalapurāṇam* of Maturakavi Vīrarākavasvāmi Ayyaṅkār. Ed. T. P. Paḻaniyappa Piḷḷai. Tirupati, 1949.

Tiruvĕṇkāṭu. *Tiruvĕṇkāṭṭuppurāṇam* of Caiva Ĕllappanāvalar. With *vacaṉam* by Tĕ. Ci. Turaicāmippiḷḷai. Madras, 1905.

Tiruveṟkātu. *Tiruveṟkāṭṭuppurāṇam*. Ed. Pūvai Kaliyāṇacuntara Mutaliyār. Madras, 1903.

*Tiruviḷaiyāṭaṟpurāṇam* of Parañcotimuṉivar. With commentary by Na. Mu. Veṅkaṭacāmi Nāṭṭār. 2 vols. Madras, SISS, 1965.

———. *Maturai kkāṇṭam*. Maturai, 1973.

———. Trans. William Taylor, *Oriental Historical Manuscripts*, Vol. I. Madras, 1835.

———. Trans. R. Dessigane, P. Z. Pattabiramin, and J. Filliozat. *La légende des jeux de çiva à Madurai d'après les textes et les peintures*. 2 vols. Pondicherry, 1960.

Tiruviriñcai. *Tiruviriñcaipurāṇam* of Ĕllappanayiṉār. With commentary by Capāpati Multaliyār. Velūr, 1928.

*Tiruviṭaimarutūr mummaṇikkovai* of Paṭṭiṉattuppiḷḷaiyār. Tiruvāvaṭuturai, 1962.

Tiruvŏṟṟiyūr. *Tiruvŏṟṟiyūrpurāṇam* of Tiruvŏṟṟiyūr Ñāṉappirakācar. With commentary by Capāpati Mutaliyār. Madras, 1869.

*Tiruvŏṟṟiyūr kṣettiratiṉ makimaiyum mahāṉkaḷiṉ stutiyum*. Madras, 1924.

*Tŏlkāppiyam. Pŏruḷatikāram*. With commentary of Nacciṉārkkiṉiyar. Ed. Ca. Pavāṉantam Piḷḷai. Madras, 1916.

———. With commentary of Iḷampūraṇar. Madras, SISS, 1961.

*Tulākkāverimāṉmiyam* of Ma. Ti. Pāṉukavi. Madras, 1917.

*Upatecakāṇṭam* of Koṉeriyappanāvalar. With commentary by Īkkāṭu Irattiṉavelu Mutaliyār. Madras, 1913.

*Upatecakāṇṭam* of Ñāṉavarotayar. Ed. V. S. Cĕṅkalvarāya Piḷḷai. Madras Government Oriental Manuscript Series no. 4. 3 vols. Madras, 1950.
*Vairavaṉkoyil stalamāṉmiyam* of Rama. Irāmacāmi Cĕṭṭiyār. Palavāṉkuṭi, 1932.
*Vaittīsvaraṉkoyil ĕṉṉum puḷḷirukku veḷūr ppurāṇam*. Kumpakoṇam, 1941.
*Vaḷḷiyammaināṭakam* of Muttuvīrakkaviñar. Ed. Mārkkaṇṭa Municāmip-piḷḷai. Madras, 1871.
*Vaḷḷiyammaṉvilācam*. Ed. Kokulāpuram Aruṇācala Mutaliyār. Madras, 1895.
*Velaimānakar caritai*. Ed. Ci. Pārttacāratināyakar. 1876, reprinted Velūr, 1909.
*Śrī vĕḷḷīsvararkoyil varalāṟu*. Madras, n.d.
Veṅkaṭācalam. *Tiruppati tirumalaiyāttirai veṅkaṭācala māhātmiyam ĕṉṉum stalapurāṇam* of I. Muṉucāminâyuṭu. Cittūr, 1928.
*Vetapuri sthalapurāṇam*. Government Oriental Manuscript Library, Madras, Mackenzie Ms. T.D. 1119.
Vetāraṇiyam (1). *Vetāraṇiyapurāṇam* of Akoratevar. Madras, 1898.
Vetāraṇiyam (2). *Vetāraṇiyapurāṇam* of Parañcotimuṉivar. Ed. Ma. Comāskantapaṭṭar. Madras, 1898.
*Vikkiramātittaṉkatai*. Ed. Pa. Vĕ. Mukammatu Ipuṟākīm Cākipu. Madras, 1938.
———. Trans. V.A.K. Aiyer. *Stories of Vikramaditya*. Bombay, 1974.
Vināyaka. *Pārkkavapurāṇam ĕṉṉum vināyakapurāṇam* of Kacciyappa-muṉivar. Ed. Ma. Ti. Pāṉukavi. Madras, 1910.
Vīraciṅkātaṉam. *Vīraciṅkātaṉapurāṇam* of Velaiyacuvāmi and Umāpāka-tevar. Madras, 1905.
Viruttācalam. *Viruttācalapurāṇam* of Ñāṉakkūttar. With commentary by Pārippākkam Muṉiyappa Mutaliyār. Madras, 1876.
*Śrī Yākñavalkiya carittiram* of S. Naracimmaṉ. Corṇāvūr, 1967.

## Secondary Sources in Tamil, by Author

Aruṇācalam, Mu. *Tamiḻ ilakkiya varalāṟu. Patiṉāṉkām nūṟṟāṇṭu; Patiṉaintām nūṟṟāṇṭu*. Māyūram, 1969.
Avināciliṅkam Cĕṭṭiyār, Ti. Cu. et al., ed. *Kalaikkaḷañciyam*. 10 vols. Madras, 1954-1968.
Cāminātaiyar, U. Ve. *Caṅkattamiḻum piṟkālattamiḻum*. Madras, 1949.
———. *Makāvittuvāṉ śrī mīṉāṭcicuntaram piḷḷaiyavarkaḷ carittiram*. Vol. II. Madras, 1940.
———. *Makāvittuvāṉ śrī mīṉāṭcicuntaram piḷḷaiyavarkaḷ carittiraccurukkam*. Vol. I. Madras, 1965.
———, ed. *Maturaittamiḻpperakarati*. Maturai, n.d.
———. *Niṉaivumañcari II*. 3rd ed. Madras, 1953.
———. *Putiyatum Paḻaiyatum*. Madras, 1949-a.

Catāciva Paṇṭārattār, T. V. *Tamil̲ ilakkiya varalāṟu* (English title: *A History of Tamil Literature*) *250-600 A.D.* 2nd ed. Aṇṇāmalainakar, 1957.
Cetuppiḷḷai, Rā. Pi. *Āṟṟaṅkaraiyiṉile.* Madras, 1961.
———. *Velum villum.* Madras, 1962.
Ekāmpara Mutaliyār, Ceñci. *See Nīlikatai.*
Irākavaiyaṅkār, Mu. *Cācaṉa ttamil̲kkavi caritam.* Māṉāmaturai, 1961.
———. *Ilakkiyakkaṭṭuraikaḷ.* Madras, 1955.
———. *Kaṭṭurai maṇikaḷ.* Māṉāmaturai, 1959.
Irāmacāmippulavar, Cu. A. *Tamil̲ppulavar akaravaricai.* 3 vols. Madras, SISS, 1959-1960.
———. *See Meṟkolviḷakka kkatai akaravaricai.*
Katiraiveṟ Piḷḷai, Na. *Cuppiramaṇiya parākkiramam.* Madras, 1906.
Kiruṣṇacāmi, Ve. *Tamil̲il talapurāṇa ilakkiyam.* Nākarkoyil, 1974.
Muttukumāracuvāmi ttampirāṉ, "Cŏllur ppĕrumaṇam," in *Tiruvaiyaṟu . . . makākumpāpiṣeka vil̲āmalar,* pp. 114-15.
Naṭarācaṉ, Tu. Co. *Citamparam aruḷmiku tillaiyammaṉ koyil talavaralāṟu.* Citamparam, 1975.
Patmanāpaṉ, Es. *Kaṉṉiyākumari.* Nākarkoyil, 1975.
Pirasaṉṉā, V. *Cucīntiram.* Kaṉṉiyākumari, n.d.
Rāmāmirtam, Lā. Ca. *Jaṉaṉi. Madras, 1952.*
Rāmanātaṉ, Aru. *Pal̲aiyaṉūr nīli.* Madras, 1954.
Raṅkarāmāṉuja Ayyaṅkār, Ār. *Śrī kiruti maṇi mālai.* Vol. V. Madras, 1953.
Śrītās (N.P.V. Rātākiruṣṇaṉ). *Kaṇṇaṉ tīrāta viḷaiyāṭṭu ppiḷḷai (pūtaṉaiyiṉ puṉita muṭivu).* Kumpakoṇam, 1975.
Tevakuñcariyammāḷ, Pālasarasvati. *Karnāṭaka yokiṉikkatai.* Madras, 1917.
Veṅkaṭacāmi, Mayilai Cīṉi. *Maṟaintu poṉa tamil̲ nūlkaḷ.* Madras, 1967.

## Sanskrit Texts, by Title

*Abhijñānaśakuntalā* of Kālidāsa. Madras, 1910.
*Agnipurāṇa.* ASS no. 41. Poona, 1957 (cited as *Agni*).
*Aitareyāraṇyaka.* Ed. and trans. Arthur B. Keith. 1909, reprinted Oxford, 1969.
*Aitareyabrāhmaṇa.* Bib. Ind. Calcutta, 1895-1896.
*Amarakoṣa* of Amarasiṃha. Benares, 1854.
———. Ed. Kuppa Bhaṭṭa. Tanjore, 1808.
*Arddhagirimāhātmya* (on Tiruccĕṅkoṭu). Ed. R. Anantakrishna Sastri. Madras, 1902.
*Arthaśāstra* of Kauṭilya. Ed. J. Jolly. Panjab Sanskrit Series no. 4. Lahore, 1923.
*Atharvaveda.* Bombay, 1895.
———. Trans. William Dwight Whitney, ed. Charles Lanman. HOS 7-8. Cambridge, Mass., 1905.
*Baudhāyanaśrautasūtra.* Ed. W. Caland. Calcutta, 1904.

*Bhagavadgītā*. Ed. and trans. R. C. Zaehner. Oxford, 1969.
*Bhāgavatapurāṇa*. Bombay, 1905 (cited as *Bhāgavata*).
*Bhaviṣyapurāṇa*. Bombay, 1910 (cited as *Bhaviṣya*).
*Bhūkailāsamāhātmya* (on Caṅkaranayiṉārkoyil). Ed. Veṅkaṭa Nārāyaṇa Śāstrin. Kumpakoṇam, 1921.
*Brahmāṇḍapurāṇa*. Ed. J. L. Shastri. Delhi, 1973 (cited as *Brahmāṇḍa*).
*Brahmapurāṇa*. ASS no. 28. Poona, 1895 (cited as *Brahma*).
*Brahmavaivartapurāṇa*. ASS no. 102. Poona, 1935 (cited as *Brahmavaivarta*).
*Bṛhaddevatā* attributed to Śaunaka. Ed. A. A. Macdonell. HOS no. 5. Cambridge, Mass., 1904.
*Bṛhaddharmapurāṇa*. Bib. Ind. Calcutta, 1888-1897 (cited as *Bṛhaddharma*).
*Bṛhadīśvaramāhātmya* (on Tañcāvūr). India Office Library, Burnell manuscripts IO 492a.
*Darpadalana* of Kṣemendra, in *Kṣemendralaghukāvyasaṅgraha*. Ed. E.V.V. Raghavacharya and D. G. Padhye. Hyderabad Sanskrit Series no. 7. Hyderabad, 1961.
*Daśakumāracarita* of Daṇḍin. Delhi, 1966.
*Devībhāgavatapurāṇa*. Benares, 1955 (cited as *Devībhāgavata*).
*Divyāvadāna*. Ed. E. B. Cowell and R. A. Neil. Cambridge, 1886.
*Gajāraṇyamāhātmya* (on Tiruvāṉaikkā). Ed. Go. Subrahmaṇya Śāstrin. Kumpakoṇam, 1901.
———. *See Tiruvāṉaikkāval māhātmiyam*.
*Gayāmāhātmya*. Ed. and trans. Claude Jacques. Pondicherry, 1962.
*Gopathabrāhmaṇa*. Ed. Dieuke Gaastre. Leiden, 1919.
*Hālāsyamāhātmya* (on Maturai). Maturai, 1870.
*Harivaṃśa*. With Hindi *ṭīkā* by Pāṇḍeya Rāmateja Śāstrin. Vārāṇasī, 1964.
*Jaiminīyabrāhmaṇa* of the *Sāmaveda*. Ed. Raghu Vira and Lokesh Chandra. Sarasvati Vihara Series no. 31, Nagpur, 1954.
*Jātakas*. Ed. Viggio Fausbøll. 7 vols. London, 1877-1897.
*Kālikāpurāṇa*. Bombay, 1891 (cited as *Kālikā*).
*Kāmākṣīvilāsa*. Bangalore, 1968.
*Kāmasūtra*. Ed. Gosvāmi Dāmodar Śāstrin. Kāśī Sanskrit Series, Benares, 1929.
*Kāñcīmāhātmya*. Ed. P. B. Ananthachariar. Śāstramuktāvali. Kāñcipuram, 1906.
*Kanyākṣetramāhātmya*. India Office Library, Burnell Manuscripts, IO B.468.
*Kāṭhakasaṃhitā*. Ed. Leopold von Schroeder. Leipzig, 1900.
*Kathāsaritsāgara* of Somadeva. Ed. Durgāprasād and Kāśināth Pāndurang Parab. 4th ed. Bombay, 1930.
———. Trans. C. H. Tawney and ed. N. M. Penzer. *The Ocean of Story*. 10 vols. London, 1924-1928.
*Kauṣītakibrāhmaṇa*. Ed. E. R. Sreekrishna Sarma. Wiesbaden, 1968.
*Kumārasambhava* of Kālidāsa. Delhi, 1967.

*Kumbhaghoṇamāhātmya*. Ed. Pāṇḍurangī L. Śrīnivāsācārya. Kumpakoṇam, 1913.
*Kūrmapurāṇa*. Ed. A. S. Gupta. Vārāṇasī, 1972 (cited as *Kūrma*).
*Liṅgapurana*. Bombay, 1906 (cited as *Liṅga*).
*Maddhyārjunamāhātmya* (*sic*) (on Tiruviṭaimarutūr). Madras, 1916.
*Mahābhārata*. Ed. Vishnu S. Sukthankar et al., Poona, 1933-1959.
———. With commentary of Nīlakaṇṭha. Bombay, 1888.
———. Southern Recension. Ed. P.P.S. Sastri. Madras, 1931-1933.
———. Trans. J.A.B. van Buitenen. *The Mahābhārata*. Chicago, 1973-.
*Mahāvaṃsa* (in Pali). London, 1908.
*Mahimnastava*. Ed. W. Norman Brown. Poona, 1965.
*Maitrāyaṇī saṃhitā*. Ed. Leopold von Schroeder. Leipzig, 1923.
*Mānavadharmaśāstra*. Bib. Ind. Calcutta, 1932 (cited as *Manusmṛti*).
*Mārkaṇḍeyapurāṇa*. Bib. Ind. Calcutta, 1862 (cited as *Mārkaṇḍeya*).
———. Trans. F. Eden Pargiter. Bib. Ind. Calcutta, 1904.
*Matsyapurāṇa*. ASS no. 54. Poona, 1909 (cited as *Matsya*).
*Nāradapurāṇa*. Summarized by K. Damodaran Nambiar in supplement to *Purāṇa* 15, no. 2 (1973), pp. 1-56.
*Nirukta* of Yāska. Ed. with commentary of Durga by R. G. Bhadkamkar. Bombay Sanskrit and Prakrit Series. 2 vols. Bombay, 1918, 1942.
*Padmapurāṇa*. ASS no. 131. Poona, 1894 (cited as *Padma*).
———. *Svargakhaṇḍa*. Ed. Asoke Chatterjee Śāstrī. Varanasi, 1972.
*Pañcatantra* (Pūrṇabhadra). Ed. Johannes Hertel. HOS no. 11. Cambridge, Mass., 1908.
———. Trans. Abbé J. A. Dubois. *Le Pantchatantra ou les cinq ruses* . . . (on the basis of three versions, in Tamil, Telugu, and Kannada). Paris, 1872.
———. Trans. Edouard Lancereau. *Pañcatantra*. 1871, reprinted with an introduction by L. Renou, Paris, 1965.
———. *See* Benfey, Theodore.
———. *See Pañcatantiram*.
*Raghuvaṃśa* of Kālidāsa. Bombay, 1891.
*Rāmāyaṇa* of Vālmīki. Ed. G. H. Bhatt et al., Baroda, 1960-.
———. Ed. Śivarāmaśarmā Vāsiṣṭha. Vārāṇasī, 1957. (Citations from the *Uttarakāṇḍa*) refer to this edition.
*Ṛgveda*. With commentary of Sāyaṇa. 6 vols. London, 1849-1864.
*Śabdakalpadruma* of Raja Sir Radhakant Deb Bahadur. 3rd ed. Chowkhamba Sanskrit Series no. 93. 5 vols. Benares, 1967.
*Śatapathabrāhmaṇa* of the White Yajurveda, with the commentary of Sāyaṇa. Ed. Albrecht Weber. Bib. Ind. Calcutta, 1903-1910.
———. 2 vols. Benares, 1938-1940.
*Satyagirimāhātmya* (on Tirupparaṅkuṉṟam). With Tamil translation. Maturai, 1931.
*Saurapurāṇa*. ASS no. 18. Poona, 1889 (cited as *Saura*).

*Śivapurāṇa*. Bombay, 1953 (cited as *Śiva*).
———. *Jñāna-, Dharma-,* and *Vāyavīya-saṃhitās*. Bombay, 1884 (cited as *Śiva*, with name of the *saṃhitā*).
*Śivarahasyakhaṇḍa* of the *Śaṅkarasaṃhitā* of the *Skandapurāṇa*. India Office Library, San. IO 1431 and San. IO 238.
———, published as *Śrīskāndamahāpurāṇa*. Ed. with Tamil trans. by Ceṅkālipuram Aṉantarāma Tīkṣitar. 3 vols. Celam, n.d.
*Skandapurāṇa*. Gurumandal Series no. 20. Calcutta, 1959 (cited as *Skanda*).
———. Bombay, 1867.
*Śrīkṛṣṇakṣetramāhātmya* (on Tirukkaṇṇapuram). Ed. and trans. into Tamil by U. Tiruveṅkaṭācāriyar. Madras, 1912.
*Śrīnāgeśakṣetramāhātmya* (on Tiruppātāḷīccaram). Ed. and trans. into Tamil prose by Ka. Ca. Kiruṣṇa Cāstiri. Madras, 1935.
*Śrīraṅgamāhātmya*. Ed. Kuppusāmi Ayyaṅkār. With Tamil commentary by Kiruṣṇayyaṅkār. Tirucirāppaḷḷi, 1908.
*Śrī svāmimalaikṣetramāhātmya*. With Tamil *vacaṉam*. Kumpakoṇam, 1935.
*Subhāṣitaratnakoṣa* of Vidyākara. Ed. D. D. Kosambi and V. V. Gokhale. HOS no. 42. Cambridge, Mass., 1957.
*Taittirīyāraṇyaka* of the Black Yajurveda. With commentary of Sāyaṇa. Ed. Rajendra Lal Mitra. Bib. Ind. Calcutta, 1872.
*Taittirīyabrāhmaṇa*. Ed. Rajendra Lal Mitra. Bib. Ind. Calcutta, 1859.
*Taittirīyasaṃhitā*. With commentary of Mādhava. Bib. Ind. Calcutta, 1860.
*Tāṇḍyamahābrāhmaṇa* (*Pañcaviṃśabrāhmaṇa*). With the commentary of Sāyaṇa. Ed. Ānandacandra Vedāntavāgīśa. Bib. Ind. Calcutta, 1869-1874.
*Tañjāpurimāhātmya*. India Office Library, Burnell Manuscripts, San. IO 492a.
*Upaniṣads*. *Aṣṭādaśa upaniṣadaḥ*. (*Eighteen Principal Upaniṣads*). Poona, 1958.
*Vājasaneyimādhyandinasaṃhitā* of the White Yajurveda. Ed. Wāsudev Laxman Shāstrī Paṇsīkar. Bombay, 1912.
*Vāmanapurāṇa*. Ed. A. S. Gupta. Vārāṇasī, 1967 (cited as *Vāmana*).
*Varāhapurāṇa*. Bib. Ind. Calcutta, 1893 (cited as *Varāha*).
*Vaṭāraṇyamāhātmya* (on Tiruvālaṅkāṭu). With Tamil *vacaṉam* by Es. Irāmacuvāmi Aiyar. Naṭukkāveri, 1898.
*Vāyupurāṇa*. ASS no. 49. Poona, 1905 (cited as *Vayu*).
*Vedāraṇyamāhātmya*. Kumpakoṇam, 1912.
*Vikramorvaśīya* of Kālidāsa. Ed. H. D. Velankar. New Delhi, 1961.
*Vīkṣāraṇyakṣetramāhātmya* (on Tiruvuḷḷūr). Tiruvuḷḷūr, 1966.
*Viṣṇupurāṇa*. With *Vaiṣṇavakūṭacandrikā* of Ratnagarbha Bhaṭṭācārya. Bombay, 1866 (cited as *Viṣṇu*).
———. Trans. H. H. Wilson. *The Vishnu Purana, a System of Hindu Mythology and Tradition*. 1840, reprinted with an introduction by R. C. Hazra, Calcutta, 1972.
*Viṣṇudharmottarapurāṇa*. Benares, n.d. (cited as *Viṣṇudharmottara*).

*Vṛṣabhādrimāhātmya* (on Tirumāliruñcolai). Ed. with an introduction by K. N. Radhakrishnan and a Tamil trans. by V. Venkatasubrahmania Sarma and Narayana Iyengar. Maturai, 1942.

WORKS IN OTHER LANGUAGES, BY AUTHOR

Adiceam, Marguerite E. *Contribution à l'étude d'AiyaNar-Śāstā*. Pondicherry, 1967.

Agrawala, R. C. "The Goddess Mahiṣāsuramardinī in Early Indian Art." *Artibus Asiae* 21 (1958), 123-30.

———. "A Rare Mahiṣamardinī Relief in the National Museum, New Delhi." *East and West* 16 (1966), 109-11.

Agrawala, Vasudeva S. *Vāmana Purāṇa—A Study*. Varanasi, 1964.

Aiyappan, A. "Myth of the Origin of Smallpox." *Folklore* 42 (1931), 291-92.

Aiyar, V.V.S. *Kamba Ramayana, A Study*. Bombay, 1965.

Aiyer (Ayer), V.A.K. *Untold Stories of King Bhoja*. Bombay, 1975.

———. *See Mataṉakāmarājaṉkatai* and *Vikkiramātittaṉkatai*.

Ananthakrishna Iyer, L. K. *See* Nanjundayya, H. V.

Arapura, J. G. "The Upside Down Tree of the Bhagavadgītā." *Numen* 22 (1975), 131-44.

Aravamuthan, T. G. *The Kaveri, the Maukharis and the Śangam Age*. Madras, 1925.

———. "The Maturai Chronicles and the Tamil Academies." *JORM* 5 (1931), 108-24, 196-214; 6 (1932), 89-105, 274-94, 322-40.

Archer, W. G. *Kalighat Paintings*. London, 1971.

Arokiaswami, M. "The Cult of Mariyamman or the Goddess of Rain." TC 2 (1953), 153-57.

Artola, George T. "Ten Tales from the *Tantropākhyāna*." *ALB* 29 (1965), 30-73.

Arunachalam, M. *Guru Jñāna Sambandha of Dharmapuram*. Tarumapuram, 1972.

Arunachalam, T. N. *Idaimarudhu, the Great and Incomparable*. Kumpakonam, 1973.

Asher, R. E., ed. *Proceedings of the Second International Conference Seminar on Tamil Studies (Madras, 1968)*. Madras, 1971.

Auboyer, Jeannine. *Le trône et son symbolisme dans l'Inde ancienne*. Paris, 1949.

Aubrecht, Theodore. *Catalogus Catalogorum: An Alphabetical Register of Sanskrit Works and Authors*. 1891 and 1896, reprinted Wiesbaden, 1962.

Baker, C. J., and Washbrook, D. A. *South India: Political Institutions and Political Change 1880-1940*. Delhi, 1975.

Basham, A. L. *The Wonder That Was India*. London, 1971.

Bazou, Leo. "Religious Landmarks in Pudukottai." *TC* 7 (1958), 370-85.

Beck, Brenda E. F. "Aṇṇanmār Katai or The Tale of the Brothers." Manuscript, 1975.

———. "Colour and Heat in South Indian Ritual." *Man* 4 (1969), 553-72.

———. "The Kin Nucleus in Tamil Folklore," in Thomas R. Trautmann, ed., *Kinship and History in South Asia*. Ann Arbor, 1974, pp. 1-27.

———. "A Praise-poem for Murugan by Cittiyananta." *Journal of South Asian Literature* 11 (1975), 95-116. (1975-a)

———. "A Study of the Structure and Basic Themes of the Skanda Purāṇa." Unpublished paper, delivered to the meeting of the Association for Asian Studies, March 1975. (1975-b)

———. "The Study of a Tamil Epic: Several Versions of the *Silappadikaram* Compared." *JTS* 1 (1972), 23-28.

———. "The Symbolic Merger of Body, Space, and Cosmos in Hindu Tamilnad." Unpublished paper, 1975. (1975-c)

Benfey, Theodore. *The Pantschatantra*. 2 vols. Leipzig, 1859.

*Bereshit Rabbah. See Midrash Rabbah.*

———. Ed. Ch. Albeck. 2nd ed. Jerusalem, 1975.

Bharati, Aghenanda. "Pilgrimage in the Indian Tradition." *HR* 3 (1963), 135-67.

Bharati, S. B. "The Pre-deluge Pandinad and Her Southern Frontier." *JAU* 5 (1935), 64-88.

Bhattacarji, Sukumari. *The Indian Theogony: A Comparative Study of Indian Mythology from the Vedas to the Purāṇas*. Cambridge, 1970.

Bhattacarya, Jogendra Nath. *Hindu Castes and Sects*. Calcutta, 1896.

Bhavnani, Enaksi. *The Dance in India*. Bombay, 1970.

*Bhojarājīyamu* of Anantāmatya. *See* Aiyer, V.A.K.

Biardeau, Madeleine. "Brahmanes combattants dans un mythe du sud de l'Inde." *ALB* 31-32 (1967-1968), 519-30.

———. "Brahmanes et potiers," article liminaire, *Annuaire de l'École Pratique des Hautes Études*, V$^{e}$ Section: Sciences Religieuses 79 (1971-1972), 31-55.

———. *Clefs pour la pensée hindoue*. Paris, 1972.

———. "Conférence de M$^{lle}$ Madeleine Biardeau." *Annuaire de l'École Pratique des Hautes Études*, V$^{e}$ Section: Sciences Religieuses 79 (1971-1972), 139-147. (1971-1972-a)

———. "La Decapitation de Reṇukā dans le mythe de Paraśurāma," in J. C. Heesterman, G. H. Schokker, and V. I. Subramoniam, ed., *Pratidānam: Indian, Iranian, and Indo-European Studies presented to Franciscus Bernardus Jacobus Kuiper on his Sixtieth Birthday*. The Hague, 1968.

———. "Études de mythologie hindoue (II)." *BEFEO* 55 (1969), 59-105.

Bolle, Kees W. *The Persistence of Religion: An Essay on Tantrism and Śrī Aurobindo's Philosophy*. Leiden, 1965.

———. "Speaking of a Place," in Joseph M. Kitagawa and Charles Long, ed., *Myths and Symbols, Studies in Honor of Mircea Eliade*. Chicago, 1969, pp. 127-39.

Bosch, F.D.K. "The God with the Horse's Head," in *Selected Studies in Indonesian Archaeology*. The Hague, 1961, pp. 137-52.

———. *The Golden Germ: An Introduction to Indian Symbolism*. The Hague, 1960.

Briggs, George Weston. *Gorakhnāth and the Kānphaṭa Yogīs*. 1938, reprinted New Delhi, 1973.

Brown, W. Norman. "Change of Sex as a Hindu Story Motif." *JAOS* 47 (1927), 3-24.

———. "The Creation Myth of the Rig Veda." *JAOS* 62 (1942), 85-98.

———. "The Name of the Goddess Mīnākṣī, 'Fish-eye.' " *JAOS* 67 (1947), 209-14.

———. "The Rigvedic Equivalent for Hell." *JAOS* 61 (1941), 76-80.

Brubaker, Richard L. "Lustful Woman, Chaste Wife, Ambivalent Goddess: A South Indian Myth." *Anima* 3:2 (1977), 59-62.

Buber, Martin. *Tales of the Hasidim: the Early Masters*. New York, 1973.

van Buitenen, J.A.B. "On the Archaism of the Bhāgavata Purāṇa," in Milton Singer, ed., *Krishna: Myths, Rites, and Attitudes*. Chicago, 1971, pp. 23-40.

———. *See Mahābhārata*.

Burnell, A. C. *A Classified Index to the Sanskrit Mss. in the Palace at Tanjore*. London, 1880.

Burrow, T., and Emeneau, M. B. *A Dravidian Etymological Dictionary*. Oxford, 1961 (with *Supplement*, 1968).

Caland, W. *Über das Rituelle Sūtra des Baudhāyana*. Leipzig, 1903.

Carr, M. W., ed. *Descriptive and Historical Papers Relating to the Seven Pagodas on the Coromandel Coast*. Madras, 1869.

Carstairs, G. Morris. *The Twice-Born: A Study of a Community of High-Caste Hindus*. London, 1957.

Chakravarti, A. *See Nīlakeci*.

Chambers, William. "Some Account of the Sculptures and Ruins at Mavalipuram, a Place a Few Miles North of Sadras, and Known to Seamen by the name of the Seven Pagodas," in Carr, pp. 1-29.

Chatterjee, Asim Kumar. *The Cult of Skanda-Kārttikeya in Ancient India*. Calcutta, 1970.

Chitty, Simon Casie. *The Tamil Plutarch*. Jaffna 1859.

Chockalingam, K., ed. *Temples of Tamil Nadu*. Vol IX, part XI-D, Vol. VII (1) of *Census of India, 1961*. Madras, 1971.

Clothey, Fred. "The Many Faces of Murugan: The History and Meaning of a South Indian God." Ph.D. dissertation, University of Chicago, 1968.

———. "Skanda-Ṣaṣṭhī: A Festival in Tamil India." *HR* 8 (1969), 236-59.

Coomaraswamy, Ananda. *The Dance of Śiva*. New York, 1918.

Cox, Arthur F. Revised by Harold A. Stuart. *North Arcot Gazeteer*. 2 vols. Madras, 1894-1895.

Crooke, W. *The Popular Religion and Folklore of Northern India*. 2 vols. 2nd ed. 1896, reprinted Delhi, 1968.

Daniélou, Alain. *Hindu Polytheism*. Bollingen Series LXXIII. New York, 1964.

Das, R. K. *Temples of Tamilnad*. Bombay, 1964.

Dasgupta, Surendranath. *Indian Idealism*. 1933, reprinted Cambridge, 1962.

Dave, J. H. *Immortal India*. 4 vols. Bombay, 1957-1961.

Davy, John. *An Account of the Interior of Ceylon and of Its Inhabitants with Travels in That Island*. London, 1821.

Day, Francis. *The Land of the Perumals, or Cochin, its Past and Present*. Madras, 1863.

Day, Lal Behari. *Folk Tales of Bengal*. 1912, reprinted Calcutta, 1969.

*The Book of Dede Korkut*. Trans. Geoffrey Lewis. Harmondsworth, 1974.

Defourny, Michel. "Note sur le symbolisme de la corne dans le *Mahābhārata* et la mythologie brahmanique classique." *IIJ* 18 (1976), 17-23.

Dessigane, R. *See Kāñcippurāṇam*; *Kantapurāṇam*; *Tiruviḷaiyāṭaṟpurāṇam*.

Dhavamony, Mariasusai. *Love of God According to Śaiva Siddhānta*. Oxford, 1971.

Diehl, C. G. *Instrument and Purpose: Studies on Rites and Rituals in South India*. Lund, 1956.

Dikshit, S. K. *The Mother Goddess*. Poona, n.d.

Dimock, Edward C. "Doctrine and Practice among the Vaiṣṇavas of Bengal," in Milton Singer, ed., *Krishna: Myths, Rites, and Attitudes*. Chicago, 1971, pp. 41-63.

———. *In Praise of Krishna*. New York, 1967.

———. *The Thief of Love: Bengali Tales from Court and Village*. Chicago, 1963.

Dorai Rangaswamy, M. A. *The Religion and Philosophy of Tēvāram*. 2 vols. Madras, 1958.

Douglas, Mary. *Purity and Danger*. 2nd ed. Harmondsworth, 1970.

Dowson, John. *A Classical Dictionary of Hindu Mythology and Religion, Geography, History and Literature*. 11th ed. London, 1968.

Dubois, Abbé J. A. *Hindu Manners, Customs and Ceremonies*. Trans. Henry K. Beauchamp. 3rd ed. Oxford, 1924.

———. *See Pañcatantra*.

Dumézil, Georges. *The Destiny of a King*. Trans. Alf Hiltebeitel. Chicago, 1973.

———. *The Destiny of the Warrior*. Trans. Alf Hiltebeitel. Chicago, 1969.

———. *Mythe et Épopée*. 3 vols. Paris, 1968-1973.

———. "La Sabhā de Yama." *JA* 253 (1965), 161-65.

Dumont, Louis. *Homus Hierarchicus*. London, 1966.

———. *Une sous-caste de l'Inde du sud: organisation sociale et religion des Pramalai Kallar*. Paris, 1957.

———. "A Structural Definition of a Folk Deity of Tamil Nad: Aiyanar, the Lord." *CIS* 3 (1959), 75-87.

Edholm, Erik A. F., and Suneson, Carl. "Kṛṣṇa's Marriage to Nīlā/NappiNNai in Sanskrit and Tamil Literature." *Temenos* 8 (1972), 29-53.

Eggeling, Julius. *Catalogue of the Sanskrit Manuscripts in the Library of the India Office*. Part VI. London, 1899.

Eliade, Mircea. *Myths, Dreams, and Mysteries*. 1960, reprinted London, 1974.

———. *The Sacred and the Profane*. New York, 1959.

———. "Spirit, Light and Seed." *HR* 11 (1971), 1-30.

———. *Yoga: Immortality and Freedom*. Princeton, 1958.

Eliot, Sir Charles. *Hinduism and Buddhism*. 3 vols. London, 1921.

Elmore, Wilber Theodore. *Dravidian Gods in Modern Hinduism*. Omaha, Nebraska, 1915, reprinted Madras, 1925.

Elwin, Verrier. *The Baiga*. London, 1939.

———. *Folk Tales of Mahakoshal*. Madras, 1944.

———. *The Muria and Their Ghotul*. Bombay, 1947.

———. *Myths of Middle India*. Madras, 1949.

Emeneau, M. B. "The Strangling Figs in Sanskrit Literature." University of California Publications in Classical Philology 13, no. 10 (1949), 345-70.

———. *Toda Songs*. Oxford, 1971.

———. *See* Burrow, T.

Fabricius, J. P. *Tamil and English Dictionary*. 4th ed. Tranquebar, 1972.

Falk, Nancy E. "Wilderness and Kingship in Ancient South Asia." *HR* 13 (1974), 1-15.

Filliozat, Jean. "Archaeology and Tamil Studies." *PICSTS* 2 (1968). I, 3-11.

———. *Étude de démonologie indienne: le Kumāratantra de Rāvaṇa et les textes parallèles indiens, tibétains, chinois, cambodgiens, et arabes*. Paris, 1937.

———. *See* Renou, Louis; *Kāñcippurāṇam*; *Tirumurukāṟṟuppaṭai*; *Tiruppāvai*; *Tiruviḷaiyāṭaṟpurāṇam*.

Francis, W. *Madura District Gazeteer*. Madras, 1906.

———. *South Arcot District Gazeteer*. Madras, 1906. (1906-a)

Frazer, James George. *The Golden Bough*. 3rd ed. London, 1927-1936.

Frere, M. *Old Deccan Days*. 2nd ed. London, 1870.

von Fürer-Haimendorf, Christoph. *The Aboriginal Tribes of Hyderabad*. Vol. I: *The Chenchus*. London, 1943. Vol. III: *The Raj Gonds of Adilabad*. I: *Myth and Ritual*. London, 1948.

Gargi, Balwant. *Folk Theatre of India*. Seattle, 1966.

Getty, Alice. *Gaṇeśa*. 1936, reprinted Delhi, 1971.

Goldman, Robert Philip. *Gods, Priests, and Warriors: The Bhṛgus of the Mahābhārata*. New York, 1976.

Gombrich, Richard. "The Consecration of a Buddhist Image." *JAS* 26 (1966), 23-36.

———. *Precept and Practice: Traditional Buddhism in the Rural Highlands of Ceylon*. Oxford, 1971.

Gonda, Jan. *Aspects of Early Viṣṇuism*. 1954, reprinted Delhi, 1969.

———. *Eye and Gaze in the Veda*. Amsterdam and London, 1965.

———. *Loka: World and Heaven in the Veda*. Amsterdam and London, 1966.

———. *Die Religionen Indiens*. I. *Veda und älterer Hinduismus*. II. *Der jüngere Hinduismus*. Stuttgart, 1960, 1963.

———. *Viṣṇuism and Śivaism*. London, 1970.

Gopinatha Rao, T. A. *Elements of Hindu Iconography*. 2 vols., 4 parts. Madras, 1914.

Govindâcârya, Âḷkoṇḍavilli. *The Holy Lives of the Âzhvârs or the Drâvida Saints*. Mysore, 1902.

Govindacharya Svamin, A. "A Lacuna in the Harivaṃśa." *Ind. An.* 40 (1911), 58-61.

Graefe, W. "Legends as Milestones in the History of Tamil Literature," in H. K. Hariyappa and M. M. Patikar, ed., *P. K. Gode Commemoration Volume*. Poona, 1960, pp. 129-46.

Gravely, F. H., and Ramachandran, T. N. "Catalogue of the South Indian Hindu Metal Images in the Madras Government Museum." *BMGM*, n.s. 1:2 (September 1932).

Graves, Robert. *The Greek Myths*. 2 vols. 1955, reprinted Harmondsworth, 1973.

———. *The White Goddess*. 1948, reprinted New York, 1975.

———, with Patai, Raphael. *Hebrew Myths*. New York, 1963.

Gros, Francois. *See Paripāṭal*.

———, with Thani Nayagam, X. S., ed. *Proceedings of the Third International Conference Seminar on Tamil Studies (Paris, 1970)*. Pondicherry, 1975.

———, with Nagaswamy, R. *Uttaramērūr: Légendes, histoire, monuments*. Pondicherry, 1970.

Gupte, B. A. *Hindu Holidays and Ceremonials*. Calcutta, 1919.

Hameed, K.P.S. "The Structural Pattern of Two Traditional Narratives in Tamil." *PICSTS* 2 (1968), Vol. II, 196-204.

Hardy, Friedhelm. "Ideology and Cultural Contexts of the Śrīvaiṣṇava Temple." *The Indian Economic and Social History Review* 14 (1977), 119-51.

Hart, George L. *The Poems of Ancient Tamil*. Berkeley, 1975.

———. *The Relation between Tamil and Classical Sanskrit Literature*, in Jan

Gonda, ed., *A History of Indian Literature*, Vol. X, fasc. 2. Wiesbaden, 1976.

———. "Some Aspects of Kinship in Ancient Tamil Literature," in T. Trautmann, ed., *Kinship and History in South Asia*. Ann Arbor, 1974, pp. 29-60.

———. "Woman and the Sacred in Ancient Tamilnad." *JAS* 32 (1973), 233-50.

Hazra, R. C. *Studies in the Purāṇic Records on Hindu Rites and Customs*. Dacca, 1940.

———. *Studies in the Upapurāṇas*. I. *Saura and Vaiṣṇava Upapurāṇas*. II. *Śākta and Non-sectarian Upapurāṇas*. Calcutta, 1958, 1963.

Heesterman, J. C. *The Ancient Indian Royal Consecration: The Rājasūya Described According to the Yajus Texts and Annotated*. The Hague, 1957.

———. "Brahmin, Ritual and Renouncer." *WZKSO* 8 (1964), 1-31.

———. "The Case of the Severed Head." *WZKSO* 11 (1967), 22-43.

———. "India and the Inner Conflict of Tradition." *Daedalus* 102 (1973), 97-113.

———. "Veda and Dharma." Paper read at the School of Oriental and African Studies, London, 1975.

———. "Vrātya and Sacrifice." *IIJ* 6 (1962), 1-37.

Hemingway, F. R. *Tanjore District Gazeteer*. Madras, 1915.

———. *Trichinopoly District Gazeteer*. Madras, 1907.

Hertel, Johannes. *Das Pañcatantra, seine Geschichte und seine Verbreitung*. Leipzig and Berlin, 1914.

———. "Uber einen südlichen *Textus Amplior* des Pañcatantra." *ZDMG* 61 (1907), 18-72.

Hiltebeitel, Alf. "The Burning of the Forest Myth," in Smith, pp. 208-24.

———. "The *Mahābhārata* and Hindu Eschatology." *HR* 12 (1972), 95-135.

———. *The Ritual of Battle*. Ithaca and London, 1976.

———. *See* Dumézil.

Hocart, A. M. *The Life-Giving Myth and Other Essays*. 1952, reprinted London, 1970.

Hooper, J.S.M. *Hymns of the Āḻvārs*. Calcutta, 1929.

Hopkins, Edward Washburn. *Epic Mythology*. Strasbourg, 1915.

Ions, Veronica. *Indian Mythology*. London, 1967.

———. *Myths and Legends of India*. London, 1970.

Jacob, K. *Folk Tales of Kerala*. New Delhi, 1972.

Jagadisa Ayyar, P. V. *South Indian Shrines*. Madras, 1920.

———. *See* Kumarasami Mudaliyar, M. M.

James, William. *The Varieties of Religious Experience*. 1902, reprinted London, 1971.

Jesudasan, C., and Jesudasan, Hephzibah. *A History of Tamil Literature*. Calcutta, 1961.

Joseph, P. *The Dravidian Problem and the South Indian Culture Complex*. Madras, 1972.

Jouveau-Dubreuil, G. *Iconography of Southern India*. Trans. A. C. Martin. Paris, 1937.

Kailasapathy, K. *Tamil Heroic Poetry*. Oxford, 1968.

Kakati, Bani Kanta. *The Mother Goddess Kāmākhyā*. Gauhati, 1948.

———. *Vishnuite Myths and Legends in Folklore Setting*. Gauhati, 1952.

Kalyanasundaram Aiyar, R. "South Indian Serpent Lore." *QJMS* 22 (1932), 424-30.

Kandiah, A. "A Critical Study of Early Tamil Śaiva Bhakti Literature, with Special Reference to Tēvāram." Ph.D. dissertation, University of London, 1973.

Kane, Pandurang Vaman. *History of Dharmaśāstra*. 5 vols. Poona, 1930-1962.

Kârâvêlane. *See Patiṉorāṉ tirumuṟai*.

Karve, Irawati. *Yuganta*. New Delhi, 1974.

Keith, Arthur Berriedale. *Catalogue of the Sanskrit and Prākrit Manuscripts in the Library of the India Office*. 2 vols. Oxford, 1935.

———. *The Religion and Philosophy of the Vedas and Upaniṣads*. HOS, nos. 31-32. Cambridge, Mass., 1925.

Kennedy, Colonel Vans. *Researches into the Nature and Affinity of Ancient and Hindu Mythology*. London, 1831.

Kincaid, Charles A. *The Tale of the Tulsi Plant and Other Studies*. Bombay, 1908.

Kingsbury, F. and Phillips, G. E. *Hymns of the Tamil Śaivite Saints*. Calcutta, 1921.

al-Kisā'ī. *Qiṣaṣ al-anbiyā'*. Leiden, 1922.

Koestler, Arthur. *The Lotus and the Robot*. London, 1960.

van Kooij, K. R. *Worship of the Goddess According to the Kālikāpurāṇa*. Vol. I. *A Translation with an Introduction and Notes of Chapters 54-69*. Leiden, 1972.

Kosambi, D. D. *The Culture and Civilization of Ancient India in Historical Outline*. London, 1965.

———. *Myth and Reality: Studies in the Formation of Indian Culture*. Bombay, 1962.

———. "On the Origin of Brahmin Gotras." *JBBRAS* 26 (1951), 21-80.

Kramrisch, Stella. *The Hindu Temple*. Calcutta, 1946.

———. "The Triple Structure of Creation in the Ṛg Veda." *HR* 2 (1962-1963), 140-75, 256-85.

———. *Unknown India: Ritual Art in Tribe and Village*. Philadelphia, 1968.

Krishna Sastri, H. *South Indian Images of Gods and Goddesses*. Madras, 1916.

Krishnaswami, T. B. *South Arcot in Sacred Song*. Madras, 1937.

Kuiper, F.B.J. "The Basic Concept of Vedic Religion." *HR* 15 (1975), 107-20.

Kuiper, F.B.J. "The Bliss of Aša." *IIJ* 8 (1964), 96-129.

———. "Cosmogony and Conception: A Query." *HR* 10 (1970), 91-138.

———. "The Heavenly Bucket," in J. Ensinck and P. Gaeffke, ed., *India Major* (congratulatory volume presented to J. Gonda). Leiden, 1972, pp. 144-56.

Kulke, Hermann. *Cidambaramāhātmya*. Wiesbaden, 1970.

Kumarasami Mudaliyar, M. M. (with Jagadisa Ayyar, P. V.). *Tirukaḻukunram (Pakshi-tīrtham)*. Madras, 1923.

Kurup, K.K.N. *The Cult of Teyyam and Hero Worship in Kerala*. Calcutta, 1973.

Leach, Edmund R. "Pulleyar and the Lord Buddha: An Aspect of Religious Syncretism in Ceylon." *Psychoanalysis and the Psychoanalytic Review* (Summer 1962), pp. 81-102.

Leslie, Charles, ed. *Anthropology of Folk Religion*. New York, 1960.

Lévi-Strauss, Claude. *Structural Anthropology*. New York, 1967.

Long, J. Bruce. "Life out of Death: A Structural Analysis of the Myth of the Churning of the Ocean of Milk," in Smith, pp. 171-207.

———. "Visions of Terror and Bliss: A Study of Rudra-Śiva in Pre-Purāṇic Hinduism." Ph.D. dissertation, University of Chicago, 1970.

Lorenzen, David. *The Kāpālikas and the Kālāmukhas*. New Delhi, 1972.

McCrindle, J. W. *Ancient India as Described by Megasthenes and Arrian*. 2nd ed. Calcutta, 1960.

Macdonell, A. A. *Vedic Mythology*. 1897, reprinted Delhi, 1971.

———. *A Vedic Reader for Students*. 1917, reprinted Madras, 1965.

Mahalingam, T. V. "Hayagrīva—the Concept and the Cult." *ALB* 29 (1965), 188-99.

———. *Mackenzie Manuscripts. I. Tamil and Malayalam*. Madras, 1972.

———. "The Pāśupatas in South India." *JIH* 27 (1949), 43-53.

Maity, Pradyot Kumar. *Historical Studies in the Cult of the Goddess Manasā*. Calcutta, 1966.

Mann, Thomas. *The Transposed Heads. A Legend of India*. Trans. H. T. Loew-Porter. New York, 1941.

Mansinha, Mayadhar. *History of Oriya Literature*. New Delhi, 1962.

Marr, J. R. "The Eight Tamil Anthologies with Special Reference to Puṟanāṉūṟu and Patiṟṟuppattu." Ph.D. dissertation, University of London, 1958.

———. "Letterature Dravidiche," in Oscar Botto, ed., *Storia delle Letterature d'Oriente*. Milan, 1969, pp. 559-626.

———. "The Lost Decades of *Patiṟṟuppattu*." *PICSTS* 2 (1968), I, 19-24.

———. "Some Manuscripts in Grantha Script in Bangkok—II." *Journal of the Siam Society* 60, part 2 (1972), 61-87.

———. Review of D. Barrett, *Early Cola Architecture and Sculpture, 866-1014 A.D.* (London, 1974), in *BSOAS* 39 (1976), 671-72.

———. Review of Kulke, *BSOAS* 35 (1972), 639-40. (1972-a)

———. Review of William Y. Willetts, *An Illustrated Annotated Annual Bibliography of Mahābalipuram on the Coromandel Coast of India, 1582-1962* (Kuala Lumpur, 1966), in *BSOAS* 30 (1967), p. 421.

Martin, James L. "Hindu Orthodoxy in a South Indian Village." *Journal of the American Academy of Religion* 35 (1967), 362-71.

Maury, Curt. *Folk Origins of Indian Art*. New York, 1969.

Meenakshisundaran, T. P. *A History of Tamil Literature*. Annamalainagar, 1965.

———. "The Lady Who Gave the Eyes." *JAU* 23 (1961), 153-56.

———. "Tamil and Other Cultures." *PICSTS* 3 (1970), 127-59.

Meyer, Johann Jakob. *Sexual Life in Ancient India*. 2 vols. London, 1930.

———. *Trilogie der Altindischer Mächte und Feste der Vegetation*. Zurich, 1937.

*Midrash Rabbah*. Tel-Aviv, 1956.

Mishra, K. C. *The Cult of Jagannātha*. Calcutta, 1971.

Mitra, Kalipada. "Change of Sex in Fiction." *QJMS* 18 (1927), 46-52.

Mitra, Sarat Chandra. "Studies in Bird-Myths No. XIII—On Three Aetiological Myths about the Spots on the Peacock's Tail-Faithers." *QJMS* 17 (1926), 145-47.

Monier-Williams, Sir Monier. *A Sanskrit-English Dictionary*. Oxford, 1899.

Nagaswamy, R. *See* Gros, François.

Naidu, Venkata Narayanaswami; Naidu, Srinivasulu; and Pantulu, Venkata Rangayya. *Tāṇḍava Lakṣaṇam, or the Fundamentals of Ancient Hindu Dancing*. Madras, 1936.

Nallaswami Pillai, J. M. *Studies in Śaiva Siddhānta*. Madras, 1911.

———. *See Civañāṉacittiyār*.

Nanjundayya, H. V., and Ananthakrishna Iyer, L. K. *The Mysore Tribes and Castes*. 4 vols. Mysore, 1931-1935.

Narayan, R. K. *The Ramayana*. London, 1973.

Narayana Ayyar, C. V. *Origin and Early History of Śaivism in South India*. Madras, 1936.

Natesa Sastri, S. M. et al. *184 Indian Tales of Fun, Folly and Folk-lore*. Madras, 1920.

———. *Folklore in Southern India*, I-III. Bombay, 1884, 1888.

———. *See Mataṉakāmarājaṉkatai*.

Neogi, Dwijendra Nath. *Sacred Tales of India*. London, 1916.

Nilakanta Sastri, K. A. *Development of Religion in South India*. Madras, 1963.

———. *Foreign Notices of South India*. Madras, 1939.

———. *History of South India*. 3rd ed. Bombay, 1966.

Oertel, Hans. "Contributions from the Jāiminiya Brāhmaṇa to the History of the Brāhmaṇa Literature." *JAOS* 26 (1905), 176-96.

O'Flaherty, Wendy Doniger. *Asceticism and Eroticism in the Mythology of Śiva*. London, 1973.

O'Flaherty, Wendy Doniger. *The Origins of Evil in Hindu Mythology.* Berkeley, 1976.

———. "The Origin of Heresy in Hindu Mythology." D.Phil. dissertation, Oxford, 1973 (1973-a)

———. *Hindu Myths.* Harmondsworth, 1975.

———. "The Submarine Mare in the Mythology of Śiva." *JRAS*, 1971, 1, pp. 9-27.

Ogibenin, B. L. *Structure d'un mythe védique: le mythe cosmogonique dans le Ṛgveda.* The Hague, 1973.

Oliphant, Samuel Grant. "Fragments of a Lost Myth—Indra and the Ants." *Proceedings of the American Philological Association* 41 (1910), LV-LIX.

Oppert, Gustav. *On the Original Inhabitants of Bharatavarṣa or India.* Westminster, 1893.

Padmanabha Menon, K. P. *History of Kerala.* 3 vols. Ernakulam, 1924-1933.

Pal, Pratapiditya. *The Arts of Nepal.* Leiden, 1974.

Parker, H. *Village Folk-Tales of Ceylon.* 3 vols. London, 1910-1914.

Patai, R. *See* Graves, Robert.

Pate, H. R. *Tinnevelly District Gazeteer.* Madras, 1917.

Pattabiramin, P. Z. *See Kāñcippurāṇam*; *Kantapurāṇam*; *Tiruviḷaiyāṭaṟ-purāṇam.*

Penzer, N. M. *See Kathāsaritsāgara.*

Percival, P. Tamil Proverbs with Their English Translation. 3rd ed. Madras, 1877.

Pfaffenberger, Bruce. "Orthodox Hindu Temples and Social Mobility in Tamil Sri Lanka." Paper, Berkeley, 1976.

Phillips, G. E. *See* Kingsbury, F.

Piatigorsky, A. *Materiali po istorii indiskoi filosofii.* Moscow, 1962.

———. "Some General Remarks on Mythology from a Psychologist's Point of View." *Semiotica* 10 (1974), 221-32.

Pillay, K. K. *The Śucīndram Temple.* Madras, 1953.

Polo, Marco. *The Book of Ser Marco Polo the Venetian Concerning the Kingdoms and Marvels of the East.* Trans. and ed. Colonel Sir Henry Yule. 3rd ed. London, 1921.

Ponnusamy, S. *Sri Thyagaraja Temple, Thiruvarur.* Madras, 1972.

Pope, G. U. *See Tiruvācakam.*

Przyluski, Jean. *La Grande Déesse: Introduction à l'étude comparative des religions.* Paris, 1950.

Purnalingam Pillai, M. S. *Tamil Literature.* Munnirpallam, 1929.

Radha Krishnan, K. N. *See Vṛṣabhādrimāhātmya.*

Raghavan, V. *New Catalogus Catalogorum.* Madras, 1969-.

———. "The Sūta Saṃhitā." *ABORI* 22 (1941), 236-53.

———. "Tamil Versions of the Purāṇas." *Purāṇa* 2 (1960), 223-46.

Ramachandra Dikshitar, V. R. *The Lalitā Cult*. Madras, 1942.
———. "Migration of Legends." *ABORI* 15 (1933-1934), 212-19.
———. *Studies in Tamil Literature and History*. London, 1930.
———. *See Cilappatikāram*.
Ramachandran, T. N. *See* Gravely, F. H.
Raman, K. V. *Srī Varadarājaswāmi Temple—Kāñchi*. New Delhi, 1975.
Ramanatha Ayyar, V. "Development of the Name and Composition of a Divine Symbol at Kāñcī." *ALB* 29 (1965), 144-75.
Ramanujachariyar, R. *Srimushna Mahatmyam*. Viruttacalam, n.d.
Ramanujan. A. K. "The Indian Oedipus," in A. Poddar, ed., *Indian Literature*. Simla, 1972, pp. 130-35.
———. *The Interior Landscape*. London, 1970.
———. *Speaking of Śiva*. Harmondsworth, 1973.
Ramesan, N. *Temples and Legends of Andhra Pradesh*. Bombay, 1962.
Ranade, R. D. *Mysticism in Maharashtra*. Poona, 1933.
Rawson, Philip. *The Art of Tantra*. London, 1973.
Redfield, Robert. *The Little Community* and *Peasant Society and Culture*. 1956, reprinted Chicago, 1969.
Regnaud, Paul. *Comment naissent les mythes*. Paris, 1897.
Renou, Louis. *The Destiny of the Veda in India*. Delhi, 1965.
———, with Jean Filliozat, ed. *L'Inde classique*. 3 vols. Paris, 1947-1953.
———. *Religions of Ancient India*. London, 1953.
Rice, Stanley. *Occasional Essays on Native South Indian Life*. London, 1901.
Rose, H. A. "Sacrifices of the Head to the Hindu Goddess." *Folklore* 37 (1926), 90-92.
Rosu, Arion. "À la recherche d'un *tīrtha* énigmatique du dekkan médiéval." *BEFEO* 55 (1969), 23-57.
Rowland, Benjamin. *The Art and Architecture of India*. 3rd ed. Harmondsworth, 1970.
Saletore, Basker Anand. *Ancient Karnāṭaka*. I. *History of Tuḷuva*. Poona, 1936.
Sambamoorthy, P. *Great Composers*. Vol. I. Madras, 1962.
Sarasvati, Bandana. "History of the Worship of Śrī in North India to cir. A. D. 550." Ph.D. dissertation, University of London, 1971.
Sarma, C. R. *The Ramayana in Telugu and Tamil: A Comparative Study*. Madras, 1973.
Sastri, P.P.S. *A Descriptive Catalogue of the Sanskrit Manuscripts in the Tanjore Mahārāja Serfoji's Sarasvati Mahāl Library*. Vol, XV, Śrīraṅkam, 1932.
———. *See Mahābhārata*.
*Sefer Ta'amei Haminhagim*. Lemberg, 1911.
Sethu Pillai, R. P. "Sacred Placenames in Tamilnad." *Proceedings of the All-India Oriental Conference, 13th Session, Nagpur, 1946*. Nagpur, 1951, III, 143-54.

Sethu Pillai, R. P. *See* Cetuppiḷḷai, Rā. Pi.

Shāstrī, Mahāmahopādhyāya Haraprasāda. *A Descriptive Catalogue of Sanskrit Manuscripts in the Government Collection, under the Care of the Asiatic Society of Bengal*. Vol. V. *Purāṇa Manuscripts*. Calcutta, 1928.

Shastri, Suryakanta. *The Flood Legend in Sanskrit Literature*. Delhi, 1950.

Shenoy, J. P. *Madura, the Temple City*. Maturai, 1937.

Shivapadasundaram, S. *The Śaiva School of Hinduism*. London, 1934.

Shulman, David. "The Cliché as Ritual and Instrument: Iconic Puns in Kampaṉ's *Irāmāvatāram*." *Numen* 25 (1978), 135-55.

———. "The Murderous Bride: Tamil Versions of the Myth of Devī and the Buffalo-Demon." *HR* 16 (1976), 120-46.

———. "Murukaṉ, the Mango, and Ekāmbareśvara-Śiva: Fragments of a Tamil Creation Myth?" *IIJ*, 21 (1979), 27-40.

———. "The Mythology of the Tamil Śaiva Talapurāṇam." Ph.D. dissertation, University of London, 1976. (1976-a)

———. "On the Prehistory of Tyāgarāja-Śiva at Tiruvārūr." *Art and Archaeology Research Papers* 13 (1978), 55-58. (1978-a)

Singaravelu, S. *Social Life of the Tamils: The Classical Period*. Kuala Lumpur, 1966.

Singer, Milton. "The Great Tradition of Hinduism in the City of Madras," in Leslie, pp. 105-66.

Singha, Rina, and Massey, Reginald. *Indian Dances, Their History and Growth*. London, 1967.

Sitapati, P. *Sri Venkateswara, the Lord of the Seven Hills*. Bombay, 1972.

Sivaraja Pillai, K. N. *Agastya in the Tamil Land*. Madras, n.d.

Sivaramamurti, C. *Naṭarāja in Art, Thought and Literature*. New Delhi, 1974.

———. *Royal Conquests and Cultural Migrations in South India and the Deccan*. Calcutta, 1955.

Sivaraman, K. *Śaivism in Philosophical Perspective*. Delhi, 1973.

Smith, Bardwell, ed. *Hinduism: New Essays in the History of Religion*. Supplement to *Numen* 33 (Leiden, 1976).

Somasundaram Pillai, J. M. *The University and Its Environs*. Annamalainagar, 1955.

Sonnerat, Pierre. *Voyage aux Indes Orientales et à la Chine*. Paris, 1782.

*South Indian Inscriptions, XVII*. Ed. K. G. Krishnan. Madras, 1964.

Spence, Lewis. *The Gods of Mexico*. London, 1923.

Spencer, A. M., and Thompson, E. G. *Bengali Religious Lyrics: Śākta*. Calcutta, 1923.

Spencer, George W. "The Sacred Geography of the Tamil Śaivite Hymns." *Numen* 17 (1970), 232-44.

Spratt, Philip. *Hindu Culture and Personality*. Bombay, 1966.

Srinivas, M. M. *Marriage and the Family in Mysore*. Bombay, 1942.

———. *Religion and Society among the Coorgs of South India*. 1952, reprinted Calcutta, 1965.

Srinivasan, K. R. "Tirukkamakottam." *Proceedings of the All-India Oriental Conference, 13th Session, Nagpur, 1946*. Nagpur, 1951, III, 50-56.

Steel, Flora Annie. *Tales of the Punjab* (with notes by R. C. Temple). 1894 (as *Wide-Awake Stories*), reprinted London, 1973.

Stein, Burton. "Devī Shrines and Folk Hinduism in Medieval Tamilnadu," in Edwin Gerow and Margery D. Lang, ed., *Studies in the Language and Culture of South Asia*. Seattle, 1973, pp. 75-90.

———. "The Economic Function of a Medieval Hindu Temple." *JAS* 19 (1960), 163-76.

Stuart, Harold A. *See* Cox, Arthur F.

Subrahmania Pillai, G. "Tree Worship and Ophiolatry in the Tamil Land." *JAU* 12 (1943), 70-82.

Subrahmanian, N. *Śaṅgam Polity*. London, 1966.

Subramaniam, K. *Brahmin Priest of Tamil Nadu*. New Delhi, 1974.

Suneson, Carl. *See* Edholm, Erik A. F.

*Tadhkirat al-Awliyā* of Farīd al-Dīn al-ʿAṭṭār. Ed. Reynold A. Nicholson. London, 1905.

Taleyarkan, Dinshah Ardeshir. "Legend of Vellur." *Ind. An.* 2 (1873), 172-75.

*Tamil Lexicon*. 7 vols. Madras, 1926-1939.

Tawney, C. H. *See Kathāsaritsāgara*.

Taylor, William. *A Catalogue Raisonée* (sic) *of Oriental Manuscripts in the Library of the (Late) College, Fort Saint George*. 3 vols. Madras, 1857, 1860, 1862.

———. *Oriental Historical Manuscripts, Chiefly Bearing on the History of the Kingdom of Madura*. 2 vols. Madras, 1835.

Temple, Sir Richard Carnac. "The Folklore in the Legends of the Panjab." *Folklore* 10 (1899), 384-443.

———. *See* Steel, Flora Annie.

Thani Nayagam, Xavier S. *Landscape and Poetry: A Study of Nature in Classical Tamil Poetry*. 2nd ed. London, 1966.

———. *See* Gros, François.

Thankappan Nair, P. "The Peacock Cult in Asia." *Asian Folklore Studies* (Japan) 33 (1974), 93-170.

Thiagarajah, M. A. "Ceranāṭu during the Caṅkam and the Post-Caṅkam Period." Ph.D. dissertation, University of London, 1963.

Thomas, P. *Epics, Myths and Legends of India*. 2nd ed. Bombay, 1961.

Thompson, E. G. *See* Spencer, A. M.

Thompson, Stith. *Motif-Index of Folk Literature*. Rev. ed. 6 vols. Bloomington, Indiana, 1955-1958.

Thurston, E. *Castes and Tribes of Southern India*. 6 vols. Madras, 1909.

Thurston, E. *Omens and Superstitions of Southern India*. London, 1912.

*Travancore Archaeological Series, IV.* Ed. K. V. Subrahmanya Aiyar. Trivandrum, 1923. (Cited as *TAS*)

Tripathi, Gaya Charan. *Der Ursprung und die Entwicklung der Vāmanalegende in der Indischen Literatur.* Wiesbaden, 1968.

Turner, Victor. *Dramas, Fields, and Metaphors: Symbolic Action in Human Society*. Ithaca, 1974.

———. *The Forest of Symbols*. Ithaca, 1967.

———. "Sacrifice as Quintessential Process: Prophylaxis or Abandonment." *HR* 16 (1977), 189-215.

Underhill, M. M. *The Hindu Religious Year*. Calcutta, 1921.

Vaiyapuri Pillai, S. *History of Tamil Language and Literature*. Madras, 1956.

Vanamamalai, N. *Studies in Tamil Folk Literature*. Madras, 1969.

———. "The Structural Pattern of Two Traditional Social Themes in Tamil Folk Ballads." *PICSTS* 2 (1968), II, 190-95.

Varadachari, K. C. *Āḻvārs of South India*. Bombay, 1966.

Vaudeville, Ch. *Étude sur les sources et la composition du Rāmāyaṇa de Tulsī-Dās*. Paris, 1955.

———. "Evolution of Love-Symbolism in Bhāgavatism." *JAOS* 82 (1962), 31-40.

Venkataraman, B. *Laddigam*. Madras, 1971.

Venkata Ramanayya, N. *An Essay on the Origin of the South Indian Temple*. Madras, 1930.

———. *Rudra-Śiva*. Madras, 1941.

———. *Trilôchana Pallava and Karikâla Chôla*. Madras, 1929.

Venkatasubbiah, A. "A Tamil Version of the Pañcatantra." *ALB* 29 (1965), 74-143.

Vogel, J. Ph. "The Head-offering to the Goddess in Pallava Sculpture." *BSOAS* 6 (1931), 539-43.

———. *Indian Serpent Lore*. London, 1926.

Walker, B. *Hindu World*. 2 vols. London, 1968.

Wariar, N. Sunkuni. "Kallil, a Famous Shrine in Southern India." *Ind. An.* 21 (1892), 95-96.

Washbrook, D. A. *See* Baker, C. J.

Wensinck, A. J. *The Ocean in the Literature of the Western Semites*. Amsterdam, 1918.

Whitehead, Henry. *The Village Gods of South India*. 2nd ed. Calcutta, 1921.

Whitney, William Dwight. *See Atharvaveda*.

Wilson, H. H. *The Mackenzie Collection, a Descriptive Catalogue* . . . 2 vols. Calcutta, 1828.

———. *See Viṣṇupurāṇa*.

Wilkins, W. J. *Hindu Mythology*. 1882, reprinted London, 1973.

Winslow, Miron. *A Comprehensive Tamil-English Dictionary of High and Low Tamil*. Madras, 1862.

Winternitz, Moriz. *A History of Indian Literature.* I. *Introduction, Veda, National Epics, Purāṇas, and Tantras.* Trans. Mrs. S. Ketkar, 2nd ed. Calcutta, 1963.

Wright, J. C. "Purūravas and Urvaśī." *BSOAS* 30 (1967), 526-47.

———. Review of Dessigane et al. (1964). *BSOAS* 29 (1966), 627-28.

Yalman, Nur. "On the Purity of Women in the Castes of Ceylon and Malabar." *Journal of the Royal Anthropological Institute of Great Britain and Ireland* 93, part 1 (January-June 1963), 25-28.

Zaehner, R. C. *Hinduism.* London, 1966.

Ziegenbalg, Bartholomaeus. *Genealogy of the South-Indian Gods.* Trans. G. J. Metzger, Madras, 1869.

Zimmer, Heinrich. *Myths and Symbols in Indian Art and Civilization.* Bollingen Series VI. 1946, reprinted Princeton, 1972.

———. *Philosophies of India.* Bollingen Series XXVI. 1951, reprinted Princeton, 1971.

de Zoete, Beryl. *The Other Mind.* London, 1953.

Zvelebil, Kamil Veith. "The Earliest Account of the Tamil Academies." *IIJ* 15 (1973), 109-35.

———. *The Poets of the Powers.* London, 1973. (1973-a)

———. *The Smile of Murugan, on Tamil Literature of South India.* Leiden, 1973. (1973-b)

———. *Tamil Literature.* Wiesbaden, 1974.

———. *Tamil Literature.* Handbuch der Orientalistik. Leiden, 1975.

———. "Vaḷḷi and Murugan—A Dravidian Myth." *IIJ* 19 (1977), 227-46.

# INDEX OF MOTIFS

The following list of major mythological motifs does not aim at completeness. Only motifs discussed in the text have been included; folklorists will find in the stories many additional motifs familiar from the Stith Thompson index.

## Motifs of Localization

*Shrine as center of the universe*



*Shrine situated on* axis mundi
*represented by*:



*Shrine connected*

MOTIFS OF REVELATION

*God appears*



*Vedas located in shrine*



*Sanctity marked*

## Motifs of Marriage

### *Incestuous love*



### *Goddess comes to the shrine*



### *Goddess subdued*

# INDEX OF PLACE NAMES AND LOCAL DEITY NAMES

LIBRARY OF CONGRESS CATALOGING IN PUBLICATION DATA

Shulman, David Dean, 1949-
Tamil temple myths.

Bibliography: p.
Includes indexes.
1. Sivaism. 2. Mythology, Tamil. 3. Temples, Hindu India—South India. 4. Sacred marriage (Mythology) 5. Sacrifice (Hinduism) I. Title.
BL1245.S5S53 294.5′513 79-17051
ISBN 0-691-06415-6